The
Book of
Welsh Saints

The
BOOK OF WELSH SAINTS

By
T. D. Breverton

Glyndŵr Publishing
Bro Morganwg

© Glyndŵr Publishing

First published 2000 by Glyndŵr Publishing

All rights reserved. No part of this book may be reproduced, stored in a retrieval system, or transmitted, in any form or by any means, electronic, mechanical, photocopying, recording or otherwise, without clearance from Glyndŵr Publishing, Porth Glyndŵr, Higher End, St Tathan, Bro Morganwg, CF62 4LW

ISBN 1-903529-01-8

Typeset and design by Glyndŵr Publishing

Produced in Wales
by
Keith Brown & Sons Ltd.,
Gwasg y Bont,
55 Eastgate,
Cowbridge,
Vale of Glamorgan
CF71 7EL

THE BOOK OF WELSH SAINTS

the 'Age of the Saints' in Wales

by T. D. Breverton

For Jane, Sophie and Alexander – sorry for the time I spent on the computer instead of being a husband and father . . .

It is bitter to know that history
Fails to teach the present to be better than the past,
For man was slave to the morning of time
And a slave he remains to the last.

Once he crawled in the barbarous gloom
As the trembling slave of theology
And to-day he moves in his sweat and his tears
As the servile fool of machinery.

It is bitter to know that all his dreams
Are roses that die to nourish the weeds,
That murder and malice and pain and grief
Are the surest traces of all his deeds.

Idris Davies, verse XVII of 'Gwalia Deserta' 1938

CONTENTS

	Page
Preamble - The 'Age of the Saints' and the Dark Ages	7
Chapter 1 - Introduction	10
Chapter 2 - Background to the Age of Saints	18
Chapter 3 - A Brief History of the Major Saints	23
Chapter 4 - The Revival of Saints' Feast days and Feast Weeks	26
Chapter 5 - Alphabetical Listing of Saints and Religious Events	34
Chapter 6 - Feast Days of the Saints	537

Appendices:

Appendix A - Derivations of Welsh Place-Names	567
Appendix B - Roman Sites associated with Wales	570
Appendix C - Timelines of the Age of Saints	571
Appendix D - A Note Upon Welsh Language Mutations	576
Appendix E - An Urgent Warning to the Welsh	577
Appendix F - The Llannau of Wales	578
Appendix G - The 28 Towns of Sub-Roman Britain	579
Appendix H - The Democratic Deficit in Parliamentary Representation in Wales	581
Appendix I - A Note on the Early British Church - Jowett's hypothesis	584
Appendix J - The Language Problem	595
Booklist	598
Addenda	602

ACKNOWLEDGEMENTS

The Wales Tourist Board has given permission to reproduce the following copyright photographs: Maen Achwyfan, Carew Cross, Llantwit Major Celtic Crosses, Strata Florida, Caerleon, Llanthony Priory, Dolaucothi, Y Gaer, Tintern Abbey, Bryn Celli Ddu, Lamphey, Pentre Ifan, Tinkinswood Burial Chamber, St Winifrede's Well, St Asaf Cathedral, Talyllyn, Children in National Costume, Coracles, St Seiriol's Well, St Woolo's Cathedral, Bangor Cathedral, Llandaf Cathedral, St David's Cathedral.

For the following photographs the author has paid a fee to CADW Welsh Historic Monuments for reproduction rights as they are Crown Copyright: Caerwent, Gwydir Uchaf Chapel, Lamphey Bishop's palace, Llangar Church, Llanthony Priory, Margam Stones Museum, Penmon Priory, Rug Chapel, Runston Chapel, St Cybi's Well, St David's Bishop's Palace, St Dogmael's Abbey, St Non's Chapel, St Winifred's Chapel, Strata Florida Abbey, Tintern Abbey and Valle Crucis Abbey.

PREAMBLE - THE AGE OF THE SAINTS and THE DARK AGES

'You never enjoy the world aright, till the sea itself floweth in your veins, till you are clothed with the heavens, and crowned with the stars: and perceive yourself to be the sole heir of the whole world, and more than so, because men are in it who are every one sole heirs as well as you. Till you can sing and rejoice and delight in God, as misers do in gold, and kings in sceptres, you never enjoy the world.'
Thomas Traherne (1637-1674) 'Centuries of Meditations'

The 5th to 7th centuries in Welsh history parallel 'The Dark Ages' of English records. It was a time when Romanised Wales held the torch of Christianity alight, when it had been extinguished in all of Europe except for a few remote Irish islands. To the early Welsh and Irish saints of this period, the Christian Church owes an unacknowledged debt – without them the history of Christianity in Europe would have been very different.

There is a real purpose to this book and calendar. In my researches for 'The A-Z of Wales and the Welsh' I came to realise that the Welsh have a 'scarred' national psyche. Its people have 'kept their heads down' for hundreds of years, so as not to antagonise a hugely more powerful neighbour. The Welsh language only held out because of a stubborn refusal to accept change that was dictated by military and political force. It was the same with religion. And Welsh Christianity was of the purest kind. Not that of military power, and payment towards salvation, but of the earlier type, closer to Christ's teachings. It was also a joyous occasion, with married priests mixing with their peers, celebrating their local saint in each village like the Breton 'pardons' and 'fest noz' events of today. What the Wales Tourist Board has realised is that people can be attracted to Wales by its culture, by its people and their traditions. If we can reawaken the feast days of the saints, and the week-long events all over Wales, just as Iolo Morganwg reawakened the eisteddfodau, prosperity and fellowship can follow, with a knowledge and consequent celebration of the past.

K. R. Dark has explained the fifth and sixth century tribal structures in Wales, after the Romans left. The king of a province like Dyfed, Gwynedd or Glamorgan was the overlord over smaller kingdoms whose kings (rhi) each ruled over a lesser territory (tud). From this we have the family of Henry VII, Elizabeth I and Henry VIII (Tudor comes from tud+rhi). This hierarchy of King, under-king and nobles was paralleled by the equivalent senior bishop, bishop and clergymen (often the sons of nobility). Baring-Gould believed that the many children of noble houses who moved into a Christian life were possibly the illegitimate offspring of the nobility. In the course of researching this book, the author found links between over one hundred related saints from the noble houses of South Wales, Cornwall and Brittany and the fabled King Arthur. It is believed that further work along these lines will give concrete substance to the existing evidence that Arthur was Arthmael ap Meurig ap Tewdrig, from south-east Wales.

A major problem was uncovered in assigning churches to the early Welsh saints, as many were renamed as part of the territorial take-over by the Normans and Angevins, leading to the destruction and removal of church records and land deeds. Other churches, of course, have simply disappeared. George Owen ('The Description of Pembrokeshire') named the following churches in Cemais, vanished even before Elizabethan times:

Place	Church
Nevern	Capel St. Fraid
	Capel Gwenfron
	Capel Gwendydd
	Capel Reall
	Capel Padric
Mynachlog Ddu	Capel Cavey
	Capel St. Silin
Newport	Capel Dewi
	Capel Curig
St. Dogmaels	Capel Carannog
	Capel Degwel
Morvil	Capel Brynach
Llanychllwydog	Capel Llanmerchan
Bridell	Capel Mewgan
Capel Wrw	Eglwys Wrw
Henry's Moat	Capel Brynach

However, Wales still has over 800 known saints of Welsh origin, and about 600 associated feast days. We can link churches by saints, for instance Ffagan was one of the earliest saints, commemorated at St Fagans, where the remnants of his church lie in the castle grounds, and at Llanmaes (formerly called Llanffagan Fach) near Llanilltud Fawr. There could be an annual sponsored walk between these sites, on his Saint's Day. He could be commemorated with a Fair, with the local cubs/guides/scouts, schools, Women's Institute, Rotary Club/Round Table, farmers' clubs, pubs, CAMRA, council, newspaper, churches, hotels, businesses, choirs, theatre groups, sports clubs and the like becoming involved.

Every week in Wales there could be fairs and events celebrating the local saints – their traditions would be remembered, trade would increase – there would be something to DO in each part of Wales throughout the year, both for locals and tourists. Wales is too wet and unpredictable to attract tourists without a thriving culture. If Cowbridge sees Llanilltud Fawr succeeding, it will follow its lead, so the whole ancient system becomes self-reinforcing. NO other country, except parts of Ireland and Brittany, has this feast tradition on such a local scale – people will learn about their locality and take pride in its history, resisting the Anglicisation of Wales. Wales can only attract people with its culture and history – a beautiful landscape is not enough. Its people have to KNOW about Wales, and transmit that feeling of 'hwyl' and 'hiraeth' to its visitors.

If any readers can add more details of saints in other parts of Wales, the author would be most grateful, and contributions mentioned in further editions of this book. It is important to pull together all the pieces of local knowledge in Wales to get a better picture of The Age of the Saints. Each edition of this book will add pieces of local knowledge. I have tried to add in all the holy wells and traditions, the standing stones, the feast-dates of this time when Wales held on to Christianity when it was extinguished everywhere else. Almost 2000 years of continuous Christian devotion is not paralleled anywhere else in the world, and the fact that Wales held on to a 'Pelagian' version of humanity and equality, rather than the formalistic creed imposed by Rome shows the basic quality of its people.

We must remember in this context the words of the superb poet Gwenallt (David James Jones), in his St David's Day broadcast of 1953:
'Wales is a Christian inheritance. In her lie the dust of St David and the early saints, the dust of monks and the abbots of the Middle Ages . . . of Ann Griffiths and Pantycelyn and Emrys ap Iwan. Our duty is to hand down to our children the inheritance which we have been given, a heritage of preaching the Gospel of the Son of God, of praying and taking action, and of making Wales a society based on Christian moral principles.'

Dean Inge wrote that *'The nations which have put mankind and posterity most in their debt have been small states - Israel, Athens, Florence, Elizabethan England.'* It is hoped that after reading this book, Wales' contribution could also be noted.

Any help to expand our knowledge of these times would be appreciated and attributed. Please contact the author at Porth Glyndŵr, Higher End, St Tathan, Vale of Glamorgan, CF62 4LW or at breverton@lineone.net or t.breverton@uwic.ac.uk

Chapter 1

INTRODUCTION

'Government, even in its best state, is but a necessary evil; in its worst state, an intolerable one.
Government, like dress, is the badge of lost innocence; the palaces of kings are built upon the ruins of the bowers of paradise.'
Tom Paine, 'Common Sense', 1776

What is the reason for a book on the early Welsh saints? Is it to re-inspire a love of an unknown history, of a Christianity that did not rely upon power structures and bureaucracy? To save what is left of the Welsh culture? To make Welsh people proud of holding the flame of Christianity aloft when it had died in Rome and all across Europe? To reinstate the marvellous local feast days, the great single holiday of the Welshman's year? To rewrite British history to show that it did not start with the Anglo-Saxon invasion of these islands? To make people freshly aware of our debt to the past, the meaning of the springs and humps in the ground soon to be swallowed up by car-parks and concrete? To undo the ravages of the Nonconformist revival and the Calvinist ideology of enjoyment equalling sin? To revive a sense of local community? To kick-start a sense of community centred around churches? To show to the world that Wales has been incredibly important in past times? To stimulate research and to help the resurgence of a culture that had held on by the skin of its teeth? To stop 'authorities' vandalising what is left of one of the wonders of Western history? To let the world know that Wales has a past unparalleled in civilised society in its attitudes towards women, socialism and pacifism? To any Welshman or Welshwoman who has seen Wales fall gently into a third-class economy in a second-class nation over the last few decades, it is for all of these reasons.

The stimulus came from my work on *'The A-Z of Wales and the Welsh'*, and the feeling that Wales was not being marketed properly to its own people, let alone potential tourists – there is more to see and do here than anyone realises. The scarred Welsh psyche, of turning the other cheek for centuries, while obstinately refusing to change into the patterns and ways of our conquerors, means that the Welsh do not trumpet their nation and achievements, unlike the Irish, Scots, English, French, Americans and most other nations. This is changing, perhaps for the better, in order that we may protect our past and rewrite the reality of British history as it was, before it was distorted by Hanoverian apologists. It is instructive to remember that the Welsh and Cornish are the original Britons of these British Isles, the descendants of the Brythonic Celts who gave us the British, now Welsh, language.

From the Celtic bardic tradition, the ancient Welsh text of *'The Eight Materials of Man'* reads:

'From the earth, the flesh;
From the water, the blood;
From the air, the breath;
From the hardness, the bones;
From the salt, the feeling;

Introduction

From the sun, that is, fire, his motion;
From the truth, his understanding;
From the Holy Ghost, that is, God,
His soul or life.'

To know the names of rivers, hills, lakes, fields, churches, stones and places in Wales, is to know its history – so much written evidence was destroyed in wars, or burned by Norman barons to give claim to their land-rights. Dorian Llywelyn points to the uniqueness of the spirituality of the Welsh people – they are *'members of a nation which has often felt itself to be simultaneously religiously distinguished and politically besieged.* There is *'a sense of nationhood **and** of belonging to the land. A Welsh sense of holy place is inseparable from a sense of belonging to a specific community of people.'* Quite apart from the sense of *'hiraeth'*, the longing for home whereby Welsh men and women tend to return like salmon to their *'bro'* or neighbourhood of birth to end their days, there is a feeling for the land and its features quite unlike many other Western cultures.

This is why the author is committed to discovering the old names of places, fields and hills. Again from Dorian Williams: *'The Celtic gods of territory were often of topographical origin: woods, rivers, mountains, springs. However, it is worth noting that these are **specific** places of holiness, each with their own numinous presence. The Christianization of such individual places was facilitated by the Christian cult of the saints: many Christian wells, for example, are of pre-Christian origin, a phenomenon which shows the anthropological roots of the Catholic-local traditions of Welsh spirituality. Such a sense of locative holiness is connected to the religious psychology in which the whole territory of a tribe is considered as a sacred place:*

View of River Cleddau from Haverfordwest Priory.   CADW: Welsh Historic Monuments. Crown Copyright.

as we have seen, national territory tends inexorably to assume a mantle of separateness and holiness.'

Miranda Green, in her 'Dictionary of Celtic Myth and Legend', points out that: *'The Celts were a very religious people. This variety and complexity is due largely to the essential animism upon which Celtic religion is based. Everything in the natural world was numinous, containing its own spirit. Thus the gods were everywhere. The topographical nature of some divine spirits is shown by the occurrence of a god whose name ties him to a particular sacred place. Of the more than 400 Celtic god-names known through inscriptions, 300 are recorded only once. Places of worship were often not built shrines, but loci consecrati or natural sacred places.'*

Place-names and saints' names intermingle across the Welsh landscape, but have often been replaced with the Anglicisation of Welsh place-names in Pembroke, Flint, Glamorgan and Gwent, the first territories of modern Wales to bear the brunt of the Norman oppression. What is not so well-known is the later re-dedication of ancient churches, which were founded when England was pagan, to different saints favoured by the Normans, for example:

Place	County	Dedication	Originally
St David's Cathedral	Pembroke	Andrew and David	David
St Dogmael's	Pembroke	Thomas	Dogwel
Stackpool Elider	Pembroke	St John the Baptist	Elider
Kilpeck	Hereford	Mary and David	David
Winforton	Hereford	Michael	Cynidr
Llanveuno	Hereford	Peter	Beuno
Llansilloe	Hereford	Peter	Tyssilio
Llangathen	Carmarthen	Michael and All Saints	Cathen
Llantoni	Monmouth	John the Baptist	David
Dyngestow	Monmouth	Mary	Dingad
Llangynyw	Monmouth	David	Cynyw
Llanegryn	Monmouth	Mary	Egryn
Gileston	Glamorgan	Giles	Mabon
Llanmaes	Glamorgan	Cadoc	Fagan
Llanfabon	Glamorgan	Constantine	Mabon
Marcross	Glamorgan	Holy Trinity	Samson
Llanbleddian	Glamorgan	John the Baptist	Bleiddian
St Donat's	Glamorgan	Donatus	Gwerydd
St George's	Glamorgan	George	Ufelwy
Llandaf Cathedral	Glamorgan	Peter and Teilo	Teilo
Northop	Flint	Peter	Eurgain
Holywell	Flint	James	Beuno
Llanegryn	Merioneth	Mary	Egryn

Wales' *'Age of Saints'* is an amazing period of history, dating mainly from the leaving of the legions around 400, as the British Celts slowly lost control of most of England and southern Scotland. Dumnonia (Devon) held out against the Saxons until around 900. The Cornish still spoke Welsh until the 18th century, and Cornwall was not annexed by England until 930. The British of Cumbria (the modern-day Lake District) until recently counted their sheep in a variation of Welsh. Cumbria was annexed to England in 1170. The Britons of Strathclyde

Introduction

('*ystrad*', or '*district*' of the river Clyde) were still counted as '*Wallenses*' or Welsh amongst his subjects by the Scots king David the Lion (1124-1153). William Wallensis, known as '*Braveheart*' was of Welsh stock. Not until the thirteenth century did the British language be replaced in the Glasgow bishopric of Cumbria by the dialect of Anglo-Saxon now known as 'lallans' or Lowland Scottish. Celtic Brittany was independent of France until the fifteenth century, had been evangelised by Welsh saints and settlers, and Welsh speakers can still be understood there. Equally, Bretons came and established dynasties of saints in Wales and helped Arthur in his struggles. Thus there are links with this book of Welsh saints with Breton, Irish, Cumbrian, North British and West Country saints. Future research hopefully will also uncover more links with Galicia in North-West Spain, another Celtic refuge and enclave.

The basic nature of Celtic Christianity was very different to the Catholic faith enforced by Augustine under Rome. The Welsh would not change to the '*new religion*'. When Augustine requested in the sixth century that they help with the evangelising of the Saxons, the Welsh and West Country bishops refused. The Saxons and other Germanic tribes were barbarian invaders, and they naturally had no desire to instruct them in the Celtic church, let alone the foreign Roman creed. As the Reverend Rice Rees pointed out in 1836, '*Bede is not explicit as to the reason why the Britons refused to have Augustine for their archbishop, nor does it appear how this point was introduced for their consideration; but the differences in discipline and ritual are proof that they did not acknowledge the jurisdiction of the Pope. No fact is more clearly asserted than that the Britons were not in communion with the Catholic Church, for it is repeated throughout the 'Ecclesiastical History' of Bede, who was himself a Catholic. The Catholics treated the British people as schismatics and heretics, and maintained that the consecration of their bishops was invalid; while the Britons on the other hand regarded the Romish clergy as unclean, and refused to eat or hold intercourse with them until they had first undergone a purification; and it is a singular argument in confirmation of British independence, that whenever terms of reconciliation were offered, the Britons refused them, proving that their separation was the **effect of choice**, and not an involuntary exclusion.*'

The Welsh Church survived right through the leaving of the Romans in 387-410 until Norman and Angevin rule in the 12th century. Like the Welsh Laws of Hywel Dda, it showed a humanity not seen in the rest of Europe. However, the Welsh nation was always defending itself and its values against vastly superior resources, as Taliesin wrote as early as the 6th century in '*The Destiny of the Britons*':

> '*Their Lord they shall praise,*
> *Their language they shall keep,*
> *Their land they shall lose*
> ***Except wild Wales***'

A subtext to this book is the **desperate** need to see churches as the centres of local communities, to find new uses for them, to make them come alive as centres of entertainment and learning. The use of demountable stages could enable schools, music groups, local theatre groups to rehearse and hold concerts. They could be used as local libraries, for farmers' meetings, for youth groups as well as religious services. The more they are used, the more hopeful the future of the church will be. Clerics need to be taught marketing of their churches and people skills, to once more be leaders of local communities. This probably sounds extreme, but a Church of England press officer ordered dioceses not to reveal the true state of church attendance recently (The Sunday Times, July 11, 1999). The article reveals that less than 2% of the population now worships at church each Sunday, and only 1% regularly take communion.

Exeter saw a drop of 36% in attendance between 1996 and 1997, and Ely diocese had a fall of 18%. The overall drop in attendance from 1995 to 1998 has been 20%. Another survey showed that half of the country's churches have no teenagers attending services. *'The same proportion of churches appear to be making no attempt to work with 15-18 year-olds.'* This is a crisis. The Church in Wales is equally suffering (report in The Western Mail, January 13th, 2000), with average weekly attendance of the over-18's dropping from 50,400 in 1996 to 48,500 in 1998. Under-18 attendance dropped from 13,400 to 12,300. The Catholic Church in Wales has an attendance of 48,500, dropping at a rate of 1.5% a year.

The new Archbishop of Wales, Rowan Williams, realises that there is a problem, but does not seem as yet to have a proactive view of solving it: *'Perhaps the important thing isn't the service of this church as an institution, but the teaching of the gospel that is important. If we put the value of the gospel first, then maybe the church will look after itself.'* The author has seen Rowan Williams preaching at St Woollo's Cathedral, and he is an excellent communicator. The problem is that many of his rectors across Wales do not have the same gifts of transmitting information and becoming a real part of the community. The church simply cannot rely upon the 'teaching of the gospel' to survive or prosper. We have seen the rapid decline in the number of Welsh chapels across the land, and churches are constantly being offered for sale. It does not appear that the church knows what to do to make Christianity attractive, and the religion is dying across Britain. New appointees to the top of the church hierarchies in Britain are now saying it is the quality of those attending church that matters, not the quantity. This is a sad dereliction of duty. In business, when a firm loses market share, it never retrieves it. The same will be true of the Christian religion, without a radical rethinking of its purpose and function in the 21st century. Unless churches become alive and used daily in their communities, for community purposes, church leaders are proposing the death of religion. All things have a life cycle, from philosophies, to empires, to hula-hoops. The church has to refresh what it is offering, to extend the life-cycle of the Christian religion by working to retrieve the heart of local communities. Hopefully, those clerics reading this book will see a way to reinvolve the church in local life, its culture and its heritage.

A final note is that this book is written, not as an academic exercise, trying to untangle cobwebs and skeins of the history of the last two millennia, but as a **celebration of Wales**. As noted elsewhere, a great mass of Welsh historical data has been dispersed, deliberately destroyed or lost. The very strength of oral tradition since Celtic times has helped to reconstruct the past, as has the absolutely remarkable survival of the Welsh language – it is difficult to think of a parallel anywhere in the world, which says much for the nature of the Welsh people. My thoughts when writing this book were that it must be *interesting* above all else – it has to stimulate people to put right my mistakes, to add to our body of knowledge about Wales as a whole. The story about a Glamorgan Militiaman of the 18th century receiving 1000 lashes, the poets, battles and injustices mentioned all mesh together to give a feeling of Wales through the ages in this book of saints.

As mentioned, the genesis of this book was my work upon *'The A-Z of Wales and the Welsh'*. With this work there was a realisation of the real meaning of *'hiraeth'* . . . why Welsh folk return home like salmon to end their lives. There is something we can almost touch, in our unbroken history of over 1500 years of Christian Democratic Socialism of the most pacifist nature. I am not a historian and for this I do not apologise. My background includes periods of management consultancy, as marketing director of a listed company, in charge of strategic planning for a multinational and as project manager on the largest construction project in the world. Non-scientific academics are trained not to explore outside their subject, but to

Introduction

specialise in a secret area of little interest to mankind as a whole. It is not their fault, but that of the educational system (and its meagre rewards) in which they find themselves. From this book it is hoped that one can see the *'big picture'* of what Wales is, what it means to be Welsh, and how the local community, centred on the church, can keep us different from a world that is evolving into one country controlled by just a few companies. Our main problem as a nation is that true Welshmen do not seek power, as we know from our history that those who want power should on no account receive it.

This is not a 'dry', academic tome, but an attempt to bring to light Wales' heritage. If there are insightful anecdotes about an area, they are included. If a saint is associated with Arthur, it is mentioned. Famous people from the saints' 'llannau' are included. Some of the answers to the following questions may be found in the following pages:

Did the 'Virgin Queen', Elizabeth I, have a secret child? (see Collen);
Why does Glasgow's city crest feature a fish with a ring? (see Kentigern and Rhydderch);
Who was King Arthur? (see Arthur and Armel);
Was Elvis Presley of Welsh origin? (see Ailbe and Addenda);
What is the link between Wales and the first house used for Christian worship in Rome? (see Claudia, Bran and Eurgain);
Did St Paul preach in London? (see Paul);
When was the first Harvest Festival? (see Mwynwen);
Where is the oldest unbroken Christian tradition in the world? (see Bran);
Who was the Patron Saint of travellers before Christopher? (see Elen);
Why was the carol 'The Twelve Days of Christmas' important for Catholics? (see Carols);
Where is the stone upon which Arthur executed Hywel? (see Hywel);
Who was Sir Gawain? (see Govan);
Which Christianity stayed unaltered from the leaving of the Roman legions around 400 until the 12th century? (see Elfod, Celtic Christianity);
What is a Kemble Pipe? (see Kemble);
Is the Holy Grail in Wales? (see Holy Grail);
Where is the original Avalon? (see Enlli);
Who is the Welsh Valentine? (see Dwynwen);
Where was the origin of 12-man juries? (see Arthur);
Who was the Welsh saint associated with rain 500 years before Swithun? (see Cewydd);
Which British King was famously pardoned by Emperor Claudius after being led in triumph through Rome? (see Caractacus);
What was the origin of the Catherine Wheel firework? (see Catherine);
Where is the only coffin-shrine in the British Isles? (see Melangell);
Who sat in front of the oncoming tide 500 years before the Danish St Canute, and floated? (see Maelgwn);
Which are the four oldest cathedrals in the British Isles? (see Cathedrals);
Where do the words 'mum and 'dad' come from? (see Mutations in Appendix);
Who was *'the first martyr of the Welsh working-class'* (see Penderyn);
Where was the first carol service held? (see Carols);
What is the link between the Pelagian heresy and Wales? (see Bangor-is-Coed and Pelagius);
Where is Europe's largest agricultural show, and the world's largest livestock exhibition hall? (see Elwedd);
Who was the 'Fisher-King' of legend? (see Bran);
From where did the tales of 'Tristan and Isolde', 'The Black Knight' and the 'Quest for the Holy Grail' come? (see Bran);

The Book of Welsh Saints

Where is *'the cradle of the Western Church'*? (see Claudia);
Why has Cardiff's National Museum one of the finest collections of Impressionist Art in the world? (see Cynon);
Who was the first British historian? (see Gildas);
How did Holywell contribute to the end of the Stuart Dynasty? (see Gwenfrewi);
Who, or what, was the original 'Black Jack'? (see Michael, Mihangel);
Why did the Venerable Bede celebrate the slaying of Welsh monks by pagans? (see Bangor-is-Coed and Celtic Christianity);
Where could be the oldest university in the world? (see Illtud);
Who wrote in the 6th century, of arrogant men *'death has entered through the windows of their pride'* (see Gildas);
Where is a mediaeval pilgrimage shrine with unbroken worship for 1300 years, the best-preserved centre in Britain? (see Gwenfrewi);
Why is the start of our financial year April 5? (see New Year's Eve);
Where is the oldest church in Britain? (see Ilid);
Was St Patrick Welsh? (see Padrig);
Where is the largest glass structure in Europe? (see Arthne);
What is the link between the mediaeval lovers Abelard and Heloise, and Wales? (see Gildas);
Why was the Scottish Assembly given more power than that of Wales? (see Appendix H);
Where can one see the first written Welsh? (see Teilo and Chad);
Which horse won Wales' principal race, then led the charges at the battles of Inkerman, the Alma and Balaclava, and survived? (see Gwladys);
Where is *'a garden lost in time'*? (see Cathan)
Why should boys born on December 5 be christened Huw William? (see Justinian);
Where are the oldest totally concrete houses in the world? (see Cynon);
Why did MP's in the House of Commons laugh at The Lord's Prayer? (see Mabon);
Which is the oldest national flag in the world? (see Cadwaladr);
Where was Britain's most authenticated UFO landing in 1974? (see Derfel);
Do we know where Arthur is buried? (see Arthur and Armel);
Where can you see a six-man treadmill? (see William Davies);
Was America named after a Welshman? (see Llan);
Where was the 'greatest relic in Britain'? (see Celtic Crosses);
Was St Timothy half-British? (see Claudia and Timothy);
Why is St Alban's Day important in Welsh history? (see Alban);
Was Oliver Cromwell Welsh? (see Isan);
Which Welshman accused the Pope of being the Antichrist, condemned the lechery of priests and stated at his 1391 trial that it was God's plan, with Welsh assistance, to overthrow the Roman church? (see Walter Brut);
Why was the Bible Society formed? (see Melangell);
Which carol was a coded rallying-cry for Bonnie Prince Charlie? (see Carols);
Where in Wales was St Buttock's Chapel? (see Budoc);
Where is one of the oldest living garden features in Europe? (see Cathan);
Which Welsh castle has accommodated the Kennedys, Churchills, Mountbattens, Lloyd-Georges, Clark Gable, Charlie Chaplin, Maurice Chevalier, Ivor Novello, George Bernard Shaw and Bob Hope?
Why has a 7th century Welsh saint been adopted as the patron saint of computer technicians? (see Beuno);
Why should the (Welsh) National Assembly be known as the British Assembly? (see The British Church);
Who made the first malt liquor in the 3rd century? (see Ceraint);

Introduction

Did Henry VIII have a son? (see Ismael);
Why should the Millennium be celebrated in March, April or May in 2006 or 2007? (see Christmas);
Was the first Pope of Rome half-British? (see Claudia);
How many Welsh saints are associated with Arthur? (see Arthur);
Where did Goering stay with Winston Churchill? (see Collen);
Which church did John Wesley call the most beautiful in Wales? (see Illtud);
Why was St Clement's Day chosen as 'No Alcohol Day? (see Clement);
Did Constantine the Great, who gave Christians the right of public worship in 312, have a Welsh mother? (see Constantine);
Which European nation had the first known uniform in battle? (see Dewi Sant);
Who invented the = and + signs, and a method of calculating square roots? (see Julian);
Where in the world was first seen the red flag of revolution? (see Lewis);
Why is the full moon called *'the sun of Llanfabon?'* (see Mabon);
Who was the *'father of modern geography'*? (see Marchell);
What is the link between Wagner, his opera Parsifal, and Wales? (see The Holy Grail);
Croeso Haf (Summer's Welcome) is which flower? (see Mary);
Why were rood screens destroyed? (see Meddwid);
What was the origin of the three balls of a pawnbroker? (see Nicholas);
Where was the ancient world's most advanced gold-mining operation? (see Romans);
Which country had the most places of Christian worship per head of the population? (see Nonconformist Revival);
Who had the first articulated artificial limb? (see Tysilio);
Where was the real Camelot? (see Tathan);
When and where is it still legal for an Englishman to kill a Welshman? (see Appendix E);
Was the British Church the first Christian Church in the world, and accepted as thus by Rome? (see Paul and Romans);
Why did the power of 2000 million atomic bombs lead to the making of modern England? (see The Yellow Plague);
Which holy well cures baldness? (see Samson);
What is the relationship between 'The Hounds of the Baskervilles' and 'The Wars of the Roses' (see Andras);
Where is there a 6th century fortified palace in a lake? (see Brychan);
Which holy well cured hangovers? (see Baruc);

There is an opportunity here, as shown in the above questions, to make history relevant, exciting and above all, interesting for the present and future generations. Also, with early retirement, there is the chance to expand upon our knowledge of the past. We all know that the Women's Institute is only open to women, and serves a useful socialising function, but there is nothing equivalent and purposive for men. There are hundreds of undiscovered and lost Celtic stones and crosses across Wales. There are thousands of memories and traditions that need recording. The author has just finished, in spare time, a history of St Tathan and the surrounding villages, and this should be carried out for all parishes across Wales, not by individuals but by teams of people from all walks of life, so we can know about the botany, flora and fauna, saints, castles, mediaeval farmhouses etc., etc. in order to protect what is valuable. Retired men could not only form village/town associations but also start a register of existing and lost Celtic stones in Wales, to be co-ordinated by a university or The Western Mail. The same activity needs to be carried out with holy and mediaeval wells.

Chapter 2

BACKGROUND to 'THE AGE OF THE SAINTS'

If ever you have look'd on better days,
If ever been where bells have knoll'd to church,
If ever sat at any good man's feast,
If ever from your eyelids wip'd a tear,
And know what 'tis to pity, and be pitied,
Let gentleness my strong enforcement be.'
William Shakespeare, 'As You Like It'.

Why has Wales so many saints, who were honoured for hundreds of years? Part of the answer lies in the genealogy – many were descended from Macsen Wledig (Magnus Maximus) and Elen, or even the semi-legendary 'old' King Coel. We must look at what the history books of England call the 'Dark Ages' before the Anglo-Saxons arrived. These 'Wasted Years' have always been known to the Welsh as 'The Age of the Saints'. In fact the history of the British Isles was rewritten by Bishop Stubbs in the 19th century to start with the invading Germanic tribes, to justify the succession of the minor German princelings who formed the Hanoverian dynasty. It is a real tragedy that historians gain knowledge by accretion rather than by original research. Received wisdom lies on top of layers of received wisdom, so that the fossils of truth are embedded out of sight. History can teach us many lessons, but unfortunately historians over the last two hundred years have made it into a construct of obscurantism.

From 43-410, Britain was effectively an outer colony of the Roman Empire, useful for gold, silver, tin and a supply of fighting men and slaves. In 383, Clemens Maximus was proclaimed emperor by his legions in Britain. Two of his three legions were centred on Wales, and would have contained many Welsh conscripts and volunteers. He assumed the title of Magnus, and as Magnus Maximus (known to the Welsh as Macsen Wledig, and remembered in the Mabinogion) set off to invade Europe. He was accompanied by his Welsh wife Elen (Helen) daughter of Eudaf.

He moved towards Paris, and the Emperor Gratian retreated to Lyon, where he was assassinated. Magnus Maximus was now in control of Gaul, with Theodosius ruling the Eastern Empire of Rome. However, Magnus now attacked Italy, was slain after the defeat at Aquileia in 388, and Elen returned to Wales. Gildas reported grimly *'Britain is robbed of all her armed soldiery, her military supplies, her rulers, cruel though they were, and of her vigorous youth, who followed the footsteps of the aforementioned tyrant, and never returned.'* Most of the legionaries were British, and the survivors seemed to have gone to Brittany under Elen's eldest son Cynan Meiriadog, or to Spain with Gerontius (Geraint).

Stilicho restored the situation in Britain after Magnus Maximus' departure, against waves of invading Picts, Scots, Irish and Scandinavian-Germanic forces. However, in 401, most Roman troops were withdrawn. Constantine III was declared emperor in Britain and in 406-407 took the remaining Romano-British forces to halt a threatened invasion by the Vandals, Swabians and Alans. His armies then moved on to Spain.

The Comes Britannorum had just a small force remaining to protect Britain, but there was a massive Saxon attack in 410. Gildas tells us that in 446 the situation was so desperate that a letter was sent to the Consul Aetius at Rome, seeking help. Gildas was born in 497, the year that Emrys Wledig, Ambrosius Aurelianus, beat the Saxons back at Mount Badon. In 'The Ruin of Britain' Gildas describes the times he grew up in '. . . *all the chief cities were razed . . . all the inhabitants, prelates, priests and people were cut down, as the swords flashed around them, and the fires burned . . . there was no burial, except in the ruined buildings . . . The wretched survivors were trapped in the mountains and slaughtered . . . Others, crushed by starvation, surrendered to the enemy. Those who were not killed at once, were enslaved . . . Some emigrated overseas (to Brittany) . . . Others resisted on their own land, though in constant fear.*'

539 saw Arthur's final British battle at Camlan. After many years of fighting the Saxons, Irish and possibly the Vandals, he may have crossed to Brittany to fight there. The year 577 saw the British kings Ithael (who may have been Arthur's nephew) and Telpald losing in battle to the Gewissae (West Saxons) at Deorham near Bath, cutting off Wales from its fellow-Britons in Dumnonia for ever. In 597, St Augustine came to try and reconcile the Celtic and Catholic Christians but failed. In 607, an attempt was made to cut Wales off from the northern British of Cumbria and Strathclyde by the Angles at Bangor-is-Coed, the great monastery of Dunawd at Bangor-on-Dee, near Chester. The Welsh were led by Brochwel (the 'Fanged'), Selyf Sarfgaddau of Powys (the 'Slayer of Serpents'), prince Bledrws of Cornwall, king Meredydd of Dyfed and king Cadfan ab Iago of Gwynedd. Brochwel escaped with his life, but hundreds of monks were slaughtered by the pagans, much to the glee of the Venerable Bede, who hated the British church and its antecedence in the religious life of Britain. The Anglo-Saxons went on to conquer Cumbria and Cornwall, leaving Wales to fend for itself at the last outpost of the British people and its independence.

664 saw the Synod of Whitby, notable for the documented lies told by Abbot Wilfred of Ripon. Abbot Colman of Holy Island (Lindisfarne) represented the Celtic Christians against the Anglo-Saxons, with Bishop Cedd of Essex acting as translator. Colman justified the Celtic Church calendar by its being handed down to him in a direct line from St John the Evangelist, who devised it. Wilfred responded that he had travelled all over the Holy Roman Empire, and that no-one used the date for Easter that the Celtic Church did. In reality, Wilfred had only ever been to Rome, and he called the Britons and Picts *'accomplices in obstinacy'* for their stand against *'the rest of the universe.'* Celtic churchmen who refused to alter their beliefs were expelled from Anglo-Saxon possessions. Colman left Lindisfarne, with the bones of St Aidan and thirty monks, and settled in Scotland. In 670 the Synod of Autun in France repeated the process, and the Celtic Church was suppressed there. It survived in Brittany until 818 when the region was conquered by Louis the Pious. The Celtic Church clung on in remote areas of Cornwall until the 12th century, and was finally exterminated in Scotland in the 14th century.

The 'Age of the Saints' in Wales, Cornwall, Cumbria/Strathclyde and Brittany dated from the leaving of the Romans around 400 until the 8th century. During this time, these regions were constantly on the defensive against invading hordes of pagans but the Christian tradition, in the truest sense, remained inviolate.

It is extremely difficult to pinpoint the ages of the secular leaders of this time, whose lives were inextricably linked with religious leaders. The noble houses usually supplied the leaders of the 'clas' system of the Celtic Church. The family or tribe of an area would claim the inheritance of a monastery. The abbot could be married, and his son or nephew would inherit the position. The following is an attempt to put these times into date order, but there will be mistakes, as even the earliest sources disagree. Nennius places Vortimer's death at 457 at the battle of Crayford, and the reign of Vortigern beginning in 425. All the author is trying to do here is to paint an overall picture of what was happening in these decades.

High King of the Britons - Pendragon or Gwledig	Reign	Born	Died	Age	Notes
Vortigern, Gwrtheyrn, Catel	c.440 - c.456	c.410	c.474	c.64	His son Categrin was King of Powys from c.456 – 458
Vortimer, Gwrthefyr, regarded as a saint in Wales	c. 456 - c.470	c.430	c.470	40	Son of Vortigern, possibly the same person as Riothamus
Vortigern – second rule	c.470 – c.472	As above			His son Pascent, Pasgen was King of Builth from 456 and King of Powys from 458
Ambrosius, Emrys	c.472 – c.473	c.417	c.473	56	Fought for kingship against Vortigern, possibly killed by Pascent
Ambrosius Aurelianus, Emrys Wledig	c.475 – c.500	c.445	c.500	55	Son of Ambrosius, and Dux Bellorum
Arthur, Arthmael, Arthwys*	c.500 – c.539	c. 475	c.539 - but could be 562/ 575	64	Led British forces at Badon, possibly the same person as St Armel. Maelgwn may have succeeded as Gwledig or Pendragon

Tewdrig ap Teithfallt ap Ninio was one of *'the three canonised kings'* of the early triads, with Cadwaladr and Gwrthefyr (Vortimer). St. Tewdrig had given over his kingdom of Glamorgan and Gwent to his son Meurig before his martyrdom in 470 near Tintern. (One theory is that Tewdrig was Ambrosius, and his son Meurig was the brother of Ambrosius Aurelianus). Meurig ap Tewdrig has been placed as Uther Pendragon, and the father of Arthur, and seems to have had Dumnonia (Devon, Somerset and Cornwall) as a vassal princedom, as Geraint ab Erbin died fighting for Arthur at Llongborth. Equally, Maelgwn Gwynedd in North Wales seems to have had Strathclyde as a vassal kingdom, under Rhydderch Hael. The final Arthurian battle of Camlan was agreed to be between British armies, and it seems that it could have been a power struggle between Maelgwn and Arthur. There seem to have been two 'overlapping' chiefs called Arthur. We have a date for Arthur's coronation of 517.

If Tewdrig died in 470, when Meurig had already taken over the crown, then perhaps Meurig had died or retired (to Pentre Meurig?) by 517, putting him at 67-72 years of age at this time (assuming he was 25-30 years old in 470.) Arthur was said to be only 15 on his coronation. We then have tentative dates of Tewdrig c.400-c.470 (he was said to be a very old man when he was martyred). Meurig ap Tewdrig could have been born c.440-445, and possibly died in 517 or handed over to his teenage son Arthur. Arthur was born in 502, was crowned (by Dyfrig?) in 517, and fought at Camlan in 539. He was a contemporary of Maelgwn Gwynedd, as we know, who lived from c.505-547. This scenario, placing the alleged 12 battles of Arthur in the time of Emrys Wledig, will allow Arthur to recover from his wounds and go to Brittany as 'Armel', while Maelgwn became 'Wledig' or 'High King' for a period before his death in 547. (Pendragon seems more linked to a military leader of the British, and may be co-terminous with Gwledig, or High-King, for many rulers when their reigns were spent in combat).

*The chronologies of Arthur and Maelgwn are still ambiguous and will be addressed in a future book upon Arthur and Wales. There was another plague in 562 which may have killed Maelgwn, and the Welsh Annals are wrongly dated, possibly in error by 33 years. Maelgwn may have still been alive at the battle of Arderydd in 573, and from the Book of Llandaf, Arthur was still alive in 575.

King of Glamorgan & Gwent	Reign	Born	Died	Age	Notes
Ninio					
Teithfallt			466?		
Tewdrig, Theodosius	440-470?	400?	470	70	Pendragon?
Meurig	470-517	440	517+	67+	Pendragon?
Arthwys, Arthur	517-539	502	539, or 562/575?	If he died at Camlan, 37	Pendragon? Went to Brittany after Camlan?

The early genealogies of the other kingdoms of Wales seem to be:

King of Powys	Reign	Born	Died	Age	Notes
Cyngen	c.500 – c.520	480	520	40	Grandson of Pascent ap Vortigern
Brochfael	c.520 – c.540	500	540	40	Son of Cyngen
Cynan Garwyn	c.540 – c.575	520	575	55	Son of Brochfael
Selyf ('the serpent of battle')	c.575 – c.610	555	610	55	Son of Cynan, killed at Chester

King of Dyfed	Reign	Born	Died	Age	Notes
Agricola	c.490 – c.520	c.470	c.520	50	
Vortipor	c.520 – c.545	c.490	c.545	55	Son of Agricola, his gravestone was found in Dyfed
Cincar	c.545 – c.565	c.515	c.565	50	Son of Vortipor
Pedr	c.565 – c.590	c.545	c.590	45	Son of Cincar
Arthur	c.590 – c.615	c.570	c.615	45	Son of Pedr, and named after Arthur

King of Gwynedd	Reign	Born	Died	Age	Notes
Cunedda					From the North of England, drove the Irish out of much of North Wales with his sons
Einion Yrth					Son of Cunedda
Cadwallon Lawhir					Son of Einion, took Anglesey from the Irish
Maelgwn Gwynedd	c.530 – c.547	c.505	c.547 of Yellow Plague (or later in 573 after becoming Pendragon?)	42 68	Son of Cadwallon, married sister of Brochfael of Powys
Brudei		c.535	c.584	49	Son of Maelgwn, King of Pictland
Rhun, Rhain	c.547 – c.570	c.525	c.570	45	Son of Maelgwn
Beli	c.570 – c.598	c.545	c.598	53	Son of Rhun, possibly killed at Cattraeth
Iacob	c.598 – c.615	c.565	c.615	50	Son of Beli
Cadfan	c.615 – c.625	c.585	c.625	40	Son of Iacob
Cadwallon	c.625 – c.635	c.605	c.635	28	Son of Cadfan, killed Edwin in 633, killed in 635
Cadwaladr			d.664		Son of Cadwallon

Chapter 3

A BRIEF HISTORY OF THE MAJOR WELSH SAINTS

They are not long, the weeping and the laughter,
Love and desire and hate:
I think they have no portion in us after
We pass the gate.

They are not long, the days of wine and roses:
Out of a misty dream
Our path emerges for a while, then closes
Within a dream.
                    Ernest Dowson (1867-1900), 'Vitae Summa Brevis'

The first known Welsh saints, St Julius and St Arvan, were martyred at Caerleon in 305, and three Celtic bishops attended the Synod of Arles in 314 and the Council of Ariminium in 359. Interestingly, of the bishops attending Arles, 11 were from Gaul, 10 from Africa, 7 from Italy and 3 from Britain. These were possibly Eborius of York, Restitutus of London and Adelfius (Elfod) of Caerleon. We can see from these dates that Christianity was thriving in Britain in the years of Roman occupation. Celtic bishops were also probably at the Council of Nicea in 325, and bishops from Britain were signatories at Tours in 461, Vannes in 465, Orleans in 511 and Paris in 555. The Welsh Triads say that Caractacus and his father Bran, after seven years' captivity in Rome, brought the religion to Wales in the 1st century, and there is a tradition that St Paul preached in Celtic Britain. St Clement's Epistle to the Corinthians, written around 95AD, states that Paul had gone to 'the very limit of the West.' It definitely seems that **Christianity reached Wales in the first century**, possibly reinforced later by waves of Christian Gauls escaping the Aurelian persecution of 177.

The teaching of Pelagius became popular in Britain, and St Germanus (St Garmon) travelled from Auxerre in 429 and in 447 to preach against the doctrine. In this second visit Garmon led the Celtic Britons against the invading Picts and Scots, defeating them with the battle cry of 'Alleluia'. Tradition has the battle placed at Maes Garmon near Mold in Flintshire.

Monasticism in Wales dates from at least 420, with the first notable saints being Dyfrig (Dubricius), Illtud and probably Tathan. The first traces of monasticism seem to be at the Roman bases of Caerleon/Caerwent. A second generation, which followed around the middle of the 6th century, were mainly taught by them, for instance Samson, Dewi, Gildas, Teilo, Catwg/Cadog, Cybi and Padarn. Many of these, with the descendants of King Brychan, also founded their own holy settlements, for instance Llandeilo, Llangybi and Llanbadarn (see Llan).

St Dyfrig died on the Isle of Saints, Bardsey Island, and his remains were moved to Llandaf Cathedral in 1120 by Bishop Urban. He seems to have been Bishop of Llandaf, and was succeeded there by St Illtud. St Illtud was possibly a disciple of St Garmon, who became head of the most famous monastery in Britain, Llanilltud Fawr (Llantwit Major), after studying at Llancarfan. His pupils included St Samson of Dol (regarded as the patron saint of Brittany), St Cybi, Gildas the historian, and Maelgwn Gwynedd. Dewi Sant was possibly educated here, also. St Illtud died around 505, and is said by some to be the model for Sir Galahad in Arthurian romance. (Others claim that Cadog was Galahad). The Life of St Samson calls Illtud *'of all the Britons the most learned in the scriptures.'* St. Samson moved on to Caldey (or more probably Barri) Island, and visited Ireland and Cornwall before going to Brittany.

Dewi Sant (Saint David) spent his life reforming the church in Wales, and fighting druidic remnants of belief. He was possibly born on the shore of St Bride's Bay, and the chapel dedicated to his mother St Non is said to mark the place, and dates from this period. Not far away is St David's Cathedral, on the spot where Dewi founded a monastery. Like Illtud, he was an ascetic with a strong sense of discipline, and a vegetarian. He was known as *'Dewi Ddyfrwr', 'David the Waterdrinker'*. Over fifty churches are still dedicated to this patron saint of Wales. A casket said to contain his bones, plus those of St. Justinian and St. Caradoc, was discovered more than a century ago in St David's Cathedral, but the bones were carbon-dated at Keble College, Oxford, and are likely to be just those of Caradoc of Llancarfan.

In 519, St David held a meeting in the church at Llanddewi Brefi to denounce the Pelagian Heresy. In this Synod of Brefi, legend says that the ground rose so that he could be heard by the crowds, and the old church stands on a prominent mound. He seems to have died between 588 and 601, and was canonised during the reign of Pope Calixtus II, around 1120. *In 1398 the Archbishop of Canterbury decreed that the Festival of St David be held on March 1st, and the Welsh continued to keep this special saint's day all through the period of the Commonwealth, when saints' days were forbidden.* **March 1st is Wales' national day**, when Welshmen all over the world wear the symbols of leeks and daffodils.

Saint Patrick (Padrig), Ireland's patron saint, was thought to have been born in Carmarthen or Pembrokeshire in 389, and was carried off by Irish raiders in 406, becoming Bishop of Armagh in AD432, consecrated by St Garmon at Auxerre. Recent evidence seems to point to his birth in Banwen, near Swansea. In St. Patrick's 'Confessio' he states he was born at Banaven Taberiar, a small-holding near a Roman fort, which could be Tafarn-y-Banwen, a farm near an old Roman stronghold. This is also on the strategically important Sarn Helen, once the major Roman road through Wales. Local custom says that Patrick came from Banwen, and there are placenames such as 'Hafod Gwyddelig' ('Irish Summerhouse') and a 'Nant Gwyddelig' ('Irish Stream'). George Brinley Evans also points to the nearby Hirfynydd Stone, the extremely rare early Christian carving of a man in prayer, surrounded by Irish symbolic patterns. (Note that 'Gwyddelig', the Welsh for 'Irish', stems from 'Goidelic'. The Welsh were the Brythonic Celts, and the Irish were the Goidelic Celts). Broadway, Cowbridge, is also strongly associated with the legend of Patrick's youth, as is Llanilltud Fawr.

St Teilo was said to have been a cousin of Dewi Sant, was born at Penally, near Tenby, and was a pupil of Dyfrig. He left his monastery at Llandeilo Fawr to escape the Yellow Plague in 547, and after seven years in Brittany returned to Llandaf, possibly succeeding Illtud. In 577, with his monks he accompanied Iddon ap Ynyr in a decisive battle against the Saxons on the banks of the River Wye. St Teilo's skull was kept by the Melchior family near Llandeilo, who up to the 1930's were offering pilgrims drinks of water from it, to cure their ills.

A Brief History of the Major Welsh Saints

St Cadog, or Catwg, was born about 497, the son of Gwynlliw and Gwladys ferch Brychan. Educated in Caerwent by Tathan, he founded the famous monastery at Llancarfan in 535, where there are still traces of the settlement. He visited Brittany, and his body was buried at Llancarfan. St Deiniol, who founded the monastery at Bangor, the precursor of the cathedral, was taught by St Cadog.

The most important saints in Brittany are the seven Founding Saints - St. Malo, St. Brieuc (Briog), St. Samson of Dol, St. Patern (Padarn, or Paternus), St. Tugdual (Tudwal), St. Pol Aurelian and St. Corentin. Of these only St. Corentin was not Welsh, being a Cornish Briton. Most were taught at Llancarfan and Llanilltud Fawr monasteries.

Mention should be made of the family of Brychan Brycheiniog, a contemporary of Cunedda and Vortigern in The Dark Ages. From his kingdom of Breconshire, many of his children became saints commemorated across Wales. His male offspring who became saints include Cynog, Clydog and Berwyn. Other sons included Arthen, Gwen, Gerwyn and Pasgen. Cynin Cof fab Tudwal Befr (Cynin, son of Bishop Tudwal) was a grandson of Brychan and a character in the Mabinogion story of Culhwch and Olwen.

Some of Brychan's many putative daughters commemorated as saints are Arianwen, Tudful (martyred at Merthyr Tudful), Tybie (Llandybie), Dwynwen (Llanddwynwen), Hawystl, Mwynen, Cain (Llangain and Llangeinor), Eleri, Ceingar the mother of Saint Cynidr (Llangynidr) and Meleri the grandmother of Dewi Sant. Other daughters included Bechan or Bethan, Ceindrych, Ceinwen, Goleuddydd, Gwen (Gwenllian or Gwenhwyfar, who may have married King Arthur), Gwawr (the mother of the poet-soldier Llywarch Hen) and Tangwystl (Ynystanglws, near Swansea). Brychan's daughter, Saint Gwladys, married Saint Gwynlliw, King of Gwent (after whom St. Woolos Cathedral in Newport is named), and their son was Saint Catwg mentioned above, who established the famous monastery at Llancarfan and churches throughout South Wales, Cornwall and Brittany.

Many churches dedicated to Welsh saints were renamed by Normans in the 11th and 12th centuries, as St John, St Peter, St Michael, St Mary, etc., but many survive, and it is interesting how many have Romano-British names.

Chapter 4

THE REVIVAL OF SAINTS' FEAST DAYS AND FEAST WEEKS

'Away with Systems! Away with a corrupt world! Let us breathe the air of the Enchanted island.
Golden lie the meadows; golden run the streams; red gold is on the pine-stems. The sun is coming down to earth, and walks the fields and the waters. The sun is coming down to earth, and the fields and the waters shout to him golden shouts.'

George Meredith, 'The Ordeal of Richard Feverel', 1959

The purpose of this book is to reinvigorate Welsh culture, and to salvage some memories before it is too late. Sources of information are too disparate for one centre to hold, but it is hoped that future editions of this book will be added to by its readers from their own local and national research. It will be a long-term haul to reinstate saints' days across Wales, but they will add so much to the local community and help Wales with desperately needed income from tourism, that it has to be done. The feast weeks were the focal point of the year for Welsh people – Christmas is a recent American invention, and 'Santa Claus' as we know him is just a hundred years old, if that. No other country save Ireland has the saints of Wales, Cornwall and Brittany – real people, unlike St George of England – real men and women who shaped the face of Wales and whose names are still remembered fifteen hundred years later. Far too much is made of Christmas, and its proximity to the New Year celebrations means huge expense rather than real enjoyment for many people. On the other hand, saints' days could be real fund-raising affairs for local communities to invest in their towns and villages. Any hope of external monetary funding for Wales will die out with the accession of Eastern European countries into the European Union, so we must work locally to reinvest in our precious communities. The Welsh identity has remained intact for two millennia – this and future generations cannot allow it to wither in the face of Anglicisation, Americanisation and McDonaldisation. The event needs to be secular to succeed, although celebrating our Christian heritage. If the local Chinese or Italian community wishes to contribute a float in a procession, or a special take-away food stall in a fair, it would be brilliant. **The point is that all the community must be involved – all ages, sexes, religions, ethnic origins and political persuasions. Once started, the event would grow and grow, and be figured into the forward planning of the local rugby club, schools, societies and churches.**

For instance, a town such as Barri is lucky to have three major saints associated with it, with Cadoc (Cadoxton), Dyfan (Merthyr Dyfan) and Baruc. Barri Island itself was once named Ynys Peirio, after yet another saint, with its monastery marked upon maps before the great dockyards were constructed. Barri is symptomatic of much of Wales outside of Cardiff, with an air of dereliction, boarded-up shops, and desperately needs to rethink how it can regenerate itself. The huge docks are being redeveloped for mixed housing, which is a start, but many of the town's fine Victorian and Edwardian buildings, like its library and old town hall have been sadly decaying for years. After discussions with the author, the Wales Tourist Board may 'pilot' the idea of feast days with the former great centres of Christianity in Wales, Bangor, St David's, Llanbadarn, St Asaf, Llanilltud Fawr (Lantwit Major), Llandeilo and Llandaf. The following is a template of what institutions can be involved, and what events could take place, in many of the places mentioned in this book. There will need to be a co-ordinator for this long-term work, or co-ordinating committee, who can work closely with the local councils. Successful events held in, say, Barri, can be replicated in Caersws, and the network of events can offer constant tourism and 'day-out' opportunities throughout the darker days of the year.

Any communities interested in starting up feast days should try to list a useful contact, address and telephone number for each of the institutions on the following list. It can be prioritised, amended, added to etc. over a period of years:

CONTACT LISTING

INSTITUTION	NAME/ADDRESS/TEL. NO.	CONTACTED TO DO:
Wales Tourist Board		Publicity
Festivals of Wales		Publicity
County Council		
Local Council		
Local MP's office		
Schools		
Colleges		
Churches and Chapels		
Rotary Club		
Round Table		
Other Clubs and Societies		
Sports Clubs		
Women's Institute		
Women's Register		
Local Shops and Traders		Publicity and sponsorship
Local Companies		Sponsorship
Choirs		
Police		
Pubs		
Restaurants		
CAMRA local branch		
Farmers		Hold farmers' fairs – gaining popularity in the West Country, an opportunity for farmers to sell their fresh produce
Young Farmers		
Museums		Information, exhibitions
Scouts,		
Guides, Cubs, Brownies		
Other Children's associations		
Local Press		

The Book of Welsh Saints

INSTITUTION	NAME/ADDRESS/TEL. NO.	CONTACTED TO DO:
Other press and magazines		
Old people's homes		Ask for memories or memorabilia to be noted of the history and traditions of the village or town
Local dance groups		
Local professions		
Local political parties		
Local history society		
Local libraries		Information, exhibitions
Councils and societies of other villages and towns which share the local saint		Twinning
YMCA/YWCA		

Again, a list can be developed, and added over the years, of festivities to hold. Some saints are celebrated at different times of the year, so there could be spring, summer and winter 'feasts'.

ACTIVITY	THEME	WHERE
Exhibitions	Local saints and traditions	At local libraries, schools, town hall, parish hall
Choirs, Folk Groups, Rock Bands	Competitions, new song-writing	
Dances – traditional, folk and modern		
Concerts – school and other		
Invite local celebrity	To 'kick off' the celebrations	
Plays and re-enactments	Prizes for best play on a local theme, to be premiered by the local dramatic society	
Fireworks/Bonfire	Rotary Club, police and fire service to contribute	Combine with food and music
Flower shows		
Animal shows		
T-shirts/cagoules/fleeces/souvenirs manufactured locally –Celebration ales, bottled 'holy water' from local saints' wells, manufacture of mead, metheglin and local cider and punches	This needs a themed logo of the local saint with the badge for 'SEINTIAU CYMRAEG' – a map of Wales with a white top half, green lower half, and outlined in red	Profits, or % of profits to go to the village fund or local hospital – as agreed by committee
Procession		From the church to the holy well, or along the High Street in traditional dress
Sponsored walk/run	For example, between Llanmaes (Llanffagan Fach) and St Fagans	
Sponsored sports matches	Link these with the saint's theme e.g. give a special St Baruc trophy in Barri to the outstanding team player in any team. Play annually for the Baruc cup.	For example 7's and mini-rugby tournaments in fields adjoining the fair. Special 'saints' ales' to be sold
Boot sales		To adjoin a local fair

ACTIVITY	THEME	WHERE
Celebratory dinner		This can be held in a restaurant, or as part of the 'feast week' on trestles with a hog-roast.
Twinning	Local saints	With other places dedicated to the local saint in Wales, Cornwall and Brittany – sharing information
Agricultural shows	There may be a local one, but try to link it to the saint's theme and extend it in time and scope	
Farmers' Fairs	Sell locally-produced foods and drink - Carmarthen Farmers' Market is on the first Friday of every month	Hopefully to become weekly or monthly events to help farming survive in parts of Wales.
Co-operative cleaning or refurbishment		Local landmarks and beauty spots, park benches
Beer and Wine Festival		To be part of the annual fair
Comedy competition		
Church services and children's Welsh carols	Church to be 'themed' for the week, with flower and other exhibits	
Revival of local customs	e.g. at weddings in Cadoxton, Barry	
Local photography exhibition and photography Research, and Joint Authorship of a book on local traditions and history, to be updated and republished every 3 years with local contributions	e.g. the author is writing a book on five local parishes for the Millennium and inviting readers to submit information and photographs for a second edition	
Mini-Eisteddfod Fancy dress or traditional dress competition etc., etc.		

All these activities can be linked to a 'Made in Wales' theme – with items available from Jeans to Cheeses. There needs to be an approved and recognisable 'national' logo for products made in Wales by Welsh-owned firms, perhaps using the colours of maroon, cream and emerald, more subtle and fashionable shades from the national colours of scarlet, green and white. The St David's Welsh kilt is an example of a home-produced item that captures the essence of Wales. (Contact Welsh Regalia, 02920-228272). From this start the designers are now offering Welsh accessories such as ties and hats, a sporran (sgrepan), the famous Welsh Dragon dresses (as worn by Shirley Bassey at the 1999 Cardiff Bay Assembly concert), and excellent red fleece jackets which are reversible to display the dragon flag. The distinctive Brithwe Dewi Sant plaid is mainly dark green, maroon and cream. Fashion is a labour-intensive industry, and start-ups should be actively encouraged by the WDA.

Carmarthen ham is now being produced which is cured like the famous 'Parma' ham. Wales could produce a cheese like 'Parmigiano Reggiana', the finest Parmesan, which costs so much to buy in Britain. Local dairies are beginning to make Caerffili Cheese in Wales again. What about producing 'ethnic' pasties like Welsh Black Beef, or lamb and laverbread? (To many of us, laverbread is preferable to caviar.) Or selling tins or frozen meals of different recipes for Cawl, and promoting it as a hearty starter, a main course, or a good healthy breakfast for winter mornings? Different county recipes and a speciality hot and spicy cawl of lamb and vegetable can be offered. 'Anglesey Eggs' and 'Glamorgan Sausages' could likewise be targeted at the vegetarian market. Welsh meads and liqueurs can make a comeback. A recent visit to Cardiff's 'Celtic Cauldron' cafe opposite the castle showed how a Welsh menu can be interesting to visitors – 'faggots and peas' is one of the most under-rated dishes in the country and would be appreciated across the continent. All too many of Wales' 'ethnic' offerings are pottery and ironwork – these are not repeat purchases that can stimulate the economy. Welsh natural, organic food rivals that of Ireland.

Recently, the author visited the lovely thatched Bush Inn at St Hilary, near Cowbridge, and bought a pint of 'scrumpy' cider and a bag of crisps. The crisps only cost 30p, cheap for a pub, and were in a smaller packet than normal. However, they tasted 'home-made', the best crisps one could remember tasting. They were made by the Real Crisp Company, a new firm based at Cwmfelinfach in Gwent, and were totally natural, with no e-numbers or artificial flavourings. Hand-cooked, they are darker than the normal crisp product, and 'Real Crisps' can now be bought at Tesco and Asda in Wales. The WDA Food Directorate has helped in this distribution, so that now the company is producing 120,000 bags of crisps a week and employing 13 staff. Make no mistake, these crisps (in several flavours) are better than any others on the UK market. Another company offering natural foods, guaranteed free from all artificial colourings, flavourings and preservatives is Black Mountains Smokery at Crickhowell, offering locally produced hampers, and smoked goose breast, duck breast, smoked Welsh trout fillets, oak roasted salmon, gravadlax, etc. The markets are there for organic produce. There is also a growing niche market for sugar-less sweets and cordials for children.

Local cheese producers have led the way in showing what can be achieved. The author first came across 'Y Fenni' cheese in Leicester's Waitrose supermarket. It is made with beer and mustard seeds, and is a delightful after-dinner cheese. Abergavenny Fine Foods only started in 1980, and make Y Fenni, traditional Caerffili, Pant-Ys-Gawn goats cheese (with or without black pepper), St Illtyd cheese with wine and herbs, and Harlech horseradish cheese. A leaflet is available from CAWS (Cheesemakers Association Wales) at Welsh Food Promotions (01222-640456) detailing all the independent cheese-makers. Buffalo Farm Cheese is made near Llandysul; traditional Caerffili with leeks and garlic at Caerfai; Cheddar in black wax on Caldey Island; Caerffili with wine and herbs and Caws Mamgu at Cenarth; Cwm Tawe Pecorino-type Cheese with onions, laver or peppers, and Ricotta at Ystalyfera; Skirrid and Lady Llanover sheep cheese and Caws Aberaeron, Merlin's Sandwich, Noson Lawen and Monks of Strata Florida cheeses at Llanon; mature Llanboidy farmhouse and laverbread cheese at Login; unpasteurised Llangloffan farmhouse cheese and red Llangloffan with chives at Castle Morris; Merlin Cheeses with olives, walnut, ginger, herb or apricots at Ystrad Meurig; Caws Nantybwla farmhouse cheeses including Caerffili at Carmarthen; Pen-y-Bont goats cheese also at Carmarthen; Penbryn organic cheese at Llandysul; Pencarreg organic soft blue cheese at Lampeter; cream cheeses from Plas Dairy near Holyhead; Caws Llyn and other cheeses from the Farmer's Co-operative of South Caernarfon Creameries at Pwllheli; and four vegetarian cheeses from the St Florence dairy. There was formerly a 'Newport Cheese' made in Wales in the 18th century, a Normandy-type cream cheese, and sage cheese was coloured by sage and spinach juice. These can easily be made again in Gwent. Incidentally, for several decades none of the famous Caerffili cheese was made in Wales because wartime regulations disallowed the used of skimmed-milk. Caerffili cheeses can thus be positioned as low-calorie organic cheeses on the European market. The taste and fullness of such cheeses mean that one eats less of them than the mass-produced bland Cheddars, thus negating any price differential, which is another selling point.

Simon Buckley has blazed a trail for Welsh beer producers. Much of the move to drinking lager has been because beer on offer is insipid or metallic-tasting. His Cwrw Haf (Summer Ale) is a delight, as are his four other brews available in the area around Llandeilo. Felinfoel's chief executive has said that at least 600 jobs could be created by independent brewers setting up. The Nag's Head, a superb old pub between Cenarth and Boncath brews 'Old Emrys', which sells at £1.40 a pint compared to around £1.90 for 'national' chemical brews like Whitbread and Welsh Bitter. Simon Buckley points out that the Welsh people drink 955,000 pints of lager and over 700,000 pints of beer a day that is imported into Wales from England's mega-breweries: *'The results are mass brewery closures, destruction of Welsh heritage, and the rape and pillage of the Welsh brewing industry by absent landlord brewers from outside Wales.'* If pubs are owned by their landlords, they are easy to convert to brew-pubs offering better and cheaper products than those sold nationally. Village pubs are dying out all over Britain, mainly because of pricing by the monolithic companies that have monopolised beer production. There is no need to pay over £2 for a pint of cider or Guinness. Local brews can be sold at a profit at £1. 40p. Local pubs can also be used as post offices and grocery shops, as in Ireland, with a little more imagination from the legislative authorities. The pub is the centre of village life with its church, and both must be kept and used to help tourism and create local jobs.

Mead and Cider were the great Welsh drinks before sugar was available. Mead Beers can be produced, using the produce of local bee-keepers, and cider-making still has a tradition on the Welsh Borders. Ralph Owen of New Radnor has the only licensed cider-making business in Wales, making 1500 gallons a year from his own orchards. Llanerch Vineyard in the northern Vale of Glamorgan is known for its excellent wines. Glyndŵr Vineyard in the southern Vale at Llanbleddian was planted with 3 acres of vines in 1982. By 1992 it was producing 12,000 bottles of excellent wine a year, and production is being doubled with another three acres being planted. Vintage sparkling wines are also produced using the Champagne method. Whiskey was a Welsh invention, and is being made in Wales again. Wales also should be making its own apple brandy, the equivalent of Armagnac, as it used to. Black Mountain Liqueurs, of Llanfoist near Abergavenny, makes an apple and blackcurrant spirit with a brandy base, and also the strong Dragon Spirit, and a Llanthony Honey Liqueur. More enterprises like this can be set up all over Wales, offering old recipes of liqueurs. Southern Comfort was a Welsh liqueur, taken by emigrants to the southern states of the USA.

Wales is good at producing raw food, but not at getting money for it. A recent headline in the Western Mail was *'We'll shoot £1 calves, say farmers'* (August 5, 1999). A farmer sold a calf for £1 at auction and after deductions received a cheque for just 5p. Why are prices this low when veal and beef are still too expensive for many families to buy in the national supermarkets? Sheep were being sold at 34 pence each for slaughter in this same month in Wales. At the same time a 'leg of lamb' in supermarkets was being sold for £10. Where is the sense? Farmers' markets are part of the answer to farmers keeping a livelihood, rather than more Welsh farms being sold as holiday homes, and the land being ruined forever. More farmers' co-operatives also are needed, but the key is a successful food-processing industry based in Wales using local products. Local food and drink are part of the total picture that will attract more visitors to Wales – it is not just about churches, mountains, beaches and castles. The infrastructure of different hospitality and entertainment will attract repeat visits, and other visits by friends of the tourists. The author has seen an 'Irish Pub' in Newquay, Cardigan, and there are a four or five in the Welsh capital as well. Cardiff has many types of theme pubs, but lacks any with Welsh singing, dancing and music. The only distinctive offerings of 'Irish' pubs, apart from restrictive drinking choices, are soda-bread and surly bouncers. At Nolton in Pembroke, there are Celtic evenings with Welsh singing and dancing – the country does not need to import an alien culture. Where can the increasing number of visitors to the Welsh capital city go to sample Welsh culture and tradition? Perhaps Brains Brewery could pilot a 'Welsh' pub in the capital of the 'Land of Song.'

Another way of attracting visitors into rural areas and boosting the local economy is by the provision of 'tourist trails' linked to mediaeval, early Christian and prehistoric sites, which can be sponsored by local councils, hotels, pubs, farm produce suppliers and the like. 'Menter Preseli' gained funding from Pembroke County Council, the WDA and the EU LEADER II Programme to fund a Heritage leaflet, newsletter and map on *'The Saints and Stones Pilgrimage: In the Shadow of the Preselis'*, including the churches of Llanfrynach, Mynacholgdu. Llangolman, Llandeilo Llwydarth, Maenclochog, Henry's Moat, Morvil and St Brynach's Well. Each church has its own informative leaflet, and visitors have trebled to these sites in the first year of the scheme (for information contact Menter Preseli at 01437-776129). Inspired by the success of the scheme, two more trails were planned, one taking in the traditional Pilgrim's Way to St David's Cathedral. *'A Pilgrim's Journey'* takes one from the Lady Stone and Llanllawer Well past St Brynach's at Pontfaen, St Justinian's at Llanstinan, the Church of the Holy Martyrs at Mathry, St Hywel's at Llanhowel, to St David's. From St David's another pilgrim's route takes one north past St Rhian's in Llanrhian, near Tregwynt traditional woollen mill, to St Nicholas church and thence to St Gwyndaf's at Llanwnda.

A similar organisation, Menter Powys (01982 552224), has been set up in Builth Wells. Its first 'church trail' is *'Where Sleeps the Dragon: on the trail of St Michael's churches in the borderlands of Powys'*, a second route is being prepared regarding the life and times of Francis Kilvert, and the third trail will be following the Celtic saints of Radnorshire. All county councils must be involved with such work, helping local communities to help themselves. It is sometimes difficult to know where to start, however. There is a democratic deficit when a community is represented at parish, town, county, Welsh Assembly, British Parliament and European Parliament levels. With six levels of bureaucracy, responsibility for progress often slips between them and can never be found. This comment is also directed at the eighty or so 'quangos' which are supposed to look after Welsh interests. Culture, tourism and inward investment all 'fit' together, and each county needs a 'leader' whose sole interest is the future of the economic welfare of the county. This future is not one where a multinational business sets up yet another 'call centre' or packing shed to 'manufacture' foreign goods by bolting together pre-assembled parts. Call centres will be replaced by the Internet within three years, and low-paid (mainly part-time female) assembly is easily moved to another country with even lower-paid workers. A man in a my local rugby club called the Welsh 'the coolies of Europe'.*

The future is one where local firms, owned by local people, create full-time local jobs with reasonable pay and a non-repetitive nature to the work. This is so important for Wales. Objective 1 funding from the EU may at last be in sight, but when the former Eastern European countries join the EU there will be no further assistance available. Eire and Brittany have shown ways to prosper. The recent Government publication 'Passport to Prosperity' showed that Wales' GDP (its Gross Domestic Product, or wealth-creating ability) is over 20% below that of the rest of Britain, 40% below Brittany's and 50% below that of Eire. In the last 20 years Wales has sunk below Northern Ireland and the North-east of England to its position as the poorest place in the British Isles. Pembroke and Conwy have a GDP level of just 55% of the rest of Britain. Welsh salaries are low, there are few real jobs outside Cardiff, and the author has shown in previous publications that 'inward investment' by Japanese companies is no answer to the nation's problems. Wales recovering and celebrating its heritage is a step on the ladder to economic prosperity, and a move towards establishing a better sense of community spirit.

Politicians will not face what happened to Wales under eighteen years of Conservative rule. With no Tory prospect of taking many Welsh parliamentary seats, the country was left to suffer. One Secretary of State for Wales, John Redwood, even refused to take European aid that was available to help Wales, while Liverpool took millions. The free market dogma of allowing market forces to rule economies is an abnegation of political and social responsibility. The author has referred it to as 'Spartan economics' where sick children were left to survive or die on mountain-sides. Swathes of Welsh industry simply vanished in the 1980's and 1990's, with nothing to take their place. There has been a terrifying decline which only the Welsh people can arrest. The following table shows that over fourteen years Welsh household income dropped from 91% of that of England to just 75%. The average Welsh family had £282 to spend compared to £375 across England in 1994-95, and the situation is still deteriorating. In case critics complain that the massive earning power in the south-east skews the English statistics, we can argue that war-torn Northern Ireland has overtaken Wales, its rise mirroring the Welsh decline. And from being 3% behind Scotland, Wales is now 22% behind. With Blair, Brown and Cook, the three leaders of the Labour Party, being Scottish, and another five Scots in the 22-man Cabinet being Scottish (Robertson, Smith, Dewar, Lord Irvine, Darling), compared to a Welsh representation of Alun Michael, there seems to be no way that Westminster will put in adequate monies to solve the problems. (See Appendix H for the democratic deficit in Parliamentary representation which has led to the Scottish Assembly having real power compared to the Welsh Assembly).

Household Income	1980-81	1994-95	Real % Change based on 1980-81
England (base)	100	100	-
Scotland	94	97	+3
N. Ireland	78	89	+14
Wales	91	75	-18

This table should be memorised by all those who care about Wales and its future. The author makes no apologies for including it in a book on Welsh saints. The nation has to build its economic strength to safeguard its heritage. The revival of feast days and encouragement of tourism is part of this process, along with disseminating the knowledge of Welsh decline. The Wales Tourist Board spends just half of its £15.36 million budget upon marketing and development, or around a quarter of what Ireland spends to attract tourists. There has been a 2% decline in Welsh tourists in 1999, in an industry which supports up to 100,000 jobs, and attracts £200 million in spending by overseas tourists. Welsh tourism, the economy, and the knowledge of its people are inextricably linked. If the people know about their fabulous heritage, and celebrate it across Wales the year round; if the people know to what extent they have been let down economically by central government; if the people realise that the wealth has been stripped out and the only way up is to set up and support indigenous Welsh companies: only then has Wales a chance of survival as a nation. The Welsh people owe it to their forefathers to take up the challenge.

*This same person discussed with the author why he returned to Wales, after 27 years of teaching in Yorkshire. He and his wife agonized about returning, leaving their friends in the North, after so long away. However, after coming back, he realised that *'it was just like coming back to a warm blanket.'* This is why *'hiraeth'* , the 'longing for home', is so strong, and why the Welsh do not form stronger communities overseas like the Scots and Irish.

Chapter 5

ALPHABETICAL LISTING OF THE SAINTS OF WALES AND RELIGIOUS EVENTS

The following listing includes approximate dates, alternative spellings, known feast days, saints' relatives, foundations of churches and traditions. The links between the holy families of Wales in the 5th and 6th centuries are particularly intriguing as they parallel the princely houses and courts. Some Cornish, Irish and Breton saints are included because of their origins in Wales or their influence in Wales. Entries headed in italics denote non-Welsh saints and miscellaneous information relevant to the book, such as the origins of All Saints Day, Christmas, Date Changes, the Romans in Wales and important historical figures of the time.

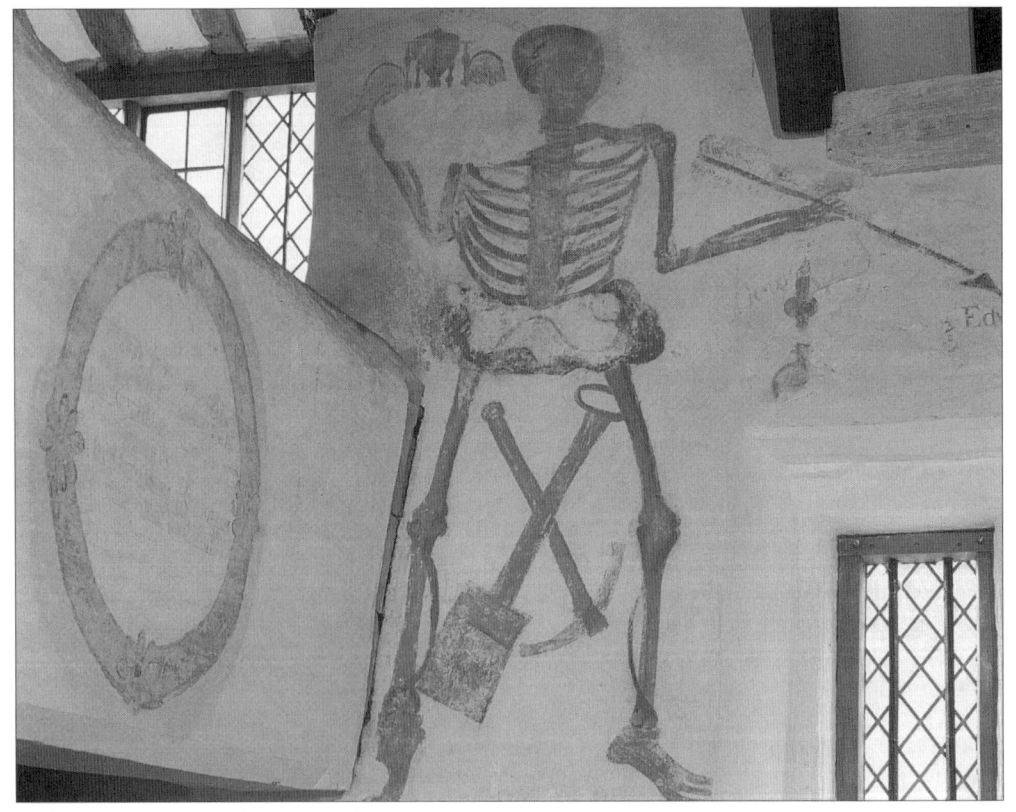

Llangar Church - Wall Painting of Death.　　　*CADW: Welsh Historic Monuments. Crown Copyright.*

Alphabetical Listing of the Saints of Wales and Religious Events

The author apologises for any errors of duplication or omission and hopes that interested readers will contribute local and national knowledge to future editions of this book. This work was written to be 'interesting' rather than academically and scrupulously correct – such a work would take a lifetime of research, but the author believes that it has been the correct approach to stimulate interest in these fascinating times which have shaped the Wales of today. (To make the book 'academically acceptable', cross-referencing would have required a tome to be the size of a small room, and consequently make it unpopular in the economic sense of the word.) It is difficult to think of any other country with such a Christian tradition in these turbulent times, known as the 'Dark Ages' in the rest of Europe but always as the **'Age of Saints'** in Wales.

A

'As to religion, I hold it to be the indispensable duty of government to protect all conscientious professors thereof, and I know of no other business which government hath to do therewith.'

Tom Paine, 'Common Sense', 1776

AARON d. after 287, before 304
ARFON
July 1 (also June 20 or July 3, same as Julius)

Julius and Aaron were among the first martyrs in Britain, executed together in Caerleon in the late third century for their Christian beliefs. However, the accepted execution date of 304 for these Romano-Britons, possibly Romanised Silures, relates to the persecution decree of Emperor Diocletian, but this does not seem to have been enforced in Britain. There were several chapels and churches around Caerleon and Newport dedicated to Julius and Aaron. St Julians, a mansion that belonged to Lord Herbert of Cherbury, stood on the site of Julian's church. St Aaron's chapel was near the Roman fortlet of Penrhos near Caerleon. According to Iolo Morganwg, Llanharan in Glamorgan was an Aaron dedication. Cressy states that they were martyred soon after Amphibalus of Caerleon. St Arvan's in Gwent was probably named after Aaron. There was a holy well in Llanreithan, Pembroke named Ffynnon Aaron.

Geoffrey of Monmouth tells us that Caerleon *'was famous for its two churches, one of these built in honour of the martyr Julius, was graced by a choir of the most lovely virgins dedicated to God. The second, founded in the name of the blessed Aaron, the companion of Julius, was served by a monastery of canons, and counted as the third metropolitan see of Britain'*. The others, also in Roman towns, were York and London. According to local tradition Aaron was buried in Penrhos, just north-east of Caerleon, where a chapel was built on a small Roman camp, an outpost of the great legionary fortress. Caerleon and its neighbouring Roman town of Caerwent have among the best Roman remains in Britain.

AARON early 6th century
AIHRAN
June 22

A saint from Wales who is venerated in Brittany, near Lamballe, at Pleumeur-Gautier and on Cesabre island near Aleth, the old name for St Malo. Malo was said to be one of Aaron's disciples. St Aaron is south of the seaside town of Le Val-Andre, near St Alban. His mass is still said at the chapel of Aaron in St Malo. There was also an Aron/Aaron in one of the earliest Welsh lists of Arthur's knights, to whom Arthur gave land. Aaron was possibly the father of St Ciwg.

ADWEN 5th-6th century
ATHEWENNA, ANNE, TANE

A virgin daughter of Brychan who settled in North Cornwall, this may quite possibly be the same saint as Dwynwen. Advent in North Cornwall was dedicated to her and St Tathan, but Tathan seems to have founded it.

AELGYFARCH 7th century

One of Helig Foel's sons, who studied with his brothers at Bangor or Enlli after the loss of their lands (the Lavan Sands) in the Menai Straits.

AELHAEARN 6th-7th century
ELHAEARN, AELHAIARN
November 1

A son of Hygarfael and brother of the saints Llwchaiarn, Cynhaiarn, Tyfrydog, Twrnog, Dier, Marchell and Tudur. He founded Llanaelhaiarn in Caernarfon and Merioneth, and Cegidfa (now called Guilsfield, near Welshpool) in Montgomery. He was a servant of St Beuno. The ascetic Beuno used to walk into a cold river to pray, and Aelhaearn followed him once, standing behind him. Beuno did not know who was behind him, and called on a pack of savage animals which tore Aelhaiarn apart. Beuno put the body together again, all except an eyebrow, which he replaced with the iron tip of his staff. Aelhaearn means *'the iron eye-brow.'*

Near Llanaelhaearn in Caernarfon lies Glasfryn Standing Stone. The legend is that a young woman who forgot to replace the well cover at Glasfryn caused a lake to form and was turned into stone. In Llanaelhaearn (Caernarfon), the *'pilnos'* or 'peeling night' arose from the practice of peeling rushes for rushlights for the winter months. In later times people gathered for this occasion to dress hemp and card wool, while stories were told. (A similar Anglesey tradition, *'pigo'r pilnos'*, helped to keep the old stories extant over the centuries.) Just 300 yards north of Llanaelhaiarn Church is Ffynnon Aelhaiarn, where the well was roofed in 1900 and now supplies the hamlet.

At Aelhaearn's holy well near Llanaelhaiarn church in Merioneth, sick people bathed in the hope of bodily restoration of which the saint is a symbol, and for resurrection after death. The 'Llanaelhaearn Stone' dates from the 5th or 6th century, and is engraved 'A LIORTVS ELMETIACO HIC IACET' which indicates contact with the British kingdom of Elmet in south Yorkshire. It was found by accident by a gravedigger in the 19th century, and is over four feet high.

ABBOT AELHAIARN 5th-6th century
ELHAIARN

He was said to have been a disciple of Dyfrig, and witnessed the grant of Penally to Dyfrig in the Book of Llandaf. He may have crossed with Teilo to Brittany to avoid the Yellow Plague. There is a St Alouarn's canonry and castle near Teilo's foundation at Plogonnec, Quimper. He is represented with Teilo in a stained glass window at Plogonnec. He may also have founded Lanherne in Cornwall.

AELRHIW
DELWFYW, AILIW
September 9

Rhiw, in Caernarfon. Ffynon Aelrhiw near the church cured cutaneous disorders, especially one called *'Man Aeliw'* (the mark of Ailiw). Tan-y-Muriau burial chamber is on the slope of Mynydd Rhiw overlooking the sea.

AERDEYRN 5th century

A son of Gwrtheyrn (Vortigern) of whom little is known.

BISHOP AFAN fl.500-542
AFAN BUELLT
November 16 or 17, October 16, 17, December 17, All Hallows

A cousin of St David, and son of Cedig ap Ceredig and Tegwedd ferch Tegid Foel of Penllyn. Afan Buallt was related to Teilo as a uterine brother as his mother was Tegwedd. He founded Llanafan Fawr in Brecon, Llanafan Fach, and Llanafan Trawsgoed on the river Ysytwyth in Cardigan. There was a Ffynnon Afan in Cardigan. He was buried in Llanafan Fawr, and his tomb reads 'HIC IACET SANCTUS AVANUS EPISCOPUS'. He was thus probably the third Bishop of Llanbadarn. Afan was the brother of King Doged, and of the royal line of Cunedda. Llanfechan chapel under Llanafan Fawr was also dedicated to him. Tradition states that he was murdered by Irish pirates or Danes at Llanafan Fawr, where there is a brook called Nant yr Sgob (Stream of the Bishop), a valley called Cwm Esgob (Bishop's Valley) and a farmstead called Derwen Afan (Afan's Oak). Ffynnon Afan was noted by Edward Lhuyd at Llanafan Fawr, as was Ffynnon Dduw (God's Well). Llantrisant in Anglesey is dedicated to Afan, Ieuan and Sannan. Lanavan in Finistere is also his foundation. St Arvan's near Chepstow may be his – see Arvan and Aaron.

Llanafan in Cardigan was the site of a famous *'toili'*, or 'phantom funeral' in 1889. Horses refused to pass the spot where the procession was seen, and two weeks later a real funeral passed that way. At the Morfa Colliery near Aberafan, in 1890 the 'Red Dogs of Morfa' a pack of hell-hounds, ran all night. Then a parade of phantom lights known as 'corpse-candles' were seen in the pit's tunnels. The sickly smell of 'death flowers' was in the air, the rats deserted the mine and ghosts of miners were seen pulling trams. Half the men refused to work, an unheard of event in those days. The braver men went down, and 87 were killed in an explosion. At Brecon's Llanafan, in the late 19th century people still remembered the practice of local boys and girls paying for dancing lessons prior to the patronal festival of All Hallows. At Cwmafan was born the great miner's leader and MP, Mabon (William Abraham). Afan was a cantref of Glamorgan, and a centre of resistance to Norman rule. However, its ruler Lleision ap Morgan Fychan 'Normanised' his name to de Avene, and when his grandson Thomas died about 1350, the region was taken over by the lordship of Glamorgan.

A 'Saying of the Wise' attributed to 'Avaon' ap Taliesin is that *'the cheek will not conceal the anguish of the heart.'* Near Aberafan, the Celtic 'Cross of St Thomas' was found on the site of a chapel endowed by William, Earl of Gloucester. Nearby Westwood noted another cross almost buried in the ground, which may have had inscriptions, but the author does not know if it has been excavated and saved, or lost.

AFARWY 5th-6th century
AFROGWY 6th century

A son of Caw.

AIDAN OF FERNS d. 626
AEDAN, AEDDAN FOEDDOG, AIDH, AIDUS, MAIDOC, MAEDDOG, MAEDOC
January 31

This possible son of Caw studied under St David in Wales, and established a monastery in Ferns, Co. Wexford where he was first bishop. (Other sources claim him as the son of Gildas ap Caw, and yet others that he was born in Connacht.) Aidan was said to be one of the monks chosen by his brother Gildas to come from Wales and re-evangelise Ireland at the request of King Ainmire in 568. A bronze reliquary containing his relics is in Dublin. St Aidan of Ferns had dedications at Llawhaden (Llanrhiadain, Llanhuadain), Nolton, Haroldston West and Solfach in Pembroke, and two churches on St Brides Bay. Maedoc, or Aidan, was supposed to have held David in his arms as he lay dying. He was with David for a long time after leaving Leinster. The Saxons invaded Britain, and the British asked David to send Maedoc to them and bless their Christian army. After his prayers and blessings, the outnumbered Britons defeated the Saxons. He then asked permission to return to Ireland. There is also a Ffynnon Faeddog at Porthmawr near St David's, and Tref Aeddan is a farm near Porth Stinan in Pembroke.

Archbishop Usher stated that Bishop Aedanus was called by the Irish 'Moedhog and Maedog'. Giraldus Cambrensis called him Maidocus, and John Of Teignmouth states that he was called Aidanus in the 'Life of St David', but in his lifetime Aidus, and in St David's Church Moedok. The Irish claim Aidan as a native, but seem to have no genealogy confirming this.

Madog is probably another saint associated with St David in Dyfed, and remembered at Llanmadog, Llanfadog and Capel Madog. See Madog ap Meurig and Madog ap Sawyl – there is confusion between Aidan and Madog foundations.

There is a new pilgrim trail linking the mediaeval estates of the Bishops of St David's, the Bishops Road trail across Pembrokeshire. It traces the ancient route along the Landsker from the Bishop's palace at Llawhaden through the vilages of Wiston, Spittal and Brawdy, which all had hospices to assist pilgrims, ending at St David's Cathedral.

AIDEN OF LINDISFARNE d. 651
August 31, October 8

Given a holy day by the Church in Wales, Bede states that he was Irish, and was given Lindisfarne as a monastery site by King Oswald of Northumbria. His predecessor had complained that he could not teach the ignorant Saxons, but Aiden perservered.

AILBE d.527-531
AILFYW, ELFYW, ELFEIS, ELVIS, ELOUIS
September 12, 13, February 27

The daughter of Cynyr of Caer Gawch and Anna ferch Vortimer was Danhadlwen (Banhadlen), the sister of Non. She married Dirdan of Brittany, and their son was Ailbe, one of the greatest figures in the Irish Church. One source states that, as St Eloius, he was confessor and bishop at Menevia, and that his saint's day was February 27. He evangelised southern Ireland, founding the see of Imlech (Emly in Tipperary). From King Angus of Munster Ailbe obtained the island of Aran for Enda. Irish legend has him being suckled by a she-wolf and retiring to the 'Land of Promise', a mixture of the happy 'other-world' of the Celts, and the paradise of Christians.

According to the 'Genealogy of the Saints', Ailfyw was the son of Dirdan and Danadlwen, but Dirdan was the son of Gynyr of Caer Gawch (see Gynyr) This makes Ailfyw the nephew of Non and thereby the cousin of St David. Baring-Gould and Fisher give the following genealogy:
'Cynyr of Caergwach married Anna, the daughter of Vortimer, who died in 457. Their children were Banhadlen, Non, Gwen, Gistlian and Sadwrn Hen. Dirdan married Banhadlen, and their son was Ailbe. Non married Sant, and their son was David who died in 589. Gwen married Selyf, and their son St Cybi died in 554. Sadwrn Hen's son was Sadyrnin. Sadyrnin, Cybi, David and Ailbe were first cousins.'

A church near St David's, called Llanailfyw or St Elfeis, was dedicated to him. St Elvis farm and St Elvis Church are near the Preseli Hills. Baring-Gould states that Ailbe *'is known in Wales as Ailfyw or Elfyw, who founded a church now a ruin, called St Elvis, in Welsh Llanailfyw, or –elfyw, near St David's, consequently near where lived his aunt, St Non.'* He remained in Menevia until David was born, and according to Welsh tradition baptised and fostered him, before going to Ireland. The remains of St Elvis Church could still be seen in the 1940's, but the name only now attaches to the farm and parish, and a few scattered islands off Solva. A farmhouse nearby is now a private house and was named Vagwr Eilw (Elvis' 'Enclosure', from 'Magwyr'). The author has not encountered any other places named Elvis, and as St Elvis lies in the foothills of the Preseli Mountains, is very tempted to place Elvis Presley as having Welsh ancestry. His parents, Vernon and Gladys, had Welsh names, and his still-born twin brother was Jesse Garon (St Caron?) Presley. The first 'Pressley' recorded in American history was a David Pressley, and Elvis' grandmother Doll was from the Welsh family of Mansell. Another ancestor was Dunnan Presley.

There are the remains of a dolmen at St Elvis Farm, near Teilo's ruined church, with two capstones, and some large nearby stones have probably come from it. See Addenda.

There is an ambiguous 'Saying of the Wise' which seems to propose the tolerance and understanding of homosexuality:
*'Hast thou heard the saying of Elvyw,
A man wise without a peer?
"Let every sex go to where it belongs".'*

Alphabetical Listing of the Saints of Wales and Religious Events

ALAN FYRGAN (White Ankles) d. 539

A son of Emyr Llydaw who escaped to Wales from Brittany, and settled at Llanilltud Fawr. Alan's three sons, saints Lleuddad, Llonio Lawhir and Llynab also studied at Llanilltud. One of the Arthurian Triads states that the host of Alan Fyrgan left the road to Camlan at night, leaving him and his servants to be killed in Arthur's last battle. There is an Alan venerated in Brittany, but this is possibly a different person. (see Arthur)

ALBAN died c.209 or 305 (Cressy gives 287)
ALBANUS OF VERULAM
June 22, 20, 17, July 22

The first martyr in Ynys Prydain, the Island of Britain. St Gildas writes about him around 540, and he is referred to in the fifth century 'Life' of St Germanus of Auxerre. A Romano-Briton, Alban was beheaded at Verulamium (St Albans) for giving shelter to a fleeing Christian in the Diocletian persecution. Bede elaborates on these details, and the Abbey of St Albans commemorates the traditional site of his martyrdom on Holmehurst Hill. Christ Church above Caerleon was formerly dedicated to Alban, and a nearby hill is called Mount Saint Alban. There is an annual rose service at St Alban's Cathedral on the Sunday of, or after, St Alban's Day, where rose petals are spread along the floor of the cathedral. His relics were taken to Ely, and captured by Danes in Canute's raid on York. They are now in St Canute's in Odense.

New research however seems to point to Alban being based on the pagan 'cult of the head', as archaeologists have found the skull of a young man at Verulamium, killed by a blow to the head, the skull being then scalped and defleshed. Churches were often placed on the site of pagan worship, and neither of the dates for Alban's martyrdom, 209 or 305, coincide with any evidence of Christianity being practised there at these times. Rosalind Niblett, after four years of excavations on St Albans Oysterfields estate, has published her findings in the Journal for the Society for Roman Studies in October 1999. Verulamium had a huge religious complex at the end of the 3rd century, with a large Celtic temple, baths and at least 50 deep pits and wells. She argues that the site celebrates a local chief or hero, and the place fits the descriptions of Alban's martyrdom. Dr Martin Henig, of Oford University, also believes that when the Christian Church came to Verulamium in the 4th century, the Church possibly felt the need for a martyr and invented the decapitation story to gain cult support.

Christianity existed in eastern Britain in the 4th and 5th centuries, but was wiped out again in the 5th and 6th centuries by Anglo-Saxon tribes from Germany. Celtic Christianity was reintroduced from western Britain and Ireland in the 7th century but had to then fight the new Roman faith, losing out at the Synod of Whitby in 664 in most of England. Wales stayed Celtic Christian, possibly from the 1st century until the 11th. New excavations at Whitby Abbey in Yorkshire should reveal the extent to which the Celtic tradition survived in the North of England against the formal pomp and cermeony of the Roman version of Christianity. The more ascetic Celtic church calculated the date of Easter in the old way, had a different form of tonsure and had different organisational and architectural traditions, although it was later a Catholic faith and accepted the power of the Pope.

June 22, St Alban's Day in 1402, was notable for one of the greatest defeats of an English army when Owain Glyndŵr's force met Roger Mortimer's larger army at Bryn Glas, near Pilleth. More than 1100 of the invading force were killed, and Roger Mortimer captured by Rhys

Gethin's soldiers. There is a mass grave still to be seen there, and Roger Mortimer joined Glyndŵr's fight for independence. A memorial should mark this spot where Wales' greatest hero won his finest victory.

ALDATE see ELDAD

ALLGO 5th - 6th century
ALLECTUS, GALLGO
November 27
The Wake of Llanallgo – first Sunday in May.

Like Eugrad, a brother of Gildas and son of Caw, remembered at Llanallgo in Anglesey, near the site of Llangadog. Llanallgo is under his brother's foundation of Llaneigrad, and near his sister Peithien's chapel at Llugwy.

He had studied at Llanilltud and Llancarfan, but was possibly forced to leave Anglesey after Gildas' insults to Maelgwn Gwynedd. In the Tale of Culhwch and Olwen he appears as Calcas ab Caw, who fights for King Arthur. Ffynnon Gallgof at Llanallgo was a curing well with a strong lime sulphate content, and Capel y Ffynnon adjoining the church was used by local people to cure chronic diseases, when they prayed there to Gallgo.

ALL SAINTS DAY, ALL HALLOWS' DAY, HALLOWE'EN
November 1 and October 31

All Hallows' Day is the feast day of all those who are in heaven, and is celebrated on November 1st. *'All Hallow-mass'* became *'Hallowmas'*, and it is now usually known as All Saints' Day. *'Hallowed'* means holy, as in the phrase in The Lord's Prayer, *'Hallowed be thy name'*, so the name meant the day that belonged to *'holy'* persons, i.e. saints. It is the day when all the saints, whose individual feast days are unknown, are celebrated, and it is a public holiday over most of Europe. The popular name for All Hallow's Eve is now Hallowe'en, also known as *'All Souls Eve'*, and it is a night of great superstition and ghostly appearances.

All Saints' Day is the start of All Hallows Summer, a traditional period of unseasonable warmth. Also known as Hollantide, the old verse is:
If ducks do slide at Hollantide, at Christmas they will swim;
If ducks do swim at Hollantide, at Christmas they will slide.

October 31 (Hallowe'en, *Nos Galan Gaeaf*) was *'Old Year's Night'* for the Celts, the night when all the witches were out and about. The Christian church made the following day All Saints' Day, to try and get away from the these connotations, but the *'witching'* tradition lives on. *'Trick or Treat Night'* has spread back across Wales by youngsters over the last few decades, having retained its popularity in Scotland and the North of England for centuries.

'Apple and Candle Night' was the local name for Hallowe'en in the Swansea area. This game was played by hanging a stick from the ceiling, with a lighted candle at one end, and an apple at the other. Without using their hands, players try to eat the apple, while avoiding the candle as the stick swings around to touch them. In one version, the player is blindfolded, and the stick

set swinging to start the game. *'Y Bwca Llwyd' (The Grey Bogey)* was made on All Hallows Eve. It was made from straw packed tightly into pieces of canvas, and formed a monster carried on the end of a pitchfork by a man hidden under the canvas. The 'beast' was paraded on All Hallows Eve, making a frightening appearance outside peoples' bedroom windows. A more common custom was the making of the *'caseg fedi' (harvest mare)* from the last tuft of corn to be cut, the equivalent of today's corn dolly. The corn dolly was kept in the house for luck until a new one replaced it the following year. The reapers' supper in some areas of Wales was *'poten ben fedi'*, a harvest pie consisting of mashed potatoes, minced beef, onions and bacon. In Pembrokeshire, it was called *'cinio cynhaeaf' (harvest dinner)* or *'ffest y wrach' (the hag's feast)*.

The reapers' supper in Carmarthenshire usually featured *'whipod'* - rice, bread, raisins, currants and treacle. In Anglesey the feast featured potatoes, turnips and oatcakes, with dancing and fiddle-playing. In Cardigan in 1760 Lewis Morris wrote that the feast was *'the contents of a brewing pan of beef and mutton, with arage and potatoes and pottage, and pudding of wheaten flour, about 20 gallons of light ale and more than 20 gallons of beer.'* In Montgomeryshire on Nos Galan Gaeaf, a mash was made of nine ingredients (three times three being doubly lucky) - leeks, potatoes, carrots, turnips, parsnips, peas, fresh milk, salt and pepper. A wedding ring was hidden in the mash, and young maids of the village would dig into it with their wooden spoons, anxious to learn their fate. The first one to find the ring would be married first. A Carmarthenshire custom also features a dish with nine ingredients, called *stwmp naw rhyw*. This was a pancake made by nine girls, who ate a piece each. Before the morning of the New Year, each would then have a vision of her future husband. 'Apple bobbing' was popular, and wassailing was also carried out, with punch being drunk from 'puzzle jugs'.

In the Vale of Glamorgan, spirits roamed the churchyards at night, and the bravest villager would don his coat and vest inside out, reciting the Lord's Prayer backwards as he walked around the church a number of times. Then he would walk up to the church porch and place his finger in the keyhole to prevent spirits from escaping (people used to be buried inside churches). It was also believed that apparitions of those about to die could be seen through the keyhole. In other parts of Wales, youths would dress up in girls' clothes, and vice-versa, and groups of young people would wander from house to house after dark, chanting verses and soliciting gifts of fruit or nuts. In more rural areas, men dressed in sheepskins and blackened their faces, and were given gifts of apples, nuts and beer. These groups were known as the *gwrachod* (hags, or witches), and were meant to bring good tidings and expel bad spirits from the household.

This last night of the old year was traditionally the time when a local *Ladi Wen* (ghost of a white lady) would appear. However, in North Wales it was more often the terrible *Hwch Ddu Gwta* (tail-less black sow). Bonfires were lit on hillsides, and great pains were taken to keep the parish's bonfire burning longer than those of its neighbours. Apples and potatoes were roasted, and the watchers would dance and leap through the flames for good luck in the forthcoming year. Stones were thrown into the fire, and as the flames died down, everyone would run home to escape the clutches of the great black pig. The next day, villagers searched for their stones in the embers. If they found them, luck would follow; if not, there would be misfortune in the family.

ALL SOULS DAY
November 2

The feast day commemorating those departed, held on November 2nd. In Pembroke, and on the Welsh borders including Shropshire and Cheshire, *'souling'* was practised on this day, when *'soul cakes'* were made and given to visiting children. Although generally replaced by money, apples, sweets and biscuits, even in the 1950's such offerings were referred to as *'soul cakes.'*

ALMEDHA 5th-6th century
EILIWEDD, ELINED, ELINUD, ALUD, AILED, LLUDD
March 17 (Cornwall), August 1 is Feast Day in Brecon (August 12 Old Style), October 9

Giraldus Cambrensis states that Almedha, a daughter of Brychan, was martyred by Saxons on a hill named Penginger near Brecon. Slwch, where there used to be an Iron Age hill-fort, was identified as the site in Jones's *'Brecknockshire'*. The stone where she died was near a mound at Pencefngaer, a mile east of Brecon, near Slwch Farm. The place was also *called 'Crug gorseddawl'* ('the hill of judgement'). Cressy states *'This devout virgin, rejecting the proposals of an earthly prince, who sought her in marriage, and espousing herself to the eternal king, consummated her life by a triumphant martyrdom. The day of her solemnity is celebrated every year on the first day of August.'* Another version is that she was escaping from an enforced marriage to a local prince. Llanelly, under Llangattock Crickhowel in Brecon, is attributed to Elinud/Almedha rather than Ellyw or Elli.

The Harleian MS. related her legend that a prince wanted to marry her, but she fled to Llanddew where she was badly treated, then moved to nearby Llanfilo where she was treated as a common thief because of her ragged clothes, then to Llechfaen where she was made to sleep in the road ever since called Heol Sant Alud. These three villages were said to have met with disasters because they refused to give her sanctuary. The prince caught up with her and she was beheaded, where a spring of water appeared on the site. Almedha's holy well is now overgrown, and the chapel has vanished, but there is a field in Llanhamlach called Clos Sant Ailed.

Giraldus Cambrensis noted the roofless condition of the Brecon chapel in the 12th century, but noted that her festival dance was still held there. The men and women came from far away for August 1st, and formed a circle around the churchyard, singing as they danced. *'Then on a sudden falling on the ground in a fit, then jumping up in a frenzy, and representing with their hands and feet before the people whatever work they have unlawfully done on feast days'.* Some mimed cobbling, tanning, spinning, weaving or even ploughing with oxen. It was the community demonstrating that they worked for the communal welfare, but also that all such work should only be done at the appropriate times and season. The 1st August was also the start of the season of Lammas, held in honour of the Celtic God, Lug. This day was also associated with the making of corn dollies in Wales. Almedha's holy well is named Penginger Well by Francis Jones, who states that she was buried at Usk.

AMBROSIUS AURELIANUS fl.500
EMRYS WLEDIG

The hero of Gildas in his invective against the weak British kings in their fight against the Saxons. He was a 'Roman' aristocrat, and said to be the founder of Amesbury. Ambrosius led his cavalry to burn Gwrtheyrn (Vortigern), the High King of Britain, out of his castle in Flint and drove him into the mountains of North Wales. He then drove back the Saxons in the north-east of his kingdom but could not dislodge them from the south-east of England. The German tribes counter-attacked and were finally halted at the great battle of Badon Hill, Mons Badonicus. Gildas does not mention Arthur as being the battle commander, but an entry of about 518 in the Easter Annals states *'Battle of Badon, in which Arthur carried the cross of our Lord Jesus Christ on his shoulders for three days and three nights, and the Britons triumphed.'* This kept the invaders at bay for years, except for the Jutish take-over of the Isle of Wight. Later, Pope Gregory sent St Augustine (not the saint who preached anti-Pelagianism) to convert the Saxons to the Italian version of Christianity and the acceptance of dominance of Rome.

Ambrosius had been smuggled to Brittany after the alleged murder of Constans by Vortigern, returned to defeat Vortigern and went on to defeat and execute Hengist and avenge the *'treachery of the long knives'*. He was poisoned by Eoppa the Saxon, on the orders of Paschent, one of Vortigern's sons.

This story is confused, as there seem to be two war-leaders called Ambrosius. The first was a rival of Vortigern around 470, and the second, with the soubriquet Aurelianus, led the British resistance from around 475 (noted by Gildas) which ended successfully at Badon Hill in 518 or 519. King Tewdrig ap Teithfallt was martyred in 470, and could be identified with Ambrosius. His son Meurig or another son could be Ambrosius Aurelianus, and Meurig's son was Arthur/Arthmael. Perhaps at Badon Hill Arthur was fighting for his father or uncle, as Gildas is remarkably silent upon Arthur's role there. Some say that Ambrosius passed on the kingship to his brother who became the high-king, Uther Pendragon, who has been identified with Meurig. Perhaps we can assume at present that Emrys Wledig was the father or grandfather of Meurig.

Gilbert believes that Emrys Wledig ('Crowned Prince') was Teithfallt, the king of Glamorgan and great-grandfather of Arthur ap Meurig ap Tewdrig ap Teithfallt. He believes that Teithfallt was a contemporary of Gwrgan Mawr of Gwent, Ewyas and Ergyng, whom he places as Ambrosius Aurelianus. Aurelius married St Ninnoca, and their daughter maried Meurig ap Tewdrig, pulling the houses of Glamorgan and Gwent together. Meurig's sister Marchell married Brychan, thus further consolidating the hold on South Wales. Meurig's children intermarried with the house of Budic II of Brittany, giving a power-base for his son Arthur in terms of fighting men.

AMLECH 5th century
ANLACH

The father of Brychan, after whom Llanhamlach may be named, and buried at Llanyspyddid. (See Brychan and Marchell). A cross there seems to represent St John and the Virgin Mary, with an inscription *'johannis moridic surexit hunc lapidam.'* It seems to be pre-Norman, and a Moridic is mentioned in the Book of Llandaf. The same *johannis* seems to be the sculptor of the six foot inscribed cross at Llanfrynach.

AMO
ANNO
May 20

Llananno or Llanamo in Radnorshire, under Llanbadarn Fynydd commemorates this unknown saint. Also Rhosyr yn Mon, now called Newborough in Anglesey was formerly called Llanamo. The Reverend John Parker eulogised over the decaying chancel screen in Llananno by the river Ithon, and made no less than fourteen drawings of it in 1828. There was a medicinal holy well, Ffynnon Llananno near Radnorshire's Knighton. Ffynnon Newydd in the same parish was used for skin complaints and scurvy, being best visited in the three months of summer. A five foot Celtic cross, the Newborough, or Brondeg Stone, was noted by Westwood on the road from Newborough to Llangaffo. Found on Brondeg Farm, it reads *'CVVRI CINI EREXIT HUNC LAPIDEM'*. It was inserted into the vestry-wall of Llangaffo Church, and there may be other inscriptions on it reading *'Vinili Filivs', 'Filius Ulrici'*.

AMPHIBALUS d.287
June 25, (July 2)

From Caerleon, he instructed St Alban, escaped to Wales on Alban's martyrdom, and was said (in a medieval fraud) to have been himself martyred at Redburn. Two of his martyred disciples were saints Stephanus and Socrates. This saint may not have existed, as his name means *'cloak'*. The '1000 Martyrs of Lichfield' were supposedly the companions of Amphibalus, martyred when fleeing to Wales after Alban's death.

AMWN DDU c.480-540.
AMON the BLACK
April 30

The son of Emyr Llydaw (King Budic II), and father of Tydecho, Samson and Tathan. He was converted by Samson, and was said to have been buried at Llanilltud. He married into Arthur's family. Amwn may be the origin of Arthur's 'Black Knight'.

ANDRAS 5th-6th century
October 1, 2

The son of Rhain Dremrudd ap Brychan and brother of Nefydd. St Andras*, now called St Andrews Major, near Dinas Powys was possibly his church. Presteigne's Welsh name is Llanandras**. It is not known for sure whether these dedications are to Andrew the Apostle or Andras. (There is a St Anne's Well just outside Presteigne, on the river Lugg, which may have been the well of Andras). Llandow is in the parish of St Andrew's Minor in Glamorgan, about fifteen miles west of Dinas Powys. (Dinas Powys was a major settlement in Arthurian times.)
The font of the ruined church of St Andrew is in Llandow church, just a half mile away, and this place was formerly called Llanandras, so the two Glamorgan dedications may well be those of Andras. Abandoned over 200 years ago, the little church is off the farm road from Llandow to the old manor of Clementstone Court. More research is needed here.

Alphabetical Listing of the Saints of Wales and Religious Events

Llandow church was built by the Normans shortly after the conquest of Glamorgan, and is dedicated to the Holy Trinity. The Franklen family lived in Clemenstone House, and eight identical crosses denote their memory in the graveyard. The Franklen family may be the descendants of the soldier who killed the last Prince of Wales. He is also associated with nearby Frampton, just outside Llanilltud Fawr. Up until last century, children were urged to go to bed as their parents *'could hear the hooves of Frampton's horse'*.

In the anti-machinery riots led by 'Captain Swing', a letter was sent to the Reverend Edward Picton, Rector of Llandow, reading:
'Newport Decr. 10th 1830
Reverend Father
No machinery no tythe to the clergy
No Bradley Agency &C (Edward Bradley of Cowbridge was the land agent who collected rents)
I have just been paying a Visit at Duffrin The Honbl W.B. Grey
I shall visit you shortly as bold as the General entered Badajoss (General Picton was a Welsh hero who fought at Badajos in the Peninsular War against Napoleon, probably related to Rev. Picton)
It is my full intention to see your house burnt down to the ground
Take this hint
Swing
PS more wages to workmen'

The letter was possibly deliberately 'illiterate' to disguise its origins. William Thomas records the death in 1766 of Lewis William of Garnill, St Andrews Major who *'was one of the vainest Jokers of St Andrews, would swear and curse the greatest lie in a Jokefull manner and had some Nick Name on all neighbours. William had a severe hard departure for an hour, for all had lingered to the very bones to a Scullaton.'*

The 'Saying of the Wise' is:
'Hast thou heard the saying of Andras,
Who suffered on the extended cross?
"Whoso distributed religion obtained heaven".'

*Gilbert makes Andras the son of Morgan ap Gwrgan Mawr, king of Ewyas, Ergyng and Gwent, and states that he built a chapel on the lands reclaimed from the sea at Castleton, on the Wentloog Levels outside Cardiff.

**The superb 14th century St Andrew's Church at Presteigne has a Tudor roof and some Saxon details remaining in the stonework. Even today, a curfew bell is rung at 8 o'clock to put the townspeople to bed. Black Vaughan of Hergest Court was beheaded after commanding Yorkist forces at the Battle of Banbury in 1469. His tomb is in Knighton Church. However, the spirit of Fychan Ddu (Black Vaughan) haunted the Welsh Borders for many years, so thirteen clergymen gathered in St Andrew's in Presteigne to put his soul to rest. All but one of the clerics fled in terror, but the thirteenth kept his wits, reduced the spirit to the size of a fly and placed him in a snuffbox which he threw into Hergest Pool. (A similar story is told at Dyserth Church). A century later the snuffbox was found and Black Vaughan's ghost was released to take the shape of a gigantic, hellish black hound. Sir Arthur Conan Doyle stayed at Hergest Court while writing 'The Hounds of the Baskervilles'. At nearby Clyro, the inn known as 'The Swan' to Francis Kilvert has been renamed 'The Baskerville Arms.'

A mediaeval tapestry that had hung in the Presteigne church for 300 years was recently discovered to be worth over £250,000. The church authorities wished to send it for auction, but the parishioners rebelled. The 14 foot by 8 foot hanging was woven in Flanders in 1511, part of a set of 12 for Canterbury Cathedral. They were hastily sent to France for safe-keeping during the Reformation, and the other eleven are in the museum at Aix-en-Provence. A wealthy local landowner bought the twelfth, and donated it to St Andras Church in 1711. Parishioners and CADW raised £170,000 and the church removed the wall-hanging from Sothebys to the Historic Royal Palaces conservation studios at Hampton Court for restoration, which began in May 1998. The glorious tapestry features Christ entering Jerusalem.

ANDREW d. c. 60
November 30, May 9

This patron saint of Scotland was a disciple of John the Baptist before becoming Christ's apostle. A fisherman, he is also the patron saint of Russia.

LANCELOT ANDREWES 1555-1626
September 26

Given a holy day by the Church in Wales, he was born in Barking and studied at Cambridge. He became chaplain to Elizabeth I and Dean of Westminster. He remained as a chaplain and adviser to King James, and was an important contributor to the 'Anglo-Catholic' school of church thought.

ANE 6th century
ANEF, ANGAR, ANGAWD, ANEU
January 13

Ane ap Caw Cawlwyd had a chapel in Anglesey, under Llanelian, called Coed Ane after him. Angawd ap Caw was one of Arthur's knights in the Mabinogion tale of Culhwch and Olwen. The ancient *'Sayings of the Wise'* contains the following lines:
'Have you heard the saying of Angar,
Son of Caw, the celebrated warrior?
"The heart will break with grief"'

ANEURIN THE BARD fl. 573 - 604

His wonderful poem *'Y Gododdin'* recounts the battle around 603 where he and only three others survived the great battle at Catraeth (Catterick in Yorkshire). Imprisoned in chains in a dungeon, he was rescued by Ceneu ap Llywarch Hen. He then went to Llancarfan to study at Cadog's monastery, and was killed by an assassin, Eiddyn ab Einygan (one of *'the three unfortunate assassinations of Britain'*). He may have been the son of Dunawd Fawr. He appears to be the nephew of Gwallawg (who was praised by Taliesin) and the brother of St Deiniol.

Alphabetical Listing of the Saints of Wales and Religious Events

Like Taliesin, Myrddin (Merlin) and Llywarch Hen, Aneirin's poems encompass the painful struggle of the *Gwyr y Gogledd* (the Men of the North) against the Scottish Picts, the Irish, and the Saxons of Deira and Bernicia. Gwenddolau died at Arderydd in 573, and Peredur in 580, and Urien Rheged was assassinated in 589. Aneirin's great poem 'Y Gododdin' recounts the last-ditch attempt by the British Gododdin tribe from Edinburgh to halt the Saxon advance at Catraeth (Catterick). Mynyddog Mwynfawr planned the expedition south carefully, and included in his war-band were men from other parts of the Brythonic world. The defeat led to Aethelfrith of Bernicia taking over Northumbria. The Gododdin has verses such as:

'Gododdin, I make this claim upon your behalf
Boldly in the presence of this crowded court:
And the song of Dwywai's son, of great courage,
May it be manifest in the one place that it conquers
Since the gentle one, the Wall-of-Battle, was slain,
Since the earth covered Aneirin,
Poetry is now departed from the Gododdin.' . . .

'Men went to Catraeth, they were famous;
Wine and mead from golden vessels was their drink for a year,
According to honourable custom;
Three men and three score and three hundred wearing gold torques.
Of those that battled after the perfect drink
None escaped save three, through feats of combat;
The two battle hounds of Aeron and Cynon the Stubborn
And I, with my blood streaming down,
For the sake of my brilliant poetry.'

One line about that *'wall of battle'*, Isag, who had *'a manner like the flowing sea for geniality and generosity and the pleasant drinking of mead'*, has been used by David Jones among others, and truly demonstrates the sorrows of war:
'His sword echoes in the heads of mothers.'

ANEURIN AP CAW see GILDAS

This son of Caw has sometimes been identified with Gildas as being the same person – Welsh genealogists make Aneurin and the Saxon 'Gildas' interchangeable.

ANHAELOG

Capel Anheilog, on the very end of the holy Llŷn Peninsula, fell into decay with the decline of the monastery at Bardsey Island (Enlli). Two fifth or sixth century Christian stones were taken from here to Cefnamlwch House. They commemorate early priests, one of whom lies *'with the multitude of the brethren'* on Enlli.

ANHUN 4th century
ANTONIUS, ANNON

Said to be the son of Macsen Wledig and Elen.

The Book of Welsh Saints

ANNA 5th-6th century
July 26

The daughter of Meurig ap Tewdrig, King of Glamorgan, and the wife of Amwn Ddu. Her children were the great saints Samson, Tydecho and Tathan. There is a St Anne's Well at Whitstone in Cornwall, and Oxenhall in Gloucester is dedicated to her. Her date coincides with that of Anne, and the wells at Trellech and Llanfihangel may well be Anna's.

ANNE 1st century
July 26

This apocryphal mother of the Virgin Mary seemed to replace Anu, the earth-Mother of Celtic paganism. Her ancient carving at St Anne's Well at Llanfihangel* (in the Vale of Glamorgan) used to feature water spouting from her nipples. The breasts were later smashed off the sculpture. St Anne's Well near Presteigne was also a famous holy well, possibly formerly that of St Andras.

Apart from the imposing St Anne's Well at Malvern Wells (former Welsh territory), there is another famous votive well dedicated to her, still in use today at Trellech in Monmouthshire. (A colleague cured seven years of psoriasis with one visit there). Also, if a stone is dropped into the waters and many bubbles rise, one's wish will come true. If there are just a few bubbles, beware the dark days to come. Trellech features the three great megaliths known as Harold's Stones, nine wells (of which four remain) and a tumulus. Anne's most famous shrine was in Buxton, Derbyshire, and the greatest density of her dedications are in Brittany, and in Canada (possibly due to Breton seamen and settlers).

*The lovely Elizabethan Llanfihangel Court overlooks the church and pond in this village, and was remodelled in the 16th century on a 14th century fortified mansion. It is haunted by two spirits. The White Lady (Y Ladi Wen) appears in the hallway at midnight, walks through the house to the terrace and screams before making her way to Lady Wood. In the early 20th century the terrace was lifted for building work, and a woman's skeleton with a bullet lodged in it was found, at the spot where the ghost screams. A small man dressed in green, with piercing green eyes appears on the stairway, where there is said to have been a fatal sword fight centuries ago. The Green Man and The White Lady are just two of hundreds of spectres across Wales.

ANNUN 5th-6th century
ANHUN, ANNON
June 9 (Madrun's date)

The virgin handmaid of St Madrun, the daughter of Gwrthefyr Fendigaid (Vortimer the Blessed). On their way to Ynys Enlli, Anhun and Madrun stopped to sleep, and both dreamed that a voice had told them to build a church there. Trawsfynydd (the home of Hedd Wynn) was the place where they founded their church. There is a ten-feet standing stone named Llech Idris, 'thrown' by the giant Idris Gawr from the summit of Caer Idris. There was a Cae Gwyn Ffynnon Annon ('field of the holy well of Annun') in the parish of Llanbeulan in Anglesey, and Llyn Anwn is near Llanystumudwy, Caernarfon, the home of David Lloyd-George.

Alphabetical Listing of the Saints of Wales and Religious Events

ARDDUN BENASGELL (Wing-headed) 6th century

The sister of St Dunawd and St Sawyl, her husband Brochwel Ysgythrog ap Cyngen ap Cadell fought Ethelfrith at the battle of Chester to defend Bangor-is-Coed. Her son was St Tyssilio. Dolarddun, an old manor-house in Castle Caereinion, was supposed to have been named after her.

ARIANELL 6th century
ARGANGELL

A deranged noblewoman from Gwent, who had to be tied up to prevent her killing or injuring herself. Her father appealed to Dyfrig, who cured her and she remained a virgin consecrated to God until her death. A stream near St Maughan's Church in Monmouth bore her name.

ARIANWEN 5th – 6th century
WRGREN, ARANWEN

A daughter or grand-daughter of Brychan, married to Iorwerth Hirflawdd ap Tegonwy ap Teon. Tegonwy ap Teon was king of Powys, and Arianwen was possibly the mother of Caenog Mawr.

ARILD
ALKELD, ARILDA
July 20, October 30

A virgin martyred at Kingston-by-Thornbury in Gloucestershire by Muncius. Her relics were taken to Gloucester Cathedral by the Normans, and her shrine was famous for miracles. Her churches were Oldbury-on-Severn and Oldbury-on-the-Hill.

ABBOT ARMEL d.c. 570 (d.552 according to Farmer)
ARTHMAEL ARTHFAEL, ARZEL, ERMEL, ERMYN, ERVAN, ARMAGILLUS
Feast Day 14-17 August, with August 16 being most popular in the Breton sources, and July 27 also noted in Vannes. June 13 is Le Passage feast day in St Armel.
Invoked for headaches, fever, colic, gout and rheumatism, and sometimes the patron of hospitals.

Abbot Armel was said to be the cousin of St Samson and St Cadfan, and from south-east Wales. Other relatives were the saints Maglorius, Malo, Padarn and Tudno. He was a member of Illtud's 'côr' (college) of monks. He went with many Welshmen to Brittany (possibly to flee the 547 Yellow Plague, and one source says that he went with Abbot Carentmail who is probably Carannog). With the assistance of King Childebert, Armel founded monasteries at Plouarmel and Ploermel. Ploermel was formerly called Lann Arthmael. With Samson, he assisted in restoring the throne of Domnonia (Britanny) to King Iuthael in 555, and the famous Samson Cross in Llanilltud records the fact.* There is St Armel south of Vannes, and another north-west of Bubry, near St Maurice (Meurig?). Plouarzel is west of St Renan, and another Plouarzel is near Lampaul. Ville Ermel is just north of Paimpont Forest, of Arthurian renown, as is Kersamson.

Another source states that Armel was a native of Morganwg, in the cantref of Penychen. King Arthur was said to have been born at Boverton in Penychen, and his uncle Pawl Penychen's Penllyn Court was just six miles north. There is a book of Breton names *'Tous les Prenoms Breton'* by Alain Stephan of Gissort University which states that Arzel/Armel was born in South Glamorgan, was connected to Childebert's court, and was a 'warrior-lord'. **There seem to be many links pointing that Armel and Arthur were the same person**. (See the footnote in the entry on Derfel Gadarn). The Iolo mss. however record him as being the son of Hywel ab Emyr Llydaw, and the brother of Derfael Gardarn, Tudwal, Dwyfael and possibly Leonore, and cousin of Cadfan, Samson, Padarn, Maglorius and Malo. However, Breton mss. would surely record the fact that Armel was a grandson of Emyr Llydaw (Budic II). Also Barber and Pykit believe that Arthmael ab Hywel Mawr was known as St Mael in Wales.

With Abbot Carentmail, Arthmael landed at Aber Benoit in Finistere and moved inland to found Plouarzel. Around 540, Jonas King of Domnonia had died and Conmore (Conmire, Conor) married his widow, forcing the rightful heir Prince Ithael (Judual, Iuthael) to flee. Armel/Arthmael left Wales sometime after Camlan (537 or 539) and went to see King Childebert in Paris to plead Iuthael's cause against Conmore. Samson's arrival compounded the religious pressure against Conmore, and together they organised an armed rising, and thus Conmore was killed in battle in 555. Arthmael was given land where he established a monastery, where the present St Armel's Church stands at Ploermel (Plouharzel) in Morbihan (seven miles south-east of Josselin). [Intriguingly, Ploermel was the chosen place for the famous 'Combat of the Thirty' in 1351. Thirty knights from the English garrison at Ploermel met 30 knights from the French garrison at nearby Josselin. Described in vivid detail by Barbara Tuchman ('A Distant Mirror'), the slaughter only ended when the English leader Bemborough died.] Many Welsh princes handed on their territories or positions and retired in middle age to monasteries (even Maelgwn Gwynedd for a time). This may have been a mechanism to ensure the survival of the princedoms, rather than seeing them split up equally by 'cyfran' (gavelkind) on the ruler's death. The strong legend that Arthur was 'unmanned' by a groin wound at Camlan may have had an effect upon his decision to seek the monastic life and hand his crown on to the son of his ally Geraint ab Erbin. His surviving son Morgan may have been too young to take over.

In the valley of Loutehel, Armel struck the ground with his staff and supplied water for the valley. He founded the monastery at Ploermel, near a lake called l'Etang du Duc. Montsaint-Armel is also named after him, and his image appears in a stained glass window at St Saveur, Dinan, with a slain dragon. He took the creature to the top of the mountain and ordered it to leap into the river below. Ergue-Armel outside Quimper was also formerly dedicated to him, as were churches at Langoet and Languedias, and four more chapels. In the Breviary of Leon, Arthmael is referred to as *'Miles fortissimus'* – *'the strongest of soldiers'*, and in the Rennes prose he is invoked as an *'armigere'* against the enemies of salvation. He founded the monastery of St Armel-des-Bochaux near Rennes.

Henry VII's glorious chapel at Westminster Abbey features a gauntleted Armel, whom Henry believed saved him from shipwreck. Armel's mutilated monument also stands on Cardinal Morton's monument in the crypt of Canterbury Cathedral. Armel is commemorated on alabaster sculptures in Stonyhurst College and St Mary Brookfield church in London, and on the reredos at Romsey Abbey. In his Anglicised form, Ermyn, he was venerated at Westminster Abbey. St Ermyn's Hotel in Westminster stood on St Ermyn's Hill, first mentioned in records in 1496 as St Armille's Hill. Armel's chapel there is now represented by Christchurch in

Alphabetical Listing of the Saints of Wales and Religious Events

Westminster. Why would a Breton warrior-monk be celebrated in London? St Erme in Cornwall appears to by Armel's only British foundation.

In the Middle Ages Armel was prayed to by people with gout and rheumatism. Sometimes a patron of hospitals, his invocation was said to cure headaches, fever, colic, gout and rheumatism. He is usually depicted in armour and a chasuble, leading a dragon with an ermine stole. He was said to have subdued a dragon – could this be the white dragon of the Anglo-Saxons rather than Conmore? As mentioned, recent researchers have placed Armel as King Arthur who went to Brittany after recovering from his wounds at Avalon (Enlli Island). If the grim Battle of Camlan happened in 539, then Arthur could have joined his Breton kinsmen to fight for them. The dragon, ermine and the placing of his saint's day in the Sarum Calendar in 1498, under the recent Tudor dynasty, mean that the links with King Arthur **must** be explored further.

In Saint Armel, the last of the saltbeds were abandoned thirty years ago, and turned over to oyster basins. The first Saturday in April sees the Miss Pearl festival at neighbouring Gildas-de-Rhuys. Gildas was Arthur's contemporary. Breton cider**, mussels and oysters are recommended. There are no known/remaining dedications to Arthmael in Wales, only the chapel in Cornwall and he was commemorated annually at Stratton. His cult spread extremely rapidly from Brittany to Normandy, Touraine and Anjou.***

The website 'Catholic Online Saints' givs the following entry: *'St Armagillus d.c. 570 Feastday August 16. Welsh missionary, called Armel, Ermel and Ervan, and a cousin of St Samson. He studied under Abbot Carentmael joining the abbot in missionary journies to Brittany, France. The missionaries founded Saint-Armel-des-Boscheaux and Plou-Ermel or Plouharzel. Connor, a local chieftain, forced them to leave the mission until 555. Connor was slain in battle that year, allowing their return. Armagillus is honoured in a Cornish church, St Erme.'* Samson's mother was Anna ferch Tewdrig, the sister of Meurig, which makes him Arthur's cousin. Arthur ap Meurig disappeared from Wales around 540 after the Battle of Camlan, and Armel was known as a warrior-saint in Brittany. The dispossessed Breton family of Amwn Ddu had married into Arthur's family, and many fought for him. Arthur had given lands to Carannog who went to Brittany with monks. Probably Carannog was Carentmael. It seems that a strong case can be made for Arthur and Armel being the same person. It would not have been in the interests of the princes of Wales and Henry VII to publicise the fact, as they were of the House of Gwynedd, not of the Silurian House of Gwynlliwg and Glwyssing.

* The Samson Cross at Llanilltud Fawr is *'in memory of Samson the Abbot and to Juthikal (Iudical) and Artmael for the sake of their souls.'* It seems absolutely certain, despite academic denial, that it records these principal actors of the 6th century.

**At the various 'Welsh Bars' in Ibiza, Strongbow cider is thought of as the national drink of Wales. In various parts of Wales, a great deal of cider is drunk because the national beers and lagers are not liked. There is a great opportunity for Welsh cider to be manufactured on a large scale in Wales, just as it brings in extra income to farms in the West Country.

***Ploermel is near the area of Brocielande and the magical Fôret de Paimpont. This has been sympathetically developed to link Arthurian legends with the site. It is where Merlin was imprisoned in a pool by Morgan le Fay, where the knights of the Round Table met at Comper Castle, where knights tramped across the wastelands seeking the Grail. Comper Castle has been made into an excellent Arthurian exhibition centre, the Abbey at Paimpont features effigies of the Welsh founding saints of Brittany, and a tree in the forest has been painted gold. Sights include a wonderful walk along the Val Sans Retour (Valley of No Return), the Fontaine de Barenton, the Fontaine de Jouvence (Spring of Eternal Youth), Comper Castle and its lake, the Etang Bleu (Blue Lake), the Etang du pas du Hout, Le Temple Helouin megalith, the Lac de Tremelin and the Tombeau de Merlin (Merlin's Tomb dolmen). Le Point-du-Secret on the southern fringe of the forest may hold the clue to the burial-place of Arthur/Armel.

ARTHEN 5th - 6th century

Fourth son of Brychan, there was a church dedicated to him in Gwynlliwg. This was the now extinct Llanarthen near Marshfield, Monmouthshire, destroyed by Saxons. He may have been the father of Cynon who lived near Llangors in Brecon. He was said to be buried in Manaw (the Isle of Man), where he was also recorded as a saint.

ARTHFODDW 6th century

A disciple of Dyfrig at Hentland and Moccas, who went to live in a hermit's cell at Lann Arthbodu on the Gower peninsula (thought to be where Pennard is today).

ARTHNE
ARTHNEU

The church of Llanarthne in Carmarthen's Tywy Valley is now dedicated to St David. A fortified mediaeval house at Lanarthen was visited by Owain Glyndŵr, and owned by Rhys ap Thomas, the warrior who was supposed to have killed Richard III at Bosworth Field in 1485.

Between Llanarthne and Porthyrhyd the National Botanic Garden of Wales is taking shape, a £44 million project at Middleton Hall, with the greatest glasshouse in Europe. Based on the parklands landscaped by William Paxton in the late 1700's, this magnificent 570-acre site was fully opened in 2000 (telephone 01558-668768 for details).

ARTHUR (see Armel/Arthmael) d. 539 after Camlan, 547* or later in 570
ARTHMAEL, ARTHWYS, ATHRWYS, ARTHUS, ADRAS, ARTHUR ap MEURIG ap TEWDRIG

At Pen Arthur Farm near St David's in Pembroke were found several ancient stones. There was a holy well (Ffynnon Arthur) and a chapel at this same site. All four stones are now in St David's Cathedral. One stone has a Latin cross with two-part terminals, another has a complex inter-laced ring-cross, and there are two fretted ring-cross slabs. One reads A7W1HS XPS GURMARC – *'Alpha and Omega is Jesus Christ, Gurmarc'*

Some historians point to King Arthur's burial place at Llanbedr-y-Mynydd (St Peter's Church) in ruins at Llanbad near Llanharan. Boverton is reputed to be his birthplace, near Llanilltud Fawr. According to Nennius, at the battle of Guinnion Fort Arthur *'carried the image of the Holy Mary, the everlasting Virgin, on his shield, and the heathen were put to flight on that day, and there was a great massacre of them, through the power of Our Lord Jesus Christ and the power of the Blessed Virgin Mary.'* The Annales Cambriae tell of the great battle of Mount Badon, where Arthur carried the cross on his shoulders. Arthur stopped the westward movement of the Germanic tribes through Britain for a generation, except for the Jutes taking the Isle of Wight.

The Easter Annals describe Arthur's final battle in 539 after 12 victories, at Camlann, *'in which Arthur and Medraut (Mordred) perished.'* However, we still are unsure if Mordred was his enemy or fighting alongside him, or indeed if Arthur died here. One of the problems with Arthur is that of the suspicion of the early Roman Church with this fabulous hero, known across Europe. As a result the Catholic monk writing the Life of Cadog describes him as being lustful and perverse, and the Life of Padarn makes him out to be a mean despot. There are other unflattering references in many of the later religious sources. Certainly his contemporary, Gildas, had no cause to love Arthur because he executed Huail, the brother of Gildas.

In the Triads, Arthur is recorded as one of the *'three red chieftains of Britain'* and also as one of the *'three heroic supreme sovereigns of Britain.'* The 6th century Llywarch Hen, one of *'the three wise-counselling equestrians of Arthur's Court'* called Arthur a great warrior, as did Nennius, writing three hundred years later. A 10th century copy of Nennius, by Mark the Hermit, called him *'dux belli'* (war leader) and *'belliger Arthur'* (warlike Arthur). All these references predate the mediaeval French romances.

'The Genealogy of Iestyn ap Gwrgan' seems to confuse Arthur with Adras:
'Adras, the son of Meyryg, was a very heroic sovereign, who frequently put the Saxons to flight; killing and destroying them. He enacted many laws and ordinances for civil and ecclesiastical government; and was the first who instituted a class of Equestrians (mounted knights), *for the maintenance of correct comportment in war, and due discipline at arms; and also to guard well the country, watch carefully its enemies, and to establish an efficient system of communications with regard to hostilities and legislation.*

Morgan, the son of Adras, called Morgan the Courteous, and Morgan of Glamorgan, was a renowned king, and an Equestrian of Arthur's court, and of the Round Table. He was Arthur's cousin; particularly handsome; extremely courteous; and so cheerfully kind and merciful, that, when he went out to war, no one, old and strong enough to bear arms, would remain at home; hence it was that he acquired the designation of – Morgan the Courteous. It was he that gave the appellation – Morganwg – to his country; which name it has retained to this very hour.'
'He erected a Court at Margam, a place which he raised to a Bishoprick; which retained that distinction during the lives of five bishops, when it became united to Llandaff.' Morgan's grave was found between Margam and Kenfig (see Cynffig).

It seems that Margam was originally called Morgan, and there is still a noble mansion there. An important but little-known fact relating to Morgan was related by Edward Mansel of Margam, a man of Norman descent, in his 'Account of the Conquest of Glamorgan' of 1591. Robert Fitzhamon was the Norman who conquered much of Glamorgan from its last prince Iestyn ap Gwrgant:
'Before the time of Robert Fitzhamon there was one Chief Lord of Glamorgan whose were the high Royalties, and he assembled the other Lords every month to his Court where all matters of Justice were determined and finally settled, these Lords sat in Judgment on all matters of Law, with twelve Freeholders from every Lordship to give opinions after what came to their knowledge, and the Bishop of Llandaff sat in the high Court as a Councellor of Conscience according to the Laws of God, this Court was formed they say by Morgan (c.515-570?) who

was Prince of the Country **after King Arthur** *in the manner of Christ and his twelve apostles, and this form of Law was kept by Sir Robert Fitzhamon according to the old usage of the Country, after the High Court was held, which lasted three days, the Courts of the twelve Lordships were held in turn, and from them an appeal might be made to the High Court in the Country, the Lord and his yeomen in the same form and manner as in the High Court.*

After the winning of the Country by Sir Robert Fitzhamon, he took to him his twelve knights to supply the places in his Courts of the Lawful and right Lords of the twelve Lordships, which caused discontent insomuch that Welsh Lords took arms under Pain Turberville and Caradock ab Iestyn and Madoc his Brother, and they came to Cardiff Castle and surrounded it insomuch that it was on the point of being taken when King Henry the first going to the top of the Raven Tower to enquire concerning the tumult which was heard, he saw the place all encompassed by fierce armed men, whereupon he called a parley when Pain Turberville told him the reason saying that if rightful orders were not made, to restore the Laws of Morgan the first, that he and Robert Fitzhamon should feel at the ears very soon of what stuff the Castle walls were of at the heart on which all in the Castle councelled together, and it was seen best to yield to the Country that request.'

This may be the origin of 12 man juries. The book goes on to say, that in 1110, after another infraction of the Laws of Morgan by the Norman lords, there was a rising by the heroic Ifor Bach:

'Ifor Petit rose up the country for that the old laws were not kept to, and at this time it was again settled for the proper Courts to be held in all the Lordships and the Lords of the Courts to join with the Chief Lord in the High Court which Laws had been a second time broke by the Norman Lords, and in this engagement as was said before the Welsh Lords won the right and it so remained till Wales and England were united in one Realm, and the Laws were altered.' It was on this occasion that Ifor Bach scaled the walls of Cardiff Castle and took captive Robert Earl of Gloucester and his wife, escaping with them back to his Lordship of Senghenydd. This was also recorded shortly after by St Caradoc at Llancarfan.

Arthur's 'Saying of the Wise' is:
*'Hast thou heard the saying of Arthur,
The Emperor, the mighty sovereign?
"There is no devastation like a deceiver".'*
He is also named as one of *'the three red ravagers of the Island of Britain'*, along with Rhun ap Beli and Morgant the Wealthy.

There are several triads referring to Arthur. From 'Gereint fab Erbin' there is:
*At Llongborth I saw Arthur's
Brave men, they hewed with steel,
Emperor, leader in toil.*

In 'Mi a Wum' is recorded:
*'I have been where Llachau was slain,
The son of Arthur, terrible in songs,
When ravens croaked over blood'*
and also:
*'What man is the porter?'
'Glewlwyd Great-Grip,
What man asks it?
'Arthur and Cai the Fair.'*

'What retinue travels with you?'
'The best men in the world.'

Arthur is also mentioned in 'Preidu Annwn', 'Cad Goddau', and finally in this marvellously evocative verse from 'Y Gododdin', the story of the British defeat at Catraeth and the oldest British poem:
'He charged before three hundred of the finest,
He cut down both centre and wing,
He excelled in the forefront of the noblest host,
He gave gifts of horses from the herd in winter.
He fed black ravens on the rampart of a fortress
Although he was no Arthur.
Among the powerful ones in battle,
In the front rank, Gwawrddur was a palisade.'

*This 547 date is intriguing, for Maelgwn Gwynedd died of the Bubonic Plague (the Yellow Death) in this year. Arthur was recorded as having a festering wound in his groin. This is one of the classic symptoms of the plague, along with the weeping yellow pustules under the armpits.

NOTE ON ARTHUR'S KNIGHTS OF THE ROUND TABLE

It is interesting to note how many Welsh saints were related to, or served, Arthur in some way. A medieval text 'Deuddeg Pedwar Marchog ar Hugan Llys Arthur' gives his 24 knights at court as: Gwalchmai (i.e. Gawain), Drudwas, Eliwlod, Gwrgi (i.e. Bors), Perceval, Galahad, Lancelot, Owain, Menw, Tristan, Eiddilig, Nasiens, Mordred, Hoel, Blaes, Cadog, Petroc, Morfran ap Tegid, Sanddef, Glewlyd, Cyon, Aron, Llywarch Hen and Bedwyr (Bedivere).
Of these, Gwalchmai/Gawain, Bors, Perceval, Galahad, Lancelot, Tristan, Mordred and Bedwyr/Bedivere are included on the thirteenth century Winchester Castle Round Table forgery.

Also of these we can count as Welsh saints Aron, Cadog, Petroc and Llywarch Hen. It is still unsure whether Arthur fought with or against Mordred at Camlan in 539. Instead, it may have been the forces of Maelgwn Gwynedd that ambushed him.

If we can cross-relate the knights mentioned above with the saints mentioned in this book with Arthurian connections, we have the following reference list:

St Alan Frygan ab Emyr Lydaw, whose troops deserted Arthur on the eve of Camlan. He married into Arthur's family;
St Allgo ap Caw appears as Calcas ap Caw in the Mabinogion, fighting for Arthur. From Glamorgan, he went to Anglesey, from which he was forced to flee by Maelgwn;
St Amwn Ddu ab Emyr Llydaw married into Arthur's family and may be the origin of the Black Knight;
St Angar, Angawd ap Caw is mentioned in the Mabinogion as Arthur's knight;
St Aron (Aaron) ap Cynfarch, father of St Ciwg, was given lands by Arthur. A saint of this name left Wales in the early 6th century and settled at St Malo;
St Baglan ab Ithel Hael is given as Sir Balan, and was related to Arthur. Baglan is culted in Brittany and therefore may have fought for Armel/Arthur there;

Bishop Bedwyn, Sir Baudwin was said to be one of Arthur's first knights, made a constable of the realm and one of the governors of Britain, but ended his life as a *'physician and hermit'* St Bedwyn was also called a 'comeregulus' (count-ruler), and Arthur had a brother called 'Comereg'. He was bishop of Cernyw (east Glamorgan/Gwent);

Bedwyr Bedrynant (of the perfect sinews) was Cai's companion and the model for Bedivere, mentioned in Culhwch and Olwen. The warrior with Cai (St Cynan) most documented with Arthur, he died fighting for him (Armel?) in France;

Bors' father was said to also be named Bors, who married Evaine, and his brother was Sir Lionel and cousin Sir Lancelot. He was said to be the father of St Elian Wyn, but Elian's father was Gallgu Rieddog. Bors has been identified with St Gwrgi.

St Brioc may possibly have been Arthur's brother Frioc, or Brioc the grandson of Brychan;

Sir Breunor ap Dunawd Fawr is the brother of Sir (St) Deiniol and Sir Dinadan, and is known as the Black Knight;

St Brynach was given land by Meurig (Arthur's father), and argued with Maelgwn Gwynedd;

St Cadfan is known as a 'warrior saint' in Brittany, and possibly helped Arthur and Samson overcome Conmire;

St Cado ap Geraint fought with Arthur at Badon Hill, was a great friend of Caradog Freich Fras (his brother-in-law), is linked with Guinevere and fought in Brittany;

St Cadog (497-577) is linked with Arthur's family and disputed lands with Rhun ap Maelgwn and Rhun ap Brychan. He sheltered an enemy of Arthur. In a 1999 Western Mail article, Lawrence Main reckons St Cadog to be Sir Galahad. He goes on to reason that *'since Cadoc's father was Gwynlliw and Sir Galahad was the son of Sir Lancelot, it seems obvious that Sir Lancelot was Gwynlliw, a neighbour of King Arthur and a notorious womaniser;*

St Caffo ap Caw, brother of Gildas, was killed by Maelgwn Gwynedd's men in Glamorgan or Anglesey;

St Cai ap Cynyr Farchog may have became Sir Kay, and Landygai is on the north Wales coast;

St Caradog Freich Fras ab Ynyr Gwent and Madrun is mentioned in the Arthurian triads, and became 'Sir Caradoc Bris Bras'. He married Amwn Ddu's sister, and became a knight of Arthur. One of Arthur's *'three cavaliers of battle'*, he fought in Brittany (for Armel?). His brother 'Turquine' wanted to kill Lancelot;

St Carannog ap Corun was given lands by Arthur, and went with Armel to Brittany;

St Cawrdaf ap Caradog Freichfras ab Ynyr Gwent is given in the Mabinogion as Arthur's counsellor. His 'côr' was near Penllin, at Miskin;

St Caw fled from his kingdom in the North of England, and has 21 children listed in the tale of Culhwch and Olwen. Many became knights of the round table in mediaeval reworkings of the life of Arthur ap Meurig ap Tewdrig, who gave some of them lands in 'Siluria', i.e. South-East Wales;

Cedwy *'of Arthur's court'* is St Cedwyn ap Gwgon Gwron ap Peredur, the half-brother of St Ceidio and Caradog Freichfras;

St Cenydd was a baby at a feast held by Arthur to celebrate Christmas;

St Cywyllog ferch Caw was the wife of Mordred, and given lands by Maelgwn Gwynedd;

St Cybi argued with Maelgwn Gwynedd, although his monastery lands were given by this king;

St Cynan Gefnhir (or Cian) ap Cynwyd may be Cyon, a 'knight-counsellor to Arthur, who in the Winchester lists is one of the 24 knights;

St Curig was a contemprary of Arthur, known as Curig the Knight, and is remembered in Brittany;

Cynan, also known as St Kea is possibly Cai (Sir Kay) ap Lleuddyn Luydog from Lothian, who died in 550, a cousin of St Beuno. He was in Brittany at the same time as Armel;

St Cynddilig ap Nwython was summoned to Arthur's coronation, with his brother Rhun;

St Cynddilig ap Gildas attended Arthur's coronation according to Geoffrey of Monmouth;

Alphabetical Listing of the Saints of Wales and Religious Events

St Cyndeyrn is mentioned as Arthur's chief bishop in the North (see Triads);

St Cyngar's father, Geraint, died fighting for Arthur;

St Cynidr appears to be the St Keneder who was with Cadog in his confrontation with Arthur;

St Cynin ap Tudwal Befr was a warrior in early triads and the brother of Sir Ifor who was linked with Arthur as a knight;

Cynlas Goch ab Owain was assassinated by Maelgwn Gwynedd when he tried to break his overlordship;

St Cynwyl ap Dunawd fawr was the brother of Deiniol, and escaped from Camlan with Sandde Bryd Angel and Morfran ap Tegid;

Cystennin (Constantine) ap Cado ap Geraint took over the High Kingship from Arthur after Camlan;

Sir Danadan was possibly St Dunawd Fawr, St Dingad or St Dunwyd;

Sir Daniel was possibly St Deiniol Fawr, with a brother Sir Breunor, known as the Black Knight. Deiniol may have been with Maelgwn Gwynedd at Llaniltud Fawr. He also witnessed a land grant by Maelgwn to Cyndeyrn;

Derfel Gadarn ap Hywel Mawr ab Emyr Llydaw survived Camlan. He was said to be the brother of Armel, and also of Christiolus, Sulien, Rhystud, Dwywan and Dwyfael;

Dewi, St David, was thought by Giraldus Cambrensis and Geoffrey of Monmouth to be Arthur's uncle. In his time, Arthur's knight Caradog Freichfras pushed the Irish out of Menevia;

Sir Drudwas could be St Trydwas:

St Dwyfael ap Hywel Mawr was one of Arthur's knights;

St Dyfrig possily crowned Arthur;

St Dywel ab Erbyn fought for Arthur, mentioned in Culhwch and Olwen and the Black Book of Carmarthen;

St Edern ap Nudd is mentioned in the Dream of Rhonabwy and the tale of Geraint ab Erbin;

St Einion's father Owain Ddantgwyn was treacherously killed by Maelgwn Gwynedd;

St Elffin was rescued from Maelgwn Gwynedd's Deganwy Castle by Taliesin;

St Elidyr fought Maelgwn Gwynedd or Rhun ap Maelgwn;

Eliwlod was one of the 24 knights, a grandson of Uther and nephew of Arthur, and perhaps the original of Sir Lancelot. Could this be St Eliquid or St Eiliwedd/Almedha?

St Endellion was said to be Arthur's god-daughter;

King Erbyn of Domnonia's sons Geraint, Dywel and Erinid fought for Arthur. Erbyn asked Arthur for Geraint to return to the West Country to take over the kingship;

St Ernin (Hernin) was linked to Conmire, who Armel fought in Brittany;

St Euddogwy was given land by Arthur;

St Eugrad ap Caw fought for Arthur in Culhwch and Olwen, as 'Ergyryat';

St Ffili is mentioned on a stone at Ogmore in connection with Arthmael/Arthur;

St Geraint ab Erbyn killed at Llongborth fighting for Arthur;

St Gildas ap Caw's brother Hywel killed Gwydre ap St Gwenafwy, so he was executed by Arthur (see Hywel, Gildas);

St Gildas arbitrated in a dispute concerning king Melwas, Gwenhwyfar and Arthur;

Gwalchmai has been associated with Gawain/Gofan (see Mabinogion), and as Arthur's nephew, killed by Lancelot or Mordred;

St Gwen has been identified with Gwenhwyfar (Guinevere);

St Gwenafwy's son was stabbed by Huail, which caused Arthur to execute Huail;

Gwenhwyfar (Guinevere, Gwenhaf) founded Amesbury Church after her affair with Lancelot (or Maelgwn Gwynedd or Medrod), and St Mylor's relics were taken there;

St Gwernabui was given land by Arthur;

Gwgan Gwron ap Peredur features in Arthurian triads and married St Madrun (see Cedwyn);

Gwrgi (Bors), the brother or son of Peredur saw the aftermath of the battle of Arderydd c.580;
St Gwrst witnessed a land grant by Maelgwn (see Trillo);
St Gwrthl was a chief elder who recognised Arthur as overlord, and was killed in Cardigan, possibly at Penbryn (Llongborth);
St Gwyddno was present when Arthur's son Llacheu was killed;
St Gwyndaf Hen married into Arthur's family
St Gwynlliw 'the Warrior' has been identified with Lancelot, and is Cadog's father;
Hywel ap Caw was killed by Arthur;
St Hywyn ap Gwyndaf was Arthur's nephew (see Meurig);
Sir Iddo was identified with the warrior-saint son of Cawrdaf but he was possibly St Iddon ab Ynyr Gwent;
Sir Ifor was the brother of St Cynin, and the son of Tudwal Befr and Nefydd;
St Idloes, with St Sadwrn was one of Arthur's knights;
St Illtud Farchog (the knight) attended Arthur's court with the warrior St Cadog;
St Kea was linked with Arthur, Gildas, Gwenhwyfar and Mordred, but may be the same saint as Cai;
St Lorcan Wyddel is mentioned in Arthurian triads;
Sir Lucan (Lorcan?) was said to be the brother of St Bedwyr;
St Llywarch Hen may be a later addition to the list, but his son was Sandde who escaped the slaughter at Camlan;
St Mabon, the brother of St Teilo, was a follower and servant at Arthur's father's court;
St Maglorius went to Brittany with Samson at the same time as Armel, and was the nephew of Amwn Ddu and nephew of Arthur;
Maelgwn Gwynedd appears to have become High King (Pendragon) after Camlan, and is mentioned as Arthur's chief elder in St David's (see Triads);
St Maelog ap Caw is one of the knights in Culhwch and Olwen;
St Maglorius was a nephew of Arthur who went at the same time as Arthur/Armel to Brittany;
St Malo, a kinsman of Arthur, had major problems with Conmire in Brittany at the same time as Armel was there;
St Marchell was Arthur's aunt;
St Mechnyd ap Sandde was a knight;
Medrod married Cywyllog ferch Caw, who was given lands by Maelgwn;
St Meugan seems to have intervened in a dispute between Maelgwn and Cadog. He was related to Arthur;
St Meurig, Arthur's father has been placed as Uther Pendragon;
St Mewan was in Brocielande, a friend of Judicael at the same time as Armel;
Morgan Mwynfawr ('gentle and great') was a knight, and Arthur's son, blessed by St Cawrdaf;
St Ninnoc was Arthur's grandmother;
Sir Nwython was probably St Nwythen ap Gildas, mentioned in Culhwch and Olwen;
Owain ab Urien Rheged was one of Arthur's knights;
St Padarn argued with Arthur and Maelgwn;
Peredur became Sir Percival, and was Pryderi ap Dolar mentioned in The Gododdin and the Arthurian triads. His son was St Dwyfael. Sir Dwyfael who fought for Arthur was probably Hywel Mawr's son;
St Petroc (Pedrog) was St Cadog's nephew, one of the *'three just knights of court'*, one of the seven knights who survived Camlan, and known as *'Paladruellt' ('splintered lance')*;
St Piran was mentioned in Arthurian legend as being appointed Archbishop of York;
Rhun ap Gildas was said to have been summoned to Arthur's coronation;
St Sadwrn was a knight and nephew of Emyr Llydaw;
St Samson was Arthur's cousin or uncle and helped Armel overcome Conmire;

Sandde Bryd Angel has been identified by some as Padarn – he escaped from Camlan;
St Talhaearn is linked in a 'saying of the wise' with Arthur and said to be the chaplain of Emrys Wledig;
St Tathan is Arthur's brother-in-law;
St Tathana's legend states that the court of Arthur's father Meurig was at Boverton;
St Tegfedd ferch Tegid Foel, of Penllyn, was with Derfel Gadarn after Camlan, and said to have been killed by Illtud so Arthur's tomb was not revealed;
St Teilo was given the land where Tegfedd was killed for settling Arthur's dispute with Cadog;
St Tewdrig was Pendragon, as was his son St Meurig, Arthur's father;
St Trillo witnessed a land grant to Maelgwn, along with Deiniol, Gwrst and Rhun ap Maelgwn;
Turquine wanted to kill Lancelot - he was the brother of St Caradog;
St Tydecho ap Amwn Ddu, the nephew of Arthur, was persecuted by Maelgwn;
St Teithfallt, Arthur's great-grandfather, is claimed to be Emrys Wledig (see Tyfodwg);
St Umbrafael, the brother of St Amwn Ddu, married Arthur's sister Afrella;
St Winnoc was the son of King Judicael, helped by Armel/Arthur to regain his throne;
St Ynyr Gwent is linked with Arthur, and went to Brittany.

Thus we have around 110 saints of the early-mid 6th century whose stories intertwine around the family of Arthur ap Meurig ap Tewdrig and the legends of King Arthur and St Armel.

Taliesin's poem 'The Graves of Warriors' gives us the following enigmatic lines:
'The grave of the horse, the grave of the Fierce-One,
The grave of Grim-Visaged red-sword,
The grave of Arthur, a mystery of the world.'
If Arthur was Armel, and went to Brittany to help his Breton kinsmen, this problem re-occurs. Armel's tomb at Ploermel is empty. Another translation of 'Englynion y Beddau' (Verses of the Graves) is:
'There is a grave for March, a grave for Gwythur,
A grave for Gwgawn Red-Sword;
The world's wonder a grave for Arthur.'
It is a difficult translation, which either means that he had a wonderful burial-place, or that no-one will ever know where he is. The 'Pointe du Secret' on the fringe of Paimpont Forest may hold a clue to this mystery.

NOTE ON ARTHUR'S SON

Lacheu fab Arthur appears in the Black Book of Carmarthen in battle against Cai Wyn. Also Gwyddno Garanhir claims he was present when Llacheu was killed. He is often mentioned elsewhere as a fearless warrior, and was supposed to have died 'below Llech Ysgar'. An early poem commemorates this:
'I have been where Llacheu was killed,
Son of Arthur, marvellous in songs,
When the ravens croaked over blood . . .
I have been where the warriors of Britain were slain,
From the East to the North;
I am alive, they are in their grave.'

Stones called the 'Sons of Arthur' may indicate that others of Arthur's offspring died, just leaving the young Morgan, causing the leadership of Britain to pass to Constans, then to Maelgwn. These two standing stones, Cerrig Meibion Arthur, stand near Cwm Cerwyn in the Preseli Hills, where Arthur fought the Twrch Trwyth and his son Gwydre and another son died. Near here is the unusually elliptical stone circle, Bedd Arthur. One tradition is that Morgan was Arthur's youngest son, born of the third of the ladies named Gwenhwyfar that Arthur married. His rise to favour irked Modred, who was Arthur's nephew, foster-son and hopeful successor. The same story tells us that Modred was the incestuous offspring of Arthur and his sister Gwyar (Morgan le Fay).

NOTE ON ARTHUR'S STONES

There are dozens of wells, cromlechs and standing stones named after Arthur in Wales. In Mynachlog Ddu there is Cerrig Meibion Arthur (The Stones of the Sons of Arthur) as well as Coetan Arthur and Cerrig Marchogion (The Stones of his Knights). On the Preseli Hills there is another Coetan Arthur, and a Carn Arthur rocking stone. A stone circle of 15 stones on the Preseli's is one of his many 'graves', Bedd Arthur. Also on the Preselis is Gors Fawr, near Mynacholg-Ddu, the most important stone circle in Wales, near the site of Stonehenge's famous 'bluestones'.

Leaving Pembroke, Arthur's Stone in Llanrhidian near Sketty is possibly Wales' most renowned prehistoric monument. Maen Ceti, the Big Stone of Sketty is referred to in the Welsh Triads as a wonder of Wales, and later writers thought that the Ark of the Covenant was concealed there. It is not the biggest dolmen in Wales, with a capstone of 14 feet by 7 feet, but is imbued with legend and tradition.

Coetan Arthur at Newport Dyfed is a fine dolmen supported by three pillars. Local farmers put white quartz on their farm gates to ward off evil spirits. This tradition may have come down from the times of Newgrange and the Welsh burial chambers where lumps of white quartz have been found. One explanation of these stones in burial chambers was the Celtic Christian burial practice – the lumps of shiny white quartz contained the new heavenly names that the deceased would acquire at the Apocalypse. Hundreds of other megaliths and dolmens are described by Barber and Williams in 'The Ancient Stones of Wales'.

ARVAN
ARUNYO

In 955, the church of St Arvan's near Chepstow in Monmouth was known as the Ecclesia Sanctorum Jarmen et Febric, but in the Book of Llandaf it was noted in the 14th century as *'Ecclesia de Sancto Aruyno'*. Wirt Sikes wrote in 1881: *'And standing in the graveyard of St Arven's, with the perfection of beautiful cultivated and hedgerowed fields all about you, yonder in the distance looms before you a scene whose grandeur is almost worthy to be mentioned in the same breath with the Yosemite Valley. Indeed as I look upon it I can almost believe myself standing once more on that rugged precipice which overlooks the mighty valley in the Sierras at whose bottom winds the silver stream of the Merced. It is the Wynd Cliff!* "What a cathedral is among churches," wrote the antiquary Fosbroke, many years ago, "the Wynd Cliff is among prospects." ' The Wynd Cliff today is the haunt of peregrine falcons, merlins and buzzards.

There is a Celtic cross-slab in the church, with decorated bird panels. A similar slab with birds can be seen in Caerleon churchyard a few miles away. It may be that Arvan was Bishop Afan. This conjecture stems from the standing stone at Llanafan Fawr in Brecon which is referred to as St Arvan's Stone. Some sources say that Bishop 'Arvan' was martyred here. Brecon's County History publication of 1910 states that the stone was in memory of Bishop Afan, Ifan or Ieuan. St Aaron is also associated with St Arvan's. Another standing stone is nearby on Fronwen Farm. It may be that Arvan was a son of Taliesin (see Afan).

BISHOP ARWYSTL mid-6th century
ARGOESTLE

A disciple of Dyfrig at Hentland and Moccas, and made a bishop by him. The Book of Llandaf notes a grant of Lancaut in Gloucester (part of Gwent Iscoed) given to him by Iddon ap Ynyr Gwent. He may have gone with Teilo to Brittany to escape the Yellow Plague, and St 'Argoestle' founded a church near Vannes (now altered to Allouestre), near the monastery founded by Gildas. He may have returned to Wales in 556 to find his church deserted, and is witness to several land grants to St Teilo at Llandaf. A contemporary of Teilo, he seems to have died around the same time, for he does not note any of the grants made under Bishop Euddogwy.

ARWYSTLI GLOFF (the lame) 6th century

A son of Seithenyn who resided at the monastery of Ynys Enlli. When Seithenyn's kingdom of Gwyddno's Plain (Cantre'r Gwaelod) was submerged by the sea in Cardigan Bay, his ten sons went to Bangor-is-Coed, from where Arwystli went to Bangor Enlli. His seven children with Tywynwedd ferch Amlawdd Wledig were the first saints at Bangor-is-Coed, who all then went to Enlli upon its destruction. Tyfrydog, Twrnog (Teyrnog), Tudur, Dier (Deifer) and Marchell were among his children. He is listed as the father of saints, rather than as a saint.

ARWYSTLI HEN (the aged) d.99
ARGUISTIL, ARISTOBULUS
March 15, 17

An Italian who came from Rome with Bran the Blessed, Ilid, Cyndaf and Mawan ap Cyndaf in the Welsh Triads. Aristobulus, according to Usher, was ordained by St Paul as first Bishop for the Britons (Welsh sources make him Bran's confessor). Cressy repeats this, based on the Greek Martyrology, saying that he was a disciple of Peter or Paul at Rome, and sent as apostle and Bishop of the Britons. He died at Glastonbury (Ynys Vitrin), where his day was traditionally March 15th. Aristobulus is mentioned in the Greek Menealogies and in Paul's Epistle to the Romans, xvi, 10: *'Salute them which are of Aristobulus' household'*. He is commemorated as an apostle of Britain in the Byzantine Calendar.

The Meniae Graecorum states the he came to Britain and *'converted many of them to Christianity; and after he had built churches and ordained deacons and priests for the island, he was there martyred.'* Hippolytus calls him *'Bishop of the British'*, and Bishop Haleca said that he was one of seventy disciples of the Lord, with his martyrdom being celebrated by the British. In 303 Bishop Dorotheus of Tyre wrote that this colleague of Paul had been Bishop of the Britons ('Synopsis de Apostol'). St Ado, the 9th century Archbishop of Vienna wrote under the date March 17th: *'Natal Day of Aristobulus, Bishop of Britain, brother of Barnabas the Apostle, by whom he was ordained bishop. He was sent to Britain where, after preaching the truth of Christ and forming a Church, he received martyrdom.'* (See also Joseph of Arimathea, who is said to have founded the British Church, and Ilid, Bran and Eurgain).

From the 4th century it is easy to show an unbroken Christian heritage in Wales, as it was never conquered by pagans, but the Joseph of Arimathea and Aristobulus links push the foundation of the Celtic Church to just after Christ's death. **This would give Wales the oldest continuous Christian heritage in the world**. Rome did not accept the faith until Constantine in the 4th century, after which it was several times over-run by non-Christian tribes. More research and publicity would help Wales to attract world-wide tourism and alleviate its present economic problems, especially when associated with the ancient Welsh traditions of Arthur, the Holy Grail, the True Cross and Merlin.

ARWYSTLI AP CUNEDDA WLEDIG 5th century

Iolo Morganwg claims that he gave his name to the district of Arwystli in Montgomery, but he is not listed in any other sources of saints.

ASAF 6th century, died early 7th century
ASA, ASAFF, ASAPH
April 30, May 1, 2 (also May 5 and 11)

Bishop Asaf was a descendant of Coel Godebog and related to St Deiniol and St Tysilio. His grandfather was the king of the north of Britain, Pabo Post Prydain. His parents were Sawyl Benuchel and Gwenaseth ferch Rhufun Rhufuniog. Asaf founded Llanasa in Flintshire, and with St Kentigern (Cyndeyrn/Mungo) established the monastery at Llanelwy nearby. Other sources say that he was taught by Cyndeyrn at Llanelwy. Llanelwy seems to have been founded in 560, and Asaf succeeded Cyndeyrn as bishop there in 573, when Cyndern went to Strathclyde at the summons of Rhydderch Hael. Rhydderch had won the great battle of Arderydd to establish himself King of Cumbria (then centred on Glasgow, it included Strathclyde and the present-day Cumbria). 665 monks went with Mungo and 300 stayed with Asaf. According to The Red Book of St Asaf, he was renowned *for 'the sweetness of his conversation, the symmetry, vigour and elegance of his body, the virtues and sanctity of his heart, and the manifestation of miracles'*.

Llanelwy was recognised and organised as a bishopric by the Normans, and renamed St Asaph. The see of St Asaph covered much of the area of the ancient kingdom of Powys. Asaf was an insubstantial figure, yet a monk writing hundreds of years later refers to him as having *'charm of manners, grace of body, holiness of heart, and witness of miracles.'* He is mentioned in the Roman Martyrology, and also remembered in Scotland and Ireland.

In his home district of Tegeingl, there is Llanasa, Pantasa (Asa's Hollow), and the second largest well in Wales, Ffynnon Asa, which was dedicated to him. (Only St Winifred's was larger). Dr Johnson described it as being covered with a building, and does Pennant *('with stone in an octagonal form')*. It was used for rheumatic and nervous illnesses. The power was strong enough to drive a mill-wheel near the source, and to form a fine waterfall at Dyserth, a

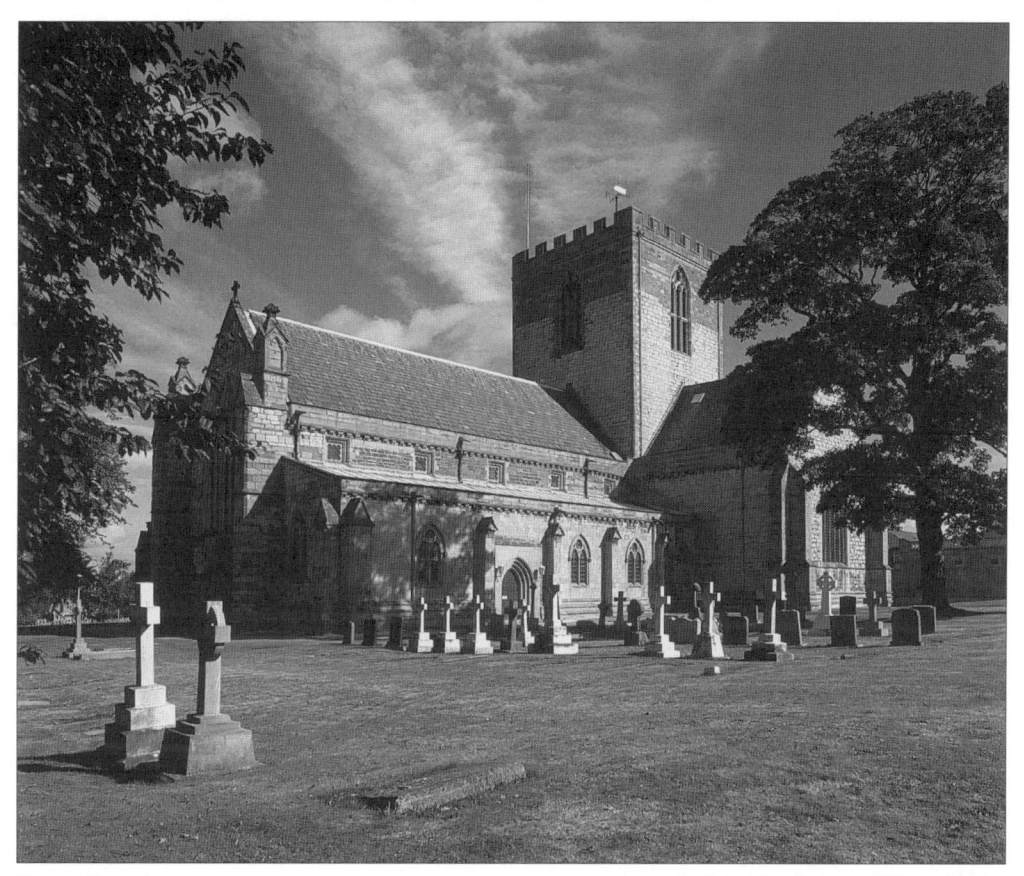

St Asaf Cathedral. © *Wales Tourist Board Photo Library.*

mile or so away. There is also a Ffynnon Asa near Llechryd, beginning a stream known as Afon Asa which flows into the Meirchion and then into the Elwy. Another holy well was in the Vale of Conwy, and yet another in Eglwys Fach in Denbigh, on the village street with a pump now attached. His fair was held on the *'eve, day and morrow'* of his feast day, May 1.

There is a double-naved parish church dedicated to Asaf and Cyndeyrn (Mungo) in St Asaf, with a hammer-beam ceiling, as well as the XIII century cathedral. The original cathedral had been destroyed by Edward I, and there is a plaque commemorating the poor workhouse boy John Rowlands, who became famous as H.M. Stanley, the explorer of Africa. It has the only mediaeval canopied stalls in Wales. The 'Translators' Memorial' on the Cathedral Green remembers Bishop William Morgan and his colleagues, who translated into Welsh the Bible and Prayer Book, thus enabling the survival of the language.

ASSER d. 909
GERAINT BARDD GLAS

Not a saint, but a Welsh bishop Geraint who was extremely important in early church history. A relative of Bishop Nobis of St David's (d. 873), Asser was brought up at the Cathedral, became bishop, and his reputation for learning spread across Europe. King Alfred the Great thus asked Asser to enter his service, but Asser delayed his answer. On his way back to Pembroke, the bishop was seriously ill, and recuperated over some time at Caerwent. He then agreed, to help Wales politically, to spend half of his time at Alfred's court, and half back in his diocese. Asser hoped that Alfred would prevent the constant attacks of King Hyfaidd of Dyfed on the see of St David's. Alfred of Wessex found Asser to be an indispensable colleague and tutor, and heaped honours on him, giving him episcopal duties in Devon and Cornwall, before making him bishop of the great abbey of Sherborne in 900. Asser's great 'Life' of Alfred, written in Latin, was never finished. Geraint was supposed to have written a Welsh grammar, and his Latin name was Asser Menevensis.

AUGULUS d.305
February 7

According to Cressy's 'Church History of Britain', a Briton who was the eighth bishop of London.

AUDE see JUTWARA

AUSTOL d.c.627
AUSTELL
June 28

The godson and disciple of Abbot Mewan, who accompanied him from South Wales to Cornwall and then to Brittany. Saint Austell in Cornwall commemorates him. He is buried with St Mewan, in the same tomb, at Saint Meen in Brittany.

B

'Brothers in humanity who live after us, let not your hearts be hardened against us, for, if you take pity on us poor ones, God will be more likely to have mercy on you. But pray God that he may be willing to absolve us all.'
Francois Villon, 'Ballade des Pendus', c.1460

BACHARIUS d.c. 460

'By Nation a Brittain and Disciple of Saint Patrick; he addicted himself to the study of litterature at Caer-leon.' – Cressy.

BAGLAN AP DINGAD late 6th century

The eldest son of Dingad ap Nudd Hael and brother of Lleuddad, Eleri, Tegwy and Tyfriog. These were all saints at Llancarfan, who went with Dyfrig to Enlli. This confessor founded Llanfaglan under Llanwnda in Caernarfon. In The Red Book of Hergest his words are *'Ffordd y Llanfaglan yd eir y nef'* (*'The way of Llanfaglan one goes to heaven'*) which roughly translated means *'None go to heaven on a feather bed'*. Ffynnon Faglan near the church had a wide stone seat and was walled. It was used for the curing of rheumatism, eye complaints and warts. For warts, they were pricked with a pin which was bent and then thrown into the well, the continuation of the Celtic tradition of bending the swords and spears of dead warriors, and offering them to the water deities. Ffynnon Dalar on Bryn Baglan was said to cure rheumatism and crutches were left at the well. A crossed stone formed the lintel of the ruined Llanfaglan Old Church, and was taken into the new church in 1854. About five feet long, it reads *'Fili Lovernii Anatemori.'* Two more crossed stones, both again around five feet in length, are used as lintels in the new church. One seems to represent a boat with a mast.

BAGLAN AB ITHEL HAEL early 6th century
BAGLAN LLYDAW (Baglan the Breton), BALAN, BALAG, BACHLA
May 1-3, Ascension Day

Educated at St Illtud's College at Llanilltud Fawr, St Baglan was said to be the son of the Breton prince, Ithel Hael. When he left the monastic college, St Illtud gave him a crozier staff as a gift, and told him to find *'a tree that bore three types of fruit, and there erect a church.'* Baglan *'Llydaw'* eventually found a wooded valley by the coast, with a tree that had a litter of pigs at its roots, a beehive in its hollow trunk, and a crow's nest in its branches. However, he did not like the sloping location, and started to build a church on the coastal plain below the tree. Every night the foundations moved to the spot where Illtud had decreed he built the church, and eventually the saint gave up and erected St Baglan's Church on the hillside, near modern Port Talbot. His well on the north of Mynydd y Dinas there was famous for curing children with rickets, but only on the first three days in May. Edward Lhuyd said that the well was best used on three Thurdays in May, one of them being Ascension Day. Baglan was associated with Cadoc in a story of him carrying fire to Cadoc in his tunic without singeing the cloth. His association with Cadog also makes him a candidate, as Balan, for one of the knights of Arthur's court.

There was a Celtic knotwork cross-stone of the ninth century in his church, with the name *'Brancuf'* incised. The decorated slab is now in St Catherine's Church, Baglan, and has an ornate circular carving of a double plait, with squared knotwork patterns. Baglan's ancient church is ruined now, but the local inhabitants had great awe of the sanctity of the place into the 1700's, and as late as 1700 Baglan's crozier survived, *'a sacred relick which had wonderful effects on the sick'*. The sad ruin of Plas Baglan in nearby woodland was the stronghold of the last native Welsh prince of Glamorgan, Iestyn ap Gwrgant. By Baglan Court, Baglan Well was used for children with rickets, and seems to be the same well as Ffynnon Pant yr Arian. A follower of Cadfan, Baglan was culted in Brittany as Bachla, and as Balag (at Penflour near Chateaulin in Finistere).

His brothers were Tanwg, Twrog, Tegai, Trillo, Fflewin, Llechid and Gredifael, most of whom accompanied Cadfan to Enlli. The Life of Lleuddad states that St Lleuddad (Llawddog) was the son of Bryn Buga of Usk, and Bryn Buga followed Baglan into a religious life.

DAVID AUGUSTINE BAKER 1575-1651
December 9

Given a Holy Day by the Church in Wales, his neice's son was the martyr David Lewis (q.v.), and he instructed the martyr Phillip Powell (q.v.) This Benedictine mystic was born in Abergafenni, and died of the plague in London. After education at Oxford, he lost his faith until he had a miraculous escape from a grave illness. In 1605 he joined the Benedictine Order at Padua, returned to Wales to minister to his dying father, and refuted the assertion that the Benedictine Order in Britain was subserviant to the Cluniac foundation, as the British order preceded it. In 1624 he was in Cambrai and in 1633 sent back from Douai to again be a missionary in England, although he was exhausted from over-work. He wrote over thirty treatises on religious matters, and requires an adequate biography. Several times he narrowly escaped imprisonment which would have led to torture and death.

BANGOR

The 'bangor' formerly meant the wattled hedge around a monastic community, but came to mean 'high choir' or a great learning establishment of monks. Thus Llanilltud Fawr was formerly called Bangor Illtud, and before that Bangor Tewdws and Bangor Eurgain. Bangor in North Wales was formerly named Bangor Fawr yn Arfon to distinguish it from Bangor-is-Coed near Chester. It was ravaged by Danes in 1073. This Bangor was the first community in Wales to conform to the Roman system, in 768 or 777. The Cornish church had also aquiesced in 768, and all the Irish church by the end of the 7th century. Although a king of Powys visited Rome in 850, it is not known if all of Wales had acknowledged Roman supremacy by the time of the Norman Conquest of England from 1066. The formal Roman Catholic parish and diocese organisation seems not to have replaced the 'clas' or mother-church system until the 14th century in most of Wales. The central village in Belle-Île is called Bangor, and Kerdavid is a hamlet on the same island.

Alphabetical Listing of the Saints of Wales and Religious Events

BANGOR-IS-COED MONASTERY – ITS DESTRUCTION
BANGOR ON DEE

The foundation of this monastery near Chester (Caerllion) by St Dunawd is described elsewhere in this book. It is important to note the importance which the Venerable Bede gave to its destruction in by the pagan Ethelfrith from Northumbria. (The author has read various dates including 603, 604, 607, 610 and 613 for this battle). When perusing the following passage, remember that the saintly Bede was describing the slaughter by barbarians of Celtic Christian monks. The refusal to follow the new ways of Rome, asking for change in the oldest continuous Christian community in the Western world, necessitated the extirpation of its greatest monastery-college. Brochwel the Fanged, the son of Cyngen who married Dunawd's sister, tried with a small force to defend the monks from attack. However, the barbarians attacked the monks before the Welsh forces, and Brochwel probably escaped to safety. His arms were three severed horse heads, supposedly a token of his previous successes against the white horse badge of the Saxons. King Selyf ap Cynan Garwyn ap Brocmael led the main force of Powys, which was too late to save the monastery and was heavily defeated at Chester. Selyf Sarfgaddau (*'the serpent of battles'*) was killed and Iolo Morganwg seems to think that he was regarded as a saint.

The Venerable Bede was an Anglo-Saxon monk, born near Sunderland in 673, and who spent his entire life in the monastery at nearby Jarrow. He completed his church history of the English people in 731 and died in 735. Bede's book describes a miracle whereby the Roman missionary to the Angles and Saxons, St Augustine, cures a blind Angle at a synod when trying to force change on the Welsh church. The Welsh delegation of bishops had failed to cure the man (it sounds like a put-up job!) so acceeded that Augustine must be right, but wished to go back and confer with their people . . .

'Without delay the blind man receives his sight, and Augustine is proclaimed by all to be the true herald of light from Heaven. Then indeed the Britons confessed that the true way of righteousness was that which Augustine preached, but **they would not renounce their ancient customs without the consent and permission of their countrymen**. *Whence they demanded that a second Synod should be held, at which a greater number of persons should meet.'* . . .

'Which being appointed, there came, as they relate, seven bishops of the Britons, and many very learned men, principally from their most famous monastery, called in the language of the Angles Bancornaburg (Bangor-is-Coed), over which Dunawd, the Abbot, is said to have presided at that time; who, being about to attend the Council just mentioned, came first to a certain holy and prudent man, who was wont to lead the life of an anchorite (hermit) in that country, to consult him whether they should forsake their traditions at the preaching of Augustine. He answered "If he be a man of God, follow him." They said, "Whence shall we prove this?"

He replied, "The Lord hath said, Take my yoke upon you and learn of me, for I am meek and lowly in heart. If therefore Augustine is meek and lowly in heart, it is to be expected that, because he bears himself the yoke of Christ, he will offer it to be borne by you; but if he is not meek but proud, it is clear that he is not of God, his speech is not to be regarded by us". They said again, "And whence shall we discover this also?" He said "Contrive that he come first, with his friends to the place of the Synod; and if he shall rise when you approach, hearken to him obediently, knowing that he is the servant of Christ; but if he shall despise you, and be not willing to rise in your presence when you are more in number, then let him be despised by you."

– They did as he had said, and it was brought to pass, that when they came, Augustine continued to sit in his chair. Seeing which, they were soon moved to anger, and charging him with pride strove to contradict every thing which he said. But he told them "Since in many things ye act contrary to our custom, and even to that of the universal Church, yet if ye will obey me in these three points; that ye celebrate the Passover at its proper time; that ye perform the service of Baptism, by which we are born again to God, after the manner of the holy Roman and Apostolic Church; and that ye preach with us the word of God to the nation of the Angles; as for the other things which ye do, although contrary to our customs, we will bear them all with patience."

But they answered that they would perform none of these, neither would they have him for an archbishop; considering among themselves, that if he would not rise up to them at that time, how much more would he despise them if they became subject to him.'

'To whom, Augustine, the man of God, is said to have foretold in a threatening tone, that because they would not have peace with their brothers, they should have war with their enemies; and if they were unwilling to preach to the nation of the Angles the way of life, by their hands they should suffer the vengeance of death. Which, by the agency of divine judgement, was so performed in all respects as he had foretold.'

'Since after this Ethelfrith (Aedilfrid), the most powerful king of the Angles, having collected a large army, made a very great slaughter of that perfidious race, at the city of the Legions, which is called by the people of the Angles Legacaestir, but by the Britons presently Caerlegion (Caerllion is the Welsh for Chester). And when, being about to give battle, he saw, standing by themselves in a place of greater safety, their priests who had come to pray to God for the soldiers engaged in the war, he enquired who were those, and for what purpose had they come hither? But most of them were from the monastery of Bancor, in which the number of monks is said to be so great, that when the monastery was divided into seven classes, with superintendents set over them, none of those classes contained less than three hundred men, all of whom were accustomed to live by the labour of their own hands. Most of these therefore, having performed a fast of three days, had come together, with others, to the before-mentioned field, for the sake of prayer, having a defender, by name Brocmail (Brochwel Ysgythrog) to protect them while still intent upon their prayers from the swords of the barbarians.

When King Ethelfrith understood the cause of their arrival, he said, "Then if they cry to their God against us, surely even they, although they do not bear arms, fight against us when they oppose us with their hostile prayers." He then ordered his arms to be turned against them first, and afterwards destroyed the other forces of that impious war, not without great loss in his own army. They relate that there were killed in that battle about twelve hundred men of those who had come to pray, and that only fifty escaped by flight. Brocmail and his troops, upon the first approach of the enemy, turned their backs, and left those, whom he ought to have defended, unarmed and naked to men who fought with swords.

And thus was accomplished the prediction of the holy pontiff Augustine, although he had so long before been raised to a heavenly kingdom; so that by the vengeance of a temporal death the perfidious people might perceive, that they had despised the counsels of everlasting salvation, which had been offered to them.'

Thus the Venerable Bede described the *'perfidious'* and *'impious'* Christians of Britain being slaughtered by the pagan German tribes. Also, this 'holy' man's account of Ethelfrith suffering

Alphabetical Listing of the Saints of Wales and Religious Events

'great loss in his own army' does not quite fit with the forces of Brochwel running away from the battle. Bede ended his 'Ecclesiastical History' with the happy reflection that all the churches of the Isles of Britain and Ireland, **with the exception of the Welsh, had forsaken their former separatism and embraced the domination of Rome.**

The seven British bishops who attended this meeting were thought to be from Menevia (St Davids), Llandaf, Llanbadarn, Bangor-is-Coed, St Asaf and probably one from Gloucester (still British with Hereford/'Ergyng'), and one from Dumnonia (Somerset, Devon and Cornwall). Somerset was still 'British' as late as 725, and Devon until the 10th century held out against the Germanic onslaught.

The account in 'The Anglo-Saxon Chronicles' (translated by A. Savage, 1995) states that Augustine arrived in 597, and the entry for the year 604 is:
'Augustine hallowed two bishops, Mellitus and Justus. Mellitus he sent to preach baptism among the East Saxons; there the king was called Saebyrht, son of Ricola, Aethelbryht's sister; Aethelbryht had made him king there. Aethelbhyrt gave Mellitus the bishopric in London, and Justus he gave Rochester, which is twenty-four miles from Canterbury.
Pope Gregory passed away, about ten years from the time he sent us baptism; his father was called Gordianus, and his mother Sylvia. Aethelferth led his army to Chester, and there killed countless Welsh; and so the prophecy of Augustine was fulfilled, when he said "If the Welsh will not be at peace with us, they shall perish at the hands of the Saxons." There also two hundred priests were killed, when they went there in order to pray for the Welsh forces. Their ealdorman was called Scrocmael (Brocmael*, Brochwel), who escaped from there, one of fifty.' (The next entry referring to Wales is in 614, when *'Cyneglis and Cwichelm fought at Beandum and killed two thousand and sixty-five Welsh.'*)

The Battle of Chester effectively cut off the Welsh from their fellow-Britons in Cumbria and Strathclyde, and from now on Wales becomes a separate and independent nation. In 577 Wales had been separated by land from Dumnonia, after the terrible defeat at Dyrham near Bath. The Anglo-Saxon Chronicles recorded that in 577 *'Cuthwine and Cealwin fought the Britons, and killed three kings, Conmail, Condidan and Farinmail, in the place called Dyrham. They took three cities: Gloucester, Cirencester and Bath'*. There was another great battle in 584 at Fethanleag, where the Saxon Cutha was killed and Cealwin was forced back.

Daniel Defoe, in his 'Tour' of Great Britain (1724-1726) calls Bangor-is-Coed 'Bangor Bridge' and recounts its fame as the birthplace of Pelagius (c.360-c.420):
'But as for the town or monastery, scarcely any of the ruins were to be seen, and as all the people spoke Welch, we could find no body that could give us any intelligence. So effectually had time in so few years, rased the very foundations of the place. I will not say, as some do, that this is miraculous, and that it is the particular judgment of God upon the place, for being the birth-place of that arch-heretick Pelagius.'

*'The Grave-Stone of Brochmael' was found between Lima and Cernioge, in the cutting of the Holyhead Railway in the 19th century. In a field evocatively named Doltrebeddw ('meadow of the home of the graves'), forty ancient tombs were discovered, cased with rough stones and lying in an area just 20 yards by 10 yards. On the underside of one of the better graves was inscribed *'BROHOMAGLI- LAM IC IACIT ET VXOR EIUS CAVNE'*. This is Brocmail, a name that figures often in the Book of Llandaf, and possibly either Brochmael Ysgythrog or his grandfather, making it 6th or early 7th century. It appears that the stone was not placed over the grave until the death of his wife Caune. Westwood states that the stone was placed in the drawing-room of Pentre Foelas Mansion in Denbighshire. (Another inscription at Pentre Foelas was found on a small tumulus called the Foel, on a pillar eight feet high. This 'Levelinus' inscription seems to commemorate Prince Llywelyn ap Sytsyllt, killed in 1021.)

BANHADLEN 5th-6th century
DANADLWEN
Daughter of Cynyr of Caer Gawch, sister of Gwen and Non, and wife of Dirdan, her son was Ailbe (Elvis). Banadlwen can be translated as the flowering shrub, white broom.

BARDSEY – THE ISLE OF 20,000 SAINTS see ENLLI

BARLOC
September 10

A hermit whose feast was kept at St Werburgh's, Chester, and of whom nothing else is known.

BARNABAS 1st century
June 11

This Jewish Cypriot introduced Paul to the other apostles. He was possibly martyred in 61 at Salamis, and evangelised Cyprus. He argued with Paul in favour of Gentiles being Christians.

BARTHOLOMEW 1st century
August 24, 25, June 13

Now the saint associated with Llanover (rather than Myfor), the 1st century apostle was said to be flayed alive before being beheaded, either in India or near the Caspian Sea. His arm was given by King Canute's wife to Canterbury Cathedral and he is the patron saint of skinners.

BARUC d. before 577 (d.700 according to Cressy, but this is too late)
BARUCK, BARUCH, BARRUC, BARNIC, BARRY, BARROG, BAROQ, BARNOC
September 26, 27, November 29

In Cressy's book he was *'a Hermite, whose memory is celebrated in the province of the Silures and the region of Glamorgan. He lyes buried in the Isle of Barry, which took its name from him'* . . . *'In our Martyrologie this Holy Hermite Baruck is said to have sprung from the Noble Blood of the Brittains, and entring into a solitary strict course of life, he at this time (700) attained to a life immortal.'*

One of St Cadoc's disciples, he died returning to Barri from Echni (Flat Holme Island). Cadoc had forgotten his codex, and sent Baruc and Gualehes back to fetch it, but they drowned. On the plaque outside Baruch's chapel it reads:
'We are told that in the year 700 the friars and monks left their Celtic monastery (Llancarfan) and walked to Barry Island, as it was then their custom, periodically to retreat from the world

for up to six weeks to pray and meditate. They took a boat from Barry Island to Flat Holm to seek solitude. On returning to Barry Island they discovered that they had left the saints' enchiridon (handbook) behind. St Cadoc sent St Baruc and St Gwalches back to retrieve the book. While recrossing they were drowned. The body of St Baruc was recovered and buried on the island. Baruc was revered as a saint for many miles around and people came flocking to the island to see his burial place which they regarded as sacred. A chapel was built here called St Baruc's Shrine.' However, as Cadog died around 577, we cannot accept 700 as Baruc's date of death. The nave measures about 20 feet by 11, and the chancel just 11 by 9 feet.

Nell's Point at the holiday resort of Barri Island was until the 1960's an unspoilt headland with holy wells, ruined medieval buildings, prehistoric burial mounds and the ancient St. Baruc's Chapel. Philistines built the sad concrete blocks of tat known as Butlin's Holiday Camp over everything but the chapel. St Baruc's had been an extremely important centre of pilgrimage. On the opposite, unspoilt Friar's Point there are surviving prehistoric mounds. In 1999, the holiday camp is being demolished to make way for housing. Great numbers of women visited Ffynnon Barruc on Ascension Day, washed their sore eyes in its water and dropped a pin in it. It also cured King's Evil, fevers and headaches. Butlins were allowed by a quiescent Barri council to 'tarmac' over the well to make a space for an extra car to park in a 300 bay car park. Another well at Barri Island was known as the Roman Well, and surrounded by a deep retaining wall when the docks were built. Votive pins and Roman coins were found in it. Just in the last thirty years at some time a café/pub (now semi-derelict) was placed upon it. The author remembers it as a source of mystery, somewhat rather different feelings than the local council. There was also a monastery marked on 19th century maps of the island, and its foundations were north of Baruc's church. Other old ruins were found near the railway station.

In 1890 Barri Island was still cut off from the mainland. It had been an uninhabited nature reserve before the building of a causeway and Barri Docks, by David Davies. In the sixteenth century, St Baruc's Chapel was the only building on the island. Gerald of Wales described the church, and noted the wondrous rock or 'blow-hole' on Nell's Point which made the *sounds 'of blacksmiths at work, the blowing of bellows, the strokes of hammers and the harsh grinding of files on metal.'* The little church was remodelled in the fourteenth century, and pilgrims travelled to St Baruc's shrine at least until the Reformation. John Leland in 1540 commented upon the well's effects on the amount of pilgrimage there. The holy well was full of bent pins thrown in by pilgrims who had sampled the healing waters. This followed the old Celtic custom of offering bent daggers and swords to the water gods. The well also appears to be the only one in Wales that was used for curing hangovers and alcoholics. Baruc is also celebrated at Fowey in Cornwall on September 27, as recorded by William Worcestre.

Barruc was linked with Bedwas, where there was a Ffynnon Farrwg in the churchyard. The parish church at Barri is now that of St Nicholas. Llanfarach Farm at Groes-faen near Pontyclun may also be linked to Baruc. Barruc was also credited with the founding of Penmark, which is now dedicated to St Mary. Penmark, in the Vale of Glamorgan, was formerly known as Penmarch Hywel. Mynydd March Hywel is near Pontardawe, where there was traditionally a great battle. An ancient custom was the burying of a human skull, or the head of a horse (horses were sacred to the Celts) – could the head of Hywel's stallion be buried at Penmark? Roman coins and signs of occupation were found at Penmark, and at nearby East Aberthaw, Nurston, Fonmon, Llanbethery and Llanilltud Fawr. Penmark is one of the largest churches in the Vale, and a November 1881 article by John Rowland in 'Yr Haul' records:
'Englishmen have held the living of Penmark as far back as the history of the parish can be traced. Dr Casberd was one of the most fortunate Englishmen. He received thousands of

Church money every year for nothing. He did not understand any Welsh; he could not administer the sacraments or pray at a sick bed in the language the people understood. His parishioners did not know him. This was scandalous and disgraceful. The appointments were nothing but a fiction. It wasn't the care of souls but emoluments which were in view. There is room to fear that the bishops, patrons and others will have much to answer for their negligence in the great day which will come. The present vicar is the Rev. Charles Fred Bryan Wood, precentor of the Cathedral Church of Cardiff. An Englishman.' This note shows just how much the English language has spread through Glamorgan in the 20th century. The constant complaints by Anglicised Welsh people in 'The Western Mail' letters page, about the uselessness of Welsh being taught in schools, seem to ignore the recent introduction of the English language in south-east Wales. Welsh was even the language of John Frost's Chartists in Newport in the 19th century (see 'The A-Z of Wales and the Welsh' under 'Chartism'.)

As one leaves Barri heading towards Llanilltud Fawr, one passes an old farmhouse turned into a chain-eatery-pub, the Cwmciddy. Not many local people know that this is a corrupion of Cwm y ci du, Valley of the black dog, which runs down to Porthkerry beach. William Thomas records on March 8th, 1763, the death of Ann Richmond *'of Cwm y ci du, of 100 years of age, some report 105. She was the mother of William Jenkin the extorter. She was buried since the 30th day of January last past and a Reported witch. All folks about dread her – and believe she could witch and the same belief is of her son, and tales of hurt she and her son made to cattle etc. And the report is that the devil before her death appeared to her with a Bull's head and offered a year longer on earth if at the end of the year she would deliver her body and all to he, which she denyed and died. Vain belief of the Vulgar, who are as credible of tales as the Indians and Negroes are, for the devil have not a moment of time to give to any, not himself, much less than a year.'*

The 'Llandawke Stone' in Carmarthen was used as a step into the church of Landawke after being in the churchyard. It reads 'BARRIVEND - FILIVS VENVBARI', and a case has been made for it meaning Baruch Vendigaid (Barri Fendigaid, the blessed). The stone is defaced, and the Ogham reads *'taqoledemu'* and *'maqi'*. (For more on Barri Island see Samson, Illtud, Pyr and Peirio).

LEWIS BAYLY (BAYLEY) d. 1631
October 25

This bishop and devotional writer was probably born in Carmarthen, and has been given the Holy Day of October 25 by the Church in Wales. After studying at Cambridge, he was vicar at Shipston-on Stour from 1597 and at Evesham from 1600, where he was also headmaster of the grammar school. In 1611 he wrote 'Practice of Piety', which had run into 71 editions by 1792. After various service, including being chaplain to James I, he became Bishop of Bangor in 1616. 'The Dictionary of Welsh Biography' shows him in an unflattering light, a vacillatory man who took on many livings to bolster his income, and showed undue preference to his relatives. Unless a major reassessment of his character is undertaken, it is difficult to understand his deserving of a 'holy day' in the church calendar. 'Practice of Piety' seems to be more of a 'do as I tell you' manual than one that promotes 'do as I do'. It is on record that Bayly persecuted Phylip Puw. Phylip Puw was with his father Robert, and the martyr William Daives, when they hid in the cave of Rhiwledyn on Little Orme for nine months, secretly printing 'Y Drych Cristianogawl.'

Alphabetical Listing of the Saints of Wales and Religious Events

BEDWAS 6th - 7th century

A son of Helig Foel, and possibly the founder of Bedwas, near Newport in Gwent. After the loss of their territories to flooding he went to Bangor-is-Coed and then to Enlli.

BEDWINI 6th century
BEDWYN, BAUDWIN

A bishop who resided at Celliwig near Cardiff and became primate of 'Cornwall'. He was associated with Arthur who celebrated Christmas, Easter and Whitsun at Celliwig, where Bedwyn was bishop. Llanmelin, the centre of the Silurian hill fort system above Caerwent, was formerly known as Llan y Gelli (church of the grove). Arthur retreated here after dealing with the threat of the Twrch Trwyth, a synonym for the Irish invaders. There is confusion between Cernyw and Cerniw (respectively the land east of Cardiff and Cornwall), and between two places named Celliwig in old history. The Triads of Arthur relate that there were *'Three throne-tribes of the Isle of Britain. The one at Celliwig in Cerniw, had Arthur as supreme king, Bishop Bedwin as chief bishop, and Caradog Freichfras as chief elder.'* As Caradog was king of Brecon, the link with Cornwall is tenuous. It may well be that Bedwin was bishop of the see at Caerleon (Celliwig in Cernyw). Bedwin Sands lie in the Severn estuary south of Caerwent, and one time were farm lands.

In 'Culhwch and Olwen', Bedwin *'blessed Arthur's meat and drink'* at his court. A 'Saying of the Wise' attributed to Bedwin goes:
'Hast thou heard the saying of Bedwini,
Who was a bishop, good and void of vanity?
"Consider thy word before uttering it" '

Sir Baudwin was said to be one of Arthur's first knights, made a constable of the realm and one of the governors of Britain (a comeregulus?), who ended his life a physician and a hermit. We should note here that 'Comereg' was one of Arthur's brothers and a son of Meurig, so Bedwyn could be Arthur's younger brother.

BEDWYR BEDRYDNANT (of the perfect sinews) 6th century
BETUVERIUS, BEDIVERE

Brother of Sir Lucan and with Cei Hir (St Cynan) the warrior most closely associated with Arthur. In Culhwch and Olwen he was *'the handsomest warrior who ever was at Arthur's court . . . although he was one-handed no three warriors drew blood in the battle field faster than he.'* At the battle of Tryfrwyd *'by the hundred they fell before Bedwr Bedrydnant.'* He was killed on the continent fighting for Arthur (Armel?). Malory makes him the knight who returns Excalibur (Caliburn) to the lake after Camlan. His father may have been Pedr ap Glywys*, and Welsh tradition is that Bedwyr is buried at Allt Tryfan, the hill of Din Dryfan. This is the ancient fortified camp where Dunraven castle was built overlooking Southerndown beach near Bridgend. The 'Song of the Graves' notes;
'The tomb of the son of Ogyryfan is in Camlan,
After much slaughter
The tomb of Bedwyr is on the steep side of Tryfan.'
There was a Ffynnon Fedwyr somewhere in north Glamorgan, but the author cannot find it.

*King Glywys Filwr was Arthur's cousin, who was given land at Ogmore by Arthur.

BELERUS 4th -5th century
PALLADIUS?

Iolo Morganwg tried to relate Theodosius to Llanilltud Fawr, which is where we first hear of the confessor Belerus. *'The religious foundation of the Emperor Tewdws (Theodosius) and Cystennin (Constantine) of Llydaw (Brittany) was Bangor Illtyd, where Belerus, a man from Rome, was superintendent, and Padrig, the son of Maewan, principal, before he was carried away captive by the Irish.'* Theodosius was sent to Britain in 368 by the Emperor Valentinian, but was beheaded in Africa in 370. His son became Theodosius I (the Great), Emperor with Gratian from 379, sole emperor from 392 and who died in 395. His grandson Theodosius II was Emperor of the Western Roman Empire from 423-425.

Constantine was proclaimed Emperor in Britain in 433, and was in power until 443. Bangor Illtud probably related to the last two emperors, and thus dates from between 423 and 443. The site of the monastery is still shown as Côr Tewdws on old maps. It may be that these emperors gave their favour and support to the monastery-college. (In 425 Theodosius II founded the University of Constantinople, and policy across Europe was to educate the nobles of conquered tribes in Roman ways). However, it may be that St Tewdrig, the King of Glamorgan and Gwent, and grand-father of Arthur, is the 'Tewdws' referred to here.

Palladius had been banished to Britain, and in 429 urged Pope Celestine to send Germanus (Garmon) and Lupus (Bleiddian) to Britain to counter the Pelagian Heresy. It may be that he left Caer Worgorn after the sacking of it to become the first missionary to Ireland and its first bishop in 431. It may never be known if Palladius and Belerus were the same person. Palladius went to Ireland with Solinus, whose stone is at Clydey (see St Clydau).

BELTANE
May 1

April 30th was Beltane Eve, a pre-Celtic festival where the Goddess of Winter is replaced by Baal, God of Summer. May-Day cakes were made in Wales, and half of them were marked with soot. The men of the community picked from a bag a cake each. Those picking the darkened cakes were forced to leap through bonfire flames, be insulted by the other men and become temporary outcasts. This was said to be a throwback to the sacrifice in flames of someone, to give thanks for the renewed strength of the sun to give crops.

BELYAU 6th century
BILIO

Llanfilo, or Llanvillo in Brecon was dedicated to this virgin daughter of Brychan. The old name of the place was written Llanbilio and Llanbiliou.

JOHN BENNETT 1550 - 1625

This priest was active in North Wales, and was born in Bryn Canellan, Cwm near Holywell. Ordained in Douai in 1578, in 1580 he was sent to Wales, and in 1582 was arrested in Gloddaith, Caernarfonshire by Sir Thomas Mostyn. Hung up on a beam by his hands in iron manacles, he was examined under torture at the same time as the martyr Richard Gwyn (q.v.). Banished in 1585, he became a Jesuit at Verdun in 1586 and illicitly returned to Wales in 1590. He ministered around Holywell, *'assistinge for the most part the poor and meaner sort of people'*, until late in life he went to London to help in the plague epidemic, where he died. It seems that Bennett was responsible for recording the suffering and martyrdom of Richard Gwyn and William Davies (q.v.).

BENNION

In Montgomery was St Bennion's Well in Carreghofa parish, and Bennion's Well was also found in both Llanymynech (a charm well until around 1880) and Llandrinio. Bennion is most likely a corruption of Beuno.

BERTHGWIN 6th century

Said to be the fourth bishop of Llandaf, and possibly the same person as Bedwini noted above.

ABBOT BERWYN 5th – 6th century
GERWYN, BRELADE, BREWARD, BRANWALATOR, BRANWALADER

St Breward's Feast is February 2 (old style January 20). Other dates given are January 19 (his translation), May 16 Brittany, July 5 Leon, February 9 and June 6 in Cornwall

This Welsh monk worked with Abbot Samson in Cornwall and Brittany, and is commemorated at St Brelade in Jersey. In 935 King Athelstan took his relics from Breton clerics and gave them to the monastery of Milton in Dorset on January 19. St Broladre in Dol and Loc-Brevelaire in Leon commemorate Berwyn. A son of Brychan, the Berwyn Hills recall his influence, and he was martyred at 'the Isle of Gerwyn', Simonsward in Cornwall. There is a Ffynnon Berwyn, a holy well in Llandyfaelog near Cidweli. Roscarrock called him Breuer or Berwine, and said that his foundation was now called St Breward or Simonsward, and that he was the brother of Menfreda (Mwynwen, Minver) and Endelentia. This makes Berwyn a son of Brychan. Near Leon in Brittany, is Berven. Many of Brychan's children have dedications near those of Peulin (Pol de Leon).

St Berwyn's Day is also the feast of Candlemas, and Thomas Hardy referred to it as the day when agricultural workers were hired at *'hiring fairs'* (in 'The Mayor of Casterbridge'). It is also notable across the world, in that people regard the behaviour of certain animals on this day as an indicator of the future weather. Germans study badgers, and Americans groundhogs, where it is known as 'Groundhog Day' (an excellent film was made with this title).

BETHAN 5th – 6th century

Possibly a daughter of Brychan who went to Manaw (the Isle of Man) with her brothers Arthen and Cynon.

ABBOT BEUNO 7th century (d. 660 according to Cressy, and d. 642 according to Baring-Gould and Fisher)
April 21 (also 20)

The son of noble parents, Bugi (Hywgi) ap Gwynllyw Filwr and Perfferen ferch Llewddyn Luydog of Edinburgh (Dinas Eiddyn). Beuno was educated at Caerwent by Tangusius. He was related to Cadog and Mungo (Kentigern). In many ways, he is the North Wales equivalent of David, although of the royal family of Morganwg.

More dedications have been made to St Beuno in North Wales than to any other saint. It seems that he moved from a base in Powys to proselytise north-west Wales. The story is that he heard a man shouting to his dog in English, and determined to move until he was out of range of the Saxon tongue. Associated with founding a monastery at Clynnog in Caernarfonshire in 616, until the end of the eighteenth century pilgrims came to his burial place, where an oratory was built over his grave. It was excavated in 1914. His relics had been translated to Eglwys y Bedd, a new church, and a place of great miracles. The land had been given by his convert King Cadfan to him (see Gwenfrewi). Other sources say Cadwallon or Cynon gave him the land. Beuno's Vita was written by the anchorite of Llanddewi Brefi in the early fourteenth century based upon older works. As an old man, Beuno instructed Gwenfrewi with St Senan, and the instruction was continued by St Deifer.

Leland stated that Beuno was buried in the chapel adjoining the church and that one could still see a stone with an incised cross, indented by the saint's thumb. There is a holy well nearby. There used to be seats around it, and it was especially recommended for children with epilepsy and rickets, as well as impotency. A cure would come if one slept on a tombstone above the well overnight. Babies were placed on a bed of rushes on the font. Pennant described seeing there *'a feather bed, on which a poor paralytic from Merionethshire had lain the whole night'* after first washing in the well water. Epileptics favoured bathing in the water, then covering Beuno's tomb with rushes and sleeping on it. People with eye diseases scraped debris from the chapel walls, and mixed it with his well water to drink. In the later 17th century it was still held that a sick person laid on Beuno's tomb on a Friday would either recover or die within three weeks.

At his church at Clynnog on the Llyn, bulls bearing a certain mark were sacrificed *'the half to God and to Beuno'*, noted by John Ansters in 1589 – *'as that people are of the opinion, that Beuno his cattell will prosper marvellously well'*. The custom finished in the 19th century. The cattle cult came down from the Celtic worship of 'Audhumla', the primal cow. In the Celtic Northern Tradition, the primal cow is responsible for the creation of the world. 'Sacred beasts' with *'Beuno's mark'* were given to the church wardens on Trinity Sunday, and the sale proceeds were placed in *'Cyff Beuno'*, *'Beuno's Chest'*, which still can be seen at Clynnog. This ancient oak chest, carved from a single piece of oak, gave rise to the local saying when someone tried to do something difficult: *'Cystal I chwi geisio tori Cyff Beuno'* – *'You might as well try to break into Beuno's Chest.'* One of the reasons for the custom of driving local bullocks to the church to dedicate them to him, was the pecuniary motive of achieving higher prices at market. The late mediaeval church of Clynnog Fawr stands on the site of St Beuno's oratory. He died there after seeing a vision of angels descending from and ascending back to heaven. The church and shrine stand on ancient megaliths, one of which can be seen in the nave floor, and others of which are in the foundations. The site may have been a standing circle.

Alphabetical Listing of the Saints of Wales and Religious Events

An early Christian inscribed stone at Llanfeuno-under-Clodock (Llanveynoe) in Archenfield (Ergyng) is close to the Roman road between Gobonium (Abergafenni) and Kenchester. The Hiberno-Saxon cross reads *'Haefdur fecit crucem istam.'* This church is now dedicated to Peter. Beuno is also remembered at Berriew and Betws Cedewain in Montgomeryshire near another Roman road to Caersws, and is said to have been a descendant of the princes of Powys of this area, centred on Mathrafal. North of here, Gwyddelwern near the Roman road to Caer Gai is also dedicated to Beuno, with his holy well. There is a late mediaeval 'waggon roof' in Gwyddelwern church. There is another St Beuno's Well at Betws Gwerfil Goch nearby (see Gwerfil). Further north, Whitford church was originally dedicated to Beuno, there was an old chapel in Llanasa, and his holy wells at Holywell and in Tremeirchion parish between Prestatyn and Denbigh. Many of these sites are near Roman remains. At Tremeirchion, the church is now that of Corpus Christi, has an 800-year-old yew, and once possessed a healing cross. Ffynnon Beuno's overflow here passes through the mouth of a carved stone head. There is mediaeval stained glass, and a remarkable 14th century canopied tomb to Dafydd ap Hywel ap Madog, Dafydd Ddu Arthro o Hiraddug (Black David, teacher of Hiraddug). This vicar of Tremeirchon was a bard, writer and sooth-saying prophet, like Sion Cent of Kentchurch. Beuno's healing well lies in a nearby hollow, with water gushing from the mouth of a roughly carved stone head of unknown age. Another interesting well was Ffynnon Nantcall in Clynnog parish – it was said to cure melancholia.

In north-west Wales, Beuno is remembered at Aberffraw (the court of the princes of Gwynedd) and Trefraeth in Anglesey, and at Clynnog Fawr, Pistyll, Botwnnog and Carnguwch on the Llyn peninsula. Aberffraw has an eleven feet dolmen called Dinas Dindryfal. There still exists Ffynnon Beuno in Malt House Lane, Aberffraw. There is also Ffynnon Bryn Fendigaid near Aberffraw, where a fish was kept for divination purposes, near some chalybeate springs where a woman named Gwladus was martyred at Croes Ladys. In Gwynedd Llanycil is dedicated to him, with another holy well, near Caer Gai roman fort, as is Penmorfa with a holy well, just off the Roman road between Segontium and Tomen-y-Mur. Ffynnon Ddeuno no longer flows, but the ruined chapel can be seen at Gatwen Farm, Broughton, Brecon. In Gwyddelwern, Merioneth, was Ffynnon Gwern Beuno. At Berriew (Aberrhiw), Powys, there is Beuno's standing stone, Maen Beuno, which was said to be Beuno's first pulpit.

One day, walking the banks of the river, he heard a Saxon calling to his hounds on the other bank. He rushed back to his monks and addressed them *'My sons, put on your clothes and shoes, and let us leave this place for the nation of this man I heard setting on his hounds has a strange language which is abominable and I heard his voice. They have invaded this land and will keep it in ownership.'* From Montgomeryshire this early Welsh Nationalist travelled north and was given the land at Clynnog.

E.G Bowen, in 'The Settlements of the Celtic Saints in Wales', draws attention to the fact that the disciples mentioned in his Vita founded churches near Beuno's. Guilsfield near Betws Cedewain, and Berriew are dedicated to Aelhaearn; Llandenan and Llanwyddelan to Lorcan Wyddel; and Llwchaearn is remembered at Llanllwchaearn and Llamyrewig. Near Gwyddelwern was an old chapel dedicated to Aelhaearn, and Cwyfan's Llangwyfan is nearby. In Flintshire, the Llyn Peninsula and Anglesey Beuno's dedications are near those of St Winifred, Gwenfrewi. In the Llyn and Arfon, saints Aelhaearn, Cwyfan, Edern, Deiniol Fab and Twrog have dedications close to Beuno's churches, and in Anglesey churches of Cwyfan, Deiniol Fab, Dona, Ceidio, Edern and Twrog are close to his dedications.

Beuno's dedications include:

Berriew (Aber-Rhiw) and Betws - Montgomery;
Llanycil and Gwyddelwern - Merioneth;
Clynnog Fawr, Carngiwch Chapel, Pistyll Chapel, Penmorfa chapel, Dolbenmaen chapel - Caernarfon;
Aberffraw chapel and Trefdraeth chapel - Anglesey;
Llanfeuno chapel to Clydog (Clodock) - Hereford;
Llanfaenor near Skenfrith in Monmouthshire should be called Llanfeuno. King Ynyr of Gwent gave Beuno three estates in Ewyas including Llanfeuno. Morgan Hen, King of Glamorgan, restored Llanfaenor in 980. A new church was built on the site in 1853.

The 'Sayings of the Wise' record:
'Have you heard the saying of Beuno
To all who resort to him?
"From death, flight will not avail".'

Clynnog has an interesting cromlech with 110 cup-shaped hollows in its capstone, called Bachwen Clynnog Dolmen, and a nearby standing stone is known as Maen Dylan. Also Penarth Dolmen stands in a field named Caer Goetan. At Berriew, Maen Beuno is a leaning standing stone on the Severn's banks. Llanycil in Merioneth is dedicated to Beuno and had three standing stones, but none seem to have survived.

The loveliest of the legends surrounding Beuno is that he dropped and lost his book of sermons walking across the Menai Strait sands from Anglesey. (The strait could have been passable at this time – it appears that water levels have risen up to forty feet in the last 1500 years). When he reached Clynnog Fawr, a curlew was in his cell, sitting by the book. Beuno prayed for God's everlasting protection of the curlew, and this is why its eggs are so difficult to find, as the colours match those of the ground upon which they have been laid.

Beuno's history of bringing back to life four or five decapitated victims has made him the 'Patron of Computer Technicians', who are frequently asked to do the impossible at once. Their web page bears the motto 'Illum Posse Dicere.'

BIGAIL
BIGEL
November 1

There are two sea rocks in Wales called Maen Bigel, one in Holyhead Bay and one in the strait between Enlli and the mainland. His church at Llanfigel under Llafachraeth in Anglesey is ruined. The Welsh name of the island West Mouse off north-west Anglesey is Ynys Bigel. The Book of Llandaf refers to a church now lost near Merthyr Mawr called Merthir Buceil, and Begelly in Pembroke may also be associated with Bigel.

BLEIDDIAN 5th century
July 29

This monk from the island of Lerins was made Bishop of Troyes in 426, and accompanied Garmon (Germanus) of Auxerre on his visit to Britain to refute the Pelagian heresy. On his return to Gaul, he was captured by Attila the Hun, and was held hostage. The story is that later he retired as a hermit in the mountains, and died in 478. However, this legend about Gaul relates to Bishop Lupus of Troyes, who probably never visited Britain. Instead Bleiddian ('young wolf') was probably a local saint who attended Llanilltud Fawr.

The parish church of Llanbleiddian (now called Llanblethian) in the Vale of Glamorgan was dedicated to St Bleddian, the Welsh form of St Lupus, but now to John the Baptist. It was known as Llanbleiddian Fawr to distinguish it from Llanbleddian Fach, St Lythans. There were chapelries to this mother church of Llanbleddian at Cowbridge, Llanquian, Llansannor and Welsh St Donats. There was also St Bleiddian's Holy Well in Llanbleiddian. However, Nicholas ap Gwrgant, Bishop of Llandaff (1148-1183) noted that Llanbleddian and its chapels had become a possession of St Mary's Abbey, Tewkesbury, and by the middle of the 13th century Llansannor was a rectory, but Welsh St Donats remained attached to Llanbleddian until the Disestablishment of the Welsh Church in 1920. In the 1896 restoration, under the crypt in the south chapel were found 200 skeletons, with some 13th century coffin lids. It is believed that they were killed at the Battle of Stalling Down between Henry IV's army and Owain Glyndŵr's troops in 1405.

His 'Saying of the Wise' is:
'Have you heard the saying of St Bleiddian
Of the land of Glamorgan?
"To possess reason is to possess everything".'

Another 'Saying of the Wise', attributed to 'Bleddyn' is:
'Hast thou heard the saying of Bleddyn
When speaking to his enemy?
"Truth is no truth without following it".'

BLENWYDD 6th century
BLENWYD

A son of Caw

BODA 6th - 7th century

A son of Helig Foel, who first went with his brothers to Bangor-is-Coed when their lands were drowned, then to Enlli after Bangor's destruction.

BODFAN 7th century
January 2, June 2 (Catholic Online Saints)

A son of Helig Foel, and the patron saint of Abergwyngregyn, commonly known as Aber, in Caernarfon, which adjoins the 'Lavan Sands' where his father's lands were. His conversion was said to date from the time he saw the formation of Beaumaris Bay in the great flood.

BRACHAN 6th century
BACHAN, BACHANUS

On Cadog's return from Ireland with his friend Finnian, he settled at Ynyspyddid near Y Gaer Roman fort in Brecon. Here Cadog learned Latin from his Italian mentor, Brachanus. Cadog saved his followers from starvation by following a mouse to a secret grain store. This could have been in the long-deserted fort. Cadog's grandfather Brychan gave him land there, and Cadog left Brachan in charge of the Llansypyddid settlement before moving to Llangadog in Dyfed.

BRÂN FENDIGAID (Bran the Blessed) 1st century

Brân ap Llyr features in the Mabinogion as Britain's 'crowned king', and was used by Iolo Morganwg to compile an early genealogy. There is little fact and much fiction in his account and the legendary Brân is not counted amongst Welsh saints. His head was supposed to be buried where the White Tower stands in London, and his name 'brân' or 'raven' has been used to explain the legend of the Ravens in the Tower of London. His head had been brought back to Britain by the seven survivors of the warband who went to Ireland to avenge the wrongs done to his sister Branwen. Bedd Branwen is in Anglesey. The author mentions (in 'The A-Z of Wales and the Welsh') the legends connecting Brân with Castell Dinas Brân over Llangollen, and he is the source for the mediaeval French romances about Bron the Fisher-King.

We know that Arthur and Merlin are integral parts of Welsh history and legend, but I am indebted to the 'New Companion to the Literature of Wales' for the entry upon Bledri ap Cydifor who delved into Welsh legend to give the world two of its most potent stories, that of 'Tristan and Isolde' and the 'Quest for the Holy Grail' in the 12th century, predating the French romances, just as Brân predated the 'Fisher-King'. The Welsh Arthurian romance 'Iarlles y Ffynnon' also gave history the legend of Owain and the 'Black Knight', plundered by Chretien de Troyes for 'Yvain' and by Hartmann von der Aue for 'Iwein'.

Tradition makes Brân the father of Caradog (Caractacus) who was taken in triumph to Rome in 51 AD but not killed. A Triad states *'Brân, the blessed son of Llyr Llediaeth, who first brought the faith in Christ to the nation of the Cymry from Rome, where he had been seven years as a hostage for his son Caradoc.'* If he was seven years in Rome, Brân could have met Paul there and returned in 58 or 59 with Arwystli, Ilid, Cyndaf and Mawan. In 59 Nero sent Suetonius Paulinus as Governor of Britain, with additional troops, and they could have travelled as camp followers across Gaul. (Arwystli was martyred at extreme age in 99 AD). Another Triad states that *'Brân brought the faith in Christ into this island from Rome, where he had been a prisoner.'* Other sources such as the Genealogy make the same claims, and Gildas afirms that Christianity was introduced into Britain before 63. (See Arwystli and Eurgain). Tre-Fran farm is supposed to be Brân's court in the kingdom of the Silures, and nearby Llanilid has a local reputation as the oldest church in Britain. Mining operations have wiped out huge areas of ancient landscape around Trefran.

BRANNOC 6th century
January 7

He sailed from Wales to Devon in a stone coffin, arrived at Braunton, and decided to build his church on the site where a sow was suckling her pigs. He took a special plough with him, the first to be used in the area, which may have been the famous 'invention' of Illtud. This may be the same saint as Brynach (q.v.)

BRAUST see TATHANA

BRENDA 7th century

A son of Helig Foel who studied at Bangor or Enlli.

BRENDAN the NAVIGATOR c. 486-c. 575
BRANDON
May 16

This Irish Abbot of Clonfert in Ireland from 559, was said to be Abbot of the famous Llancarfan in Glamorgan before this time. He may have visited Brittany with St Malo, and is remembered in Brittany, Ireland, Scotland and Wales. The story of his missionary travels in a coracle across the seas was fictionalised in the 11th century in the 'Navigation of St Brendan'.

BRETON FOUNDER SAINTS

Of the seven 'founders' of Christianity in Brittany, it seems that six were Welsh – Malo, Briog (Brieuc), Samson of Dol, Padarn (Paternus), Tudwal (Tugdual, Tudy) and Peulin (Pol Aurelian). Only Saint Corentin cannot be linked to Wales, but is (Welsh-speaking) Cornish. To these saints, pilgrimages were regularly made at Easter, Pentecost, Michaelmas and Christmas throughout the Middle Ages.

The whole of northern Brittany from earliest times to the French Revolution was divided into five bishoprics founded by Welsh monks, Dol, St Malo, St Brieuc, Treguier and St Pol de Leon.

BRIAC d.570
December 17

An Irish monk who came to Wales under the tuition of Tudwal, with whom he went to Brittany. Tudwal founded the monastery of Lanpabo, and was granted land by prince Deroc ap Rhiwal which is the present town of Treguier. Briac founded Bourbriac near the prince's palace at Castel-deroch. He was invoked to cure insanity, and lunatics were locked up in a cell near his tomb and holy well.

BRIAVEL
BRIGOMAGLOS (in Old Celtic)
June 17

A hermit in the Forest of Dean, who possibly gave his name to St Briavels in Gloucestershire on the Welsh borders. However, the foundation may be that of Brioc. The festival date of

Briavel is different, but the author of the first 'Life' of Brioc called him Briomagl which changed into being called Briomail then Briafael. The church of St Briavel's in the Forest of Dean dates from around 1120 with 13th century additions.

BRICE 4th - 5th century
BRITHIUS, BERRYS, BERRES, BREWYS, BREWIS, BRISE
November 13

Eglwys Brewys church is dedicated to St Brise, a 5th century bishop. It is a small church inside the airbase of St Athan, and has been subject to a great deal of vandalism despite being on a site sealed from the general public. The RAF authorities have consequently been asked by the church authorities to help in its repair. *'All the windows have been smashed and an attempt has been made to set fire to the main door . . . 'the slates seem to have been pulled from the roof and a wall has been knocked down'* according to the Llantwit Gem newspaper. The Archdeacon of Llandaf proposes to place a fence around it, to protect it from the families of RAF personnel. Its name may come from one of the ruling Norman families, de Braose.

Llanferres in Denbigh is definitely attributed to Brice, and he was said to have been a disciple of Martin of Tours, whom he succeeded to the bishopric. St Brice was said to have been raised by Martin of Tours at Marmoutier and was known for his haughtiness and ambition, before he asked Martin for forgiveness. He succeeded as Bishop in 397, but reverted to his old ways of arrogance, and was exiled to Rome for seven years. When the administrator of his see died, he returned to Tours as a chastened, humble man once more, and was venerated as a saint by the time of his death.

The wake of this bishop at Tours, and that at Llanferres is the same date of November 13. Eglwys Sant Berres lies between Mold and Ruthin, with a 'jolly lantern' dovecote, and adjacent is the Druid Inn. A remarkable legend concerns Llanferres. It had a place called Rhyd y Gyfartha (Ford of the Barking), where dogs would always bark. People were afraid of investigating further until the great Urien Rheged came upon a woman washing there. The dogs fell quiet, and she told him that the blessing of God had brought him there. It was her destiny to wash at the ford until a Christian approached her. She told Urien that she was the daughter of Annwn, King of the Underworld, and when Urien returned as instructed, a year later, she presented him with Owain and Morfudd, his son and daughter.

Near Avranches are St Brice, and St Brice-de-Landelles. St Brice-en-Cogles is near Fougeres. The 13th century Eglwys Brewis Church is to the north of the St Athan (Tathan) airfield and is possibly the 'crudest and smallest' in use in the Vale of Glamorgan, being only 35 feet by 19. There is a Norman font, and a 1643 tombstone in the floor dedicated to the 12-year-old Mary, daughter of Miles Bassett. The de Braose family held lands in Llanmaes, and may have been its founders, as stated above. William de Braose was Bishop of Llandaff from 1266-1287. In 1254 the church was valued at £2, and in 1535 at £4-0s-2d. Known as Eglis Priwes in the Taxatio of Norwich in 1254, its first recorded cleric was Ricardus de Egluspirwys in 1443. Bettws Perwas under Llanrhuddlad in Anglesey was known as Llan Berwas, and Leland called him a *'swete servant.'* No-one yet seems to have made the link between Perwas and 'Egluspirwys'. (Eglwys is the Welsh for church, from the latin Ecclesia). There are wall-paintings in the church, and its structure, save for some remodelling of the nave in the 15th century, is essentially as it was in the 13th century.

Alphabetical Listing of the Saints of Wales and Religious Events

As an interesting footnote to the history of the little hamlet of Eglwys Brewys, a Cardiff trial noted the following in 1564: *'Gwenllian Morgan of Cowbridge and Johanna Thomas of Eglwysbrewis. That on 25 June 5 Elizabeth (1563) they maliciously gave a certain poison called Ratsbane mixed up with a certain pudding called Whitepott to Maurice Dee the husband of the said Gwenllian at Cowbridge aforesaid of which the said Maurice languished till the 1st day of July and then died. They are found guilty of the felony, they have no goods or chattels, and the said Gwenllian and Johanna shall be burned to ashes.'* The crime of poisoning a husband was 'petty treason' so the perpetrators had to be boiled or burned to death, rather than hanged. At this same time Meyrick Bruton of Llangyfelach was found guilty at Cardiff in 1566 of murdering David William with a knife valued at two pence. He escaped with a branding, as did John ap Boweyn of St Andrews two years later. John ap Boweyn had smashed Phillip Colen's head in with an iron shovel. Both claimed *'benefit of clergy'* which meant branding on the palm of the left hand for a serious offence. The method used to prove the *'benefit'* was if the accused person could read a passage from a book. One law for men and another for women?

BRIDE see FFRAID

ABBOT BRIOC c. 440-c. 530 (or 410-510)
BRIOG, BRIEUC, BREOKE, BREOCK, BRIAC, TYFRIOG, BRIOMAGLUS
April 30, May 1
Patron saint of purse makers

Possibly born in 440 in Cardigan (Ceredigion), where he founded a monastery, he ministered in South-West Britain before becoming a missionary in Brittany. Coritica (Cardigan) was his province, according to Cressy. An Ogham tombstone in Bridell churchyard, north Pembrokeshire, reads *'NETTASAGRU MAQUI MUCOI BRECI'*, which indicated the monument of Nettasagrus of the tribe or family of Brec, or Brioc. Also in south Cardigan is Llandyfriog*, with the prefix of Ty (house) of Briog. The Rickardston Hall stone, found near Brawdy in Pembroke reads *'Briac Fil . . . '* and the Llandefaelog stone near Brecon reads *'Briamail Flou', ('The Cross of Briomaglus Flavis')*. Thus the family of Brioc seems to have spread across Wales from Cardigan. Some attempts have been made to link him with Arthur's brother Frioc.

He was said to be a disciple of Garmon, along with Illtud and Patrick. Breoke or St Breock in the Forest of Dean on the Welsh borders is dedicated to him. Brioc was founder of the great monastery near Treguier in Brittany which became St Brieuc, Cote-d'Armor's biggest town, with St Stephen's Cathedral. He had converted Conan, the local ruler. Because St Brieuc was so vulnerable to Viking raids, his relics were taken to Angers around 850. Some bones were given back in 1210. In 1166, he was translated in the presence of King Henry II. Brioc became the patron saint of purse-makers because of his reputation for great works of charity. A founder–saint of Brittany, St Brieuc and several other towns commemorate him, lands being given by his 'cousin' Riwal (Hywel) Mawr, Prince of Domnonee. Hywel Mawr was a kinsman of Arthur, so the placing of Brioc as Arthur's brother Frioc may be correct. However, Welsh legends state that Frioc was killed by Morgan ap Arthur to claim his inheritance of Glamorgan and Gwent.

The stone in Brawdy Church could denote Brioc's burial place (see Ffraid). One of the *'peregrini'* or wandering holy men, he is associated with St Briavels, but Briavel's feast day is different, so he may have been a different saint. St Breoke near Bodmin, and thirteen dedications in Brittany are his, such as St Brieuc-des-Iffs between St Malo and Rennes, and St Briac-sur-Mer east of Dinard and St Malo.

May 1st was also known as *'Evil May'* or *'Ill May Day'*, from the occasion in 1517 when the London apprentices rioted against *'privileged foreigners, whose advantages in trade had occasioned great jealousy.'* The main source of discontent were the Welshmen who had flooded into London in the years following Henry Tudor's victory at Bosworth Field in 1485. May 1 was also a major celebration in the early Celtic calendar.

*It strongly appears that Brioc is the son of Dingad ap Brychan, and is sometimes confused with Tyfriog ap Dingad ap Nudd Hael whose date is also May 1. Tyfriog was given as the son of Dingad ap Nudd Hael and Tenoi, and was supposed to have founded founded Llandyfriog in Cardigan. If Tyfriog is a separate saint, his brother Tygwy is the patron of the neighbouring Llandysgydd. 'Ty' is the prefix of endearment to Briog, or meaning 'the house of' Briog. His cult was said to survive at Little Lidney near St Briavel's on the Welsh borders. A Romano-British dedication near there to 'Nodens' is possibly to Nudd Hael. Perhaps readers can suggest whether Tyfriog merits a separate entry in future editions of this book.

THE BRITISH CHURCH, OR PRIMITIVE CELTIC CHURCH

This survived the leaving of the Roman legions between 380 and 410, and in the next few decades Christianity was wiped out all over the rest of Europe except for a few anchorites living on islands off Ireland. However, Celtic Christianity survived in Wales. Later writers such as Bede resented the survival of this church when the rest of Britain was finally Christianised, as its power would reduce that of Rome in Britain. (See Bangor-is-Coed). Apart from the form of tonsure and the timing of Easter, the other major difference was that the Welsh would have nothing to do with the new 'Italian' faith of the Saxons. The Germanic tribes had over-run England, and cut off Wales, which had been fighting the barbarian Irish, Scots, English and Vikings for centuries. Why should the Welsh give up their faith and take up that of their enemies? Although the Irish took up a Welsh type of Christianity in the 6th century, and relations improved considerably, the other invaders were still alien and so was their faith. A letter by Aldhelm, the Saxon catholic priest, later Bishop of Shelborne, to Geraint King of Cornwall survives. It shows that the differences were small, and Cressy's translation reads:
'But beside these enormities (The Tonsure and the Paschal cycle) there is another thing wherein they do notoriously swerve from the Catholic Faith and Evangelical Tradition, which is, that the Priests of the Demetae, or South-West Wales, inhabiting beyond the bay of Severn, puffed up with conceit of their own purity, do exceedingly abhor communion with us, inasmuch that they will neither join in prayers with us in the Church, nor enter into society with us at the Table; yea moreover the fragments which we leave after refection (dining) they will not touch, but cast them to be devoured by dogs and unclean Swine. The Cups also in which we have drunk, they will not make use of, till they have rubbed and cleansed them with sand or ashes. They refuse all civil salutations or to give us the kisses of pious fraternity, contrary to the Apostolic precept, "Salute one another with a holy kiss." They will not afford us water and a towel for our hands, nor a vessel to wash our feet. Whereas our Saviour having girt Himself with a towel, washed his Disciples' feet, and left us a pattern to imitate, saying "As I have done to you, so do you to others." Moreover if any of us who are Catholics do go among them to

make an abode, they will not vouchsafe to admit us to their fellowship until we be compelled to spend forty days in Penance . . .'

'Since therefore the truth of these things cannot be denied, we do with earnest humble prayers and bended knees beseech and adjure you, as you hope to attain to the fellowship of Angels in God's heavenly kingdom, that you will no longer with pride and stubbornness abhor the doctrines and Decrees of the Blessed Apostle St Peter, nor pertinaciously and arrogantly despise the Tradition of the Roman Church, preferring before it the Decrees and ancient Rites of your Predecessors . . .'

As regards the place of Wales in the *'British'* Isles, a recent letter in the 'Western Mail' pointed out that *'The English and Scots were known as the English and Scots prior to the 16th century; only the Welsh have always been Britons. In view of the desire expressed in the English press for explicit national identities,* **perhaps the (Welsh National) Assembly should be known as the British Assembly.'** (K. Vivian, Garnant).

BRITO d. 386
BRITONIUS
May 5

Probably British, this Bishop of Trier in Germany opposed Priscillian heretics and worked to convert them. He refused to hand them over to state authorities because he did not wish to see fellow-Christians persecuted.

BRITTANY

Prydein Fychain (Little Britain) has a similar language to the Welsh of Great Britain, and there was considerable movement between Brittany, Cornwall and Wales in the Age of Saints. The West Country (Domnonia) was a useful crossing area for both nations. Noted throughout this book we see the influence of Breton saints, and the families of the sons of Emyr Llydaw (King Budic of Brittany) fighting for Arthur ap Meurig when dispossessed by the Franks. The *'Armorican Mission'* of saints coming to Wales in the 6th century is detailed under Cadfan's entry in this book.

The waves of the British movement into Brittany began with the *'first migration'* of 388, of the remnants of Macsen Wledig's legions. Cynan Meiriadog and Gadeon were Elen's brothers and thus Macsen's brothers-in-law. After staying loyal to Rome as Duke of Armorica (Brittany) for some time, Cynan claimed independence for Brittany in 409, dying in 421.

From 440-450 there was migration from England as the Saxons pressed through the country, and 458-460 saw the *'second migration'* of British nobles and their followers, led by the fabled Riothamus. In 469 Riothamus led a British army trying to help the emperor Anthemius but was heavily defeated by the Visigoths.

The *'third migration'* was from 530-550, a mass emigration from the west of Britain, when Armel and Samson fought Conmire to restore Iuthael to the Breton crown. In 547, many Welsh saints fled to Brittany to avoid the Yellow Plague.

KING BROCHWEL YSGYTHROG (The 'Fanged') 6th-7th century

The son of Cyngen ap Cadell and Tudglid, probably a grand-daughter of Brychan, his great grandfather was king Brochwel of Powys. Brochwel's sister Sannan married Maelgwn Gwynedd. A version of his name, Brohomagli, was found on a 6th or 7th century inscribed stone at Voelas Hall. He married Arddun ferch Pabo Post Prydain, and their children included St Tyssilio and King Cynan Garwyn. Brochwel led an armed escort for the monks of Bangor-is-Coed at the Battle of Chester in 607 (or 603), when only 50 of 1250 monks escaped murder by the pagan Ethelfrith. Some sources state that he died there, and others that he escaped or fled. Before this terrible battle, Pengwern (Shrewsbury) was the capital of the kingdom of Powys, and its palace was said to have been where St Chad's Church stands now. A fountain there, which for centuries supplied fresh water to the town, was called Ffynnon Frochwel, Brochwel's Well.

BROTHAN ap SEIRIOL 6th century

This saint appears only to be mentioned by Iolo Morganwg.

BROTHEN 6th – 7th century
October 14 (also 15 and 18)

One of the twelve sons of Helig ap Glannog. He is buried at Llanfrothen in Merioneth, which now has only one house standing near it. The church was later dedicated to the Festival of the Assumption. Sir John Wynn believed that he was buried at Dwygyfylchi with his brother Gwynin. Ffynnon Frothen stood outside his church, and is probably the holy well now named Hen Ffynnon (Old Well).

WALTER BRUT (fl. 1390-1402)

This intriguing layman is included because of the nature of his trial recorded before the Welshman John Trefnant, Bishop of Hereford, in 1391. He took a Pelagian stance in the value of faith as the means for justifying action, and declared that the Brythonic Christians, from whom the Welsh were descended, took their Christian doctrines directly from the East, and not through the 'European filter' of Rome. He condemned the lechery and greed of priests, and their granting of indulgences. Not content with this, the Pope was condemned as the Antichrist, and Brut refreshingly accused the Roman church of fomenting wars for no good reason and against the will of Christ. It was God's plan, with Welsh assistance, to overthrow the Antichrist, i.e. the Pope and his supporting clergy. After this testimony, Bishop Trefnant surprisingly released Brut without him making a full recantation.

KING BRYCHAN c.390-450
April 5, 6

Son of the Irish prince Amlech and the Welsh St Marchell, he was born at Bannium, the Roman town and camp now known as Y Gaer in Brecon. His father was buried near the door of Ynyspyddid Church. In the churchyard is the ancient monument always known as 'The Cross of Brychan Brycheiniog', and the church is dedicated to Cadog, his grandson. The inscription 'Broccagni' was found on a fragmented stone at Capel Mair, Llangeler, Carmarthenshire, and also at Porthqueene, near Camelford in Cornwall. He was a contemporary of Cunedda and Vortigern.

The first king of Brecon (Brychan Brycheiniog) after the Romans left, he was the founder of a long line of saints, including his daughters or grand-daughters Gwladus (who married Gwynlliw), Arianwen, Bechan/Bethan, Tanglwst (Ynystanglws, near Swansea), Mechell, Nefyn, Gwawr (the mother of the soldier-poet Llywarch Hen), Gwrgon (who married Cadrawd), Eleri, Lleian, Nefydd, Rhiengar, Gwenddydd, Tybie (Llandybie), Elined, Ceindrych, Gwen (Gwenllian or Gwenhwyfar, who may have married King Arthur), Cenedlon, Cymorth, Clydai, Dwynwen, Ceinwen, Tudfyl (martyred at Merthyr Tydfil), Enfail, Hawystl, Tybie, Callwen, Gwenfyl, Ceingar (the mother of Cynidr), Goleuddydd, Meleri (the grandmother of Dewi Sant), Ceneu, Ellyw, Keneython, Nectan, Mwynen, Cain (Llangain and Llangeinor), Endellion, Clether and Morwenna.

Among his sons or grandsons, Arthen, Berwyn, Clydwyn, Clydog, Cynog, Gwen, Gwynau, Gwynws, Cyflefyr, Rhain,Dyfnan, Gerwyn, Cadog, Mathaiarn, Pasgen, Neffai, Pabliali, Dedyn, Llecheu, Cynbryd, Cynfran, Hychan, Dyfrig, Cynin, Dogfan, Rhawin, Rhun, Clydog, Caian and Dingad were saints. Many of his children went to Cornwall from Brecon, where they were venerated. There are many lists extant of his descendants, but all vary. Brychan's family forms one of the *'Three Saintly Tribes of the Isle of Britain'*, along with those of Caw and Cunedda. Brychan is depicted in a stained glass window at St Neots in Cornwall. His wives were said to be Eurbrawst, Proestri and Rhybrawst.

Gerald of Wales talks of Brychan's 24 daughters, *'dedicated from their youth to religious observances'*, who *'happily ended their lives in sanctity'*. Michael Drayton in 'Polyolbion' refers to the legend of Brychan's 24 daughters remaining virgins and being transformed into rivers flowing into the Severn (Hafren) on their deaths, no doubt a tale linked with the Celtic river goddesses of folk memory.

The descendants of Brychan, with those of his instructor Byrnach, and of Gastayn, (the spiritual advisor of Brychan's eldest son Cynog), are responsible for over fifty ancient church sites in Wales. About 22 are in Brecon and on its borders. There are around 16 in Carmarthen and Pembroke, at that time occupied by the Gwyddyl Fichti (Irish Picts). There are 5 churches in Anglesey, 3 on the Isle of Man, and others in Denbigh. Leland, in his Life of St Nectan, listed the influence in Dumnonia – *'Nectanus, Joannes, Endelient, Menfre, Dilic, Tedda, Maben, Weneu, Wensent, Merewenna, Wenna, Juliana, Yse, Morwenna, Wymp, Wenheder, Cleder, Keri, Jona, Kanane, Kerhender, Adwen, Helic, Talamanc. All these sons or daughters were afterwards holy martyrs and confessors in Devon and Cornwall, where they led an eremetical life.'* It seems that there was a missionary movement from Brycheiniog along the Roman roads in the 5th and 6th centuries.

Llangors Lake in Brecon is now known as Llyn Syfaddan, but was called Breccanmere in the Anglo-Saxon Chronicle. The only known crannog (fortified island) in Wales is here, and is held to be the place of Brychan's court. Crannogs are well-documented in Ireland. In 916 it was raided by Aethelflaed and King Tewdwr's wife and 33 captives taken. Nearby is the ancient church of St Paulinus. (See Gastayn). There was a place-name near Pol-de-Leon named *'Brochana pars'*, and Doble notes how many of the dedications of Brychan's descendants are near those of Peulin. There was also a place seven miles west of Llanddeusant named Llys

Brychan (Brychan's Palace), which is surrounded by the foundations of Brychan's children at Llandingad, Capel Tudyst, Capel Cynheiddon, Llandybie, Llanceinwyry, Llanlluan and Llansteffan (Cynog).

ABBOT BRYNACH d. c. 570
BRYNACH WYDDEL (The Irishman), BERNACH, BYRNACH, BRANACH
April 7

A chaplain and instructor of the warlord King Brychan, some sources say that he married Cymorth (Corth), one of his daughters. (However, Gerwyn seems to have married Corth). Another story says that the daughter of a ruling nobleman tried to seduce Brynach with a love-potion made from wolfs-bane, but he fled from her advances. She then sent men to capture or kill him. He was wounded and cured at a sacred fountain called the Redspring. Most of his dedications are clustered on the routes to Ireland, mainly in Pembrokeshire. Perhaps he left Brychan's Brecon court to be nearer Ireland for an easy escape-route. Like many other saints, he argued with Maelgwn Gwynedd. His 'Life' says that he travelled to Rome to see the shrines of Peter and Paul, and sailed to Milford Haven via Brittany on a 'stone', which probably means that he possessed a portable altar. In Pembroke he was met by 'propositioning' women and also by assassins engaged in a purge of Irish settlers. He escaped first to Llanboidy, a cowshed being his only shelter, and then to Cilmaenllwyd ('the shelter of a grey stone'). South of Llanboidy was a medicinal well known as Ffynnon Foida. West of the church there is Ffynnon Frynach, with a small well chamber. At Llanfrynach he then bult an oratory near a spring at Trehenry Farm. Thence he travelled to Henry's Moat and then to Pontfaen, finally reaching the end of his pilgrimage at Nevern, which became a great centre of pilgrimage and learning. There is a tradition that he died at Braunton in Devon, where the church is dedicated to St Branach (see Brannoc).

In Cwm-yr-Eglwys* (Valley of the Church), just on the neck of Dinas Head peninsula (between Fishguard and Cardigan), lies the beautifully sited remains of St Brynach's Church. A huge storm in 1859 demolished most of the building, and another in 1979 took away some of the graveyard. St Brynach was said to talk to angels on the prehistoric hill fort that tops nearby Carn Ingli (Rock of Angels). The hill was thus called in mediaeval times 'Mons Angelorum'.

Just inland from Cwm-yr-Eglwys, standing above the beautiful Gwaun Valley, is Pontfaen, with its tiny church dedicated to Brynach. According to his 'Life' he fled from here, pursued by evil spirits, to settle at Nevern (Nanhyfer, or Nyfer in Welsh). There are two 6th-9th century pillar stones in the Celtic circular churchyard. Just a few miles west of here, also on the 'Pilgrim's Trail', is Llanllawer Well, enclosed by a vaulted chamber of rough masonry. It was especially eficacious in curing eye ailments when pins and coins were offered. It also was used as a 'cursing well', with pre-Christian traditions, and there is a superb view from here down Trecwn Gorge. There is a cromlech on Mynydd Llanllawer, another standing stone near Rhos Isaf, and seven standing stones in alignment in The Field of the Dead (Parc y Merw) at Trellwyn.

In Nevern Churchyard, the magnificent twelve foot high Celtic cross is associated with St Brynach – he is supposed to have swapped it with St David for a loaf of bread. The are three Ogham stones in Nevern churchyard, an Irish tradition associated with the 'cil' or 'kil' of a saint (the 'llan'). One of his wife's family, Clether, gave him the land at Nevern, around the River Nyfer to make his foundation. This Clether may be related to the 5th century 'Clutar' who is named in Irish and Ogham inscriptions on a stone that is used as a window-sill in the eastern nave of Nevern church. Westwood, however, says that Meurig, 'regulus' of the country (and Arthur's father) gave Byrnach lands for churches. Westwood noted that a Celtic stone pitched on the end of Nevern church was inscribed 'St Iohannes', another was inscribed *'Vitaliani Emeret . . . '*, and yet another *tb-wi-mi-im'*. He states that the Vitalianus stone had 'disgracefully' been stolen from the church to be used as a gatepost on Cwm Gloyn Farm. Blackett and Wilson (in 'Artorius Rex Discovered') believe Vitalianus not to be Vortigern (Gwrtheyrn) but Gwythelin, a brother of King Tewdrig.

'The Bleeding Yew' in Nanhyfer (Nevern) churchyard has a story that a monk was hanged from it, and he swore that it would bleed ever after to remember the injustice. The yew's trunk still oozes red resin. Near Nevern is Trellyffant Cromlech (Toad's Town), recorded by Giraldus Cambensis as having this name because the chieftain buried there was eaten by toads. Also close to Nevern is the famous Pentre Ifan (Coetan Arthur) cromlech, with a huge capstone, and a stone circle on the Preselis known as Waun Mawr. Two more standing stones are just south, called Carreg Meibion Owen, and there is another, Y Garreg Hir, outside Tre-fach.

A lovely legend was recounted in George Owen's Elizabethan history of Pembrokeshire. On April 7th, the feast day of Brynach, the priest would never begin to say mass until the cuckoo arrived, as it always came on that day, perching on the great cross of Brynach at Nanhyfer (Nevern). One year it was late, and the priest and people waited patiently for several hours. When the cuckoo eventually appeared, it was so exhausted that it dropped dead before it could sing. According to the people it had battled its way against storms, never resting, because it knew it could not fail its ancestors who had the honour of starting Mass on Brynach's day. This was a pagan site, and this legend of the first cuckoo to sing in mid-Wales to herald the Spring may come from a pre-Christian tradition. St Brynach's Cross is made of Preseli dolorite for the shaft and sandstone for the wheelhead. It is probably 10th century, and stands thirteen feet high with rich carvings on its side panels, with a totally decorated cross-head.

Brynach is counted as the founder of Llanfrynach in Brecon, Llanfrynach which is now called Penlline in Glamorgan, Llanfernach at Dinas, Pembrokeshire, Nefern in Pembroke and Llanboidy in Carmarthen. The Llanboidy Stone was said to read *'Lvharch (Llywarch?) Cocc . . . '*. Henry's Moat and nearby Pontfaen in Pembroke were also his, but ascribed to Bernard by the Normans. At Llanfyrnach in Pembroke, the church was referred to as 'Ecclesia Sancti Bernachi de Blaentaf in Kemeys' in the 12th century, and became the property of the Knights Hospitaller of St John of Jerusalem. St Brynach's Church is unusually sited on a raised circular mound surrounded by a slight embankment and a ditch. Opposite the church, in the farm of Rhyd y Garth, is a 7th century stone with a Latin ring cross. Two miles away at Glandwr, inside the gate of the 1712 Baptist Chapel is an Ogham stone to *'effessangus asegnus.'* It is 5th-6th century with a Latin wheel-cross over-inscribed in the 7th-9th centuries. The stone Maengwyn Hir at Llanfrynach was said to have been thrown from the summit of Frenni Fawr by St Samson. There is a cromlech known as Gwal y Filiast at Brynach's Llanboidy on the river Tâf.

St Brynach's Church at Henry's Moat (Castellhenri) is close to an Iron Age encampment and a castle motte, and included in the 'pilgrim's trail' of churches. There is a seven foot standing stone in a field called Parc Maen Hir, and the remains of a stone circle with 13 boulders near Bernard's Well, formerly called Ffynnon Frynach. Near Henry's Moat, just off the Maenclochog road in Pembroke are these ruins of St. Brynach's Well. A Dark Age stone has been removed from there and placed in Henry's Moat Church, and the little chapel next to the holy well has almost disappeared. The well is featured in the Menter Preseli 'In the Shadow of

Pentre Ifan Cromlech, Newport, Dyfed. © *Wales Tourist Board Photo Library.*

the Preselis' pilgrim's trail, and still gushes forth from a stone-built arch under a hedge, where there are traces of a well-chamber.

There are another three holy wells in Pembroke associated with Brynach. Nearby is Morvil, with the church of St John the Baptist, but on a Celtic circular site, possibly Byrnach's foundation. There is a 10th century cross there, but the church is now on farm property. Between Henry's Moat and Morvil, the pilgrim's trail leaflet recommends visiting the Iron Age fort of Cas Bwch on Castlebythe Mountain. *'There the pilgrim commands a view which extends from St Anne's Head in the south, taking in the peaks of Ramsey Island, Carn Llidi, Pen Beri, on St David's Head, Garn Fawr on Pencaer, to where the peak of Carn Ingli, St Brynach's mountain of the angels, rises over the shoulder of Cilciffeth.'*

Lavernock on the coast between Penarth and Barri is dedicated to St Laurence, but was possibly Llanfyrnach previously. St Laurence (August 10) was broiled in a gridiron in the 3rd century. By all accounts his last words were:
'This side is toasted, so turn me, tyrant, eat,
And see whether raw or roasted I make the better meat.'
Rather strangely, Laurence is the patron saint of confectioners, bakers and cooks.

The parish church of Llanfrynach, near Cowbridge in Glamorgan, is dedicated to the 6th century Irish saint, who established the first church on this site. It fell into disuse in the 17th century because it was remote from the village, but occasional services are still held here. It lies under the large Iron Age hillfort of Caer Dynnaf, and the church is next to the ploughed-out remains of a Romano-British farmstead, only discovered in 1976. 1982 excavations around the churchyard found the remains of two large medieval buildings, possible belonging to a grange of Margam Abbey.

'The Merthyr Mynach Stone' is now fixed as a seat in the rebuilt church of Merthyr Mynach (Monk's Martyrdom), near Dwrt Derllys outside Carmarthen. It was found in the 19th century by a sexton digging a grave, and reads *'CATVRVG - FILI LOVERNAC'*. It is suggested as the gravestone of Cadwr ap Ednyfed ap Macsen Wledig, and also as of Cadwr ap Bernach.

*A hundred years after the great storm wrecked St Brynach's church, Waldo Williams wrote a hymn which ends:
'Frynach Wyddel, edrych arnom,
Llifed ein gweddiau ynghyd,
Fel y codo'r muriau cadarn
Uwch tymhestloedd moroedd byd.'
*(Brynach the Irishman, look upon us,
May our prayers flow together,
That the strong walls may be built
Above the storms of the world's seas.)*

BUAN late 6th century
August 4th

He founded Bodfuan in Caernarfon, and was the son of Ysgwn ap Llywarch Hen. When he fled with his family from the invading Angles in the north, he stayed for some time at the court of Cynddylan, Prince of Powys. This was probably Viriconium, or Wroxeter in Shropshire, the superb Roman town.

BUDDWAL 5th century
BUDDWALAN

Mentioned in the Book of Llandaf, with the grant of land to the church of Lann Budgualan in Ergyng, i.e. Ballingham near Hereford.

BUDIC see EMYR LLYDAW

BISHOP BUDOC OF DOL 6th century
BUOC, BEUZEC, BUDEAUX
December 8 (9 in Brittany)

This Welsh missionary monk is honoured in Pembrokeshire, Cornwall and as St Budeaux in Plymouth. In Brittany he is known as St Beuzec, and is the saint of the church at Plourin. Buzec is west of the lovely fishing village of Douarnanez. He asked his disciple Illtud to cut off his arm when he died, and a finger is still in a reliquary in Plourin. As abbot in the monastery on the Isles of Brehat, he taught Gwenole (Winwaloe). In Cornwall, Budock on Falmouth Harbour and Budoc Vean both have churches commemorating him, as does St Budeaux in Devon. 'Catholic Online Saints' gives his genealogy as being the son of a king of Brittany and of Azenor, the daughter of the ruler of Brest. Azenor was exiled in a cask and Budoc born at sea, being raised in a monastery at Waterford, attended by St Brigid. After becoming abbot there, he moved to Dol.

Farmer notes that Budock faces Mawes across Falmouth Harbour, while Mawes' Breton monastery was also close to Budoc's. In Pembrokeshire a Tironian monastery was dedicated to him at Pill, and Steynton church of St Botolph's is his foundation. Nearby there was an old chapel called St Buttock's on Hubberston Pill. There was also a pre-Norman dedication near the site of Oxford Castle. A kinsman of Samson and Maglorius, he succeeded Maglorius at Dol where he was bishop from 586-600.

BUDOC d.c.560
November 24

A Welsh disciple of Gildas, they co-founded a monastery at Castanec in Brittany. Gildas later left for his main foundation in Rhuys. Budoc was martyred on November 24 by a local chief, and in Beuzy churchyard is a portion of his stone bell.

BUGI 6th century
HYWGI

Beuno's father, and the son of Gwynlliw ap Glywys, he gave his lands to God and Cadog and became a saint with his brother Cadog at Llancarfan. The Vita of St Beuno has a different story, where Beuno gave his father the last rites at a place called Banhenig in Powys, near the river Severn.

THOMAS BURGESS 1756-1837
February 19

Given the Holy Day of February 19, the day of his death, Burgess was a Hampshire man who became Bishop of St David's in 1803. He instituted reforms in the diocese, and was instrumental in the foundation of St David's College at Lampeter in 1822. He showed a remarkable interest in Welsh culture and eisteddfodau before his translation to Salisbury in 1825.

C

*'**C**hristianity is the most materialistic of all the great religions.'*

Archbishop William Temple, 'Reading in St John's Gospel', 1939

CADELL early 7th century
CATLEU?

The son of Urien Foeddog ap Rhun Rhion ap Llywarch Hen, he possibly founded Llangadell in Glamorgan. This is now called Llancadle (Llancatal), and his little church is now a farm outhouse. It may well be however, that Llancatal was dedicated to Cadog (Cathmael). The hamlet is just upriver from Aberthaw. [The history of Aberthaw (Aberddawen), Sain Tathan (Llandathan), Flemingston (Flimstwn, Llanelwan), Eglwys Brewys and Gileston (Llanfabon-y-fro) has been published by this author for the Millenium Celebrations in the five parishes.]

A 'Saying of the Wise' is:
'Hast thou heard the saying of Cadell,
The prince whose better was never found?
"Not much good will come much deceit".'

This village, with 'The Green Dragon' pub and about fifteen houses, was variously known as Talcatlon and Llandili. St Catlon and St Cadell have been associated with it, but possibly it was once known as Llan Gadfael. Catlon was a witness to the Llandaf Charters, and he is another contender for the founder of the church. Cadell of Powys, the father of Cyngen and son of Brochmael, is noted on the famous Pillar of Eliseg (see Collen).

There is also a legend of the Romans or Normans fighting on the bank of the nearby river Kenson. Cad-lle means place of battle. Some of Cromwell's soldiers are also said to be buried in the field leading down to the river, and there is a tradition that he worshipped in the church. The chapel was visited by the vicar of Llancarfan until about 1925.

In proof-reading this book (which could easily be 2000 pages long with another 2000 pages of attributions), the author came across the 'Llan Vaughan Stone'. Over six feet high, it stood in a hedge at the ruined Llanfechan House near Llanbyther in Cardigan. Westwood translates its inscription as *'TRENACATUS IC IACIT FILIVS MAGLAGNI'*. However, the Ogham carving reads 'Tren and Catlo' who are identified with Trenecatus and Catleu. Catleu is the same person as Catlo, so we may have the founder of Llancadle. Again, Vortigern (Gwrtheyrn) has also been called Catel, which is another possibility for the founder. The author has also just found a 19th century map which denotes a chapel ruins on the other side of the River Dawen (Thaw), on Flemingstone Moors. It is between the hamlets of Castleton and Flemingston (both with Norman remains), in the valley under a field today known as Chapel Field, and some stones remain.

CADFAN 5th-6th century
CADMAN, CATMAN, CATAMANUS
November 1st
Patron of warriors

A Breton who emigrated to Gwynedd and founded Tywyn church and the monastery on Bardsey Island. The son of Eneas Lydewig and Gwen Teirbron ferch Emyr Llydaw. Cadfan was the leader of what was known as the 'Armorican Mission' into Wales. He was half-brother to Winwaloe and Padarn's cousin. Cadfan's noble and princely companions are said to have included Cynon, Padarn, Tydecho, Trinio, Gwyndaf, Dochdwy, Mael, Sulien, Tanwg, Eithras, Sadwrn, Lleuddad, Tecwyn and Maelrys. It seems that they escaped from the invasion of Clovis and the Franks into their territories in Armorica (Brittany). King Einion gave Cadfan Ynys Enlli (Bardsey Island) to found a monastery, where traditionally he was the first abbot. Llangadfan in Montgomery is Cadfan's foundation. Ffynnon Gadfan at Llangadfan in Merioneth was narrowly saved from destruction by the efforts of the curate in 1850, and an arch now carries a road over it.

His main settlement was Tywyn between Dolgellau and Aberdyfi, and his monastery there flourished until at least the thirteenth century, when a bard described his church as being *'near the shore of a blue sea'*. This was still standing in 1620. There were many miracles at his holy well, which now lies in the grounds of the National Westminster Bank. The well was said to cure rheumatism, and scrofulous and cutaneous illnesses, and it still attracted people seeking a cure even after wells were proscribed in the Reformation. There were baths and changing rooms, but by 1894 it was disused and converted. The owners could no longer afford to pay a 'well-keeper' as the number of pilgrims decreased. The Cadfan Stone, the Celtic pillar in Towyn Church, records his burial place *'Beneath a similar mound lies Cadfan, sad that it should enclose the praise of the earth. May he rest without blemish'*, with the inscription *'Cadfan the king, the wisest and most renowned of all kings.'* (See Cadwaladr). It also notes the burial of Cyngen (q.v.).

The Celtic stone known as the 'Tywyn Stone' has probably the earliest example of the Welsh language recorded on stone. It is probably 8th century, and the half-uncial script has been deciphered as:
*'Ceinrwy wife of Addian (lies here) close to Bud (and) Meirchiaw
Cun, wife of Celyn: grief and loss remain
The memorial of four
This is a memorial of the three'*

It seems that Cadfan died at Enlli but his remains were then taken back to Tywyn, his initial settlement. Near Abergynolwyn we can find Pistyll Cadfan, Llwybr Cadfan and Eisteddfa Gadfan. From Tywyn via Abergynolwyn one comes to Llangadfan in Montgomeryshire. There is a Llangadfan in Merioneth also, near his disciple Tydecho's church at Garthbeibio.

In Finistere and Cotes du Nord there is a cult of Cadfan, and a church in Poullan near Douarnanez is dedicated to him. A statue in Briec shows Cadfan in armour, as does one near Juimpier. He is the patron of warriors in Brittany, so it seems that he fought heroically against the Franks before escaping to Wales.

Baring Gould and Fisher ('The Lives of the British Saints') claim that the following saints were led by St Cadfan from Brittany into Wales – Baglan, Cynon, Cristiolus, Dochwy, Eithras,

Fflewyn, Gredifael, Gwyndaf, Henwyn, Ilar, Llechid, Lleuddad, Llyfab, Llywen, Mael, Maelrys, Meilyr, Padarn, Rhystud Sadwrn, Sulien, Tannwg, Tegai, Tegwyn, Trillo, Trinio and Tydecho. Many of these can be traced back through Cadfan to his maternal grandfather Emyr Llydaw (Emyr of Brittany), and their churches are clustered near his. However, few of these saints except Cadfan, Baglan and Sulien are followed in Brittany. It may be that Cadfan and Baglan went to Brittany with Arthur/Armel to fight Conmire. The author will follow this line of reasoning with a forthcoming book upon Arthur.

CADFAN fl. 620

Not a saint, but this prince was a descendant of Maelgwn, and the son of Iago ap Beli, who died in 613. He features in the legends of Beuno and Gwenfrewi, and (unfortunately) sheltered Edwin of Northumbria. His main place in history is as the father of St Cadwallon, the British military leader, and his tombstone is in his grandson St Cadwaladr's foundation at Llangadwaladr.

CADFARCH mid 6th century
October 24th

The son of Caradog Fraichfras and brother of Cawrdaf, and the founder of Penegoes in Montgomery and Abererch in Caernarfon. Penegoes was called Llangadfarch, and there was a healing well there, Ffynnon Gadfarch used for healing rheumatism. Two other healing wells are next to each other at Penegoes, one supposedly having a higher temperature which was used for different complaints.

His son was St Elgud, and his brothers the saints Medrod and Iddew. There is a burial chamber at Four Crosses, Abererch and also a standing stone. In Abererch parish is a well dedicated to Cadfarch's brother Cawrdaf, and there is also Ffynnon Gadfarch near Llangedwydd. Water from Cadfarch's well was carried to the church for baptisms. Ffynnon Gadferth holy well is on the road from Cammarch to Cefn Treflis in Llangammarch parish, Brecon.

'Y Saith Gefnder' (The Seven Cousins) were supposed to be Beuno, Cybi, Seiriol, Deiniol, Cawrdaf, David and Cadfarch, who went to Rome to pray for rain after a three-year drought, *'ar dafn cyntaf a syrthiodd ar lyvr Cadfarch Sant'* (-'and the first drop fell on St Cadfarch's book' (Henken - 'The Welsh Saints'). This drought could possibly be linked with the conditions which caused the Yellow Plague (q.v.)

CADFRAWD 4th century

Possibly the bishop of Caerleon who went with the bishops of London and York to the Council of Arles in Gaul in 314. British bishops also attended the Council of Sardica in Illyria in 347 and Ariminium in Italy in 359. His brothers Gwerydd and Iestyn, and his sons Cadgyfarch and Gwrmael were also saints, but little is known of them. It may be, however, that Gwerydd was the founder of St Donat's church, previously called Llanwerydd.

CADGYFARCH 4th century

The son of Cadfrawd.

CADIFOR d. 883

The tenth abbot of Llancarfan, who Lifris tells us sent six learned men to instruct the Irish.

CADO 5th-6th century
CATAW, CADWY, CADRWS, CADIR, CADWR

The son of the martyr King Geraint, who succeeded him as King of Domnonia. He was the brother of St Iestyn (Jusinian). Arthur was Cado's cousin and Over-King, and they fought the Saxons on many occasions. At Badon Hill, Cado's force chased the invaders back to their boats. His great friend was Caradog Freich Fras and he helped him in battles in Brittany. There are two places named St Cadou in Brittany, south-east of Sizun and south of Landivisiau. Kercado is outside Vannes, and St Cado is on the Riviere d'Etel north of Carnac.

Cado's subordinate King Melwas of Glastenning (Somerset) kidnapped Guinevere but Cado restored her to the throne. He is said to be buried at Condolden (Cadon) Barrow in Cornwall. Geoffrey of Monmouth called Cadwr the Duke of Cornwall, and stated that he fostered Guinevere. Cado's son Cystennin took over the crown of the isle of Britain after Arthur's defeat at Camlan.

CADOG c.497– 577 given by Pennick. (Cressy states that he died in 500, but this was Cadog the Elder)
CATWG, CADOC, CATHMAEL, CADFAEL
September 25 and February 24
Patron of the deaf in Brittany

An important Welsh saint and missionary, who like Dyfrig, Teilo, Beuno, Gwenfrewi and Padarn could have been Wales' patron saint. Venerated in South Wales, he probably visited Cornwall (but less likely Scotland), and was influential in Ireland because he instructed Finnian at Llancarfan. He seems to have been a contemporary of Gildas, David and Samson. According to Cressy he was taught by Tathan at Caerwent. He was associated with Arthur, and was said to have attended his court with the warrior-saint Illtud.

His parents, King Gwynlliw (Gunleus) and Gwladys, lived at Stow Hill in Newport, where St Woolos Cathedral (a corruption of Gwynlliw) now stands on the remains of a Celtic fort. Cadog was first named Cadfael (Battle Prince) and has been associated with Galahad. Cadog was asked to take his father's crown when Gwynlliw was converted. There are two versions of his death. One is that he was killed fighting the Saxons at Weedon* in Northants, where there is now a huge church. A more plausible story is that the Welsh hid his relics during the Norman invasion of Glamorgan, and used this story as a smokescreen when the great monastery of Llancarfan was placed under St Peter's of Gloucester. Gwynlliw is said to have left his kingdom to Meurig, the son of King Tewdrig. Meurig had married into Gwynlliw's family, and was the father of Arthur. According to Lifris, Cadog's successors as abbot at Llancarfan were

Alphabetical Listing of the Saints of Wales and Religious Events

Elli, Pawl, Concen, Iascob, Sulien, Dagan, Gnauon, Elisael, and Cadifor, who died in 883. Lifris was probably the last abbot, and also archdeacon of Glamorgan.

There are at least fifteen dedications to Cadog in South Wales, and one in Cornwall. Most are found around his foundation of Nant Carban (Llancarfan) in what was Glywyssing, (east Glamorgan), and around Llangattock-nigh-Usk** in Gwent. Near Llangattock-nigh-Usk were Llangattock Lenig, Llangattock Lingoed and Llangattock Feibion Afel (Llangattock Vibon Avel – referring to the sons of Abel or Afel). Pendeulwyn (Pendoylan) in Glamorgan, Llangattock (just outside Cardiff's Pontprennau estate), Llancarfan with its four chapels at Llanfeithin, Garnllwyd, Treguff and Liege Castle, Pentyrch, Llanmaes, and Cadoxton-juxta-Barri are sites of his. 'Cattwg's Monastery' at Llanfeithyn was marked upon O.S. maps until a century ago. There are also churches at the Roman sites of Gelli-gaer (with a chapel at Brithdir) and Caerleon. Other dedications include Llangadog Crucywel, Llanysbyddyd outside Brecon, Llangadog near Llandovery and Cadoxton-juxta-Neath. The latter church had chapels at Aberpergwm and Creinant. Furthest west, there is a St Cadog's chapel in Llawhaden (Llanrhiadain). Cadog's churches are also to be found north of Cydweli and in Cheriton and Portheinon on the Gower Peninsula. Penrhos under Llandeilo Crosseny in Monmouth, and Trefethin under Llanofer in Monmouth also were his. Penrhos came for a time to be under St Michael, but somehow soon returned to Cadog, and the place was known as Llancaddoc Penrhos in a list of Abergavenny churches in 1348. St David is now the patron saint of Raglan church, but again this is considered a Cadog foundation. Raglan has a superb battlemented tower, and the tombs of the Marquises of Worcester and Dukes of Beaufort. Many of the Somerset family monuments there were destroyed by Cromwell's forces after the siege of Raglan Castle in 1640.

There are few remains of Llangadog near Amwlch in Anglesey, but a church in Cambuslang near Glasgow is still dedicated to Cadog – probably another Cadog. He had a large chapel near Harlyn Bay near Padstow, now in ruins, with one of Cornwall's most famous holy wells. There was also a holy well in St Just near the river Fal, once called Fenton Cadoc (Ffynon Cadoc) and now called Venton-Gassick.

He is celebrated in Brittany, from the Lannion Peninsula to Vannes, with a famous monastery on the Ile de Cado, off the Quiberon peninsula. A beautiful islet with a 12th century chapel on the Etel estuary in Brittany was named Saint-Cado after a 6th century *'prince de Glamorgant'*, who returned to Wales and was martyred. He was the patron saint of the deaf, and those afflicted used to lie on a stone 'bed' inside his chapel. The church at Pleucadeuc east of Vannes is Cadoc's. The prefix Pleu (or Plou, or Plo) dates from before the eighth century and indicates an early centre of Celtic Christianity, much as Llan often does in Wales. This Cadoc may be the son of Brychan however.

Llancarfan Church is dedicated to St Cadoc who founded the 6th century Nant Carban monastery here. Here he instructed Finnian of Clonnard, and prayed with him on the island of Flat Holm. Lifris wrote that the rocks around the island, known as the *'wolves'* were real wolves who were turned to stone when they swam across the water to try and take Cadoc's sheep. Llancarfan church was given to the Abbey of St Peter, Gloucester, by Robert Fitzhamon around 1107. Cromwell's soldiers broke the churchyard cross. It is very odd that only a fragment of ancient stone has been found here, unlike at nearby Llanilltud Fawr and Llandough. Perhaps crosses were moved at some time, or are still to be discovered in the vicinity of Llanfeithyn, Gowlog and Garnllwyd. There is just one Celtic stone in Llancarfan Church, being used as the sill of a window with some interlaced ribbon-work and a few letters visible. Cadoc was baptised Catmail, and it is thought that the ruined church of Lancatal (Llancadle) near Aberthaw was his foundation.

Llanmaes (Llanfaes) Church is an old Celtic foundation, now dedicated to Cadoc, as is Cadoxton juxta Neath and Cadoxton juxta Barry (formerly Tregatwg). At Cadoxton-juxta-Neath, Cadog found on the banks of the river Nedd a wild boar, bees in a hollow tree, and the nest of a hawk at the top of the tree. He sent these as gifts to King Arthfael (Arthur) who granted him land to build a church. However, Llanmaes was previously dedicated to Fagan, and was called Llanffagan Fach. The parish register of Cadog's church at Llanmaes records several centenarians, including Elizabeth Yorath, who died in 1668 aged 177. Another record reads *'Ivan Yorath buried Saturdaye ye XVII day of June anno dni 1621 et anno regni vicessimo primo anno aetatis circa 180. He was a sowdiar in the fight at Boswoorthe and lived at Llantwit major and he lived mostly by fishing.'* So this soldier was a veteran 44 year-old in Henry VII's Welsh forces in 1485, and lived another 136 years !

Cadoc's Life, by Lifris, is the most complete of all the Lives written in Wales. Lifris' father was Bishop Herwald (1056-1104) and it is probable that Lifris was the last abbot of the great Llancarfan foundation before the Normans stripped it. Gildas is said to have copied the 'Life' when he stayed with Cadoc, and Caradoc of Llancarfan, who wrote Gildas' Life, states that it was still in the great church of Cadoc in 1150, covered with silver and gold. This original was probably destroyed to hide land ownership details by the Normans. Cadoc is linked to Arthur by giving sanctuary to a man who killed some of Arthur's men. Nine of the ancient breed of Glamorgan cattle were given in settlement (black, with a white stripe along the backbone – their red cousins can still be seen at Margam Abbey Park. This herd is not Glamorganshire as claimed, but Gloucestershire. The last Glamorgan cattle were at Treguff in the late 19th century, bred by the Bradleys and Thomases.) Cadoc also argued with Maelgwn Gwynedd and Rhun ap Maelgwn, and Rhain Dremrydd ap Brychan. These were times of the men of North Wales pillaging in the south, after Arthur's fateful battle at Camlan.

In the 6th or 7th century, Ilias ap Morlais, with the approval of King Ithael, gave a mansion in the middle of Abermynwy (Monmouth) and land to Dyfrig, Teilo and Euddogwy, and in the hand of Bishop Berthgwyn, the fourth Bishop of Llandaf. However, in 1075 Withnoc founded a priory there and mentions the church of Cattwg in Monmouth, and this may be the same church originally dedicated to the three saints. It seems to have been in the priory churchyard, but the present building is dedicated to the Virgin Mary. Heth, in his description of Monmouthshire, says that the school now stands on the site, and that it was known as Geoffry's Chapel – a beautiful bay window there is still called Geoffry's Window. It was a catholic chapel until the middle of the 18th century, and is believed to have been where Geoffrey of Monmouth studied.

Between Llangaddock and Bethlehem is a six feet standing stone supported by two others. At nearby Sythfaen is a ten feet Neolithic standing stone, and Coitan Arthur lies at Pont-yr-Aber also near Llangaddock. It is said to have been thrown here by Arthur from Pen Arthur Isa Farm on Cerrig Pen Arthur. Cadoc's memorial may have been at Landyfaelog Fach, where there was once a stone inscribed CATVC.

At Llangatwg in Brecon is Ffynnon Gatwg, near the church. Francis Jones also notes his Glamorgan wells at Gelligaer (near the Roman camp), Pendoylan church, Aberkenfig, 'Kibwr' Castle and Court Colman. Near Llancarfan is Dyfrig's Well and the healing well Ffynnon y Fflamwydden (Flamebearer's Well) for erysipelas (fever with an infectious skin disease). Seven streams meet in Llancarfan, under the brooding Iron Age encampment, and it is an area noted for wells. Francis Jones gives several sources to study, and mentions pin and rag wells to cure King's Evil, and a rag well still used in the early 20th century where a paste was made from soil and well water to cure erysipelas. John Aubrey of nearby Llantrithyd mentions seeing crutches by wells in Llancarfan. The Breach Well was still being used for erysipelas before the Second World War, where rags and pins were used as well as bathing. Probably his most famous well is that just outside Pendoylan Church.

* This attribution to Weedon in Northampton, with its remarkable church, comes from the fact that it seems to have been called Beneventum. However, the Breton writer Albert le Grand places Beneventum as Venta, or Caerwent, where Cadog was originally taught by Tathan. Barber and Pykitt have also noted Professor Bury's identification with Caerwent in his edited 'Muirchu's Life of St Patrick.' Perhaps, therefore, Patrick came from Caerwent as it was possibly the earliest major centre of Christian learning in Britain. Barber and Pykitt also hypothesise that Beneventum may have been mis-attributed from *'Lan bent nant auan'*, or Nant Naduan, the valley of the River Thaw (Dawen) near Llancarfan. They believe that Cadog may have been buried in his silver coffin at the monastery of Llan Synnwyr, now Llansannor, where a new church was raised over his shrine. Llansannor is sometimes called City Llansannor and is near the source of the Thaw. Lifris stated that Cadog was murdered during mass by the lance of a hostile party and was buried in a silver coffin with a great basilica raised over his tomb. No Briton was allowed to enter Civitas Beneventana as it was feared that the people of Llancarfan would try to take Cadog's remains home. It this should occur, a fountain in the rampart would overwhelm the church. The Rev. Wade-Evans associated *'monasterium Sancti Sophia'* where he was martyred with Llansynnwyr (Llansannor) as Sophias was another name for Cadog. He further stated that *'Civitas Beneventana'* was Civitas Ben Nant Avan (the settlement at the head of the Avan Valley). Nant Nadavan was an early form of the river name Dawen (Thaw).

** The US consul to Cardiff in the late 19th century, Wirt Sikes, knew how much history there was in every field and wood in Wales:

Abergavenny, however, is but a fair specimen of a Welsh town in matters of interest to the stranger. It would be impossible to find in all Wales a community of 5000 inhabitants without its rich mine of legend, centring round its crumbling ruin, its ancient landing-place, its mystic well, its historic cave, or something of the sort; and in general these relics of antiquity are counted by threes and fours in the neighbourhood of every town you visit. If you were to be shot out of a catapult – a violent supposition certainly – and should drop in any inhabited part of Wales, you might ask the first person you met where the castle was, with the utmost confidence that he would immediately point it out to you. He might, indeed, ask you which castle, but he would be most unlikely to answer that he knew of none in the neighbourhood; the worst that would be likely to happen would be the offer of a ruined abbey or palace in lieu of a castle.

Leaving Abergavenny, and wending our way down the river to the town of Usk, we pass unnoticed ruined castles, old-fashioned hamlets, ancient churches, and mouldering abbeys: the Cistercian Abbey Dore, near Llangattock, with its five eastern chapels and procession path; Raolstone Church, with its swinging brackets and quaint sculptures; and other venerable ruins, whose very names are unrecorded, standing alone and forsaken of all save their clinging parasites, the mistletoe and the ivy. There is hardly a rod of this ground which would not yield curious and interesting details for the pen of the writer. At Llangatock-juxta-Usk I encountered an old man with astonished eyes, who, if I may judge from his own account of things, inhabits a centre than which none on earth is more fascinating.

"Not seen Llangattock Church, sir!" he exclaims, in excess of wonder. "Woy, 'tis one of the ancientest churches in Wales. The gentry comes from far about to see Llangattock Church. Not goin' to stop in Llangattock at all! 'Deed sir, but you ought. There is finer farms about Llangattock – well, you'll go far, beggin' your pardon, sir, afor you'll see finer farms than Parc Lettice, Llewyn Cecil, and Bryn Cainge. Not been to Llangattock Lingoed! Oh, sewerly, that's strange. Woy, 'tis there the schoolmaster o' Devauden was born. Never 'eerd o' the schoolmaster o' Devauden – the idol o' the poor o' Monmouthshire! Sir Thomas Phillips did write his life in a book, an' what's more, sir, he did help to bear the pall at schoolmaster's funeral. Ah, you must 'ave come from far parts, sir, never to 'ave 'eerd o' James Davis, the schoolmaster o' Devauden: from Lunnon, perhaps, sir? **From America**!" And I leave him with a new wrinkle of astonishment on his forehead, which surely had no need of more.

Cadog's 'Saying of the Wise' was *'let the heart be where the appearance is.'*

A NOTE ON CADOG'S FOUNDATION OF LLANCARFAN

Seven small streams meet under Llancarfan's great hillfort, the Whitewell, Greendown, Gowlog, Coed-Abernant, Whitton Bush, Walterston and Moulton, forming the small river Carman with its (often-flooded) ford. One tradition states that the stream and settlement were named after a saint 'Garman', the 'Apostle of Britain'. Both Germanus and Dyfrig are associated with the foundation, which appears to have been called Bangor Garman. Another legend is that the river was called Nant-Carw, the stream of the stag, because Cadog was assisted by two stags dragging timber from the forest to build his church. Dubricius (Dyfrig) was said to have lived at Garnllwyd monastery, a mile north of Llancarfan, so he could be near Cadog, and Ffynnon Dyfrig holy well is still in the woodlands here. Llancarfan Well in the Culvery (Calvary?) Field cured many illnesses, and several other local wells cured King's Evil, the skin disease. Stan Awbery wrote a lovely little book on Llancarfan in 1959, in which he records:

'The chief festival of the year was called the "Mabsant" or the "Gwyl Mab-Sant". It was held in January each year. Marie Trevelyan tells us that it was held in a large building on the hill at the rear of Llanveithin. (Llanfeithyn, just a mile from Llancarfan, is dedicated to Tathan, whose feast date was December 26th and 30th until the 12-day date change, so this must have originated from Tathan rather than Cadog, whose feast day is in September and February). *It was forty feet long with one room above and two below. The back of the building was against the side of the hill with the eaves resting on it. The revels were held in this until it became too ruinous for use. A road led from the village and farm to this place along which the villagers went to the festival. It must have been the rallying place for all the people of the parish on festival and great occasions. The Mabsant was the principal event of the year in all Welsh villages. It was the local saint's day. Sometimes the festivities continued for several days. All the villagers turned out, old and young, rich and poor. There were games, cockfighting and drinking. One of the villagers was decorated with ribbons and made mayor for the period. His face was painted and a cabbage hung around his neck as a badge of office. The crowd marched around the locality to the principal farms, where in a friendly and humorous manner they demanded, and were always given, a liberal supply of beer . . .*

One of the prevalent customs of the vale was the scattering of black earth on tombs, especially those without headstones. It was usual among farmers to obtain this black soil from what were considered to be sacred or important places. They held a superstitious belief that it had power to avert evil. They used it for sprinkling the stables and pig-sties and even inside their houses.

Portions of it were strewn over coffins and graves of relatives and friends. At funerals it was frequently thrown over the next of kin of the person being buried. In Llancarfan it was taken from the garden of St Cadoc, and in Llantwit Major from beside the cross of St Illtud or from Côr-Eurgain, which was the site of the old college to the north of the Church. Another custom was the placing of primroses and white flowers on every grave in the churchyard on Palm Sunday. None was forgotten by the villagers, even if there were no relatives of the dead left alive to do it. Evergreens were also placed with the flowers as a symbol of everlasting life. The flowers, which spring from the dead seed in the spring of the year, typified the resurrection after death. This custom has not quite faded out but it is likely to do so in a generation or two.' The Reverend Louis Nedelec visited Llancarfan in 1870, and retold a Breton tradition about the *'seven wise men of Llancarfan'*, the saints Talhaiarn, Teilo, Gildas, Cynan, Eidden (Aidan?), Estayfan (Ysteffan?) and Taliesin *'the chief of bards.'*

CADOCUS d.490
SOPHIAS
January 24

Son of Guilleicus, prince of the Ordovices, he was consecrated bishop of Beneventum in Italy. He is often confused with Cadog of Llancarfan, who in the 'Life' by Lifris of Llancarfan is transported in a white cloud to Benevenuto in Italy, where he met a martyr's death while celebrating mass. Caradoc's Life of Cadoc has him taking the road to Bienvenuto and dying a natural death. It is said that no access to this Italian grave has ever been allowed to British pilgrims, for fear that they would steal his relics. (This legend also is attached to the previous Cadog). There is also a Briton named Cadog celebrated at Tarento in Italy - see Appendix I

CADOG 5th – 6th century
RHEIDIOG, RHYDOCH, REIDOC, IUDOC
January 24

A son or grandson of Brychan, buried in France. Llanyspyddid in Brecon and Llangadog Fawr in Carmarthen are said to be his foundations rather than those of Cadog ap Gwynlliw. Cadog went to France and died at a place variously mentioned as Tomriwch, Reidoc or Twmbreidoc.

CADOG 7th century
CAIDOC
May 30

He crossed to the land of Morini at the end of the 6th century, converted Ricarius and founded the Abbey of Centule in 627, where he was buried. His epitaph was composed by St Angilbert, Abbot of Centule. There is much overlapping between the legends of the four saints named Cadog.

CADRAWD 6th century
CADROD CALCHFYNYDD

This son of Cynwyd ap Cynfelin, descended from Coel, was the brother of the saints Clydno Eiddyn, Cynfelin Drwsgl and Cynan Genhir, all disciples of Cadoc at Llancarfan. There is a Maes Cadrod near Bridgend. He married Gwrgon ferch Brychan, who may have been quite a woman, for the 'Sayings of the Wise' refer to him thus:
'Hast thou heard the saying of Cadrawd,
Of Calchfynydd, of great meditation?
"The best woman is without a tongue".'

KING CADWALADR ap CADWALLON d. 664
CADWALADR FENDIGAID
November 12, October 9

He was the last king to hold the title of Gwledig, 'High King' of Britain. His father was King Cadwallon, the son of Cadfan ap Iago ap Beli. In 633, allying with the Anglian King Penda of Mercia, King Cadwallon's army had defeated and killed Edwin King of Northumbria at Heathfield. Cadwallon, 'the last hero of the British race' was later killed in the last of his sixteen battles and forty skirmishes at 'Heaven's Field' (Catscaul) in 635 by Oswald (see 'The A-Z of Wales and the Welsh'). By this battle, with great losses on both sides, the British were finally pushed out of Northumbria. The Venerable Bede, who despised the Christian British, and always took the side of the pagan Anglo-Saxons in his accounts, said that Cadwallon tried to 'cut off all the race of the English within the borders of Britain . . . Nor did he pay any respect to the Christian religion which had newly taken root amongst them; it being to this day the custom of the Britons not to pay any regard to the faith and religion of the English.'

Although Cadwallon's son's nick-name was 'Cadomedd'*, 'battle-shunner', Cadwaladr led the British against invaders from Wessex from 634, after his father was killed fighting Oswald of Bernicia. Cadwaladr was forced to lead his people to a bad defeat, against Cenwalh, King of the West Saxons, at Peonne in Somerset in 658. There are churches dedicated to Cadwaladr in places named Llangadwaladr as far apart as Bishopston (also known as Bishton or Tref Esgob, and formerly called Llangadwaladr) under Llanwern in Monmouthshire, Llangadwaladr under Llanrhaiadr in Mochnant in Denbighshire, and Llangadwaladr in Anglesey. Magor (Magwyr) in Monmouth has been rededicated to the Virgin Mary. Michaelston-y-Fedw in Glamorgan was rededicated to Michael. There was also a Capel Llangadwaladr under Llanddeiniol Fab in Anglesey.

The Anglesey church, Eglwys Ael, contains a stone with a Latin epitaph to his grandfather, King Cadfan. It was a lintel on the old church of Llangadwaldr. The 7th century inscription reads
'CATAMANUS REX SAPIENTISIMUS OPINATISIMUS OMNIUM REGUM'
('Cadfan the King, wisest and most renowned of all kings')
Cadfan died in 625, and his grandson Cadwaladr built the church in his honour. Cadwaladr died of the plague in 664, and was called by the bards 'Bendigaid', and one of the three blessed sovereigns of Britain. On Cadfan's tomb there are three intertwined fish, and a single fish on either side of a carved cross.

Cadwaladr's 'Saying of the Wise' is:
Have you heard the saying of Cadwaladr,
King of all Wales;
"The best crooked thing is the crooked handle of a plough."

The mediaeval 'Chronicles of the Princes' begins with the death of Cadwaladr, misplaced by sixteen years:
'Six hundred and eighty was the year of Christ when there was a great mortality throughout all the island of Britain . . . And in that year, Cadwaladr the Blessed, son of Cadwallon ap Cadfan, king of the Britons, died in Rome on the twelfth day of May, as Myrddin had before that prophesied to Gwrtheyrn Gwrthenau. And from that time forth the Britons lost the crown of the kingdom, and the Saxons gained it.'

'The Red Dragon' of Cadwaladr was the standard borne by Henry VII on his way to Bosworth Field, and earlier used by Owain Glyndŵr as a mark of the kingship of the Britons. Gildas referred to it, the 'Insularis Draco', being carried earlier by another Gwedig, or High King, Maelgwn Gwynedd. **It is the oldest national flag in the world.** (See 'The A-Z of Wales and the Welsh' for full details). Cadwaladr is regarded as the Patron saint of the contemporary Orthodox Mission in Wales, according to the website orthodox.co.uk.

* Note that Ellis Peter's name for her Welsh monk in the series of books on Cadfael alluded to his crusading past. *'Cadafael'* means *'battle-seizer or battle-prince'*. Cad means battle, or army; cadfarch is war-horse; cadfywall is battle-axe; cadlong is warship; cadlys is camp or headquarters; and cadofydd is a strategist.

ABBOT CADWALADR
October 18

A disciple of Cadoc who followed Cadoc to Brittany, and was placed in charge of a foundation on an island. He is still remembered in the pardon (annual procession) at St Segal near Chateaulin. This is also St Luke's Day, traditionally a lucky day for a lady to choose a husband.

ROGER CADWALDR 1566 -1610
August 27

Born at Stretton Sugwas in Hereford, he entered the seminary at Reims in 1590, and was ordained at Valladolid in 1593. He became a missionary in Hereford and Gwent, but was arrested in 1610. In prison he was visited by the Jesuit Superior, Father Robert Jones, the day he was condemned to death. Jones wrote an account in Italian of the martyrdom at Leominster.

CADWALLON LAWHIR see CASWALLON

CAEMAN 6th – 7th century
CYMMUN
November 3

Remembered at Eglwys Gymmun in Carmarthen, he became Abbot of Antrim in Ireland. At this place, called the 'Ecclesia de Sancto Cumano' in Edward III's time, was found an inscribed stone with 'CUNIGNI' written on it (Cynan). However, there are also two early stones in Llandilo in Pembroke, one of which is inscribed 'COIMAGNI FILI CAVETI'.

CAENOG MAWR 6th century
August 27

This saint's history, or lack of it, is very confused. He may have been the founder of Clog-caenog (Clocaenog) in Denbigh, and the son of St Arianwen ferch Brychan. However, another saint, Beddwid or Meddwid appears to have been venerated at Clocaenog upon August 27. The nearby Bryn y Beddau (Hill of the Graves) had an early monument in Ogham and Latin, reading SIMILINI TOVISACI, probably meaning Prince (Tywysog) Similinus. An alternative reading is Prince Aemilianus, or Emlyn. Westwood states that the stone was moved by Lord Bagot to Pool Park. It was on a mound commonly known as 'Bedd Emlyn' (Emlyn's Grave), and another stone was still standing next to the tumulus in the 19th century. Hundreds of tumuli across Wales have still not been excavated, and the author knows of several in the more arable areas that have been 'ploughed out' while the authorities have done nothing. At Pool Park was also a rough stone chair, taken away from near Bedd Emlyn, and known as Cadair Brenhines (The Chair of the Queen). Near its original location was an oblong embankment with excellent views, known as 'Llys Brenhines', the Queen's Palace. Westwood believes that this chair is like the coronation chair of the O'Neills, carefully preserved at Rathcarrick. In Archaeologica Cambrensis, 1855, there is more information upon stone saints' chairs.

However, it seems that neither the Wales Tourist Board, nor the nascent British Assembly in Cardiff, nor individual county authorities see any major value in using a superb Christian heritage and culture to resurrect tourism in Wales. Perhaps we could promote the unusual and original concept of 'ethical tourism.' People who go to China and dozens of other countries are actively supporting totalitarian regimes which still practise torture, have practised genocide (as in Tibet) and have no interest in human rights. Christian Aid and Amnesty International believe that two-thirds of the world's countries have institutionalised torture. Others have a record of constant aggression. Wales has had 2000 years of defending itself, with a Christian heritage, probably the world's most advanced attitudes to women for well over a millennium, and has no record of torture, unlike the Norman/Angevin/Plantagenet conquerors of Britain.

CAFFO 6th century
November 1 (The Wake of Caffo, popular until the rise of Nonconformism)

The brother of Gildas, son of Caw, and a cousin and follower of Cybi. He seems to have studied at Llangenys, Cyngar's foundation in Glamorgan. Gildas had offended Maelgwn Gwynedd, so Maelgwn ordered Cybi to send Caffo away from Anglesey. Caffo then settled at Rhosyr (Newborough) and founded a community, but Maelgwn's men murdered him, and the district became known as Llangaffo (Llangaffo chapel was under Llangeinwen in Anglesey).

He was apparently killed by servants of Maelgwn's wife, and the place was known as Merthyr Caffo for many years.

There are several ninth century stones in the area. Crochan Caffo (Caffo's Cauldron) was a well where young cockerels were sacrificed (a sacred bird of the Celts). This was supposed to stop babies crying, and the cockerels were given to the guardian of the well. The well has since vanished, but the farmhouse there is still called Ffynnon Gaffo. Llangaffo in Anglesey was the site of a large Celtic monastery. In the porch of Llangaffo Church is the lower half of an ornate Celtic wheelhead, and some broken parts of its pillar can be seen in the churchyard. In the walls of the churchyard wall are several stones with Latin-type crosses, and the sacristy contains a 7th century stone inscribed *'Gvernin son of Couris Cini set up this stone'* (see also St Amo). Westwood noted that a portion of the cross was taken away to Denham by the Rev. Prichard in the 19th century.

Francis Jones records another well at Langaffo, Ffynnon Pechod ('the well of the sin, or offence'), where sinners washed away their past misdeeds after being 'whipped' from Y Chwipyn ('the whipping place') crossroads.

CAI 6th century

A reputed son of Brychan, whose church at Aber Cai was destroyed by Danes. Another Cai, of Caer Gai (the Roman fort near Bala) appears to be the Cai Hir of the Mabinogion. This son of Cynyr Farchog was celebrated as Sir Kay, Arthur's loyal companion. In 'Culhwch and Olwen' Cai is the leading knight in conquering the obstacles in the search for Olwen (see Kea). Llandygai ('Llan tŷ Cai', the holy place of the house of Cai) is on the coast near Penrhyn, but is associated with Tegai (q.v.). However, a crossed stone was found at a small holy well near Resolven, then used as a pump-stone in a colliery manager's house on the tramway at Bryn Cefneithin. It may now be in Neath, and has a large cross, with the remaining letters *'prop aravi tgaic'*, which may have been *'Preparavit Gai crucem hanc'*. The reader should also check the entry on Kea - this may be the same saint associated with Arthur.

CAIAN 5th-6th century
September 25th, (November 1 and November 15 are given for the festivals at Tregaian.)

Possibly a grandson of Brychan, the chapel of Tregaian under Llangefni in Anglesey is commemorated to him.

CAIN 5th-6th century
KEYNE, CENEU, KEINA, KENYA, CEINWYRY (Cain the Virgin), CEINWEN (Cein the Holy)
October 8 (also October 7)

A daughter of Brychan, this beautiful hermit went to Cornwall and later met her nephew Cadog at Mount St Michael, who asked her to return to Wales, where she died. At St Keyne's Well in Cornwall, the tradition was that the first to drink water from it after marriage would attain mastery over the other partner. One man left his bride on the church porch to drink the water first, whereupon she quickly produced and drank a bottle that she had hidden under her

wedding dress. This well, near Liskeard, was so famous that it inspired Robert Southey to write:
'I hastened as soon as the wedding was o'er
And I left my good wife in the porch,
But i'faith she had been wiser than I
For she took a bottle to church'

Near this well are the foundations of her brothers, Clether, Cynog and Cynin. The same powers of spouse dominance were said to be bestowed by Keyne on the stone seat in the castle at St Michael's Mount.

Associated with South Wales and Herefordshire, Cain was supposed to have been an itinerant evangelist, who moved between Brecon and St Michael's Mount. Llangeneu (Llangenny) in Brecon is ascribed to Ceneu, the daughter or grand-daughter of Brychan, but others place it earlier with Ceneu ap Coel. Her feast day is the same as that of her sister Ceinwen. Cressy recorded that *'when she came to ripe years, many nobles sought her in marriage, but she utterly refused that state; having consecrated her virginity to our Lord by a perpetual vow; for which cause she was afterwards by the Britons called Keyn wiri (Cein-wyryf), that is Keyna the virgin: at length she determined to forsake her country and find out some desert place, where she might attend to contemplation. Therefore directing her journey beyond the Severn, and there meeting a woody place, she made her request to the prince of that country, that she might be permitted to serve God in that solitude. His answer was, that he was very willing to grant her request, but that the place did so swarm with serpents that neither man nor beast could inhabit it: but she constantly replied, that her firm trust was in the name and assistance of Almighty God to drive out all that poisonous brood out of the region. Hereupon the place was granted to the holy virgin, who presently prostrating herself to God obtained of him to change the vipers and serpents into stones; and to this day, the stones in that region do resemble the windings of serpents through all the fields and villages, as if they had been framed so by the hand of the engraver.'* The religious community at Keynsham on the Avon near Bristol was said by Camden to be founded by Cain, on account of the number of 'snakes', ammonite fossils found there which she destroyed. However, the name comes from 'Caega's Hamlet', although its church was dedicated to Keyne before St John.

Her nephew Cadog ap Gwynlliw made a pilgrimage to the Mount of St Michael just outside Abergavenny, where he met Ceneu, and the local inhabitants wanted her to stay in the region. However, she later returned to her Brecon birthplace where she built an oratory on the top of a mountain and prayed to God who provided a spring there. Last century the traces of her oratory and holy well Ffynnon Geneu (St Geney's Well) could still be seen near the church of Llangeneu in Brecon, a chapel under Cadog's foundation at Llangattock Crickhowel. The well water cured sore eyes, and the first of a newly-married couple to drink its waters would be 'dominant' in the marriage, the same tradition as in her Liskeard foundation. When her oratory was demolished around 1790 a farmer found an ancient iron hand-bell used to call people to church (a 'bangu').

At Llangeneu, Golden Grove Standing Stone is between Druid's Altar and the Dragon's Head public house. Nearby is 'The Growing Stone', almost 14 feet high, surrounded by oak trees. Kentchurch in Hereford was formerly called Llangain, then Keynechurch, and its priest was the famous Welsh 'magician' and cleric Sion Cent. He was said to be buried half-in and half-out of his church. Llangeinor* in Mid-Glamorgan is also associated with Cain. Its original name, Llan Gain Wyryf, means the Church of Cain the Virgin, but it is dedicated to Ceinwyr**. St Kenya's

Church, Runston, is in the care of CADW and is freely accessible near Chepstow. The ruined church is in the centre of a deserted village of twenty-two houses, and the site of a medieval manor house can be made out. At Cilcain in Clwyd, in Penbedw Park, there still stands a Neolithic stone circle with five stones, in an oak copse.

Apart from Llangeinor in Glamorgan, Cain was associated with Llan-gain and Capel Cain Wyry (in the parish of Talley) in Carmarthen, Llangeinwen in Anglesey, and perhaps Machen in Monmouthshire. There are churches in Hereford, Somerset and Cornwall. The once-popular Welsh name, Gaynor, comes from this saint.

*There may have been a saint named Ceinor. There is a Ffynnon Geinor holy well noted at Pontsian near Llandysul in Cardigan, and Ceinor was once a popular female name in that county.

**The beautifully restored church Norman church at Llangeinor is part of a conservation area of the village on the mountainside. The 18th century financial genius, influencer of the American Revolution and one of the greatest Welshmen was born here, Dr Richard Price. *'The most original thinker ever to come out of Wales'* anticipated Kant's work in the philosophy of ethics, and pioneered work in statistics which enabled life assurance to develop. A leader in civil and religious freedom, this 'Apostle of Liberty' was honoured by the new, republican, American and French governments.

CAIN 6th century
CANNA, CANNAU

This daughter of King Caw was the patroness of Llangain in Carmarthenshire, although it has been attributed to Cain ferch Brychan. As 'Candida', she may also be associated with the abbess of Scaere in Finistere. Tregain is south of Chateaulin in this region. Ffynnon Gain is near Bletherstone in Pembroke. Near Llangain School are three large standing stones known as Merlin's Quoits, and another two stones near the main Carmarthen to Llansteffan road are also marked as Myrddin's Quoits.

CAIN ferch MAELGWN, see EURGAIN

CAIO

There are manors known as Upper Llancaio and Lower Llancaio in Gwehelog near Usk.

CALAN HEN
OLD NEW YEAR

In 1752, the only place in the British Isles which did not adopt the new date for New Year's Eve was the beautiful and secretive Gwaun Valley, which winds up from Fishguard to the Preseli foothills. The close-knit Welsh-speaking community held out for the 'old' New Year, and still celebrates it upon January 13th. Indeed, not only did they 'keep' the eleven days lost in the change, but one day was added 'for luck'. The celebrations included children singing at the various farmhouses, and receiving food and apples, and were centred on the inn, the Dyffryn Arms. However, Fife Robertson came with the BBC 'Tonight' TV team in the 1960's and the resulting fame forced much of the celebration 'underground.' Bessie Davies has run the pub for half-a-century and remembers the great days of the past. Because of the 1752 date change, it is often difficult to state which is the real 'saint's feast day' in many areas of Wales.

CALLWEN 5th – 6th century
April 20, November 1 (with Gwenfyl)

One of the many daughters of Brychan, her Capel Callwen was under her brother's church of Defynog in Brecon. According to Edward Lhuyd, Cellan in Cardigan is hers, and a spring there was called Ffynnon Callwen or Ffynnon y Forwyn. On a nearby hill is a funeral mound named Bedd y Forwyn, The Virgin's Grave. At Cellan is the site of a Roman camp (SN 641 493), with the only example of an uncompleted Roman camp in Britain just a thousand metres away (SN 647 485). There is also a circular earthwork, Carreg y Bwci there, which may have been used by the Romans to guard the road between Llanio fort and Pumsaint where they mined gold. Cellan is now dedicated to All Saints, which used to be celebrated upon April 20th until the eleventh or twelfth century, so we can assign Callwen this feast date. Her sister Gwenfyl was the patron of nearby Gwynfil. Defynog Church has a mutilated inscribed stone, high above the ground, which may read *'RUGNIAVTO (fi)LI VENDONI.'*

On the Roman road Sarn Helen, between Loventium (Llannio) and Llanfair-y-bryn, was an inscribed Maen Hir outside Llanycrwys, Cellan. Another menhir was blasted to repair Sarn Helen, and another lies prostrate in a stone circle nearby.

CAMMAB 6th century

Very late sources name him as the son of Gwynlliw Filwr and brother of Cadog and Cammarch.

CAMMARCH 6th century
October 8

The son of Gwynlliw and founder of Llangammarch in Breconshire, although it is dedicated to St Tysilio. 'Cammarch' means 'crooked horse' and was a nickname of Cynog ap Brychan, so the church may not have been founded by Cammarch. The river Cammarch joins the Irfon nearby. A fragment of a decorated Celtic slab has been built into the porch at Llangammarch church.

Llangammarch Wells was one of only two Barium water spas in Europe, and very popular with Germans and their sympathisers like Charles Lindbergh. It was one of the four major Welsh spa towns, the others being Llandrindod, Llanwrtyd and Builth. In the visitors' book of the Lake Hotel at Llangammarch once can read the signatures of Sir James Hill-Johne's VC, W. Bird *'late 8th hussars, and one of the 600'* who took part in the Charge of the Light Brigade, Ernest Blofeld (the origin for the 'James Bond' character?) and Prince Munster. Prince Munster was one of the titles of Kaiser Wilhelm II, who stayed there in 1912 to take the waters. (I am indebted for this information to 'The Kaiser in Wales', an article by Byron Rogers in that

St Kenya's Chapel, Runston.   *CADW: Welsh Historic Monuments. Crown Copyright.*

excellent glossy magazine, 'Cambria'. Any person with a love of Wales should subscribe to this bi-monthly at £2.95 a copy by contacting Cambria Publications, PO Box 22, Carmarthen SA32 7YH).

CANDIDA (see NINNOC)

CANDLEMAS
February 2

This feast celebrates when Jesus and Mary gave sacrifice for their first-born. Zephaniah 1:12 reads *'I will search Jerusalem with candles'*, and it was occasioned with a candle-lit procession. The early church seems to have used Candlemas to mask the pagan fire festival of Imbolc, or Wiccan, which celebrated the coming of spring, when there was a torch-light procession to purify and fertilise the fields for the new year's crops. An old saying is:
'If Candlemas Day be bright and clear
There will be two winters in a year.'

In Brecon a local rhyme gave advice upon which wood to burn at different times of the year:
'Gwern a helyg hyd Nadolig,
Bedw os cair hyd Gwyl Fair,

Cringoed y caeau o hyn hyd Gla'mai,
Briwydd y fran o hynny ymla'n.'
(Alder and willow until Christmas,
Birch, if available until Candlemas,
Withered branches from the fields until May Day,
The small twigs of the crow from then on.)

'Candlemas singing' took place in Anglesey and other parts of Wales, many examples of which were recorded by Richard Morris in the 18th century. The custom involved verse contests, with singers outside houses and a 'chair carol' after the choir had entered a house. A young girl with a child on her knee represented Mary and the baby Jesus.

CANNA 6th century
October 25

The daughter of Tewdwr Mawr ab Emyr Llydaw and wife of Sadwrn, who was considerably older than her. After Sadwrn's death, she married Gallgu Rieddog (Alltu Rededog), and by him was the mother of Elian Geimiad, Cybi's friend who was assisted by King Caswallon. According to Westwood, she was Illtud's cousin and sister-in-law.

The parish church of Llangan (previously called Llanganna) in Glamorgan is dedicated to St Canna, the mother of St Crallo, and has a very special 9th century sculptured cross protected by a wooden shelter. Disc-headed, it has a very rare Welsh example of the Crucifixion, with the lance-bearers Longinus (q.v.) and Stephaton featured. Christ is dressed in a loin-cloth, with the sponge-bearer and lance-bearer on either side. Below the cross is a very worn figure with extended arms, holding in the left hand an inward-curving bow or horn, and in the right hand a small cylindrical object. This could be either St David, St Peter or Mary Magdalene with a phial of ointment. Glamorganshire contains around half of all the sculptured Celtic monuments in Wales, and it appears that there were schools of sculptors at Margam, Merthyr Mawr and Llanilltud Fawr, all near to each other. (The only other major concentrations seem to be around St David's in Pembroke and Penmon in Anglesey, but there are more crosses still to be discovered in Wales). There is also a beautiful 15th century churchyard cross, the only survivor of the Reformation in the Vale of Glamorgan along with that of St Donat's.

Llangan adjoins Llangrallo, the foundation of her son, where there is a stream still called the Canna. Canton in Cardiff used to be called Treganna, before it was pulled into the Cardiff boundaries, and the neighbouring suburb is Pontcanna, the Bridge of Canna. Canna's Farm, now called Canon's Farm, is in the next area of Cardiff, Llandaff. In Llangan is a stone shaped like a seat called St Canna's Chair, with Canna inscribed on it. It is near Ffynnon Ganna, which cured the ague and stomach illnesses. The patient had to throw pins into the well, then drink its waters or bathe in it, then sit in the chair. If he fell asleep in the chair, a cure was more certain. The treatment had to be kept up for fourteen days. The well disappeared around 1840, but the unique megalith is still there.

The beautifully situated Llangan Church and Celtic circular graveyard at Henllan Amgoed, near Whitland on the Carmarthen-Pembroke border, is for sale for £20,000 at the time of writing.

The human representation on the Llangan Cross is only replicated in Wales in four other places. At Llandyfaelog (q.v. Maelog) in Brecon is a kilted figure with a short club, the 'baculum' or sign of kingship similar to that carried centuries later by William the Bastard at Hastings. There is also a kilted figure now in Swansea Museum, with its arms raised in prayer. This was one of the stones gathered for the Gnoll Estate grotto in the early 19th century by Lady Mackworth. At Llanfrynach (q.v. Brynach) in Brecon is another figure with outstretched hands in 'orans' appeal to God, and there is also a human figure on the Llanhamlach stone.

CANNEN 6th century
CANTEN

The son of Gwyddlew ap Gwynlliw Filwr, he is presumed to have founded Llanganten near Builth. He has also been credited with Llangan in Glamorgan, but that is more familiarly associated with Canna.

The circumstances of Llywelyn ap Gruffydd's death at Aberedw near Builth point to the fact that he was lured there by the Marcher Lords. After his death, Edward I carried out 'systematic slaughter' in many parts of Wales to reduce Welsh manpower. 3000 footsoldiers who surrendered when Llywelyn died were executed between Llanganten and Builth, and while Edward was at Rhuddlan he carried on the genocide, even killing priests. He was reproved by John Pecham, Archbishop of Canterbury, who had been involved in peace negotiations with Llywelyn. These 'details' of history appear in no history taught in British schools or universities. The Wales Heritage Campaign, PO Box 22, Carmarthen SA32 7YH, has been set up to lobby for the commemoration of Welsh heroes, to defend Welsh heritage and work to ensure the proper teaching of history in Welsh schools.

For a growing number of Welshmen, a knowledge of the past is important to pass on to the future. The author has seen his mother's village become Anglicised in the last fifty years, and is aware of the problems of North Wales becoming a retirement and holiday home area for people who have made vast profits upon selling their homes in England. However, the problem is now endemic in that immigration is killing culture. At a village of around forty houses in Cardigan, the last ten have been bought by English people. This type of movement in Cardiff or Bridgend does not matter much in the long run. As mentioned in 'The A-Z of Wales and the Welsh', the children of new families have replaced people leaving Wales for work and eventually 'turn' Welsh in the sense of regarding themselves as Welsh people. However, in a small Welsh-speaking village there are massive implications. These people do not usually come to work, except those foolishly seeking the small-holding 'Good Life.' One Englishman in the village has been supported by local farmers with knowledge and information for ten years to eke a living out of his smallholding. He and his newcomer friends have made no attempts to learn Welsh *as it's a dead language* and the village pub is now deserted by locals as the 'Essex fringe' props up the bar wishing they were back in England, only now they cannot afford it. Others who come to retire bring no benefits to Wales but represent a drain upon the over-stretched health services of the nation. The English language, a Franco-German hybrid, dates in understandable form from Shakespeare's time, four-hundred years ago. The Welsh language is at least four times as old in its current form, and people who come to live in Wales must make the effort to understand its value. Many English pensioners and others who live in Wales treat it as the retirees in the Costa del Sol treat the Spanish and their language. Arrogance is the façade of the charlatan and the ignoramus.

Dr Roger Geary commented in an article called 'The Dragon and the Flame' on the internet site welshdragon.net: *'By 1979 . . . Gwynedd, the heartland of the Welsh language, was recording some 7,600 holiday and second homes; eight per cent of the total housing stock. In some popular seaside villages, such as Abersoch and Llanbedrog on the Llŷn peninsula, the total was approaching a staggering 50%. By 1988 Welsh Office statistics revealed that there were more than 20,000 holiday homes in Wales with the majority located in the northern and western Welsh speaking areas. The effect of this buoyant holiday and second home market has undoubtedly been to inflate property prices in parts of rural Wales to a level that is well beyond the reach of local people. To many, it must have seemed particularly unjust for so many of these second homes to be left empty for the greater part of the year, creating virtual ghost villages, when local authority housing departments had over-subscribed lists of local people. In addition to the growth of second home ownership, the rate of immigration into north and west Wales also increased dramatically in the 1970's and 1980's. During the period **from 1981 to 1990 some 600,000 people, nearly all from the rest of the UK settled in Wales**.* (note that the population of Wales was under 3,000,000, and this process was repeated in the 1990's - the situation is worse than critical, and seemingly politicians turn a blind eye to the destruction of the fabric of Wales).

The major attractions of rural Wales for these "white settlers", as they rapidly became known, seemed to be the promise of a more relaxed and environmentally friendly life-style in landscapes of great natural beauty together with relatively cheap property prices. At this time it was possible to sell a semi-detached property in London or the Home Counties and buy a modest farm in Wales with the proceeds. Many of the newcomers used their superior purchasing power to buy up small local businesses, hotels, guesthouses, cafes, garages, supermarkets and newsagents. The very infrastructure of many small rural communities seemed to be changing hands during this period. **At the same time many young local people were being forced to leave their villages.** *Employment opportunities in rural Wales have never been plentiful and deteriorated further during the recessions of the 1970's and 1980's. This two-way traffic, monoglot English settlers moving in and bilingual Welsh moving out, inevitably diluted and in some areas actually obliterated several small Welsh-speaking communities.'* This is 'cultural cleansing', driven by economic forces.

Note: as this book was going to the printers, the author noted an article in The Western Mail (March 15th, 2000), whereby house prices in the picturesque seaside village of Newport, Cardiganshire rose 25% in the last three months of 1999. The population in Newport triples every summer. One two-bedroomed bungalow there sold for over £200,000. A one-bedroom flat in Tenby sold in a morning for £75,000, and a three-up, two-down cottage in Little Haven in need of restoration sold for £100,000. These are not prices that local Welsh people can afford.

CANNICE c. 525-c. 600
CANICUS, KENNETH, CAINNECH, CANICE, CENNECH, MACMOIL
October 11

This Irish monk, the son of a Derry bard, is remembered in the church at Llangennech near the Gower Peninsula. He was a favourite disciple of Cadog, who ordained him in a chapel on Cefn Mamoel near Bedwellty, called Ecclesia de Massmoilo in the 12th century. At Pentre Mamoel there is still a house named Tŷ'r Capel. One of Ireland's greatest saints is thus commemorated by place-names on a Welsh hillside 1500 years later.

Cannice was educated with Finnian, as a pupil of Cadoc at Llancarfan, where he was ordained. A Llancarfan charter, dating from Cadog's lifetime, notes that Cadog *'built a church for Macmoil, his disciple, and secured it with a rampart and built an altar in the same.'* (source - 'Wales in the Early Middle Ages', Wendy Davies, Leicester, 1982). When plague attacked his monastery at Glasnevin, he had come to Llancarfan for some time, before returning to establish monasteries in Ireland and Scotland. At Inchkenneth on Mull he formally admonished the local seabirds for their noise on Sundays, and banished all mice for eating his sandals. He frequently visited his friend St Columba on Iona.

CANOC see CYNOG

CANWG

The superb late medieval church dedicated to St Canwg in Llandanwg, Gwynedd, is slowly being buried beneath shifting sands, so the interior cannot now be entered. He is possibly the same saint as Cynog.

CARACTACUS 1st century
CARATACUS, CARADOC, CARADAWG

The king, captured and shown by Claudius in the famous triumph in Rome, was not recorded as a saint, but has an important place in the legends of early Christianity in Wales. His father Brân was supposed to have been kept hostage at Rome for 7 years, and returned with the saints Ilid, Cyndaf, Arwystli Hen and Mawan who preached the gospel in the 1st century from around 58. His daughter Eurgain, or Eigan, was recorded as the first female saint in Britain, who founded its first monastery at Llanilltud Fawr. (See Brân, Eurgain, Claudia, Illtud and Llanilltud Fawr). Another daughter, Gwladys Claudia may have been extremely influential in the early Christian church in Rome. Caradog was said to have returned with Eurgain to his base at Dunraven Castle or St Donat's, and there is an ancient farm, Cae Caradog, near Dunraven. Caradog's great-grandson Lleurwg ap Cyllin was said to be the saint who erected the first church in Britain, at Llandaf, and sent to Rome for Elfan, Dyfan, Medwy and Fagan to evangelise Britain. Whatever the truth, Christianity was well-established in Wales in the second century, and remained as the religion through the Dark Ages of England and the rest of Europe. It seems more likely, however, that the father of Caractacus was the Cymbeline recorded by Shakespeare (Cunobelinus, King of the Catuvellauni). Suetonius called Cunobelin son of Tasciovanus, 'Rex Britanniorum', and he was friendly with Rome. Unfortunately his death led to a power-struggle between his sons Caractacus, Togodumnus and Adminius, because of the *'cyfran'* principle of inheritance (gavelkind). Adminius appealed to Rome, as did the ousted Verica, King of the Atrebates. This partially led to the Roman invasion of 43 AD.

Caractus' fight against the Romans was well-documented by Tacitus. Many sources place him as the son of Cunobelinus, the fabled Cymbeline, and some equate him with Arvigarus, and even Arthur. His tribe, the Catuvellauni were pushing hard against their neighbours, the Atrebates, whose king Verica asked the Emperor Claudius for military assistance. In 43 AD Caractacus and his brother Togodumnus were defeated by Claudius' army on the river Medway in Kent. Publius Ostorius Scapula became governor in 47AD, and attempted to force the Celtic tribes into a 'proper' state of submission to Rome. Caractacus again fought against Rome with the Trinovantes in the south-east of England, but was forced back to join the Silures in south-east Wales. The Iceni of the east coast rebelled and were defeated, then Scapula marched against the Deceangli of North Wales, fighting them until he had to head north to deal with the Brigantes in Yorkshire. The great fort of Gloucester (Caerloyw) was built to push back the belligerent Silures. Next Scapula returned to try to take Caractacus, who using guerrilla tactics retreated with the Silures to join up with the Ordovices of Powys. Eventually, Caractacus believed that he had found an excellent defensive position, described by Tacitus as following:

Then Caractacus staked his fate on a battle. He selected a site where numerous factors – notably approaches and escape routes – helped him and impeded us. On one side there were steep hills. Wherever the gradient was gentler, stones were piled into a kind of rampart. And at his front there was a river without easy crossings. The defences were strongly manned . . . The British chieftains went around their men, encouraging and heartening them to be unafraid and optimistic, and offering other stimulants to battle. Caractacus, as he hastened to one point and another, stressed that this was the day, this the battle, which would either win back their freedom or enslave them forever . . . Then every man swore by his tribal oath that no enemy weapons would make them yield – and no wounds either . . .

This eagerness dismayed the Roman commander disconcerted as he already was by the river-barrier, the fortifications supplementing it, the overhanging cliffs, and the ferocious crowds of defenders at every point . . . After a reconnaissance to detect vulnerable and invulnerable points, Ostorius Scapula led his enthusiastic forces forward. They crossed the river without difficulty, and reached the rampart. But then, in an exchange of missiles, they came off worse in wounds and casualties. However, under a roof of locked shields, the Romans demolished the crude and clumsy stone embankment, and in the subsequent fight at close quarters the natives were driven to the hill-tops. Our troops pursued them closely.'

Caractacus managed to escape with his family and took refuge with Queen Cartimandua of the Brigantes, who treacherously handed him over, in chains, to Scapula. He was led in triumph before the Emperor Claudius in Rome, usually the precursor to a public execution of captured opponents. However, Tacitus records the famous sparing of his life by the emperor, noting Caractacus' defence:

'*Had my lineage and rank been accompanied by only moderate success, I should have come to this city as a friend rather than prisoner, and you would not have disdained to ally yourself peacefully with one so nobly born, the ruler of so many nations. As it is, humiliation is my lot, glory yours. I had horses, men, arms, wealth. Are you surprised I am sorry to lose them? If you want to rule the world, does it follow that everyone else welcomes enslavement? If I had surrendered without a blow being brought before you, neither my downfall nor your triumph would have become famous. If you execute me, they will be forgotten. Spare me, and I shall be an everlasting token of your mercy.'*

Many experts place the hill-fort of Old Oswestry as the place of battle, but it may have been Clunbury Hill, the Breiddin near Welshpool or Cefn Carnedd near Llanidloes. Caractacus will feature in future editions of 'A Hundred Great Welshmen' by this author, and any new knowledge on the probable site would be welcome. The *'exceptionally stubborn'* Silures kept on resisting Rome, forcing a legion to be based at the new fort of Isca (Caerleon). The Deceangli and Ordovices rose again and were almost exterminated. Huge forts had to be built at Uriconium (Wroxeter) and Deva (Chester) to attempt to subdue the Welsh tribes, and the Romans cut through to Anglesey, the heart of European druidism in 60 AD. A garrison was established on this holy island but Boadicea (Buddug) led a revolt in England, so the Romans could not consolidate their gains in Wales. In 71, Petilius crushed the Brigantes, and between 74 and 78 the might of Rome turned once more against the Silures of Glamorgan and Gwent.

The Silures had fought Rome from 49 and were regarded by Tacitus as courageous, stubborn, powerful and warlike. Ostorius Scapula had said that they must be annihilated or transplanted. When he died, *'worn out with care'*, the Silures destroyed a Roman legion. However, the construction of Caerleon in 75 meant that the Silures came to an accommodation with the governor, leaving their hillfort capital of Llanmelin and settling in the new Roman town of Caerwent. The Silures became the most Romanised of the Welsh tribes, paving the way for Meurig and Arthur to become Pendragons in the years after the Romans left Britain. With south-east Wales secure, Agricola moved north to avenge a Roman defeat by the Ordovices and *'cut to pieces the whole fighting force of the region'*. Again, Anglesey was ravaged. The next 300 years were by no means peaceful in Wales, but the great stone forts at Chester, Caerleon, Carmarthen (Moridunum) and Caernarfon (Segontium) controlled a semi-quiescent people until the legions left around 400 AD. Unlike more 'settled' colonies of Rome, very few Roman villas have been found in Wales, and those that have are mainly attributed to Romano-Celts. Professor Euros Bowen noted that several Roman villas were found near the sites of Cadog's Llancarfan, Illtud's Llanilltud and Dyfrig's foundations. Tathan was also active at Caerwent, which leads to Bowen's conclusion, that the group of Celtic saints largely confined to south-east Wales represent a church that was locally established in late Roman times. This was the only part of Wales where Roman urban and country house culture was rooted, and Romano-British estates carried on the Christian tradition rather than relied on missionaries from Gaul.

An interesting link with Caradoc may be the inscribed stone noted by Edward Lhuyd in Gibson's Camden: *'in Panwen Brydhin, in the parish of Llangadoc, about 6 miles from Neath, is the Maen dan Llygad yr ych, two circular stone intrenchments and a stone pillar, inscribed M. CARITINI FILII BERICII.'* About 1835, Lady Mackworth of the Gnoll estate in Neath, collected all the inscribed stones and crosses in the neighbourhood to make a grotto, and the stone was damaged on its way there. The grotto later gave way in a storm and the stone disappeared for a time. People in the area thought that this was the revenge of the fairies, who *'had been constantly seen dancing on a fine evening'* in the charmed circles from where the stone was stolen. Marcus Coritanus is a Roman name, and there was a Berice, Prince of the Coritani who had a feud with Caradog. Treachery by the Coritani (Corinaid) supposedly broght Caradog his final defeat. Westwood notes that Berice had a son named Marcus Collatinus (see Appendix I).

CARADOG FREICHFRAS (Strong-Arm) 6th century
May 3

This son of Ynyr Gwent* and Madrun lived at Caerwent and succeeded his father. He married Derwela, a sister of Amwn Ddu. Caradoc was one of Arthur's knights, and on May 3, Rood Day, a young noble is said to have brought a golden cloak into his court, which would only look good on a faithful woman. In the old Cumbrian ballad Sir Cai's wife tried it, but it would not fit properly. Lady Briefbras (Tegau) wore it well, having confessed that she kissed Caradoc twice before she married. The young man then called Arthur a cuckold, and Gwynhafar (Guinevere) *'a bitch and a witch and a whore bold.'* He then produced the head of a freshly-killed boar, saying that only a man with a faithful wife could cut it. Again, only Caradoc could do it. Finally, the boy said that all the cuckolded knights would spill their drinks, which they did except Caradoc. It seems to have been an allegory to prove Guinevere's unfaithfulness with Maelgwn Gwynedd or Modred (Medraut).

Caradog is also counted as the son of St Gwenllian, a daughter or grand-daughter of Brychan. The Triads call him one of the *'three beloved chiefs of Arthur's court'* who could never bear a superior in their families, and of whom Arthur sang:
'These are my three cavaliers of battle –
Mael the tall, Llydd the armipotent,
And the pillar of Cymru, Caradoc.'

In a triad he is said to be the son of Llyr Marini, who cast a spell upon Tegau Eurfron ferch Nudd Llawhael, the king of North Britain. In another triad his horse was Lluagor and he was one of the *'three Battle-Horsemen of the Isle of Britain'*. In the 'Dream of Rhonabwy' from the Red Book of Hergest', Caradog was virtuous, proud and the chief counsellor and cousin of Arthur. The Life of Padarn makes him important in the settling of Britons in Brittany and conquering the Vannetais, and the Life of Collen states that he injured his arm at the Battle of Hiraddug. He is also mentioned in the 'Life' of Tathan.

It seems Caradog's main court was at Caer Gwent, but he gave the city (the Roman Caerwent) to Tathan to found a monastery. Caradog moved to Porthskewett, possibly the Roman outpost of Sudbrook fort, which was more easily defended than the walled Roman town. Sudbrook was later dedicated to the Holy Trinity by the Normans and lies in ruins on the edge of the Severn. Erosion by the sea has taken away much of the adjoining massive hill-fort, where there are remains of a mediaeval village. It is surprising that more visitors to the great Roman fort at Caerleon do not travel another three miles or so to walk around the walls of Caerwent. St Caradec north of Pontivy, and St Caradec-Tregomer west of Pontivy may be his.

There was a holy 'rag well', Ffynnon Garadog near Llanilid, but the patron may be Caradog of Llancarfan, or even Caractacus (q.v.) In Cheriton, Glamorgan was another holy well known as Scraddock's Well (St Caradoc's Well). A 'Saying of the Wise' attributed to Caradoc is:
'Hast thou heard the saying of old Caradoc,
When he lost half a penny?
"The full knows not the grief of the needy".'

Gilbert and others make Caradog the son of Gwrgant Mawr and St Ninnoca.

CARADOG FYNACH d. 1124
April 13, 14, May 16

The 'Life' of this recluse was written by Giraldus Cambrensis but has been lost. This hermit-saint from Brecon was harpist and keeper of the hounds to Prince Rhys ap Tewdwr in the eleventh century, but lost the dogs. He then fled from Dyfed and Rhys ap Tewdwr to Llandaf Cathedral and was ordained. The histories attribute miracles to him, healing tumours by touching, turning fish into coins for the poor, and halting a chasing Viking longship. His tomb-effigy can now be seen in St David's Cathedral. For many years after his death, his body did not decay and laid in state in the cathedral. William of Malmesbury recounts trying to steal a finger of Caradoc as a relic, but the hermit jerked his hand away. Bones were recently analysed in the hope that they were those of David and Iestyn, but were dated at around 1000 years old, so may be those of Caradog.

Caradog built an oratory, now in ruins, on the island of Burry Holms, and refounded the shrine of St Cenydd at Llangennith (Llangenydd) on the Gower Peninsula. He then moved to Menevia (St Davids), settling at Llanrhian (known as Ynys Barri, there is a Barry Island Farm in Pembroke today). Some say that he retired to an island off the Pembroke coast, but 'ynys' does not always mean an island surrounded by water. Because of harassment from Vikings, he finally moved to the cell of St Ismael in Rhos (St Isell's, Haroldston) where he died on Low Sunday (April 13). He may be associated with the *'Caradog, a very learned man'*, who visited Ynys Enlli around this time. Early in the reign of Henry I, Flemish settlers forced out the local population from Rhos district, and Caradog's relations with his new neighbour, the Norman Tancred of Haverfordwest, deteriorated badly. Haroldston East and Lawrenny in Pembroke are dedicated to him, and there was a holy well in Haroldston. Lawrenny, on Milford Haven has a St Caradog's church. Haroldston West has a menhir called the Hang Davy Stone, but Harold's Stone seems to have been destroyed.

St Caradoc's Chapel at Newgale near St David's is now a mere hollow in the sands above the beach, but was still standing at the start of the nineteenth century. It was possibly built to commemorate Caradoc's funeral procession across the sands to St David's Cathedral, when Gerald of Wales recounts that a storm failed to wet the coffin. A letter survives of Pope Innocent III in response to a request by Gerald to have Caradoc canonised. He is one of the few Welshmen to have been officially sanctified by Rome, along with Dewi, Sadyrnin, Cyfelach and Gwryd, before the martyrs of the Middle Ages. Giraldus Cambrensis took the 'Life' to read it to Pope Innocent III in Rome, to get Caradog canonized. The Pope apponted the abbots of Whitland, St Dogmael's and Strata Florida as a commission to inquire into the case, upon May 8, 1200.

There was a holy well called Sanctus Cradokus near Padstow in Cornwall, which killed worms in people. His hermitage may have been at Portfield, common land in St Thomas parish, Haverfordwest, where around Caradog's Well festivities were held on Easter Monday or in Whitsun week. It was near St David's Well, and was visited by lovers on the morning of Easter Monday Fair.

CARADOG of LLANCARFAN fl. 1135
CARADOC

It seems that Caradog and Geoffrey of Monmouth knew each other, for Geoffrey said that he would leave the history of the Kings of the Welsh to Caradog of Llancarfan, and the history of the Kings of the English to William of Malmesbury and Henry of Huntingdon. Whether Caradog completed his history is difficult to tell, as so much early material has been destroyed. He is known in history, however, for his Life of Cadog, the founder of Llancarfan. It seems that Caradog moved to Glastonbury because of the Norman despoiling of Llancarfan, and it is said that he died in 1156.

CARANNOG 6th century
CARANWC, CARENTOC, CARANTOC, CERNACH, CARANTACUS, CARENTMAIL?
May 16. His feast was held in Llangrannog in Cardiganshire upon May 27th for centuries.

'Vita Carantoci' tells up that Carannog was the son of Ceredig ap Cunedda Wledig, but 'Bonedd y Saint' states that he was the great grandson of Cunedda, Carannog ap Corun ap

Ceredig ap Cunedda Wledig. (Sometimes, as with the Brychan family, the 'ap' refers to the grandparent or great-grandparent rather than the father, especially when the ancestor is famous). His background certainly seems to be from the noble house of Ceredigion (Cardigan), but other sources claim that he was an Irish monk. He was said to be St David's uncle, and the brother of saints Tyssul, Pedyr, Tydiwg and Ceneu, so it seems probable that his father was Corun.

His 'Life' relates three lessons. Firstly, Carannog had an altar of a colour that could not be described. He followed it from Wales across the River Severn and destroyed a serpent that King Arthur had been chasing. Arthur and King Cado of Domononia then gave him land to build a monastery at a place called Carrov or Carrum (Carhampton). The saint is linked with Cornwall. The second lesson tells us that Carannog refused to take over the kingship from his father, who was old and weary of fighting the invading Irish. Instead he disguised himself as a beggar, and followed Padrig (Patrick) to Ireland, where he built another monastery. The third lesson describes Carannog curing the leprosy of Saint Tyrnog in Ireland.

He returned from Ireland to Ogof Grannog (Carannog's Cave), near Llangrannog in Dyfed. Eisteddfa Grannog (Carannog's Seat) is a rock above the local harbour shaped like a chair, and an old cottage has been called Llety Carannog (Carannog's Lodgings). The holy well near Llety Carannog was possibly dedicated to him, but renamed Ffynnon Fair (Mary's Well) by Norman landlords. Llangrannog Church is dedicated to the saint, and local tradition says that Carannog fled his father's kingdom disguised as a pauper. He decided to build the church at Llangrannog because a dove carried off wood shavings from his staff and showed him the site. There was also a pilgrimage chapel near St Dogmaels known as Capel Cranog, and at Egremont (near Lawhaden) was found a stone incised with 'Carantacus'. Ffynnon y Groes is near Llangrannog Church in Cardigan and the tradition is that pilgims went there and made the sign of the cross, as Carannog used to after drinking from the well. There may have been a stone cross here.

His Life also states that Carannog prayed for disfigurement to discourage the attentions of the king's daughter. From Wales it appears Carranog went with a group of monks to evangelise Cornwall, and then they went on to Brittany. He also evangelised Ireland, where he was known as Cernach, and was buried at Chernach, where he died on May 16th. Carannog is associated with Carentec and Tregarantec in Brittany. These towns are both in the jurisdiction of the Church of Leon, and its Breviary honours Carannog on May 16, calling him variously Carantoc and Caradog. Carannog was supposed to have killed a dragon in a cave by Carentec. Crantock near Newquay in Cornwall, where a stained glass window commemorated him. Llangrannog in Cardigan is his. In Llandudoch there was a chapel and an ancient well dedicated to Carannog. There was also a Ffynnon Garadog between Aberystwyth and Bow Street.

The 'Saying of the Wise', for Carannog's father or grandfather Ceredig, is appropriate for these days of a growing 'underclass' across Europe:
Hast thou heard the saying of Ceredig,
A wise and select king?
"Everyone has his foot on the fallen".'

'Carentmail' went with Armel from Wales to Brittany. More research is necessary to link Arthur with Armel, and Carentmail may be a useful starting point in Breton historical data. A problem is that Iolo states that Armel went with Cadfan, and the author cannot at present disentangle Carentmael from Carannog and Cadfan. However, it looks more likely that

Carranog was Carentmael, as it appears that Cadfan did not return to Brittany. A stone inscribed *'D.M. BARRECT - CARANTI'* was found at Tomen y Mur Roman fort, which was probably to a Roman called Carantos. Another six inscribed stones were found here in Merioneth but have been dispersed. One went to Tan y Bwlch Hall.

CAROLS

These are a recent innovation in Christian tradition which used to be banned for their paganism and subversion. The earliest carols were pagan chants and dances associated with fertility rites and the passing of the winter solstice. Their performance was condemned by church councils as late as 1435. The songs concentrated on the pleasures of feasting and drinking and made little reference to Jesus. Carols were banned by Cromwell's regime, and in the 18th century the only carol allowed to be sung was 'While Shepherds Watched'. 'Adeste Fideles' was written by an English supporter of Bonnie Prince Charlie as a coded rallying cry for all Jacobites and Catholics. Later, 'Hark the Herald Angels' was allowed to be sung in churches. The established Church of England thought that carol-singing was a dangerous superstition, and disliked the wassailers* who went from house to house over the Christmas holiday.

The very first carol service was held in Truro, Cornwall, at 10pm on Christmas Eve, 1878. In the late 19th century, 'Away in a Manger', 'O Little Town of Bethlehem', 'We Three Kings', 'Good King Wenceslas' and 'Ding Dong Merrily' were all written to satisfy the new fashion. However, some old carols remain popular – 'I Saw Three Ships' seems to celebrate the transport of the skulls of three kings to Cologne Cathedral. 'The Twelve Days of Christmas' has an interesting history. From 1588 and the attempt to invade England by the Spanish Armada, it was forbidden to openly practise the Catholic faith in England and Wales until 1829. Without the assistance of regular church-going, the carol was made up to help children learn the elements of their faith. *'True love'* in the song is God, and Jesus is the *'partridge in a pear tree'*, who will risk its life to save its children, by feigning injury and drawing predators away from the nest. Thus *'On the First Day of Christmas my true love gave to me a partridge in a pear tree'* refers to God giving us his brave son. The other symbols are as follows:
'Two turtle doves' – Old and New Testaments;
'Three French hens' – Faith, Hope and Charity;
'Four calling birds' – the gospels;
'Five golden rings' – the first five books of the Old Testament, recording man's fall from grace;
'Six geese a laying' – the six days of the Creation;
'Seven swans a swimming' – seven gifts of the Holy Spirit;
'Eight maids a milking' – the eight Beatitudes;
'Nine ladies dancing' – nine choirs of angels;
'Ten lords a leaping' – the Ten Commandments;
'Eleven pipers piping' – the eleven faithful Apostles; and
'Twelve drummers drumming' – the twelve points of belief in the Apostles' Creed.

Victorian writers set Jesus' birth in the *'bleak midwinter'* with snow scattered over his humble stable. Having often worked in the Middle East, this author can state that snow would indeed be a miracle, except on the mountains of Iran. Moreover, Jesus was probably born in the summer in Palestine, and the unthinking acceptance of this 'tradition' in our Christmas festivities is rather sad. Traditions are best when rooted in reality. The above information comes from Ian Bradley's 'The Penguin Book of Carols', published in 1999. (See 'Christmas' for other doubts about this festival).

The 'snow on the crib' scenario was described in Bishop Lancelot Andrewes' 'Sermon 15, Of the Nativity' in 1622 as follows:

'It was no summer progress. A cold coming they had of it, at this time of the year; just, the worst time of the year, to take a journey, and specially a long journey, in. The ways deep, the weather sharp, the days short, the sun farthest off in solstitio brumali, the very dead of Winter.'
This is not quite the way that Thomas Cook describes its winter holidays in Israel.

It is worth noting the famous 'saint' King Wenceslas in relation to our Christmas celebrations. The author has recently returned from Prague, and the carol is a recent reworking of a medieval song 'Tempus Adest Floridum'. Born in 907, Duke Vaclav (Wenceslas) was never a king, and the St Agnes fountain, where *'yonder peasant dwelt'* was not built until the 13th century. Local Christians persuaded Vlacav's younger brother, Boleslav the Cruel, to stab Vlacav/Wenceslas to death, three months before the feast of Stephen, in 929. The chapel of St Wenceslas in St Vitus Cathedral (inside Prague Castle) is now usually closed to the public, but his skull is sometimes on display.

Of more religious, moral and ethical import is the spot on Wenceslas Square where Jan Palach self-immolated in 1969 in protest against the Russian occupation and imprisonment of Dubcek. Nearby the spot is marked where 30 years previously Jan Opletal was killed when the occupying Nazis opened fire upon unarmed protesters. And several others followed Jan Palach's example, for instance Jan Zajic, who set fire to himself in the same place upon February 26th, 1969, the anniversary of the Russian-backed communist coup. Intriguingly, Vlacav Havel received the last of his prison sentences for laying flowers at the impromptu martyrs' shrine here, in January 1989. Since the November 1989 revolution, there is now a simple memorial cross there to the victims of communism, with photos of Palach and Zajic, and a constant presence of fresh flowers. Despite the crowds of curious tourists, it is a far more moving monument to faith than the gilded tomb of Duke Wenceslas. Prague has overtaken Lisbon as the cheapest capital city in Europe for tourists, but like Barcelona is a rats-nest of pickpockets, especially at the Museum metro station at the top of Wenceslas Square.

*'Wassail' comes from the Anglo-Saxon 'Waes Hael' or 'good health'. Originally it was a drink made from mulled ale, curdled cream, roasted apples, eggs, cloves, ginger, nutmeg and sugar, and served from huge bowls.

BISHOP CARON 7th century?
March 5, and the fair was celebrated at Tregaron on March 15, 16 and 17

'Nos Ffair Caron' was held on the evening of March 16th at Tregaron. On this evening, the maid symbolically handed a candle back to her mistress, as from then the family would retire to bed before darkness came. It was the end of the *'amser gwylad'*, the night vigil which began in September. George Owen also placed Caron as the founder of Llanreithan in Pembrokeshire. At Glanbrenig Farm, Tregaron, children came with cups on Easter eve to mix sugar with well-water from Ffynnon Garon. On Easter Day, sweethearts gathered there and gave each other white bread which they drank with well water.

Caron seems to have been an Irish saint. A small pillar-stone, two feet high, is now in the National Museum of Wales. This Tregaron stone is marked with a cross derived from the chi-rho symbol, and there is an inscription to Enevir. The half-uncial form of lettering was derived from previous Roman capitals, so the stone dates from the seventh to ninth centuries. Some

Irish sources believe that this was the Irish saint Ciaran. There is a great deal of difficulty in deciding the truth of this matter – much ecclesiastical history was written late in Ireland, and destroyed in Wales. Rhygyfarch's 'Life of David' certainly overstated his influence in Ireland, but it was also written late and was an attempt to prove the supremacy of St David's amongst Welsh churches.

During 19th century restoration, several Celtic inscribed stones were removed from the church at Tregaron. The crossed stone mentioned above was placed in the wall of the chapel at Goodrich Court, and bears the inscription ENEVIRI. Another important stone went to Goodrich, the 'Potentina Stone', reading *'potentina malher'*, the equivalent of *'Bod yn yna Mael hir'*, dedicated to Prince Mael Hir of the 6th century. However, Dr John Jones, in his 'History of Wales', believed it to be the stone of Maelor ap Peredur Gam, killed in battle at Dinerth in Cardigan in 907. Jones also believed that Heraidd ap Caron ap Illtud was commemorated at Llanwnnws. Whether Caron was the son of St Illtud is a matter of conjecture.

CARWYD early 5th century
CARWED

A brother of St Dunawd Fawr, and son of Pabo Post Prydain who spent his life in the monastery at Bangor-is-Coed.

KING CASWALLON LAWHIR (long-handed) d.517
CADWALLON LAWHIR

Maelgwn Gwynedd's father, and the son of Einion Yrth ap Cunedda Wledig. Caswallon was probably not counted as a saint, but his victory over the Irish Picts (Gwyddl Fichti) drove them out of Anglesey and Gwynedd, where they had settled (as in Pembroke and Carmarthen) in the times after the Romans left Wales. He was a grandson of Cunedda, and with his brothers Meigyr and Meilyr won fame and territory by defeating the Irish. Caswallon was said to have slain Serigi, the Pictish leader, with his own hand, then expelled the Irish from Gwynedd. A chapel called Eglwys y Bedd, or Llangwyddl existed near Holyhead which was erected over Serigi's grave (see Cybi). The 1775 History of Anglesey recorded that *'the ruins of it a few years ago were removed in order to render the way to the church more commodious. Here formerly was the shrine of Serigi, who was canonised by the Irish. It seems to have been held in exceeding great repute for several very wonderful qualities and cures: but according to an old Irish chronicle, it was carried off by some Irish rovers, and deposited in the cathedral of Christ Church, Dublin.'* None of the ecclesiastical staff at Christ Church knew this story, however, when inquiries were made by the author.

Caswallon was a strong patron on Anglesey of Cybi, Seiriol and especially Eilian, and the remains of his court, Llys Caswallon, were near Llaneilian. Caswallon ap Beli Mawr features in the Mabinogion wearing a magic cloak of invisibility, killing off the six Principal Officers left by Bran to guard Britain when he attacked Ireland to avenge his sister. The seventh, Caradog ap Beli, was frightened to death. The name Caswallon appears to come from Casivellaunus, who led the Catuvellauni and other British tribes against Julius Caesar in 54 BC.

CATHAN late 6th century
CATHEN
May 17

The son of Cawrdaf ap Caradog Freichfras, who founded Llangathen in Carmarthen. Ffynnon Gathen was marked on Allt y Gaer Farm, but seems to have vanished. Ffynnon Capel Pen Arw near Llangathen, at Allt y Capel, cured rheumatism and sore eyes and still flows but the well building has gone. Pistyll Llwyfen was a healing well near the church. The hundred of Llangeithien in Carmarthen is supposed to have been named after him. His brothers were Medrod and Iddo. Cathan may be buried at Caldey Island (see Dyfrig).

At Llangathen in the beautiful Tywy Valley is Aberglasney, *'a garden lost in time'*, the only surviving 16th-17th century garden in Britain. As early as 1471, Lewis Glyn Cothi had praised Aberglasney's white-painted court, surrounded by nine gardens, orchards, vineyards and oak trees. The Bishops of St Davids built the gatehouse and cloister garden from 1600 onwards. The fabulous yew tunnel may be over a thousand years old, and is therefore one of the oldest living garden freatures in Europe. One of the hall's residents, John Dyer, wrote the famous poem 'Grongar Hill' about the nearby hillfort. There was a television series documenting the restoration of the house and gardens in late 1999 and a family ticket to visit only costs £9. 85p (01558-668998).

CATHEDRALS

The four oldest cathedrals in the British Isles are St Asaf (founded 537, a bishopric in 560), St David's (550), Llandaf (c.560) and Bangor (founded 525, a bishopric in 560). (Wales also has cathedrals at Newport [St Woolos], Brecon and St David's Roman Catholic Cathedral at Cardiff). The four early foundations were based upon the tribal territories of the Celtic tribes. The Deceangli controlled Gwynedd, with Bangor; the Ordovices ruled in Powys, with the bishopric of St Asaph replacing the destroyed monastery at Bangor-on-Dee and the tribal capital of Shrewsbury (Pengwern); the Demetae ruled Dyfed and Ceredigion, with St David's at its south-western perimeter; and the Silures of Morganwg and Gwent replaced Caerleon with Llandaf near Cardiff as their religious centre. The earliest English cathedral, at Canterbury, was founded in 601 by Augustine who became its first archbishop after converting Ethelbert of Kent. Not one British history book has ever mentioned this predating of Canterbury by Welsh cathedrals.

There is a threat at present facing the wonderful Llandaf Cathedral, just north of Cardiff. In 1874 Thomas Nicholas noted Dean Conybeare's description *'the Western façade of our Cathedral is a very beautiful and characteristic specimen of the transition between the later Norman and early pointed styles contemporaneously with the age of our Richard Coeur de Lion . . . exquisitely beautiful . . . nearly unrivalled for the elegance and simplicity of its compostion and execution . . .'* The art critic of The Daily Mail recently wrote that *'the west front of Llandaf cathedral, both inside and out, is one of the great architectural set pieces, not only in Wales, but in Europe . . . it is probably the oldest see in Britain . . . other cathedrals are similarly sited . . . but none compares with the picturesque drama of Llandaf.'* (Western Mail, February 21st, 2000). In an article entitled 'Threat to a Historic Wonder of Wales' the author criticises in the most severe terms the Dean's avowed intention to obscure the West front by a massive concrete ramp, despite the fact that *'Llandaf Diocese's own expert advisory committee has already refused to countance the plans.'* With great difficulty, the former dean and chapter were persuaded not to go ahead with a great glass box 'visitor centre' stuck of the West façade. Anyone reading the full-page article should write to politicians to ask them to oppose such unwarranted and permanent vandalism.

CATHERINE 4th century
November 25

Nothing is known of this saint of Alexandria until the 9th century at Mount Sinai. The legend was that she was tortured on a wheel – the origin of the 'Catherine Wheel' of firework displays – and then beheaded. Crusaders brought her dedication back with them, and in Worcester on 'Cathern Day' young women made merry, *'catherning'*. A *'Cathern bowl'* of wine and spices was prepared for the students at Worcester college. She is included in this book as a typical example of the mythical saints like George, favoured by the French-Normans, who replaced the native Celtic saints.

CATLON

A witness in the Llandaf Charters, possibly the founder of Llancadle.

CAW 5th century

This saint had over twenty sons, all of whom were heroes or saints. 21 of his children are listed in the tale of Culhwch and Olwen, and many became Knights of the Round Table in the mediaeval rewritings of the stories of the real-life Arthwys ap Meurig ap Tewdrig (see Armel, Meurig and Tewdrig). These *'victorious warriors'* were Angawd, Ardwyat, Kalcas, Kelin, Koch, Konnyn, Kynwas, Dirmyc, Ergyryat, Etmic, Gildas, Gwarthegyt, Gwyngat, Iustic, Llwybyr, Mabsant, Meilic, Neb and Ouan. Caw's daughter Cwyllog married Mordred (Medraut). Tradition places Caw's wife (or mother) as a native of Anglesey, from 'Twr Celyn'.

He appears to have been king of a territory called Cwm Cawlwyd or Cowllwg in the North of England, or Scotland, but to have been dispossessed by invading Picts and Scots (Gwyddyl Fichti). He settled at Twrcelyn in Anglesey, where lands were given to him by Maelgwn Gwynedd. It is said that King Arthur also gave lands to Caw's children in 'Siluria', south-east Wales that was the kingdom of the Silures. His children probably included Hywel (killed by Arthur), Aneurin (the author of the great 'Y Gododdin'), Caffo, Ceidio, Aeddan Foeddog, Cwyllog, Dirynig, Cain, Eigrad, Samson, Eigron, Gildas, Gwenafwy, Gallgo, Peirio, Cewydd, Maelog, Meilig, Gwrddelw, Gwrhai and Huail. One Triad refers to this as 'the third Holy Family of Ynys Pridein'.

Caw was credited with founding Llangewydd (dedicated to Cewydd, his son), and Laleston, both in Glamorgan near where Caw and his brothers (Cado, Selyf, Iestyn and Cyngar) studied at Llancarfan. However, Laleston appears to also have been called Llangewydd. There are two standing stones in a field just north of Laleston called Cae'r-hen-Eglwys (Field of the Old Church).

There is a difficult 'Saying of the Wise', for which the author's translation could probably be improved:

'A glywaist ti chedl y Caw?
Cyt bei hawd datrhewi rhew,
Byd anhawdd datrywiaw rhyw'
'Hast thou heard the saying of Caw?
"Athough it is easy to unfreeze frost,
It is difficult to understand sex".'

CAWEY

George Owen noted Capel Cawey and Capel Silin at Mynachlog-ddu, as pilgrimage chapels of the middle ages, but only Dogmael's church remains here.

CAWRDAF mid 6th century
December 5, November 12

King and the son of Caradog Freichfras of the line of Coel, and of Tegau ferch Nudd Hael. He succeeded as ruler of Brecon, and is remembered in the Triads for his courage in battle and the fact that the whole country followed his call to arms. The Triads call him one of the three *'Cynweisiaid', 'chief or prime ministers of the Isle of Britain'*, and the Mabinogion's 'Dream of Rhonabwy' names him as a counsellor of Arthur. His brothers were the saints Cadfarch, Tangwn and Maethlu. He retired to study at Llanilltud monastery, and founded Llangoed under Llaniestin in Anglesey with his brother Tangwn. Perhaps Llanwrda in Carmarthen is his foundation – the wake held there was on the old-style All Saints Day, November 12th. However, more likely St Gwrdaf was its founder.

Gelli Gawrdaf, near Miskin Manor in Glamorgan is where he had his 'côr' of 300 monks. This monastery is still marked upon O.S. maps. At Abererch in Caernarfon, (formerly Llangawrda), there is a Ffynnon Gawrdaf healing well near the church, and also a large boulder with a seat cut out, called Cadair Gawrdaf (Cawrdaf's Seat). His shrine and holy bells were there for centuries. A megalith named Caer Cawrdaf also stands near here.

An 1856 record of Abererch reveals *'A curious custom prevailed in this parish within the memory of persons still alive. On the eve of St Cawrdaf's festival all the children brought into the church a number of candles, which they had been making themselves, or had bought – one candle for each member of their family in whom they were particularly interested, and which they had called after their names. They knelt down, lighted them, and muttered any prayer they recollected as long as the candles continued burning; but, according as the candles became extinguished one after the other, they supposed that the person whose name was attached to the candle that burnt out first would certainly die first; and so on in the order of successive extinctions.'*

His 'Saying of the Wise' is:
'Have you heard the saying of Cawrdaf,
Son of Caradog Freichfras, the chieftain?
"Let the work of the cautious hand prosper."

Morgan Mwynfawr, the king of Morganwg, was said to have been blessed by Cawrdaf to live to a long age, and Morgan's father was Arthur (Arthrwys ap Meurig). Morgan's court was probably at Penllin (following Pawl Penychen) or at nearby Pentre Meurig, just a couple of miles south of Cawrdaf's monastery at Miskin.

CEDOL
November 1

Llangedol, or Pentir Chapel, under Bangor in Caernarfon is his foundation.

CEDWYDD

Nothing is at present known by the author, except that the ruins of Llangedwydd chapel are in Abererch parish in Caernarfon (see Cadfarch).

CEDWYN 6th century
CEDWEN, CEDWY

His mother Madrun was a saint married to Ynyr Gwent, but he was her child by Gwgon Gwron ap Peredur. This is the same warrior mentioned as Gwgawn Gwrawn in the Triads of Arthur. Llandegwyn in the Tanad valley near Llanrhaeadr-ym Mechain and Llanyblodwel was his. This chapel was under Llanrhaidr in Montgomery. There was also a Llandegwyn in Brecon, since lost. The Cedwyn stream runs into the Ely at Leckwith near Cardiff, and between Leckwith and Llandough is Cwm Cedwyn, a wooded valley. This half-brother of the warrior saint Caradog Freich Fras (by Madrun's marriage to Ynyr Gwent) was known in Arthur's court as Cedwy.

Ffynnon Gedwen is a holy well at Trefeglwys in Montgomery, now dedicated to Michael. Edward Lhuyd commented that *'The water of it was of such vertue being boyled and put in milke breaks it into possett.'* It is tempting to attribute Trefeglwys to Cedwyn. There is an unfinished manuscript, possibly in Newtown or Aberystwyth library upon the history of Trefeglwys and perhaps some reader could assess the possibility. The author's mother remembers this well as being just past a 'haunted' house, where children used to fill up bottles to drink, as it was better water than that of the village pump. The 'ghost house' seems to be Dol Gau, where the magician Ifan Huw was said to have raised demons in 1781, causing a man to ride to the authorities in Llanidloes to request aid. T. Gwynn Jones notes that poor people were buried in a shroud, but after a shroud gave way, burial without coffins was prohibited at Trefeglwys Church. There is a Cedwyn dedication in Montgomery, so Trefeglwys could well have been Llangedwen.

CEIDIO AP CAW 6th century
November 18

Rhodwydd Geidio under Llantrisaint in Anglesey was founded by this son of Caw.

CEIDIO AB YNYR GWENT 6th century
CETIAU
November 3 (and 6)

A prince of Gwent, whose mother was St Madrun, daughter of Vortimer the Blessed (Gwrthefyr Fendigaid). He studied at Llancarfan, and his brothers Cynheiddon, Caradog and Iddon, and sister Tegiwg, were also saints. His foundation of Ceidio on the Llŷn Peninsula lay under the hill of Carn Madryn, named after his mother. The legend is that when Vortimer's palace near Tre'r Geiri was burnt, Madrun fled with the infant Ceidio to a hillfort on Carn Madryn.

He may have succeeded Teilo as Bishop of Llandaff, and is said to be buried in a barrow in a field called Cefn Ceidio near Rhayader in Radnorshire. Rhayader (Rhaedr), Llangeidio on the Llŷn and Ceidio near Llandyrnog are his foundations. Ceidio took his sister Tegiwg to evangelise the West Country and she died at Minster. Ceidio was associated with sanctuary-seeking deer, as his horse was one of the *'cloven-hoofed horses'* of Britain.

CEIDIO AB ARTHWYS

He is only mentioned in Iolo Morganwg's manuscripts, the father of three Llanilltud saints called Gwenddolau, Nudd and Cof.

CEINDRYCH 5th century
CEINDREG, KERDECH

This virgin daughter of Brychan lived at Caergodolaur, a place now unknown. However, she seems to have been associated with Llandegwyn in Merioneth. There is also a possibility that she founded Cedris near Abergynolwyn.

CEINOR see CAIN

CEINWEN 5th-6th century
CEIN
October 8

A daughter or grand-daughter of Brychan, who founded Llangeinwen and Cerrig Ceinwen in Anglesey. At Cerrig Ceinwen her holy well was still in place in the early 1900's, formerly famed for healing. This is the sister of Ceneu (Cain or Keyne) although some authorites state that she is the same person because the feast date is shared. A standing stone with a cross and scrollwork has been incorporated into a church buttress at Llangeinwen. A rare lead sarcophagus was found at Rhyddgaer Mansion near Llangeinwen in 1878. Probably 5th century, there is a raised Latin inscription which is translated as *'here lie the bones of Camuloris'*. The fragments are now in Bangor Museum. Llanceinwyry near Llanddeusant is given by Doble as Ceinwen's foundation. Llangeinor (see Cain) is attributed to Ceinwyr, so as mentioned these saints may be the same person.

Alphabetical Listing of the Saints of Wales and Religious Events

ABBOT CEITHO 6th century
August 5 and All Saints Day. 'Pumsaint' was also celebrated on January 7.

One of the five saintly sons of Cynyr of Cynwyl Gaio, Llangeitho in Cardiganshire is named after him, and Llanpumsaint in Carmarthenshire commemorates Ceitho and his brothers, Gwyno, Gwynoro, Celynin and Gwyn. At Llanpumpsaint is Ffos y Maen standing stone in a field known as Parc y Maen Llwyd. Ffynnon Geitho at Llangeitho is said to have cold water in summer and luke-warm water in winter. Daniel Rowland, the great Methodist preacher, died aged 82 in Llangeitho in 1790.

Large numbers of 'Jumpers' were first seen in Llangeitho in 1762. These Methodist Revivalists leapt and danced as an expression of their spiritual joy. The practice occurred across parts of Wales well into the 19th century.

CELER 7th century?
CELERT
June 21, 22 and up to June 29

Martyred at Llangeler in Carmarthen, known as Martir Keler in the Taxatio of 1291. The nearby Ffynnon Geler was a medicinal well. Beddgelert was previously called Bedd Kelert, and may mark his grave, although the burial mound is probably much older. The local legend there, of Llywelyn ab Iorwerth's faithful hound, predates Richard III's death in 1485. Beddgelert Church is now dedicated to the Virgin Mary. Ffynnon Fair near St Mary's Priory ruins was also probably Celer's original well. (There are many holy wells dedicated to Mary in Wales that have not been included in this book, as they are probably later attributions). There was also a Ffynnon Angau near Felindre, and a Pistyll Nefol in Llangeler parish. There is a ten feet standing stone known as Crugiau on a moated mound in a field known as Parc Garreg Llwyd, near Llangeler.

Ffynnon Geler drew pilgrims to bathe in its waters into the 18th century. Edward Llwyd described it in his 'Parochalia':
'Not far from the church at the bottom of a steep hill issueth a fountain. Over the fall thereof a little chapel is erected. Hither every summer infirm people make a frequent resort, but particularly from the 21st of June to the feast of St Peter (29th) there will be such a concourse of people that no fair in Wales can equal it in multitude, out of an opinion that the saint imbued it with such a virtue as will cure all infirmities. The tradition obtains that about two years since, some infirm persons left their crutches behind in the church in memory of their being cured by bathing in this well. But I doubt there was in this much of the monkish poae fraudes. However, there are persons alive this day that saw the crutches. In the churchyard there is a place which I may properly call a cemetery (in Welsh it is called Llech) where after bathing, the infirm must lie down to sleep, which as many do are persuaded will recover, otherwise not.' It was thought that the stone slab, or llech, lay over Celer's grave. It was said to be more popular than any fair in Wales, and probably the spring is the one at the foot of Allt Celer, near a house named Plas Geler, but the well chapel has vanished.

'The Llangeler Stone' at Capel Mair, Llangeler was near the spring dedicated to Celer. One account is that a farmer demolished it to stop people trespassing to see it, and another is that the inscription was entirely effaced and it still stands there, or went to Traws Mawr. The inscription read: *'deca barbalom (n-) filvs Brocagnl'*, or *'deccaibanvalbdis'* in Ogham.

CELESTINE 5th century
CAELESTIUS

Not a saint, but the British (probably Irish) companion and colleague of Pelagius (q.v.), he was called 'open-hearted' but 'obstinate' by St Augustine in Rome. In 411 he left Italy for Carthage when Alaric sacked Rome. When Pelagius left for Palestine, Celestine tried to have himself made a presbyter at Carthage, but his plans were frustrated by the deacon Paulinus of Milan. Paulinus submitted to Bishop Aurelius a memorial in which six theses of Celestine were branded as heretical. They were:
Even if Adam had not sinned, he would have died.
Adam's sin harmed only himself, not the human race.
Children just born are in the same state as Adam before his fall.
The whole human race neither dies through Adam's sin or death, nor rises again through the resurrection of Christ
The Mosaic Law is as good a guide to heaven as the Gospel.
Even before the advent of Christ there were men without sin.

Because of these doctrines, containing the quintessence of Pelagianism, Celestine was summoned before a synod at Carthage in 411, but refused to retract them. He stated that the inheritance of Adam's sin was an open question and hence its denial was not heresy. As a result his theses were condemned, and he was excluded from ordination. He moved to Ephesus and became a priest there. Pelagianism was seen as a threat to the fabric of the Roman Church, so Pope Zosimus held the famous Council of Carthage on May 1, 418, with 200 bishops attending to discuss the 'heresy'. As a result, Pelagianism was branded as a heresy in 9 canons, as follows:
Death did not come to Adam from a physical necessity, but through sin.
New-born children must be baptised on account of original sin.
Justifying grace not only avails for the forgiveness of past sins, but also gives assistance for the avoidance of future sins.
The grace of Christ not only discloses the knowledge of God's commandments, but also imparts strength to will and execute them.
Without God's grace it is not merely more difficult, but absolutely impossible to perform good works.
The saints refer the petition of the Our Father, "Forgive us our trespasses", not only to others, but also to themselves.
The saints pronounce the same supplication not from mere humility, but from truthfulness.
Not out of humility, but in truth must we confess ourselves to be sinners.
Children dying without baptism do not go to a "middle place" (medius locus), since the non-reception of baptism excludes them both from the "kingdom of heaven" and from "eternal life".

CELLAN see CALLWEN

CELTIC CHRISTIANITY

Richard Davies wrote 'The Letter to the Welsh' as a preface to the 1567 Welsh New Testament, in which he wrote:
'There was a great difference between the Christianity of the Britons and the false Christianity

which Augustine of Canterbury gave the Saxons. The Britons kept their Christianity pure and immaculate, without admixture of human imaginings. Augustine's Christinaity veered rather from the matchless purity of the Gospel, and was mixed in with much superficiality, human opinions and vain ceremonies, which did not accord with the nature of the kingdom of Christ.'

The Celtic Church predated the 4th century, as British bishops were at Arles in 314 and Rimini in 359. It was based upon Wales and its borders, the West Country, Northumbria, Ireland and the west of Britain through Lancashire to Cumbria and Strathclyde. It seems that Breton and Welsh saints were the driving force for evangelism in the 5th and 6th centuries, with Irish missionaries becoming predominant in the 7th century. However, the Southern Irish had joined the Church of Rome in 632, followed by Northumbria in 664, Northern Ireland by 695, and Scotland about 717. Domnonia (Somerset, Devon and Cornwall) acquiesced in 768. The first diocese in Wales to accept the rule of Rome was Bangor in 768 or 777, but the Celtic Church seems to have lasted until the late 11th century in much of Wales, including St David's and Llanbadarn. Indeed, the 'mother-church' and 'clas' system survived across Wales until the 14th century and Anglo-Norman reorganisation.

It is interesting to study the work of the Breton philosopher Ernest Renan (1823-1892) as regards the interlinking ethnicity and attitudes of the Celts. His entry in 'The New Companion to the Literature of Wales' includes the following lines: "*In his view the Celtic nature was reserved, inward-looking, lacking in inititative or political aptitude, fatalistic and given to defending lost causes, yet redeemed by a sensitivity and deep feeling for nature and all living creatures, exhibited in Brittany by the cult of forests, springs and wells. He emphasized the close bonds of blood-relationship which are manifested among all the Celtic peoples and are expressed in their 'backward look' – their faithfulness to their past and to the memory of their dead. He described The Mabinogion as 'the real expression of the Celtic genius' and regarded it, with the legend of Arthur, as the source of all the romantic creations which in the twelfth century had 'changed the direction of the European imagination'. In spite of the threat of modern industrialized civilization, Renan believed firmly that the Celtic peoples had not yet 'said their last word' but might still have a mature and unique contribution to make to European life and culture.*"

CELTIC CROSSES

Many have been destroyed, some of which were recorded by Edward Lhuyd (Llwyd), but there are still around 450 ancient sculptured stones, crosses and allied monuments in Wales. The three major Glamorgan workshops of Llantwit Major, Merthyr Mawr and Margam account for around half of all known crosses, the characteristic being the 'panelled' or 'cartwheel' slab, of which the prime example is the Conbelin cross in the excellently refurbished Margam Stones Museum. By comparison, those inside Llanilltud Fawr church are shoddily displayed and prone to damage. There are several excellent publications with photographs of remarkable sculptures like the Irbic Cross at Llandough, the cross of King Mareddud at Carew and the like, but the author would like to draw attention to *'the most holy Celtic Cross of Wales'*, the *Cross Gneth*.

This was a jewel-studded reliquary which enshrined a small part of the True Cross (itself said to have been brought to Wales). With the rest of the betrayed Llywelyn II's possessions, it was taken by Edward I from Aberffraw in 1283. When Edward III founded the Order of the Garter in 1348, he gave the Cross Gneth to the chapel of the order at Windsor Castle, where it was given its own shrine as the **greatest relic in Britain**. The cross was taken from St George's

Carew Celtic Cross. © *Wales Tourist Board Photo Library.*

Chapel in the 1548 Reformation for the value of its gold casing. A stone roof boss in the chapel shows Edward I and his perfidious Archbishop Beauchamp (Pecham) of Canterbury (instrumental in Llywelyn's capture), kneeling before the relic. It was a classic Celtic cross, taller than a man. 40 days' pardon for sins was granted to anyone kneeling before the cross. There have been many Celtic crosses 'lost' since the days of the saints, some of which were noted by Edward Lhuyd, others unforgivably covered by roads (recently near Miskin, for example), and a new work is need to find and record all the Welsh crosses. Westwood's work 'Lapidarium Walliae' is a start, and non-intrusive churchyard and field boundary surveys will uncover more of Wales' heritage and history. Perhaps politicians may see benefits to Wales in exploiting its past, rather than in supporting the building of temporary temples to Mammon, such as the appallingly tacky Blair-o-Dome on the golden streets of London. (Incidentally, there was a 'dome' at the 1951 Festival of Britain on the South Bank of the Thames. The author possesses the guidebook, and the dome featured themes on the sea, polar regions, the living world, the physical world, the land, the earth, the sky, and outer space, with a polar theatre. All the greatest minds in London got together to plan the failure of the contents of the dome, when a successful exhibition layout was already available in a fifty year-old catalogue which cost two shillings and six pence).

CELTIC SAINTS

British history was rewritten in the 19th century to date from the Germanic invasions of the Saxons and Jutes. Before that were the 'Dark Ages' before Germanic civilisation came to the Isle of Britain. It is interesting that in British (not English) history, this period has always been known as 'The Age of the Saints'. (For those who wish to know why the history of Britain was rewritten, and how, please consult 'The A-Z of Wales and the Welsh' by this author). In 1903, Baring-Gould and Fisher eloquently expressed what these forgotten people gave to the heritage of Britain:

'For centuries, partly due to the sneer of Bede, and partly to the proud contempt with which the Latin Church regarded all missionary work that did not proceed from its own initiative, the English Church has looked to Augustine of Canterbury as the one main source from whom Christianity in our island sprang, and Rome as the mother who sent him to bring our ancestors to Christ. That he did a good and great work is not to be denied; he was the Apostle of Kent, where the Britons had all been massacred or from whence they had been driven. But Kent is only a corner of the island. And it was forgotten how much was wrought by the Celtic Church, even for the Teutonic invaders, **far more than was achieved by Augustine**.

It was the Church in Wales which sent a stream of missionaries to Ireland to complete its conversion, begun by Patrick . . . It was from Ireland that Columcille went to Iona to become evangelist to the Picts. From Llanelwy went forth Kentigern with 665 monks and clerics to restore Christianity in Cumbria, which extended from the Clyde to the Dee. It was from Iona that the missioners proceeded who converted all Northumbria, Mercia, and the East Saxons and Angles. Honour to whom honour is due, and **the debt of obligation to the Celtic saints in the British Isles has been ignored or set aside hitherto**.

But they did more. To them was due the conversion of Armorica. Evidence shows that nothing, or next to nothing, was done for the original inhabitants of that peninsula by the stately prelates of the Gallo-Roman Church. They ministered to the city populations of Nantes and Rennes and Vannes, and did almost nothing for the scattered natives of the province. They were left to live in their heathenism and die without the light, till the influx of British colonists changed the whole aspect, and brought the people of the land into the fold of Christ.'

The Irish connection, with the Welshman Patrick and contributions from the way of Christianity in Wales, has never been truly assessed. The Irish, with their flair for publicity, can publish books like Thomas Cahill's *'HOW THE IRISH SAVED CIVILIZATION: the Untold Story of Ireland's Heroic Role from the Fall of Rome to the Rise of Medieval Europe'* (Sceptre 1995 paperback) – a Welsh book could have been written with the same title and probably more validity. (The book's title capitals are reproduced exactly). It totally ignores the fact that the Irish church was basically a Welsh construct upon a formerly heathen population. The church in Wales lasted from the earliest days of Christianity in the Western world through to the present day. **In all other European countries the Christian church was extinguished at some time**, including Ireland except for a few hermits clinging to rocks in the Atlantic. The survival of Christianity in Wales is as amazing as the survival of its language over this period, with such close proximity to England. In Ireland and Scotland, the language has all but died, despite their relatively greater distance from the power of the government of the south-east of England.

CELTS

Herodotus (c. 485-425 BC) wrote of the Celts of Spain, fifty years or so after Hecataeus of Miletus had described Massalia (Marseilles) in Liguria in the land of the Celts. It seems that they originated around 1200 BC in the Danube Basin, the Alps and parts of France and Germany. Their assorted tribes slowly pushed across Europe, from the great walls of Thessaloniki to Portugal. Around 600 BC they intermarried in the Iberian Peninsula, where they were known as the Iberian Celts. Upon July 18, 390 BC, the Celts sacked Rome, and in 273 BC Delphi suffered the same fate.

In terms of British history, there were two distinct tribes of Celts. The Goidelic Celts were the first to arrive in southern Ireland, around 400 BC, quickly taking over all of the rest of Ireland, then moving into the Isle of Man and Scotland. They came from Spain and Portugal, the Iberian Celts. From these Goidels comes the Gaelic language. Shortly after this migration, the Brythonic Celts came from France, Bretons closely related to the Frankish Gauls. These moved into England and Wales, and thus the British languages of Brittany, Cornwall, and Wales are closely linked.

CELYNIN 7th century
CELYNEN
November 2 Caernarfon (November 20 Merioneth)

The son of Helig Foel, he founded Llangelynin in Merioneth and also in Caernarfon. St Celynin's church, on the coast between Tywyn and Fairbourne in Merioneth, is used only in the summer months. Ffynnon Gelynin in Caernarfon had a roof and three sides of stone seats. Sickly children were immersed in it, wrapped in a blanket and allowed to sleep. The children's clothes were washed in the well – if they floated the child would recover, if not it would die. Children were also baptised in this well, which used to be housed in a building measuring around 15 feet by 12 feet. Ffynnon Gwynwy was also near his Caernarfon church. To cure warts a bent pin had to be dropped in the well before bathing, or the forgetful sufferer would 'catch' the warts that had dropped off previous bathers.

Capel Celyn, drowned under Liverpool's reservoir at Trywerin, may be Celynin's church. Plaid Cymru developed a scheme to dam a tributary of the Trywerin to give Liverpool its water with no inhabitants displaced, but the village and farms of the valley had to go under the waters after a Parliamentary vote. Only one of the Welsh MP's sided with the Government, and in 1957 the bill was passed by 175 votes to 79. The opening of Llyn Celyn reservoir was disrupted by angry crowds in 1965. London-based democracy has never worked for Wales – the Welsh have the lowest standards of living in the British Isles. Perhaps the new Welsh Assembly can vote to dam the Thames and flood London – it is the same principle at work. Probably no other event in the 20th century sparked the resurgence of Welsh nationalism as much as this reservoir. The fact that the Welsh pay far more for their water than the English also does not help the situation. There is an appeal fund to erect a huge sculpture of a bird rising from the shores of

Llyn Celyn, and contributions can be sent to the Ymddiriedolaeth Tryweryn Memorial Fund at Ty Newydd, Llanuwchllyn, Y Bala, Gwynedd LL23 7TL. Professor Hywel Teifi Edwards launched the appeal with the words *'The event was a watershed in our history and we certainly have an opportunity in this project to establish Tryweryn as a symbol of our determination as a nation to demand our rightful responsibilites. We shall rise with confidence above the reservoir waters.'* Sadly, Liverpool's need for the water has all but disappeared, with the demise of its manufacturing industry.

In 1940 a huge area of the Brecon Beacons, Mynydd Epynt, was compulsorily requisitioned by the Ministry of Defence as a firing range, destroying an organic, Welsh-speaking community. Fifty-four Welsh-speaking families were ejected from their ancestral lands within days in 1940 to use the land as a firing range. Other war-related take-overs of Welsh land occurred at Pendine, Penbre, Castlemartin, Llandathan and Penyberth, the last-named causing prison sentences for the founders of the Welsh Nationalist party*. There is absolutely no reason for a Christian-Socialist country, which has never declared war on another country in its history, to have imposed upon it the machinery of war.

It is worth repeating the fact that a Welsh jury in Caernarfon refused to convict the 'Penyberth Three' in 1936. The trial was therefore transferred to the Old Bailey to achieve the 'right sentence', which took just a few minutes. The British legislative system demanded an immediate form of 'justice', as in the case of many wrongfully imprisoned Irish victims in the last few decades. The British are the most heavily 'propagandised' nation in the Western world – we are told that our legal system is the fairest (which it is, if you are rich); that our society is best (with the highest teenage parenthood, dirtiest streets, most prisoners per head of population and highest crime rates in Europe); our education is outstanding (this is laughable, it is one of the worst); our National Health Service is the envy of the world (with fiddled statistics, and early death rates); our employment rate is the best in Europe (again only because of changed statistics, with part-time jobs being included, and older people transferred onto sickness registers); our standard of living is excellent (it is for politicians); our economy is an example to the world (it is foreign-owned by multinational companies who pay no British corporate taxes, thus forcing the higher loading of indirect personal taxation); our taxes are low (they are not – they are hidden, causing higher prices for petrol and thousands of items compared to Europe); our food is cheap (it is expensive compared to Europe, where take-home pay is higher, because of the greed of the major supermarket chains); and that our political system is an exemplar (read about Trywerin again). Politicians in positions of power know absolutely nothing about real families and their socio-economic problems outside the prosperous south-east of England, and seem not to want to know. The next 'flash-point' in Welsh history may be the plan to dump nuclear waste at Trecwn outside Fishguard. If this is given approval, in a country which has never declared war on another in its 2000-year-history, then the path to independence will be shortened.

'An Uprooted Community – a History of Epynt' by Herbert Hughes is available from Gomer Press. 'Tal y Llyn' by Dafydd Jenkins, published in Welsh in 1937, has been reprinted by the Welsh Academic Press as 'A Nation on Trial', and tells the awful story of Penyberth.

CELYNIN 6th century
January 7 and All Saints Day

One of the five saintly quintuplets of Llanpumsaint and the ruined Capel Pumsaint under Caio in Carmarthen. There was also a Lann Celinni in Archenfield, Hereford noted in 1100 - see Ceitho and Cynyr.

CENAU

This saint was said to be a cousin of David

CENEDLON see ENDELENTIA

CENEDLON 7th century?

Daughter of Briafel, she married Arthfael ab Ithel, King of Gwent and is said to have founded Rockfield near Monmouth, although it became dedicated to Kenelm. St Michael's Well in Rockfield parish had stones spotted with red 'blood', and Lhuyd recorded that a saint had been beheaded there, which indicated that it predates the Michael dedication. Franciscan friars from Rockfield made annual pilgrimages to Priest's Well in Darran Wood, a curative well under an ancient oak tree.

CENEU 5th century
June 15

A warrior, son of Coel Godebog and Ystrafael (Cadrawd's sister). He was a saint in Brecon, and is supposed to have founded Llangeneu under Llangattock, which also had his famous holy well. In an ancient chapel nearby was found an ancient iron bell weighing seven pounds, typically shaped like the old 'bangu' with two iron plates hammered together. It is now in the Library of University College, Cardiff, but should be displayed in the National Museum of Wales. His son was St Mor, and his grandson was Cynllo. In 1851, it was noted that the Celtic stone at Llangeneu had disappeared 'quite recently'. It was marked on old maps in a field between Crickhowell and Llangeneu.

CENEU ferch BRYCHAN see CAIN

BISHOP CENEU GWYNCENEU late 6th century

Bishop of Menevia when Euddogwy was bishop of Llandaf, he founded Llangeneu, a church in Pembroke which did not survive the Fleming settlements in the south of that county, although it is mentioned in the Laws of Hywel Dda. Probably the son of Corun ap Ceredig, and the third or fourth Bishop of St David's. There is a Geneu'r Glyn in Cardiganshire, whose vicar John Davies wrote in 1656 of 'death omens'. Everyone in the district, including himself had seen them, and they took the form of lights, which were white, becoming red or sometimes blue.

They appeared outside but sometimes entered houses, and were seen indoors. When one walked towards them, they vanished, but reappeared behind one. If the light was small, a baby or child would die; if larger, an adult was sure to expire soon. The number of lights seen gave the number of imminent deaths. Rev. Davies had seen such lights at Llanrhystud. His wife's sister, Jane Wyatt, saw five lights together in a room in Llangathen. That night five servants were suffocated by a burning lime and coal mix, when sleeping there. His wife's mother, Catherine Wyatt, saw twin lights on her own body shortly before she gave birth to two still-born children in Tenby. He gives many other examples, noted in T. Gwynne Jones' seminal work on Welsh folklore. Many people saw a light hovering over the river at Llanilar, a few weeks before a girl drowned trying to cross it.

CENYDD 6th century
CENNYDD, KYNED, KENED, KENETH
July 5 (Llangennith Mabsant), August 1, June 27

The son of Gildas and grandson of Caw, he married and fathered two sons before becoming a monk under St Illtud at Llanilltud Fawr. Other sources state that he trained at nearby Llancarfan. His saintly brothers were Madog, Dolgan, Nwython, Gwynno and Garci, and his sister was Dolgar. He then founded a religious society, Côr Cennydd, where there is now the church of Llangennydd (Llangennith) on the Gower peninsula. It was said that he founded a great church north of Cardiff, which gave its name to the district of Seinghenydd, i.e. Senghenydd. He then travelled to Brittany, where Ploumelin is the centre of his cult. St David was said to have cured Cenydd of a deformity, but Cenydd asked for it to be restored as he was not a vain man.

A legend tells us that Cenydd was cast adrift in the Loughor Estuary, a baby in a wickerwork basket, by parents who were trying to conceal their adultery. This was at a feast to celebrate Christmas, held by King Arthur. He then grew up, fed by gulls, on the Worm's Head near Rhossili on the Gower Peninsula. An angel told him to establish a church at Llangennith (Llangenydd) on the nearby mainland, but he later retired and lived as a hermit upon the nearby island of Burry Holms. The island, with a Mesolithic settlement, a Bronze Age cairn and an Iron Age fort, can be reached at low tide. Neither St Cenydd's hermitage nor St Caradoc of Rhos's oratory and cell survive. Norman remains lie over Cenydd's shrine, which itself is among Iron Age dwellings. Archaeologists have found a complex of church buildings including a church, large hall, rounded and square chancels and a schoolroom or scriptorium. It is likely that the Reformation ended the flow of pilgrims to Cenydd's shrine, and as monies dried up, the settlement fell into decline. His sons were Ufelwy and Ffili (Caerffili is named after this saint, and there is a nearby Bryn Cenydd, and a ruined chapel at Senghennydd. However, Blackett and Wilson believe that Ufelwy and Ffili are the same person). There is an elaborate Celtic sandstone slab in St Cenydd's Church in Llangennith, Gower, referred to as 'Cenydd's Stone', and supposed to mark his burial place. It used to be in the centre of the chancel floor, and appears to have been used in conjunction with the saint's skull which was venerated here until the Reformation. Two more incised cross-slabs are in the wall of the vestry.

Near the church is Llangennith Well, with a capstone which bears an incised cross. Ilston Well (Ffynnon Genydd) which cured sore eyes, is on the Gower near his chapel. Ilston (Illtud's Town) has the oldest Baptist Chapel in Wales (1650) but unfortunately it was built with stones from Cenydd's well-chapel. The Baptist Chapel eventually decayed and the holy well destroyed. There is also a Ffynnon Gynydd near Glasbury in Radnorshire, which may be Cenydd's. As late as 1910 a well-house was erected over this holy 'wishing well'.

In Brittany he settled at Languidic near his father's great monastery at Castanec. There are five avenues of upright stones there, said to be pagans who pursued the saint and were turned to stone. Nearby Kervili is the equivalent of Caerphilly in Wales. He is also remembered at Ploumelin and Plaintel in Brittany. At the great Llangennith Mabsant, a huge cauldron of flour and milk was boiled up and the *'white pot'*, also called *'milked meat'* was drunk. This commemorated the legend that Cenydd was brought up on does' milk sipped from a holy bell, the *'cloch dethog'*, or *'titty bell'* as described by Baring-Gould and Fisher.

A 'Saying of the Wise ' given to Cenydd ab Aneurin (Gildas) is *'none is void of care but the religious.'*

CENWYN

Possibly a saint of Llanbadarn Fawr in Cardigan, and he may be the founder of nearby Cilcennin (Cennin's Retreat), although it is now dedicated to the Holy Trinity.

CERAINT AP BERWYN AP MORGAN AP BLEDDYN 3rd century

Not a saint, but included for his far-reaching effects upon mankind. According to the Genealogy of Iestyn ap Gwrgan, Prince of Glamorgan, King *'Ceraint the Drunkard, the son of Berwyn, was the first who made malt liquor properly: and the commencement was thus:- After he had boiled the wort, together with field flowers and honey, a boar came there, and, drinking of it, cast in his foam, which caused the liquor to ferment. The beer thus prepared, was superior to any known before; and thence arose the practice of putting barm in wort. Having attained this knowledge, Ceraint gave himself up entirely to drunkenness; in which state he died.'*

CERI 1st - 2nd century
Midsummer Day?

A prince of Glamorgan, the son of Caid ab Arch, after whom Porthceri (Porthkerry as it is known today, with 'c' and 'k' being interchangeable in old Welsh) is probably named. He was said to be Caradog's nephew, who took over the Silure kingdom when Caradog was taken to Rome. Even in Norman times there was a Porthceri Castle, where Castle Rock can sometimes be seen at very low tides. Porthceri was a port (now a country park) and Ceri 'Longsword' was said to have constructed warships to defend the Glamorgan and Gwent coastlines. Edward Mansel mentions that the Normans invaded via this port. Two miles west of Porthceri is Fontygari, a village now joined to Rhoose, next to Cardiff Wales airport. This seems to stem from Ffynnon Ceri, Ffynnon Tŷ Ceri or Geri, and there was an ancient well in East Aberthaw nearby. There is also a well marked on 1885 maps at the opening to Fontygary beach. (Both wells appear to have disappeared, the former recently covered by 14,000,000 tones of ash from a power station.) William Thomas in 1788 calls the place Fondegary, which seems to confirm it as Ffynnon Tŷ Geri. There was also a Caer Ceri (Castell Ceri) in Llanilid, Glamorgan, mentioned by Nennius and in the Triads. Ffynnon Ceri was near the field called Castell Ceri, and a paved causeway was found there three hundred years ago. Gwyl Geri was held for several days in Midsummer between the churchyard and a tumulus called Y Gaer Gronn (circular fortress). Perhaps future editions will be enlightened by contributions from readers on the link between Curig and Ceri, as the holy well named Ffynnon Geri at Llanilid was associated with Curig. Ceri's relatives Caractacus, Eurgain and Bran of the 1st century are also linked with Llanilid.

Mentioned under St Corbre is 'the grave of Ceri', and Blackett and Wilson place his burial in a large boat-shaped grave at Nash Point in Glamorgan. The ancient site here is still called 'Hen Eglwys' (Old Church), as in the Corbre triad.

On the 9th September, 1762, two men of the Glamorgan Militia allowed 30 French prisoners to escape from custody in Bristol, for which they each received 1,000 lashes, given in instalments of 400, 300 and 300. The 19 year-old William James of Fontygary died in June 1763 from the effects of the whipping, and is buried in neighbouring Penmark churchyard. William Thomas records that it was Edward James of Porthkerry that suffered, with another man from Carmarthen, however. He states that a collar was placed around their necks for the whipping, then they were to go to London to be shot, but were reprieved. They were both of Captain Jones of Fonmon's Company of Grenadiers, and Thomas unsympathetically notes *'Our Militia are a reproach to our shire.'* On September 17th he wrote *'Our Militia very rude and neglecting duty by drinking and whoreing, that the Evening past Thomas Robert received 50 lashes for drinking. He was the son to Hary Robert, late of Sparrow's house in St Faggans. Also Edwards James . . . and the other . . . received 300 lashes each and were this evening to receive 300 each more and to be drummed out. The French, by our Militia giving them freedom for money, is gone very bold, that one of them was shoot dead a few days past from the wall and another run through etc. Jack of the Hendy has been lashed, but not drumed out as the report came. Our Militia, wherever they goes is a shame to our Shire, that Earl Talbot of Hensol, the Colonel, have send a letter to send them away somewhere, and 400 invalids are send to Bristol in their stead to guard the Franch prisoners and the report is they will soon come home.'* War prisoners were kept on rotting men-of-war, the 'hulks' in Bristol Docks. *'Welchmen these few years past have almost fill Bristol, that oftenly two Welchmen can be found to one Englishman, for the English goes abroad and the Welchmen fill England in their stead.'*

A day after this entry, there were riots in Bristol between the Glamorgan Militia and sailors, where several were injured and two sailors killed. William Thomas then noted that Edward James received a warrant from London, after his 1000 lashes *'to shot him to death. Our Militia have made the City of Bristol, as they did Exeter, a Brothel. Of all the militia in the kingdom the most vicious . . . '* On October 5th, 1762, a further entry is *'Also heard that Edward James of Porthkerry, one of our Militia men were not shoot, but lashed in such condition that the surgeon had work to clean his bones, for he was lashed till the bones naked and the other with him that left out the French.'*

Kerry* in Montgomery (of sheep breed fame) is named after a person called Ceri (also see Michael, after whom the church is now named). This church has a blocked North door, which used to be opened to allow the devil to escape during baptisms. The Neolithic stone circle at Kerry Hill (OS ref. 157860) is one of the three most important such sites in Britain, *'as its compound ring led to the Avebury construction.'* There are only 8 stones remaining with one in the centre, and one pair of stones on the east side of the circle has small circular hollows containing a circle of six dots. The same pattern can be seen on the stone east of Arthur's Stone at Reynoldston.

The nearby Llanrhaeadr stone circle is based on the sun and the 1st magnitude star, Spica. Built some 2000 years BC, it is of particular interest as it has an avenue of stones, 180 feet long leading to it. Tradition is that this site, Rhos y Beddau (Moor of the Graves), was where Owain Gwynedd's dead warriors were laid out after fighting the English army which came up Ffordd y Saeson (English Way) from Maengwynedd. Forced to retreat by the weather, King Henry blinded all his Welsh captives, including two sons of Owain Gwynedd. The 12 feet high standing stone, Post Coch, in Llanrhaeadr, was set up to destroy a dragon. It was draped with red cloth and studded with spikes, and a dragon repeatedly attacked it until it died on the spikes. (This information is from Phillips 'A View of Old Montgomeryshire').

*A letter sent from Kerry to Henry III in 1259 shows how the ancient Celtic social control mechanism of 'galanas' (a compensation payment paid by the kinship group) was breaking down in Wales:
'The men of Kery, both great and small beg that the laws of the King of England's realm should be granted to them everywhere throughout Wales and the March that is - that the innocent be not punished for the guilty, and that if a member of a kin-group should commit a murder or theft or sedition then it should not be blamed on that kin-group itself. They also ask that when cases have been adjudged in the King's court and their own, then the King's bailiffs should not try to try the case a second time. In witness wherof the following persons of the men of Kery, great and small, have set their seals to this letter.
Einion Grug, Maredudd ap Hywel, Raldulphus ap Maredudd, Einion ap Hywel, Cadwgan Goch, Gruffydd ap Goronwy, Gruffydd ap Grogenau, Iorwerth Fychan . . . '

CERNYW see DIGAIN

CERWYDD 7th century
CEWYDD?

The ruined St James's Church at Lancaut, north of Chepstow, lies in a loop of spectacular scenery flanked by the river Wyndcliffe, near Offa's Dyke. It is claimed to be the smallest parish in England, and the church was founded around AD700, and dedicated to St Cerwydd, who had other church dedications in this River Wye area. All this area was Welsh-speaking, and Welsh was still the predominant language here until 1450. The Normans rededicated the church to James shortly after 1066, but it was not until the late Middle Ages that the local population officially took any notice and abandoned their saint. A stone Saxon font from Lancaut now lies in The Lady Chapel at Gloucester Cathedral. The Norman church was abandoned in the 1860's. 'Cerwydd' is the name given by Davis and Lloyd-Fern ('Lost Churches of Wales and the Marches'), but it seems this saint may be Cewydd. The imposing Chepstow Castle (the first stone castle in Britain) is just a mile away, and an Iron Age promontory hill-fort and deserted village are near Lancaut.

Alphabetical Listing of the Saints of Wales and Religious Events

CEWYDD 6th century
HEN GEWYDD Y GLAW, (Old Cewydd of the Rain)
July 15 (and July 1, 2), second week in July

This son of Caw founded Aberedw and Dyserth (Diserth) in Radnorshire, and also the church (now vanished) at Llangewydd near Bridgend in Glamorgan. There are many place names associated with Cewydd near it, and the author has just discovered that the beautiful woodland walk from Monknash to Traeth Mawr, is in a valley known as Cwm Cewydd. Laleston in Glamorgan was known as Llangewydd, according to Fisher.

Gerald of Wales, in his 'Speculum Ecclesiae' noted the destruction wrought by the great abbeys when they took over parish churches *'All the monasteries in Wales are involved in one and the same vice . . . for they are wont to occupy the parish of mother and baptismal church, and either in large measure diminish their extent or obtain complete control over them, expelling the parishioners and leaving the churches empty and deserted.'* He stated that the monks from the Margam Grange of Llangewydd took the church from the parson and then proceeded to evict the parishioners. At night, upon instruction from superiors, they demolished the ancient church dedicated to St Cewydd, and took away all the building materials so that no trace remained. The field is still called *'Cae'r Hen Eglwys' (Field of the Old Church)*. It is so important to list and ascribe all the old field names in Wales before they are only known by numbers, as legally required by EU law at present. The monastic grange at Monknash was owned by Margam Abbey, so there is a further link with Cewydd, and perhaps Monknash Church was his foundation. This may be an opportunity for Andrew Davies, the celebrated owner of Wales' best pub, the Plough and Harrow at Monknash, to throw one of his famous festivals.

This 'rain saint' was known in Glamorgan as *'Hen Gewydd y Gwlaw' (Old Cewyd of the Rain)*, and his tradition was transferred to St Swithun by the Saxons. July 2nd was the traditional date, replaced by July 15th over time, partly because of the '12 days' date change. At Dyserth Cewydd's wake was held on the first Sunday after St Swithun's Day (July 15), and at Aberedw in the second week in July. Gwyl Gewydd y Glaw was held at Llancarfan on July 1st and 2nd. July 15 in the 19th century was known in South Wales as *'Dygwyl Gewydd'*, with the similar belief to Swithun's Day that 40 days of rain would follow rainfall. This echoes some pre-Christian belief. In Dyfed, there was a tradition that Noah's Deluge started on July 15.
His 'Saying of the Wise' was:
'Have you heard the saying of St Cewydd
To his numerous relatives?
"There is no true friend but the Lord." '

The St Swithun's tradition dates from the transferrence of Swithun's relics into Winchester Cathedral on July 15th, 971. This former bishop had died in 862. The occasion was marked by heavy rainfall, so it seems more than likely that the Cewydd tradition of 500 years earlier was picked up. In Brittany however, Gildas became their 'rain saint'.

There was a Ffynnon Gewydd near the church of Dyserth. 'Disserth', by W. H. Howse, contains the following tale about the ghost of a dishonest tanner in the 18th century: *'Parson Jones summoned the spirit to meet him in Disserth church, and there with three other parsons he faced the spirit, his awed congregation crowding into the churchyard. They saw four parsons enter, armed with books and candles. Presently three of the parsons, paralysed with fear, joined the crowd outside: the devil had blown out their candles. Parson Jones saved his light by hiding it in his top-boot and . . . At last he emerged triumphant, carrying in his hand a silver snuff box, in which he said was the evil spirit . . . reduced to the size of a blue-bottle fly. It was tied to the top of an iron bar and forced into the depths of the quaking mire.'*

Cusop, near Hay on Wye (Y Gelli Gandryll) is also dedicated to Cewydd.

CHAD d. 672
CEADDA
March 2

This British saint is included because he founded Lichfield, which was claimed as part of the episcopacy of St David's by Owain Glyndŵr. The superb illuminated manuscript in Lichfield Cathedral, known as the Book of St Chad, is in fact the Chartulary of Llandaf, formerly in Llandeilo, and was taken from Llandaf cathedral. It should be returned – Wales has been stripped of too many of its treasures. Chadwell is a holy well near St Chad's in Hanmer, Denbighshire, and there is also a Chadwell near Clun in Radnor.

The Gospel predates the Book of Kells, and has many 8th and 9th century entries in Welsh minuscule script, denoting its ownership by a Teilo foundation. When it was taken from Wales is uncertain. Incidentally, it seems that when the court at Aberffraw was ransacked after the death of Llywelyn in 1282, gold and jewels were taken to bolster the Crown Jewel collection in the Tower of London. The most holy relic in Britain, a fragment of the True Cross, was also taken, with Llywelyn's crown. The court and church were destroyed. The rapacity of the Normans meant that anything Welsh was taken or burnt as they slowly took possession over lands belonging to Welsh princes. There are also indications of genocide after 1282 in parts of Wales.

CHRIST

Early dedications to Jesus, Christ or the Holy Cross are almost non-existent in Wales – they came with Norman and later influences. Capel Crist at Llannarth in Cardigan may be one of the older dedications.

CHRISTMAS – the Mass (Religious Festival) of Christ
GWYL GENI CRIST, Y NADOLIG
December 25 (January 6, Old Style)

This is a fairly recent festival that in many ways displaced all the various saints' feasts and traditions in Wales (see Carols). According to Luke, Mary gave birth during a population census, ordered by Cyrenius, the Roman governor of Syria. Judaea was a dependency, where Herod was King. This census took place in AD 6 or 7, i.e. some 12 - 13 years after the accepted birth of Jesus in 6 BC. Thus Jesus may have never lived to be thirty, and possibly died in his mid-20's. Christian scholars have never fully resolved their problems – whatever the truth of Christ's birth year, it is certain that the Millennium festival was being celebrated in London, at enormous cost to the rest of Britain, in the wrong month about six years too early. The Millennium Dome is an order of political folly and human aggrandisement not being replicated in any other country in the world. A billion pounds being distributed to the underclass of

Alphabetical Listing of the Saints of Wales and Religious Events

Britain would have been a more Christian act, than the building of a temporary temple to Mammon in the acknowledged European centre of capitalism and greed. The 'socialist' party of Mr Blair has moved a long way in the last decade, from its proximity to the working classes outside the south-east of England. Mr Blair is notoriously 'computer-illiterate' for a man of his age and education, but he can surely do 'sums'. With a family ticket costing £56, and over £100 to take a family by train to London, plus the additional costs of a day out, plus possibly 8-10 hours travelling time there and back, what normal Welsh family will visit the Dome?

Until the 4th century, the most common dates given for Jesus' birth were March 28, April 18 or May 29. Then the established Church decided that Jesus had lived for exactly 30 years. From the moment of Incarnation, he lived for exactly 9 months in Mary's womb, then lived on Earth for another exact 29 years and three months. The fathers of the Church agreed that Jesus' date of execution was April 6, so took away 29 years and 3 months to give his birth-date as January 6. This is still the accepted date in the Eastern Orthodox Church, known as Epiphany (Greek for 'appearance'), when the Son of God descended to earth. So we have the probable date of Jesus' birth, by tradition, as March, April or May, with a later imposed date of January.

However, nothing is simple in history. As Christianity advanced throughout Europe and North Africa, it came up against the great pagan festival of Sol Invictus, falling on December 25. This was when the virgin goddess of heaven (sometimes called Isis) gave birth to the sun god (Horus). On December 25, Winter had reached its peak, and Isis peeped over the horizon, preparing for Spring. The Roman Empire allowed the belief to flourish. Emperor Constantine was persuaded to absorb the attributes of this hugely popular cult into Christianity. Isis 'became' the Virgin Mary, and the sun god Horus 'became' Jesus. The Nativity, which was actually in Spring, was used to fuse the two faiths together. Thus only from the the fifth century, December 25 was the Mass of Christ, the religious festival to commemorate His birth. During the Middle Ages, the festival began upon December 25 and ended upon Epiphany, January 6, giving us the 'Twelve Days of Christmas.' So we can see that Christ was born in March, April or May in the year 6 or 7, which was first altered to January 6 in the year 0, then to December 25. The fact that 'nothing' happened historically in the year 0, is beyond this author's powers of explanation. The West moved from 1BC, missing out the year 0, straight into 1AD.

The above facts are taken from an article by the Welsh author Gordon Thomas ('Faith and Fact', The Western Mail, December 19, 1998). A well-known 'thriller' writer, born in Ammanford, he has written several books on theology and Christianity, the latest being 'Mary Magdalene', published in 1998. The purpose of this explanation is to emphasise the importance of our saints' days. Much about Christmas – the presents, carols, snow on the stable, dates, etc., etc. - is simply bogus. It is a time of excess, a time of spending, not of 'giving'; a time of great stress on many people to meet the demands of a materialistic world; a time of absurd over-indulgence that creates financial problems for many. Most of the traditions associated with Christmas come from America in the late 19th century. Clement Moore (1779-1863) wrote the seminal *'The Night Before Christmas'*, inventing St Nicholas with his reindeer (Dasher, Dancer, Prancer, Vixen, Comet, Cupid, Donder and Blitzen) flying through the night sky. He also invented a chubby St Nicholas coming down the chimney *'dressed all in fur'* with a sack of toys on his back, *'filling stockings'*. The fat, pink, father Christmas also comes from this American children's poem - *'His cheeks were like roses, his nose like a cherry'*. In the 1860's, shop Santas were invented in America to encourage more spending, and the British stores followed this habit in the 1870's. In 1931, Coca-Cola used Santa Claus in its winter advertising campaign, building on Clement Moore's model and adding black boots and the red tunic with fur trim that we all recognise today. (Until the middle of the 19th century, the active ingredient of Coca-Cola was coca-leaf extract, which led to a mild form of cocaine addiction, possibly suffered by the illustrator, Haddon Sunblom). Another American trend that has not so far hit Britain is that started by the First Church of the Nazarene in Little Rock, Arkansas. In 1999 there was a 'drive-thru' Nativity for drivers to experience *'the true meaning of Christmas without leaving their cars.'*

The Christmas tree is also a fairly modern innovation in Britain. The Welsh phrase for Father Christmas, Sion Corn, only dates from the 20th century. Another 20th century innovation, 'political correctness', recently manifested itself in Shropshire. Its council decided that Santa's beard in its libraries frightened children, and substituted a Mother Christmas. At least in Britain we do not have the worries of choosing presents that they must have in Latvia. There, Father Christmas brings presents on the 12 Days of Christmas, starting on Christmas Eve.

St Nicholas' Day is December 6 – he was a Turkish saint of the 4th century. Dutch immigrants in New York called him Sinter Klaas, from where we have Santa Claus. Christmas Cards did not occur until the first Penny Post service began in 1840, and started to be manufactured in large numbers in the 1860's. Hanging stockings is a Victorian invention, where stockings were hung up to dry overnight in a fireplace to catch any coins or baubles that Father Christmas dropped when descending the chimney. It was based on the legend of St Nicholas throwing bags of gold through windows. Any gift from an unknown source was thereafter attributed to him.

The hanging of greenery around a house (holly, ivy and mistletoe) is a pre-Christian tradition, to lift winter spirits and remind people that Spring was approaching. Sprigs of holly were placed on beehives, as it was believed that bees hummed in honour of Jesus on the first Christmas. Holly came to represent the crown of thorns of Christ and its red berries his drops of blood. Mistletoe was formerly used by the druids as it had mystical powers to bring good luck and ward off evil spirits. The fir tree was added to the 'green' element in relation to a legend of St Boniface in Germany. It was first used in Britain when the German princeling, Albert of Saxe-Coburg-Gotha, set one up in Windsor Castle in 1841 for Queen Victoria and their children. The habit was first taken up by German industrialists working in Manchester in the 1840's. Candles represented stars on the tree, and an American telephonist solved the fire risk by inventing electric Christmas tree lights. Christmas Crackers were invented in 1850 by Tom Smith, a London sweet-manufacturer, as a way of selling more sweets and gifts.

The Yule Log is generally thought to be a medieval Nordic custom, where a huge log was fed into a fire over the twelve days of festivities. However, its burning was an old custom in Wales when recorded by Guto'r Glyn and Tewdwr Aled in the 15th century. The *'cyff Nadolig'* was placed behind the fire, and at Llanfyllin and Llansanffraid-ym-Mechain a portion was kept as a charm to mix with the crop seeds for the following spring. A description survives of the custom in Shropshire, when the yule-log was burned over several days, being placed *'at the back of a large square hearth, the fire for general use being made up in front of it, the embers raked up to it every night, and the log carefully tended that it did not go out. During the twelve days of Christmas no light must be struck, given or borrowed.'*

In some areas of Wales such as Dyfed, New Year's Day was a far more important day than Christmas, even in the early 20th century (see Cynwyl). Christmas was just another Sunday. In many parts of Wales, such as Llanfyllin (see Myllin), Christmas meant staying up overnight, or rising early for the 'plygain' service that was celebrated in the church between 3am and 6am.

Alphabetical Listing of the Saints of Wales and Religious Events

This was still celebrated in Llanllyfni, Caernarfon in the 1940's, but discontinued at Llanfair Dyffryn Clwyd during the 1939-1945 war and ended at Llansannan and Llancynfelyn around 1900.

Cromwell's followers abhorred Christmas, and in Canterbury on Decenber 22nd, 1647, its abolition was proclaimed by decree of the English Parliament. It was known to Puritans at this time as *'Heathen's Feasting Day.'* A little-known fact is the origin of 'Boxing Day', St Stephen's Day, December 26. The locked alms boxes kept in churches were opened on the day after Christmas, and the donations distributed to the poor and needy of the parish. Traditionally, this was the only day of the year that household retainers and servants did not have to work and could spend time with their families. There is a relic of this mediaeval custom of opening alms boxes, in the 'tips' (the 'Christmas box') we give to delivery boys, postmen and refuse collectors today.

In the four weeks preceding Christmas, 2.5 billion letters and parcels are posted in Britain. If we assume that 2 billion are Christmas Cards, then the cost of postage and cards is probably in the order of 2 billion times 30 pence, or £600,000,000. Perhaps if/when these transactions are replaced by e-mails, there can be a scheme of charity donation to take the place of Christmas posting.

CIAN 7th century
December 11

The servant of St Peris, commemorated with Peris at Llangian, under Llanbedrog in Caernarfon. Yr Allor Dolmen, with a capstone measuring twelve feet square, is on Foel Gron Hill, Llangian, and there is a standing stone at Pandy. There was a holy well on Mynydd Mynytho in Llangian parish. An ancient stone in Llangian churchyard stands almost four feet high, and is inscribed *'MELI MEDICI FILI MARTINI JACET'*.

CIANAN 6th century
February 25

From Glamorgan, a disciple of St Jaoua, who accompanied him to Brittany and settled at Abbot Judual's Landevennec. Around 567, Jaoua (Jouvin) succeeded his uncle Pawl as Bishop of Leon, and sent Cianan to Plouguerneau, where he is remembered.

CILLO

There is a Norman church dedicated to Peter at Llancillo in Hereford, next to Llancillo Court, but nothing further as yet is known of its foundation.

CIWA see KEW

CIWG 6th century
June 29

Ciwg ab Aron ap Cynfarch was descended from Coel Hen and founded Llangiwg in Glamorgan. His father was given lands by Arthur, according to Geoffrey of Monmouth. His 'Saying of the Wise' is:
'Have you heard the saying of Ciwg,
The truly wise bard of Gwynhylwg?
"The possessor of discretion is far-sighted." '

CLASAU – MOTHER CHURCHES IN WALES

A 'clas' was a body of canons, usually hereditary, attached to a mother church. The Normans destroyed the 'clas' system of the Celtic Church by suppressing the clasau and transferring their endowments to monasteries in England or on the Contintent. Thus, the possessions of Llanilltud Fawr passed to Tewkesbury. To accelerate their break-up, Latin-type monasteries were introduced into Wales, the first being established by the Benedictines. Built under the shadow of Norman castles, they never flourished in those parts of Wales which were for any length of time in Welsh hands. Throughout their existence, the Black Monks of the Benedictine Order were suspected by the Welsh, and were recruited from a non-Welsh population. The Rule of St Benedict had been associated with the destruction of Celtic practices such as the type of tonsure, the marriage of clergymen and the date of Easter. 'Europe Day' has been assigned to St Benedict's feast day by the EU bureaucrats, for his 'beneficial' effects across Europe. However, the Benedictine monasteries hold no good memories for the people of Wales, being more associated with the greedy placemen of the Norman barons.

The Cistercians, or White Monks, were popular with the Welsh, however, being unassociated with alien conquest. They built their abbeys in the remote Welsh heartlands, and the abbeys became allied with the Welsh princes over time. Their clergy flocked to join Owain Glyndŵr's revolt, and the Abbot of Llantarnam was killed fighting for him. The Cistercian Margam Abbey was also destroyed by the Anglo-French at this time. The Franciscan Grey Friars* and the Dominican Black Friars were also well accepted in Wales.

The following is a partial list of the clasau across Wales:
Anglesey – Caer Gybi, Penmon, Ynys Seiriol
Gwynedd – Aberdaron, Clynnog, Bangor, Tywyn
Denbigh – Abergele, Llanelwy (St Asaf), Llanynys, Llanrhaeadr
Flint – Bangor-is-Coed
Cardigan - Llanbadarn Fawr, Llanddewi Brefi
Merioneth - Llangurig, St Harmons
Montgomery - Meifod, Llandinam
Brecon - Glascwm, Glasbury
Hereford and Worcester - Moccas, Dewchurch, Garway, Welsh Bicknor
Monmouth - Caerwent
Glamorgan - Llandough, Llancarfan, Llanilltud Fawr, Llandeilo Ferwallt (Bishopston), Llangyfelach
Carmarthen - Llandeilo Fawr, Llanarthne
Pembroke – Penally, Tyddewi (St David's)

The monastic system (clas) was based upon families, where members were hereditary, and wives were also members. After the Normans came, the clas developed into the chapter in the cathedrals, but still the Welsh clergy refused to agree with celibacy, and it was not generally enforced until the Reformation. The word 'clas' is recalled in former British monasteries such as Glastonbury, Glasgow, Glasnevin (near Dublin), Glasserton (in Cumbria), Glassbhein (Inverness) and Glasbury (the 'clas' on the Wye).

*The City of Cardiff unforgivably allowed an office block to be built upon Cardiff's Grey Friars site, because of its commercial value in the city centre. Because of this, the vista from the main shopping area Queen Street, to one of the finest civic centres in the world, has been lost.

CLAUDIA 1st-2nd century
GWLADYS
August 7

Many authorities claimed she was the daughter of Caradog (Caractacus), and wife of Pudens, as Caradog was taken with his wife and daughters in chains to Rome. Her sister was Eurgain, who was said to have brought the gospel back to Britain. (Another theory is that Eurgain and Gwladys* were the same person). Claudia was said as a child to have been baptised by Joseph of Arimathea. Claudia died at Pudens' villa in Sabium in Umbria, Italy in 110. Her body was taken back to Rome to lie alongside his. However, Tacitus calls her the daughter of the British king Cogidubnus. A marble tablet discovered at Chichester notes that Pudens, under the sanction of Cogidubnus, erected a temple to Neptune and Minerva. (Whether she was the daughter of Cogidubnus or Caractacus may be uncovered in future editions of this book – suffice it to say that this British woman was extremely important in the very early Christian church in Rome, three centuries before Rome officially stopped its persecution of Christians). The house of Pudens in Rome was the first to be used for Christian worship, and the church of St Pudentiana now stands on the site. Claudia and Pudens were the parents of the saints Timothy, Pudentiana and Praxedes, and Claudia and Pudens were said to have received St Peter into their house (see Appendix I).

Her brother Cyllin was also said to be a saint of this time. Other sources reckon that she was Gwladys Ruffyth, Romanised to Claudina Ruffina, and born in Penllyn Court, Glamorgan. Much more research is needed upon the legends concerning Wales and first century Rome, but it may be well to elucidate what is known to the author. From 51 AD Caradog was in Rome. His father Brân also seems to have been held hostage with him for seven years (see Brân and Arwystli). Around this time St Paul was in Rome, and was executed in 67 or 68. Paul converted a wealthy Roman couple, Quintus Cornelius Pudens and Priscilla, and the faithful, including St Peter, assembled at their house (now in Via Urbana) for worship. Quintus Pudens was martyred and Priscilla had a catacomb, still known by her name, made as the family cemetery.

Their son Cornelius Pudens appears to have been in Britain in the reign of Claudius. The stone found at Chichester reads:
'The College of Artificers and they who preside over sacred rites or hold office there by the authority of King Cogidubnus, legate to Tiberius Claudius Augustus in Britain, dedicated this temple to Neptune and Minerva for the welfare of the Imperial Family, Pudens the son of Pudentinus giving the ground.'

Pudens seems to have returned to Rome as a member of the imperial household around 65, and like Gwladys (Claudia) and Eurgain probably came into contact with Paul and was baptised. It is thought that Gwladys took the name Claudia at baptism in gratitude to the Emperor Claudius for sparing her father's life. (A Roman tradition was that those given mercy or pardon took the name of their benefactor). Cornelius Pudens married Claudia, and Martial wrote several odes to her in 66:

'From painted Britons how was Claudia born?
The fair barbarian how do arts adorn?
When Roman charms a Grecian soul commend,
Athens and Rome may well for her contend.'
  (Book II, Epigram 54)

'My Pudens, with the stranger Claudia wed,
Demands thy torch, O Hymen, light to shed,
Then rare cinnamon with spikenard join,
And mix Thaesean sweets with Massick wine.'
  (Book IV, Epigram 13)

In The Roman Martyrologies, Pudens and Claudia had six children: Pudentiana, Potentiana, Praxedes, Linus, Timotheus and Novatus. St Paul in his Second Epistle to Timothy at Ephesus (iv.21) reads *'Eubulus greeteth thee, and Pudens, and Linus, and Claudia, and all the brethren.'* Timotheus and Novatus held services in Rome at the baths they had built. It was said that St Timotheus came to Britain, and a letter from Pastor Hermas telling him of death in his family still exists. He returned to Rome and was martyred. When Justin the Martyr was forced to tell the place where Christians assembled he answered *'in the baths of Timotheus.'* Linus, according to the Apostolic Constitutions, was made first Bishop of Rome, so Peter's successor, like St Timotheus, was half-British.

When her five siblings were all dead, Praxedes asked Pope Pius I to erect a church on the site of her brothers' baths. The church was eventually founded around 145 in Pudens' house and dedicated Pudentis. Rebuilt around 780 by Hadrian I, it has been called *'The Cradle of the Western Church.'*

The extended entry on Llanilltud Fawr, under Illtud, explains more about Côr Eurgain, the putative foundation of Claudia's sister near Llanilltud Fawr.

*There was a sister of Caradog named Gwladys, who went with him to Rome and married Aulus Plautius. Like her neice, she changed her name, and was known to history as Pomponia Graecina Plautius (the name Graecina refers to her fluency in Greek). Tacitus records her as being tried for *'foreign superstition'*, i.e. being a Christian. Fortunately the presiding magistrate was her husband.

CLEER 5th-6th century
CLETHER, CLANIS, CLARUS
August 19, October 23, November 3 and 4

One of Brychan Brycheiniog's progeny, he settled in Cornwall at Clether in the Inny Valley. There is a superb oratory and holy well (rebuilt in the 15th century) at Clether church, and St Cleer's church a few miles south is named after him. St Clear's in Pembrokeshire may also be his foundation. 'The Hurlers' is a stone circle near St Cleer. It is said that the saint saw some locals playing a hurling match on a Sunday, and turned them to stone.

CLEMENT d.100
November 23, 24
Emblem – an anchor
Patron of blacksmiths, sailors and lighthousemen

Not a Welsh saint, but celebrated in Tenby on this day of 'Old Martinmas'. He had been tied to an anchor and drowned, and angels made an undersea tomb for him, uncovered once a year by exceptionally low tides. He is the patron saint of blacksmiths, who had an annual procession with torches, mock anvils and an effigy named *'Old Clem'*. He is also the patron of lighthousemen and celebrated by sailors. At Tenby, the fishing-crews rounded off their *'Clementing'* celebrations on this day with a meal of roast goose and rice pudding, provided by the boat-owners. There were also 'Clemeny Songs' which need detailing and reviving. *'Oranges and Lemons say the Bells of St Clement's'* led to a popular drink made up of half lemon juice and half orange juice. Because of this, it has been suggested that St Clement's Day becomes a national *'No Alcohol Day.'*

CLOFFAN early 5th century

There is no sign remaining of a church at Llangloffan in Pembroke, but Cloffan was said to be an early bishop at the time of Cystennin Fendigaid (Constantine the Blessed).

CLYDAU 5th century
CLYDAI
November 1

A virgin daughter of Brychan Brycheiniog, who founded Clydey (Clydai) in Pembroke. Ffynnon Halog is in the parish. Later, Saint Cristiolus was associated with this church in the 6th century. Her sisters Cymorth and Cenedlon also lived around Newcastle Emlyn. Clydai means 'shelter her'. Clydey is just north of St Brynach's church in Llanfrynach, and Brynach was possibly married to Cymorth. There were three 5th – 6th century inscribed stones in the churchyard with Ogham and Latin dedications, one of which was super-inscribed with a Maltese-style ring cross of Irish type. The 'Solinus Stone' reads *'Solini Filivs Vendoni'*. This son of Vendonus was supposed to be the Irish companion of St Palladius/Belerius. Another stone is figured *'Etterni fili Victor'*. St Ettern features in the Martyrology of Donegal as Bishop Ethern. 'The Dugoed Stone' was taken from Clydai churchyard to Dugoed farm, and built into a stone stairway into the granary. It was mainly buried in the ground when Westwood saw it, but he managed to read *'Dob Filivs Evolenc-'*. Evolengi is also on a stone at Llandyssilio (see Tyssul), and Dubhuan was a Bishop of Kildare in 900. The Ogham that could be seen was translated as *'DOFOTMAQIS'*.

CLYDNO EIDDYN 6th century

A son of Cynwyd, and with his brothers a disciple of Cadog at Llancarfan. Originally from Edinburgh, he is said to have invaded Arfon to avenge Elidyr Mwynfawr's death, and there is a Cefn Cludno there mentioned in the Mabinogi of Math and Mathonwy.

KING CLYDOG d.492
CLEDOG, CLODOCK, CLITAUCUS, CLITANC, CLINTANC
August 19 (martyred), November 3

This son of Clydwyn and grandson of Brychan Brycheiniog was King of Ewyas (modern Hereford and Worcester). His brother was St Dedyn (Neubydd) and sister St Pedita. The Book of Llandaf records how a noble's daughter fell in love with him, and a jealous suitor killed Clydog with a sword while hunting. The body was carried on a cart to the river Monmow, but the oxen refused to ford the river as the yoke broke. This was considered an omen, a church was built on this site at Clodock (Merthyr Clytauc) and the king buried there. He was a king of *'straight justice, a lover of peace, and of pure chastity, and of straight and perfect life that was cruelly slain by a false traitor.'* His tomb was said to be a place of great miracles. The chapels to Clodock were Llanfeuno, Longtown (St Peter) and Cresswell (St Mary). Clodock became the ecclesiastical centre and motherchurch of Ewyas, and in the time of King Ithael ap Morgan (c. 750) it was acquired by the see of Llandaf. Fenton believed that 'Clydawc' also founded Llanerchlwydog rather than Llawddog.

KING CLYDWYN 5th century
CLEDWYN
November 1

The second or third of Brychan's sons, who was said to have conquered south Wales as a warrior. More likely he subdued the Gwyddyl Fichti (Goidelic Irish Picts) who still remained in Carmarthen and Pembroke. Llanglydwen (Llancledwyn) lies on the borders of these counties. He possibly succeeded his father as king of Brecon. There is an early Celtic Cross at Llanglydwen.

COELBREN

No saint of this name is venerated, but the author was intrigued by a sandstone slab in Swansea Museum. The sandstone carving was found near Capel Coelbren on Cefn Hirfynydd near Neath. A belted kilted figure is praying in the 'orans' position of both arms raised. He has a round 'Celtic' head and moon-shaped eyes, and is probably the remains of a disc-headed slab cross. Another 'orans' carving has recently been found at Blaenowen in Pembroke, but few others are known in Wales. Obviously Capel Coelbren has some Celtic Christian history.

COEL GODEBOG 4th – 5th century
COEL HEN

This saint was a chief (from Cumbria or Strathclyde/Ayrshire) whose descendants included the North Wales saints Asaf, Cenau, Collen, Cynfarch, Cynwyl, Deiniol, Deiniolen ap Deiniol, Dunawd, Gwrst, Gwynnin, Maethlu, Nidan and Pabo Post Prydain. The saints Ceneu, Elen and Gwawl were his children. He is said to have founded the church of Llandaf. The dynasties of Urien Rheged, Llywarch Hen and Gwenddolau, the kings of the North of England, came from Coel.

COF see CEIDIO AB ATHRWYS

COFEN

Llangofen in Monmouth, possibly St Govan's chapel in Pembroke – see Govan and Cwyfan.

COLLEN late 6th century
COLAN
May 21 (May 31 after the change of style), 2nd Sunday in August (Langolan)

Collen founded the churches at Llangollen in Denbigh, where he slayed an evil giantess, at Colan in Cornwall and Langolen in Finistere. Castell Collen near Llandrindod Wells was a Roman fort where he may have had a chapel – its stones were used to build Capel Maelog, about a mile away. His mother may have been Ethni Wyddeles, daughter of the Irish chief Matholwch. Some sources state that his father was Gwynog of the line of Caradog Freichfras, and others that his father was Petrwn of the line of Rhydderch Hael. Until the 18th century his tomb-shrine, 'the old church' survived in the churchyard but was demolished to provide stone for the present tower of the Church of St Collen. There is a superb pair of hammer-beam roofs in the three-aisled church. Llangollen was the mother church for the whole of the commote of Nanheudwy. Castell Dinas Bran, built by Gruffydd ap Madoc, overlooks the town, with breathtaking views over the Vale of Llangollen. Ffynnon Oerog near Llangollen was much used by rheumatic patients until the early 20th century.

Llangollen is a beautiful place from which to tour Wales. However, one piece of notoriety will always be attached to it. At the Royal National Eisteddfod there in 1858, the organisers awarded each other the best prizes and ran away with the profits. It has always since been known as *'The Thieves' Eisteddfod'*. Nearby is Plas Uchaf, linked forever with the Welsh 'Helen of Troy', Nest ferch Rhys ap Tudor. In the 12th century she was placed into the care of Henry I of England as a royal ward, but he seduced her and her son was made the Duke of Gloucester. She was then given by Henry in marriage to Gerald de Windsor, Earl of Pembroke. The earl maintained an uneasy truce with Prince Cadwgan of Ceredigion and Powys, but Owain ap Cadwgan saw the beautiful Nest at his father's eisteddfod and resolved to elope with her. From his manor at Plas Eglwyseg near Llangollen he broke into Pembroke Castle, fired it, and escaped with Nest. Cadwgan was ordered to restore Nest to the earl, but Owain refused his father's wishes, and Norman barons eventually wrenched Powys and Ceredigion from Cadwgan. They closed in on Owain, who escaped to Ireland, and Nest returned to Gerald de Windsor. He later killed Owain in battle before dying at Carew Castle. (Giraldus Cambrensis was one of their children). Nest then married Stephen, the Constable of Caernarfon Castle, and then the Sheriff of Pembroke, having sons by both of them. Thus the great families of Fitzgerald, Carew, Barry and Fitzstephen were descended from Nest. Plas Eglwyseg is now named Plas Uchaf, near the quaintly named World's End, and according to a previous owner, Goering and Churchill stayed there on a shooting holiday in 1936-37. More intriguingly still, there is a very strong local tradition that Elizabeth I, the Virgin Queen, bore a baby there. (There has always been a strange rumour that Sir Francis Bacon was the offspring of Elizabeth and Sir Francis Drake). A large inscription upon the present Tudor building reads LX III ELIZABETH REGINA.

The 8-acre gardens of Plas Newydd at Llangollen are being restored with a £600,000 grant from the Lottery Heritage Fund. Lady Eleanor Butler and Miss Sarah Ponsonby, the 'Ladies of Llangollen' lived here, and Ponsonby's journal is being used to recreate the landscapes they planned. The women are buried with their hot-tempered Irish servant, *'Mollie the Bruiser'*, under a memorial in the church of St Collen. Walter Scott, Wellington, Castlereagh, de Quincey, Wordsworth and Southey visited these eccentric Anglo-Irish spinsters. When their finances dried up, Molly the Bruiser bought the freehold of Plas Newydd, and left it in her will to the ladies. Lady Eleanor Butler's Journal entry for August 14th, 1789 reads breathlessly:
'Light airy Clouds - purple mountains - lilac and silver rocks - hum of Bees - rush of Waters. Goat, Sheep. Cattle. Melody of Haymakers. What Weather ! What a country !'

Rhiwabon (Ruabon) Parish Church was formerly dedicated to St Collen, but the Normans rededicated it to St Mary. At Capel Collen field near Ruabon stood his chapel and a cross where his wake was kept 'on the third week of summer'. He is also remembered at Glastonbury, where he is said to have had a cell on Glastonbury Tor, and at St Colan in Cornwall. At Langolan south-west of Chateauneuf du Faou in Brittany, his pardon is held on the second Sunday in August.

Just outside Llangollen is Carreg-y-Big, a nine feet high Neolithic standing stone near Ffynnon Arthur and Llety Ifan. There was also Ffynnon Gollen near the town, where the saint washed his wounds after slaying the cannibal giantess Cawres y Bwlch. Just two miles from Llangollen is the lovely Valle Crucis (Valley of the Cross) Abbey, named after the 9th century cross known as the Eliseg Pillar. It celebrates Concenn (d. 854) and Elise, kings of Powys (the added 'g' on Eliseg was a 17th century transcription error). The existing pillar is over 7 feet high, and the broken top near it is around six feet in length. It was broken in two in the Civil War, and Edward Lhuyd fortunately managed to write down the (now faded) inscription of 31 lines in 1696. This is exceptionally long, and mentions Macsen Wledig, Vortigern and Garmon who are all included in this book:

+ Concenn son of Catell, Catell
son of Brochmail, Brochmail son
of Eliseg, Eliseg son of Guoillauc
+ Concenn therefore being great-grandson of Eliseg
erected this stone to his great-grandfather
Eliseg + It is Eliseg who annexed
the inheritance of Powys . . .
throughout nine (years?) from the power of the English,
which he made into a sword-land by fire
+ Whosoever shall read this hand-inscribed
stone, let him give a blessing on
the soul of Eliseg. + It is Concenn

who ... with his hand
... to his own kingdom of Powys
... and which ...
...
the mountain
...
... The monarchy
Maximus ... of Britain ...
Concenn, Pascent, ... Maun, Anna.
+ Britu, moreover (was) the son of Guorthigirn (Vortigern),
whom Germanus blessed and
whom Severa bore to him, the daughter of Maximus
the King, who slew the king of the Romans.
+ Conmarch painted this
writing at the command of his king
Concenn
+ The blessing of the Lord (be) upon
Concenn and all the members of his family
And upon all the land of Powys
Until the Day of Judgment. Amen.

COLLEN

It may be that another saint is commemorated at the Roman site of Castell Collen near Llandrindod, and at Trallwng Gollen, the township of Welshpool.

COLMAN of DROMORE late 5th century
November 20 (June 7 in Scotland and Ireland)

The original saint of Fishguard, according to Wade-Evans. Croeswell holy well in the town has now been lost. This Irish saint is said to have come to stay at Sant and Non's house, where Non had given birth to the still-born St David (Dewi). Colman 'the Elder' brought him back to life and is commemorated at the nearby North Pembrokeshire churches of Llangolman near Maenclochog, and Capel Golman subject to Llanfihangel Penbedw. At Capel Golman (Capel Colman, near Boncath) a crossed stone was used as a gate-post and called Maen-ar-Golman (the Stone-on-Colman), indicating that it had been his burial marker. Llangolman is included in the Pembroke pilgrim's trail, and stands on high ground, suuposedly above the old Roman road from Llanglydwen to Maenclochog, with wonderful views of the eastern Cleddau valley. There is a gravestone with a carved wine glass for Martha Thomas of Pomprenmaen, who died in 1820, having brewed wine for all the local gentry.

COLUMB 6th century
December 13

An associate of Carannog, Briog and Pedrog, St Columb Major and St Columb Minor in Cornwall commemorate him, as does Plougoulum in Brittany.

CONBELANUS 1st century
CYMBELINE, CUNOBELIN

Said to be the father of Caractacus, this fabled king's name is remembered in the famous Cross of Conbelanus, found in a hedge next to a stile on Whiting Farm, on the footpath from Merthyr Mawr to Laleston. Decorated with interlaced ribbonwork, the remaining lettering was transcribed by Westwood as *'(Con)belani possuit hanc crucem pro anima ejus seigliuffi herte(i?)bo et fratris eui . . . et pater eius a me prepara tus (est?) st(c?)il(g?)oo . . .'* The inscription is ascribed to 600 AD. The 'Great Cross' at Merthyr Mawr is over seven feet tall, commonly known as the 'Gobblin Stone', and Westwood transcribed it as *'i nomine di pat rif et fili fperi tuf . . . a . . . eus . . . post . . . caifto . . . gre ciam ad pro prium . . . In diem iudici'*. Iolo Morganwg believed that this much defaced cross referred to a prince of Glamorgan called Eric, who lived in the 2nd century, making it the oldest British inscription.

KING CONSTANTINE 6th century c.520-c.589
CYSTENNIN AP CADO
March 9 (also 13) and March 11 in Scotland

This King of Dumnonia (the Celtic kingdom of Somerset, Devon, Dorset and Cornwall) broke the law of sanctuary by killing two of Mordred's sons in churches in Caerwent and possibly London. They had allied with the Saxons against him. His contemporary Gildas (writing around 540) is the authority, who approved of the killing, but not the place. Later in his life, around 589 Constantine became a monk and lived a holy life at Menevia (St David's). Cystennin's grandfather Geraint had died fighting the Saxons for Arthur, his father Cado fought for Arthur, and Arthur was said to have left the High Kingship of Britain to the young Cystennin. Because Cystennin was so young when Arthur left after Camlan, perhaps Maelgwn Gwynedd took over as overlord until his death in 547 or later.

In the Life of St Petroc, Constantine was baptised by Petroc after chasing a stag near Padstow. This legend relates that Tewdrig had been King, and was succeeded by his son Meurig, which seems to confirm that Meurig was Uther Pendragon, the father of Arthur. There was a ruined church of St Constantine next to St Constantine's bay near Padstow, and his feast is held in St Merryn on March 9, in which parish the church lies. The nearby Holy Well now just forms a marsh. Constantine also seems to have founded, on his conversion, Constantine in the deanery of Kerrier and Milton Abbot on the river Tamar in Devon. He then went to St David's to study on his way to Ireland. Milton Abbot was dedicated to David's mother Non, and lies just across the river Tamar from Landue (Llan-Dewi). There are also Constantine dedications at Dunsford, Devon and Illogan, Cornwall. Towards the end of his life, Kentigern (Cyndeyrn) asked him to come as a missionary to Galloway, and he was slain by pirates on the Mull of Kintyre. His arm was cut off and he bled to death, becoming Scotland's first martyr.

CONSTANTINE THE BLESSED see CYSTENNIN FENDIGAID

EMPEROR CONSTANTINE THE GREAT d.337
May 21, September 14 (Holy Cross Day)

Cressy commemorates him as Bishop of Rome, and as a saint of the British Church. His father was Constantius (Constantine Chlorus), the Roman general who reconquered Britain in 296 after Carausius* had usurped Rome's authority. Constantius defeated Allectus, the successor of Carausius. He then married Elen ferch Coel, a British woman and their son was Constantine. Constantius does not seem to have strongly enforced the Diocletian Persecution in Britain in 303. Constantius became Emperor of Rome, Constantine I, and the legend related by Eusebius is that he gauged the loyalty of his Christian troops by asking them to give up God or accept his vengeance. He then retained the soldiers who would not forsake God, as they had showed that they would not betray their faith. Henceforth, Christianity was allowed in the Roman Empire, he fought under the Chi-Rho of Christ and he issued the Edict of Milan giving Christians liberty of public worship in 312.

He was succeeded by his son Constantine II, known to history as Constantine the Great. Christianity owes its survival to the fact that it was adopted by Roman emperors in the 4th century, from which event the Roman domination of the faith remains. Christians were still being persecuted across the empire, when the young Constantine fortunately won the Battle of Milvian Gate. Before the battle, there was the shape of a cross in the clouds. Some Christian supporters told him that it was a sign that their God was on his side, and he could overcome overwhelming odds. Constantine won the battle, then overcame each of his rivals in turn and seized Rome. He established Christianity as the Empire's most favoured religion, and his mother Elen and his sons carried on the work. **It was this period, from Constantius leaving Britain with a British Christian wife, to their son's death in 337, which enabled the rise of Christianity as a great faith across Europe, rather than remain as an underground movement everywhere except in Britain.** This may seem to be a sweeping statement, but it is difficult to trace major monastic settlements or traditions for this time in the 'traditional' homes of catholicism.

However, the last member of Constantine's family was Julian, who succeeded in 361 and began to restore the old cults, before he was killed in a skirmish with Persians in 363. A Christian general was chosen by the troops to succeed him, and the Empire stayed Christian until 391 when the usurper Eugenius conquered the western provinces. In 395, however, the Emperor of the East, Theodosius the Great overcame him, and Christianity was thereafter the faith of Rome. There is much entanglement between the stories of the Constantines and Cystennins in the 4th and 5th centuries – the author would appreciate any enlightenment before the next edition of this book.

September 14 is celebrated as Holy Cross Day, the Exaltation of the Holy Cross, when the vision appeared to Constantine. It was also known as Holy Rood day, and the Jews in Rome were forced to hear a Christian sermon on this day.

*Carausius is probably commemorated at Penmachno in Caernarfon, where a monument reads CARAUSIUS LIES HERE IN THIS STONY MOUND. He took control in Britain from 287-293.

CONSTANTINE AP RHYDDERCH HAEL 6th-7th century
March 11?

His conception was assisted by a blessing from Kentigern, as his mother Langueth was thought to be sterile. He succeeded Rhydderch as King of Cumbria in 600, and successfully kept the 'Northern Cymru' from Cumberland to Strathclyde safe against their barbarian neighbours in England and Scotland. He is listed as a Scottish saint, and died around 630. There is confusion concerning the March 11 feast date for both Constantine ap Rhydderch and Constantine ap Cado.

CONSTANTINE THE TYRANT d. 411
CYSTENNIN

This Constantine was elected Emperor by his troops in Britain in 408, and killed in 411 with his son Constans. Also known as 'Constantine the Usurper', he had led the remaining British legions into Gaul, aided by Geraint (Gerontius). (Macsen Wledig had similarly denuded Britain of its legions 30 years previously). He lost a battle againt Stilicho, and sent Constans to Spain to take it from troops loyal to the Emperor Honorius. Honorius accepted Constantine as co-Emperor, and Constantine entered Italy but had to return to Spain as Gerontius defected. Gerontius killed Constans and besieged Constantine in Arles until Honorius raised the siege. Honorius then put Constantine to death near Ravenna. The 'Brut Dingestow' states that Constantine succeeded his father as King of Britain, with Roman help conquered Macsen Wledig and was received in Rome by the Emperor. Gerontius appears to have retired to Spain (Galicia?) with his British troops.

CÔR

This now means 'choir', but in earliest times meant college or congregation, and translated into Latin as 'monasterium'. The Triads relate that there were three 'high choirs', Bangor-is-Coed (Dunawd), Bangor Illtud and Bangor Henllan (Dyfrig). According to Bede, who wrote just a hundred years after the destruction of Bangor-is-Coed (at Bangor-on-Dee), such an institution had no less than 2,100 members. 100 monks were employed every hour to praise God throughout every hour of the day. Bede was no friend of the Celtic church, but even allowing for hyperbole, these were certainly large foundations as present remains show. Bede stated that Bangor-is-Coed at the time of its sacking had 2100 monks, divided into 7 classes. Old sources state that Dyfrig had over 1000 followers at Henllan. Another manuscript claimed that Llanilltud Fawr had 7 halls and 400 houses for its saints. On a smaller scale, Cadog at Llancarfan had 100 ecclesiastics, and also cared for orphans, widows, paupers, strangers and guests at his own expense.

CORBRE 6th century?
November 19 or 22

Hen Eglwys in Anglesey was formerly known as St Corbre's Church. A stone from the old church, taken down in 1845, was placed in the new church, and reads in part *'filivs cv . . . Anima requiescat.'* In the 'Verses of the Graves' in the Black Book of Carmarthen, we read:
'The grave of Ceri Gleddyfhir (Long-sword) is in the confine of Hen Eglwys,

On the gravelly cliff:
Tarw Torment (the Bull of Conflict) in the cemetery of Corbre.'

The church was dedicated to the saints Faustinus and Bacellinus, Roman priests, so it may be a very old foundation dating from the 4th century. There was a saint Faustus, but it may be that Bacellinus was a misnomer for Marcellinus, who with Marcellus is the co-founder of Llanddeusant in Anglesey. (See Llwydian).

CORDULA d.453
October 22

A British virgin, martyred with Ursula.

BISHOP CORENTIN b. 410, d.c. 490-500
CORENTINUS, CURY
May 1 (Exeter), November 2 (Cury), December 11, 12 and September 5 (Brittany)

This Cornish Celtic hermit was the only one of the seven founding saints of Brittany who was not from Wales. He became a recluse in Plomdiern, then Bishop of Cornouaille. His feast day is celebrated in the beautiful Breton city of Quimper every year with presents of blessed cakes. King Grallo (Gradlon) visited him in Brittany, where Corentin's name was invoked to cure paralysis. Quimper is the capital of the ancient diocese, kingdom and then duchy of Cornouaille and is well worth visiting for its magnificent cathedral and network of mediaeval streets. The Festival of Cornouaille started in 1923, and Celtic countries join in music, theatre and dance in the third week of July. Corentin is also remembered at Cury in Cornwall. Tregurentin lies north-west of Ploermel, and St Corentin is north of Carhaix-Plouguer.

CORNELY?

At Carnac the *'cattle traditions'* of this British saint are still observed. (see Beuno). Also at St Herbot's church in Huelgoat, cattle tails were offered. At his pardon, cattle are driven around the church, then led to his holy well to drink its water. Water from the well was then taken home to cure sick cattle. Huelgoat is one of the great tourist attractions of Finistère, a magical valley of moss-covered boulders and water-falls. Cornelly, near Porthcawl, may have some link with this saint.

CRALLO
August 8

The son of St Canna and St Sadwrn, he probably came from Brittany with his parents, to study at his uncle St Illtud's school, and is the founder of Llangrallo, now called Coychurch outside Bridgend. He was buried at Llangrallo, where a now illegible stone cross is said to mark his grave. At the east end of the church, 'Ebissar' can be made out on it, the same name as on Samson's cross at Llanilltud Fawr. The name of Samson was also said to be on the Coychurch stone, according to Westwood.

Falling masonry broke his ten feet high Celtic cross into three parts in the early 19th century, but it has been restored and placed inside the church. This is known as 'The Wheel-Cross of Ebisar', and the carvings are similar to those of stones at nearby Merthyr Mawr. There is also a five feet high shaft with plaitwork inside the church, but its inscription is illegible. Crallo's holy well is just south of the church. There was also Ffynnon Court Gwilym near it, a 'moated well' that even in Edward Lhuyd's time was in ruins.

The saying *'Yr hen Grallo'* was used even in the early twentieth century in Glamorgan, to signify someone who was a little crazy. A *'Saying of the Wise'* is:
'Have you heard the saying of Crallo,
When there was nothing stirring?
"It is easy to make the crooked-mouthed weep" '.

William Thomas notes a sad case of rabies in 1785, when *'was lately smothered to Death at Pencoed, Llangrallo, being in great rage from the bite of a Mad Dog, a child, vizt. a maid from five to six years of age. Had first bitten her mother and the other children.'*

CRISTIOLUS 6th century
November 3

The son of Hywel Fychan ap Hywel Farchog ab Emyr Llydaw, cousin of Cadfan and brother of Sulien, he is said to have founded Llangristiolus in Anglesey, and the churches of Eglwyswrw and Penrydd (Penrieth) in Pembroke. Llangristiolus has Henblas Dolmen, which has been called *'the most gigantic cromlech in Britain.'* ('Archaeologia Cambrensis', 1866). There was an ancient semi-cylindrical stone near the well at Henblas Mansion, but it appears to have vanished. Many Celtic stones were used as animal rubbing posts and farm gates in Anglesey, so have lost their carvings and inscriptions over the years.

CRONWERN
CRUNWEAR

There is a church of a Celtic saint at Crunwear in Carmarthenshire.

CUHELYN 6th century
CYHELIN

A son of Caw, also known as Celyn Moel, who studied at Llancarfan.

CUNEDDA WLEDIG 5th century

He was not a saint, but through Einion Yrth to the sixth generation he was the progenitor of the 'royal' saints Eurgain, Edeyrn, Meirion, Seiriol and Einion Frenhin. Also the royal line of Gwynedd claimed descent from this 'Dux Brittaniae', or 'Gwledig' (Over-King). Welsh traditions state that he came with his sons and 900 mounted troops from the North (Cumbria/Strathclyde) in the early 5th century and drove the Goidels out of most of North Wales. They may have been invited by Vortigern, just as he invited the Saxons to act as

mercenaries in the south-east of England. Cunedda's new lands were said to be divided by his son Meirion amongst his sons as following:
Meirion – Merioneth;
Ceredig – Ceredigion;
Dunod – Dunoding (Ardudwy and Eifionydd)
Mael – Dinmael, Denbigh;
Arwystl – Arwystli;
Oswail – Osweilion (the areas around Oswestry, now Shropshire);
Einion Yrth – Caer Einion;
Dogfail – Dogfeiliog, Denbigh;
Edeyrn – Edeyrnion;
Rhufon – Rhufoniog, Denbigh;
Coel – Coeleion, Denbigh

Cunedda's 6th century great-grandson, Maelgwn Gwynedd, was also regarded as Gwledig, which seems to have led to the great battle of Camlan between Arthur of South Wales and his Breton/West Country allies, and Maelgwn of the North with his Cumbria/Strathclyde relatives. At present this is hypothetical, but this battle appeared to be between Celts, rather than Saxon against Celt, for the overlord-ship of Wales and the West Country. A stone in the church at St Dogmael's may commemorate Cunedda's family (see Dogmael).

CURIG d.c.550
CURIG LWYD (Grey, or Blessed), CURIG MARCHOG (The Knight), KIRIK, CIR
June 16 (Wales), February 17 (Brittany)

He lived at the time of Maelgwn Gwynedd, and forsook a military career to become a monk. Curig argued with Maelgwn, and blinded him and his men until Maelgwn gave him lands. Maelgwn's sons Mael, Arwystl and Ceredig gave him the lands around Llangurig where their boundaries met. Curig's cell became the church at Llangurig, but many of his dedications were replaced by the Normans with ones to St Cyriacus, the boy martyr. The Reverend Parker lamented the destruction of Llangurig's beautiful chancel screen in the early 19th century in the so-called name of progress – *'Oh ! What pearls we have cast before swine.'* There is a rock on the nearby mountain at Llangurig, where he sat, still called Eisteddfa Gurig. He may have become a bishop of Llanbadarn Fawr. To the Bretons he was Kirik. Curig died at Landerneau, was buried at Locquirec, and several other Breton churches remember him.

Curig was said to have been consecrated by Paul Aurelian. He studied with Tudwal at Llanilltud Fawr. Giraldus Cambrensis states that his cross was covered with silver and gold, and was kept in Harmon's Church in Radnorshire, just a few miles from Llangurig. A penny was charged for the application of the holy staff to cure glandular and tumorous swellings. Commissioners took it away in the Reformation and burned it. Apart from Llangurig in Montgomeryshire, there is Capel Curig in Caernarfonshire, and Eglwys Fair a Churig in Carmarthenshire. (The Normans added the dedication to Mary). Capel Curig, a pilgrimage chapel near Newport, Pembrokeshire, no longer exists. St Curig's Chapel at Cat's Ash, between Newport and Caerleon, is the ruined *'capella Sancti Ciriaci'* mentioned in 'The Book of Llandaf'. It is now linked to a farmhouse, and used to be under the jurisdiction of the Benedictine Priory at Goldcliffe from 1113. There is a Porthkerry Church in Glamorgan, on the cliff above the drowned castle, dedicated to St Curig. (see Ceri, however). Llanilid in

Glamorgan is dedicated to Ilid and Curig. At Llanilid is a well known as Ffynnon Geri, and the parish wake, Gwyl Geri, was held in mid-summer to commemorate Curig.

In Llandegai parish, Brecon*, Ffynnon Gurig cured warts, and a curse befell the man who closed the well. At Llanengan in Caernarfon there were two adjacent holy wells near Curig's chapel, where blind people could be cured. People bathed in the large well and drank from the small one. Ffair Gurig used to be held at Ffynnon Gurig near the castle in Newport, Pembrokeshire.

*At Abercar in Brecon, Westwood had been informed of a Celtic cross in the lintel of a beast-house by Taliesin Williams (Iolo Morganwg's son). Near Capel-Nant-ddu, on the Cwm-Car (valley of the Car brook), Westwood found the visible part of the inscription as: *'S CVRI IN HOC TUMULO'*. If the stone could be uncovered, this may be another Brecon link with Curig, or perhaps with Prince Ceri of Glamorgan.

CWRDA
COWRDA
February 21

There are the remains of a chapel called Bron Llangowrda in Cardigan, and the church of Jordanston in Pembroke is dedicated to St Cwrda (Jordanston was formerly called Tre-Cwrdan). St Cawrdaf or St Gwrdaf may also have founded these sites.

CWYAN

Llanguian, with its castle remains on Stalling Down near Cowbridge, possibly had a church with this obscure saint's dedication. There may also have been a chapel at Llanquian near Llanblethian. There is a 'Llanquian Aisle' in Cowbridge's Church of the Holy Cross, and this church used to be a chapel of ease to the major church of the parish of Llanblethian.

CWYFAN d.618
CWYFEN, KEVIN, COEMGEN
June 3

This saint founded the communities of Llangwyfan or Llangwyfen in Denbighshire and Anglesey, and Dyserth in Flint. (Cewydd is also associated with Dyserth). Tudweiliog chapel on the Llŷn peninsula was under Llangwynodl and dedicated to Cwyfen. In 1669 Edward Lhuyd wrote of Dyserth that *'their Cwyfan and wakes were held ye next Sunday after ye second of June'*. Ffynnon Gwyfan there cured the ague and sore eyes. Warts were pricked with pins which were thrown into the well. Near the church, this holy well once contained trout. Some sources call Cwyfan a Breton, for he was the son of Brwyno Hen ap Dyfnog, and descended from Caradog Freichfras. His mother was Camell of Bodangharad in Denbigh.

In Anglesey, Cwyfan's church is on a small islet, Ynys Gwyfan, connected at low tide by a 200 yard causeway. It was built on this single acre of land about 605, but the present church is twelfth century. In the winter, when conditions made it impossible to cross to the church, services were held in a room in the great house of Plas Llangwyfan on the mainland. The rector

Maen Achwyfan Celtic Cross. © *Wales Tourist Board Photo Library.*

could claim from the owner of the 'plas' ('great house') hay for his horse, two eggs, a penny loaf and a half pint of beer instead of taking the tithe on the property. There is a nearby stream called Afon Cwyfan, and the bay is named Porth Cwyfan.

Eglwys Sant Cwyfan in Denbigh is in a lane on the slopes of the Clwydian hills, with stocks in the churchyard. Thankfully, there has been no Victorian 'restoration', and the Georgian interior has box-pews painted green. At Dyserth, his Holy Well no longer operates because of the changes in the water table caused by lead mining. Dyserth means a deserted place, or hermitage, and this Flint church is now dedicated to St Bridget and St Cwyfan, being first recorded in the Domesday Book of 1087. There is a nearly complete Celtic churchyard cross, now inside the church, where there is also a beautiful stained-glass east window. The upper 'tracery' dates from 1450, and the lower 'Tree of Jesse' is from the 1530's. How it escaped destruction is unrecorded. Cwyfan may also be the saint Cofan venerated at Llangoven in Monmouth and responsible for St Govan's Chapel in Pembroke.

Gerald of Wales mentions St Kevin's Apples, fruit that grew on a willow tree at his centre of Glendalough and which were sought after all over Ireland. It is now one of the four principal pilgrimage sites in Ireland. A yew tree said to have been planted by him near the cathedral was cut down in 1835. All Irish and Latin Lives which refer to him date from the 11th century, and were written to further the claims of Glendalough monastery and attract more pilgrims. They make the Welsh-Breton Cwyfan an Irish saint, but earlier Welsh writings make him a saint who evangelised Ireland.

Not far from Dyserth, at Whitford is Maen Achwynfan*, the 'Stone of Lamentations', the tallest disc-headed cross in Wales at twelve feet above the ground, and carved from one block of stone. It features Christian and pagan orthography, with representations of a man, dog, donkey and coiled serpent, with some beautiful ribbon-plait carvings. The stone should be mentioned in this book, and apart from its proximity to Dyserth, Chwyfan is the aspirate mutation of Cwyfan, so it may have one time been dedicated to the saint. According to Barber's book on 'The Ancient Stones of Wales' it is sometimes called St Cwyfan's Stone. This book also mentions the ubiquitous Forestry Commission blowing up a six feet stone, Carreg Wen, at nearby Cynwyl Elfed in order to make a fence. How permission is given for such vandalism is unknown. There are two other dolmens in this area as well as the destroyed white quartz stone, (named Cerrig Llwydion and Arthur's Quoit), so the site must have been an important one.

At Llangwyfan is the world-famous Barclodiad y Gawres (The Apronful of the Giantess), on Mynydd Cnwc headland. This chambered cairn was said to have been formed when a giantess dropped an apronful of building stones. Just below is Arthur's cave, where he was supposed to have sheltered while fighting the Irish pagans. At Bettws Disserth in Radnor, there is a stone circle with a dozen small stones, on Gelli Hill.

*The author keeps coming across references to Boudicca's fateful last stand against the Romans being at Newmarket in Flint, just two miles from this Stone of Lamentations, which stood at a junction of the Sarn Helen Roman road and the Holywell road. Perhaps others can research further into this site. With Carew Cross and Penmon Cross it is the largest such structure in Wales. From Westwood's 'Lapidarium Walliae' we read:
'The Maen Achwynfan is here seen with its top towering over the hedges of the field in which it stands, far removed from any village or any remains either of a religious or civil nature, and devoid of any tradition on the spot which would give a clue to the reason of so remarkable a monument being placed in such a situation. The surrounding district, however, has been the scene of many conflicts. Close to Newmarket is the Cop'r'leni, with an immense carnedd of limestones on its summit. On the brow of another adjacent hill is Bryn Saethau ("the Hill of Arrows". Near to this is Bryn y Lladdfa ("the Hill of Slaughter"). Below this, again, is the Pant y Gwae ("the Hollow of Woe"); and, indeed, says Mr Pennant, the tract from this place to Caerwys was certainly a field of battle, as no place in North Wales exhibits an equal amount of tumuli; - all sepulchral, as is proved by the urns discovered in them.' (See Appendix I).

CWYLLOG see CYWYLLOG

Alphabetical Listing of the Saints of Wales and Religious Events

ABBOT CYBI d.c. 554
CUBY
November 6 or 8, but some parts of Wales celebrated on the 5 and 7. The festival usually lasted 3 days. The last Sunday before July 25. In Cornwall, August 13.

The son of Selyf ap Geraint ab Erbin, his mother was Gwen ferch Gynyr, and he was a younger contemporary of David. He was said to have been present at the Synod of Brefi, and the church of Llangybi is next to Llanddewi Brefi. Cybi founded the monastery at Holy Island, Ynys Gybi, off Holyhead (Caer Gybi) in Anglesey. This was near the spot where Caswallon Lawhir had slain Serigi, over whose grave a chapel was built. It was still a famous collegiate church through the Middle Ages.

A friend of Seiriol, he is with him Anglesey's most famed saint. The story about Cybi meeting Seiriol at Clorach is replicated with his weekly meeting of Elian at Llandyfrdog, halfway between Holyhead and Llanelian. There were two healing wells at Clorach, Ffynnon Seiriol and Ffynnon Gybi, but Cybi's was destroyed when a bridge was built around 1840. Seiriol's Well still flows, however. The megalith near there, Carreg Leidr, has been taken into Llandyfrydog Church, and was once known as Lleidr y Frydog. It appears that the land for Cybi's monastery was granted him by Maelgwn Gwynedd, and Cybi's Holyhead church was situated inside the remains of the Roman fort, like the foundations of many of the earliest saints.

A small island off Dyfed's Pencaer peninsula is also called Ynys Gybi, and there is another Llangybi on the Teifi river. Llangibby on Usk, near Caerleon, is an important church with Ffynnon Gybi just outside the churchyard. Usk is the Roman town of Burrium, and Llangibby Castle and Park are still extant. King Ethelic was struck blind by Cybi for trying to eject him and his monks off some land. When Cybi cured him (and raised his horse from the dead) the King gave Cybi Llangybi (on Usk) and also land at Tredunnock. The hounds at Llangibby Castle have been famous since at least 1720, and the local farmers' Christmas toast was:
Iechyd da I'r Cymro sydd yn byw ar y mynydd draw,
Iechyd da I'r crefftwr sydd yn byw ar waith ei law,
Iechyd da I'r ffermwr sydd yn hau a 'redig yr yd,
Iechyd da I'r helwr sydd yn galw ei gwn ynghyd.
(Here's a health to the Welshman who lives on yon mountain,
To the craftsman who lives by the work of his hand,
To the farmer who sows the wheat and ploughs,
To the huntsman who calls his hounds together.)

The use of Welsh stopped in this Monmouth church, apart from funerals, around 1850. The old Welsh custom of whitewashing the walls is still practised there. In some villages such as Flemingstone in Glamorgan, the whole village was whitewashed to share the protection of the church. (However, buildings outside villages were often painted pink by adding ox-blood, to keep out evil spirits).

Cybi had travelled from Cornwall to settle at Llangybi on the Usk, and then went west to Menevia. One 13th century Life tells us that he could read at 7 and aged 27 made a pilgrimage to Jerusalem. He left Menevia to go to Ireland with Enda* (March 21), but had an argument and returned to Wales in a coracle. He argued with Maelgwn Gwynedd, possibly because his companion Caffo was the brother of Gildas, who hated Maelgwn.

St Cybi's Well.   *CADW: Welsh Historic Monuments. Crown Copyright.*

There were dedications at Llangybi in the Teifi valley, and another at Llangybi near Pwllheli on the Llŷn. At the latter is the remains of a beehive cell, about 400 yard from the present church, and near the present St Cybi's well still used for baptism and healing. It was used to assess the fidelity of one's partner. If a handkerchief floated north, the lover was faithful; if it headed south, infidelity was suspected. The well also used to contain eels embodying the power of the water. If they wrapped themselves around one's legs, feet and leg ailments would be cured. The impressive well was roofed, with a separate building for its 'caretaker', and was useful for curing lameness, warts, blindness, scrofula, scurvy and rheumatism. The well water was carried away for use as medicine. This well was near the graveyard with its ancient Celtic cross. In Holyhead (Caergybi) parish, Ffynnon y Gorlles was a famous well inside Capel y Gorlles. Another nearby holy well, Ffynnon Llochwyd was visited on Cybi's Day (the last Sunday before July 25th), prior to two weeks of festivities. Also at Caergybi was a holy well said to cure scrofula, scurvy and rheumatism, and crutches were left at the well building in the 18th century. At Llangybi in Caernarfon is an unusual eight feet standing stone with a pointed top.

In the Cardigan Llangybi the sick washed themselves in Ffynnon Gybi (Ffynnon Wen), then slept under Llech Gybi nearby. The bath had seats around it for bathers, and was still in reasonable condition before World War I. Landauer Guir, also on the Usk, is now known as Tredunnock and dedicated to Andrew, but seems to be a Cybi foundation. However, some believe that Llandauer Guir is Panteg at Llanddowror in Carmarthen. He is also remembered at Llandulph, Tregony, Cuby, and Duloe near Liskeard in Cornwall.

Between Llangybi Church and the river Usk is a six feet standing stone. Near Caergybi (Holyhead) are several ancient monuments, Coetan Arthur Standing Stone near Trearddur Bay, a group of standing stones on Holyhead Mountain called Meini Moelton (Bald Stones), a burial chamber called Trefignath Dolmen, and two ten-feet standing stones near Plas Meilw called Meini Hirion.

In the 1740's at Holyhead, attempts were made to stop the celebration of Cybi's feast. His bones were carried through the town on three successive Sundays during the wakes (*Suliau'r Creiriau – Sundays of the Relics*). Courting couples gathered at this time and walked from the church to his well. Water was then carried in the mouth and gravel or sand in the hand, from the holy well back to Cybi's chapel to divine marriage prospects. If no sand nor water was spilt, marriage prospects were good. Football matches, boat races and horse racing occurred during the three Sundays of the Relics.

The 'Saying of the Wise' is:
'Hast thou heard the saying of St Cybi
Of Anglesey, to the son of Gwrgi?
"There is no misfortune like wickedness".'

*This pioneer of Irish monasticism may have studied under St David as well as at Ninian's foundation at Whithorn, Galloway.

CYDIFOR

Brut y Tywysog notes under 883 that Cydifor, Abbot of Llanveithyn (Llancarfan) died, *'a wise and learned man, and of great piety, who sent six learned men to Ireland to instruct the Irish.'* Danish raids had almost wiped out the Irish Church at this time. Some Irish monks escaped to Whithorn in Wigtownshire, to Ninian's Candida Casa.

CYFELACH d. 927
March 1

Bishop of Llandaf from 880-927. St David's older foundation was given Cyfelach's name at Llangyfelach in Glamorgan. He was one of the rare Welshmen officially sanctified by the Church of Rome. Caradog of Llancarfan also recorded the death of another Cyfelach, Bishop of Morganwg, in the Welsh victory over the Saxons at the second Battle of Hereford in 754. There was also an abbot Cyfeilliog of Llanilltud Fawr, but we do not know which of these three was commemorated at of Llangyfelach, now jointly dedicated to Cyfelach and David. The feast day there was March 1, David's Day.

The tower is all that remains of St Cyfelach's Church at Llangyfelach near Swansea, as a storm wrecked the old church in 1803. The circular churchyard denotes the site's antiquity, and may well be the boundary of the monastery founded here by Dewi, St David, in the sixth century. There are three Celtic stones here. A cross-stone of 600-800 is placed above the north door of the tower, another stone now inside the church is carved CRUX-XPI 'The Cross of Christ', and there is also the decorated base of a tenth century cross, presumably smashed up in the Reformation. Nearby was the medicinal holy well known as Ffynnon Fydw or Ffynnon Saint. Ffynnon y Fil Feibion is next to the church. In the parish is Carnllechart, a stone circle with an entrance and a cist-faen (flat stone-topped chest) in the middle.

In the 'Life of David' a church was built by David at Llangyfelach in the Gower. A monastery was also said to be on the site, in which David placed the altar sent by Pepiau which cured the blind King of Ergyng. The holy altar there was said to have been sent to David by the Patriarch of Jerusalem.

CYFFIG

St Cyffig's church lies upstream from Tre Vaughan in Carmarthenshire

CYFLEFYR 6th century

Probably the son of Dingad and grandson of Brychan, he was martyred at a place called Merthyr Cyflefyr, perhaps in Cardigan.

CYFLEWYR 6th century

A son of King Gwynlliw and brother of Cadog.

CYFYW 6th century

The brother of Cadog, and an elder in his monastery in Llancarfan. Llangyfyw near Caerleon was named after him. He must be the same saint as Cynfyw.

CYHYLYN 6th century

The son of Tewdrig ap Teithfallt, and thus Meurig's brother and Arthur's uncle.

CYLLIN 1st century

The putative son of Caractacus, and brother of Eurgain and Claudia (Gwladys Ruffina). There is a Glamorgan tradition about a saintly prince called Owain ap Cyllin who was captured by the Romans but was brought back to Wales to be buried. (See Appendix I)

CYMORTH 5th century
CORTH

A daughter of Brychan who lived in Emlyn, the district between the present-day counties of Carmarthen and Pembroke. She was the wife of Brynach Wyddel and the mother of Gerwyn and his three sisters, Gwenlliw, Gwennan and Mwynen. There are several Brynach dedications in this area.

CYNAN see KEA

CYNAN GEFNHIR 6th century

The son of Cynwyd and brother of Cadrod Calchfynydd, he was said to have studied under Cadoc at Llancarfan and to have been a knight-counsellor to Arthur. There is a Bryn Cynan near Llangynwyd, his father's foundation. A stone inscribed *'Cunigni'* was found at Eglwys Gymmun in Carmarthenshire.

Iolo Morganwg's 'Sayings of the Wise' refers to Cynan (or possibly Kea):
'A glywaist ti chwedl Cynan
Wledig, Sant da ei anian?
Dryccai bob ammhwyll ei rann.'
'Hast thou heard the saying of Cynan
Wledig, a Saint of good disposition?
"Every rash person spoils his fate".'

CYNAN MEIRIADOG d. 421
CYNAN AP EUDAF

There are many legends about the flower of the British army that went to help Magnus Maximus become Roman emperor by defeating Gratian. Known in Brittany as Conan Meriadoc, this British prince was given lands in Armorica by Magnus as a reward for assisting him. Upon Magnus' death in 388, Cynan stayed as Duke of Armorica ('Brytein Fechan', Little Britain), submitting to Emperor Valentinian II.

In 409 he claimed independence for Brittany and died in 421. Cynan lived at Castel Meriadoc (Plougoulm outside Morlaix), *'divided the land into plous and trefs and thenceforth by the grace of God the country was called Little Britain'*. He seems to have also settled near Nantes. Cynan features in the 'Dream of Macsen Wledig' in 'The Red Book of Hergest', as the son of Eudaf ap Caradog and thereby the brother of Elen Luyddog, the wife of Magnus Maximus (Macsen Wledig).

CYNBRYD 5th century
March 19

A son of Brychan, he founded Llanddulas in Denbigh, near his brother Cynfran's foundation at Llysfaen. Prince Cynbryd was martyred by Saxons at the pass still known as Bwlch Cynbryd.

CYNDAF 1st century

A converted Jew, 'a man of Israel' who is said to have accompanied Caractacus' father Bran, and Ilid, from Rome. His name as 'Cunotami' is found on a stone inscribed in Latin and Ogham at St Dogmael's outside Cardigan.

CYNDDILIG late sixth century
CYNDDELW
November 1

The son of Cenydd or Nwython ap Gildas, his memory was celebrated at Capel Cynddilig, Llanrhystud in Cardigan. *'The Festival of Cynddilig, within the parish of Rhystyd, where indulgences were granted from midday on All Saints' Eve until midday on All Saints Day, and cocks were offered for the cure of whooping cough.'* There was a hiring fair at Llanrhystud on November 11. He was one of Arthur's men at his coronation, according to Geoffrey of Monmouth.

CYNDEYRN 6th century
July 25
August 5 and 6 Llangyndeyrn Fair

Of the line of Cunedda, and the son of Cyngar ab Arthog ap Ceredig, Llangendeirne (Llangyndeyrn) in Carmarthen is dedicated to him. His father Cyngar was said to have established a foundation at Llangenys in Glamorgan. Llangendeirne district possesses several Neolithic monuments. There are three standing stones at Coed Walter, one near Cloigyn Fawr, one on the Ffrwd road, and Llech yr Ast (The Bitch's Stone) is in a field called Canllefas. Bwrdd Arthur is a megalith on Mynydd Llangendeirne.

When the church at Llangyndeyrn was restored, no less than 497 adult skeletons were found closely packed in layers five deep. With no wounds, it appears that they died of the plague, possibly the Yellow Plague that killed Maelgwn in 547.

CYNDEYRN - see **KENTIGERN**

CYNFAB
November 15

Capel Cynfab under Llanfair ar y Bryn in Carmarthen.

CYNFALL 6th century?
CYNFEL

Merthyr Cynfall is recorded in the Book of Llandaf, and now is called Llangynvil, near Monmouth. 'Llangunville' near Skenfrith (Ynys Cynfraith) was known as Llangynfel. In the 7th century, Grecielis was Bishop of Llandaf, when the church of 'Merthyr Cynfel' was given to him by Brithgon Hael. It was taken from Llandaf and given to Hereford in 1100, but there are no remains.

CYNFARCH OER KINEMARK 5th century

This disciple of Dyfrig founded Llangynfarch (St Kinemark, in the boundaries of which lies Chepstow), and was said to be descended from Coel. He was mentioned by Spenser in 'The Faery Queen'.

CYNFARCH AP MEIRCHION 6th century
September 8

Not the same saint as Cynfarch Oer, there were some dedications in North Wales, and the church at Llanfair Dyffryn Clwyd once depicted 'Sanctus Kynfarch' in a stained glass window. The church is now dedicated to Mary and Cynfarch, Eglwys y Santes Fair a Sant Cynfarch, and has a splendid 14th century effigy of the knight Dafydd ap Madoc. Cynfarch married St Nefyn (Nyfain), a daughter of Brychan and their son was the great Urien Rheged. Iolo Morganwg thought that he founded Llangyngar in Maelor (now known as Hope, in Flint) destroyed by the Saxons in the battle of Bangor in 603. However, this is a Cyngar dedication.

His 'Saying of the Wise' is:
'Hast thou heard the saying of Cynvarch,
The bold and active warrior?
"Whoso respects thee not, respect not him".'

Some authorities put Merchianum ap Gurgust (Meirchion) as the first King of Rheged, succeeded by Cynfarch, who lived from c.500-555. This genealogy gives Elidr (Elidyr, q.v.) as Cynfarch's son, who married a daughter of Maelgwn Gwynedd, and was slain in Gwynedd, possibly by Rhun ap Maelgwn around 560. Elidyr was succeeded as King of Rheged by Urien Rheged, his brother, whose son was Llywarch Hen, who in turn lost the kingdom of South Rheged to Aethelfrith and came to Wales. Urien's other sons were Rhun and Owain. Rhun's daughter Rhieinfellt married King Oswy in 633.

CYNFARWY
November 7, 8, 10 or 11

Llechgynfarwy (Llangynfarwy) in Anglesey. He was the son of Awy ap Llenog, a prince of Cornwall. Maen Llech Gwern Farwydd (the Slate Stone in the Alder Grove) was a nine foot memorial stone next to the church but was broken up for wall-building. Perhaps the pieces can be found and any inscriptions recorded.

CYNFELIN 6th century
January 17, All Saints Day

Descended from Cunedda, and a son of Bleiddyn ap Meirion, he was a monk at Bangor Deiniol. He founded Llangynfelyn in Cardigan, and a church at Trallwng (Welshpool)* in Montgomery, where his brother Llywelyn had formed a religious society. Aneurin's 'Stanzas of the Months' says:

'Truly says Cynfelyn,
"A man's best candle is reason." '

The Cross of Conbelin, Margam Stones Museum.
CADW: Welsh Historic Monuments. Crown Copyright.

A 15th century Welsh poem has been translated thus:
'The month of January, the valley is smoky,
The cup-bearer is weary, the wondering poet is in distress,
The raven is starving, the hum of bees is rare,
The barn is empty, the kiln is cold;
Degraded is the man who is not worthy to be asked for anything;
Woe to him who loves his three enemies
Cynfelin spoke the truth
The best candle for a man is good sense.'

Sarn Gynfelin, the natural causeway over the lost kingdom of Cantre'r Gwaelod in Cardigan Bay, may be named after him (see the author's 'A-Z of Wales and the Welsh'.) There is a Roman fortlet at Llangynfelin only discovered during the 1976 drought, just seven miles from Pennal Roman fort and a similar distance from Pen Llwyn fort. It was abandoned around 130 AD, and was possibly sited to exploit local silver and lead deposits. It may be that Cynfelin, like many other Welsh saints, used a Roman site for his religious foundation. Churchgoers bathed their feet in Ffynnon Gynfelin in Llangynfelin churchyard, and took its waters away in bottles to use as medication.

*Mike Salter gives its dedication as 'Matu' or Cynfelin.

CYNFELIN DRWSGWL (the Clumsy) 6th century
CONBELINUS?

One of the 'Three Pillars of Battle' of the Isle of Britain, he saw the *'funeral pile of Gwenddolau's host'* at the battle of Arderydd in 567. He was probably a warrior more than a saint, but with his brothers Cadrawd, Clydno and Cynan is said to have studied under Cadog at Llancarfan. Cynfelyn ap Tegfan is a Gwynedd warrior mentioned in the Book of Aneirin, along with Tudfwlch ap Cilydd who died at the slaughter at Cattraeth. Wilson and Blackett believe that the Cynfelin commemorated at Margam was the brother of King Tewdrig, not the 1st century legendary King Cymbeline.

The great wheelcross, the 'Cross of Confelyn' is in the Margam Stones Museum, with the inscription CON/BELIN FUIT, knotwork, fretwork and interlaced carvings. Other Celtic stones here include one to CANTUSUS (see Peulin).

A six-feet high disc-headed cross reads CRUX XPI + ENNIAUN GUORGORET (*The Cross of Christ + Einoin made it for the soul of Gourgoret*). Einion (q.v.) is noted on the Pedigree of the Saints as a king in Llyn and Seiriol, the son of Owain Danwyn ab Einion Yrth ap Cunedda. 'Guagnorit' was a witness with Samson, Abbot of Llanilltud of a land grant of the village of 'Congworet' to the Abbot of St Cadoc's monastery in Llancarfan in the early 6th century.

A slab cross was made by Grutne* for the soul of Anest (*In nomine dei summi crux Christ preparavit Grutni pro anima ahest ...*), and there are radial cross slabs dedicated to Ilquici and Ilci. The six feet sculptured 'Cross of Ilquici' was for centuries used as a footbridge on Court y Dafydd farm before its removal to Margam Chapter-House. The smiliar 'Cross of Ilci' partially reads *'ilci Fecit hanc cruce m. in nomine. di summi'*. Other broken wheel crosses can be seen here.

The Cross of Grutne, Margam Stones Museum. CADW: Welsh Historic Monuments. Crown Copyright.

Cadw has re-built the museum to better show these magnificent stones, and Margam Park and Abbey can be visited at the same site. Another pillar to 'CONBELANI' can be seen at Merthyr Mawr, only a few miles east (see Glywys).

*A triad in the Myvyrian Archaeology reads *'The three brave chieftains of the Isle of Britain, Grudnet, Henbrien and Aednawg. They would never leave the field of battle escept on their biers, and they were the three sons of Gleisiar of the North and Haernwedd Vradawg (the treacherous) their mother.'* If this is the same Grutne, it is a 6th century cross.

CYNFFIG
CINFIC, CYNFIG

With Mirgint, Huui and Eruen, one of the four saints of Llangwm in Monmouth, recorded in 1056. There are two Llangwm's in Monmouth, Llanwgm Isaf and Llangwm Uchaf, with churches now dedicated to Jerome and John respectively. Kenfig near Pyle is now dedicated to Mary Magdalene. Ffynnon Llygad near Kenfig Castle (now being excavated from the drifting sand dunes) cured eye illnesses. A standing stone between Margam and Kenfig was called Bedd Morgan Morganwg, and Westwood noted it as the murdered Prince Morgan's sepulchre, showing Ogham and Latin inscriptions. Morgan was supposedly Arthur's son.

This stone was found on the Via Julia Maritima, near Pyle Station, and is now known as the Pompeius Stone, from its Roman inscription PVMPEIVS CARANTORIVS. Bishop Godwin of Llandaf noted in a letter to Camden that *'the Welsh Britans (sic) . . . make this interpretation* (anagram) *"Pim bis an car Antopius", i.e. 'The five fingers of our friends or neighbours have killed us.'* This was the first Welsh stone upon which Ogham writing was noticed. Blackett and Wilson believe that this stone possibly commemorates Hywel Mawr, the Breton saint and prince who fought for Arthur, and who was also known as Pompeius Regulus. Between Kenfig and Margam is Eglwys Newydd, now known as the Nunnery Farm, just 200 yards north of the Pompeius Stone. A Celtic cross noted by Westwood was found here.

CYNFOR 6th century
CYNFWR

The monastery at Bishopston in the Gower was founded by Cynfor for his master Teilo. Its name in Welsh was Llandeilo Ferwallt, Mergualdus being its first abbot. Llangunnor (Llangynwyr) in Carmarthen may also be his foundation, and there was an extinct chapel called Capel Cynnor near Pembrey. He may have been one of the Britons who fled to Brittany in 547 to avoid the Yellow Plague, and who lived in St Senoux. There was a hermit named Cynfor who improved the church at Clodock in Hereford with his brother after Clydog was martyred, who may also be this saint.

CYNFRAN 5th century
November 11 and 12

Llysfaen (formerly called Llangynfran) in Caernarfonshire and Llysfaen in Rhos, Denbigh have churches dedicated to Cynfran, a son of Brychan. Edward Lhuyd described Ffynnon Gynfran, where offerings were made to procure the saint's blessings on cattle. The invocation *'Rhad Duw a Chynfran Lwyd ar y da'*, 'The blessing of God and Holy Cynfran be upon the cattle' was used. It is interesting to note that the word 'da' is used for cattle here. Da means 'good', and cattle were tradeable commodities before money, so 'goods' were bartered. Llangynfran was destroyed by Saxons, and his brother Cynbryd is the patron of the neighbouring Llanddulas. Bishop Maddox around 1740 compared the well to that of Montpellier because on the 12th of November *'the Common People formerly offer'd here for their horned cattle.'*

CYNFYW 6th century
CYNYW

A son of Gwynlliw Filwr, who founded St Cynyw's Church, in Llangyniew (Llangynyw) in Montgomery. Llangyfyw, now called Llangeview near Usk is also his church. It is claimed that he was his brother Cadog's registrar at Llancarfan. (See CYFYW)

CYNFYN

The church at Ysbyty Cynfin (the Hospice of Cynfin) in north Cardigan may have been built inside a former megalithic circle. The churchyard wall contains at least four large standing stones, the largest of which is eleven feet high. The characters marked on them had become defaced by the 19th century.

CYNGAR 6th century
CONGAR, DOCCUINUS (teacher), DOCWIN, DOCHAU, DOCHDWY, DOGWYN, DOCCO
November 7 and 27, March 7 at Llangefni, May 12 Brittany

Cyngar may have come from Llanwngar near St David's in Pembrokeshire, and was one of the missionaries who went from Wales to found Christian communities in Devon and Somerset. He left his homeland to escape an undesired marriage. Son of Geraint, King of Dumnonia, he is supposed to have been buried at Congresbury in Somerset, his body having been brought back from a Jerusalem pilgrimage. King Ina founded a church there, and gave Cyngar's name to the place of his grave. A yew tree grew from Cyngar's staff that had been buried with him. His monastery there is mentioned in Bishop Asser's Life of King Alfred, and from the 11th century Congresbury church claimed his body. He was also celebrated in great feast days at nearby Dunster Priory and at Muchelney Abbey near Langport, both in Somerset.

His brother was Selyf, Saint Cybi's father. When Cyngar was old and unable to eat solid food, Cybi bought him a cow in calf to ensure that he had an ample supply of milk. The calf strayed on to the lands of Cybi's rival, Fintan, who would not release it. The power of Cybi's prayer helped the calf to uproot the tree it was tied to, and return to its mother, so that the cow could go on producing milk for the starving Cyngar. Other sources state that Dochdwy/Cyngar escaped from Brittany with Cadfan to Ynys Enlli where he was ordained bishop. When Cadfan died, Teilo went to administer Enlli, and Cyngar cared for Llandaf in Teilo's absence.

The parish church of Llandough-by Cowbridge is dedicated to St Cyngar, who founded a small cell or church here in the 6th century. The church stands in the precincts of Llandough Castle. At Llandough just west of Cardiff is the famous Irbic Cross. This ten feet high pillar cross is similar to one at Llandaf, and it is elaborately carved out of Sutton stone from near Ogmore. There are figures of people on all four panels of the rectangular pedestal, but the cross-head has disappeared. Westwood was told in the late 19th century that the cross-head had been rolled into the river or buried in a mound of rubbbish. Llandough was a 'clas', or mother church of, among other places, Llanddyfrdwy (on the site of Tredunnock* in Monmouth), Bishopston (also in Monmouth), and a cell in Cardiff. The church at Llandough near Cardiff grew into a noted monastery, but was eclipsed eventually by the spiritual growth of Llancarfan and Llanilltud Fawr, and the political growth of Llandaf.**

Cyngar is also remembered at Badgworth in Somerset, and is the patron saint of Hope (formerly Llangyngar) in Flintshire and Llangefni in Anglesey. His father Geraint was killed by the Saxons, as was his brother Selyf. St Cyngar is associated with Llangefni in Anglesey, and Ynys Gyngar is near Cricieth. In Llangefni a stone was found in 1824, when the old church was taken down. The inscription reads *'CVLIDORI IACIT ET ORVVITE MULIER SECVNDL'*. Another reading is 'Celidon Iacit', Celidon Wood being a battle site of Hoel Mawr. Cyngar is also the patron saint of Llanwngar near St David's.

St Kew in Cornwall was previously known as Lan Docco, from the monastery of Cyngar (Docco) which he founded there. There is a farm called St Ingonger with a holy well and chapel, just 2 miles south of Bodmin in Cornwall. The Cornish version of the story is that Docco and his sister Kew came from Gwent and first landed at Lan Docco, which St Samson later made his first place to visit in Cornwall. Cyngar's foundation at 'Llangenys' in Glamorgan is probably Llandough-juxta-Cardiff, formerly known as Bangor Cyngar and Bangor Dochau. In Brittany he is remembered at Lanlivet and St Congard in Morbihan. Baring-Gould and Fisher noted that at the latter's Pardon, *'women get taken with a convulsive affliction, and bark like dogs.'* There were two other Cyngars, ap Caw and ap Garthog and these may be their dedications, however. St Congard is south of Armel's Plourmel, on the road to Redon.

Cyngar's 'Saying of the Wise' is:
Hast thou heard the saying of Cyngar,
To those who derided him?
"Longer endures anger than sorrow".'

*A Roman stone was found fastened by four pins to the foundations of Tredunnock Church, and is now fixed to a wall. It reads *'D.M. JULIANVS/MIL LEG II AVG STIP: XVIII ANNOR XL/HIC SITVS EST/CVRA AGENTE/AMANDA/CONJVGE.'* Legend placed it as the gravestone of St Julian (q.v.), who was martyred at nearby Caerleon.

**In 1979, the Glamorgan-Gwent Archaeology Trust undertook emergency excavations at Llandough near Dinas Powys, uncovering a substantial Romano-British villa, with evidence of 'Dark Age' activity. The site was then used as a monastic grange in the Middle Ages. Originally a late Iron Age farmstead with a defensive ditch and round timber huts, the Roman villa was constructed around 120-130 AD. In the early 3rd century it was extended and an elaborate bath complex was added. The iron collars that connected the wooden hot water pipes were still intact. By the middle to late 4th century it had fallen out of use and was used as a burial ground. This was probably Cyngar's monastic site – many other early saints are associated with Roman sites as the local Roman-British nobility took them over. Part of the villa was still standing in the 13th and 14th centuries, and a medieval dovecot was also found in the buildings, the foundations of which were used for the building of the grange for Tewkesbury Abbey. This exciting complex is now covered by a series of identical boxes known as modern housing. Archaeologists, with very limited funds, were only allowed eight weeks to excavate the site before the bulldozers charged in. Why do planners always bow to builders?

CYNGAR ferch BRYCHAN 6th century

Francis Jones claims a daughter of Brychan of this name who lived in Brecon, and is associated with Ffynnon Gyngar in Eastyn (Queen's Hope, Denbigh), Flint and Penginger Well in Brecon (see Almedha). This is possibly the Cyngar noted above, however, who is the patron of Hope in

Denbigh. The differing feast dates of Cyngar show the confusion surrounding this saint. Perhaps readers can elucidate the matter further for a future edition of this book.

CYNGEN 6th century

The son of Cadell Deyrnllug and of Gwawrddydd, one of Brychan's daughters. Cyngen succeeded as prince of part of northern Powys, and gave most of his lands to saints and the church. He gave the lands at Bangor-is-Coed in Flint for the great monastery and college of Dunawd. There was a church dedicated to him in Shrewsbury, but it no longer exists. His son Mawan was a saint, and his other son Brochwel Ysgythrog, Brochwel the Fanged, vainly fought the great battle to defend Bangor-is-Coed from destruction. The name Cyngen occurs as *'Cunocenni'* on an inscribed stone at Trallwng near Brecon. The famous 'Pillar of Eliseg' near Valle Crucis Abbey was placed by Cyngen ap Cadell, the last King of Powys, who was murdered at Rome in 854 or 855. His territories passed to Rhodri Mawr. The stone celebrates his great grandfather Elise as the deliverer of Powys from the English (see Collen for the full text).

The Stone of St Cadfan at Tywyn Church is philologically the most important of all the Welsh stones, as all its four sides contain examples of the oldest from of Welsh in the country. The Cadfan inscription on the seven feet cross is noted in the St Cadfan and St Cadwaladr entries, and another side reads: *'CYNGEN CELAIN AR TU RHWNG DYBYDD MARCIAU'*, *'The body of Cyngen is on the side where the marks will be.'* It is possible that this is the burial stone of Cyngen, and Westwood believes that Cadfan was a nephew, Cyngen's sister's son. However, the 'Marciau' inscription is weathered and may have read Marciaun (Meirchion).

CYNHAEARN (see AELHAERN) late 6th century

A son of Hygarfael. Ynys Gynhaiarn, a chapel *'under Cruccaith'* on the Llyn peninsula was dedicated to him. At Ynyscynhaearn was born the great harpist and composer David Owen, Dafydd y Garreg Wen, who died in 1741. Only six stones remain of the thirty-eight that composed a stone circle at nearby Cwm Mawr.

CYNHAFAL early 7th century
October 5

The son of Elgud ap Cadfarch ap Caradog Freichfras and of Tubrawst ferch Tuthlwyniaid, he founded Llangynhafal in Denbigh. There is a circular Celtic churchyard with magnificent views of Moel Famau. The hammer-beamed church is a treasure-house of antiquities, with a large painted swan-like pelican on her nest above the south altar. The carving dates from 1690. Cynhafal's holy well near the church is in an enclosure measuring 18 feet by 10 feet, and was used up to a century ago. Arched over, with steps down, it was used for curing warts and rheumatism. The wart was pricked with a pin, which was then thrown in the well.

Alphabetical Listing of the Saints of Wales and Religious Events

CYNHEIDDION 6th century

A son of King Ynyr Gwent and Madrun, the daughter of Vortimer. The brother of saints Ceidio and Tegiwg, and of the future king Iddon.

CYNHEIDDON 5th century
KENEYTHON, RHYNEIDON

A virgin daughter of Brychan. The hamlet of Capel Llangynheiddon at Llandefeilog, near Cydweli, remembers her name, but the chapel appears to have vanished. Nearby Mynydd Cyfor and Cydweli were also associated with her. However, an alternative spelling of Llangynheiddon was Llangenedlon, and Cehedlon was another of Brychan's 'daughters'.

CYNIDR 6th century
ENODER
December 8, April 4

The son of Gwynlliw and Gwladys, and Cadog's brother. Cynidr probably went to Cornwall with Cadog. He is buried at Glasbury and there were several churches in Brecon dedicated to him, but all have been rededicated to Mary or Peter. Glasbury was his most important foundation, with his holy well, Ffynnon Gynidr, and was formerly known as Y Clas ar Wy (the monastery on the Wye). Llangynidr and Aberyscir in Brecon still commemorate him jointly with Mary, but nearby Llanywern under Llanfihangel is now only dedicated to the Virgin. Kenderchurch in Hereford was formerly called Lanncinitur. His hermitage at was at an island on the Wye at Winforton, but Winforton Church in Hereford is now dedicated to Michael.

Near Llangynidr Bridge, on the banks of the Usk, is the famous 'Fish Stone.' It is the tallest standing stone in Wales at 18 feet high, of red sandstone and shaped like a fish. On Midsummer Eve it is said that it jumps into the river for a swim. As it appears to have been moved from ancient workings on the other side of the Usk, this may be a folk memory of the great stone block being transported. Carreg Wen Llech is a monolith near Llangynidr Mountain, with strange lines of holes running down two of its four sides. Cynidr may be the saint Keneder in the Life of Cadog who accompanies Cadog in his confrontation with Arthur.

CYNIDR 6th century
April 27

The son of Rhiegar and Ceingar ferch Brychan, and commemorated in Maelienydd, Radnorshire. There is some confusion between the dedications of the two Cynidrs.

CYNIN 5th – 6th century
CUNIGNUS
November 24. Llangynin Fair was held on January 7, and later on the 18th when dates were changed in 1752 (see Dates)

The son of Tudwal Befr, by Nefydd a daughter of Brychan, and the founder of Llangynin near St Clears in Carmarthen. St Clears may also have been previously a Cynin foundation, where he may have been counted as a bishop. Nearby is Afon Cynin, three farms named after him, and a stone inscribed *'Cunegni'* (probably his gravestone) was found at Newchurch and is now at Traws Mawr. In the graveyard at Eglwys 'Gummun' a stone was found inscribed in Ogham and Latin, commemorating Cynin's daughter Avitoria: 'AVITORIA FILIA CUNIGINI'.

The holy well at St Clears was medicinal and called Ffynnon Gaing, which may indeed be a 'Normanised' corruption of Cynin. His brother was St Ifor. Known as Cynin Cof (of great memory), he featured as a warrior in early Triads and poems, and with his brother is linked with Arthur.

CYNLAS GOCH 6th century
CUNEGLASUS

The king of Rhos (East Gwynedd), and eldest son of King Owain Ddantgwyn who was assassinated by Maelgwn Gwynedd. Gildas calls him *'you Bear, rider of many and driver of the chariot of Dineirth'* (Din-Arth hillfort above Llandrillo-yn-Rhos). Cynlas was accused of starting a civil war as he tried to shake off Maelgwn's overlordship. He was possibly not a saint but is recorded as the patron of Penmon Church and founder of its priory. There was a Carn Cynlas noted in the parish of Llantrisant, Glamorgan in 1655.

CYNLLO early 5th century
July 16 and 17, Gwyl Gynllo was August 8

King Cynllo was the son of Mor, and of the line of Coel Godebog. Other sources place him as the son of Usyllt ab Hywyn Dwn, and the brother of Teilo.

Pistyll Cynllo, a famous spring, is in North Radnor's Llanbister, and it seems that he was also the patron of Rhayader church, now dedicated to Clement. St Cynllo's parish church at Nantmel was the mother-church to Llanfihangel Helygen and Llayre in Radnorshire. He also founded Llangynllo in Radnor and Llangoedmor in Cardigan. In Llangynllo parish, Ffynnon Lwli on Ffynnon Wen Farm, cured diarrhoea. Also in the parish is the holy well known as Pistyll Cynwy, which cured children's coughs and possibly lumbago. Parc Ffynnon Haiarn was also a field name in Llangynllo. At Llanbister were three *'black sulphurous mineral springs'* used to cure skin diseases.

As patron of Nantmel, Llangynllo, Llanbister and Rhayader in Radnorshire, and of Llangynllo and Llangoedmor in Cardigan, we can see Cynllo's influence across almost all of Maelienydd and Gwerthrynion. Llangoedmor was a mother church of which the 'clas' included Cardigan. Llanbister was one of the three richest churches in its diocese in 1291. Mount and Llechryd churches, later dedicated to the Holy Cross, used to be under Llangoedmor. In Llangoedmor is Ffynnon Cynllo, which was famous for curing rheumatism. Nearby is his cave, with 'Cerwyni Cynllo', his brewing tubs, round cavities formed by eddies of water on the rocky bed of the river. Earthworks in the parish are known as Cynllo Faes, and nearby are the imprints of his knees, and of his horse's hooves in the rocks. In Cwm Wernddu, Llangynllo is Ffynnon Fair which cured whooping cough. This is possibly one of the dozens of reattributions to Mary from an existing saint.

Alphabetical Listing of the Saints of Wales and Religious Events

ABBOT CYNOG d.492
CYNAWG FERTHYR, CANOC
October 7,8,9, 10, 11 and later in the month, February 11, January 24 (Padstow)

One of Brychan's sons by Banhadlwedd, and a claimant to be the eldest, was celebrated at Defynnog, Ystrad Gynlais, Merthyr Gynog and Penderyn in Brecon and Llangynog in Montgomery. In Brecon, Battle chapel and Llangynog under Llanganten were also his chapels, as was Boughrood in Radnor. Just south of Battle Church is a twelve foot menhir on a small tumulus. There are two Llangunnocks, in Hereford and Monmouthshire, also associated with him. Cwrt Brychan is near Llangunnock on the Pill Brook in Monmouthshire. He was supposed to have been murdered by Saxons or Irish Picts upon Van mountain (Y Fan Oleu) in Brecon, in the parish of Merthyr Cynog*, where the church of Merthyr (the Martyr) was built over his grave. However, it is more likely that he was killed in a skirmish between Brychan's Irish tribe and other local chieftains, after which many of the family of Brychan fled to Cornwall. His name is seen on a 7th century inscribed stone near Tremadoc, as CUNACI.

Giraldus Cambrensis described the armlet that Brychan gave to Cynog:
'*I must not be silent concerning the collar which they call St Canauc's; for it is most like to gold in weight, nature and colour; it is in four pieces wrought round, joined together artificially, and clefted as it were in the middle, with a dog's head, the teeth projecting. It is considered by the inhabitants so powerful a relic, that no man ventures to swear falsely upon it when laid before him. It bears the marks of heavy blows, as if made by an iron hammer; for a certain man, it is said, endeavouring to break the torque for the sake of the gold, experienced divine vengeance, was deprived of his eyesight, and lingered out the rest of his days in darkness.*'

Baring-Gould and Fisher note Hugh Thomas' description of Cynog in 1702:
'*In his youthfull days forsaking this World for the next, he retired from his Father's Court to a Cott or Hermitage not far from the high Roade betweene Brecknock and Battle, about a mile from Carevong, his father's Metropolitan City . . . where he travilled up and down in a poor miserable Habit and made himself a heavy boult or Ring of Iron for his head roughly twisted togather like a Torce or Wreeth insteed of a Crowne of Golde . . . This rendered him . . . he Scorne and Derition of all that saw him from which he was nick named Kynog Camarch that is the Dispised King.*'

At Defynnog his Gwyl Mabsant was commemorated at the time of Cynog's 'Ffair a Bwla' on the second Thurday in October. At this fair, purchases were made for his wake, on the following Sunday. The wake lasted a week, with feasting and celebrations taking place in front of the Bull Inn. (The custom finished in 1835, except for several decades after there was a goose fair on the Sunday.) On the Monday, 'Dydd Llun Gwyl Gwynog', there was a custom of '*carrying Cynog*' where a stranger or local volunteer was dressed in a suit of old clothes, carried through the village, and thrown into the river. He was jeered at by the crowd as he tried to clamber out. The last record was of a drunken farmer being carried in 1822. On Tuesday, a tithe was taken of cheese, which was brought to the churchyard, displayed on the gravestones, and sold for the benefit of the church. Defynnog has a tall Celtic pillar-cross with Latin and Ogham inscriptions which are now illegible. Cynog is also remembered at Llansteffan (see Ystyffan).

He went with Cadoc to Cornwall, where their joint feast was held at Padstow on January 24, and he set up a great church at Pinnock, next to Boconnoc, also named after him.

Cynog's 'Saying of the Wise' is:
'Hast thou heard the saying of St Cynog,
Chief of the land of Brecon?
"The one half of learning is (already) in the head".'

At Ystradgynlais, on Cribarth Hill is Saith Maen, Seven Stones, a line of stones pointing one way to another Seven Stones, and the other way to Cerig Duon stone circle. The other Saith Maen is on Y Wern, and six stones appear to be remaining. Two Celtic stone fragments are in Ystradgynlais Church, one reading *'ADIVNE',* and the other simply *'hic iacet'.*

*When the church of Trallong, between Brecon and Defynnog, was rebuilt around 1830, an inscribed and Oghamic stone was discovered being used as a window support. The inscription had been hidden, but reads:
'cvnocenni filius
cvnoceni hic jacit'
The Ogham reads *'cunacenni? fi? ilffeto'* and has been damaged, and a goidelic traslation is *'Cu nac, a warrior pierced by many wounds, lies beneath in silence'.* Cynog ap Cynog does not appear in Welsh records, but it may be an infant son of St Cynog, and the Rev. H.L. Jones believed it to be definitely connected with the saint (see Westwood).

CYNOG d.606
March 14

The second bishop of Llanbadarn who was raised to the archbishopric of St David's on David's death. He was succeeded shortly after there by Teilo, David's fellow student and friend. The chapel of Llangynog in Carmarthen was his dedication, or that of Cunog ap Brychan. Ffynnon Gynog was on Parc Gynog Farm there, and Ffynnon Ddagrau was not far from the church. Many of the churches of the bishopric of Llanbadarn were destroyed by Saxons in 720, and later the weakened see was merged with St David's. At Llangynog is a dolmen known variously as Arthur's Table or Twlc y Filiast, near Ffynnon Newydd, a holy well which cured Judge Vaughan of Derllys (as noted in Francis Jones' 'The Holy Wells of Wales').

At a cottage called Maenhir, on Bodfeddan Farm in Anglesey, was found a 5th-6th century stone reading *'CYNOGVSI HIC IACIT.'* Mentioned by Westwood, the author does not know its present whereabouts, but it could be Cynog's burial site.

CYNON 6th century
November 9

He accompanied Cadfan from Brittany to Ynys Enlli, and was appointed first chancellor of the monastery. He had first studied at Llancarfan and Llanilltud. Capel Cynon near Llandyssilio Gogo in Cardigan commemorated him, and he is reputed to have founded Tregynon church in Montgomeryshire. Near Llanbister in Radnor was an old mansion called Croes Cynon, supposedly where his cross was. A nearby rock (Craig Cynon) was his hermitage and he drank fresh water from Nant Cynon. His 'Saying of the Wise' is:
'Have you heard what Cynon sang
When avoiding drunkards?
"Good ale is the key of the heart" '
(Cwrw [da] yw allwedd calon).

St Cynon has a well at Langynwyd, the remarkable village near Maesteg. The first person to drink out of the well after a wedding ceremony would inevitably have the upper hand in the marriage. Trinity Well lies on the borders of Tregynon and Bettws Cedewain in Montgomery, and until recently its water was mixed with brown sugar and drunk on Trinity Sunday. *'The people afterwards retire to a green spot for dancing, etc. An old Welsh calendar said that on the eve of Trinity Sunday it is customary to wash or bathe to prevent the tertian ague.'* (Rev. John Foster, 'The Welsh Calendar' 1895).

Tregynon, a village of 503 people, has its own website, but puts Cynon's church as a 12th century site, confusing its foundation with the hospital of the Knights Templar nearby. A mile away is the superb black and white Gregynog Hall, a University of Wales building now, and a centre of printing excellence. One of the owners, Henry Hanbury-Tracy, built 'concrete cottages' in the driveway in 1870, believed to be the oldest totally concrete houses in the world. Tregynon has no pub, because the Davies sisters who lived there from 1924-1964, closed down 'The Dragon' and replaced it with a 'Temperance House', still to be seen in the centre of the village. The sisters left their fabulous collection of impressionist art to the National Gallery in Cardiff.

CYNON OF MANAW 5th-6th century
November 9

One of Brychan's family, a confessor who seems to have settled on the Isle of Man with his kinsfolk Arthen and Bethan. Other sources state that this son of Brychan was the Cynon who founded Capel Cynon in Cardigan. They have been given the same feast date.

CYNUDYN 6th century

The son of Bleiddyd ap Meirion, and a dean at Llanbadarn college. There is a stone in the churchyard at Llanwnws in Cardigan inscribed *'Canotinn'* which may be a monument to this saint.

CYNWYD early 6th century
September 28 (Browne Willis), October 15 Feast day (Edward Lhuyd)

Cynwydd Cynwyddion was a saint in Llancarfan, and the son of Cynfelyn ap Garthwys. He founded Llangynwyd Fawr, near Bridgend in Glamorgan. He was a 'warrior from the North', and his links with Llangynwyd would be tenuous but for the fact that two large farms there, Bryn Cynan and Maes Cadrod, recall his sons' names. Ffynnon Gynwyd (which cured gout, especially when used in May) is near the church, as is Ffynnon Gynon and Ffynnon Caerau, a pin well in which one bathed to cure rheumatism. Another healing well was Ffynnon Wrgan at Llwyni Farm, named after one of the princes of Glamorgan or St Eurgain. Several other healing wells are noted by Francis Jones in Llangynwyd parish. The Corner House pub in Llangynwyd often has a *'Noson Lawen'* (a happy evening of singing) upon a Friday night. This village is unusual in its retaining Welsh traditions and language in a heavily 'Normanised' part of Wales. The thatched Yr Hen Dŷ (The Old House) is one of the oldest inns in Wales.

November 31 in Llangynwyd sees a form of *'wassail'* known as the *'Mari Llwyd' (Grey Mare)*, or *'Y March' (the Horse)* which still takes place here. The festivities take place around the old thatched *'Yr Hen Dŷ' ('Old House')* pub. A man is covered with a white sheet and carries a decorated horse's skull, wrapped tightly in a white sheet and decorated. Until recently the octogenarian Cynwyd Evans masterminded the ceremonies from midnight onwards. The Mari and its party of followers go from farmhouse to farmhouse, gaining entry and refreshment by outsinging the householders. There is a *'battle of the bards'* where challenges, insults and jokes are exchanged, some traditional and some improvised. On New Year's Day, the skull is replaced by the original. This 'Mari' or skull is so precious that it is kept for most of the rest of the year in the Museum of Welsh Life in St Fagan's, Cardiff. This is a Celtic festival, predating Christianity and remembering horse-worship. It can also be seen between late December and early January around Llantrisant and Pontypridd in Glamorgan, Ystradgynlais further west and Ammanford in Dyfed. In the 18th century, Methodists made New Year's Eve their 'Watch Night', singing hymns until a few minutes before midnight, when there is a silence before the bells ring out.

A 'Stanza of the Hearing' states:
'Have you heard what Cynwyd sang
And heard said?
"The most excusable of injury is the evil of war." '

Iolo Morganwg placed him as a saint at Llancarfan, and a 'Stanza of Achievement' reads:
'The achievement of Cynwyd Cynwyddion
Was the advancement of goodly institutions,
And the establishment for corau of wise regulations.'

One of the most beautiful and haunting Welsh tunes is 'The Maid of Cefn Ydfa.' It is based on the legend of the bard Wil Hopcyn and his tragic love Ann Thomas, who are both buried in Llangynwyd churchyard. Westwood notes an ancient stone found in the chancel wall, with a cross-socket, and of a hard stone not found in the area. He presumes it was placed during the 1688 church restoration.

CYNWYL 6th century
April 30 (Rice Rees), January 5 at Cynwyl Elfed, January 8 at Cynwyl Gaio and November 21 at Aberporth (Browne Willis).

A son of Dunawd Fawr and brother of Deiniol, he lived under the protection of David at Brefi, and founded Cynwyl Gaio, the church nearest to Llanddewi Brefi. Aberporth in Cardigan and Cynwyl Elfed in Carmarthen are attributed to the saint, and he was the patron saint of Penrhos (formerly Llangynwyl), a chapel under Abererch in Caernarfonshire. With his father and brothers he helped found Bangor-is-Coed.

He is yet another saint associated with Arthur. In 'Culhwch and Olwen' 'Cynwyl Sant' is *'the third man that escaped from the Battle of Camlan, and he was the last who parted from Arthur, on Hengroen his horse.'* The other two were Sandde Bryd Angel and Morfran ap Tegid.

At Cynwyl Gaio, there is a place in the River Annell where he used to kneel in the cold waters and pray. For centuries, farmers scooped water from the hollows made by his knees, to pour over the backs of their cattle to protect them from disease. At Cynwyl Elfed, Carmarthen, a mock trial was held as late as 1865 where a *'ceffyl pren' (wooden horse)* was tried and burnt. The 'ceffyl pren' was a social control mechanism to punish adultery. T.M. Owen quotes from Emlyn Jenkins' 'Cofiant Elfed':

'In Cynwyl Elfed, Carmarthenshire, in the 1860's, Christmas did not mean much to its inhabitants. "It was half Sunday and half work-day, a colourless day. People were afraid to work and avoided amusing themselves at all costs . . . Its chief importance was that it was within a week of New Year's Day, the biggest day of the year for us children." The Christmas Season was more important than Christmas Day and the cessation of work made prolonged festivities possible.' (see Christmas, Carols).

Also in Cynwyl parish was Ffynnon Ffos Anna, which seems to have had a stone circle around it and which was noted for healing cripples. In 1881 Wirt Sikes noted of Cynwyl Gaio, near the Roman gold mines, *'There is a Roman type, too, among the Welsh women. Many inhabitants of Cynwil Gayo parish, Carmarthenshire, are said to pride themselves on their Roman descent, and Roman names prevail among them. I have heard of two families in Wales of the name of Aurelius, and another of the name of Cornelius, whose features in both cases closely resemble the ancient Roman type. The resemblance holds good in both the men and the women.'*

CYNYR OF CAER GAWCH 5th century
GYNYR

The grandfather of St David, and father of the saints Non, Sadwrn Hen, Gwen, Banhadlen and Gwestlan (Giustlianus). The son of Gwyndeg ap Seithenin, he gave his all lands in Menevia to the church.

He was the chief of the territory later called Pebidiog or Dewisland, where St David's is situated. His first wife was Mechell (Marchell), a daughter of Brychan, and their daughter was Banadlwen who married St Dirdan. His second wife was Anna, the daughter of Gwrthefyr Fendigaid (Vortimer, High King of Britain). Their son Giustilianus was a saint, as were their daughters Non (mother of St David) and Gwen (mother of Cybi). Giraldus Cambrensis states that Cynyr's son Gistlianus was bishop of Menevia, before David.

CYNYR FARFDRWCH 6th century
CYNYR FARFWYN, CYNYR CEINFARFOG

From Cynwyl Gaio in Carmarthen, he was the father of the saints Gwyn, Gwynno, Gwynnoro, Celynin and Ceithio, alleged quintuplets. Cynyr was the son of Gwron ap Cunedda. Llanpumsaint in Carmarthen commemorates the five saints, and Pumsaint in Caio parish formerly had a chapel of ease dedicated to them. Their day was All Saints Day.

CYRUMO

Nothing is known by the author of this saint except that he is noted as the patron of Llangoedmore in Cardigan by Mike Salter.

KING CYSTENNIN GORNEU d. 443 or 448
CYSTENNIN FENDIGAID (the BLESSED), CONSTANTINE

The son of Magnus Maximus and St Elen ferch Eudaf, and the brother of St Peblig, he is remembered at Llangystennin in Caernarfonshire, and at Welsh Bicknor in Herefordshire, which was formerly called Llangystennin Garth Benni. Near the former is Llangernyw, the Church of the Cornishman. It is dedicated to the saints Erbyn and Digain, who were Cystennin's sons by the daughter of Peibio, King of Ergyng. He seems to have been the first 'Pendragon', or warleader, to assume the actual monarchy of Britain. Other sources say that he was a prince of Armorica. Welsh Bicknor (Llangystennin/Garthbenni) had a notable monastery between 575 and 866, possibly the seat of Dyfrig's original bishopric.

Macsen Wledig's son Constantine was murdered in 448 by Vortigern, and was avenged by Emrys Wledig (Ambrosius Aurelianus). Cystennin was the great-great-grandfather of the saints Cybi and Gildas. Much of this story overlaps with Constantine. Geoffrey of Monmouth made Cystennin the father of Uther Pendragon and grandfather of Arthur. At Caernarfonshire's Llangystennin is Ffynnon Llangystennin (near Llandudno Junction).

On the outskirts of Caernarfon (Segontium Roman town) is Llanbeblig, said to have been founded by Peblig, a son of Macsen Wledig and Elen. Nennius wrote that the *'son of the great, the very great'* was buried at Segontium, i.e. the son of Magnus Maximus. Matthew of Westminster informs us that in 1283, the body of Emperor Constantine was transferred to Llanbeblig, the mother church of Caernarfon, on the orders of King Edward I.

CYWAIR
GOWER
July 11

Llangywair (Llangower) near Bala commemorates this female saint, and her holy well is there, with a stone inscribed with a cross known as Llech Gower. Ffynnon Gower was used to cure children of rickets. There is an ancient legend that her other holy well was not capped one night as it should have been, and flooded the ancient town of Bala to form Wales' largest natural lake. (See Gwyar)

CYWYLLOG 6th century
CWYLLOG
January 7

A daughter of the fugitive King Caw, who was given lands on Anglesey by Maelgwn Gwynedd, she founded Llangwyllog in the centre of the island. The wife of Medrod, she took up the religious life when her husband was possibly slain by Arthur at the terrible battle of Camlan. However, Medrod may have been on Arthur's side. (Why historians persist in placing Camlan in the West country, when it was a battle between the Britons of north and south Wales, on a known site in Wales, is beyond this author's comprehension. Arthurian links with the West are tenuously adopted from writers of the Middle Ages, following the Glastonbury fraud, and have been seized upon to exploit tourism in England. Some 'historians' even have made Arthur a Saxon-German, and another a Scot.)

D

'Diogenes struck the father when the son swore'

Robert Burton, 'Democritus to the Reader', c.1630

DANIEL see DEINIOL

DARERCA d. 518
MONENNA, BLINE
July 6

Welsh authorities state that this was Patrick's Welsh sister whose sons who were saints including Mel, Rioch (who was consecrated a bishop in Ireland by Patrick), Sechnallus (Secundinus), Menni and Auxilius. Mel was consecrated Bishop of Ardagh by his uncle Patrick, and is recorded as a British evangelist in Ireland, celebrated on February 6. Irish sources however make Darerca a virgin, closely associated with Patrick and Bridget, and the foundress of Killeevy in County Armagh. (See Ffraid Leian).

DATES

It is difficult to place the correct Saint's Feast Day at times, because many records are not replicated, and often we do not know whether the date relates to before the great calendar change of 1752, or after it. The Vatican had ruled that ten days be taken out of the year in 1582, and by the time Britain agreed to the same new dates as the rest of the Continent, another day was needed for adjustment (see Duncan's marvellous book, 'The Calendar').

In 1752, people woke up on September 3rd and discovered that it was September 14th, and the 'Calendar Riots' broke out across Britain. The crowds wanted their 11 days of life (and wages) given back to them. In the Gwaun Valley near Fishguard, people have kept on celebrating the 'old date' of New Year until the present time. January 11 is 'Old New Year's Eve' there. The festival of 'Hen Galan' is still held there on January 12th, where children in the valley go around houses singing for presents, and in the evening there is a *'noson lawen'* – food and beer at local farmhouses, with stories and songs. There is also a Hen Galan service in Llandysul church near Cardigan, with a local style of singing known as 'pwnc' chanting. When the dates went back 11 days at Glastonbury, crowds gathered to see the Glastonbury Thorn which always flowered on Christmas Day. It flowered on January 5th, Twelfth Night, instead.

Incidentally, until 1752 and the Gregorian Calendar replaced the Julian one, **March 24 was New Year's Eve across Britain.** The 'new' January date was chosen because it coincided with Christ's circumcision (at least four Italian cathedrals claim to have the relevant relic of Jesus). In actuality, because Jewish practice was to carry out the operation 8 days after the birth, the Feast of the Circumcision, and the New Year, should fall on January 2. However, the start of the month appealed more to the relevant authorities, and 'Old New Year's Eve' became April 5, not 11 but 12 days on from March 24. (Just 11 days had been 'lost', but many dates moved by an extra day). Another point to this intriguing little discursion is that **April 5 marks the boundary between old and new financial years even now.** London bankers protested *'give us back our 11 days'* as they were losing interest monies, and refused to pay their taxes on March 25 as Parliament had decreed when it scrapped September 2 -14. Unfortunately, the present near coincidence of the dates of Christmas and the New Year, changed by the order of church authorities, has given the Western world a period of over-indulgence spread over just six days every year (see Christmas).

Incidentally, Caesar has created a *'year of confusion'* in 45 BC by adding 80 days to the year. Out of jealousy of Julius Caesar's 31-day July, Augustus named the month of Sextilius after himself in 14 AD, robbing a day from February to achieve the equivalent number of 31 days. In 532 AD, the astronomer Dionysius Exiguus confused the world forever by declaring the date of Christ's birth to be 1 AD rather than 0 AD, so a year disappeared from our reckoning of dates. Thus even today, people argue about the 'true' date of New Year's Eve, 2000. To complicate matters even further, a letter in the Western Mail (by Chris Williams) pointed out that *'The inhabitants of Gwaun Valley have celebrated the Julian New Year a day too early. The current Gregorian calendar is now 13 days out of line with the old Julian calendar. The Julian New Year's Day was January 14, 2000. When the Gregorian calendar was adopted by Britain in 1752 we were 11 days out. The two extra days are accounted for by the fact that in the Julian calendar 1800 and 1900 were leap years while in the Gregorian calendar they are not.'*

One strange consequence of Pope Greory XIII's original date change of 1582, starting a new calendar that began January 1st, instead of April 1st, was that many people refused to believe the change, and still celebrated New Year on April 1st. Wiser citizens called them 'April Fools', and played tricks on them. Some of the April Fool's Day hoax stories in 'The Western Mail' are as follows. In 1977, because of dwindling supplies of laverbread, scientists had invented a synthetic substitute. In 1993, Pwllheli council came to an agreement with the inventors of Russia's proposed space mirror, to send 15 hours of sunshine a day to the resort, thus making it a contender for the 2000 Olympic Games. In 1996, EU officials told Oakwood Park officials that their Megaphobia ride had to run anti-clockwise for increased safety. And in 1997 a leaked Welsh Rugby Union document informed us that the new Millennium Stadium had been designed to give the Welsh rugby team an unfair advantage, with a positive magnetic field in the Welsh team's changing room..

DAVID – see DEWI

JOHN DAVIES 1567-1644
May 15

Dr John Davies of Mallwyd is one of the greatest Welsh scholars, given a Holy Day by the Church in Wales. Born in Llanferres, the son of David ap John ap Rhys and Elizabeth ferch Lewis ap David Lloyd, he graduated from Jesus College in 1593. He was close to Bishop William Morgan of Llandaf, whom he helped translate the Bible. He gained his divinity degree and doctorate from Lincoln College Oxford in 1608 and 1616 respectively. From 1604 he was rector of Mallwyd, and also gained the rector's post at Llan-ym-Mawddwy in 1614. He surrendered the sinecure of Darowen for the sinecure of Llanfor in 1621. From 1617 he was the prebendary of Llanefydd in the cathedral church of St Asaf. Davies is best known for his great Welsh-Latin Dictionary of 1632, which he compiled during his time as Rector at Mallwyd. His

Welsh grammar, 'Antiquae Lingua Britannicae', was another magisterial work dating from 1620, and it is supposed that he was an active contributor to Richard Parry's Welsh Bible of 1620. He stayed at Mallwyd for 40 years, and his contribution towards the survival of the Welsh language cannot be underestimated.

RICHARD DAVIES 1501-1581
RHYSIART ap DAFYDD
November 7

This bishop and translator is given the Holy Day of his day of death. His father was Dafydd ap Gronw, curate of Gyffin, and Davies was forced to follow the change in law by 'Anglicising' his surname. Educated at Oxford, he was a curate in Buckinghamshire, but summoned to the Privy Council in 1553 upon the accession of Queen Mary. Davies was deprived of his livings, and went with his family to exile in Frankfurt until 1558 and the accession of Elizabeth. In 1559 he led a royal commission visiting the dioceses of Hereford, Worcester and Wales, and in 1559 was elected bishop of St Asaf. In 1561 he became bishop of St David's. He criticised 'self-seeking' clergy, and tried hard to reform the church for the better. His greatest contribution to Wales was his collaboration with Willam Salesbury (q.v.) at the Bishop's Palace at Abergwili to translate the Prayer Book and the New Testament into Welsh. This was part of his plan to expedite the translation of the Bible into Welsh, but supposedly the two quarrelled before its completion (see William Morgan). Near Abergwili, at Felin Wen was found a Celtic cross marked *'Corbagnus, filius A--'*. It was being used as a sharpening stone in the 19th century, and formerly stood in a nearby ancient chapel in Hen Llan lane.

WILLIAM DAVIES d. 1593
July 27

A Catholic martyr from Croes-yr-Eirias, Colwyn (near Llandrillo-yn-Rhos, Denbighshire). After attending Douai, he went to the seminary at Rheims in 1582. With three other Welshmen, he was ordained by Cardinal Guise in 1585. Just two months later he went as part of the 'English Mission' heading for his native district, where a Catholic community was forming under Robert Puw (q.v.). He lived for most of 1586 in Rhiwledyn Cave on the Little Orme, reprinting Richard Gwyn's 'Y Drych Cristianogawl', probably the first book to be printed in Wales. Around this time, the President of Wales was the second Earl of Pembroke, who was actively persecuting Catholics. Davies was captured in 1592 by Foulk Thomas at Holyhead, along with Robert Puw, as they were escorting four young Welshmen who wished to go to a Spanish seminary in Ireland. He confessed to Bishop Hugh Bellot of Bangor, but refused to implicate his travelling companions, one of whom was the young Robert Gwynne (q.v.).

Davies was separated from his fellows and thrown into the *'dark, stinking dungeon'* of Beaumaris Gaol*, where he refused all offers to recant his faith. After a month's solitary confinement, his imprisonment eased, and he celebrated mass for Catholic vistiors. He was offered several chances of escaping by Robert Puw, but refused them all. Judge William Leighton pronounced Davies guilty of treason, but postponed sentence, hoping that the saintly Davies would recant. The Council of Ludlow did not wish him to die and become a focus for discontent, and he was also held in Bewdley prison before being returned to Beaumaris. He again refused an offer to escape, and for six months he 'ruled' a Catholic community in the gaol.

Despite difficulties in obtaining a hangman from the hostile local population, William Davies was executed on July 27. A chapel was erected at Beaumaris in 1909. Gwilym Pue described him as *'Syr William, seren ei wlad' (Sir William, star of the home country),* and T. P. Ellis called him *'one of the most appealing of all the Welsh martyrs.'* His disciples included the fathers Robert Edmonds and William Robins, both ordained at Valladolid.

*Beaumaris Gaol can be visited as a tourist attraction these days, and has a unique treadmill dating from 1867. Six prisoners were made to climb it for a period of 15 minutes on and 15 minutes off, for 8 hours a day. Every quarter of an hour they were replaced by a second batch of prisoners. They had to stand on the outside platforms of the wheel, with no place to rest their arms or upper bodies, and failing to step would mean serious injury from the wheel, as it moved over the prisoner's fallen body in the wheel-pit. The wheel pumped water into a tank on top of the prison.

DAYS

When the Saxons and Angles of England were converted, Caesar's calendar was reintroduced into the island, with some Anglo-Saxon modifications. The Germanic goddess Eostre was used to name Easter, which is still officially called the Feast of the Passion by Catholics, and Y Pasg in Welsh. Pope Gregory had told Augustine:
'The idols are to be destroyed, but the temples themselves are to be aspersed with holy water, altars set up in them, and relics deposited there . . . In this way, we hope that the people, seeing that their temples are not destroyed, may abandon their error and, flocking more readily to their accustomed resorts, may come to know and adore the true God. And since they have a custom of sacrificing many oxen to demons, let some other solemnity be substituted in its place, such as a day of Dedication or the Festivals of the holy martyrs whose relics are enshrined there . . . For it is certainly impossible to eradicate all errors from obstinate minds in one stroke.'

In this spirit, Augustine allowed the Saxons to keep their gods' names in weekdays in order to help win over their 'obstinacy.' The Welsh, however, had adopted Romano-Christian days centuries before:

Day	Anglo-Saxon	Roman	Welsh (dydd)
Sunday	Sun	Sul	Sul (Sun)
Monday	Moon	Luna	Llun (Moon)
Tuesday	Tiw	Mars	Mawrth (Mars)
Wednesday	Woden	Mercurius	Mercher (Mercury)
Thursday	Thor	Jupiter	Iau (Jupiter)
Friday	Freya	Venus	Gwener (Venus)
Saturday	Saturn	Saturnus	Sadwrn (Saturn)

DEDYN 6th century
NEUBYDD

The brother of the martyred Clydog and grandson of Brynach.

Bangor Cathedral. © *Wales Tourist Board Photo Library.*

DEGEMAN d.706
DECUMANUS
August 27 (August 30 in Norwich and Cornwall)

A hermit-saint of noble birth from south-west Wales, he is the patron saint of Rhoscrowther in Pembroke, and of the extinct chapel of Llandegeman under Llanfihangel Cwm Du, near Tretower Court in Brecon. Rhoscrowther, where he was possibly born, was formerly called Llanddeygman and Eglwys Degeman. The villagers have slowly been moved out by the owners of the local petro-chemical complex, which will leave the present church in time to decay and die.

Decuman sailed across the waters of the Bristol Channel, landing at Watchet in Somerset, where he made a hermitage, living off milk from his cow. A robber cut off Degeman's head, but the saint carried his head to his well where he washed it, thus sanctifying the waters. His day was the principal festival in the calendar of the monks of Muchelney Abbey, near Langport. He was also culted at Wells Cathedral. Near the church in Watchet dedicated to Degeman lies the holy well. Its waters fall over three terraced basins.

Just outside Rhoscrowther Church, St Degman's holy well had curative properties. The Welsh legend is that after he was beheaded in Somerset, Degeman crossed the seas to Rhoscrowther where the well gushed forth for him to wash his head, and he was then buried at the place of his birth. Doble believes that Degeman's origin was in Brecon: *'We have every reason to associate the establishment of these and other churches dedicated to the children of Brychan with an early diffusion of Celtic Christianity from Brycheiniog in the 5th and 6th centuries . . . Now we know that from Brecknock went forth numerous missionaries who evangelised Hereford to the east and Glamorgan, Carmarthen and Pembroke to the south and west . . . Thus it looks as if St Decuman belonged to a group of Brecon saints who founded monasteries in south-west Wales, from which missions to Somerset and Cornwall were sent out . . . he may have been associated with the great saints of Cardigan and Pembroke, Carantoc, Petroc and Brioc, who did such important work in Somerset, Cornwall and Brittany.'*

BISHOP DEINIOL fl. 550
DEINIOL WYN, THE BLESSED, DEINIOL AIL, DANIEL
September 10, 11, 21, 22, December 10, possibly November 21

Deiniol was a hermit who lived on Daniel's Mount in Mynyw in Pembroke, who became Bishop of Bangor. He was said to have been uneducated and illiterate, and suddenly became endowed with complete religious knowledge when he said his first mass in the cathedral. However, his parents were the famous Dunawd Fawr and Dwywe ferch Gwallog ap Llenog, which made his illiteracy unlikely. He probably assisted his father in the foundation of Bangor-is-Coed. Deiniol and Dyfrig were said to be the two clerics who persuaded David to take part in the Synod of Brefi in 545, which makes him an extremely important figure in the early Christian church. If Gildas is correct in his description of Illtud (*'praeceptorem paene totius Britanniae magistrum elegantem'*), Deiniol was educated at Llanilltud Fawr with Maelgwn Gwynedd.

He founded Bangor Fawr (Bangor Deiniol) on the Menai Straits, where the cathedral is dedicated to him. He was the abbot but Maelgwn Gwynedd raised the place to an episcopal see, and Deiniol was the first bishop of Gwynedd, possibly receiving the consecration from Dyfrig. He was buried on the Isle of 20,000 Saints, Bardsey (Enlli). Annales Cambriae give his death date at 584, but as the years seem to be twelve years 'out' for Kentigern and David, he probably died in 572.

As founder and first Bishop of Bangor in Arfon, his diocese covered Gwynedd, and there is a dedication in Denbigh at Marchwiel outside Wrexham. Churches are also associated with Deiniol at Llanuwchllyn, and at Llanfor near Bala in Merionethshire. Wakes were held at Llanfor on September 11, and a great fair at Llanuwchllyn on September 22 until this century. Itton in Gwent was formerly called Llanddeiniol. St Deiniol's Ash is in Clwyd. Llanddeiniol in Cardiganshire is near Llanddewi Brefi, where Deiniol was associated with St David. Hawarden in Flint is dedicated to Deiniol, and there were chapels at Worthenbury in Flint, and St Daniels

Bryn Celli Ddu Burial Chamber. © *Wales Tourist Board Photo Library.*

under Monktown (Monkton) in Pembroke. Hawarden Fair was held on September 10th, and on the 21st when the dates changed in 1752. Near Deiniol's church at Llanuwchllyn, Bala, is the Roman fort of Caer Gai, where a stone was found reading *'Hic jacet Salviaunus Bursocavi, filius Cupetian.'* This Romano-Celtic monument seems to have vanished.

Gwynfardd wrote about the privileges of St David at Brefi, that he had such joy:
'To have around him, about his plains,
Men liberal and kindly disposed, and fair towns;
He ensured protection to a quiet people,
The tribe of Daniel, highly exalted, their equal
Exists not, for lineage and morality and courtesy.'
(*'A bod o'I gylchyn, cylch ei faesydd,*

Haelon, a thirion, a theg drefydd;
A gorfod gwared lliwed llonydd,
Llwyth Daniel oruchel, eu hefelydd
Nid oes, yn cadw oes, a moes, a mynudydd.')

At Bod-Deiniol farmhouse on Anglesey is Bedd Branwen, also sometimes called Bod-Deiniol. This is said to the burial-place of Branwen, whose tale in the Mabinogion involves the invasion of Ireland and the death of Bran. There is a Daniel's Well in Bangor, Caernarfon, Ffynnon Ddeiniol was in Penbryn parish, Cardigan, and Ffynnon Ddeiniol was in Bangor Monachorum parish, Denbigh. In Flint there was a Ffynnon Daniel in Bangor-is-Coed parish, and another near Llanfor churchyard in Merioneth.

Deiniol fled the Yellow Plague in 547 and is remembered in Brittany at St Denoual and Plangenoual in the Cotes du Nord. Ploudaniel is south of Lesnevin, Kerdaniel is near St Fiacre south of Guincamp, and Pleu Daniel lies between Paimpol and Treguier.

DEINIOLEN 6th - 7th century
DEINIOL FAB (son of Deiniol)
November 23 and 22

The son of Deiniol Ail and grandson of Dunawd. He was a member of the monastery of Bangor-is-Coed under his grandfather until he fled from its destruction, and moved to Bangor, his father's foundation, where he succeeded him as abbot. In 616 he founded Llanddeiniolen in Caernarfon. Llanddeiniolen has a stone circle, consisting of around 20 stones and called Cairn Glyn Arthur, near Arthur's Kitchen Well. Ffynnon Ddeiniolen cured rheumatism, scorbutic diseases and warts, and is now covered with stone slabs in the garden of Hen Gapel, half a mile from Llanddeiniolen Church. It is near the famous chalybeate spring known as the Well of Arthur's Kitchen (Ffynnon Cegin Arthur), which has a thin film of oil on the surface of the water, which probably explains this naming.

There was also a chapel called Llanddeiniol Fab, under Llanidan in Anglesey. Llanddaniel Fab has the superb burial chamber of Bryn Celli Ddu, one of the finest chambered cairns in Europe. Inside there are snake-like spiral carvings like those at Newgrange in Ireland. There is a curious 'patterned stone' outside the grave. In Llanddeiniolfab also was Ffynnon Ddaniel, a well said to cure warts.

DEINST

According to Mike Salter's 'Parish Church' series, Llangarran's 14th-15th century church in Herefordshire is dedicated to this saint, but it is probably a corruption of Deiniol.

DERFEL GADARN (the Mighty) 6th century
DERFAEL CADARN
April 5

The son of Hywel Mawr ab Emyr Llydaw. His father was said to be buried at Llanilltud Fawr. His brother Arthfael is supposed to have gone with Carentmael to Brittany in 547, where he was known as Armel*. Derfael and Arthfael both are said to have studied at Llanilltud Fawr. Other sources state that his brothers were Sulien, Rhystud, Dwywau and Cristiolus.

On a remote hillside above Cwmbran in Gwent, the ruined Llanderfel Chapel was founded in the sixth century by Derfel Gadarn. Llanderfel Farm still exists near there, as does a place named Penllan-gwyn. Derfel was one of the few survivors of the dreadful final battle of Camlan in 537 or 539 where King Arthur was wounded and Mordred (Medrod) killed. Llanderfel was known as 'the old abbey' in 1291 documents, to distinguish it from Llantarnam Abbey which took it over.

Derfel became a monk after the battle and seems to have later been Abbot of Bardsey (where Arthur is said to have recovered from his wounds). He founded the church of Llandderfel, near Bala in Gwynedd. The remains of his staff and famous wooden statue can still be seen at Llandderfel. The effigy depicted Derfel mounted on a horse and bearing a staff. It was a mechanical device with a 'voice', and attracted up to 500 people a day (and assorted livestock to be cured) in the early 16th century. In 1538, Thomas Cromwell's agent Dr Ellis Price wrote to him *'the people have so much trust in him that they come daily on pilgrimage to him with cows or horses or money, to the number of five or six hundred on 5th April. The common saying was that whoever offered anything to this saint would be delivered out of hell by him'*. Bishop Barlow also wrote to Cromwell about Derfel Gadarn *'and such other Welsh gods, antique gargels (gargoyles) of idolatry.'* The large wooden figure protected both men and cattle, rescued souls from purgatory and inflicted disease upon enemies. Disgusted with such superstition, Cromwell ordered the statue to be taken to London. Locals offered the vast bribe of £40 not to take the horse and effigy away, and just the statue of Derfel was taken to London.

Henry VIII had ordered Catherine of Aragon's confessor, a Franciscan friar named John Forest, to be burned to death for not recognising Henry's claim to be 'Supreme Head of the Church in England'. Derfel's *'huge and great image'* was therefore taken to the gallows and set on fire under the recalcitrant priest. A story was attached to the wooden effigy that *'the Welsh had a prophecy that this image should set a whole forest afire; which prophecy now took effect, for he set this friar Forest on fire and consumed him to nothing.'*

Hall's Chronicles relate that *'upon the gallows that he died on was set up, in great letters, these verses following:-*
David Darvel Gatheren
As sayth the Welshman
Fetched outlaws out of Hell;

Now is he come with spere and sheld,
In harnes (armour) *to burne in Smithfield,*
For in Wales he may not dwel.

And Forest the Freer,
That obstinate lyer

That wilfully shal be dead,

In his contumacye
The Gospel doeth deny
The Kyng to be supreme head.'

The ghoulish Bishop Latimer ensured that he preached at the execution, to prevent Forest receiving the Sacrament before his death, and asked for his stage to be built as near to the funeral pyre as possible, so that Forest could hear his speech. The friar was suspended in chains with Derfel underneath him, and perished slowly in the flames. Jan Morris writes ('The Matter of Wales') that the remains of the horse and effigy look *'less like a holy relic than a long-cherished rocking horse from a medieval playroom.'* The ceffyl, or horse, is in a bad condition, after a dean ordered its head to be cut off in 1730, and Derfel's staff has lost most of its gilding. The horse was taken in a great procession every Easter Tuesday and children were allowed to 'ride' on it. This sequence of events could be re-enacted on Derfel's feast day on Bryn Sant. Derfel also had a holy well 500 yards from his church. Two ruined chapels in Monmouth may remember Derfel, Llanderfil (St Derval's) and St Dial's.

Llandderfel in the Berwyn Hills has the most authenticated UFO siting in Britain in January 1974, which deserves a documentary or book to commemorate it. Witnesses from as far apart as Llangynog and Bettws-y-Coed commented recently upon the army 'swarming' all over the mountain. By all accounts, four or five alien bodies were taken in two long coffins to Porton Down chemical warfare research station. *'The craft was domed, about fifty feet in size and metallic with an orange glow.'* The report in 'Wales on Sunday', June 13th, 1999, quotes an American army officer reporting the journey to Porton Down: *'We received orders to proceed to Llangollen and wait. On arrival, our unit was split into four groups. There was a great deal of ground and aircraft activity. Myself and four others were ordered to go to Llandderfel. When we reached our objective we were ordered to load two large oblong boxes, which we were warned not to open, and proceed to Porton Down military facility. We set off south with our cargo and during the journey stopped for a drink. We were immediately approached by a man in civilian clothes who produced an ID card and ordered us to keep going and not to stop again. When we arrived the boxes were opened by staff in our presence. We were shocked to see two creatures which had been placed in decontamination suits. When the suits were opened it was obvious that the creatures were not of this world and when examined, were found to be dead. The bodies were about five to six feet tall, humanoid in shape but so thin they looked almost skeletal. Although I did not see a craft at the scene I was informed that a large craft had crashed.'* The mountain was cordoned off from villagers for days by the army.

The bedridden Gaenor Hughes (1745-1780) was said to have lived for nearly six years on nothing but water from a spring near her cottage at Bodelith, Llandderfel. She saw visions and was visited by Thomas Pennant among others. Ffynnon Dderfel near Llandderfel Church has a small bath about four feet across.

* Armel has been placed by modern writers as the same person as Arthur, after Camlan. The author will try in a future book to research further into this link. It may be that 'brother' was meant in the form of kinsman, or kindred warrior, and Derfel was related to Arthur and fought for him. Barber and Pykit place this Arthmael ap Hywel as St Mael, and it is believed that Arthmael ap Meurig was the real Arthur.

Alphabetical Listing of the Saints of Wales and Religious Events

DEWI SANT dates of birth are variously given between 460 and 520, death between 544 and 589 (Annales Cambriaea gives 601 for his death date)
DAFYDD DYFRWR, AQUATICUS, DAVID PATRON SAINT OF WALES
March 1, July 10 in Brittany, March 12 (Gwaun Valley)
Canonised 1119 or 1124 by Pope Calixtus
Emblem - a dove
Flag – a gold saltire on a black background
David is the only Welsh saint canonised and culted in the Western Church.

Dewi ap Sant (Sanctus) ap Ceredig ap Cunedda was the great grandson of Cunedda who came from the North Country to conquer North Wales, and the grandson of the founder of Ceredigion. Geoffrey of Monmouth believed that he was King Arthur's uncle, as did Giraldus Cambrensis. He was possibly born in Henfynyw in Cardigan, where the church is dedicated to him. Ffynnon Ddewi lies nearby. It seems that his original monastery, on land inherited from his father, was at Henllan in Dyfed, and Dewi moved to Menevia, St Davids, later. The Irish 'Catalogue of the Saints' of 730 records that Irish monks **'received the mass from Bishop David, Gildas and Teilo'**, and they influenced monastic development in Ireland. In 800, the 'Martyrology of Oengus' records his feast date as March 1. His uncle was St Carannog and his aunt St Ina. His cousins were said to be saints Cenau, Dogfael, Pedr, Gwynlle and Afan.

Bishop's Palace at St David's Cathedral.   *CADW: Welsh Historic Monuments. Crown Copyright.*

Legend says that his father Sant was told by an angel to save some land for David, thirty years before he was born. Also at this time St Patrick was going to settle in Glyn Rhosyn (Vallis Rosina, Vale of Roses) near the sea in Pembrokeshire, when an angel told him to leave it, as the place was reserved for a boy to be born in thirty years' time. Patrick was so upset at his God preferring an unborn child to him, that God had to take Patrick to a cliff rock still known as Eisteddfa Badrig (Sedes Patricii, Patrick's Seat), to show him that God wanted him to look after all of Ireland instead.

Many sources state that Dewi was born on the site of St Non's Chapel, baptised at Porth Clais, and educated at Hen Fynyw or Henllwyn (Vetus Rebus), with St Teilo, studying under Peulin (Paulinus). St Illtud's Life however says that David, Gildas, Samson and Paulinus studied under Illtud. Dewi is said to have founded twelve monasteries, from Croyland to Pembrokeshire, and including Glastonbury and Bath.

It was claimed that Dewi made a pilgrimage to Jerusalem, where he was made a bishop, and took a principal part at the councils of Brefi (in Cardigan) and Caerleon. At Brefi he was recognised as primate of all Wales to replace Dubricius (Dyfrig), and he moved the see from

St David's Cathedral. © *Wales Tourist Board Photo Library.*

Caerleon to Menevia (Mynyw, or St Davids in Pembrokeshire). Much of this information stems from a document of around 1090 which attempted to make St David's independent of Canterbury, but may not be reliable. All sources agree, however, that his principal seat was at St David's, where he died. There is a legend that he died in the arms of his pupil and great friend, Maedoc of Ferns. The great Irish saints claimed to be taught by David included Maedoc, Finnian of Clonard, Senan of Scattery Island, Findbar of Cork and Brendan of Clonfert.

The most famous tradition about David is that the ground rose at his feet at the Synod of Brefi in 545. David had never preached before, but was persuaded by Deiniol and Dyfrig to do so, where the church now stands at Llanddewibrefi. He was heard as clear as a bell, as far away as Llandudoch (St Dogmael's). He was known traditionally as *'The Waterman'* as he and his monks were ascetic teetotallers and vegetarians. His last words were said to have been *'Lords, brothers and sisters, be happy and keep the faith, and do those little things you have seen me do and heard me say.'*

The story that David went with Teilo and Padarn on pilgrimage to Jerusalem, is mentioned in the Lives of all the other saints. It was recounted that the Patriarch John III of Jerusalem advanced him to the Archbishopric of Mynyw, Menevia, and gave Dewi the gifts of a staff, bell, golden tunic and portable altar. In David's Welsh Life, however, he is consecrated Archbishop in Rome when Peulin tells the Synod of his holiness. The 'Brut Dingestow' says that at this time there were just three archbishoprics in Britain and David succeeded Dyfrig (Dubricius) at Caerleon, not Mynyw (Menevia, or St David's). The other two cathedrals were London and York. One of Merlin's prophecies was that *'Menevia shall be dressed in the shadow of the City of the Legions'*. Geoffrey of Monmouth agrees with this, but one (later?) Triad tells us that the three Archbishoprics of 'Ynys Prydein' (the Island of Britain) were St David's, Canterbury and York.

Dewi is culted in Hereford, Gloucester, South Wales, Devon, Cornwall and Brittany, where he seems to have travelled after the great plague of 547. He was invoked to cure sick children in Brittany. David was recognised as patron saint of Wales only when the bones of Gwenfrewi were removed to England. Bishop Asser's Life of Alfred, written around 893, mentions the famous monastery and parish of Holy David. About 1120 Pope Callistus II approved David's cult. A letter sent by the Chapter of St David's to Rome around 1125-1130 claims that St David's had been a metropolitan see since the beginnings of Christianity in Britain. Two pilgrimages to David at Mynyw equalled one to Rome, and three equalled one to Jerusalem. St David's Cathedral was rebuilt in 1275, largely from offerings taken at his shrine, which William the Conqueror, Henry II and Edward I and Queen Eleanor had visited.

David is associated with over fifty known churches in South Wales, most in the south-west. Glastonbury was claimed to be founded by David. At Llanddewi Brefi, possibly Dewi's original monastery, are four stones. Two are cross-marked, and one inscribed to Dallus Dumelus. Another inscribed stone reads:
HIC IACET IDNERT FILIUS IACOBI QUI OCCISUS FUIT PROPTER PRAEDAM SANCTI DAVID
'Here lies Idnert son of Jacob who was killed because of the despoiling of St David'.
A 1693 recording fills in the words David and Jacob. This stone dates from around the 7th century, possibly carved after St David's was ransacked. One of the stones has been 'Christianised' and is called St David's Staff, which Dewi and Dyfrig leaned upon at the famous Synod of Brefi. At St David's Cathedral are also a number of Celtic cross-slabs. One

stone had been used as a gate-post and has an inscription to 'Gurmarc'. They came from a holy well at Pen Arthur Farm a few miles away.

The church of St Mary and St David in Kilpeck in Herefordshire was formerly dedicated solely to St David. Its amazing carvings and rare 'sheel-na-gig' draw visitors from all over Britain. The present church dates from around 1140, but some Saxon stonework survives. In Cardigan Blaenpennal, Capel Dewi (Llandysul), Henfynyw, Llanarth, Llanddewi Aber-arth as well as Llanddewi Brefi are David's churches. At Llanddewi Aberarth, just north of Aberaeron, there are two Celtic stone fragments embedded in the wall of the west porch. Probably 10th century, they were found in the 1860 rebuilding of the church, and are parts of what has been called the *'finest cross in Wales.'* The inscription is faded on one, and the other stone has key patterns and intricate Celtic knotwork. In the church is an 11th century *'hogback'* stone, the only one in Wales and of a type only found in 'Viking' Yorkshire. 'Bangu' was David's portable bell and was kept in Glascwm Church, one of the first twelve churches he founded.

The following dedications can be noted:
Pembroke – St David's cathedral, Whitchurch, Brawdy, Llanychllwydog, Llanychaer, Maenor Deifi, Bridell, Llanddewi Velfrey, Hubberston, Prendergast;
Carmarthen – Abergwili, Bettws, Henllan Amgoed, Abergorlech, Llanarthney, Llangadock, St David's Carmarthen, Llanycrwys, Meidrim;
Glamorgan – Llanddewi in Gower with a holy spring, Llangyfelach, Ystalyfera, Bettws, Laleston;
Monmouth – Llanddewi Fach, Llanddewi Skirrid, Bettws, Raglan, Llanthony (formerly Llanddewi Nant Honddu), Llangeview, Trostre;
Hereford – Much Dewchurch, Little Dewchurch, Kilpeck, Dewsall;
Cardigan – Bangor Teifi, Henllan, Bangor, Blaenporth, Henfynyw, Llanddewi Aberarth, Llanarth, Llanddewi Brefi, Blaenpenal, Capel Dewi;
Brecon – Garthbenni, Llanfaes, Llanwrtyd, Llanddewi Abergwessin, Llywel, Trallwng, Maesmynys, Llanynys, Llanddewi y'r Cwm, Llanddulas;
Radnor – Creguna, Gladesbury, Glasgwm, Llanddewi Ystrad Enny, Llanddewi Fach, Heyope (Llanddewi Heiob), Whitton (Llanddewi yn Hwytyn).

Many churches were rededicated to David after he became patron saint of Wales, but there are no North Wales dedications to him in the traditional 'Six Counties', and precious few in Catwg's territory of Glamorgan, Glywyssing. In Monmouthshire there is Capel David near Abergafenni, Raglan, Llanddewi Rhydderch, Llanddewi Fach and Llanddewi Ysgryd. Llanarthne is now rededicated to David, and St Llywel's church at Llywel now also has dedications to David and Teilo. Near the great Carreg Cennen Castle, at Trapp on The Black Mountain, are earthworks and stone rubble of an ancient chapel dedicated to David.

It seems that David travelled to Ireland, and also that he and Teilo evangelised parts of Cornwall and Brittany. Near Llanfeuno in Hereford, Kilpeck, Dewsall, Little Dewchurch and Much Dewchurch are all dedicated to David. In Devon (Dumnonia was still British until around 900), there were dedications at Tilbruge (Thelbridge), Ashprington and Painsford, St David's chapel to Heavitree in Exeter, and also in Cornwall at Dewstowe (Davidstow). His mother Non had a dedication at Altarnon, and at Plenynt (Pelynt, Plint) in Cornwall and Bradstone in Devon.

The political power of the bishops of St David's probably swayed the choice of Dewi as the patron saint of Wales – as stated there is not one dedication to him in North Wales. Research by the Reverend Rice Rees in the 1830's showed that *'in the original Diocese of Llandaff he has but two chapels, and only three in what is supposed to have been the original Diocese of Llanbadarn; all the rest, including every one of his endowments, are in the district of which, as Archbishop of Menevia, he was himself the Diocesan. The Cathedral of St David's is in the territory of his maternal grandfather, the neighbourhood of Henfynyw appears to have been the property of his father, and Llandewi Brefi is situated on the spot where he refuted the Pelagian heresy.'* The patron saint of Wales might well have been Gwenfrewi, if not for the removal of her relics to Shrewsbury. Better claims as patron saint can possibly come from Dyfrig (especially), Beuno, Teilo, Illtud and Cadog. His fight against the Pelagian Heresy probably assisted in his canonisation by the Roman church in the 12th century. Some of these Pelagian saints' foundations were later rededicated to David, such as Llangadog in Carmarthen. To the author, Pelagius was a far more attractive religious thinker than any popes of his knowledge – Christianity based on equality and natural goodness, rather than referent and political power, would have caused fewer deaths over the centuries.

There is a tradition that Arthur allowed Dewi to move the seat of his archbishopric from Caerleon to Menevia. Geoffrey of Monmouth states that he was honourably buried on the instructions of Maelgwn Gwynedd in Menevia, soon after Arthur's death, whom he thought died in 542. Archbishop Usher thought that David died in 544 aged 82. Maelgwn Gwynedd, according to the Annales Menevensses, died in 547 during the great plague. In David's times Caradog Freichfras (the son of a grand-daughter of Brychan) recovered Brecon from the Picts, and featured as Sir Carados Bris Bras in later Arthurian romances. Urien Rheged cleared out Pictish and Irish settlers from the lands between the rivers Towy and Neath, and his descendants ruled these territories. He was known as Sir Urience in Arthurian mythology. It seems that David took the opportunity in establishing churches in these reclaimed territories.

February 28 is St David's Eve, and one of the favourite nights for the Cwn Annwn (Hounds of Annwn, the Underworld) to take to the skies. They race and howl across the firmament, and are the souls of the damned, hunting for more souls to feed to the furnaces of Hell. Anyone who hears them will soon meet death. Sometimes they are seen as huge dogs with human heads. This is a pre-Christian belief that lasted in rural Wales until the nineteenth century. There was a mass sighting of this spectral pack of dogs (probably geese) in Taunton, Somerset in 1940.

In the Gwaun valley in Pembrokeshire, Old St David's Day (March 12) was the occasion where the wax candle on the table was replaced by a wooden one, signifying that supper could be eaten without candle-light. Like the custom at Tregaron, it was a symbol of the end of the winter nights. At this time, farm workers were also entitled to three meals a day, until Michaelmas when this right reverted back to two meals.

Some old sources say that it was David who convinced the Welsh to wear a leek* in their caps to identify each other in battle. David's spirit visited King Cadwallon's army at Hatfield Moors in 633, telling the army to put leeks in their hats, so they could recognise each other in the battle, and Edwin of Northumbria was beaten. Certainly the Welsh had the first uniform, (green and white) in European warfare (see the author's 'The A-Z of Wales and the Welsh'). Michael Drayton, in his 1612 'Polyolbion' however puts the Welsh leek into perspective in that David was a vegetarian water-drinker:
As he did only drink what crystal Hodney yields,
And fed upon the leeks he gathered in the fields.
In memory of whom, in each revolving year,
The Welshmen, on his day, that sacred herb do wear.'

In Shakespeare's 'Henry V', Pistol threatens the Welshman Fluellen:
'Tell him I'll knock his leek about his pate upon St Davy's Day',
but later Fluellen forces him to eat the leek. In the same play, Fluellen refers to the Welsh service to the Black Prince at the battle of Poitiers:
'If your Majesties is remembered of it, the Welshmen did good service in a garden where leeks did grow, wearing leeks in their Monmouth caps; which your Majesty knows to this hour is an honourable badge of the service; and I do believe your Majesty takes no scorn to wear the leek upon St Tavy's day.'

Shakespeare described the habit of Welshmen wearing leeks and daffodils on St David's Day as *'an ancient tradition begun upon an honourable request.'* An interesting correlation between the leek and St David's Day is found in Hone's 'Every-Day Book, Table Book and Year Book' (four Volumes, 1839) in which March 1st is the flowering day of the leek. The traditional Welsh daffodil will flower on March 7th.

Dewi's 'Saying of the Wise' is as follows:
'A glywaist ti chwedl Dewi
Gwr llwyd llydan ei deithi
Goreu defawd daioni.'
'Hast thou heard the saying of St David,
The venerable man of extended honour?
"The best usage is goodness".'

There are evocative remains of palaces of the bishops of St David's at Lamphey, St David's and Abergwili. William Barlow, the monoglot English bishop from 1536-1548, tried to have the see moved to Carmarthen. He therefore stripped the roof of his palace at St David's to pay for his daughters' marriages, and built the 'new' palace at Abergwili. Intriguingly, Owain Glyndŵr in his Pennal document to Charles VI of France in 1406, wanted St David's to be accepted as a metropolitan church. Its authority would have covered the other Welsh dioceses, plus those of Exeter, Bath, Hereford, Worcester and Lichfield. Also, appropriation of Welsh churches by English monasteries would be annulled, only Welsh-speakers were to be appointed to ecclesiastical office in Wales, and two universities were to be established in North and South Wales. (The difficulties of transport and communication between the north and south in Wales are still in existence because of the nature of Welsh geography).

Maen Dewi, an eight-foot menhir was on the edge of Dowrog Common in 1912, standing by a cottage known as Drws Gobiaeth (The Door of Hope). There was also a rocking stone, now destroyed, near St David's still intact in 1919. Other notable monuments in the area of the abbey include a stone circle inside the prehistoric camp on St David's Head, Trecenny Standing Stone, and two dolmens of the slopes of Carn Llidi. A seven feet Christianised standing stone can be found in Dewi's church at Bridell, made up of porphyrite greenstone from the Preselis, with Ogham and cup markings. It is inscribed 'Nettasgru Maqui Mucoi Breci' (Nettasagus son of the descendants of Breci) and was probably carved in the 5th or 6th century. Llanarth in Cardigan is David's, and has a crossed stone which seems to read 'HENRICUS' with also some Ogham c's and s's decipherable. In 1874, Professor Rhys claimed that the cross-shaft named 'Gwrhir's Cross'. Gwrhir (q.v.) founded Lisvane in Cardiff.

David's dedication at Abergwili in Dyfed is surrounded by standing stones such as Pentre Ynis, Pant y Glien and Merlin's Stone. The last two are both in fields called Parc y Maen Llwyd (Grey Stone Park). Carreg Fyrddin (Merlin's Stone) carried Merlin's prophecy that a raven would drink human blood off it. In the 19th century a man digging for treasure was killed when the stone fell on him. At Dewi's Hubberston, there is also a standing stone.

David had many holy wells in Wales, and the author is indebted to Francis Jones' seminal work for the following listing:
Anglesey: Llangammarch; and near Llanddewi Abergwesin Church;
Cardigan: Capel Dewi, Llandysul (used for brewing beer for the fair); Llandygwydd; near Llanarth on the ford of Afon Ffynnon Ddewi; Henfynyw; and near Gogoyam, Llanddewi Brefi, where the well was in a cottage itself called Ffynnon Ddewi; Llandysilio-go-go;
Carmarthen: Llwyn Dewi healing well near Whitland; and Pistyll Dewi near Llanarthney;
Glamorgan: Llangyfelach; Southerndown; and Newton Nottage (where there was also his chapel and Dewiscwm has been renamed The Rhyll);
Pembroke: near St David's; near St Lawrence; Mabws Fach Farm in Mathry; Llanrheithan; St Dogwell's parish (formerly called Llantydewi); Brawdy, Whitchurch; Fishguard; Llanychllwydiog; Maenclochog; Manordeifi; Llanddewi Velfrey; Pistyll Dewi at the Cathedral; Porthclais where David was baptised; Newport; Haverfordwest; Cosherston; Harglodd Isa Farm;
Radnor: Ffynnon Ddewi in Llanbadarn Fynydd.

There are many traditions associated with these wells, and many are noted in Jones' work. The author wished to take photographs of many of these sites and their associated ruins, but finance and publishing deadlines did not allow it. Perhaps such work would stimulate the authorities to refurbish some of these shrines – they represent over 1400 years of history which few other countries can show.

St David's Cathedral and its Bishop's Palace are in a hollow below the City of St David's, and it was thought that the bones of David and Justinian were still there. However, they were possibly destroyed when the shrines were smashed in the Reformation, and the remaining relics were analysed as being only 1000 years old, which means that they may be those of St Caradog Fynach. The tombs of Edmund Tudor (Henry VII's father), Bishop Gower and Rhys Grug can be seen, as well as those attributed to the great Lord Rhys and Giraldus Cambrensis. There is a Millennium appeal to restore the cloisters, West Front stonework, organ and 14th century gatehouse, for which over £4 million is needed (telephone 01437-720204).

*There is a note on the virtues of the leek in the 13th century herbal manuals of the physicians of Meddfai, 'Meddygon Myddfai':
'The juice is good against the vomiting of blood. It is good for women who desire children to eat leeks. Take leeks and wine to cure the bite of adders and venomous beasts. The juice of leeks and women's milk is good against pneumonia. The juice with goat's gall and honey in equal parts, put warm into the ear, is good for deafness. It will relieve wind of the stomach, and engender strange dreams.' This fascinating cornucopia of mediaeval Welsh recipes gives another cure, for excessive vomiting, of placing one's testicles in vinegar. For irritability it recommends frequent partaking of celery juice, to relieve the mood and induce joy.

DIER d.664
DIHEUFYR, DEIFERUS, DEIFER, DEIFAR
March 7, 8

The successor of St Beuno in instructing Gwenfrewi. A son of Arwystli Gloff, he founded Bodfari in Flint, now dedicated to Stephen. In the legend of Gwenfrewi he is named Deiferus. Gwenfrewi was directed to go to him at Bodfari when her head was cut off at Holywell. His brothers were Tewdwr, Teyrnog and Tyfrydog, saints of Bangor-is-Coed and then Ynys Enlli. His sister was St Marchell. He had a divine spring, Ffynnon Ddier, at Bodfari, and he was buried in the church there. Chickens were pricked with a pin, and the pin thrown into the well, as at Tegla's well in Denbigh. The church at Bodfari is now dedicated to Stephen, and 'St Diefar's Well' (Ffynnon 'Ddeier') was also where children were dipped three times to prevent their crying at night. There is still a well in view in the 'Well Bar' at the nearby Dinorben Arms which may be Dier's.

His well was diverted to supply water to the village. Edward Lhuyd recorded that on Dier's Gwyl Mabsant, held on St Stephen's Day, *'it is a Custom for ye poorest person in the parish to offer Chickens after going (with them) nine times around ye well. A Cockrell for a boy & a Pullet for a girl. The child is dipt up to his neck at three of ye corners of ye Well. This is to prevent their crying in ye night.'*

KING DIGAIN early 5th century
November 21

The son, with Erbyn, of Cystennyn Gorneu, and to whom Llangernyw in Denbigh was probably dedicated ('The church of the Cornishman'). A 'pillar' stone was placed over, or in, a grave, and a good example can be seen in Llangernyw's churchyard. There is an incised cross with 'crutches' at the end of each arm and dots, and it was probably copied from a manuscript. This type of cross dates it to between the seventh and ninth centuries. Without the cross it could be mistaken for a Celtic menhir or standing stone. In Brittany it was common practice to engrave crosses upon sacred stones, but this does not appear to be the case here, although it is recorded that St Patrick cut a cross in a stone venerated by pagans. Ffynnon Digain is in Coed Digain, a mile from Llangernyw Church.

DILIC

A Cornish church was dedicated to this saint, and Ffynnon Dilic is in Cilybebyll (near Pontardawe) on Drymma Hill. One of the Peniarth mss. (118) notes Bedd Dilic Gawr, the saint's grave over 30 feet long, between Llan Sawel (Briton Ferry) and Baglan. In the hills near Cilybebyll are many tumuli, tracks and traditions of great battles, and an ancient farm called Hendrecaradog. Mynydd Marchywel and this area needs a huge input of archaeological expertise to discover its secrets. In the author's view, the funding of projects such as this, or the uncovering of the Roman villa at Llanilltud would be cost-effective research, as the end result would be increased tourism and knowledge.

DILWAR
February 4

A female saint of whom nothing is known except her feast day.

DIMET 4th-5th century

Possibly the son of Macsen Wledig and Elen.

DINABO

Llandinabo Church in Herefordshire is dedicated to this saint. More information would be welcome upon any history attached to the foundation of the church.

DINGAD 5th century
DINGAT
November 1

One of Brychan's sons, he founded Landovery, which was formerly known as Llanddingat, in Dyfed. He is said to be buried at Llandovery. There is also Llandingad in Carmarthen, with two chapels to Peulin under it. His son Cyflefyr was martyred, and according to Doble, another son was St Brioc. Dingestow in the hundred of Raglan was also known as Llanddingat. The castle mound there was the scene of the revenge attack of the Welsh after William de Braose's treachery of seven years previously. In 1184 the castle's builder, Ranulph de Poer, sheriff of Hereford was killed, but de Braose escaped. Giraldus Cambrensis related the story that two English soldiers, firing at the Welsh from the rear, penetrated the castle's oak door with their arrows. The door was four inches thick. The church was given in the time of Bishop Nudd (about 800), by Tudmab for the soul of his father Pawl, to Llandaf. The nearby Ffynnon y Cleifion ('spring of the sick people') was obviously used in the past, but only a pool remains. At Pen-y-Gaer near Llandingad is Ffynnon yr Army, a holy well near an Iron Age camp which was levelled in the 19th century. Near Crickhowel was the Turpilian Stone, which commemorated Dingad's children.

Westwood read the Turpilian Stone as:
TURPILLI IC IACIT PUUERI
TRILUNI DUNOCATI

This stone was nine feet long, having been moved from Ty-yn-y-wlad farm to Wern-y-Butler Farm, and being overgrown with brambles.The Ogham marks were also decipherable. Dunocati is Dincat in the Book of Llandaf, so this stone may mark the sons of St Dingad. Acording to Westwood, Lluni is the equivalent of Llwni.

DINGAD ap NUDD HAEL mid 6th century

His sons were the saints Llawddog, Baglan, Gwytherin, Tygwy, Tegwyn, Tyfrydog and Eleri. It is not known for definite whether Dingestow, formerly Dingat's Stowe in Gwent was founded by this Dingad, by the previous Dingad, either one of whom could have been king of Bryn

Buga (Usk). Dingad was said to be buried here, so we may assign Dingestow to either. He is also patron of Llandingad in Gwent.

There is a 'Saying of the Wise' attributed to Dingad ap Brychan or Dingad ap Nudd:
'Hast thou heard the saying of Dingad,
When rebuking the son of a wicked father?
"Soon the duck's son will learn to swim".'

DIRDAN 5th century

The husband of St Banadlwen ferch Cynyr, who was the sister of Non, David's mother. He was said to have been a 'nobleman of Italy' (of Roman stock?) and was the father of Ailfyw. Ffynnon Ddurdan, at Nant near Aberdaron commemorates him, near the old mansion of Bodwrda (also see Elaeth).

DOCHDWY
DOCHEU
August 18

He came from Brittany with Cadfan and stayed at Llancarfan and Llanilltud before presumably going with Cadfan to evangelise Gwynedd. (Possibly Cyngar is the same saint, but the feast day is different.)

DOCHDWY see CYNGAR

KING DOGED FRENIN fl. 500-542
April 7. One account gives his feast days as 9 days before May and 9 days before August. Another source gives the 24th day before May 1. A second wake was held on the 24th day before August 1.

He was the son of Cedig ap Ceredig ap Cunedda Wledig, St David's cousin, the brother of St Afan, and the founder of Llanddoged church in Denbighshire. Mentioned in the Mabinogion tale of Culhwch and Olwen, Doged was killed by the rival King Cilydd, who wanted his wife and daughter. Because King Doged was murdered defending his wife and family, he was regarded as a martyred saint. He was probably killed at Llanddoged in west Denbigh, where there used to be his statue in the church. At Ffynnon Ddoged is a walled well, just 60 yards from the church, where the water was used to cure eye ailments.

DOGFAN 5th-6th century
DOGWAN, DOEWAN, DWYWAN
July 13 – Fairs were held in Llanrhaiadr-ym-Mochnant upon July 23 and 24.

Martyred by Saxons at Merthyr Dogfan in Pembroke, where a church was built, but the site of it is no longer known. He is also the patron saint of Llanrhaiadr-ym-Mochnant in Denbigh (with its holy well), to which are subject the churches of Llanarmon Mynydd Mawr (Garmon),

Llangedwyn (Cedywn), Llanwddyn and Llangadwaladr (Cadwaladr). At Llanwddyn is a holy well dedicated to Dogfan.

Possibly a brother of Berwyn and son of Brychan, his old church and graveyard are at Buarth yr Hendre in the parish of Llanrhaiadr-ym-Mochnant. The valley in which it is situated is Cwm Doefon, and there is a Ffynnon Ddoefan there. The cloudberries that grow on parts of the nearby Berwyn Mountains were called *'Mwyar Doewan', 'Doewan's Berries'*. Anyone giving the parson a ripe quart of them on the morning of Doewan's festival had his church payments waived for a year. This very rare plant has also been found recently at Fenn's Moss, a nature site near Wrexham, 30 miles from the upland Berwyn Hills. There is another Ffynnon Ddogfan used for curing eye problems, near Llyn Fyrnwy in Llanwddyn parish, Montgomery.

Inside the church at Llanrhaiadr-ym-Mochnant in Clwyd is a tall slab with a wheel-cross, variously dated between the ninth and eleventh centuries. Along with plaited interlacing, fret-patterns and spirals in spandrels, there is a faded Latin inscription that is believed to have been to a Gwgan who died in the eleventh century. The letters XRI and a small equal-armed cross is used on similar slabs in Pembrokeshire, symbolising the Cross of Christ. Post-y-Wiber, The Dragon's Post, is also near here, a twelve-foot standing stone that killed a dragon from Cwm Cothy. There is also another ten-foot standing stone near the school, which is said to have come from Rhos Maes Criafal in Maengwynedd. A stone circle near Llanrhaiadr, with an avenue known as Rhos-y-Beddau (Moor of the Graves) had 13 boulders.

DOGMAEL
DOGWEL, DYGWEL, DOGFAEL, TEGWEL, TOEL d. 500 or early sixth century
October 31 (June 14 at the chapels of Dogwel/Tegwel, now extinct, in Pembroke and Anglesey)

A cousin of St David, Dogwel ab Ithel ap Ceredig ap Cunedda Wledig has dedicated churches in West Wales, including Dogwel near Fishguard, and probably St Dogmael's which is also now one of his churches, although it used to be known as Landudoch. There was a chapel also at Llanddogwel in Anglesey, which was under the jurisdiction of Llanrhyddlad then Llanfechell. The cross, Croes Dygwel, near this chapel seems to have disappeared. According to the Reverend Rice Rees, he was the patron of St Dogwels in Pebidiog, Mynachlog Ddu and Melinau (Meline), all in Pembrokeshire. Mynachlog Ddu may have been another saint's foundation (Silin or Cawey?), and it has a Celtic circular churchyard, bounded on several sides by small streams falling down to the Eastern, or Black, Cleddau river (Cleddau Ddu). It is dedicated to Dogmael because in the 12th century it was a chapel of the Abbey of St Dogmael, a daughter house of Tiron under Benedictine rule. It appears as the 'Capella Nigra Grangea' in the 1291 Taxatio, hence its attribution to the black monks. Mynachlog-ddu is thought also to have come from the Welsh name for black monks. Nearby is the great fortified camp of Foel Drygarn, and the Neolithic quarries of 'bluestone' which went to Stonehenge 4000 years ago. Cwm Cerwyn has associations with Arthur, and there is a stone circle at Gors Fawr. There is a simple memorial at Mynachlog Ddu to Waldo Williams, the great Welsh poet and Christian pacifist without peer.

There seems to have been a pre-Norman monastery and cemetery on the site of the post-Norman Benedictine abbey ruins at St Dogmaels, with two cross-marked stones, two inscribed stones and two cross-slabs being found here. In St Dogwel's Church is one inscribed stone in Ogham and Latin which reads HOGTIVIS FILI DEMETI (Hogtivis son of Demetus). As Dyfed was the kingdom of the Demetae, this has special importance. The other inscribed stone

St Dogmael's Abbey. © *Wales Tourist Board Photo Library.*

reads SAGRANI FILI CUNOTAMI (Sagrani son of Cunotamus, the Latinised form of Cunedda. Cunedda was Dogmael's great-grandfather). This was being used as a footbridge until the 19th century. The Ogham on the stone reads *'Sagramni maqi Cvnatami'*.

It seems that Dogmael also travelled to Brittany, where St Dogmeel or Toel has many churches, and prayers to St Dogmeel were invoked to help children learn to walk. St Dogmel is near Lanmerin, south of Perros Guirec in Brittany. His holy wells include Ffynnon Ddygfael in Anglesey (which seems to have disappeared) and Ffynnon Ddegwel in St Dogmael's. There was also a Ffynnon Ddegfel between Brawdy and St Elvis parishes in Pembroke. Here, warts were bathed on Sunday before dawn, then on the following seven days, until the early twentieth century. A legend is that Dogmael, on pilgrimage to St David's, bathed his eyes here. Ffynnon Dogmael is adjacent to Meline churchyard in Pembroke, and its water was used for baptisms in the church.

St Dogmael's has the lovely legend of the mermaid who saved Peregrin and his fellow fishermen off Pen Cemaes (Cemaes Head). The men of Nefyn in Caernarfon also claimed this mermaid belonged to them. Drayton, in his 'Battaile of Agincourt' noted the mermaid on a rock in Cardiganshire's armorial bearings.

Alphabetical Listing of the Saints of Wales and Religious Events

Anyone who is interested in Welsh history and culture should read the journals of Gerald of Wales, Giraldus Cambrensis. Aged almost 60, and seeking the bishopric of St David's, he was thrown into prison in Chatillon-sur-Seine. He was freed by the Seneschal of Burgundy, who put his accuser, John of Tynemouth, in his place. Gerald then saw King John to protest against the possible election of the abbots of St Dogmaels and Whitland, and Reginald Foliot, on the grounds that the first was illiterate, the second was illegitimate, and that the third was a notorious fornicator.

DOLGAN mid 6th century

The son of Gildas, a saint of the college of Catwg at Llancarfan.

DOLGAR

A daughter of Gildas ap Caw.

DOWROR?

Llanddowror in Carmarthenshire

ABBOT DUNAWD 6th century
DUNAWD FAWR
September 7

According to Giraldus Cambrensis, Dunawd is the man who Padrig raised from the dead before sailing to Ireland. There is also a story in the Life of David where David's enemy Boia has a wife who takes her step-daughter to Glyn Alun to look for nuts. With the daughter's head in her lap, she kills her, whereupon the curative fountain known as Ffynnon Dunawd or Merthyr Dunod springs forth, near St David's. Dunawd's wife was St Dwywe ferch Gwallog ap Llenog. His brothers were the saints Sawyl Benuchel and Carwyd, and his sister St Arddun. Her husband, Brochwel, defended Bangor is Coed against the pagans.

The college and great monastery at Bangor-is-Coed was supposedly founded by him with his sons Deiniol Wyn, Cynwyl and Gwarthan. He was a warrior saint, and the poems of Llywarch Hen show him engaged in battle against the sons of Urien Rheged around the middle of the sixth century. Dunawd Fawr's father was Pabo, of the line of Coel Godebog, and in the Triads Dunawd is called one of the 'three pillars' of his country in battle. After fighting the sons of Urien, he fled from invading Picts and sought the protection of Cyngen ap Cadell, Prince of Powys, and then founded his great monastery on the banks of the River Dee in Flint. He is the patron saint of Bangor Iscoed in Flint, his only foundation. Many of the wise men who attended the conference with Augustine around 599 - 603 came from Bangor, which was destroyed around 603 – 613 (see Bede). Ffynnon Dunawd was near Cae'r Dyni Farm, Criccieth. The Annales state that he died in 595, but Bede states that he was still abbot of Bangor when the seven Welsh bishops met Augustine in 602 or 603.

DUNWYD d.874 or 876
DONAT, DONATUS, DINO
Feast day August 22, 17
Patron Saint of Storm-Tossed Sailors

The parish church of Welsh St Donat's is dedicated to St Donat, and was attached to Llanbleddian Chuch as 'Capella Sancti Donati'. It was called Eglwys Llanddunwyd or Welsh St Donat's to distinguish it from St Donat's on the coast, called English St Donat's or 'Sancto Donato Anglicana'. At the end of the nineteenth century, Welsh St Donat's was notable in that it was the last church in the Vale of Glamorgan to hold services in Welsh.

Hidden in a valley under St Donat's Castle, St Donat's Church was probably originally dedicated to St Gwerydd, the original name being Llanwerydd.* This is the place where Caractacus is said to have lived, whose daughter Eurgain brought Christianity from Rome, where she met St Paul. Dunwyd or Donatus was an Irish or Scots saint, who on a pilgrimage to Rome was made Bishop of Fiesole in Northern Italy. It is thought that the de Haweyes, the Normans who built the castle, chose Donat for rededicating the church because of their frequent trips across the Bristol Channel to their Somerset lands. A nearby old farm called Splott is called because the Knights Hospitallers also held lands here. St Donats is a lovely church, with an original mediaeval calvary (reminiscent of some in Brittany) dating from the fourteenth century.

Dunwyd, Cadoc and Tathan were the three saints who allowed their oxen to take building materials for a new church. The animals were not driven, but where they stopped, on a hill between two woods, was the site of the church. There is obvious confusion here between a local saint who may have been the founder of St Donat's, and the Donatus/Dino whom the de Haweyes imposed upon the church. (Also see Gwerydd).

One of the most prominent recusants in Wales was Sir Thomas Stradling (1499-1571). On March 20th, 1559 an old ash tree in St Donat's park was struck by lightning, and in the split stump was found the clear impression of a cross fourteen inches long. Stradling made a drawing and had four pictures painted. By 1561, news of the miracle reached Elizabeth's minister, the Welshman Cecil. Fearing that the cross would become a rallying point for the 'old faith', he had Stradling thrown into the Tower of London, but he was later released, and never signed the Act of Uniformity.

An entry in St Donat's burials register records *'William John of Wick – an idiot who rode a blind horse over the cliffs – a tremendous death'*, and he was buried here on 5tth October 1817 aged 21 years. There was a holy well, Ffynnon y Capel, just north of St Donat's village, and a healing well for erysipelas on the cliff below St Donat's Castle.

The castle is remarkable in that it was renovated by William Randolph Hearst (the prototype for 'Citizen Kane'), features a fabulous ceiling from the church of 'Boston Stump', and includes the hall of Bradenstoke Priory. Enfys McMurry's recent book lists just some of the guests of Hearst and his mistress Marion Davies (an Irishwoman, originally named Douras). At various times the remarkable swimming pool in the grounds overlooking the Bristol Channel saw all the members of the Kennedy family (Including Joe, Jack, Bobby, Edward and Rose), the Churchills, David and Megan Lloyd-George, Clarke Gable, Charlie Chaplin, Maurice Chevalier, Elinor Glyn, Bob Hope, Anita Loos, Ben Lyon and Bebe Daniels, the Mountbattens, Ivor Novello and George Bernard Shaw.

*St Donat's stream, which flows past the church in the dell, is known as Nant Werydd. A half-mile upstream from the church is the site of an ancient village, and it is thought that St Donat's Castle is constructed upon an Iron Age hill-fort. It was called Llanwerydd by the old Welsh, the 'parish of the Atlantic', and the present Atlantic College keeps this connection. It was known as St Dunwydd on the 1877 map, and only as St Donat's in the 20th century.

DURDAN 6th century
DWRDAN

A companion of Cadfan, and regarded as a presiding saint of Ynys Enlli.

DWNA 6th - 7th century
DONA, DONA
November 1

This son of Selyf ap Cynan Garwyn ap Brochwel founded Llanddona in Anglesey. His father Selyf Sarffgadau (the 'Serpent of Battles'), King of Powys, died at the battle of Chester in 603 or 613. All Saints Day was celebrated as the Wake of Dona. Dwna's grandfather was Brochwel, King of Powys (not Brochwel the Fanged, who also fought at Chester). From Bangor Deiniol monastery, Dwna went to Anglesey and lived in a cell on the north-east shores, in the area now known as Llanddona. He was associated with Crafgoed in the district, and at Mynydd Crafgoed there is a rock formation above his church still known as Dona's Chair. Near Knighton in Radnorshire is Craig Dona, where people used to drink from Dona's spring on Sunday evenings.

The three 'Witches of Llanddona', Lisi Blac, Siân Bwt and Bela Fawr are among Wales' most famous. They met near Ffynnon Oer (the Cold Well) to chant curses, one of which is translated as: *'Let him wander for many centuries; and at each step a style; on each style a fall; in each fall a breaking of bone; neither the largest nor the smallest but the neck bone every time.'*

There is a large standing stone not far from Cremyn Dolmen at Llanddona, and another one surviving (of two originals) just 300 yards away. In the outer wall of the nave of the church is an ancient figured stone from an earlier church.

DWYFAEL 6th century

Dwyfael ab Hywel ab Emyr Llydaw was the brother of the warrior saints Derfel, Sulien and Arthfael, and travelled with Cadfan from Llanilltud Fawr to Bardsey Island, Ynys Enlli.

DWYFAEL 6th century

The son of Pryderi ap Dolor, of Deira and Bernicia. His father was mentioned in the Arthurian Triads as one of the 'Three Strong-limbed Ones of the Isle of Britain', and *'Pryderi's Host'* is mentioned in the Gododdin also.

DWYNWEN 5th – 6th century
DWYN, DONWENNA, DUNWEN, DONWEN
January 25
Patron Saint of Lovers

A daughter of Brychan, this virgin moved to Anglesey and her name is commemorated at Llanddwyn and Porthddwyn. A young man called Maelon Dafodrill wished to marry her, but she refused him and prayed for deliverance. She then dreamed that a drink cured her of her longings and turned Maelon to ice. Dwynwen thus prayed for three things: that Maelon was unfrozen; that all true lovers should succeed in their quest for love, or be cured of their passion, and that she should never wish to become married. She then became a nun. Her church was a focal point for young men and women, and for the sick.

St Dwynwen bult an oratory and hermitage in the sixth century. Another legend is that this was after she had been turned down in love. She has become a Welsh 'Valentine', with cards being sent on her feast day. The ruins of 'St Dwynwen's Abbey', on Llanddwyn Island, are cut off at high tide from Maltraeth Bay in Snowdonia. A rock shaped like a bed on the island is known as 'Gwely Esyth', and those who slept on it would be cured of rheumatism if they carved their names on the surrounding turf when they awoke. Another boulder on the cliff edge has a strange 'spy-hole' in it, which opened for the dying Dwynwen to finally look at the magnificent sunset over the Irish Sea.

St Dwynwen's Well on Llanddwyn Island (since renamed Ffynnon Fair, Mary's Well) had a sacred eel. Pilgrims to it sprinkled breadcrumbs on the surface of the water, and covered them with a piece of cloth. If the eel took the cloth as well as the crumbs, the pilgrim's loved one was unfaithful. Another version is that if bubbles appeared during the 'ceremonies', lovers would find happiness. Because of the fame of the well, Llanddwyn became rich. Ffynnon Ddwynwen was also known as Crochan Llanddwyn (Llanddwyn's Cauldron), but it was mainly destroyed by Calvinistic nonconformists in the 19th century. There was a custom of invoking Dwynwen to cure sick animals, which also lasted until the 19th century, probably because Llanddwyn (near Newborough) was formerly a fairly remote island. There was also a Ffynnon Dafaden holy well on the headland near her church.

In 'The Sayings of the Wise' there are the lines:
'Hast thou heard the saying of St Dwynwen,
The fair daughter of Brychan the Aged?
"There is none so loveable as the cheerful" '

Dafydd ap Gwilym wrote a famous cywyd that he read to her image, asking her to take the message to his beloved Morfudd:
'Dwynwen, beautiful as tears of frost,
In your candle-lit choir
Your golden statue knows well
How to soothe the pain and
Torment of sad men.
He who keeps watch in radiant holiness
In your choir, shining Indeg,
Can never depart from Llanddwyn
With love-sickness nor a troubled mind.'

At Tresilian Cove in Glamorgan, where the notorious Breton pirate Colyn Dolphyn was buried up to his neck to face the incoming tide, is a huge fissure known as the cave of Dwynwen. There is a natural archway in the cave, called her Bow of Destiny. Local people used to throw a stone to pass over the arch. If it took ten times to achieve this, it would be ten years before one married. If one was married, it would be ten years before one's partner died. Marriages were also celebrated in this cave. A scribbled note by John Prosser of St Athan was that Colyn Dolphyn's cries could be heard *'especially on the nights of the February full moon. However, Tresilian Bay has also been the scene of more pleasant happenings. In her book "Land of My Fathers" Miss Edith Picton-Turberville asserts that the parents of her famous ancestor, General Thomas Picton, were actually married in Tresilian Caves. The bridal couple were Miss Cecil Powell of Llandow and Thomas Picton of Poyston.'*

DWYWAU 6th century
DWYARAW
September 14

Patron saint of Llanddwywau, a chapel under Llanenddwyn in Merionethshire. He was a son of Hywel ab Emyr Llydaw, and the brother of Sulien and Derfel Gadarn.

DWYWE 6th century
DWYWAI

The wife of Dunawd Fawr, and mother of the saints Deiniol, Cynwyl and Gwarthan. In Llanddwye-is-y-Craig at Pont Fadog (Madog's Bridge), on the side of the river Ysgethin are Cors y Gedol dolmen remains, sometimes called Arthur's Quoit (like so many other cromlechs across Wales). The capstone measures 12 by 10 feet.

DWYWIG 6th - 7th century

The son of Llywarch Hen, and said to have a church in Ewyas (Hereford). He is mainly notable for being the direct ancestor of the great Rhodri Mawr, who was killed in 877.

DYDDGEN and DYDDGAU

These saints had adjoining chapels in Llangyndeyrn and Llanelli in Carmarthenshire.

DYFAN d.193
DAMIANUS, DIRUVIANUS
May 24 (with Fagan), April 8

Dyfan, the saint sent by Pope Eleutherius with Fagan in 180 AD, is buried at Merthyr Dyfan Church, where many Roman remains have been found. There was a holy well there, later called Ffynnon Mynwen. It is believed that Teilo founded this church in memoriam of Dyfan in the 6th century. A stone at Llangwarren in Pembroke was inscribed Dobagni and Dovagni, and may commemorate Dyfan. He and Ffagan were also supposed to have been the first bishops of

Congresbury in 167, returning to Rome in 186. Merthyr Dyfan is between Cadog's foundations of Llancarfan and Cadoxton, and Llandyfan is near Llangadog and Llandeilo. There is also a Llandefand (now Llandevaud) in Llanmartin in Monmouth. The parish church of Landevant in Britanny is near Cadog's famous monastery on the Sea of Etel, and now dedicated to St Martin.

Dyfan's 'Saying of the Wise' is:
'Hast thou heard the saying of Dyfan
The Martyr, in the day of slaughter?
"God is superior to ill foreboding".'

A 12th century deed from William, Earl of Gloucester and Lord of Glamorgan, gave three acres of the Welsh mainland to the brothers at the religious house dedicated to *'Sancto Michael et Sancto Cadoco et Dolfino'* in the island off Penarth. This has to be Flat Holm, but there was a St Michael's priory on Steep Holm also. It seems that Dolfino was the Latinised version of Dyfan, as there are no alternative saints known. Another of Earl William's charters gave the Bristol Abbey of St Augustine *'Platam Holmam....with the chapels....on that island.'* In yet another deed he gave the advowson of the church of Rumney, Cardiff, for the use and sustenance of the Augustinian canons of Flat Holm (- see Gildas and Tewdrig). The Anglo-Saxon Chronicle records that, after Harold's defeat at Hastings, his mother Queen Githa, or Glytha, and her ladies fled to Bradanreolice (the Broad Burial Ground, or Flat Holm. They then went for sanctuary to the monastery of St Omer).

At Landyfan Forge, near Trapp and the fabulous Carreg Cennen Castle, William Lewis used a cannon ball to grind indigo to make dye. It was bought by Carmarthen Museum in 1892. Different herbs were used to dye Welsh costumes, explaining the regional variations in colours. Welsh black wool was very popular for stockings as it did not fade. The following is from Ken Etheridge's lovely little book on 'Welsh Costume' (published by Christopher Davies, 1977):
Each area specialised in its own kind of cloth; Gwallter Mechain tells us that blue cloth was woven on Anglesey and sold at Chester Fair; while the people of Caernarfon produced two kinds of cloth – a blue cloth to sell in Merioneth, and a grey (called "brethyn Sir Fon" – the cloth of Anglesey) to sell at the Anglesey fairs. The finest flannel was made in the district between Dolobran and Llanidloes, which was called the Welsh flannel country. A kind of slate-blue flannel was produced in the Carmarthen district, while the coastal regions of Gower, Llanelli and southern Glamorgan specialised in the production of a brilliant scarlet cloth; in Pembroke it was dark red, almost claret; in Gower it was more scarlet; in Carmarthen and Llanelli (Penclawdd) it was more of a crimson colour; all were sometimes striped with narrow lines of black, cream, white or dark brown. In Montgomery cloths of blue, drab and brown – all with stripes of darker self-colour – were produced.

Perhaps this choice of colour had a good deal to do with local products; the red, obtained in earliest times from the cockle, was a colour predominating near the coast; while blacks and browns from rock lichens were the colours worn by shepherds and their families in the mountain regions. The relation between dye and the vegetation of the locality was probably much more distinct in the olden days of restricted communications. With the advent of industrial amenities the local idiosyncrasies tend to vanish ...

The wool then passed to the weaver, who was a craftsman venerated by all for his skill, which took a lifetime to learn. He was practised not only in the weaving, but also in dyeing and fulling the cloth. The dyeing varied in different regions (as indicated above); checks and stripes were also peculiar to certain localities and not to others. Checks were popular in eastern parts of the country and in the northern parts of Cardigan, while plaid patterns were prevalent in Gwent. Altogether South Wales patterns and colourings were considerably gayer: scarlet, crimson, blues and orange and bright brown were seen; while in the North drab greys and black, with greens, Prussian blues and violets (in the Bangor area) were more prevalent. Herbs, plants and wild fruit, such as blackberry and bilberry were used; onion skins gave a rich brown; indigo gave a variety of blues and greens; chemical dyes superceded the vegetable, but it is doubtful whether any more beautiful or lasting colours were achieved.'

The present crisis in farming in Wales has much to do with the collapse of the price of sheep-skins. The USSR used to buy all Wales could sell at £8.50 each, but the collapse of its economy has meant that hill-farms have lost income that meant the difference between survival and bankruptcy. We need to 'brainstorm' a new use in Wales for sheepskins – a Welsh slipper factory? Also in Etheridge's fine book he notes the individual specialities across Wales that we could well emulate today to get into niche markets: *'Caerphilly wove yard-wide cloths and broad-cloth; Bridgend produced serge, plush, plains and kerseys from the fine wool of the Glamorgan vales; while other items were manufactured at Denbigh (shoes and gloves), Monmouth (caps), and Mold (cotton goods); Holywell produced silks and cottons, while boots and shoes were produced at Narberth, Haverfordwest and Lampeter.'* The author has recently found a book with a picture of the plaid associated with Glynneath in past times. Welsh kilts and costumes are now being made.

This principle could also apply to Welsh organic foods, such as canned or frozen Cardiganshire 'cawl' or Glamorgan sausages (vegetarian) and laverbread cheeses. The lie of cheap food in Britain has been exposed by foreign travel. Food prices may be similar in parts of Europe, but European pay is considerably higher. On the whole, however, all food is cheaper in Europe because four companies control the British market. (The arrival of Walmart from the USA and its takeover of Asda will soon lessen the margins of Marks & Spencer, Tesco and Sainsbury, and at last force UK prices down, however. The directors of these major stores have been ennobled by successive governments despite the greatest profiteering on food margins in Europe). What Wales needs is local producers serving local markets as a countervailing power to large operators, offering higher quality food and drink at lower prices. Of course, one problem with this argument is that successful small operations are swallowed up by large firms, and the status quo is re-established. Perhaps the Robert Owen idea of co-operatives could be re-implemented.

Finally, the Welsh universities could combine around Swansea Institute's expertise to design a 'people's car' to be built in Wales at a reasonable price. The car multinationals charge more for their cars in Britain than anywhere else in Europe. In relation to GDP per capita, Welsh people pay more for everything than consumers in the rest of Britain. Wales needs to start producing again, rather than be a low-paid assembly centre for transnational corporations which neither pay British business taxes nor create 'real' jobs. Wales needs to process its own organic food in Wales and resist foreign take-overs of such projects. Ty-Nant is now French and Rachel's Dairy has been sold to an American company. Wales has to help itself. The targets set by Welsh politicians to reach 90% of England's GDP are impossible to achieve by present methods. Call-centres are the worst possible answer to an endemic problem, depressing wage levels still further with unskilled jobs.

DYFANOG see TYFANOG

DYFNAN 5th century
April 21, 22, 23 and 24

A son of Brychan, the founder of Llanddyfnan in Anglesey where he is buried. Its chapels, all now dedicated to Mary, were at Llanbedr Goch, Pentraeth and Llanfair ym Mathafarn Eithaf. There is a burial chamber known as Arthur's Quoit there, and a standing stone leaning at an angle of 45 degrees near Llanddyfnan Rectory.

DYFNIG 6th century
DOMINICUS
May 1

A companion of Ust (Justus) from Brittany, they jointly founded Llanwrin in Montgomery. This could be the Difwng noted as a son of Emyr Llydaw.

DYFNOG early 7th century
DYFYNOG
February 13

Patron of Llanrhaeadr-yng-Nghinmeirch, south of Denbigh. His holy well, Ffynnon Ddyfnog cured and healed supplicants. He was an ascetic, living on bread and water, wearing a horsehair shirt and a heavy iron belt. He used to stand under the holy spring, in the well tank, for long periods as a penance.

Dyfnog was celebrated at Ddyfynog in Brecon, although it appears that this was originally founded by Cynog ap Brychan. His father was Medrod ap Cawrdaf ap Caradog, or Cawrdaf. Llanrhaiadr-in-Cinmerch was formerly known as Llanddyfnog. Edward Lhuyd commented of its well *'some say it would cure ye pox'*. The well could cure not only *'scabs and the itch'*, but also smallpox, dumbness and deafness. It was still used in the 18th century, when the bath *'provided with all conveniences of rooms for bathing built around it.'*

Many other travellers have commented upon Ffynnon Ddyfnog, west of Llanrhaeadr-yng-Nghinmeirch church. Leland said that it was held in great regard for healing scabs and itches, with some believing that its waters cured 'pox'. Pennant described the fountain as being enclosed in an angular well-house, decorated with *'small human figures.'* Fenton described it thus: *'arched over, from which the Water used to fall through a Pipe in the Wall into a Bath, whose bottom was paved with Marble, with a building round it and roofed, but now exhibiting one shapeless ruin.'* The 'Tree of Jesse' window in the church is the finest in Wales, and preserved from destruction in the Civil War by being buried in the massive dug-out chest which still stands beneath it. Both naves have hammer-beam roofs, and the church is well worth visiting for many other features.

Alphabetical Listing of the Saints of Wales and Religious Events

BISHOP DYFRIG c. 465 – c. 546
DUBRICIUS, DEVEREUX
November 4 and 14 (translation May 29), March 11 (Whitchurch near Monmouth)

In the Life of Dyfrig (Vita Dubricii), his mother is Eurddil or Eurduila, daughter of King Peibio of Ergyng (Archenfield district in Herefordshire). His father was said to be a king of Ergyng called Pepiau, so his genealogy is confused. As Pabiali ap Brychan was also known as Papai, this may then be justified. Dyfrig may have been born in Madley on the Wye near Hereford, which was Welsh-speaking until the eighteenth century. Other sources say that he was born at Mochros (Moccas) on the Wye in the same county, or on the banks of the Gwaun near Fishguard (Abergwaun) in Pembroke. He was of the line of Brychan, probably a grandson. King Peibio was known as 'King Dribbler', and when he discovered that Eurddil was pregnant threw her into the river in a sack. Three times the current threw her back on the shore. He then decided to burn her, but she was found next morning unharmed, cuddling the infant Dyfrig.

Dyfrig's own estate was called Ynys Eurddil, or Ynys Ebrdil (also Miserbdil) which was probably Mochros. Most sources say that his first foundation was at Archenfield (based on the Roman city of Ariconum). Another version is that he wandered along the Wye looking for the best place, and saw a wild white sow with piglets in a meander of the river. He called the site Moch-rhos, or Mochros (Moor of the Pigs), modern-day Moccas. Associated with St Illtud and St Samson, Dyfrig was extremely important in south-east Wales and Herefordshire, and it appears that David succeeded him as primate of Wales. He had religious centres at Hentland*, Whitchurch, Ballingham, Madley, Moccas and Caldey Island**. His chief church was centred at Hentland (Henllan), just outside Ross-on-Wye, and the village itself rests on a Roman site. At a farm called Llanfrother there, were found traces of an ancient establishment. In Archenfield (modern Herefordshire) the church at Whitchurch, and chapels at Ballingham and Hentland are dedicated to him. It seems fairly certain that he and his disciples moved west after the battle of Dyrham, when Gloucester, Bath and probably Caerwent were destroyed. Their monasteries in Ergyng and Ewyas were wasted, and they sought refuge at Llandaf with Teilo, and at Llanilltud Fawr and Llancarfan.

In the 7th century Life of Samson, Dyfrig is a famed churchman. (Many of the details of the Welsh saints come from the Breton Lives, as Welsh records were destroyed during the four-hundred year fight against Anglo-French domination. Destruction of land titles and deeds, usually recorded on church manuscripts, allowed Norman and Angevin lords to take over Welsh territories legally). Known as 'papa' Dubricius in the Book of Llandaf, he was said to have ordained Samson as a deacon at Llanilltud Fawr. Some sources say that Dyfrig was taught himself by Germanus of Auxerre but Dyfrig was a century too late, so this may mean that he was a follower of Garmon's teaching. Certainly, he seemed to have been a strong opponent of Pelagianism and persuaded his friend David to preach against it at the Llanddewi Brefi synod. Samson's Life claims that Dyfrig was an abbot at Enlli, and Geoffrey of Monmouth claimed that he crowned the 15-year old Arthur at Silchester. Geoffrey of Monmouth states that there were 200 philosophers in his college at Caerleon, studying science and astronomy.

Other later mediaeval records place him as bishop of Caerleon from 490 on succeeding Tremorinus, the founder of Llandaf and again as the saint who crowned Arthur***. On Caldey Island was found a stone inscribed *'Magl Dubr' (tonsured servant of Dubricius)*, where it seems Dyfrig was for some time the abbot. There are also dedications to him at Gwenddwr, south of Builth in Breconshire and at Porlock in Somerset. Porlock was formerly 'ecclesia

Saint Dubricius' in a deed of 1476. There are at least six churches clustered in Archenfield dedicated to Dyfrig. Hereford's Saint Devereux is a corruption of Dubricius.

Dyfrig retired to Enlli, but a Norman bishop of Llandaf had his bones translated to Llandaf in 1120 for the greater honour of his cathedral, where he was one of the four titular saints. The relics reached the Llyn peninsula mainland on May 7 and arrived at Llandaf on May 23, where his reliquaries (his head and one arm encased in silver) drew pilgrims until the Reformation. They were removed in 1538 and lost. Tennyson called him *'Dubric the high saint, Chief of the church in Britain'*.

Dyfrig's most famous well is near the ancient monastery site of Garnllwyd at Llancarfan, where Cadog was presiding at this time. Ffynnon Dyfrig can still be found in the woods known as Coed Ffynnon Dyfrig, and nearby at Llanfeithyn he had another healing well. These survivals certainly seem to authenticate his stay, possibly with Teilo, at Llancarfan. A menhir near Cefn Gelli Gaer, Caerffili, was noted by Edward Lhuyd in 'Archaeologica Britannica'. He records *'we find the British name DYVROD inscribed on a stone TYFRAU TI. In the notes on Glamorganshire, in Camden, I have read this inscription, supposing it might have been Welsh "Deffro iti" (mayst thou awake); but having found afterwards that the names anciently inscribed on monuments in our country are very often in the genitive case, as Conbelini, Severini****, Aimilini, etc., and most, if not all, in Latin, I now conclude it has to be a proper name, and the very same that is otherwise called Dubricius.'* The stone was later vandalised, so no letters were legible, but alternative theories upon the menhir's provenance are found in Westwood's 'Lapidarium Walliae'.

There is a case to be made that Dyfrig founded the colleges of Llancarfan, Caerworgan (Llanilltud Fawr) and Caerleon, and that he should have been made the patron saint of Wales for the effects that these monasteries had upon Celtic Christianity. His effigy still lies in Llandaf Cathedral.

*Traditionally, Dyfrig's community moved about a mile and a half from Henllan to Llanfrodyr ('the Church of the Brethren', also known as Llanfrother), but the Book of Llandaf tells us that he *'retained two thousand clergy for seven successive years at Henllan, on the banks of the Wye, in the literary study of divine and humane wisdom; setting forth to them in himself an example of religious life, and of perfect charity.'* It seems that he also had a great monastery at Welsh Bicknor (Llangystennin-Garthbenni), which was active from around 575 to 866 and Saxon incursion. Canon Doble noted Dyfrig's place as *'one of the chief figures in the creation of Christian Wales.'*

**An inscribed slab from the Caldey Priory ruins was used as a window-sill, then in 1810 found in a garden before being built into the wall of the chapel. Westwood translates it as *'Et signo crucis in illam finxi rogo omnibus ambulantibus ibi exorent pro anima Catuoconi.'* He believes that it remembers St Cathan (q.v.). The monastery at Caldey has received lottery funding to help with repairs, and the island is one of Wales' most attractive tourist features.

***The Book of Llandaf states that Dubricius *'summus doctor'* was appointed archbishop of all of *'Southern Britain'*, being elected by the king and the whole *'parochia'*, with his see being based at the monastery of *'Lanntam'* (Llandaf), founded in honour of St Peter, with the consent of King *Mouricius* (Meurig). Meurig was Arthur's father.

Alphabetical Listing of the Saints of Wales and Religious Events

****There was a pillar inscribed *'Severini fili Severini'* on the roadside at Llan-Newydd, between Carmarthen and Cynfel. It was said that the Romans under Severinus, son of Severus, the Roman governor of Britain, fought a great battle here in 72 AD, where Severinus was killed. It was moved to Traws Mawr farm. Other stones moved to Traws Mawr were one inscribed CVNEGN (Cynon?), and another crossed stone of before the 10th century.

E

> *'Education . . . has produced a vast population able to read but unable to distinguish what is worth reading.'*
> **G. M. Trevelyan, 'English Social History', 1942**

EASTER

One of the major differences between the Roman and Celtic churches was the date of commemoration of Easter. The Irish and Welsh churches followed for at least two hundred years the original date known in Western Europe. However, in 457 the Bishop of Rome had issued the 'Victorinus table' changing religious dates to those practised in Alexandria. The Frankish bishops in Europe adopted the new dates, but they were not accepted in Britain. St Columbanus argued cogently for the British case based on the Jewish calendar, while the Latin Church changed to the days celebrated in Africa. The British version was based upon the date of the Jewish Passover, but its bishops were anathematised by the Nicene Council for keeping this pre-Roman belief.

Sir John Edward Lloyd, in his 1911 'History of Wales' pointed out the problems: *'Easter forced itself on men's notice as a visible sign of discord, since the sudden transition from the gloom of Holy Week to the rejoicings of the Day of Resurrection was an event in the Christian year to catch the attention of the most careless, and to see one Christian still keeping the Lenten fast while another at his side was in the midst of the Easter revels brought out in the clearest fashion how far they were from dwelling as brethren in unison together. In this way it came about that as the result of one rule, the Celtic Easter often anticipated the Roman by a week, while occasionally, through the operation of another, it would fall no less than four weeks later. Among the Celts 25th March was the earliest possible Easter Day, 21st April the latest, while at Rome the range of oscillation was from 22nd March to 25th April. As a result of these conflicting calculations, it was the exception for the two Easters to coincide.'*

Easter Day now occurs between March 22 and April 25 each year, and is particularly associated with eggs, which used to be decorated and sometimes rolled down slopes. The Church explains that the eggs are symbols of the resurrection (new life), but they seem to be a continuation of pagan fertility rites. Easter Monday is a Bank Holiday. Hock Day was the second Tuesday after Easter, also known as Binding Tuesday, and villagers collected money for their parishes by light-hearted methods such as collecting forfeits. Shrove Tuesday was '*Ynyd*', and it was customary to make annual payments to the landlord called '*ynyd*' or '*gieir ynyd*', which usually consisted on one hen and twenty eggs. The Welsh Land Commission in 1856 noted a payment of two fat geese and forty eggs.

The Celtic Church of Spanish Galicia conformed to the reformed Easter at the Council of Toledo in 663, and Louis the Pious ordered the Abbot of Landevenec, in the Crozon Peninsula of Brittany, to adopt the Roman tonsure and Rule of St Benedict in 818, but Brittany held out longer than all the other Celtic areas in altering Easter. Wall gives the adoption of Roman Easter by the Celtic Church as follows:
Southern Ireland 634; Northumbria 664; Strathclyde 688; North Ireland 692; Somerset and Devon 705; Iona 710; Picts 710; North Wales 768; South Wales 777 to 850; and Cornwall 925-940.

Stan Awberry writes of the nineteenth century: *'The Easter Monday Festival was held in most of the villages including Llantwit (Llanilltud). It was the holiday of the year especially for young people. It was not only a day of liveliness and laughter, it was supposed to be symbolic of the resurrection on the third day. The young men of the village dressed in colourful clothes, and decorated a chair which they carried on their shoulders. The first girl they met would be placed on the chair and raised above their heads three times. She was then released and kissed each of the men. They in return made a gift to her which was usually a small coin. The festival ended at noon. The colourful decorations of the men indicated the purple robe, the lifting of the chair was the raising and nailing to the cross, the kiss implied the betrayal, the gift of coins denoted the pieces of silver, the price which was paid. This festival, like many others of a similar character, has been discontinued for many years.'*

Francis Kilvert wrote lyrically of Clyro's 'Easter Eve Idyll' custom of decking graves with flowers, on April 16th, 1870:
'More and more people kept coming into the churchyard as they finished their day's work. The sun went down in glory behind the dingle, but still the work of love went on through the twilight and into the dusk until the moon rose full and splendid. The figures continued to move about among the graves and to bend over the green mounds in the calm clear moonlight and warm air of the balmy evening. At 8 o'clock there was a gathering of the Choir in the Church to practise the two anthems for tomorrow. The moonlight came streaming in broadly through the chancel windows. When the choir had gone and the lights were out and the church quiet again, as I walked down the Churchyard alone the decked graves had a strange effect in the moonlight and looked as if the people had lain down to sleep for the night out of doors, ready dressed to rise early on Easter morning. I lingered in the verandah before going to bed. The air was as soft and warm as a summer night, and the broad moonlight made the village almost as light as day. Everyone seemed to have gone to rest, and there was not a sound except the clink and trickle of the brook.'

EDERN 6th- 7th century
EDEYRN
January 6 Bodedern, December 2 Edern

This son of Nudd ap Beli was a bard, who took up the monastic life and founded Bodedeyrn under Holyhead in Anglesey. There are dolmens near here at Presaddfed near Llyn Llywelyn. He also founded Llanedern, Edern, on the Llŷn peninsula. Up until 1880, the custom at Edern was to break the eggs of magpies, crows and blackbirds on May-Day, the eggs being collected and kept for this purpose.

Edern ap Nudd ap Rhun ap Maelgwn features as one of Arthur's knights, and is mentioned in the 'Dream of Rhonabwy' and in 'Geraint ab Erbin' in the Mabinogion tales. In Cardiff he won the jousting tournament two years in succession, and a third victory would have given him the title *'Knight of the Sparrow-hawk'* but Geraint wounded him badly. However, Edern is too late – Arthur was a contemporary of Maelgwn Gwynedd. Maelgwn Gwynedd and his son Rhun both came into conflict with St Cadog, and one of Cadog's followers was St Edeyrn ap Gwrtheyrn. Possibly the venomous hatred of Gwrtheyrn (Vortigenn) engendered by Gildas substituted Edern ap Nudd for Edeyrn ap Gwrtheyrn.

Edern in Brittany is counted as a local saint, symbolised as a stag, and Lannedern near Huelgoat is 14 north east of Chateaulin. Stags feature in decorations all over the church and calvary, referring to the legend of Edern and his sister Genovefa. The village of Edern is outside Briec.

EDEYRN 5th - 6th century
FAUSTUS?
November 11, November 23 at Llanedeyrn

The son of Gwrtheyrn (Vortigern), and a saint in Catwg's community at Llancarfan, Edeyrn founded a large religious community on the banks of the Rhymni at Llanedeyrn (on the northern outskirts of Cardiff). His saintly sons (or brothers) were Aerdeyrn and Elldeyrn. Nennius seems to refer to Edeyrn as Faustus, and he may have been the warrior in Arthur's court, rather than Edern ap Nudd. (See Faustus).

Upon July 5 1762, William Thomas recorded *'Report came of the death of Thomas Hedges of Laneddern, Brother of John Hedges the great herb Doctor, by a sting from a snake in his ear and under his chin by sleeping in mowing hay the 29th of June last. But the report was not true for he went as soon as stinged to his sister (to she he mowed the hay) and she with a cord tyed his throat as hard that the sting went not down, and lanched under his chin and he have since recovered.'*

EDI
EDITHA, EDITH
November 8

There are five Saxon saints of this name, and one may be remembered at Llanedy in Carmarthen. Ogof Gwyl Edi is near the church, a large cave for a giant man in legend, whose bed, Gwely Edi is a stone slab in the cave. Brynrhyd Stone near the church is around eight feet high and contains white quartz.

EDMUND d.870
November 20

Edmund Ironside, King of the East Angles, was a Christian and was horribly martyred by Danes. He is remembered at Crickhowell, Crughywel. As the Saxon kingdoms of England became Christian in the 6th and 7th centuries, Edmund the Wuffing's was perhaps the greatest saintly cult in England. However, William Fitzrobert's Norman Conquest saw the start of a process of cultural imperialism, whereby the illiterate Normans portrayed the Saxons as backward, destroying their cathedrals and decanonising their saints. At Senlac Hill (The Battle of Hastings) William had carried a papal banner to justify his 'crusade'. Thus in future years a mythological Lebanese became England's patron saint, George. The recent groundswell in the English press to celebrate St George's day with a holiday is out of focus. If England wishes to celebrate its nationhood, surely other dates such as November 20th would be far more appropriate, commemorating the Angles and Saxons who founded the modern English nation. A Celtic stone found at Llanhetty near Crickhowell is almost five feet long and reads '+ *GURdon + sacerdos'*.

EDNYFED 4th - 5th century

The son of Macsen Wledig, his brothers were the saints Owain Ffinddu, Gwythyr, Cystennin and Peblig. His sons were also saints.

EDREN
EDRIN
November 26

St Edren's, subject to St Lawrence in Pembroke is dedicated to this unknown saint. Two places near St David's, Carnedren Uchaf and Carnedren Isaf also are associated with him or her. In St Edren's churchyard, local people paid for the grass, which they would eat with bread and butter. This was recorded as going on in 1818, in Carlisle's Topographical Dictionary of Wales. There had been a well in the churchyard, famed for curing hydrophobia (rabies), but a wicked woman washed clothes in it on a Sunday, so it dried up. Its healing virtues were then transferred to the grass around it. St Edren's has an early Christian inscribed stone.

A scaly serpent flew one night from the tower at St Edren's Church to Rholwm marsh near Grinston, where it sleeps at the bottom of Grinston Well. There are several megaliths in the district. The remains of Clunffrwn Dolmen and Tre Hywel Dolmen, and Penlan Mabus Uchaf Burial Chamber are nearby.

EDWARD THE CONFESSOR d.1066
January 5 and October 13

This penultimate Saxon king is remembered at Knighton in Radnorshire.

EDWEN 7th century
November 6

Llanedwen in Anglesey is devoted to her. King Edwin of Northumbria was brought up in the court of King Cadfan in Caerseiont (now called Caernarfon). His virgin daughter or niece was Edwen, and it appears that this Saxon princess stayed in Wales after Edwin's departure. Eglwys Fach in Cardigan, dedicated to Michael, used to be known as Llanfihangel Capel Edwin. At Llanedwen is one of the most important dolmens in Wales, in Plas Newydd Park. There is also another burial chamber in the park, called Bryn-yr-Hen-Bobl (Hill of the Old People) Dolmen.

EDWIN OF NORTHUMBRIA 6th-7th century

This king is included because of the debate with his nobles whether to accept Christianity in 627. A member of his council made the following memorable speech, which has become Bede's most famous piece of writing:

'The present life of Man, O King, seems to me, in comparison with that time which is unknown to us, like the swift flight of a sparrow through the room in which you sit at supper round the fire, while the wind is howling and the snow is drifting without. It passes swiftly in at one door and out through another, feeling for the moment the warmth and shelter of your palace; but it

flies from winter to winter and swiftly escapes from our sight. Even such is our life here, and if anyone can tell us certainly what lies beyond it, we shall do wisely to follow his teaching.'

EFENGYLAU TEILO 8the century

This is one of the most beautiful illuminated gospels in the British Isles, earlier than the Book of Kells, which contains in its margins some of the earliest examples of written Welsh. In legend, Gelhi gave his best horse to Cingal for the book, which Gelhi then presented *'to God and Teilo'*. The volume was placed on Teilo's altar at Llandeilo Fawr. It notes many land-grants in Glamorgan and Gwent, because it was taken to Llandaf Cathedral, presumably because Llandaf claimed Teilo's relics. Somehow it was taken to Lichfield Cathedral where it is now known as the Lichfield Gospels, or the Book of St Chad.

The Welsh Heritage Campaign is calling for the return of the gospels to Wales, but Lichfield Cathedral's Librarian insists that they were written by a scribe trained in Lindisfarne about 700AD, at the cathedral. W.M. Andrews of St Andrew's University has stated that there is a *'Welsh style'* to these *'Welsh Elgin Marbles',* and the author sees little case for Lichfield keeping them. The similarly dated Lindisfarne Gospels are being returned to the north-east of England (near Tony Blair's constituency), so perhaps the Welsh nation needs a Welsh Prime Minister to effect the deed.

EFFYDD see NEFYDD

EFRDDYL 5th century
EBRDIL, EURDYL
August 6 and July 7

This daughter of Pepiau ab Erb was the mother of Dyfrig. She was the patron saint of Madley (Lann Ebrdil) in Hereford, where Dyfrig was born. There was a Ffynon Efrdil or Eurdil near the Monmow river in Monmouth (at Llangynvil, near Welsh Newton).

EGRYN early 7th century

The founder of Llanegryn in Merioneth, and the son of Gwrydr Drwm of the line of Cadell Deyrnllug. He was a monk at Llanilltud Fawr. Croes Egryn near his church has disappeared, but there is a large farm known as Egryn Abbey on the site of a mansion. His church is now dedicated to Mary the Virgin. On the site of the original church, the Cistercian monks from Cymmer Abbey built the present church (and a hospital) in the 13th century. Just before the Dissolution of the Monasteries, they took Cymmer's magnificent rood loft and screen and placed them in Llanegryn. Egryn was associated with strange lights, which some associated with fairies, and others with the rare natural phenomenon we know as 'will o' the wisps'. Near Llanegryn is the standing stone known as Bryn Seward. Ffynnon y Fron in the parish cured rheumatism and other illnesses. A Celtic crossed stone is built into the south wall of Llanegryn Church.

EGWAD early 7th century

He founded Llanegwad and Llanfynydd in Carmarthen, and was the son of Cynddilig ap Cenydd ap Gildas.

EIGION (see IGON)
First Sunday after September 20

Llaneigion, also called Llanigon is near Hay on Wye in Brecon. Ffynnon Eigion is nearby.

EIGRAD see EUGRAD

EIGRON 6th century

A son of Caw, said to have founded a church in Cornwall.

EILIAN GEIMIAD (the Pilgrim) 6th century
ELIAN, HILARY
January 13 and 14
Llaneilian Wakes were held on the first three Friday evenings in August.

A contemporary of Cybi and Seiriol on Anglesey, where he founded Llanelian. He was the son of Gallgu Rieddog and Canna, the daughter of Tewdwr Mawr of Llydaw. Canna was the widow of St Sadwrn. His uncle was St Tegfan, who settled in Anglesey. There were miraculous cures at St Elian's shrine in Anglesey, where offerings were placed into Cyff Eilian, his old oak chest. Ffynnon Eilian is half a mile from the church, near the shore, and blessings were made for crops and livestock there. Water passes though a rock fissure into a square stone well chamber. The water also cured fits, scrofula and the ague. In the 1750's the practice of divination flourished at Llanelian. A person entered a small semi-circular cupboard in the chapel next to the church, and turned around thrice within it, to ensure his or her survival through the coming year.

Near Llanelian church in the parish of Llandrillo-yn-Rhos, Denbigh, the well of Ffynnon Elian was popular up to this century. It had changed from a healing well to a 'cursing well', near the church and Colwyn Bay, *'the most dreadful of all the Welsh Holy Wells'* (Baring-Gould and Fisher). The *'guardian'* of the well, for a sum of money, offered to put someone under the evil influence of the well. A pin was dropped into the well, with the name of the victim being uttered, as well as a piece of paper with the victim's name or initials on it, folded up in a thin sheet of lead. Those *'put into the well'* got to hear of it, and wasted away. If someone fell ill, he often rushed to the well to have the spell lifted by a different ritual, just in case he had been cursed. Again, money exchanged hands. John Edwards was fined 15 shillings in 1820 for *'pulling Edward Pierce out of Ffynnon Elian'* and the authorities had it filled in 1829. It appears that King Cadwallon had offered Eilian as much land for his church as Eilian's tame doe could run in a day, but the deer was pulled down and killed by a greyhound. Eilian cursed the inhabitants and had condemned them to a life of poverty. There was also a Ffynnon Elian in Merioneth and in Llanrhaiadr-ym-Mochnant in Montgomery.

Another description gives the procedure followed by another keeper of the well:
'Even in this present age (the well) is annually visited by some hundreds of people, for the reprehensive purpose of invoking curses upon the heads of those who have grievously offended them. The ceremony is performed by the applicant standing on a certain spot near the well, whilst the owner of it reads passages of the sacred scriptures, and then, taking a small quantity of water, gives it to the former to drink, and throws the residue over his head, which is repeated three times, the party continuing to mutter his imprecations in whatever terms his vengeance may dictate.' (Lewis's 'Topographical Dictionary of Wales', London 1843).

Even Thomas Pennant was threatened with the curse of Eilian on his tour of Wales, but it was also a famous rag well. Rags were tied to nearby bushes with raw wool. It was thought that if one wished to get rid of warts, say, one must pick up wool which the sheep has dropped, then prick each wart with a pin. The pin was then rubbed on the wool, then bent and thrown into the well (a relic of the Celtic bent sword tradition). The wool was then placed on the first whitethorn bush the sufferer encountered, and the wind was left to 'scatter' the warts. At other places the warts were bathed with greasy rags which were then hidden under a stone at the well's mouth. Another variation was to use the cloth to bathe the affected parts where the skin was diseased, and then tie up the rag to a branch, while also making an offering to the well.

EILIWEDD see ALMEDHA

EILW

Llan Eilw was a church in Pebeidiog, four miles from St David's. There is also a site two miles away called Fagwr Eilw (Aelfwy's Enclosure). This holy man may be the St Ailbe who was Bishop of Munster at the time, or St Eilfyw – both these names are given as the saint who baptised the infant St David, possibly at the spring that runs under Capel-y-Pistyll, near St David's Key in Porth Glais (Portclais).

EINION FRENHIN 6th century
ENGAN, KING EINION
February 9, 10 and 12, August 5

This king was the brother of King Cynlas, St Meirion and St Seiriol, and founded with Cynlas the monastery of Penmon on Anglesey, where he made Seiriol principal. Einion was the son of Owain Ddantgwyn (White-teeth) ab Einion Yrth ap Cunedda. He also gave the holy island of Enlli (Bardsey) to St Cadfan, and with Cadfan he founded the monastery there. After Einion's death there were frequent miracle cures at Llanengan church, also called Llaneinion Frenhin, in the Llŷn Peninsula. He ruled the sub-kingdom of Afflogion after his father's treacherous murder by Maelgwn, while Cynlas ruled the small territory of Rhos but tried to throw off Maelgwn's yoke.

His gilded statue was at his burial place of Llanengan church, and Leland referred to a great pilgrimage there, where the old oak chest known as Cyff Engan held pilgrims' offerings. Cilau Dolmen is on the coast at Llanengan, with a fallen capstone of 12 feet by 9 feet. Pistyll Einion holy well near Cellan, Cardigan, may be his. Ffynnon Dduw, between Llanengan and Llanbedrog, was the centre of great festivities upon three successive Sundays each July, with

Penmon Priory. *CADW: Welsh Historic Monuments. Crown Copyright.*

Tinkinswood Burial Chamber. © *Wales Tourist Board Photo Library.*

sports and ball games. It has two adjacent wells, one for bathing and curing rheumatism, and a smaller well for invalids to drink from. Ffynnon Sarff on nearby Mynydd Mynitho had a 'snake' living in it, hence its name of Serpent's Well.

EINYDD 6th - 7th century?

Charles Shepherd makes St Nicholas, the pretty village heading west out of Cardiff towards Bridged, the dedication of St Einydd . . . *'he is reputed to be the son of Ithel, probably King Ithel (c. 600 AD) who was thrown from his horse while riding across the land of Guowf which is thought to be Wenvoe.'* ('The Winding Trail', in Stewart Williams' 'Vale of Glamorgan Series - Volume I'). The village and church were burned in the Owain Glyndŵr rebellion, and a mile away is the fabulous Tinkinswood cromlech, with the largest capstone in the British Isles.

EITHIN

At Capel Eithin in Anglesey there is a prehistoric site with a small square stone buiiding of Roman date. An inhumation cemetery of 97 graves lies just north of it. The building was described as a 'cella memoria', a structure around a martyr's tomb.

EITHRAS 6th century

A companion of Cadfan, who travelled with him from Brittany to Ynys Enlli. He may have been a son of Ithel Hael, and the brother of Tanwg, and Roscarrock associates him with Llandanwg in Merioneth, where there was a Capel Eithras.

ELAITH FRENHIN mid 6th century
KING ELAETH, ALECTUS
November 10

This son of Meurig ab Idno was driven from the North of Britain to find refuge in Seiriol's college at Penmon in Anglesey, and is said to have founded Amlwch on the island. There is a nine feet standing stone just outside Amlwch church. The ruins of Capel 'Elaethin' have disappeared. Another Elaeth (Allectus) murdered Carausius (q.v.) near Caernarfon in the early 4th century, to take over the legions in Britain.

Amlwch used to be known as Llan Elaeth Frenin, and his holy well, Ffynnon Elaeth was famous. A 'priest' used to foretell the future by the movements of an eel in the well. Two short poems are attributed to Elaith in the Black Book of Carmarthen, and some of his bardic verses are recorded in the Myvyrian Archaiology. The Cefn Amlwch Stones in Caernarfon were noted by Westwood. They came from the burial ground of an ancient church between Gors and Aberdaron around 1850, and it has been surmised that they were brought there from Bardsey Island after the closure of its monastery. The farm at Gors is near Bodwrdda and the holy Ffynnon Ddurdan, so the church may have been that of St Dirdan (q.v.). One stone reads *'SENACVS PRSB HIC IACIT CVM MVLTITV DINEM FRATRVM : : : FRE ET . . .'*. One suggestion is that Senacus was the abbot in charge of a community of brothers who were wiped out with him. The second stones reads: *'MERACIVS* (or Veracius) *PBR HIC IACIT'*.

ELDAD early 7th century

Eldad ab Arth ab Arthog Frych was saint at Llanilltud Fawr. A 'Saying of the Wise' is:
'Hast thou heard the saying of Eldad,
When counselling his countrymen?
"To the pious, God gives grace".'

BISHOP ELDAD d.577
ALDATE
February 4

Son of Prince Geraint ap Carannog of Ergyng, and bishop of Caer Lliw (Gloucester), he studied at Llanilltud Fawr. After the fateful battle of Dyrham in 577, when the British kings Conmael, Farimael (Farnmail) and Cynddylan were defeated by the Saxons, Gloucester was sacked and burned. It is believed that Eldad was martyred then. His brothers were the saints Ustig (Usted) and Mewan, and Mewan escaped to found the great monastic settlement of St Meen in Brittany. Eldad is remembered in Gloucester and Oxford churches. The disaster at Dyrham effectively cut off the Welsh from their neighbours in Domnonia (the West Country).

ELEN LLUYDDOG 4th century
HELEN OF CAERNARFON, ELEN FERCH EUDAF, ELEN OF THE HOSTS
May 22, August 25
Saint of Travellers

This saint is supposed to have been the daughter of King Coel ('Old King Cole'), and is often confused with the Elen who *'brought the True Cross to Wales'*. This latter saint was St Helena, the British mother of Constantine the Great, responsible for his conversion to Christianity. Much Welsh legend also interlinks Elen ferch Eudaf, the British wife of the Emperor Maximus (Macsen Wledig), with St. Helena. Elen ferch Eudaf was the mother of Cystennin (Constantine) and Peblig (Publicius), and the progenitor of the Royal House of Dyfed.

When Magnus Clemens Maximus led his British legions to become emperor of Gaul, Britain and Spain from 383, he held his Imperial Court at Treves (Trier), and was in contact with St Martin of Tours. In 388, he died at Aquileia trying to become Emperor of Rome. Some of his Welsh troops then seem to have gone to Brittany to settle there. One tradition is that Elen had stayed in Caernarfon (Segontium) with her son Owain Finddu. There are North Wales churches dedicated to Elen and also the extinct Llanelen near Llanrhidian in Gower, and Llanelen near Abergavenny in Monmouthshire. There was a Capel Elen in Penrhosllugwy in Anglesey, and Bletherston Church in Pembrokeshire is a dedication. Bletherston is now St Mary's, but the village was known as Tref Elen. Bletherston Church has two holy wells, one used for children's ailments and one for baptismal water. There is also Elen's Well in nearby Lawhaden (Llan Aidan). Ffynnon St Elen was a famous well near her ruined chapel in the Roman fort of Caernarfon (Segontium).

Another tradition is that she returned to Wales on the death of Macsen Wledig, with her sons who became saints, Cystennin (Constantine) and Peblig (Publicius). Other records show that Elen had other sons - Owain Finddu, Gwythyr and Ednyfed also were counted as saints. Even more sons may have been Anhun (Antonius) and Dimet. (see Macsen Wledig).

From tradition, Elen's father Eudaf held Caernarfon (Segontium) for Rome. She married Macsen before he left for Gaul, and her brothers Cynan Meriadog and Gadeon went with them. The 'Notitia Dignitatum' of 429AD records a regiment of the Segontientes serving in Illyricum, and the other claimant for Macsen's wife is Helen 'of Illyricum', so we have the Mabinogion tale based upon ancient facts. Recent evidence also backs up the Mabinogion story of Cynan Meriadog completing his service for the Emperor and settling in Europe, with the discovery that he settled near Nantes.

Sarn Helen, Ffordd Elen and Llwybr Elen are associated with her, and she is the Celtic patron of travellers, the (older) Welsh equivalent of St Christopher. There is a Ffynnon Elen in Cwm Croesor, on Fford Elen in Snowdonia. A giant called Cidwm is supposed to have killed her favourite son with an arrow where the well sprung forth. Castell Cidwm is the name of the crag on the Cnicht Mountain, near Nantmor, from where Cidwm loosed the arrow. When Elen heard she shouted *'Croes awr – croes awr i mi !'* (*'Cursed hour – cursed hour to me !'*). She suspected a jealous elder brother of killing her son. The spot was called Croesawr or Croesmor ever after, and the small village that grew up around the well was called Croesor. The spring was diverted to make a water-supply for Croesor village, but its mossy mouth can still be seen, and after heavy rain it still flows. It is on the side of Sarn Helen, the Roman road in Llanfrothen parish, Merioneth.

Near the Seiont river at Llanbeblig is Ffynnon Helen, approached by steps as the ground around it has been raised. Jones noted that it was still being used by people who filled bottles for use as medicine in the 1950's, and that there once was a Capel Helen near the well. There was also a Ffynnon Elin holy well near Llanilar in Cardigan, and St Ellen's Well near Cydweli in Carmarthen. St Helen's Well has given its name to a district of Swansea, and was a chalybeate spring said to cure wounds and cancers, still regularly used in the 1850's. There were two holy wells in Pembroke named Ellen's Well, one near Angle and one near Llawhaden. As stated, Blethersone, the neighbouring parish to Llawhaden, was originally Tref Elen. Over the years Trefelenstown became Bletherstone in this part of 'Little England Beyond Wales.'

There are several old Roman roads and pathways known as Sarn Elen. One leads down to the Roman camp at Nidum (Neath), there is another near Festiniog and another near Dolwyddelan. Llwybr Cam Elen runs between Llandderfel and Llangynog. The 'baldmoney' (spignel, meum) plant is known as Amranwen Elen Lluyddog (Elen's whitewort) or Ffenigl Elen Lluyddog (Elen's fennel).

ELEN
HELENA, HELEN c255-326 or 328
August 18 in the West, May 21 (with Constantine) in the East

Possibly the British wife of the Emperor Constantius Chlorus from 270, their son was Constantine the Great, born in 274. Constantius repudiated her in 292 for political reasons when he was proclaimed Emperor of Britain and Gaul. In return he had to marry Theodora, the daughter of the Emperor Maximian.

However, Elen's son Constantine was proclaimed Emperor by his legion at York in 306. After winning the Battle of Milviam Gate, he followed his mother's religion from 312. Elen then proselytised Christianity, founding churches throughout Europe, and visiting the Holy Land where she died. Coins were minted for her in 330, and she was buried in Rome. Her son Emperor Constantine, who died in 337, is commemorated in the British Church. (See Constantine, Cystennin).

She is particularly associated with the finding of the True Cross near the Hill of Calvary, when the Emperor Constantine built a church there. She brought it back to Wales. The Princes of Gwynedd always claimed to have a fragment of the cross, and a recent book (Adrian Gilbert's 'The Holy Kingdom') states that it is still in Wales. Most sources say that Helen was born at Drepanum (Helenopolis) in Bithynia, but if the above details are true, this is an important Welsh fulcrum in the survival of Christianity in Europe. She certainly beautified Drepanum in the honour of St Lucian before returning to Rome, where she died, but this is her only known link with the town. Readers must remember that the early history of the Christian Church has been confused because of political and economic considerations. It has never been in the interests of a church centred upon Rome, to give credence to a small country upon the outskirts of Europe in terms of its contribution to Christianity. A case can be made for Wales having a far longer Christian tradition than Rome, Britons being involved in the first century fight to keep the faith alive in Rome, and for the pro-Christian Roman emperors of the 4th century being influenced by the Welsh.

ELERI late 6th century
HILARIUS, ILAR
June 13

The son of Dingad ap Nudd Hael, he lived at Pennant, near his brother Tyfrydog's foundation at Gwytherin in Denbigh. Eleri became abbot at Gwytherin, where he invited Gwenfrewi to join the nuns there under Theonia. Winifred (Gwenfrewi) succeeded Theonia as abbess. Gwytherin church was dedicated to Eleri until the 12th century, when it was rededicated by the Normans to James.

His 'Saying of the Wise' is:
'Hast thou heard the saying of Eleri,
Where there was not a bestowing hand?
"It is not almsgiving that causes poverty".'

ELERI 5th century

Brychan's daughter who married Ceredig ap Cunedda and thus was St David's paternal grandmother.

ELERIUS fl. 650
Cressy states that he was the abbot of a monastery in the Vale of Clwyd.

ELFAN 2nd century
ELVANUS
September 26

Cressy states that Elvanus succeeded Theanus as second Bishop of London, and his companion was Medwinus. Theanus was bishop around 185. Lleurwg Mawr ap Cyllin ap Caradog had asked Bishop Elutherius of Rome to send help in evangelising Britain. The British saints Dyfan, Elfan, Ffagan and Medwy were sent by Rome. Ffagan and Dyfan seem to have stayed in the Silurian kingdom of Glamorgan at this time. Elfan may have been associated with Medwy in founding Michaelston-y-Fedw. 'Côr Elfan' is an ancient Welsh song.

The author is unsure of the connection, but there is a St Elvan's Church in Aberdare, whose steeple makes a fine view on the approach to the town. The local council has approved permission for McDonalds to put their famous illuminated trademark on a twelve foot pole, to give motorists their first view of Aberdare, obscuring the church. There is a McDonalds on a corner of the beautiful mediaeval square in the centre of Bologna. Its windows are dark, the sunblinds are chocolate and deep gold, and it looks more like a high-class jeweller's than a fast-food-burger-outlet. It fits in perfectly with its surroundings, and does not allow people to carry food out of the shop. Why do British councils allow multinationals to dictate to them? The architecture of our city centres and villages has been ruined by plate glass Americanisation. People must learn to walk looking upwards, to see what their surroundings used to be like. So few people actually 'see' the remarkable Victorian buildings of Cardiff's Queen Street and St Mary Street, the capital's main shopping areas. With such awareness, we can stop the building of edifices which have no match with their surroundings. The modern 1950's and 60's utilitarian square blocks that mar cities and towns all over the country could never be built if children were taught culture, heritage and art appreciation in schools. Just one hour a week could expand people's horizons for the rest of their lives.

ELFFIN 6th century

A son of the Gwyddno who lost his lands in Cardigan Bay around 520. He features in the legend of the birth of Taliesin. Later in life Taliesin repaid the favour by securing his release from Maelgwn Gwynedd's clutches in Deganwy Castle, as described in the Mabinogion. He was possibly a saint of the great college of Illtud, but this is not known for sure. Thomas Love Peacock wrote 'The Misfortunes of Elphin' from the legend. Ffynnon Gwyddno in Llanfachreth, Merioneth is near the church, but is now called Ffynnon y Capel and said to have been formed by St Machreth.

ELFFIN 6th century

A son of Urien Rheged (q.v.) and grandfather of Grwst (q.v.), he is the patron of Warrington in Lancashire.

ELFODD d.809
ELBODIUS, ELBODUGUS
March 22

The Archbishop of Bangor, said to have been appointed by the Pope, who forced through the changes to the Primitive Church of Wales to adopt the new Catholic date of Easter. Elfodd's work was recognised by the Catholic church which officially sanctified him along with Sadyrnin, Cyfelach, Caradog and Gwryd. (This date alteration was the only important change in Celtic Christianity in most of Wales from the 5th to the 12th century.) However, the bishops of South Wales did not agree and stayed outside the pale of the Roman church. A Saxon army, said to have invaded to enforce the change, was defeated at Coed Marchan, but there was some acceptance of it by 777. After the death of Elfodd, the new date was still not accepted all over Wales until the middle of the 9th century.

Elfodd may also have been bishop of Holyhead (Caer Gybi). Ffynnon Elwad near Tregaron, in Cardigan, was used for the relief of sore breasts, and the farm there was named Maes Elwad. There was a Ffynnon Elwoe in Abergele where pins were offered, and people used to gather in crowds at Easter to drink its waters and practise 'hydromancy' (to know how long they would live). Ffynnon Elwoc near Abergele in Denbigh was probably Elfodd's holy well, a pin well that was still known in the early 20th century, but it seems to have disappeared. Nennius, the author of 'Historia Brittanorum', states that he himself was a pupil of Elfodd.

ELFYW see AILBE and EILYW

ELGUD late 6th century

The son of Cadfarch ap Caradog Freichfras

ELICQUID 6th century
ELIQUOD

He features often as a witness in the Book of Llandaf, and it is suggested that Leckwith near Cardiff was his, but it is now dedicated to James. There was a Ffynnon Elichguid near Mathern, mentioned in a land grant by Meurig ap Tewdrig in the mid 6th century, which was used as a boundary mark. Elgud (above) or Eliwlod (q.v.) may be the same person.

ELID
LIDE, ELIDIUS
August 8

The remains of a hermitage hut and tomb were found on the Scilly Island now known as St Helen's. In the middle ages, Tavistock Abbey granted a seven-year indulgence to anyone visiting the shrine on St Elid's Day, August 8, or at Christmas, or on John the Baptist's Day (Midsummer Day). This Elid could be the Elidon commemorated at St Lythans. Pirates were warned that if they raided her shrine they would be instantly excommunicated. The Scilly Isles in legend are the mountains of Lyonesse, the kingdom that sank into the sea in Arthurian times. 'Friday in Lide' was the first Sunday in March, celebrated as a holiday by Cornish tin miners.

ELIDON
ELIDAN
June 16, September 1 at St Lythans

Llanelidan church in Denbigh is his foundation, a 15th century church with barrel-vaulted 'canopies of honour' over the altar, old box pews and a wonderful mediaeval rood screen. Although St Lythan's Church in Glamorgan is dedicated to St Bleddian, a charter copied by the Book of Llandaf records that the church of Elidon was granted to Bishop Euddogwy by King Ithel ab Athrwys in the last quarter of the 7th century. Llaneliddon is the Welsh for St Lythan's, and the Anglicisation of the mutated 'dd' is easy to understand. St Lythan's in Welsh was later known as Llanfleiddian Fach to distinguish it from Llanfleiddian Fawr, Llanblethian outside Cowbridge. This latter village was also once called Llan Elidan or Llan Leiddan, so there is no Bleiddan or Lupus attached to either village. William Thomas in his 1762-1795 diary constantly refers to St Lythans as Lanlithens, and recorded the death of John Humphrey the blacksmith in 1778 – *'He was buried under the Ewe from his own desire, being he slept there this two years past or more in drink and dreamed as if one said to him he was there to be buried.'* William Thomas also notes the gruesome death of William John of Hamston, Lanelidan (St Lythans) in 1767. He died of a *'Cancer which eated his lower jaw to his throat, that the meat taken in one way would come out another way.'*

The nineteenth century gravestones in Welsh, in this village just outside Cardiff, remind us of how quickly the Welsh language was wiped out in Glamorgan. In another church near Cardiff at Sully, the English vicar, a W.D. Conybeare, was responsible for substituting the English language for Welsh in the services, although Welsh was the predominant language of the parish. This was repeated all through Wales in the nineteenth century, supported by the heinous use of the 'Welsh Not' in schools (see T. D. Breverton's 'The A-Z of Wales and the Welsh', published by Christopher Davies Ltd.)

The cromlech that stands at St Lythan's (not far from the superb Tinkinswood site and magnificent Dyffryn gardens), has an ancient raised circle of oak trees near it, with a stone in the centre. There may be a path that can be delineated from Tinkinswood through St Lythan's to the pillow mounds now covered up by Barri's Atlantic Trading Estate. Like many other burial sites in Wales (such as Michaelston-y-Fedw), the St Lythan's cromlech is known as 'Gwal y Filiast', or 'Llech y Filiast' which modern translations tell us is the 'Lair of the Greyhound Bitch'. However, the Romans referred to the Dog-Star Sirius as Canicula (the little dog or bitch). The Greek poet Aratus, in the 3rd century BC described the Dog Star chasing the constellation Lepus (the Hare) through the heavens for eternity. There may have been some astronomical reason for such sites, as in Newgrange in Ireland and Stonehenge in England. I am indebted to 'Place Names of the Welsh Borderlands' by Anthony Lias for this information. He also makes the point that the word 'greyhound' comes from Old Norse *'grey'* (bitch) and *'hundr'* (hound). The capstone measures 14 feet by 10 feet, and the field in which it stands is called the *'cursed field'* because little will grow there. It has always been used for sheep rearing in the author's lifetime.

Just the other side of Duffryn House and Gardens from St Lythans is the magnificent Tinkinswood Long Barrow, with the heaviest capstone in the British Isles, possibly in Europe. Twenty-two feet long, fifteen feet wide and three feet thick, it weighs around 46 tons. It is known as a 'cromlech', from the Welsh 'cromen' (roof) and 'llech' (stone). This area is known as 'Dyffryn Golwg', the 'Vale of Worship'. Somehow, morons have given planning permission for a huge electricity pylon next to this remarkable site. Courses upon cultural appreciation should be mandatory for the faceless bureaucrats who make such decisions. There are other Neolithic remains nearby as well as ancient field systems.

There is a seven feet high cross-shaft with excellent Celtic decoration in Cardiff's National Museum, dedicated to EIUDON. It was moved from Llanfynydd Church in 1910, but had previously come from a *'field of stones'* at Aberglasney. Aberglasney Manor, with the oldest formal gardens in Britain, is being renovated and will be a highlight of any tourist trails across Carmarthen. If anyone can pinpoint the 'findsite' of the stone, the author would be grateful.

ELIDYR MWYNFAWR (the Courteous Pilgrim) 6th century

Mentioned in the Triads as a 'Man of the North', his great horse Du y Moroedd (the Black Stallion of the Seas) carried seven persons from Penllech Elidyr in the north, to Penllech Elidyr in the south of Anglesey. He was killed at Elidyr Bank in the Elidyr Mountains near Llanberis. He married Eurgain, the daughter of Maelgwn Gwynedd.

Maelgwn's son Rhun led a counter-attack against the 'Men of the North' who had ravaged Arfon and killed Elidyr. However, a more recent tradition is that Elidyr had attacked Maelgwn to dethrone him, as Elidyr was Maelgwn's illegitimate son.

ELIDYR GODDSGORFAWR 6th century

There was a church at Llaneliver near Bettisfield in Flint.

ELIDYR 8th century

Not a saint, but notable as the great grandson of Llywarch Hen and the heir of South Rheged, who married the heiress to Ynys Manaw (the Isle of Man). He transferred his family from Powys, and his grandson Merfyn Frych stabilised Gwynedd.

ELIWLOD 6th century

Probably not a saint, but noted here as the son of Madog ab Uther, and thus said to be Arthur's nephew. He was suggested as the original 'Lancelot' and after his death in battle appeared to Arthur in the guise of an eagle. (See Eliquid and Almedha).

ELLDEYRN 5th century
February 1

Possibly a brother or son of the High King Vortigern, and who founded Capel Llanilltern, under St Fagans, in Glamorgan. Possibly Lansallos in Cornwall is his also, as he appears to have left Wales after Gwrtheyrn (Vortigern) was slain.

ELLI 6th century
January 23 (Carmarthen), August 1 Brecon (August 12 old style)

Said to have founded Llanelli, where he had a healing well, next to Llangattock in Carmarthen. The Vita Cadoci states that Cadog landed on a group of islands called Grimbul, and their queen implored him to cure her barrenness. When she gave birth to a son, she entrusted the infant Elli to the care of Cadog. Llanelli in Brecon is probably not his foundation, but that of Almedha. There were two Fynnon Elli in Carmarthen. Cadog taught him from childhood, and appointed him as his successor, as abbot of Llancarfan. Elli lived at Albium Atrium, the White Court, probably Whitton (Hwytyn) nearby, which was the site of a Romano-Celtic villa. Lifris noted the charter to found a monastery given by Cadog to Elli: *'Elli, disciple of the blessed Cadog, having been diligently educated by him from an early age and eminently instructed in sacred literature, was the dearest to him of all his disciples. And Elli declared, saying, "Lo, I have built a church and houses in the name of the Lord, and I and all my successors of the familia of Cadog will be obedient, subject and kindly disposed to the familia of Cadog."*

His old style birth date of August 12 was *'ffest y bugeilaid'* (the shepherds' feast') across Wales, also known as *'ffest Awst'* (the August feast). Boys herding sheep and cattle, across a wide area, in the summer months congregated for a feast on a hilltop or bank on Elli's Day.

ELLYW 5th-6th century
ELYW
July 14 or 17

Llanelieu in Brecon has been attributed to a grand-daughter of Brychan named Ellyw or Elyw

ELOI 6th century

A Welsh saint, who was invoked for sick horses with Gildas and Herbot (Huerve) in Brittany. He is probably not the French St Eloi (Eligius c.588 – 660) Bishop of Noyon, known as a goldsmith, whose cult flourished all over Europe. There are many villages called St Eloi in Brittany, e.g. near St Brieuc and west of Guincamp.

ELWAN 6th century

Only noted by Iolo Morganwg, who states that the original name of his home village, Flemingston, the Vale of Glamorgan, was Llanelwan. Iolo (Edward Williams) is buried there. He also refers to the village as Llanfihangel-y-Twyn, and the 14th century church is still dedicated to Michael in this beautiful hamlet, with Flemingston Court nestled in the ruins of the castle. The Fleming family had a castle at St George's which was destroyed by Llywelyn Bren in 1318. They then built a castle at Wenvoe, and a brother of the Lord of Wenvoe married the heiress to Llanfihangel-y-Twyn. They built St Michael's castle at Flemingston, but it was mainly destroyed by Owain Glyndŵr in 1410. The Flemings built Flemingston Court on the site in 1430. However, William Randolph Hearst bought the medieval wooden panelling from the Court and shipped it to America where it still remains in storage somewhere. (For more information on Flemingston, see the author's 'The Secret Vale - the story of St Tathan, Gileston, Eglwys Brewis, Aberthaw and Flemingston.')

ELWEDD

It is not known at present if there was a saint of this name, but it is included because Llanelwedd, the north part of Builth Wells, is the home to the week-long Royal Welsh Show every July. This is a fabulous occasion, the biggest agricultural show in Europe held on this purpose-built site since 1963. The Royal Welsh Exhibition Centre opened in October 1999, the largest livestock exhibiition hall in the world at 102,000 square feet.

There was also a famous healing well at St David's, now lost, called Ffynnon Eliud (see Gistlianus), near Ffynnon Gwestlan. Perhaps Elwedd and Eliwlod are the same person. Then again, Elwedd may be derived from the Welsh for 'reconciliation'.

ELWYN
ELVITUS

Noted by Roscarrock as Confessor at *'Llhan Hamelac'* (Llanhamlach) in Brecon, now dedicated to Illtud and Peter. Llanhamlach has a Celtic pillar with a male holding a book, and a female with her arms raised in the 'orans' praying attitude. It seems to be inscribed to Iohannis, and Moridic erected it.

EMERITA d.193 or 201
December 4

A sister of Lleurwg (Lucius), she was martyred at Trimas near Curia in Germany.

EMRYS WLEDIG see AMBROSIUS

EMYR LLYDAW (Emperor of Brittany) c.460 – c.546
BUDIC II, BUDIG, BUDICIUS

The father of Amwn Ddu, Alan, Gwen Tierbron, Gwyndaf Hen and forced to flee Brittany to live under Cadog at Llancarfan. He is said to have founded Pendeulwyn (Pendoylan) in Glamorgan, which is now dedicated to Cadog. His children married into the family of Meurig ap Tewdrig, and many appear as Arthur's 'knights'. According to some genealogies, his children by Elain ferch Gwyrlys were Hywel Mawr, Alain Frygain (White Ankles), Amwn Ddu, Madoc, Owain, Pedrwn (Petrwn), Gwyddno, Dyfynwg (Difwng), Ffedin, Gwyndaf Hen, Gwen Tierbron and 'Lancelot du Lac'.

From Cornuaille (Cornwall province) of Armorica (Brittany), this nobleman went first to Pembrokeshire, where he was welcomed by Prince Aercol Lawhir. He married St Teilo's sister, Anauwed ferch Enlleu (Ensic), and their children Tyfei and Ismael devoted themselves to religious works. Ismael followed Teilo as the bishop of Menevia. After some time, ambassadors came from Brittany requesting Budic to return as king over all Armorica, not just Cornuaille. There, he had another son, Oudoceus (Euddogwy), who later became Archbishop of Llandaf.

An internet site 'Biographies of the Kings of Brittany and the Princes of Cornouaille', states that Budic (Emyr Llydaw) married Anna, the sister of the High-King of Britain, before marrying Anauwed. However, it seems that his son Amwn Ddu married Anna. Anna was Arthur's sister, and the daughter of Meurig ap Tewdrig. During Budic II's reign, Breton armies became invincible on horseback – perhaps because his followers had learned the use of cavalry during their support of Arthur's mounted troops in Britain.

At Margam Abbey, the 'Bodvoc Stone' reads: 'BODVOC - HIC IACIT - FILIVS CATOGIRNI PRONEPVS ETERNALI VEDOMAV', *'Here lies Bodvoc, son of Catotigirnis, great-grandson of Eternalaus Vedomanus'*. Budic I of Brittany appears to have been aided by Arthur's grandfather Tewdrig to reclaim his kingdom in Brittany, just as Arthur later assisted Budic II (Emyr Llydaw). Westwood found the stone, commonly called Maen Llythrog, on top of the mountain above Margam Abbey. It stood near a small tumulus called Crug Diwlith (the dewless rock), where the bards of Tir Iarrl met on the morning of every June 24th. The river Kenfig rises from a small marsh near this spot. Coins with the name of Bodvoc have been found, and the name Bodvogatus is mentioned in Caesar's 'Gallic Wars'. The cross on the five foot stone shows that Bodvoc was a Christian of the 5th or 6th century.

ENDA d. 530
March 21, 31

This Irish abbot was taught at St David's monastery, and went on to found the first Irish monastery on Aranmore in Galway Bay. Farmer notes that he was taught at Whithorn by Ninian. Aranmore was regarded as *'the capital of the Ireland of the Saints'*, and he preceded the influential Finnian (q.v.) in Irish evangelism.

The Bodvoc Stone, Margam Stones Museum.   *CADW: Welsh Historic Monuments. Crown Copyright.*

ENDDWYN
May 14

Near Llanenddwyn Church in Merioneth is Ffynnon Enddwyn. Her well was famous for 'scrofulous disorders' and had to be regularly emptied of pins. Moss from the well was applied to skin diseases, and it also cured eye diseases and glandular infections. Enough remains of the well and bath to restore it. There are two large dolmens near Bron-y-Foel in the parish, and at nearby Duffryn Ardudwy school are two more burial chambers, called Carreg Arthur.

ENDELLION 5th – 6th century
ENDELIENTA, CENEDLON
April 29

A daughter of Brychan who lived a holy life near her sisters Cymorth and Clydai, on the *'mountain of Cymorth'* near Newcastle Emlyn. She was a virgin who is commemorated at St Endelion's just west of the Celtic monastery of Tintagel in Cornwall. Part of her tomb still exists, and two holy wells are named after her. There is a chapel at Tregony where she is said to have lived, and also one on Lundy Island, opposite her brother Nectan's foundation at Hartland. She only survived on the milk of one cow, which was killed by the lord of Tregony when it trespassed on his lands. Her 'godfather' then killed the lord, whom Endellion miraculously revived. Arthur was said to be her godfather.

Part of her church survives at St Endellion near Wadebridge in Cornwall, and there are also two wells there named after her.

ENFAIL 5th-6th century

Possibly a daughter of Brychan, martyred at Merthyr Enfail in Carmarthenshire, the place now known as Merthyr outside the county town of Carmarthen.

ENGHENEDL 7th century
ANGHANELL
Qinquagesima Sunday

Son of Cynan Garwyn of Powys, and grandson of Brochwel Ysgyrthog, he founded Llanenghenel under Llanfachraith in Anglesey.

ENLLI

Enlli, or Bardsey Island, is *'the Isle of Twenty Thousand Saints'*, the holiest place in Wales, where Merlin guards the *'Thirteen Treasures of Wales'*. There was a Celtic monastery here in the Dark Ages, then an Augustinian abbey, but only the abbey tower and two Dark Age cross-stones remain. (See *'The A-Z of Wales and the Welsh'*, and Pykit and Barber's *'Journey to Avalon'* for more details). The saints Dyfrig, Padarn and Beuno lie here, and many pilgrims came here to die and be buried, which probably accounts for the hyperbole of 20,000. Islands, being surrounded by water, were sacred to the Celts, and this tradition carried on through early Christian times.

The Life of Dubricius tells us:
'The blessed man, seeing that his vital powers sufficed not for himself and for the people too, oppressed by certain infirmities and by old age, resigned the laborious task of the episcopal office and (resumed) the hermit's life, in company with several holy men and with his disciples, who lived by the labour of their hands, he dwelt alone for many years in the island of Enlli and gloriously finished his life there. It has been for ages a proverbial saying among the Welsh that this island is "the Rome of Britain", on account of its distance - it is situated in the extremity of the kingdom - and of the danger of the sea-voyage, and also because of the sanctity and charm of the place: sanctity, for twenty thousand bodies of saints, as well confessors as martyrs, lie buried there: and charm, since it is surrounded by the sea, with a lofty promontory on the eastern side and a level and fertile plain, where there is a fountain of sweet water, on the western. It is entirely free from serpents and frogs, and no brother has ever died there leaving one older than himself to survive him.'

The holy island is about four miles long and a mile wide, and a ferry leaves Pwllheli once a week. Hostel accommodation for bird-watchers can be booked on 01626-773908, and Bardsey Island Trust houses can be rented on a self-catering basis on 01758-730740. Enlli seems to have been a 5th century ruler who was a follower of Pelagius. From Mynydd Enlli (548 feet high) one can see Ireland, Anglesey and the Welsh coast as far as Pembrokeshire. Up to a hundred seals can be seen near the island's slipway. St Mary's Abbey ruins can be explored, and there are many hut circles. Several inscribed stones have been found on the island, but there are probably many more unrecorded.

'Enlli' refers to the treacherous currents between the island and Aberdaron on the Llyn Peninsula. Previously it was called Ynys Afallach, perhaps after Afallach ap Beli Mawr. Much later it was called Ynys Afallon, and may well be the place that Arthur was taken after Camlan, a place of safety to recover from this wounds in the care of monks. The renaming and movement of Avalon to Glastonbury was William of Malmesbury's invention, followed by Giraldus Cambrensis. The entry upon Ynys Afallon in 'The New Companion to the Literature of Wales' explains the importance of the island and its place as the original and real Avalon in more detail.

ENODOC
GUINEDOCUS
March 7 (feast) and July 13 (dedication)

A Welsh hermit who founded his church on the north coast of Cornwall, near St Minver. (See Gwethenoc).

EPIPHANY
GWYL YSTWYLL
January 6

The 'Twelfth Night' of Christmas, but Christmas Day itself before the date change of 1752. It is called 'Gwyl Ystwyll' or 'Yr Ystwyll', from the Latin 'stella' (stars). The name 'Festum Stella' was peculiar to the Celtic Church and has been replaced in the Welsh Prayer Book by 'Seren Wyl' or 'Star Festival.' The first Monday after 'Twelfth Day' was called 'Dydd Gwyl Heiliau', 'The Festival of the Sheepfolds'. An old Gwent saying was *'Dydd gwyl Geiliau, at y bara haidd a'r bacsau'*, *'Plough Monday, resume ordinary fare and working clothing.'* On the day after Twelfth Day, the Christmas 'greenery' was taken down in East Cornwall, but it was considered unlucky to burn it.

ERBIN mid 6th century
ERBYN
January 13, May 29

King of Cornwall, the son of Cystennin Gorneu, and father of the famous Geraint. His sons also fought for Arthur – Dywel and Erinid are mentioned in Culhwch and Olwen, and Dywel also in the Black Book of Carmarthen. The Gelli-Dywell Stone stood near Newcastle Emlyn, inscribed *'Cvrcagn - Fili - Andagell -'*. Erbin asked Arthur to allow Geraint to return to Cornwall to take up its kingship from him. Erbistock (Erbin's Stockade) in Flint was his church, but he has been superseded by Hilary there. It lies in the Vale of Erbine. He is the patron of St Ervan in Cornwall.

ERFYL 6th century?
EURFYL
July 6

A virgin saint, possibly Padarn's daughter. Near Anglesey's Llanerfyl, Ffynnon Erfyl has now been drained, but was used for baptisms, and on Wake Sunday and Easter Monday the water was sweetened with sugar before dancing. At Llanerfyl in Montgomeryshire was found one of the earliest Christian stones, with inscriptions arranged in horizontal lines in the classic Roman fashion. (There is a similar stone at Bodafan in Gwynedd). Llanerfyl's stone reads HIC (IN) TUM(V)LO IACIT R(O)STEECE FILIA PATERNINI AN(N)IS XIII IN PA(CE) – 'Here in this tomb lies Rosteece, daughter of Paternius (aged) 13 years. In peace'. Could Rosteece be Erfyl's sister?

ERGYNG

J. E Lloyd wrote in 1911 that *'Ergyng was bounded by the Wye, the Worm and the Monnow, though so close to the gates of Hereford, it was a stronghold of Welsh customs and ideas as late as the end of the twelfth century. The Welsh saints were honoured throughout the district, and among them St David had a great church at Much Dewchurch, and Dyfrig, who was (if we may believe his legend) by birth and residence a man of Ergyng, a group of churches which commanded the allegiance of the dwellers along the winding banks of the Wye . . . This ancient cantref was the subject of contention between Llandaf and Hereford in the twelfth century, as in evidenced in the Book of Llan Dav. It was eventually retained within Hereford.'* Between Gwynllwg and Ergyng lay Gwent, the country between the rivers Usk, Wye, Monnow and the sea. After the Act of Union in 1536, Gwynllwg and Gwent were joined together to form Monmouthshire, while Ergyng became English.

ERNIN 6th century
HERNIN, HOIERNIN, ISARNINUS
Patron saint of headaches
November 2, First Monday in May (Brittany)

This was the son of Helig, whose lands opposite Anglesey were flooded (it used to be believed that Llys Helig could be seen beneath the waters of the Menai Straits). Upon losing his inheritance he became a monk on Bardsey, and then probably travelled to Brittany, settling as a hermit at Duault near Carhaix. A British chief gave him land there. A stag took refuge with him, and the hounds refused to attack it. He was buried at Locarn, and Count Conmire of Domnonia ordered a church to be built there. Ernin's head and one arm are still enshrined there as relics. Other Breton sites are Morbihan, St Hernin outside Guincamp and at Lesernin. Another St Hernin exists south-west of the Roman town of Carhaix-Plouguer. There was an extinct chapel called Llanhernin under Llanegwad in Caernarfonshire, and Cilhernin under Llanboidy in Carmarthenshire was his (see Gwbert).

ERTH 6th century
ERC
November 2, October 31

The brother of Ia (q.v.), he became Bishop of Slane in Ireland. He founded St Erth in Cornwall

ERUEN

Llangwm in Monmouth, see Huui.

ETHBIN 6th century
EGBIN
October 19

Educated by Samson after his father died, he travelled from Wales to Brittany, where he became a disciple of Gwenole. After the destruction of the monastery, he retired to spend the last two decades of his life as a hermit in Ireland. His relics are claimed at Montreuil and Eure (Pont-Mort). His name is Anglo-Saxon rather than Celtic.

ETHERN
ETTERN

The Bishop is noted in the Martyrology of Donegal and may be Welsh. A stone *'Etterni fili Victor'* was found at Clydai in Pembroke.

EUDDOG

A saint of Anglesey, who had a chapel called Llaneuddog near Llanwenllwyfo. A nearby farm is still called Llaneiddog. (See EUDDOGWY).

BISHOP EUDDOGWY c. 546-615
OUDOCEUS
July 2

Nephew of Teilo, with Dyfrig (Dubricius), Peter and Teilo he was a co-titular head of Llandaf Cathedral, and succeeded Teilo as its third Bishop. The Book of Llandaf states that he came from a princely Breton family, and was born in Wales around 546. His father was Budic, King of Armorica, his mother Anawed (sister of Teilo), and his brothers the saints Tyfei and Ismael. The Saxons cut off Wales from the West Country at the battle of Dyrham in 577, when Euddogwy was a monk at Llandogo. When at Llandogo he is said to have come into conflict with Gildas, who came into the forests to collect timber for building. Euddogwy became bishop in 580, and asked the abbots of Llanilltud Fawr, Llandough and Llancarfan to combine against a local prince. This was the beginning of the see of Llandaf, where his shrine was revered and remained a centre of pilgrimage until 1540 when it was stripped and destroyed.

Teilo is strongly linked with Emyr Llydaw (Budic) in Brittany, and was said to have brought Euddogwy (Budic's youngest son) back to Wales in 556. Arthrwys ap Meurig, King Arthur, granted Euddogwy lands *'by his authority'*, which may mean that he was still alive (after Camlan) in Brittany at this time. King Einion granted Euddogwy lands at Llaneuddogwy, now called Llandogo, in Monmouth, which was also known as Laneinion centuries ago. His 'Vita' in the Book of Llandaf describes his journey to Rome, and his removal of relics from Llandeilo-fawr and St David's to Llandaf. It may well be that Eudoce, a 9th century bishop of Glamorgan, has been confused with Oudoceus. (See EUDDOG).

EUGRAD 6th century
EIGRAD, ENGREAS, EGREAS, EGRAT
January 6, June 8

Like Gallgo, a brother of Gildas and son of Caw, whose foundation at Llaneugrad in Anglesey is near that of his brother's at Llanallgo and of the site of Llangadog. He was taught by St Illtud at Llanilltud Fawr, and features as a knight of Arthur named Ergyryat in 'Culwch and Olwen'. He may have flown from Gwynedd following Gildas' denunciation of Maelgwn, and be remembered as Egrat in Brittany. His skull and holy well are at Treouergat in Leon.

'Egreas, moreover, with Allaecus (Gallgo), his brother, and Peteona, their sister, a virgin consecrated to God, in like manner leaving their father's estate; and renouncing all worldly pomp, withdrew to the farthest part of that country, where, not far from each other, they built their several monasteries, placing their sister in the midst.'

EURGAIN 1st – 2nd century

According to Iolo Morganwg's 'Genealogy of Iestyn ap Gwrgan', *'Caradog built a palace, after the manner of the Romans, at Abergwerydwyr, called now Llandunwyd Major, or St Donat's. His daughter, Eurgain, married a Roman chieftain, who accompanied her to Cambria. This chieftain had been converted to Christianity, as well as his wife Eurgain, who first introduced the faith among the Cambro-Britons, and sent for Ilid (a native of the land of israel) from Rome to Britain. This Ilid is called, in the service of commemoration, St Joseph of Arimathea. He became principal teacher of Christianity to the Cambro-Britons, and introduced good order into the côr of Eurgain, which she had established for twelve saints near the place now called Llantwit; but which was burnt in the time of King Edgar. After this arrangement, Ilid went to Ynys Afallen in Glad yr Haf, where he died and was buried.'* Côr Eurgain, or Côr Worgorn, appears to be the Romano-Celtic villa outside Llanilltud Fawr. Whether Iolo knew it actually existed, as it was covered by grass, is open to doubt. (See Claudia, Bran, Caradog, Illtud, Ilid, Joseph of Arimathea and Paul).

EURGAIN 6th century
June 29

The daughter of Maelgwn Gwynedd, she married Elidyr Mwynfawr who was killed near Caernarfon. She founded Llaneurgain in Flint, now known as Northop. Her body is supposed to lie under a tumulus at Criccin, near Rhuddlan. Westwood noted that the shaft of a cross surmounting the burial mound was missing its head, which was in the pool of an adjoining farm. Perhaps it could be rescued? Westwood also gives Eurgain's alternative name of Cain.

EURYN 6th-7th century
August 23

A son of Helig Foel, known as Euryn y Coed Helig (of the Willow Wood), he was a monk at Bangor-is-Coed then at Ynys Enlli.

PHILIP EVANS 1645-1679
October 25, July 22 executed

Born in Monmouth, Evans was educated at St Omer, joined the Jesuits in 1665 and was ordained at Liege in 1675. As 'Captain Evans' he stayed with Thomas Gunter and preached in Welsh in his chapel in Cross Street, Abergavenny, where *'100's goe to Mass there when not 40 goe to the Church.'* After the Popish Plot, a reward of £250 was offered for him by John Arnold of Llanvihangel Court near Abergavenny. Evans was arrested at Christopher Turberville's Sker House near Porthcawl in 1678. (The evocative Sker House, with its priest holes, is fortunately being renovated after being semi-derelict for some years). The authorities could find no-one to testify that he had practised as a priest before his five month incarceration in Cardiff gaol, until at last a poor woman and a dwarf spoke against him. He was joined in the dungeon by John Lloyd.

The two were not accused of complicity in the fabrications of Titus Oates, but with unlawfully entering the realm as priests. The dwarf and the woman lied to say that they had seen Father Evans celebrating mass, so Justice Owen Wynne told the jury to give a 'guilty' verdict. The execution was delayed, and Evans was allowed to play tennis in much improved conditions of imprisonment. When given his notice of execution, he answered *'What hurry is there? Let me first play out my game.'* He was butchered to death upon July 22nd at Cardiff, and for some hours before played his Welsh harp. His final words were: *'I die for God and religion's sake; and I think myself so happy that if I had ever so many lives, I would willingly give them all for so good a cause.'* Upon climbing the gallows, he is reputed to have said *'Sure, this is the best pulpit a man can have to preach in'*. These statements seem to have incensed the executioners, who performed the drawing and quartering with particular skill and relish on the still-living martyr. After witnessing this ghastly event, poor John Lloyd was killed by the same method shortly after, at Gallows Field, at the north-east of Richmond Road in Cardiff. This is where Richmond Road and Albany Road meet Crwys Road and City Road. Prisoners were traditionally hanged at major cross-roads and left there as a warning to travellers.

EWRYD 5th century
EURIDIUS
January 31

The patron saint of Bodewryd in Anglesey, now dedicated to the Virgin Mary. He was the younger son of Cynyr Ceinfarfog, and the brother of the saints Non, Gwen and Banhadlwen.

F

'For we are strangers before thee, and sojourners, as were all our fathers; our days on the earth are as a shadow, and there is none abiding.'
Chronicles: 29:15

FAIRS

Holy days, when no work must be carried out, helped break up the year into units and made it easier to know when annual tasks had to be carried out. The Yorkshire farmer, Henry Best, recorded his tasks in the mid-17th century. Lambs conceived at Michaelmas would be born before Candlemas, and ewes should *'go into tup'* at St Luke's Day. Servants were traditionally hired at Martinmas fairs, and hay fields should not be grazed for a fortnight after Lady Day, itself when rent was traditionally paid. Lambs were weaned by the days of St Philip and St James. Wheat had to be sowed before Hallowmas Eve. Saints' days often marked the times of paying rents, so many remained on the calendars, although they were from Elizabethan times no longer celebrated as holidays. As almost all the annual fairs occurred on saints' days, the old saints' names survived in many Welsh calendars. The nature of Wales' landscape, leading to difficult communications, meant that the local nature of the fairs was preserved at certain dates, rather than days being designated across the whole country for celebration.

There is a lovely description of the fairs of the 19th century given by Cardiff US Consul, Wirt Sikes, in 1881. Almost Dickensian in tone, the following passage is well worth including in this book, if only to show how recently fairs were an important and regular feature of Welsh life:

VII.VII

Pleasure-fairs are of frequent occurrence in every nook and corner of Wales, and at short intervals throughout the year. They were, originally, in rural parts, religious feasts in honour of some saint, and were so incessant of occurrence that laws were passed in the 16th century to regulate and restrain them. Dissipation and licentiousness had grown to be their leading feature, and these vices were especially practised in the churchyards. From an old MS. legend of St. John the Baptist (quoted by Dugdale) this passage: "In the beginning of holy Chirche, it was so that the pepul cam to the Chirche with candellys brennyng, and wold wake and coome with light to the Chirche in their devocions; and after that they fell to lecherie and songs, daunces, harping, piping, and also to glotony and sinne, and so turned the holynesse to cursydnees." But laws were not equal to their suppression, at least in Wales, custom proving stronger than law; and it is not until very recent years, animated by the spirit of modern progress towards good morals, that the pleasure-fairs have been made the comparatively decorous holidayings they now are.

The cattle-shows, horse-races, agricultural exhibiitions, etc., which we call fairs in the United States – and which as local exhibitions are perhaps the finest in the world – are for the most part confined to the months of July, August, and September . . . **But in Wales there is no limit to the time of year for fairs***; like death, the fair has "all seasons for its own"; they occur in every month of the year. Notwithstanding the general bad name borne by the climate of the British Isles, that of South Wales is so far tolerable that one may usually enjoy the open air every day all the year round. The grass is green and the flowers bloom out of doors from January to January again. On the 18th of December, 1877, strawberries were growing ripe along the lanes* of Ystradowen, Glamorganshire; and roses grew all winter on the sunny southerly wall of my garden in Cardiff. Yet the climate is not at all enervating; there are storms enough, and snow-storms are among them.

Before large towns existed, where the necessaries of life can be bought in shops, all sorts of goods and commodities were sold chiefly at fairs, periodically held. To these everybody went, and the so-called "great" fairs, like that of Llandaf, were the scene of a prodigious display, to which half the people of Wales would go. The age of Llandaf fair is very great; tradition dates its origin to the first century, A.D. At the most prosperous period of its career it was prolonged for many days. Monks and laymen alike come to this fair, sometimes from a hundred miles away. Llandaf churchyard was one scene of buying and selling, in tents and booths. Nowadays, booths are not set up in the churchyard, but they occupy the streets of the decayed cathedral city, even to the very walls of the bishop's palace – Punch and Judy, Cheap John and all. In the old days, fairs and markets were held on Sunday more often than any other day, and remnants of this custom still exist in Wales. At Llantwit Major (Llanilltud Fawr), an extremely ancient little town in Glamorganshire, the people have for centuries past gathered for purposes of barter on Sundays, before or after church service, and, unless it has very recently become extinct, this antique custom still prevails.

VII.VIII

The religious tone of Welsh towns and villages is notable. All respectable people are church-goers or chapel-goers, even more so than in America. I am told that there are a greater number of Methodists in Glamorganshire than in any other county of its size in the world. The observance of Sunday is rigidly oppressive. Yet the most anomalous customs are not unknown, like this regarding Sunday fairs. Llandaf "great" fair occurs at Whitsuntide, and lasts three days, ostensibly. **Whitmonday is the great holiday of Wales**; the feast of Whitsuntide is characterized everywhere by fetes and galas, and is a ceaseless round of pleasure; but Whitmonday is the one day of the year when the people go holidaying en masse, as they do at no other time of the year. The great fair of Llandaf legally begins on Monday, concluding on Wednesday night. But in point of fact the revels commence with Sunday. The merry-go-rounds, the Aunt Sallies, the candy booths, etc., are set up, and throngs of people gather. The hammering of the booth-builders echoes through the aisles of the solemn cathedral where the usual congregation is gathered. The voice of the minister expounding the doctrines of Christianity within the venerable walls which have stood for centuries, mingles with the noisy revelry of the crowd which is gathered in the little green in the heart of the town, close to the cathedral gates. In front of the ruined gatehouse of the ancient episcopal palace the Saturnalia proceeds; people lean shamelessly against its very walls, and after nightfall they lean there drunk. All this goes on in defiance of the law, while ostensibly in obedience to it. No cries of hawkers rend the air, but a thriving trade is done in oranges, nuts, and gingerbread, all the same. Keepers of shows surreptitiously take pence and pass people quietly into their tents to see the African serpents, the waxworks, and the rest. As the hours pass matters grow worse. After dusk the beer begins to flow, and with the falling darkness the licence becomes greater. At midnight there are uncountable crowds on the scene.

The following morning the fair ostensibly begins; before noon it is roaring with bustle; Punch and Judy squeak; hawkers howl; exhibitors of curiosities bawl at the highest pitch of their voices. There are curiosities enough here, at least – fat women, living skeletons, waxworks, pigmies, giants, performing dogs and monkeys, an endless array of idle and profitless diversions. Merry-go-rounds whirl their laughing, shrieking freight through the air – "warranted to make you sea-sick for a penny." Shooting-galleries, and even perambulating *photograph-galleries, are there. "Come and get your picture pulled, Sally," is a favourite form of treat offered their sweethearts by lads of the labouring class. There is a sparring-booth, before which a burly touter roars with stentorian lungs: "Now then, gents, now is yer time fer to witness some of the most renowned and scientific and ekally celerbrated crushers of the prize ring; walk right up; in h'our establishment we do not wish to 'ave the fun h'all to ourselves, ho, dear, no; we allows any gent who feels disposed to put on the gloves to any of hus; yes indeed we does – walk right up gents; wots more, we offers any gent a shillin' who will do it, Hi ! Hi ! Now's yer time !" By nightfall the scene becomes a sort of pandemonium. In the most "successful" Whitsuntide fairs of recent years the streets of Llandaf have been given up to a huge mob, crushing and swearing and tearing, and whose only idea of fun was to sustain one prolonged and lingering yell, of a sort to split the ears of the very tenants of the graveyard close at hand.*

The above paragraph is a record of a time so recent that I prefer to leave it as originally penned (in 1878) although the evil it depicts has ceased. Modern influences served to make the Whitsunday gathering at Llandaf a scandal, and a strong public feeling was at work which led to the abolition of the fair entirely. The wonder was that it had not long ago been abolished, for it seemed to violate in every way the Welsh character. Some explanation of the contrasts it presented to the more rural pleasure-fairs of Wales may be found in the fact that Llandaf is practically a suburb of Cardiff, where the population is more English and Irish than Welsh, and where there is also a large floating population of foreigners, especially Italians, Frenchmen, Spaniards, Portuguese, etc., of the lower classes. The fair was a source of pecuniary profit to one gentleman, namely, the lord of the manor, who "owned" it, as the right is phrased. This gentleman (recently deceased) naturally objected to its being done away with, especially as he was of a sporting turn, and accustomed to the moral licence of the Derby, a race he had at times won with his own horses. The law by which the Llandaf pleasure-fair could be abolished was so worded that all depended on this gentleman's individual will. The Dean of Llandaf publicly appealed to him in the matter in 1876, but without immediate result. The people still gathered; but whereas eight or ten years ago they gathered in thousands, they were now present only in hundreds, each year fewer in numbers, and more quiet, gradually giving way to the pressure of public opinion, until in 1879, on visiting the spot at Whitsuntide, I found the little green almost deserted, and no booths, nor shows, nor noisy hawkers to be seen.

VII.IX

Some Welsh fairs combine the original office of the fair as a place of barter with the idea more common in America, viz., as an opportunity for competitive exhibition, like our State and county fairs, as we call them. Of this class are the Welsh horse-shows, flower-shows, Christmas-shows, fat-cattle-shows, poultry-shows, etc., which are sometimes also fairs. Others bear unique names, as Warm Fair, Winter Fair, Midsummer Fair, Martinmas Fair, St Luke's Fair, Michaelmas Fair, October Fair, April Fair, Dish Fair, Pear Fair, et id genus omne, a list without end. They are named after the towns, the seasons, the saints, the months, the articles originally sold at them, and the traditions or legends out of which they arose; many of the last are quaint and interesting in the highest degree. There is not, indeed, a fair in Wales that has not its history and traditions, its records and strange tales, some of which are poetical, some patriotic, others superstitious. The only sort of fair I ever heard of which is not included in the Welsh domain is the fighting-fair. The last of these was at Donnybrook, the abolition of which broke almost as many Irish hearts as its existence formerly broke Irish heads . . .

VII.X

The hiring-fair is a peculiar institution, which still lingers in Wales. But this, too, is a relic of ancient days, which will not much longer exist, for it is exciting the active animosity of the better sort of farmers and country gentlemen. From time immemorial the custom has been to hold these fairs in every important centre of a farming district, their sole purpose being to bring servants and masters together. To these fairs troop men and maidens in vast numbers, on fun and profit both intent. To them also troop the farmers, in search of human toilers on their farms for the coming year. Sometimes, and originally I believe always, these hiring-fairs were held on Martinmas-day, known as the servants' saint's day. At present the hiring-fair is not confined to that day, but is held on different days in different towns, usually either in October or November.

At these fairs, there is undoubtedly a considerable consumption of cwrw da (good beer); a temperance or teetotal fair would hardly thrive. The men are of a certain bearish roughness, which would, beyond question, prove uncomfortable to those of us as have been gently bred. It would be no joke to the average reformer of the period, I fear, to have a blackthorn cudgel thwacked across his back, with all the power of an arm accustomed to farm work, or to be hustled in the prodigiously vigorous way the grinning Welsh peasants at Kidwelly have of shouldering one another in groups, for a lark. It would be rough and tumble fighting if they were Irishmen, and whisky had them in their clutches; heads would crack, blood would flow, the air would ring with hurroos of defiance and debate. But where every man's face is at a broad grin, where the air echoes but roars of laughter, and half the pushers and strugglers have got their hands shoved deep down in their pockets – it may be rough, and it might break bones not overlaid with muscle, but it is not likely to do much harm. **Beer is not a quarrelsome beverage, at least in Wales; it moves a Welshman's feet to dancing, not his fist to mauling**, and he grins instead of growls. The Cambrian proverb is "I wedd calon cwrw da" (Good ale is the key of the heart).

Having stood waiting in the market-place till they have found masters who will pay them for the coming year the small wages they demand, and so laid out for themselves twelve months of good hard work, Sion and Mairi feel like celebrating their success. So when the shades of evening fall, the serious work of the day being done, the merriment waxes furious. The streets are so densely thronged with people that it is almost impossible to move among them. Vehicles cannot go about at all, and this is not attempted. Torches light up the scene; drums beat; hawkers and Cheap Johns bawl; Punch and Judy add their squeaking to the din; and any Mairi or Catti whose waist is not encircled by the arm of a Twm or Sion, is a reproach to the traditions of her race. The "fair-day arm" of a Welsh hiring-fair is said to be an entirely unique feature, by persons who have visited fairs in Ireland, Scotland, Cumberland, Lancashire, etc. Annexation is the common lot, and every Catti has her own. Thus amicably linked, the couples rove about, side by side, laughing, chaffing, chuckling, roaring at Punch, hustling and shouldering each other in merriest kind; while down upon the noisy scene looks with solemn face the ivied front of a hoary castle, whose towers have stood thus dark against the starry background for half a thousand years.

VII.XI

The farming class is divided in opinion as to the good and bad effects of hiring-fairs*; progressive men want to see them abolished, and describe their evils feelingly. The habit of holding the fairs on different days is condemned. Thus for example Narberth, in Pembrokeshire, will have its hiring-fair on a Thursday; Haverfordwest will follow on the ensuing Saturday; St Clear's, Carmarthenshire, the Saturday succeeding; and Llanboidy and Carmarthen a week or two later. As all these towns are within short distances of each other, and may be reached afoot by such vigorous trampers as Welsh peasants are, it is easy to see that the servants are able to go about from one to another, in case of not finding an employer at the first attempt. One abuse growing out of this is, that unscrupulous servants, boys especially, will sometimes go from fair to fair, hiring out to several masters in turn, and then giving them all the slip; the hiring pennies paid to him forming no insignificant sum for a boy of a larky and unreliable sort, aiming to get something for nothing, pocketing pence for doing no work, and having "all the fun of the fair" besides . . .

VIII.XII

A quiet example of a local fair in the heart of Old South Wales is a cattle-fair in the old town of Carmarthen. Carmarthen anciently was the capital of Wales, for centuries the seat of kings and the home of the Welsh Parliament. It is now a dull old agricultural town of 10,000 or 15,000 inhabitants. Its streets are busy only on great market and fair days, and are dark and stony of aspect; but it is surrounded by a landscape of fairy-like beauty, and its woods and rivers are as rich with legend as fairyland itself. The enchanter Merlin was born at Carmarthen, and this was the centre of his magical exploits. Quaintly set upon a hill, the old stone town looks out over a sylvan valley, through which winds the river Towy in graceful undulations.

The most striking peculiarities of the Carmarthen fair are its utter rusticity and its pronounced Welshiness. No language but Welsh is heard about you. The characteristic tall beaver hats abound on the heads of women, who by this sign advertise their back-country residence. The women of the towns – even this old Welsh town – are less given to the shining and stubborn beaver than to a sort of calash peculiar to Wales, fitting the head snugly. The two old women standing near you, with cheeks pressed close together, whispering sleepily in each other's ears, telling some story of corpse-candle or cyhirraeth, could not be thus intimate with their secrets if their hats were the rigid beavers of the farmer-wives. There is no single specimen here to be found of the characteristic cockney fair-frequenters who so abound, as a rule, in every part of the British Isles, Wales included. There are no balladists singing English songs; no hawkers crying their wares in English; no gymnasts vaunting their own powers in English; no gamblers, no Aunt Sallies, no shooting-galleries – nothing whatever uttering itself in English. There is fun enough, but it is Welsh fun – scuffling, laughing, chaffing. There are hawkers enough, but they cry in Welsh, and they conduct their trades in Welsh. To beat down the price seems to be the rule with every purchase, be it nothing more than a pennyworth of sweets. To go to a fair or market and buy without chaffering is mere infantile greenness, from a Welsh point of view.

The persistent enquirer in that direction hears a great many strange tales of superstition in connexion with the old-established Welsh fairs, and Carmarthen is particularly rich in this regard. You cannot avoid noticing at Carmarthen fair a singular class of cattle, which are as characteristically Welsh as any Welshman here. These are the black cattle of Wales, which, if they cannot trace their ancestry back through forty centuries, are at least peculiar to the country they inhabit. This strange breed is sometimes seen in other parts of Great Britain, but they are everywhere known by the name of Welsh black cattle. In Carmarthenshire and the adjoining regions they abound. When beheld in a drove together, browsing in a field, or pouring through a gate like ink out of a bottle, they present a spectacle as uncanny as one can imagine of anything innocent and eatable. The first time one sees this sight it is nothing less than startling; for, it must be understood, there is not a spot of hide in the whole drove that is not black, from hoof-tips to nose-tips. The suggestion of something eerie and elfin in their disposition is irresistible . . .

XII.XIV

The antiquity of most of the existing fairs is very great. Some have records in black and white to prove their age; others are more matters of tradition, but tradition amounting almost to the value of written testimony, in this part of the world. The charter of the borough of Kidwelly, granted in the reign of James 1, speaks thus: "3 fairs are now holden and kept from time of which the memory of man is not to to the contrary accustomed and kept yearly in several diverse places, one within the walls of the said borough on the feast of St Magdalene, another at Llangendeirne within 3 miles of the said borough and within the circuits and liberties therof on the feasts of St James the Apostle and the 3rd within the walls of the said borough upon the feast of St Luke the Evangelist."

There are numberless little local fairs whose fame has never got abroad, which have been held regularly for hundreds of years. They are not celebrated throughout Wales, like the fairs of Llandaf and Kidwelly, though they stir up their own neighbourhood with a periodical excitement like that of the proverbial cwd poten, and set whole parishes agog. Such a one is the Waun Fair, held near the town of Merthyr on stated days throughout the year, the largest being the "Apple and Pear Fair" of September 24th – not confined by any means to apples and pears, of which the natural growth of the region is anything but fine, but including horses and ponies, which latter favourite animals are sold in Wales in great numbers, between the eggs and the apples. The fair is known to have been originated by Iestyn ap Gwrgant, who was sovereign of this region at and before the time when William the Conqueror sat on the throne of England.

* My recently deceased neighbour, 94 year-old Arthur Hammett, who lived at the remarkable West Orchard Farm in Sain Tathan, pointed out an odd set of external stairs at the back of the farm. They were built around 200 years ago to prevent the 'hired men' using the internal stairs to get to their bedrooms. The internal stairs, of course, were used by the hired female servants to get to their own bedrooms, and it was not thought wise for the young men to meet the equally young women on the stairs when retiring.

FAUSTUS c. 408 - 490
September 28, January 13, 16

He may be the same person as Edeyrn ap Gwtheyrn, and was a Briton according to St Avitus of Vienne. Faustus lived around 400-490, and became friends with a fellow-Briton Rioc (Riocatus), at Lerins. He gave Rioc two of his anti-Arian treatises when Rioc returned to Britain around 450. Faustus was Abbot of Lerins from 433, and was made Bishop of Riez in 459 or 462, succeeding Maximus. However, he was forced into exile by the Visigoth King Euric in 481, returning to Riez on Euric's death three years later. An attractive character and a preacher of great eloquence, he fiercely opposed Augustus' doctrine of predestination (the precursor of the Calvinism which took much of the joy and culture out of Welsh life over a millennium later). Faustus knew that this creed made a nonsense of Christ's teaching of the power of redemption. In a response to a criticism by Benedictus Paulinus, he is quoted as saying *'I am asked whether the knowledge of the Trinity in Unity suffices to salvation in things divine; I answer, a rational grasp of the faith is not all that is required of us, there must be the reason for pleasing God. Naked truth without merits is empty and vain.'*

He was savagely attacked by Mamertus and Fulgensias for his belief in a 'Christian' approach to religion. This humane saint is still venerated at Riez on September 28, and also celebrated on January 16. The village church at St Faustus near Pau was rededicated to John the Baptist after its restoration. Nennius claimed that Faustus was a son of Vortigern, brought up and educated by Garmon. (See Edeyrn – they may well be the same saint, or brothers, and the feast dates are different.) His works *'De Gratia'* and *De Spiritu Sanctu'* were condemned by the Council of Orange in 529.

FEAST DAYS

These were the saints' days and associated more with 'fetes' or sporting activities than the 'feasts' or medieval banquets that we think of today. The Latin for holiday was 'festus' (which gives the Spanish 'fiesta'). Thomas Hughes, in 'Tom Brown's Schooldays', gives the best description:
'They are literally, so far as one can ascertain, feasts of the dedication, i.e. they were first established in the churchyard, on the day on which the village church opened for public worship, which was on the wake or festival of the patron saint, and have been held on the same day in every year ever since that time. There was no longer any remembrance of why the 'veast' had been instituted, but nevertheless it had a pleasant and almost sacred character of its own. For it was than that all the children of the village, wherever they were scattered, tried to get home for a holiday to visit their fathers and mothers, bringing with them their wages or some little gift from up the country for the folks.' After this passage, he notes that his own village feast, in the vale of Berkshire, died out from the 1830's because of the lack of contributions for prizes by the local farmers and gentry. Many feasts lasted longer in England than in Wales because the spirit of Calvinist purity (and probity) did not take a hold as it did in Wales.

FEBRIC

With Iarmen, he featured in a grant of land noted in 955 in the Book of Llandaf at Lann Bedeui (Penterry, Monmouthshire), as being the patron of 'Sanctorum Iarmen et Febric'. The church is now known as St Arvan's. A case could possibly be made be made for Garmon of Man being Iarmen.

NICHOLAS FERRAR 1592 or 93 - 1637
December 1

Given a Holy Day, aged 34 he founded a religious community in Little Gidding which was visited by Charles I. George Herbert was a friend of the community. Upon Ferrar's death, leadership of the foundation passed to his brother John, who was visited by the king twice more. Another visit, with the Prince of Wales, seems to have occurred after the defeat at Naseby. The community was forcibly broken up by Parliamentary soldiers in 1646. T.S Eliot used the events as the backdrop to his 'Four Quartets', written in the Second World War where the future of Britain was uncertain.

ROBERT FERRAR d. 1555
March 30

The English Bishop of St David's from 1548, and the first to be consecrated in the English language there. At Oxford University he became an Augustinian canon, but was one of a group of students found trafficking in Lutheran literature in 1528, and was forced to recant. A leading reformer and favourite of Lord Somerset, he was accused by Somerset's enemies, imprisoned in Southwark, and deprived of his bishopric for heresy and marriage in 1554. In Queen Mary's time he refused to disavow Protestantism in front of Bishop Gardner. Ferrar was then arraigned before his successor at St David's, Bishop Henry Morgan, in Carmarthen. Showing great fortitude, Ferrar was burned at the stake in Carmarthen on March 30th. Henry Morgan, born at Dewisland in Pembroke, was in turn deprived of the bishopric by Queen Elizabeth in 1559, and retired to Wolvercote in Oxfordshire, where he died that same year.

FESTIVALS

Some ancient sites, such as St Davids, Llanfyllin, Caernarfon and St Asaf have annual festivals celebrating music or poetry. Erddig outside Wrecsam has an Apple Festival (which Merthyr Tudful also used to celebrate). There is nothing stopping any localities in Wales organising such functions, at any time of the year, using churches, church halls and club-houses. 'Festivals of Wales' is based in Newtown (01686 640766) and produces a free leaflet for each season. The following list is not all-inclusive, as the author knows that some of the St Donat's festivals are excluded, such as the July story-telling fair, but lists many of the major events in Wales as follows:

April (8 days) Llanddewi Brefi Cambria Arts Festival – painting, sculpture, music, poetry, film
May (9 days) Wrecsam Arts Festival – performing and visual arts
May (9 days) St David's Cathedral Festival – classical music concerts in the Cathedral
May (6 days, venue changes) Urdd National Eisteddfod - Europe's largest youth festival
June (3 days) and July (3 days) Llanfyllin Festival - chamber music in the church
June (2 weeks) Carmarthen Festival – opera, jazz, rock, art 'in all its forms'
June (1 week) Gwyl Criccieth – music, fireworks, crafts, sculture, walks
June (2 days) Tregaron Music Festival – folk, jazz, rock, classical and choral music
July (month) Chepstow Arts and Community Festival – 60 events, son et lumiere at the castle
July (9 days) Aberystwyth Poetryfest
July (6 days) Llangollen International Music Eisteddfod – the largest such event in the world
July (9 days) Cardiff – The Welsh Proms – at least 6 classical concerts and a jazz prom
July (2 days) Fishguard Mediaeval Experience – mediaeval environment with battles
July (2 weeks) Gower Festival – concerts in Gower churches
July (1 day) Aberaeron – Cardigan Bay Seafood Festival
July (4 days) Royal Welsh Show at Builth Wells – largest agricultural event in Europe
July (2 weeks) Aberystwyth Musicfest – outstanding chamber music from Europe
July (8 days) Caernarfon Festival – circus, performing arts, music and theatre
July-August (4 weeks) Swansea Dylan Thomas Festival – open air events
July-August (8 days) Fishguard Music Festival – orchestral, choral, recital, jazz
July-August (2 weeks) Abergavenny Arts Festival – music, drama, literature, folk, art
August Bank Holiday (2 days) Caerphilly Big Cheese – funfair, encampments, cheese market, folk dance, the end of the Summer Festival of two weeks
August (2 days) Erddig Gala Weekend – near Wrecsam in the gardens, proms and fireworks
August (9 days, venue changes) National Eisteddfod of Wales – 170,000 visitors a year
August (3 days) Brecon Jazz – the best jazz concerts in Britain
August (5 days) Machynlleth Equilibre Horse Theatre – dancers and horses in a wooded valley (this is under threat of closure on economic grounds)
August (10 days) Newtown Mid-Wales Opera Festival – new productions with international soloists
August (3 days) Pontardawe Festival – music and dance on 5 stages, torchlight procession
August (9 days) Llandrindod Wells Victorian Festival – 200 events and 100 street theatre performances
August (8 days) Machynlleth Festival – classical music, jazz, art
August (3 days) Ruthin Festival – free outdoor concert with Celtic bands

August-September (5 days) Presteigne Festival of Music and the Arts – string quartets, choirs, opera
September (month) Swansea Literature Proms – readings, talks, lectures
September (1 week) Barmouth Arts Festival – various arts events in the theatre
September (9 days) Conwy Festival – performing arts and street entertainment inside the City Walls
September (9 days) Tenby Arts Festival – all inclusive arts and music
September (8 days) St Asaf North Wales International Music Festival – in the Cathedral
October (3 weeks) Swansea Festival of Music and the Arts – concerts in the Brangwyn Hall
October (8 days) Anglesey Oyster Fayre – music, gourmet events
October (2 days) Erddig Apple Festival – cider tasting, music, children's events
November (10 days, formerly at Aberystwyth, now Cardiff) – Welsh International Film Festival

We may note from the above that there are only two major festivals in the six months between October and May. Thus there are many opportunities to put new 'covered' events on the schedule. Two week-long Welsh food and drink fairs could easily be held at the new Millennium Stadium during this time. There is enough room for exhibits in the walkways without using the pitch surface, and the WRU shows no sign of having a strategic plan to pay off its debts by utilising the stadium properly.

In the early 1970's, Bretons launched an arts festival in protest against de Gaulle's treatment of the Breton language, and this small beginning has grown to one of the world's biggest festivals of its kind. Around half a million people saw the 1999 Inter-Celtic Festival. Artists, musicians and dancers from the eight Celtic nations perform and compete. Under Charles de Gaulle*, probably the most pompous and over-rated war leader of all time, people were imprisoned for playing Breton instruments or christening their children with Breton names. The French had the same attitudes to the Breton language as shown by the use of the 'Welsh Not' in school in Wales. Its survival is as remarkable as that of Welsh. The author recounted in 'The A-Z of Wales and the Welsh' supporting France against England at rugby in a Finistère bar. The local villagers watching the game on television were vociferous in their support for England against France. Plus ça change . . .

*The famed 'Resistance' against German occupation was a virtual myth in most of non-Vichy France except Brittany. France, like England and Germany, is a prime example of a nation which seeks 'la gloire' at every opportunity and wants a strong 'leader' like de Gaulle/Mitterand, Thatcher/Blair or Adenauer/Kohl. The Welsh, Cornish and Bretons are extremely suspicious of powerful führers, preferring a consensus approach to politics.

FFAGAN d.193
FAGAN, FUGATIUS, PHAGANUS,
August 8, May 26, February 10, May 24 (with Dyfan)

The foundations of St Fagan's Chapel can be seen near the castle at The Museum of Welsh Life, just outside Cardiff. It appears that, like many other Celtic churches, Côr Ffagan was built upon a prehistoric burial site. The actual parish church of St Fagans is now dedicated to St Mary. Leland (1506-1552), in his 'Itinerary of England and Wales' notes *'The Paroch Church of S. Fagan is now of our Lady, but there is yet by the village a Chapelle of S. Fagan sumtime the Paroch Church.'* His holy well was a spring under a yew tree, and Richard Symonds, when with Charles I at St Fagans in 1645 wrote: *'many resort from all parts to drink it for the falling sickness which cures them at all seasons. Many come a yeare after they have drank and relate their health ever since.'*

According to the Lucius legend, Ffagan was sent with Dyfan by Pope Eleutherius in 180AD, at the request of King Lleuwrg, to preach the holy gospel and baptise the Cymry. Some sources say that their fellow-Britons Medwy and Elfan were sent with the request to Rome, and returned with Fagan and Dyfan. Ffagan died in the same year, 193, as Dyfan, and is commemorated on the same date. There was also a 'Phagan' who is said to have succeeded Joseph of Arimathea in 82 in Glastonbury, according to Cressy. It may be that Ffagan was in Glastonbury after Cressy's date.

Llanmaes (Llanfaes), in the vale of Glamorgan, was once called Llanffagan Fach to distinguish it from Llanffagan Fawr near Cardiff, and is now Cadog's foundation. Ffagan's 'Saying of the Wise' is: *'where God is silent it is not wise to speak.'*

The diary of William Thomas, a schoolmaster of Michaelston-super-Ely, is now lost, but was copied by David Jones, the great antiquarian. He notes an interesting anecdote about St Ffagans:
'1765, October 25th. This day the Excisemen searched the house of Isaac David of St Faggans for distilling liquors clandestine as he have this 12 months past newly bought a worm for distilling liquors for he had a Limbeck yrs. before and distilled water and sold it and now sold liquor at 2 shillings the Qt.' He had been informed upon by a neighbour, but escaped prosecution as *'None can prove yt. He distill but Lees, wch. has pay duty before and herbs wch. is free of all duty.'*

Willam Thomas disapproved of the old custom of raiding the 'May Pole' between villages. This seems to have been a pre-Christian rite, and he records the famous fight when St Ffagan's villagers stole Llandaff's 'painted wooden god' from the green in June 1768. The pole was set up in St Ffagan's, *'with much vain Pomp and Rejoycing and Watching it with guns'*. In turn there was a raid by 50 people from St Nicholas, intent on taking it to their own village green. However, they were outnumbered and forced to retreat, threatened with guns and clubs. More men were set to guard the pole as there were reports that *'Penmark, Lancarvan and St Nicholas folks were to come and steal their wooden god . . . '* Several men received fines of 52 shillings each at Cowbridge magistrates for their part in the affray.

A note from Thomas' diary, for July 13, 1762, not only shows the survival of 'mab' or 'ap' (meaning 'son of') in the Cardiff area, but makes us give thanks for medical progress:
'Was buried in Llandaff, Miles Morgan, a Taylor and a Shopkeeper, called Miles mab Gladys, of a year or more lingring from first a sore Toe, which swelled and putrified at last up to his secret parts and body, that his thighs and hips were rotten and black as pitch. He might be about 60 years of age and wealthy and he left all to his wife'. A remark by William Thomas shows us that Welsh was the main language at Cardiff and St Fagans in 1762, whereby *'Elsbed Gydyn Gwyn* (Elspeth with the lock of white hair) *. . . broke into St Faggans Mill and stole therefrom five podorans of wheaten meal, one podoran of potatoes and two and a half of barley . . .* (a podoran was a quarter of a hundredweight)'.

FFILI late 6th century
February 12

The son of Cenydd ap Gildas, who founded Rhossili on the Gower peninsula, formerly called Rhos Ffili. It is now dedicated to the Virgin Mary. Lamphil (Lan-Ffili) in Glamorgan was also his, as was Kervili in Brittany. This was near his father's foundation at Languidic and that of his grandfather at Castanec. Caerphilly, Caerffili, was formerly known as Senghenyd after his father. The Mabsant at Rhossilli lasted for 3 days, the eve, day and morrow of Ffili, and was noted for the *'bony clobby'*, a plum pudding made and sold on these days. Bishop Ffili is mentioned on a stone found at Ogmore (see Glywys).

From Peniarth MSS, No 118, probably written by John David Rhys, the author of the Welsh Grammar published in 1592, we have another source for the origin of Caerphilly:
Bwch is the giant abode in the place which is still called Castell Bwch between Caerlleon on Usk and Llantarnam, and he also dwelt in the other castle of Bwch between Pentre-bach and Henllys in the country of Gwent. And Bwch had sons, namely Ernallt the giant, his dwelling was in the place still called Castell Ernallt in Llangattwg Dyffryn Wysg. Clytha the giant in the parish of Bettws Newydd, his dwelling was in the place called the Trenches of Clytha Fortress (the fort and camp of Coed-y-Bonedd). *And this land is called today the land of Clytha in the parish of Llanarth. Buga the giant, his dwelling was in the place still called Castell Bryn Buga* (the Roman fort now known as Usk, the 'Castle at Buga's Bridge' in Welsh). *Trogi the giant abode in the castle which is still called Castell Trogi near Wentwood* (The little stream known as the Troggy gave its name to the ruined fort of Cas Troggy, near the Silurian hill-fort capital of Llanmelin above Caerwent). *All these were the sons of Bwch the giant of the country of Gwent. And some say that Phili was a giant and son of the above Bwch; his dwelling was at Caerphily in the country of Morganwg. Their father had his head cut off in the country of Morganwg above Llantrisant in the place still called Pen-Bwch.*

There are places in Brittany called Kerfili and Bois de Kerfili, but also St Bily and Bois de St Bily, so it is dificult to attribute Ffili to them. The Green Lady of Caerffili Castle is one of the most famous of Welsh ghosts. The wife of Gilbert de Clare, Princess Alice of Angouleme, fell in love with Gruffudd, the Lord of Senghenydd. A monk betrayed their relationship, and Gruffudd hung him at Ystrad Mynach (The Vale of the Monk). De Clare tracked Gruffudd down and killed him. When the news was brought to Alice at Caerfilli, her heart broke and she died instantly. She has been seen throughout the centuries pacing the ramparts, looking for her lost lover. (N.B. Some have placed St Ufelwy as the same person as St Ffili).

FFINAN see FINAN

ABBOT FFINIAN, FINNIAN OF CLONARD b. c. 472-475, d. c. 547-550
December 12, February 23

He studied at Llancarfan under Cadoc, where he had a chapel. Ffinian went often with Cadoc and Gildas to Echni (Flat Holm* Island), and left Cadoc around 520 after 30 years in Wales. Cadoc had originally brought him from Ireland, with the other saints Macmoil and Gnawan (q.v.), to study at Llancarfan. His monastery at Clonard in Meath, founded in 533, was on the pattern shown him by Cadoc, David and Gildas. Close to the Welsh church, Ffinian was the leading saint in Ireland after Patrick's death, and initiated the strict monastic order following the Llancarfan pattern. He visited St David at Menevia about 530, and was said to have remained in Britain for some years, when he built three churches. He combined a life of study with the Welsh form of monastic life. According to his Life, he came to Wales aged 30, and stayed for 30 years. Also the Life states that he chose David above Gildas as primate of Britain - Cadog could not decide who should rule the church, and asked his great friend Finnian to be an impartial judge. He died of the Yellow Plague that killed Maelgwn Gwynedd, but not before he had instructed St Columba of Iona, Brendan the Voyager and St Ciaran of Clonmacnois. The Welsh Calendars state that he founded Nantcarfan and Melboc in Wales. Nothing is known of Melboc, but the Nant Carfan reference is probably his chapel at Cadoc's Llancarfan (Nant Carban).

Father John Ryan ('Irish Monasticism: Origins and Early Development', London, 1931) noted the influence of Cadog on Finnian, who was the saint responsible for the development of Irish monastic schools, and thereby the Irish missionary movement across Europe. *'Finnian, under the influence chiefly of Cadoc, transformed Clonard, founded originally . . . after the loose Patrician pattern, into a monastery strictly so called . . . British monasticism . . . laid stress on study, particularly sacred study, as part of the daily round of duties. Finnian adopted this principle, and the monasteries founded by him and his disciples soon rivalled, if they did not surpass, the schools of secular learning.'* He also noted that Cadoc's tutelage left its imprint in *'the peculiarly British way in which Latin was pronounced in Ireland,'* and stated that the monasteries of Llancarfan, Llanilltud and possibly Miskin supplied the new Irish monasteries with books. Thus from Llancarfan stemmed the notable Irish intellectual movement of the end of the 6th century. Finnian's most famous pupil was St Columba, whose Scottish monastery on the isle of Iona became *'one of the most important centres of learning in north-western Europe'* ('Columba', Ian Finlay, London 1979).

*'Holm' is Scandinavian for an island in an estuary. In the Bristol Channel, Flat Holm is Welsh and its neighbour Steep Holm is English. The island was an important sanctuary and monastery for Welsh monks, and is mentioned in 917 in the Anglo-Saxon Chronicle: *'In this year a great pirate host came over hither from the south of Britanny under two jarls, Ohtor and Hroald, and sailed west about until they reached the estuary of the Severn, and hamed (ravaged) at will everywhere along the Welsh coast. They seized Cyfeiliog, bishop of Archenfield and took him to their ships, but King Edward ransomed him afterwards for forty pounds. Then after this the whole host went inland with the intention of renewing their raids in the direction of Archenfield: they were opposed by the men from Hereford and Gloucester and from the nearest fortresses who fought against them and put them to flight. They slew the jarl Hroald and the other jarl Ohtor's brother and a great part of the host, and drove them into an enclosure and besieged them there until they gave them hostages and promised to depart from King Edward's dominion . . . The king had arranged that the coast should be guarded all along the southern shore of the Severn estuary* (the north shore was of course Welsh), *from Cornwall in the west eastwards as far as the mouth of the Avon, with the result that they dared not land anywhere in that region. However, they landed secretly by night on two separate occasions, once east of Watchet and again at Porlock, and on each occasion the English struck them so that only those few escaped who swam out to the ships. They encamped out on the isle of Flatholm until the time that they were short of food, and many perished of hunger, since they were unable to obtain provisions. They went thence to Dyfed, and then out to Ireland, and this was in the autumn.'* There are also traditions from this time of Vikings being trapped in the old Iron Age fort on Sulli Island near Penarth, when they attacked Glamorgan, and starving to death there.

Two graves were discovered and excavated in 1942 on the monastic site on Flat Holm, near the old farmhouse. Three skeletons were found, and the legend was that they were the knights who killed Thomas a'Becket in 1170. Of the four knights, Hugh de Morville was the only one who did not aim a blow at Thomas, and he seems to have gone on crusade as a penance, then returned to Knaresborough Castle, being buried in Kirkoswald, Cumbria in 1204. Sir Hugh left William de Tracey's sword to Carlisle Cathedral. Wiliam de Tracey died in Sicily in 1173, on his way to the Holy Land. Reginald Fitznurse may have fled to the Welsh Black Mountains with the others directly after the murder, but seems to be buried in Jerusalem *'before the door of the Templars' church'*. It is also claimed that Hugh de Morville is buried here. Three knights thus have links with the Crusade after Thomas' martyrdom, leaving Richard le Breton as a possible candidate for one of these graves.

According to old maps, there was a friar's garden on the island. Bob Jory's book on Flat Holm (Wincanton Press, 1995) gives us the uses of some of the plants found on the island which may have been there from the time of Gildas, Barruc and Cadog. Flat Holm is a Site of Special Scientific Interest, and can be visited, with the interesting phenomenon of many white-flowering plants which flower elsewhere as pink or blue. Plants that can be eaten are Sorrel, Dandelion, Hawthorn, Elder and Sloe, and the Wild Leek, which is rare on the mainland. Plants with medicinal properties are St John's Wort, Nettle, Chickweed, Yarrow, and Cleavers. The roots of Henbane were once used as a teething necklace, and although poisonous in quantity, it has a narcotic effect. Salad Burnet, Violet, Mint, Wild Thyme, Daisy and Cowslip were all used as strewing herbs. Bracken was used for bedding and dye, and Bluebells for glue or starch for laundering. Burdock leaves could be butter wrappers, while Great Mullein leaves were used as tinder, wicks or tobacco.

FFLEWYN 6th century
December 11 and12

The son of Ithael Hael, and brother to Tanwg, Gredifael, Tecwyn, Tegai, Trillo, Twrog, Baglan and Llechid. He is the saint of Llanfflewyn, a chapel of Llanrhuddlad in Anglesey. Fflewyn was one of the superintendents at Pawl Hen's monastery at Whitland, with his brother Gredifael.

FFRAID c.450-c.525
BRIGID, BRIDGET, BRIDE, MARY of the GAEL
February 1 (also March 24)
Patron of poets, blacksmiths, brewers, cooking and kitchens, and healers

St Brigid, 'The Mary of the Gael', is revered second only to Patrick in Ireland. Probably born in Faughart, she died as Abbess of Kildare. She was the initiator and abbess of Ireland's first community of nuns at Kildare, and was known in Wales as Ffraid Santes. The church of St Bride's Major in Glamorgan is dedicated to this saint, as is St Bride's-super-Ely in the same county. The people of the latter St Brides were once known as *'cacwns Sant y Brid'*, *'the hornets of St Brides'*, a reference to an 18th century tragedy when two children disturbed a nest and were stung to death. St Bride's Bay in Pembroke emphasised the passage of Welsh and Irish clerics between the two countries. There are many Llansantffraid place names in Wales. According to Cressy, she visited Britain in 488 and died at Down in 502.

At Llansanffraidd Deuddwr in Radnorshire, the church was moved and rededicated to St Gwenfrewi (Winifred) in 1778, so two feast days can be celebrated there. Brawdy Church in Pembrokeshire, near Brawdy hill-fort, was probably an early Christian burial site, and the church was originally dedicated to Bridget. At the hill-fort was found a stone inscribed in Ogham, reading *MAQI QUAGTE, 'the son of Quagte'*, which dates from the 5th or 6th century. From Brawdy Farm and probably originally from the church, is another 'Irish' stone inscribed: *MACUTRE ( ) FILI CATOMAG ( ), Macutrenus son of Catomaglus'*. Macutrenus is an Irish name. Two more local stones read *VENDAGNI FILI V( )NI (Vendagnus son of V . . . nus)* and *BRIAC( ) FILI ( )GI, Briacus son of ( )gus*.

Could Briac be St Briog?* The large number of dedications to Ffraid in Wales are thought to occur because she replaced the Celtic Goddess of fire of earlier times, as her cult seemed to spread from Scotland through Cumbria, Wales, Ireland, Devon and Cornwall to Brittany.

Giraldus Cambrensis recounts that a perpetual fire was kept burning at Kildare for nearly 1,000 years. It was surrounded by a circle of shrubs and no man was allowed to aproach it. It burned until 1220 in a shrine near her Kildare church. This follows on from a pagan custom. Her feast on 1st February is also the night of the pagan fire festival of Imbolc, which marks the return of light after the darkness of winter, and the lactation of ewes. It seems that Ffraid was superimposed upon the Celtic mother-goddess of fire and song, Brighde, which accounts for the fact that the cult is so widespread. In Ireland, only Patrick has more dedications. The fire festival was called Brigantia or Imbolc, replaced by Candlemas in the Christian tradition.

Bishop Cormac in the 9th century described Ffraid as a *'goddess that the bards worshipped, for very great and noble was her perfection. Her sisters were Brigid, the woman of healing, and Brigid, the smith-woman'*. Like Beuno, she was associated in Wales with the cattle cult, and horned cattle and sheep were eaten at feasts in her honour. In mediaeval times, Welsh travellers, before setting out, would pray *'St Ffraid, bless us on our journey.'*

Early in the nineteenth century, there were still 19 dedications to Ffraid or Ffraid Leian remaining in Wales, at the following locations:
Flint – Diserth**;
Denbigh – Llansanffraid Glyn Conwy and Llansanffraid Glyn Ceiriog;
Radnor – Llansanffraid yn Elfael, Nantgwyllt chapel and Llansanffraid Cwmmwd Deuddwr
Montgomery – Llansanffraid yn Mechain*;
Merioneth – Llansanffraid Glyndyfrdwy;
Brecon - Llansanffraid
Anglesey – Capel Sanffraid (a chapel to Holyhead, in ruins);
Pembroke – St Brides (a ruined chapel);
Cardigan – Llansanffraid chapel near Llannon;
Glamorgan – St Brides Major near Wick, St Brides Minor upon Ogmore, a ruined chapel near Ogmore and St Brides super Ely (Elai)
Monmouth – Llansanffraid (now called St Brides), Ysgynfraith (now called Skenfrith), St Brides in Netherwent and St Brides Wentloog.

Other known 'British' dedications are:
Shropshire – Kinnerley church, which is now dedicated to the Virgin Mary.
Devon – Bridestow and Bridgerule
Somerset – Breane and Chelvey
Cumberland – Bridekirk, Kirkbride, Brigham and Bassenthwaite
Cheshire – St Bride's church at Chester (now demolished)

In Brittany there are almost thirty dedications known in Finistere and Morbihan, with more in the Cotes du Nord.

Like Ffraid of Cil-Muine, Fraid of Kildare (Cill Dara, the Church of the Oak) is associated with rushes. While she was explaining the passion to a dying pagan, she wove a cross from the rushes on his floor. The St Brigid Coss is still made of rushes today and placed on the rafters of cottages on February 1st, her day of death. The emblem protects the home from evil and want. They are hand-made from rushes from the river Shannon to the same traditional design and cost around £3.50 in Irish gift shops. Cribau Sant Ffraid (St Bride's combs) is the Welsh name for the plant known as wood betony.

*A major problem is unravelling early Welsh history is the cost of travelling to find information – there is no central source. A largely unexplored area is the existence of old Welsh place names, especially field names. Unfortunately, European law has forced Wales to give its field numbers instead of names. However, if we can find out the original field names across all of Wales, before it is too late, we can establish patterns of events. For instance the name Maescadlawr – the 'field of the floor of battle' on Mynydd Baeddan near Bridgend has possible links with Arthur's battle of Badon Hill. Equally, Llansanffraid-yn-Mechain is supposed to be the site of the great Gruffydd ap Llywelyn's disastrous battle against Earl Harold Godwinsson shortly before Hastings. Nearby place-names are Wyddigoed (Shouting Wood), Cae Caethas (Field of the Enslaving) and Gwern y Ciliaw (Swamp of the Retreat). Harold and Tostig chased Gruffydd to Snowdonia, where he was supposedly killed by his own men, but the Saxons never conquered Wales. A study of tithe maps held in Aberystwyth will help to preserve field names, but they need to be available electronically.

Official funding to the sum of £400,000 has been found to pay for the production of a Welsh Encyclopaedia, which could have been far better used to examine the actual fabric of our history, its local place-names, rather than pay the chosen few to regurgitate the Anglicised history they have been taught. This author's 'A-Z of Wales and the Welsh' took seven years' unpaid work, including constant applications for publishing assistance to every Welsh authority, before a (Swansea) publisher could be found. The idea of a Welsh heritage database has been constantly pushed to the Welsh Office, WTB, WDA, Welsh Arts Council, University of Wales, political parties, etc., etc. by the author. It is interesting that the private publication of the 'A-Z' coincided with state and lottery money being diverted into a competitive offering.

This present publication upon Welsh saints, pushing Wales into remembering and restoring its heritage, is also a labour of love which has opened up a new avenue of exploration into the reality of King Arthur. The forthcoming 'Hundred Great Welshmen' and another book upon Welsh pirates, buccaneers and seafarers have equally received no support from any of the dozens or so quangos and institutions which have been set up to serve the interests of Cardiff rather than Wales. It is this author's intention to constantly write books of Welsh interest to educate our own people as well as tourists. The work is done at week-ends and evenings, with no financial support, but any assistance from readers of this book in matters of fact would be appreciated. Future purchasers of the Wales Encyclopaedia, assuming a 20,000 print run, may like to know that each book has been subsidised by the public to the tune of £20. The University of Wales Press, which will print it, also receives public funds. (The author also approached large local companies for assistance with the funding of printing a Millennium book for St Tathan council on the parishes of Aberthaw, Gileston, Flemingston and Eglwys Brewys, for which he is receiving no payment. National Power, which is one of the worst acid rain producers in Europe and has covered the beautiful harbour of Aberthaw with waste dumps, refused. So did all the operators at Cardiff Wales Airport, including TBI, and BAMC which disfigured the Vale of Glamorgan with its huge repair building. So did the RAF, responsible for the dereliction of Eglwys Brewys Church, the requisitioning of a huge area of land, and constant noise. So did DARA, the privatised RAF repair agency. So did Blue Circle Cement at Aberthaw. These are huge companies, to whom a couple of hundred pounds represents a good meal for their directors. There is little support from either the public or private sector for initiative and community in Wales).

**A cross in the churchyard may have vanished. It appeared to have been re-inscribed centuries later when it was moved from a nearby hill to the church. The inscription was said to be to Einion ap Rhirid Flaidd, who was killed by an arrow when Llywelyn ap Gruffydd stormed Diserth Castle in 1260.

ABBESS FFRAID LEIAN OF CIL-MUINE 6th century
November 12

This virgin saint of Cil-Muine, another name for Menevia, is often mixed up with the Irish 'Bride', and may have been her sister. She was sent by St Darerca to St David's to learn the rules of the monastic life, and crossed the sea with Bride, Luge and Alethea, landing at Capel Sant Ffraid, near the present church of Llansantffraid Glyn Conwy. The original chapel near Deganwy Castle was almost washed away by 1740, and can no longer be seen. Ffraid Leian (Ffraid the Nun) was extremely popular in medieval Wales, her cult being only surpassed by those of David, Michael and the Virgin Mary. Dedications to Ffraid in the south-west of Wales may be those of Ffraid Leian rather than Ffraid of Kildare. In a time of famine, Ffraid threw rushes into the Conwy river which became 'brwyniaid', boneless smelts, for which the river is still famous. At Llansantffraid-Glyn-Conwy is a cromlech known variously as Hendre Waelod, Morloch's Altar and Allor Moloch. There was a Ffynnon Lluan and Capel Lluan near Lanarthne.

FFRAID

This Irish nun is said to have landed by herself near Holyhead, on a sandy beach still called Tywyn y Capel. She founded Capel Sant Ffraid on a dolmen (both now vanished), but this is either Ffraid Leian or yet another Ffraid. Bishop Cormac noted three sisters all named Bride.

FFWYST

Probably the saint who founded Llanfoist in Monmouth, now dedicated to St Faith.

FINAN 6th century
FFINNAN WINNIN
September 14, March 18, (possibly January 14)

An Irish disciple of St Cyndeyrn (Mungo, Kentigern), who founded Llanffinan under Llanfihangel Ysgeifog near the Menai Straits. He left Llanelwy (St Asaf) to go to Scotland in 573, with Cyndeyrn to evangelise the Picts. He is remembered at Lumphanan in Aberdeen.

FLOWERING SUNDAY
Palm Sunday, the Sunday before easter

Graves are decked with flowers, especially daffodils, as has been the custom since at least the 15th century. Francis Kilvert describes the practice at Clyro in Radnoshire in the 1870's. The decoration also used to occur at Christmas and Whitsunday. The tradition is still relatively common, especially in the former industrial areas of South Wales.

FORTY MARTYRS OF ENGLAND AND WALES
October 25

These were Roman Catholics who were martyred between 1535 and 1679, canonized by Pope Paul VI on October 25th, 1970. Welsh saints included were Philip Evans, Richard Gwyn, John Jones, David Lewis, Nicholas Owen and John Roberts.

Cardiff Gaol had a terrible reputation for the mistreatment of Catholic recusants, of whom around 40 died in its confines between 1594 and 1598. These were men and women who refused to attend Church of England services. About five or six were members of the Turberville family from Sker House and Llysworney. William Thomas, the diarist noted that even in later years it was a terrible place: *'March 1st, 1783. Was buried in Cardiff about Christmas he that broke jail and runid away with Jack Philip and Will Rees August last but he was caught afterwds. and brought in and there dyed. He was at ye Quarter sessions condemned to be Transported for stealing bread and cheese from his own brother . . . and the reports is that Jack Oram the jailer now after he was caught starved him in giving him to eat raw beef liver with grains. He was not very sharp in his senses – of 25 yrs. of age.'*

FOUNDER SAINTS OF BRITTANY

The *'pères de la patrie'* were all British, with six being of Welsh origin and Corentin being of British-Cornish stock. There were Corentin (Quimper), Padarn (remembered as Patern at Vannes), Briog (St Brieuc), Samson (Dol), Pol Aurelian (Pol-de-Leon), Tudwal (known as Tugdual at Treguier) and St Malo. All these 6th century evangelical saints founded monasteries and now have mediaeval cathedrals dedicated in their honour. A motoring tour of Brittany taking in these sites is thoroughly recommended, starting from St Malo.

FRACAN 5th – 6th century
October 3

This may also be the name Brychan – he was the second husband of St Gwen Tierbron, and their sons were the saints Gwethenoc, James (Iago) and Winwaloe. A cousin of Cado, Duke of Cornwall, he went with his twin sons Gwethenoc and Iago to Brittany around 460. A battle was recorded of Ffracan repelling invaders off the coast of Leon. Other colonists followed him into Leon and Domnonia from Wales and the West Country. Plou Fragan outside St Brieuc and St Fregan near Lesneven commemorate this saint.

FRYMDERI see NEFYDD

G

*'**God** and the doctor we alike adore
But only when in danger, not before;
The danger o'er, both are alike requited,
God is forgotten, and the Doctor slighted.'*

John Owen (1560-1622), 'Epigrams'

GALICIA

Wales, Brittany, Strathclyde, Cumbria, Eire, Cornwall and Galicia in Spain all have remnant Celtic populations. The Celts settled in Galicia around 1000BC, before they came to the British Isles. The kingdom of Galicia was destroyed by the Visigoths in 585, and had a city called Brigantia. Its Celtic monastery of Santa Maria de Bretona, near Montonedo, was listed as a British bishopric, and Bishop Mailoc (Mailocus/Maelog ap Caw?) is noted as the *'Britonensis Ecclesiae episcopus'* who endorsed the acts of the Council of Braga in 572. Mailoc was the suffragan to Archbisop Martin at Braga. When the Council of Lugo was held in 596, the British see in Galicia under Bishop Madoc was an established fact. The British form of tonsure prevailed in Galicia until abolished by the Council of Toledo in 663, when the British bishop Metopius conformed to the ruling. British bishops of Bretona signed the decrees of the Council of Toledo in 646, 653, 683 and 693, and the see was not united with Oviedo until 830.

The region has numerous megaliths like the Welsh cromlechs, called 'medorras' or 'mamoas', and also large numbers of Celtic hill-forts, known as 'castros'. The Romans brought Christianity, in their exploitation of Galicia's mineral wealth, and Galicia has its own language, Gallego. Pabai, Nefei and Pasgen appear to have gone to Spain in the 5th - 6th century, and attempts have been made to make Iago the founder of Santiago de Compostella – Welsh/Galician connections would be an intriguing line of research. Perhaps these links were the reason that Compostela was the favoured pilgrimage from mediaeval Britain. North-west Spain is the most remote of the Celtic fringes of Europe – Strathclyde in south-west Scotland, Cumbria in north-west England, Wales, Cornwall in south-west England, Brittany/Cornouaille in north-west France all share 2000 years of history. Intriguingly both the tips of Britanny and Galicia are known as Finisterre – the end of land, just like Cornwall's Land's End.

GALLGO see ALLGO

GARAI 5th – 6th century

Iolo Morganwg thinks that this saint was founder of Llanharri near Llantrisant, and is a son of Cewydd ap Caw, but he may be Gwrhai, or Gwrai ap Caw. The church was known as Llanarrai, and is now dedicated to St Illtud.

GARCI 5th – 6th century

The son of Cewydd ap Caw, he had a church dedicated to him somewhere in Glamorgan.

Alphabetical Listing of the Saints of Wales and Religious Events

GARMON d. 448
GERMANUS OF AUXERRE
July 31, August 1

From 418 this Roman Gaul was bishop of Auxerre, and was asked by the British to come over (with Bishop Lupus of Troyes) to refute Pelagianism in 429 at the Conference of Verulanium. He returned in 435 or 447 to deal with the revival of Pelagianism with Severus, Bishop of Trier, and its leaders were banished. He then led the British forces in the famous victory at Llaniarmon yn Ial near Wrexham, at the battlefield still named Maes Garmon.

Pilgrimages and offerings were made to his statue at Llaniarmon. He had led the Celtic army against a combined Pict and Saxon force, and defeated them by asking the British to shout *'Alleluia!"* with such power that the attackers were terrified and fled. The next year he was in Ravenna, pleading to the Holy Roman Emperor for the rebelling Bretons. He died there in 448 and his body returned to Auxerre for a great funeral. Auxerre became a great centre of pilgrimage.

Castell Caereinion with its round churchyard (signifying a pagan site, like Llanerfyl) is dedicated to Garmon and is intriguingly the place where Pelagius is said to have started preaching.

GARMON c.410-c.475
GERMANUS OF MAN, GARMON ap GORONWY
July 31, October 1, 12, (Isle of Man July 3), May 27, 28, July 13, 14, August 1, 31

This is Garmon ap Goronwy of Gwaredog, and a saint of Beuno's côr at Clynog. He is often confused with Garmon of Auxerre, and it seems that the Welsh feast dates have come to coincide with the other saint's feast day and translation day. Garmon was a Breton who stayed with Patrick in Ireland and then came to Wales and lived in the monastery Côr Tewdws (later Llanilltud Fawr) with St Brioc around 460. He then went to Gaul, but returned to meet Patrick in Britain around 462 where he had a *'magic contest'* with Gwrtheyrn (Vortigern) of Wales. (Was this a confused folk-memory, of an attempt by the other Garmon to move the High-King from his Pelagian leanings?) Garmon eventually became bishop of the Isle of Man in 466.

There are dedications to Garmon in the counties of Caernarfon, Radnor, Montgomery and Denbigh. Which of these were originally Garmon of Auxerre are not known, but there is a Llanarmon Dyffryn Ceiriog in Denbigh, St Harmon's in Radnor and Llanfechain church in Montgomery, all dedicated to Garmon. Ffynnon Armon healing and baptismal well was near his church at Llanfechain, and the churchyard contains a mound called Twmpath Garmon.

The following chapels were also his: Llanarmon Fach under Llandegfan, Capel Garmon under Llanrwst and Bettws Garmon under Llanfair Isgaer in Denbigh, and Llanarmon under Llangybi in Caernarfon. Capel Garmon Neolithic cromlech near Capel Garmon Church was once used as a stable. There are nearby remains of standing stones called Maen Pebyll at Nebo. At Llanarmon, in Plasdu Farm yard, there was a huge standing stone, but it is not known if it is still intact.

There was a 'Gwyl Armon' held in the months of May (27 and 28), July (13, 14) and October. Gwyl Armon yn Ial was October 1, and his fair was held in Llanfechain and Castell Caereinion on October 12. The Caernarfon parishes celebrated him on July 31, and Yale on August 1. In St Harmon's Radnor, the first Sunday after August 31 commemorated him. At Plougastel-Saint-Germain his feast was the first Sunday in July, and the first Sunday after Easter his pardon was held. At Pleyben there is a fine statue of Garmon, and his pardon is the first Sunday in August, but at Riec the first Monday in July.

A mile west of Betws Armon Church in Caernarfon is Ffynnon Armon, on the slopes of Moel Smythan. It is near the ruins of an old chapel and cured rheumatism and skin diseases. There was also Ffynnon Garmon in Llanfihangel Yoreth parish in Carmarthen. Ffynnon Armon is near a field called Cae'r Saint in Llanarmon and effected miraculous cures. Another Armon's Well was in Castell Caereinion in Montgomery.

Local traditions say that Garmon came to the area in 447 and sought refuge at the mountain stronghold of Benlli Gawr, a giant chieftain but was refused admission. However, Cadell took pity on him and gave the saint food and shelter. Garmon then warned Cadell to leave the fort, before it was destroyed, and it was struck by lightning, killing Benlli the Giant. Cadell became the new chieftain and gave Garmon land at Llanarmon yn Ial, Llanarmon Dyfrryn Ceiriog and probably the original Celtic church at Llanbedr Duffryn Clwyd. A stone showing a human figure blowing a trumpet was found there in 1870, similar to stones found at Valle Crucis Abbey near Llangollen. At St Harmon's there was a standing stone near Pant-y-Dwr, destroyed sometime in the 1950's, and another two are on the banks of the Dulas at Gwenfron, one of which may also have disappeared since the 1950's. Another can be seen at Henrhiw, but has toppled. It was in a row of inscribed stones which appear to have been destroyed in the last fifty years. Thus history vanishes for no good reason in our lifetimes. If any reader can enlighten the author further upon the saints named Garmon, please contact at the publisher's address.

GARTHELI

Capel Gartheli in Cardigan.

GASTAYN 5th – 6th century

This is possibly the saint who baptised Cynog, Brychan's eldest son. His church was on the side of Llyn Syfaddon (Langorse Lake), at Llangasty Tal-y-Llyn (End of Lake). Parts of the mediaeval rood screen remain. Legend makes him the son of Myfig, the last prince of the drowned realm of Syfaddon, under the lake. The crannog at this lake, unique in Wales, gave rise to legends of a hidden city under its waters.

GAVELKIND

This Welsh inheritance principle, known as *'cyfran'*, serves to explain much of Welsh history, especially the fragmentation of landholdings and the system of saints. Because land and property were shared equally upon death, the stability of society could be affected. To some extent it was easier when there was common land available to take over, but it often led to internecine warfare between the sons of Welsh princes, leading to weakness against the Norman (and other) invaders. To some extent, the removal of some competition by the inheritance of churches and monasteries by those children designated for, or wanting, a religious life, helped ease the situation. In 1536 it was abolished in Wales.

It may be that illegitimate children were encouraged to join the church in early times. Certainly the early church and Brittany offered some sort of outlet for the children of nobles as the Celtic world shrank with encroaching invaders. It also appears to the author that the practice of Welsh kings and princes for centuries, of retiring to monasteries in their later years, was a holding mechanism to ensure the survival of their lands. By designating a successor, not necessarily the eldest son, there was a period when the father's authority helped the continuing existence of the kingship, without family strife, before he died.

GENEALOGIES OF SAINTS

The *'three saintly tribes of Britain'* were those of Cunedda Wledig, St Brychan and Caw. Brychan Brycheiniog's children and descendants included dozens of saints – see the entry on Brychan. Cunedda Wledig's line includes David, Teilo, Seiriol, Gwen, Cybi and Ailbe.

Cystennin Gorneu (Constantine the Tyrant) produced Dyfrig, Gildas and other saints.
Cadell Deyrnllwg's son was Saint Cyngen, and his great grandson St Beuno, and also included in the family were Cadog, Ystyffan, Eigion, Elvis and Gwyddloyw. From Gwrtheyrn Gwrtheneu we have the saints Edeyrn, Elldeyrn, Eurdeyrn and Faustus.

The noble house of Eudaf also gave Wales many saints. St Elen Luyddog, the daughter of Eudaf, was the wife of Magnus Maximus, the Macsen Wledig of the Mabinogion. From their line comes the great Tudwal, and the saints Gwerydd, Iestyn, Cadfrawd and Gwrmael. King Arthur also belongs to this genealogy, as do 20 other saints including Owain Finddu, Lleuddad, Baglan and Collen. Maximus and Elen had seven children, Ednyfed, Cystennin, Gwythyr, Owain Finddu, Peblig, Dimet and Antonius.

From the descendants of Coel Godebog (*'Old King Cole'*) we have Deiniol, Gwenddoleu, Asaf and King Pabo Post Prydain (the saint known as the *'Pillar of Britain'*). From Coel through Gorwst Ledlwm come Kentigern, Cadell and Mordred (the cousin and enemy of Arthur). Also related to Arthur through his grandfather Amlawdd Wledig were the saints Tyfrydog, Teyrnog and Tudur.

The family of Emyr Llydaw (late 5th century) gives us Germanus (the Armorican) known in the Isle of Man, Gwen Tierbron (Three-Breasted) the patroness of nursing mothers and her sons James, Gwethenoc and Winwaloe. Emyr's children were Gwen Teirbron, Hywel, Amwn Ddu, Petrwn, Alan, Gwyndaf Hen, Difwng, Tewdwr Mawr and Gwyddno, all flourishing around the time of Arthur. Emyr's grandchildren included the saints Cadfan, Derfel Gadarn, Dwywau, Cristiolus, Rhystyd, Sulien, Tydecho, Samson, Tathan, Padarn, Lleuddad, Llonio, Llynab, Meugan, Hywyn, Trinio, Canna, Meilyr and Maelrys.

According to Baring-Gould and Fisher, the Saints of Wales belong to *'eight great families'*:
'1. That of Maxen Wledig, or Maximus the Usurper, 383-388. He is held to have married Elen, daughter of Eudaf, a petty prince in Arfon, and Aurelius Ambrosius probably claimed descent from Maximus. From the same stock came Rhydderch Hael, the prince who established himself supreme over the Cumbrian Britons; also Ynyr Gwent prince of Gwent, who resided at Caerwent. This family would seem to have represented the Romano-British civilisation. The

pedigree has been disturbed by confounding Elen, the wife of Maxen, with St Helena, the wife of Constantius and mother of Constantine the Great.

2. That of Cunedda, which came from the North, from the defence of the Wall, and which had been seated in the ancient Roman Valentia. This family is said to have expelled the Gwyddyl from Gwynedd, Ceredigion and Môn, and to have also occupied Merioneth, Osweilion and Denbigh. From it proceeded the royal line of Gwynedd, which only came to an end with the last Llywelyn. From this family proceeded those important saints, Dewi and Teilo.

3. That of Cadell Deyrnllwg in Powys, which sent out a branch into Glywyssing. Cadell became prince of Powys with his seat at Wroxeter or Shrewsbury, in the fifth century, in consequence of a revolt of the Romano-British and Christian subjects of Benlli against their prince, who favoured paganism. Cadell was grandfather of Brochwel Ysgythrog. This family died out in the male line in Cyngen, murdered in Rome in 854. It produced several saints, notably St Tyssilio of Meifod; and its branch in Glywyssing afforded the still more illustrious St Pedrog and St Catwg.

4. That of Brychan, king of Brycheiniog. This was an Irish family. Anlach, father of Brychan, made himself master of Brecknock. The family produced an incredible number of saints, who are found not only in their native district, but also in North-east and East Cornwall.

5. That of Caw of Cwm Cawlwyd in North Britain. Caw, however, was son of Geraint ab Erbin, Prince of Devon. Owing to the inroads of the Picts, the family of Caw was forced to abandon Arecluda and fly to Gwynedd, where they were well received by Cadwallon Lawhir (v. Life of Gildas), and Maelgwn, his son, who gave them lands, mainly in Môn, but apparently with the proviso that they should enter religion, so as not to form any small principalities which might be politically disadvantageous to the interests of the crown of Gwynedd. To this family, which never after its expulsion from the North obtained any secular importance, belonged Gildas, the famous abbot of Rhuys.

6. That of Coel Godebog. According to Skene, he was king in North Britain, and from him Kyle now takes its name. He was ancestor of a large and important family, of Llyr Merini, prince in Devon and Cornwall, of Urien Rheged, and of the poet Llwyarch Hen. From him descended a great many saints, but none of any great importance. Pabo Post Prydyn, and Dunawd, and Deiniol of Bangor, are the most conspicuous.

7. That of Cystennin Gorneu, a stock that, like the family of Maxen Wledig, derived from an usurper of the purple, Constantine the Tyrant, 408-411. It was from this stock that issued the family of Caw, given above. It would seem to have supplied Domnonia (Devon and Cornwall) with princes, who were called either Constantine or Geraint. The saint of this family that proved most remarkable was St Cybi, unless we prefer the notorious Constantine whom Gildas denounced for his crimes and immoralities, but who was afterwards converted.

8. That of Emyr Llydaw from Armorica. The Welsh pedigrees derive Emyr from Cynan, son of Eudaf and brother of Elen, wife of Maximus. But this is certainly imaginary. All that we really know of Emyr is that probably, on account of an usurpation by one of his sons, the others had to fly from Armorica and take refuge in South Wales, where they were well received by Meurig, king of Morganwg, who gave to several of them his daughters in marriage. The Bretons pretend* that his eldest son, who sent his brothers flying, was Llywel, or Hoel, "the Great".

From Emyr proceeded some men of great mark, such as St Samson, St Padarn, and, by a daughter, St Cadfan and St Winwaloe.'

* It seems certain that Llywel (Hywel) was Hoel Mawr, king of Brittany. Emyr Llydaw was King Budic II of Brittany.

GENYS 6th century?
GENNYS, GENESIUS. GWYNUS
May 2 and 3, translated July 19

This is possibly Gwynws ap Brychan, who has St Gennys Church at Trigg Minor, Cornwall. This is surrounded by dedications ot the other children of Brychan. He was celebrated at Launceston. December 13 is the feast of Gwynus at Llanwnws, so we may account him as a separate saint.

GEORGE d.303
April 18, 23

This patron saint of England was a semi-mythical Palestinian or Lebanese martyr whose popularity grew enormously after the Crusades, because of the dragon-slaying tale. He had replaced Edward the Confessor and Edmund of East Anglia by the 16th century, as the most popular English saint.

GERAINT AB ERBYN 5th - 6th century
GERENT, GEREINT, GERONTIUS
May 16

In the Book of Llandaf, Geraint founded the church at Magor near Newport. There is also Gerrans in Cornwall dedicated to Geraint, but this may be another saint *. A martyr who died in battle, St Geraint is remembered in the old text 'The Sayings of the Wise':
'Hast thou heard the saying of Geraint,
Son of Erbin, the just and experienced?
"Short-lived is the hater of saints." '

King Geraint ab Erbyn was killed fighting for Arthur at Llongborth, and his sons Selyf, Cyngar, Iestyn and Cado were also saints. Llywarch Hen records his death in the wonderful 'Elegy for Geraint' in the 'Black Book of Carmarthen':
In Llongborth I saw hard toiling
Amidst the stones, ravens feasting on entrails,
And on the chieftain's brow a crimson gash.

In Llongborth I saw a confused conflict,
Men striving together and blood to the knees,
From the assault of the great son of Erbyn.

At Llongborth was Geraint slain,
A strenuous warrior from the woodland of Dyfnaint (Devon),
Slaughtering his foes as he fell.'

The Anglo-Saxon Chronicle places Gereint's death in 501, when *'Port and his two sons, Bieda and Maegla, came to Britain at the place called Llongborth, and slew a young Welshman, a very noble man.'* Some think, following Bede's mis-dating of the coming of the Saxons by 20 years, that this battle was actually fought in 480. Others believe that it was fought in 510. Welsh tradition places Llongborth at Penbryn beach, near Aberporth in Cardigan rather than Portsmouth. (Llongborth means 'harbour' in Welsh). A farm inland is called Perth Geraint (at Bedd Geraint, Geraint's Grave) where he was said to be buried after the battle. Nearby is a standing stone inscribed *'Corbalengi iacit Ordovs'* denoting Corbalengus of the Ordovices tribe. In this parish John Jones wrote that there is a Llech yr Ochain (the Stone of Grief), near a well named Ffynnon Waedog (the Bloody Well). However, Barber and Pykitt place the battle on the Severn Estuary, near Magor (and Port-is-Coed, or Porthskewett to where Geraint moved his court). Merthyr Gerein (Geraint's Martyrdom, or Shrine) was an ancient chapel on a hillock known as Chapel Tump near Magor.

Geraint may have held lands in Wales as well as the West Country, as there was a castle ruin named Dyngeraint (Dinas Geraint). Just seven miles from Penbryn is Cilgerran (Geraint's Retreat), with its magnificent castle overlooking a bend in the River Teifi. Provisions could be brought by boat to this site from Aberteifi (Cardigan). Cilgerran castle was known as Dyngeraint up to 1130 when Gilbert de Clare, first Earl of Pembroke, completed his Norman castle there.

Some claim that Geraint was the grandfather of Gildas, and of Geraint who is mentioned in the Life of Teilo. A cousin or kinsman of Arthur, in legend Geraint defeated Edern ap Nudd in revenge for his slight on Gwenhwyfar (Guinevere), and married Enid, the daughter of Yniwl Iarll. In Arthurian legend, it was Geraint who encountered the 'Sparrow-Hawk Knight'. Chretien de Troyes wrote the mediaeval poem 'Erec and Enide' about Geraint's marriage. Geraint's son Cado carried on fighting the Saxons for Arthur after his father's death.

* Another King Geraint of Domnonia was supposed to have founded a church at Caerffawydd (Hereford). A letter dated 705 from Bishop Aldhelm (639-709) is still extant to this Geraint, telling the Celtic Church of Domnonia (Somerset, Devon and Cornwall) to comply with the doctrine of Rome as outlined by the Synod of Whitby. This King Geraint (born c. 680) fought the Saxons for twelve years to push them back out of Domnonia.

GERAINT d.556

A grandson of Geraint ab Erbyn, who may be the saint at Pentraeth in Anglesey, once known as Llanfair Bettwes Geraint. He may have died in Teilo's arms. The church is now dedicated to Mary.

KING GERAINT of DOMNONIA d. 598
GERREN, GERRANS, GEREINT, GERONTIUS

He joined with King Mynyddog Mwynfawr of Din-Eidyn (Edinburgh) and King Cynon of Gododdin (Lothian) to fight the Saxons who had taken over Bernicia, and was said to have died at the terrible battle of Cattraeth (Catterick). However, he is also said to have died in Teilo's arms, but Teilo died in 580. He is remembered as Gerrans in Brittany and possibly at Magor in

Gwent. Perhaps Geraint ab Erbyn was buried at Bedd Gereint in Cardigan, and King Geraint at Magor's Chapel Tump (see Geraint ab Erbyn).

Geraint's brother Bledric took over the kingdom and died around 610 or 613 at Caer-Legion (Chester) fighting with the forces of Iago of Gwynedd and Selyf Sarfgaddau of Powys against Aethelfrith. Geraint's son Clemens was then attacked by Cyneglis of Wessex in 614, at Bindon, Devon. However, the High-King Cadwallon of Gwynedd arrived to help push back Cyneglis and King Penda of Mercia.

GERWYN 5th-6th century

The son of Brynach Wyddel who married Corth, a daughter of Brychan. This may be the same saint as Berwyn.

ABBOT GILDAS BADONICUS c. 498 – c. 570 or 583
GILDAS THE WISE, GILDAS-DE-RHUYS OF MORBIHAN, GWELTAS
January 29 (also January 28)
The 'rain-saint' of Brittany – see Cewydd

Gildas, son of Caw, wrote *'De Excidio et Conquesta Britanniae' ('Concerning the Ruin and Conquest of Britain')* in 540, which was extensively used by Bede. His epithet 'Badonicus' came from the fact that he was born in the year of the great victory over the Saxons at Mount Badon. **Gildas was the first British historian**, and it seems more than likely that he wrote 'De Excidio' at Llanilltud Fawr or nearby Caer Worgan. In 'De Excidio' is quoted the letter from the Britons to Aetius in Gaul asking for assistance against the pagans. He drew lessons from the Roman occupation of Britain, and denounced five contemporary 'tyrants', the kings named as Constantinus (Cystennin) of Domnonia (Devon and Cornwall), Aurelius Caninus, Vortipor of Dyfed (whose burial marker has been found), Cuneglasus of Clwyd, North Wales and the basest of them all, Maelgwn Gwynedd (Magloconus). [It is interesting that Blackett and Wilson believe that Aurelius Caninus is Conan Aurelian, also known as Meirchion, who controlled Wiltshire, Gloucester and Somerset. They go on to state that he was the ambitious Conmore or Count Conomorus, who seems to be the same Prince Conmire that usurped the throne of Brittany and whom Armel (Arthur?) fought.]

Gildas wrote accusingly that the decadence of British rulers and clerics had led to Anglo-Saxon successes in Ynys Pridein, the Island of Britain. After the remaining Roman troops left in 410 to protect the Empire in Europe, the Romanised Celts of the island were increasingly subject to attacks by the Picts of Scotland, Scots of Ireland (Goidels) and Saxons of Germany. During these disintegrating and troubled times, the British were increasingly pushed back westwards into the areas now known as Strathclyde, Cumbria, Wales and the West of England. The brunt of the attacks on Celtic Wales in this period were from the sea-borne Goidels, and from the Germanic tribes pushing ever westwards.

Gildas was taught (with David, Paul and Samson) by St Illtud at Llanilltud Fawr, and visited Ireland, influencing the development of its church. The Irish High King, Ainmire was so concerned about the decline of Christianity in Ireland that he had requested Gildas to organise its revival in 570. Gildas took monks from St David's (Menevia) and Llancarfan to carry out the task, including (his brother?) St Aidan, who joined the King of Leinster's retinue. Gildas was known as **'the second apostle of Ireland.'** St Columbanus wrote to Pope Gregory the Great about *'Gildas auctor'* who was asked to give advice on church doctrine to *'Vennianus auctor'* (probably Finnian of Clonard). Finnian founded the monastic order in Ireland before his death in 548. Cadog possibly refused to arbitrate between Gildas and David for the see of Menevia. Cadog went with Gildas to Ronech and Echni (Steep Holm* and Flat Holm). Possibly the wild leek and entire-leaved paeony still found there are remnants of these early monastic settlements. On Steep Holm, where Gildas is said to have stayed, there is a well and chapel, and he lived on birds' eggs and fish. In 530-534 he stayed at Glastonbury, where he was said to have arbitrated in a dispute between Arthur, and King Melwas of Somerset who had taken Gwenwyfar – he halted Arthur's siege.

He returned when he heard that his eldest brother Huail (Hywel) had been killed by King Arthur**. He was reconciled with Arthur, who asked for his pardon, then went to Armorica for ten years where it is claimed that he wrote his 'Epistle' admonishing the British kings for their vices***. There are also claims that it was written in Glastonbury around 540-544. It certainly seems to date from around the time of Camlan and Arthur's possible death. When Gildas returned from Brittany, Cadog asked him to direct the studies in Llancarfan for a year. Like Cadog, he then went to a small island (perhaps Flat or Steep Holm, or even Barri Island), intending to spend the rest of his days in prayer, but was disturbed by pirates. His lack of reference to Arthur is legendarily excused by the story that he threw the pages concerning the King into the sea after Huail's death. However, it could be that the main purpose of the book was to chastise the retreating Welsh chiefs rather than praising the good who fought for their country. There is also doubt that Arthur was present at Badon Hill – 498 may be too early, and it seems that Ambrosius led the British forces, possibly assisted by another chieftain called Arthmael. Arthur may have been around 16 at this time, probably old enough to fight (when life expectancy was far shorter) but too young to assume any real battle command.

According to Breton tradition Gildas ended his days in Brittany, founding the monastery near Rhuys near Morbihan, and dying on the Island of Houat. Gildas-de-Rhuys neighbours Saint Armel, which again shows his links with Arthur. Exiled from Paris, Pierre Abelard was abbot at Gildas-de-Rhuys in 1126, writing to Heloise *'I live in a wild country where every day brings new perils'*. Showing remarkable acuity, he quickly fled as he realised that his brother monks were trying to poison him.

On the Gulf of Morbihan Gildas was known as a 'Breton' monk called Gweltas, and there is a 'Bonnes Fontaine' under the Grand Mont where his Romanesque abbey-church is situated. This well is where Gildas first stepped on the mainland. The Rhuys Peninsula, 17 miles south of Vannes, has an exceptionally mild climate, and was renowned for its wine and its 6th century monastery. The Ile St Gildas, off Treguier on the Cotes-d'Armor, has St Gildas' Chapel, two dolmens and a shrine to St Roch. In 919, because of Viking raids the monks at Rhuys fled to Locmine with the body of Gildas. The Isle of Houat, off Quiberon in Brittany, also has a church dedicated to St Gildas. With fellow Welsh saints Herve and Eloi, prayers were given to Gildas in Brittany for sick horses. His feast day is still celebrated in Vannes, and in Carhaix his festival has assumed the character of Cerwydd's and is a fateful rain-day. Some other dedications include St Gildas south of Chateaulin, St Gildas-des-Bois north of St Nazaire, St Gueltas between Lamballe and Plancoat, and St Gildas north of Carhaix-Plouguer.

Llanildas near Llanilltud Fawr became Y Wig Fawr (The Great Wood) and is now known as Wick. It seems a pity that our first historian is not remembered in his own country, and perhaps Wick could re-assume its original name. His brothers were said in his Life to be St Allgo

(Allectus), St Eugrad (Egreas), St Maelog, Guillin and he had a sister Peithien (Peteona). Old Welsh sources claim he had five sons, Cenydd, Maidoc (Aidan), Dolgan, Nwython and Gwynno. The sons of St Cenydd were St Ffili and St Ufelwy.

A fragment of one of his letters remains:
'*Abstinence from bodily food is useless without charity. Those who do not fast unduly or abstain overmuch from God's creation, while being careful in the sight of God to preserve within them a clean heart (on which, as they know, their life ultimately depends), are better than those who do not eat flesh or take pleasure in the food of this world, or travel in carriages or on horseback, and so regard themselves as superior to the rest of men: to these **death has entered through the windows of their pride.**'*

He also left a 'lorica', a kind of charm prayer for every part of the human body, asking for protection of the teeth, tongue, mouth, throat, uvula, windpipe, root of tongue, etc., etc. Gildas' 'Saying of the Wise' is: 'fortune will never favour the hateful'. It is well worth quoting parts of 'De Excidio' to show the feeling with which Gildas wrote of his times. Interestingly he calls Vortigern 'unlucky' in the first extract (from Chapters 23 and 24), when he invited the Saxons into Kent to act as mercenaries, against the constant attacks from Ireland and Scotland. In the second extract, from Chapter 25, we can see his great admiration for Emrys Wledig, Ambrosius Aurelianus, who pushed back the ravaging Saxons for a time:

'*They first landed on the eastern side of the island, by the invitation of the unlucky king, and there fixed their sharp talons, apparently to fight in favour of the island, but alas ! more truly against it. Their mother-land, finding her first brood thus successful, sends forth a larger company of her wolfish offspring, which sailing over, join themselves to their bastard-born comrades. From that time the germ of iniquity and the root of contention planted their poison amongst us, as we deserved, and shot forth into leaves and branches*' . . . '*For the fire of vengeance, justly kindled by former crimes, spread from sea to sea, fed by the hands of our foes in the east, and did not cease, until, destroying the neighbouring towns and lands, it reached the other side of the island, and dipped its red and savage tongue in the western ocean . . .*

So that all the columns were levelled with the ground by the frequent strokes of the battering-ram, all the husbandmen routed, together with their bishops, priests and people, while the sword gleamed, and the flames crackled around them on every side. Lamentable to behold, in the midst of the streets lay the tops of lofty towers, tumbled to the ground, stones of high walls, holy altars, fragments of human bodies, covered with livid clots of coagulated blood, looking as if they had been squeezed together in a press; and with no chance of being buried, save in the ruins of the houses, or in the ravening bellies of wild beasts and birds; with reverence be it spoken for their blessed souls, if, indeed, there were so many found who were carried, at that time, into the high heaven by the holy angels. So entirely had the vintage, once so fine, degenerated and become bitter, that, in the words of the prophet, there was hardly a grape or ear of corn to be seen where the husbandman had turned his back.'

'*Some, therefore, of the miserable remnant, being taken in the mountains, were murdered in great numbers; others, constrained by famine, came and yielded themselves to be slaves for ever to their foes, running the risk of being instantly slain, which truly was the greatest favour which could be offered them; some others passed beyond the seas with loud lamentations instead of the voice of exhortation. "Thou hast given us as sheep to be slaughtered, and among the Gentiles hast thou dispersed us." Others, committing the safeguard of their lives, which were in continual jeopardy, to the mountains, precipices, thickly wooded forests, and to the rocks of the seas (albeit with trembling hearts), remained still in the country. But in the* meanwhile, an opportunity happening, when these most cruel robbers were returned home, the poor remnants of our nation (to whom flocked from divers places round about our miserable countrymen as fast as bees to their hives, for fear of an ensuing storm), being strengthened by God, calling upon him with all their hearts, as the poet says, - "With their unnumbered vows they burden Heaven," that they might not be brought to utter destruction, took arms under the conduct of Ambrosius Aurelianus, a modest man, who of all the Roman nation was then alone in the confusion of this troubled period left alive. His parents, who for their merit were adorned with the purple, had been slain in these same broils, and now his progeny in these our days, although shamefully degenerated from the worthiness of our ancestors, provoke to battle their cruel conquerors, and by the goodness of our Lord obtain the victory.' It is hardly surprising from this contemporary writing, that the Celtic Church refused to evangelise the Saxons in later years, incurring the wrath of Bede.

Gildas also wrote 'Ormesta Britanniae', and other works. Some astute detective work in 'The Dictionary of Welsh National Biography' places 504 as the last possible date for the Battle of Badon, which coincided with Gildas' birth, with a possible birthdate for Gildas of 500, the writing of De Excidio in 545 (before the death of Maelgwn Gwynedd), and the death of Gildas around 570.

* On Steep Holm, on the beach near the monastery ruins, was found a Celtic 'god-head', whose 'shouting aspect' signifies a symbol of life. It could have been placed in a wall as a talisman or fixed into the mouth of an island spring which emerges from the cliff face. It may have been venerated by some of the Celtic soldiers who made up the Roman garrison there. Steep Holm was known as Ronech in Gildas' time, and Flat Holm as Echni. Barri (Ynys Peirio) was also a hermit island. Gildas and Cadoc probably used the Roman ruins on Steep Holm as a base for their hermitage. They were said to live on fish and the eggs of sea-birds. The edible plant known as Alexanders still grows on the island, as do wild leeks and nettles, which would have complemented their diet. A few times a year one can travel to Steep Holm by the world's last ocean-going paddle-steamer, and walk around for a few hours. Flat Holm can be reached most days of the summer from Barri harbour.

The Saxons renamed the islands Bradanreolice and Steopanreolice ('Broad', and 'Steep Place of Burial'). Isolated offshore islands around Wales were regarded as sacred burial sites by the early Welsh. John Leland (c.1506-1552) quoted from an old document, now lost, that Saint Cadoc the Wise stayed on Flat Holm (*'Echin'*, sic) and Gildas on Steep Holm (*'Ronnet'*, sic) respectively. Leland also states that on Steep Holm Gildas began writing 'De Excidio'. There was a Roman signal station upon Steep Holm, in sight of the Roman harbour of Cardiff, and also within site of the Roman supply base of Classis Britannica, the Roman fleet, at Cold Knap in Barri. This latter Roman naval defence base, protecting the Channel from Irish attacks, is of great historical importance, and some remains can still be seen.

Steep Holm has the remains of a mediaeval priory, and Mary Collier's 1972 book on the 'Ghosts of Dorset, Devon and Somerset' repeats a 19th century recollection: *"But although the religious house at Glastonbury was once his home, his ghost haunts Steep Holme. Maybe he loved the little island. He is not seen, but on moonlight nights he is heard nearby the ruin of the Priory, just the slow footsteps of somebody walking along, which are called 'St Gilda's Tread'."* The '*tread*' has also been heard throughout the 20th century, a noise like the 'slow crunching of gravel', although there are no gravel paths, and the reports predate the introduction of Muntjac deer in 1977.

** In Ruthin today, Maen Huail in St Peter's Square is supposed to be the stone upon which Huail was executed by Arthur. It seems that Arthur may have given lands to atone for this deed, as Gallgo, Maelog, Eugrad and Peithien all had foundations in Radnorshire. Rowland's 'Mona Antiqua' makes Caw the father-in-law of Modred, which again would place Gildas with his kinsmen antipathetic to Arthur.

*** The tone of Gildas' attack upon the remaining kings of the British people can be seen in the following extract:

Britain has kings, but they are tyrants; she has judges, but unrighteous ones; generally engaged in plunder and rapine, but always preying on the innocent; whenever they exert themselves to avenge or protect, it is sure to be in favour of robbers and criminals; they have an abundance of wives, yet are they addicted to fornication and adultery; they are ever ready to take oaths, and as often perjure themselves; they make a vow and almost immediately act falsely; they make war, but their wars are against their countrymen, and are unjust ones; they rigorously prosecute thieves throughout their country, but those who sit with them at table are robbers, and they not only cherish but reward them; they give alms plentifully, but in contrast to this is a whole mountain of crimes which they have committed; they sit on the seat of justice, but rarely seek for the rule of right judgment; they despise the innocent and the humble, but seize every occasion of exalting to the utmost the bloody-minded, the proud, murderers, the concubines and adulterers, enemies of God, who ought to be utterly destroyed and their names forgotten. They have many prisoners in their gaols, loaded with chains, but this is done in treachery rather than in just punishment for crimes . . .'

GIRALDUS CAMBRENSIS 1146? - 1223
GERALD OF WALES

Not a saint, but an extremely important figure in Welsh church (and social) history. His father was William of Manorbier, and his mother was Angharad, the daughter of Gerald de Windsor and the famous Nest. He was educated by his uncle David Fitzgerald at St David's, at St Peter's Gloucester, then at the University of Paris. As archdeacon of Brecon, he was the favourite to succeed his uncle at St David's in 1176, but Henry II refused to recognize his nomination by the Welsh canons and enforced the election of the Englishman, Peter of Lee. Bitterly disappointed, Giraldus returned to France and became a lecturer in the University of Paris. He mediated in a dispute between Rhys ap Gruffydd and the king, and accompanied Prince John to Ireland in 1185, when he wrote 'Expugnatio Hibernica' and 'Topographica Hibernica.' 1188 sees him with Archbishop Baldwin touring Wales to recruit for the Crusade, the journey of which is recounted in 'Itinerarium Cambriae'. In 1194 he completed 'Descriptio Cambriae', left the Crown service and went to Lincoln to further his studies.

Giraldus was offered the bishoprics of Llandaf and Bangor, and those of Ferns and Leighlin in Ireland, but he only wanted St David's. On the death of Peter de Lee in 1198, yet again the King and the Archbishop of Canterbury opposed the appointment of Giraldus, although the chapter wanted him to succeed. The dispute widened to one where Giraldus wanted the recognition of St David's as a metropolitan see separate from Canterbury, and three times in five years Giraldus took the arduous journey to Rome to see the Pope and plead this case. His Welshness, energy, learning and intelligence were seen as a dangerous combination by the Plantagenets, a French-speaking illiterate dynasty not noted for subtlety. Giraldus never succeeded in his ambition, but was buried in St David's. He appears to have been a friend of Walter Map and Geoffrey of Monmouth, and is one of the more attractive figures in British history.

GISTLIANUS 5th century
GUISTILIANUS, GWESLAN, GWESTLAN
March 2 and 4

The son of Cynyr (Gynyr), said to be bishop of Menevia before David, his nephew. His sisters were Non and Gwen. According to Rhygyfarch's 'Life of David', Guistilianus instructed David at Hen Fynyw. Euros Bowen noted the site of Hen Fynyw in Ceredigion as *'typical of so many such monasteries, around the coasts of Wales in the time of David. We note the narrow steep-sided valley running down off the coastal plateau with the monastic site in the upper reaches of the valley (like Llanilltud Fawr), where the land opens out, set in an excellent position by way of the narrow valley cleft to maintain direct communication with the coast. The sea, we recall, was the chief means of movement and the highway of traffic for people and goods at this time.'* The sea was also a source of potential attack, which is why all the early churches were 'hidden' from the view of boats. There was a Ffynnon Gwestlan near St David's, near Ffynnon Eluid. The saints prayed during a drought and these wells formed, which cured the blind, crippled and diseased. It is not known where the wells are now.

On March 4, Gwestlan's Day in 1800, was born the notable pacifist, Chartist, socialist, nationalist, free-thinking, vegetarian, libidinist doctor and druid who pioneered cremation in Europe, Wiliam Price of Llantrisant.

GLASTONBURY

One of the most famous hoaxes in British history was the Arthurian connection with Glastonbury. The Abbey had burned to the ground in 1184, and Henry II died five years later. Abbot Henry de Sully needed a miracle to restore his incomes from pilgrims and rebuild his church. Thus a leaden cross was found, inscribed, according to Giraldus Cambrensis *'Here in the Isle of Avalon lies buried the renowned King Arthur, with Guinevere, his second wife.'* Naturally next to it were two coffins, and the lage numbers of pilgrims to see the holy relics financed a new Glastonbury. The French Cluniac monks, as well as Arthur's tomb, claimed to have the bodies of the saints Joseph of Arimathea, Patrick, Gildas and David, and claimed that they had converted Beon, Patrick's successor as Irish primate. On Joseph of Arimathea's 'tomb' was inscribed *'I came to the Britons after I buried Christ. I taught. I rest.'*

Henry de Sully's family, inspired by their success at Glastonbury, went on to discover the Holy Blood of Christ in two lead caskets, inside a fig tree in France. This was at the Norman abbey of Fecamp, which also then gained tremendous wealth from influxes of pilgrims from all over Europe. Through the ages, corruption has affected religious leaders as much as secular ones. A recent book claims that the 'True Cross' is hidden in Wales – the Welsh problem is that it has never been able to market itself properly. In Adrian Gilbert's 'The Holy Kingdom' it is claimed that the True Cross is in a sealed cave at Nevern, where there are the crosses of Maelgwn Gwynedd, King Hywell Dda and Vortimer the Blessed. In the book it is claimed that Edward I after vanquishing Llywelyn in 1282, demanded a piece of the True Cross, as carried by Arthur at Badon Hill. It is said that a forgery was given him in a silver casket, and Edward II gave it to his favourite Piers Gaveston from where it possibly passed to the Templars in France.

Alphabetical Listing of the Saints of Wales and Religious Events

GLYWYS 6th century
GLUVIAS, CLIVIS, GLYWYS CERNYW
May 3

The son of Gwynlliw Filwr, king of Gwent, and brother of Cadog. This Welsh monk was said to be the nephew of St Petroc, and is the patron of St Gluvias, near Penryn in Cornwall. He was also identified with Coedkernew (Coed Cernyw) in Gwent and with Merthyr Clivis, mentioned in the Book of Llandaf, where he may have been martyred (Newton Nottage). Merthyr means either holy shrine or place of martyrdom. St Glywys may be buried in St Roque's Chapel at Merthyr Mawr, according to the smaller Celtic stone there (see Samson and Teilo). In St Roques Chapel a four feet high sandstone block was inscribed CONBELANI (sketched by Edward Lhuyd in 1697). The cross was erected by him, *'for his soul, for Saint Glywys and his brother and father.'* More carved crosses are in St Teilo's Church at Merthyr Mawr. Another stone, now in the National Museum of Wales, was found near Ogmore Castle and links Glywys to his cousin Arthur: *'Be it known to all that Arthmail has given this field to God, to Glywys and to Nertart and to Bishop Fili.'* Nertart may have been the wife of Glywys.

May 3 was also Crouchmas Day. Gluvias in Cornwall celebrated the saint on the first Sunday in May.

GLYWYS ap TEGID 5th - 6th century

The grandfather of Glywys Cernyw, King Glywys ap Tegid was said to have founded Machen, and owned the lands between the rivers Tawe and Usk known as Glywyssing. This area between Swansea and Usk has sometimes been used as a synonym for Morganwg (Glamorgan) but that early kingdom (formerly the territory of the Silures) also included Gwent. Some ot it was known as Cernyw. His son was Gwynlliw Filwr.

GNAWAN 6th century
GNAVAN

A disciple brought back from Ireland by Cadog to Llancarfan (with Ffinnian and Macmoil) after his evangelical visit with Gildas. Manerwawan is now Manorowen in Pembroke. There is also a Kilnawan near Llanboidy, and Kilawen at St Issell's near Tenby. This is probably the abbot 'Gnouan' noted at Cadoc's altar at Llancarfan.

GOFOR (see MYFOR)

This saint is probably Myfor, but according to Iolo Morganwg Gofor was the patron of Lanover, now dedicated to Bartholomew, in Monmouth. There is a large tombstone there with a poorly carved cross. There were also eight wells, all flowing into a bath known as Ffynnon Over or Gofor. Gwyl Ofer was celebrated on May 9, but the Book of Llandaf informs us that the previous spelling of Llanover was Lanmouor, which gives us Myfor as the saint. Previous spellings of Merthyr Mawr also are Merthyr Myour, Mouor and Momor.

GOLEU 5th – 6th century
GOLEUDDYDD

Goleuddydd ap Brychan is given in old manuscripts as the founder of Llanhesgyn in Glamorgan. Goleuddydd means 'perfect day.' (See Nefydd ferch Brychan.)

GONERI 6th century
GONERY
April 4, 7 (also July 18, 19)

A Briton who went to Brittany, and who induced Tudwal to sail with him there. They crossed in a 'stone' boat (probably referring to a portable stone altar), and Goneril is invoked by Breton sailors. Buried at Plougrescent, he is remembered at churches at St Gonery near Pontivy, Langoat, Locarn and chapels at Plougras and Ploezal. He may be the same person as Gwynnoro, one of the five saints of Llanpumsaint.

GORAN 5th century?
GWRAN
April 7

Possibly Gwran ap Cunedda, with a holy well in Bodmin churchyard. There is also a Goran near St Austell.

BISHOP GOULVEN 6th century
July 1, 7, 8

Of British parents, Glaudan and Gologwen, who emigrated to Leon in Brittany, he is remembered at Goulien and has a holy well at Goulven.

GOVAN 6th century
GOWAN GOFAN, GAVAN, GOBAN, GAWAIN?
Feast Day June 20 (also March 26)

Between Pembroke and Castlemartin, near the famous Bosherston Lakes, is a tiny chapel built into the sea-cliffs. Old legends link the site with Gawain, King Arthur's nephew, who was killed by Sir Lancelot and buried here. (A case has been made for Maelgwn Gwynedd being Sir Lancelot). Other sources say that the Irish Abbot of Dairinis Monastery, County Wexford, was chased here by pirates in the sixth century, and spent the remainder of his life ministering to local people in Dyfed. The hermit's chapel is similar to the cell described in Bede's 'Life of Cuthbert', where only the sky is visible. The fresh water well is now dry and covered with a stone. In the nearby cliffs are red clays that are said to heal skin lesions.

At the back of the chapel, Bell Rock is supposed to have his magical silver bell embedded in it. There is also a cleft in Bell Rock, which Govan is said to have backed into to escape from pirates. The rock closed behind him and protected him, and ridges in the opening are said to have been caused by the impressions of his ribs. If one squeezes inside the fissure, it is claimed that one may experience a feeling of closeness to God and nature. It is also said that one's wishes will all come true within a year, as long as one is firm and decisive and turn around each time a wish is made. (This may be in modern terminology the power of positive thinking, in 'neuro-linguistic programming' – *'if you always do what you've always done, you'll always get what you always got.'*) He seems to have been a disciple of Elfyw/Ailbe, and is probably not the saint associated with Llangovan in Monmouthshire.

The spring near the entrance to his chapel was a healing well, and the waters were traditionally sipped from a limpet shell. The well just below the chapel is now dry, but used to cure rheumatism, failing eye-sight and lameness. A poultice was made from the red clay in the 160 foot high cliffs here, mixed with holy water and applied. Those cured used to leave their crutches on the altar as testimony to the saint's miraculous water. There are 52 steps down to the well, and like many other stairways, it is said that the number counted always varies going up compared to coming down.

Gwalchmai ap Gwyar was one of Arthur's knights, known in English as Gawain and in French as Gauvain. In Culhwch and Olwen, he is a nephew of Arthur. His horse was Ceingaled ('diamond-hard', translated in French romance to Guingalet) according to the Black Book of Carmarthen. William of Malmesbury wrote that he was buried in Rhos, and there is a commote known as Castell Gwalchmai in Rhos in Dyfed. He features strongly in the Welsh Triads and Arthurian legends, and it was said that he died fighting the traitor Modred. His mother Gwyar was the sister of Arthur, and Gwalchmai was Arthur's nephew and most faithful supporter. Some said that Modred was his foster-brother and others that Modred was the incestuous offspring of Arthur and Gwyar. Gawain's grave was discovered in 1125 at Rhos in Pembrokeshire, near a stream that runs to the sea from Castell Gwalchmai (Walwyn's Castle). In French romances his name changed to Walwen, Gualganus and Gawain.

H. G. Bohn in 1836 says that the tomb of Arthur found at Ross-on-Wye in 1082 was in fact the grave of Gawain, under a fourteen foot sepulchre. *'That place of sculpture still exists under the name of St Gowen's chapel.'*

GRAID
GREAIT

A saint buried on Ynys Enlli, the Isle of 20,000 Saints.

GREDFYW 6th century
July 6, November 11

Llanllyfni in Carmarthenshire is dedicated to Gredfyw ab Ithel Hael, not St Rhedyw. At the covered well, Ffynnon Redyw, infants were baptised. The saint is said to be buried at Bedd Rhedyw at Llanllyfni. There is a defaced effigy to him in the church, and a nearby house called Eisteddfa Redyw and a cottage named Tyddyn Rhedyw. His Wake was celebrated by a fair where one could buy harvest implements, horses and cattle, and was held on July 6, but Gwyl Redyw was November 11 (see Redyw).

GREDIFAL 6th century
GREDIFAEL
November 13, 14, 22 or 30

Gredifael ab Ithael Hael was with his brother Fflewyn appointed superintendent of Tygwyn ar Daf (Whitland), the monastery of Paulinus. He founded Penymynydd in Anglesey, which was formerly known as Llanredifael, and is near his brother Fflewyn's foundation. Bedd Gredifael is in the church, and a sick person had to lie on it for a night to be cured of illness. At Ffynnon Gredifael in nearby Cae Gredifael, one picked one's warts with a pin until they bled, then threw the pin into the well to cure them.

ANN GRIFFITHS 1776-1805
August 12

Given this Holy Day by the Church in Wales, she was notable hymn-writer from Dolwar Fach, Llanfihangel-yng-Ngwynfa, Montgomery. She converted to Methodism in 1797, married in 1804, and died after the birth of a child in 1805. Her cottage can be visited at Llanfihangel, and she is commemorated in the church. Griffiths wrote hymns which she recited to her maid, Ruth Evans. When Evans married John Hughes, he wrote them down in two notebooks which he passed on to Thomas Charles of Bala. They were published in 1805 and in later years. The hymns are characterised by deep religious and mystical feeling and the use of bold metaphors. For more information on Ann Griffiths, see the author's 'The A to Z of Wales and the Welsh', and the forthcoming '100 Great Welsh Women.'

DAVID GRIFFITHS 1792-1863

Unlike his fellow-missionaries, David Johns (q.v.) and David Jones (q.v.), Griffiths is not given a Holy Day by the Church in Wales, but is worth noting in this book. Born at Glanmeilwch near Gwynfe in Carmarthen, he began to preach aged 20, in 1812. In 1814 he attended Wrexham Academy and then in 1817 went to Missionary College in Gosport. He and his wife sailed for Madagascar in 1820, arriving in 1821. He evangelised on the island for 15 years, despite persecution. He was condemned to death, but the sentence was commuted on his paying a ransom and quitting Madagascar. All his possessions and property were confiscated. Griffiths then spent time on the African coast, helping Christians escape from the island, before returning to Wales and settling in Hay-on-Wye in 1842. He helped translate the Bible and 'A Pilgrim's Progress' into Malagasy, as well as writing a Malagasy grammar, a hymn book, catechisms and 'Hanes Madagascar' ('A History of Madagascar'). After moving to Machynlleth, this saintly man died upon March 21st, and is buried in Capel y Graig graveyard.

A book should be written upon Welsh missionaries in India, Africa and across the world. David Griffith's daughter Jane married Dr Griffith John (1831-1912), a Swansea man who wished to go to Madagascar, but was sent to China instead.They arrived in Shanghai in 1855, visited Soochow, planted Christian stations in Sung Kiang and founded a permanent base in Hankow. In 1868 alone he travelled 3000 miles touring the provinces. Jane Griffiths died in 1873, returning to China from a visit home. Griffith John published many tracts, and wrote the New Testament in the Wen-Li dialect. Elected chairman of the Congregational Union of England and Wales in 1888, he declined the offer. In 1889 the University of Edinburgh conferred a D.D. upon him, and in 1905 he celebrated his fifty-year Jubilee at Hankow. Through ill-health,

Griffiths returned to Wales, but was in China again in 1907. Returning to Britain in 1912, he died in London on July 25th, and is buried in Sketty, Swansea. The University of Wales had resolved to give him a D.D. in 1911, but bureaucracy prevaricated and he died before its award. Some things never change.

GUALCH 6th century
GWALCH, GWAHELES, GWALEHES, GWALCHES

According to Camden, the Holm islands were famous for the '*Burial of Gualch a Britton of Great piety whose disciple Barruk gave his name to Barry Isle on ye Opposite Welsh Shore.*' There seem to have been burial sites on both Flat Holm (Echni) and Steep Holm (Ronech - see Gildas). He died with Baruc when sent back by Cadog to fetch his 'enchiridon' (holy manual) from Echni. A simple tombstone found on Flat Holm in the 19th century was conjectured to be his.

BISHOP GUDWAL d. 603
GURVAL, GALLWELL, GODWALD
June 6 (in Cornwall, June 4 or 7)

This Celtic abbot may have come from Ewyas (Hereford and Worcester) as he was venerated at Worcester cathedral and the church at Finstall is dedicated to him. In Cornwall, Gulval church is also a dedication. With Cadog, he took monks to Brittany and evangelised Finistere. They were probably forced to leave Wales by the Yellow Plague of 547. His hermitage and monastery seem to be on the islands of Locoal and Guer near Morbihan. Apart from his church near Penzance, some scholars believe that Trewidwal near St Dogmaels was connected with him. He is associated with Flanders, where he spent the latter part of his life. According to Cressy, the feast of the translation of his body to the monastery of Ghent is celebrated on the third day before the Nones of December. Gudwal was claimed as the first bishop of St Malo. He is possibly the same saint as Gurwal.

GUENHAF

The wife of Usyllt (Enlleu) and mother of Teilo, remembered at Penally, which was previously known as Llan Geneu (also as Eglwys Gunniau or Eglwys Guiniau). This is where Teilo was born (see Tegfedd, who may be the same woman).

GUINGUINUS 6th century

A disciple of Dyfrig, a member of the clergy who appointed Euddogwy as Bishop of Llandaff.

GURGUARE 6th century

A disciple of Gwernabui at Welsh Bicknor (see Dyfrig), who founded Lann Enniaun, now called Llandogo in Monmouth.

GURMAET 6th century

A companion who accompanied Teilo on his return from Brittany, and who founded a church on land given by Rhydderch ab Iestin to Llandaf at Llandeilo'r Fan in Brecon. The church was named Languruaet or Llangurmaet (see Llywel).

GURWAL 6th century
June 6, 12

A Briton related to Samson and Malo, who went to Guer near Ploermel. It seems that he is the same person as Gudwal.

GWAINERTH

Lann Sant Guainnerth is now St Weonards in Monmouth.

GWALCHMAI see GWYAR, GOVAN and GWAWR

GWARTHAN 6th century
GUARCHAN

The son of Dunawd ap Pabo Post Prydain, he was killed at Cattraeth. 'Y Gododin' mentions him as '*Guarchan ap Dwywei*' (his mother), '*of gallant bravery.*' He helped establish the monastery at Bangor-is-Coed.

GWAWR 5th – 6th century
JULIA

Probably a grand-daughter of Brychan, married to Elidyr Lydanwyn, and the mother of Llywarch Hen. Gwawr (Latinized into Julia) means '*the hue of dawn*'.

GWAWR FERCH CEREDIG AP CUNEDDA WLEDIG 5th – 6th century

The mother of Gwynlliw Filwr and grandmother of Cadog. In some stories she seems to associated with the 'Gwyar' who is the mother of Gwalchmai/Gawain (see Govan).

GWBERT 6th century

One of the 'peregrini', wandering saints who crossed to Cornwall and Brittany. Doble demonstrated that Gwbert was one of a number of Welsh saints commemorated in the New Quay, Padstow and Bodmin area of mid-Cornwall, who were all somehow connected to each other. The saints included Briog, Cadoc, Carantoc, Collen, Congar, Gwbert, Hernin, Petroc and Mawgan. All have church dedications in Wales, most also in Brittany, and four are commemorated in Somerset. Gwbert on the Cardiganshire coast is near the foundations of Llangrannog (Carannog) and Llandyfriog (Briog). Near Gwbert is a cave known as Ogo'r Eglwys, Church Cave. Gwbert lies in Ferwig parish, dedicated to Pedrog.

GWEIRYDD AP BROCHFAEL ninth century

This King of Glamorgan ruled through an age of *'calamitous wickedness'*. Iolo Morganwg claimed that he built Llanweirydd, now called Caerau, in western Cardiff. The church, on the site of a Roman camp inside a hillfort, is now dedicated to Mary, and in grave danger of demolition. Perhaps the quarry site known as Llyswerry, just north of Aberddawen (Aberthaw) was his court. (See Gwerydd).

GWEN OF CORNWALL d. 544
WENNA, WENEP, WENN, WENNAP, WYNUP
October 18

Possibly one of Brychan's children, or more probably the daughter of Cynyr and sister of Banhadlwen. She founded Lanwenep, now Gwennap in Cornwall. St Wenn in Cornwall also commemorates her, as does Morval church near East Looe in the same county. The wife of King Selyf of Cornwall and mother of Cybi, her sister was said to be Non, David's mother.

GWEN TIERBRON 5th – 6th century
GWEN ferch EMYR LLYDAW, WITA, CANDIDA
June 1

The patroness of nursing mothers, Gwen took on the attributes of a former Celtic goddess, and was known throughout Britain as Candida, Wita or White. Nursing mothers used to offer flax and a distaff to her in the prayer for adequate nursing milk for their babies. However, many of her statues were destroyed by puritanical Breton priests in the 1870's. 'Tier bron' means 'three breasted', the traditional mark of a witch or of a spiritual woman. However, the Celts used this term when a woman had children by different husbands, so the epithet *'four-breasted'* is also known. A coffin attributed to Albanus, or White (Gwen is Welsh for white) at Whitchurch Canonicorum in Dorset was opened in 1900. The bones were those of a 40-year-old woman. By Eneas Lydewig she bore St Cadfan. Then by Fracan, Gwen bore the saints Iago, Gwethenoc and Winwaloe (Gwenole).

GWEN 6th century
GWENLLIAN*, GWENDELINE, GWENDOLINE, GWENHWYFAR?
October 18

A grand-daughter of Brychan, wife of Llyr Merini and said to be the mother of Caradog Freichfras. She was buried at Talgarth** in Brecon, and was possibly murdered by Saxons. She has also been identified as the Gwenhwyfar (Guinevere) who married Arthur (various accounts give Arthur three marriages to women named Gwenhwyfar). St Gwendoline's Church in Talgarth, her legendary burial place, is also the burial place of Howel Harris, the 'founder' of Welsh Methodism.

Near Peterstone-super-Ely (west of Cardiff), there is the village known of Llanwensan (Llanwensol). There may have been a saint called Gwensol, but it may also be a corruption of Llan-Gwen-Sant. Further research is needed. Llanwyddelan in Montgomery celebrated Gwendolina on October 18, but it is also attributed to Lorcan Wyddel or Gwyddelan.

*Gwenllian is also the name of Wales greatest heroine. Sister of the great Owain Gwynedd (q.v.) and daughter of the warrior Gruffydd ap Cynan, King of Gwynedd, Gwenllian was born in 1098, when Wales was under unceasing attack from the Normans. Owain Gwynedd had succeeded his father in leading the Welsh defence against the Marcher Lords, and Gwenllian married Gruffydd ap Rhys ap Tewdwr and lived in Dinefwr, with her four sons, Morgan, Maelgwn, Mareddud and Rhys. On New Year's Day, 1136, her husband joined other Welsh forces in an attack upon the Norman invaders.

Gruffydd ap Rhys was away in North Wales, trying to gain assistance from Gwenllian's father, Gruffydd ap Cynan. Maurice de Londres, the detested Norman Lord of Cydweli (Kidwelly) attacked the Welsh in South-West Wales. Gwenllian led the few defenders that were left in the area, although her youngest son, Rhys, was only four years old. Giraldus Cambrenis stated that *'she marched like the Queen of the Amazons and a second Penthesileia leading the army'*. In 1136, Gwenllian led her army against the Normans at Cydweli. A Norman army had landed in Glamorgan, and was marching to join the force of Maurice de Londres. Gwenllian stationed her rapidly assembled volunteers at the foot of Mynydd-y-Garreg, with the river Gwendraeth in front of her, and Cydweli Castle just two miles away. She sent some of her forces to delay the oncoming invasion force, but it evaded them and her remaining army was trapped between two Norman attacks.

One son, Morgan, was killed, another, Maelgwn, imprisoned, and towards the end of the fighting, Gwenllian ferch Gruffydd ap Cynan was captured and executed, over the body of her dead son. She had pleaded for mercy, but was beheaded on de Londres' express order. The battlefield is still called Maes Gwenllian, a mile from the castle, and a stone marks the place of her death. She left a 4-year-old son, to be known as The Lord Rhys, the grandson of Rhys ap Tudwr who was slain by the Normans at Brycheiniog in 1093, and the nephew of the great Owain Gwynedd. Her daughter Nest married Ifor ap Meurig, the Welsh hero Ifor Bach who scaled the walls of Cardiff Castle, to kidnap Earl William and regain his stolen lands. Gwenllian's husband partially avenged her death in defeating the Normans at Cardigan a year later.

Dr Andrew Breeze (' Medieval Welsh Literature') believes that the author of 'The Four Branches of the Mabinogion' is Gwenllian, around 1128, making her the *first British woman author*. The battlefield has still not been fully explored, and should be preserved as a heritage site.

Another Gwenllian was the tragic daughter of the 'Last Prince of Wales', Llywelyn ap Gruffydd. After his death by treachery at Builth Wells, Edward I had her kidnapped and incarcerated in Sempringham Convent, Lincolnshire on December 11, 1282. She was Llywelyn's only daughter, as her mother died in giving birth to her. The little girl was taken to ensure that the bloodline of the princes of Gwynedd was exterminated as a focus for Welsh discontent. Gwenllian died fifty-five years later, on June 7 1337, and the Gwenllian Society recently placed a plaque in the ruins of Sempringham. However, Llywelyn's brother Rhodri had been allowed to live in peace in England. His grandson Owain took up the service of the King of France in 1350, and Owain Llawgoch (Red-Hand) became with Bertrand de Guesclin the most famous warrior on the continent of Europe. Once he tried to invade Britain to reclaim the Welsh throne, but was called back when he had taken Guernsey. He was known as Yvain de Gales in Europe and fought from Spain to Switzerland before he was assassinated on the orders of the English Crown. A payment in the Rolls of the Exchequer for December 4, 1378 notes the payment of the fortune of £20 to John Lambe of Scotland *'for killing Owyn de Gales.'* He was thought to have been killed before he married, but research by the Owain Llawgoch Society indicates that he may have married a Breton woman, so the line of the Princes of Gwynedd may still exist in France. The next hero to try and claim Wales was the great Owain Glyndŵr, on the basis of his descent from the House of Powys on his father's side and of Deheubarth on his mother's. His grave is possibly at Monnington Court, after the Scudamore family divulged its secret to the Owain Glyndŵr Society in 1999, around 600 years after Glyndŵr's disappearance.

** Wall notes a St 'Given' martyred at Talgarth in about 492.

GWENAFWY 6th century
GWENABWY
Whit Sunday

A saintly daughter of King Caw, the sister of Cywyllog who married Mordred. Gwennap in Cornwall commemorates her or Gwen of Cornwall. Her feast was Whitsunday. In 'Culhwch and Olwen', it was her son Gwydre who was stabbed by Huail, which caused Arthur to execute him and gain the enmity of Gildas.

GWENASETH late 5th century

The wife of Pabo Post Prydain and daughter of Rhufon ap Cunedda.

GWENDDOLAU see CEIDIO ab ARTHWYS

GWENDYDD and GWAWRDDYDD 5th century

Gwendydd (White, or Holy Day) daughter of Brychan, the wife of Cadell Deyrnllug and mother of St Cyngen. She was remembered at Tywyn in Merioneth, where she was buried with her sister Gwawrddydd. There was a Capel Gwenfydd at Nevern in Pembroke. (See Pasgen).

GWENFAEL 5th – 6th century
GWENFIL

Llanllywenfel is now Llanlleonfel in Brecon, and Gwenfael may have been a 'daughter' or descendant of Brychan. She is associated with Llanillteyrn. A stone was found at Llanillterne (Llanillteyrn), Cardiff, with the words *'Vendumagil hic jacet'*. Another stone reading *'Vinnemagli fili senemagli'* was discovered at Gwytherin in Pembroke. She may be the same saint as Gwenfyl. Iolo Morganwg read the Llanillteyrn stone as *'-ven-duc-arti'*, which may explain the tradition that Gwenhwyfar, one of the wives of Arthur, was buried here, just three miles from Llandaf. A stone in the churchyard at Llanfihangel-yr-Arth, Carmarthen, reads *'Hic Iacit Vlcagnus Filvs Senomagll'* (*'here lies Ulcacinus the son of Senomagli'*), giving a possible link with the Gwytherin stone. A few miles from Padstow is another stone, *'Vlcagni fili Sever-'*.

GWENFAEN 6th century
November 4, 5

A daughter of Pawl Hen. Little is known of this saint of Rhoscolyn (once Llanwenfaen) in Anglesey, but half a mile away are the remains of her holy well inside a small square building, similar to the ruins left by Seiriol and Cybi. The bath has two triangular seats and was used for curing mental illnesses, with two whitespar pebbles being thrown into it. The white stones tradition probably comes down from the cromlech builders via the Celts, where they contain one's name in the afterlife, but also Gwenfaen means 'white stone'.

GWENFOE
November 3

Iolo Morganwg noted this saint at Gwenfo, now Wenvoe, outside Cardiff. William Thomas recorded at the end of April 1793, the death at 92 of Thomas French of Wenvoe, from *'a decline in Age'* – *'a very knowing man in several branches of Knowledge, as clock and watch work, etc. Also a fidler and by trade a Glazier'*. Thomas then notes the deaths of Maud Purcel of Cardiff, aged 105, Frances Lewis of the Hall in Cardiff aged 99, Griffith of Whitehall in Penmark aged 97, Gwenllian Joseph of Merthyr Dyfan aged 94, and John Thomas of St Donats aged 116. Over a period of a few days *'in all the ages of the six is 603 years, a very rare thing.'* They were immediately followed in the diary by the death of Lewis John of Llantrithyd, aged 92.

GWENFREWI 6th - 7th century
WINIFRED, BREWI (Gwen Brewi = Gwenfrewi)
November 3 feast of her death, June 22 feast of her martyrdom (also November 4 and September 19 and 20)

Daughter of Prince Tefydd and Gwenlo. Legend is that she suffered from the unwanted attentions of Prince Caradog ab Alan, from Hawarden (Penarlag in Flintshire). On Midsummer's Day, she fled from him but he caught up with her at the church door before she could gain sanctuary. Because she had spurned him, he cut off her head, whereupon the earth opened up and swallowed him. Her uncle, St Beuno, restored her head to her shoulders and she lived the rest of her days as a nun at Gwytherin in Denbighshire. Where her head fell to the earth at Holywell (Treffynnon, Welltown), a spring of water gushed forth. Some sources say that she became abbess of a nunnery at Holywell, and others that she followed Beuno to Clynnog, then moved on to Bodfari, Henllan and finally became a nun under St Eleri in Gwytherin near Llanrwst. She died fifteen years after her head was restored to her body.

A legend says that Beuno asked Gwenfrewi to send him a rain-proof woollen cloak each year on the feast day of John the Baptist, the anniversary of the day upon which she was brought back to life. She placed it on a stone in the river, and each year the stone would sail down the river and across the sea to her uncle, and reach him in a perfectly dry condition. St Beuno's chapel was erected just above where St Margaret's Chapel now stands in Holywell, but the site is now dedicated to St James.

In 1138, her relics were removed from Gwytherin and enshrined in Shrewsbury's Benedictine Abbey church (Pengwern)*. Partially as a result, St David became patron saint of Wales in her stead. Her cult was confined to North Wales and the Marches, and to Ewyas and Ergyng in South Wales until 1398. From Dafydd ap Llywelyn's gift of 1240, the Cistercian monks at nearby Basingwerk Abbey were in possession of the well and church at Holywell until the Dissolution of the Monasteries. In 1398, Archbishop Roger Walden of Canterbury ordered Winifred's feast to be kept in the province of Canterbury. In 1415 Archbishop Chichele of Canterbury commanded that she be registered as one of the more important feasts, along with those of David and Chad. In Wales, a famous pilgrim route was from St David's through the Cistercian monastery of Ystrad Fflur with its Holy Grail, to Holywell. In 1416 Henry V walked on foot from Shrewsbury to Holywell, to give thanks for his victory at Agincourt. In 1427 Pope Martin V entrusted indulgences to the monks for all who visited the chapel. The Earl of Warwick in 1437 ordered an effigy of himself made of twenty pounds weight of gold be placed at the shrine. In 1439 his wife gave her velvet gown to clothe the image of Gwenfrewi. Edward IV is said to have made a pilgrimage there in 1461 just before the great battle of Towton Moor, and placed some soil on his crown. Richard III paid for a priest to maintain the well until his death at Bosworth in 1485.

Because the cult spread that the well waters cured disease, Henry Tudor's mother, Margaret Beaufort, enclosed it in a stone shrine in 1490. Her son Henry VII had some years before had a lucky escape from Richard III at Mostyn after visiting the shrine. The window he fled through can still be seen. It seems that the shrine was not smashed up during the Dissolution as Margaret was Henry VIII's grandmother, and because the waters were seen as 'medicinal'. Over 1500 Roman Catholics gathered at the well on November 3, 1629. In 1686 King James II and his Queen Mary of Modena visited, desperate for an heir to the throne. Soon after the queen became pregnant. To achieve a wish, they had to duck under the water and kiss the wishing stone, 'Beuno's Pillow', near the steps. Unfortunately for James and the Stuart dynasty, the consequent birth ten months later of a male Catholic heir, hastened his expulsion from England, never to return.

Father Gerard, one of the few men to escape from the Tower of London, bathed in the well on November 3, 1593. In 1605 'Little John' (see Nicholas Owen) made a pilgrimage with the Jesuit Superior, Henry Garnet. Both were executed within two years, as was Edward Oldcorne, who had come to Holywell in 1601 to cure cancer of the tongue. Interestingly, throughout the Reformation and after, pilgrimages never ceased, despite sporadic attempts at suppression. Pilgrims still travel to the well, which has been described in two poems by Gerard Manley Hopkins. It is the best-preserved medieval pilgrimage centre in Britain. Some of the stones in this holy shrine have strange red marks, said to be the blood of Gwenfrewi.

The Welsh bard Tudur Aled of Llansannan (c1465-c1525) wrote:

'In the earth, red-marked stones,
Musk and balm within the world,
A pure white stone with a pure place,
Stones marked with the blood of a white neck.
Which mark endures forever?
The band of her blessed blood.

A shower of tears like rose-hips,
Droplets of Christ,
From the wounds of the Cross;
It is good for a man's body –
To accept tears of blessed water;
Bloody droplets, like water and wine,
Bringing miracles of laughter.
The laughter of the seething sweet water
Is a sign of health – the bells of the water.
A burning stream from the fiery foam,
The powerful support of the Holy Ghost,
The waters of baptism are
The life support of the world,
It is the fountain of the oil of faith.'

Caxton wrote that the well *'heleth al langours and sekenesses as well in men as in bestes'* and in August 1774 Samuel Johnson witnessed people bathing in its waters. He remarked also that it turned no fewer than nineteen mills as Afon Wenfrewi rushed the mile from the spring to the sea. The bell in Holywell's church was dipped in the well, then wrapped in a christening robe, before being mounted, to keep lightning, evil and storms away from the site. The well was the most copious natural spring in Britain, but the rate of flow is now restricted to a fifth of its previous flow into the well. Its flow was 100,000 gallons per minute in 1917, but it was diverted in 1917. The water is a chilly ten degrees Centigrade, all the year round.

Open morning to dusk, pilgrims are expected to pass through the water three times, perhaps a derivation of the old Celtic custom of triple immersion (three was the holy number). By a miracle, the shrine was not destroyed in the reformation, only the sacred images, but a priest remained to guard the well. Not until 1688 did Protestants sack the chapel and expel the guardian priest. However, people continued to use the well and in 1851 and 1887 popes granted indulgences to pilgrims using the well. Unfortunately Gwenfrewi's great tomb and shrine at Shrewsbury were destroyed in the Reformation. Nearby to Holywell was Basingwerk Abbey, whose monks used to guard the well, and it was smashed to its foundations. ** *'Oh Winifred'* was a popular expression in the 1890's, meaning disbelief, and stemming from the reputed miracles at Holywell.

It is fairly certain that Daniel Defoe never went to Wales, but he records the toleration shown to Catholics at Holy Well:
'*The stories of this Well of St Winifred are, that the pious virgin, being ravished and murthered, this healing water sprung out of her body when buried; but this smells too much of the legend, to take up any of my time; the Romanists indeed believe it, as tis evident from their thronging hither to receive the healing sanative virtue of the water, which they do not hope for as it is a medicinal water, but as it is a miraculous water, and heals them by virtue of the intercession and influence of the famous virgin, St Winifred, of which I believe as much as comes to my share ... There is a little town near the well, which may, indeed, be said to have risen from the confluence of the people hither, for almost all the houses are either public houses, or let into lodgings; and the priests that attend there, and are very numerous, appear in disguise. Sometimes they are physicians, sometimes surgeons, sometimes gentlemen, and sometimes patients, or anything as occasion presents ... Nobody takes any notice of them, as to their profession, though they know them well enough, no not the Roman Catholics themselves; but in private, they have their proper oratories in certain places, whither the votaries resort; and*

St Winifred's Chapel and Holy Well.   *CADW: Welsh Historic Monuments. Crown Copyright.*

good manners has prevailed so far, that however the Protestants know who and who's together; no body takes notice of it, or enquires where another goes, or has been gone.' (from 'The Tour of the Whole Island of Great Britain' published anonymously in 3 volumes between 1725 and 1726)

Large pilgrimages were undertaken to the well at Holywell in the 17th century. When a man was found dead near the well in 1603 after denigrating its powers, a local jury brought a verdict of *'death by divine judgement.'* Until recently, when the authorities clamped down, it was customary for those cured to leave their crutches and calipers on the wall at the back of the well. Thousands still take the waters every year, from countries as far as Australia and Canada. More people should know about the shrine – there is nothing like it in Europe – over ***1300 years of unbroken pilgrimage*** has taken place here. We can compare the shrine favourably to Lourdes, dating from a vision by a 14-year-old shepherdess named Bernadette in 1828. From the anti-Semitism of the shrine's early political supporters, via the need for income in a poor part of the Pyrenees, Ruth Harris describes the manipulation by the church for Bernadette to achieve sainthood, and for the place to become a centre of pilgrimage. The following anecdote tells us as much about the 'holiness' of Lourdes as any of the 'glow-in-the-dark' plastic Madonna cigarette-lighters on sale there: *'At the height of the sentimental hysteria surrounding the new shrine of Lourdes in the late 19th century, a priest called Pere Ricard who was visiting the shrine asked for a drink. Not ordinary water – instead, he asked a Lourdes stretcher-bearer*

St Winifred's Statue at her Holywell. © *Wales Tourist Board Photo Library.*

to fill his glass with the infected blood and scabs of sick pilgrims. He made the sign of the Cross and drank it. "The water of the good Mother of Heaven is always delicious", he said with a beatific smile.' (Ruth Harris, 'Lourdes' Penguin Press 1999, from an article by Cristina Odone, 'The Times, April 1, 1999)

One can stay at another St Winifred's Well, hidden away in the woods at Woolston near Oswestry. Her body was taken in the 12th century from its Denbighshire grave by the monks of Shrewsbury Abbey – they believed that more people would receive benefit from her relics being in a greater centre of population, and of course this would bring greater revenues to their abbey (a theme explored by Ellis Peters in her 'Brother Cadfael' stories). The story is that the saint's body was rested at Woolston, where a spring gushed forth, just as it did Flintshire's Holywell. The well has been venerated for centuries, and the innermost pool, with a niche for a statue, is presumably the medieval well chamber. A mediaeval timber well chapel stands over it, which was adapted for use as a Court House until 1824, when it became a cottage. The well had been enlarged to form a bath, open to the general public, but conduct became so riotous that it was closed to them in 1755, together with the ale-houses which had opened nearby. The Woolston well is in the care of the Landmark Trust, and can accommodate two people. Being near to Shrewsbury, Sycharth (Glyndŵr's Court), Wroxeter Roman City, Valle Crucis and Llangollen, it is a perfect place to take a vacation.

It is worthwhile noting one of the lesser-known poems by Gerard Manley Hopkins (1844-1889), a beautiful verse called simply 'St Winefride's Well':
Oh now while skies are blue, now while seas are salt,
  While rushy rains shall fall or brooks shall fleet from fountains,
While sick men shall cast sighs, of sweet health all despairing,
  While blind men's eyes shall thirst after daylight, drafts of daylight
Or deaf ears shall desire that lipmusic that's lost upon them,
While cripples are, while lepers, dancers in dismal limb dance,
  Fallers in dreadful frothpits, waterfearers wild,
Stone, palsy, cancer, cough, lung-wasting, womb not bearing
  Rupture, running sores, what more? in brief, in burden,
As long as men are mortal and God merciful,
  So long to this sweet spot, this leafy lean-over,
This dry dene, now no longer dry nor dumb, but moist and musical
With the uproll and the downcarol of day and night delivering
Water, which keeps thy name, (for not in rock written,
But in pale water, frail water, wild rash and reeling water,
That will not wear a print, that will not stain a pen,
Thy venerable record, virgin, is recorded)
Here to this holy well shall pilgrimages be,
And not from purple Wales only nor from elmy England,
But from beyond seas, Erin, France and Flanders everywhere,
Pilgrims, still pilgrims, more pilgrims, still more pilgrims
What sights shall be when some that swung, wretches, on crutches
Their crutches shall cast from them, on heels of air departing,
Or they go rich as roseleaves hence that loathsome came hither!
Not now to name even
Those dearer, more divine boons whose haven the heart is.
  As sure as what is most sure, sure as that spring
primroses shall new-dapple next year, sure as tomorrow
morning, amongst come-back-again things, things with
a revival, things with a recovery,
Thy name Winefride will live.'

* There is still recounted in Holywell the following story about Gwenfrewi's relics. When Shrewsbury's 'Black Monks' (disliked by the Welsh, unlike the Cistercians) tried to find Gwenfrewi's coffin, only one monk at Gwytherin disclosed its whereabouts. The bones were reverentially disinterred and placed in a fine coffin to be ceremonially transferred to Shrewsbury. That night, the monk who betrayed her resting-place was poisoned and placed in the coffin, while Gwenfrewi's bones were once again interred at Gwytherin. However, two of her finger-bones were left in the new coffin by accident. Holywell claims one finger bone as a relic, and the other was allowed to stay with the body of the treacherous monk and is in Shrewsbury Cathedral. In the Dissolution of the monasteries, the Shrewsbury finger-bone was taken to Powys Castle, then to Rome, only returning to Shrewsbury in 1852. However, the Holywell bone was not known about by Henry VIII's agents, and has been venerated in Britain for centuries.

** The Brittannia website tells us that Sir Gawain may have stayed at Basingwerk Abbey when searching for the Green Knight, when Holywell was known as 'Holy Head', before he went on to the Wirral Peninsula.

GWENFYL 5th century
November 1, 2 (July 6 with her sister Callwen)

A daughter of Brychan, an extinct chapel was named Capel Gwenfyl, under Llanddewi Brefi in Cardigan. There was a Capel Gwenfyl in Llangeitho which fell down in the 17th century. Ffynno Wenwyl (or Wenfyl) was on a farm of the same name near Llaniarmon yn Ial, and cured sprained limbs. Gwynfil in Cardigan is hers (see Gwenfael).

GWENGUSTLE see NINNOC

GWENLLWYFO
November 30

Llanwenllwyfo in Anglesey

GWENNOG
GWENOG
January 3rd, but Fair Wenog was later held on January 14th

The virgin founder of Llanwenog in Cardigan. Ffynnon Wenog near the church was used for children with weak backs, who were immersed in its waters before sunrise. Other medicinal springs in the parish were Ffynnon Meredith and Ffynnon Ddafras. Llanwenog sheep are a very old native breed. A stone from Capel Wyl at Llanwenog reads in Ogham:
TRENACCATLO, and in Latin TRENACATUS IC IACIT FILIUS MAGLAGNI (Trenacatus lies here son of Maglagnus). Ffynnon Wenog was a holy well in Trefethin parish, Monmouthshire.

ABBOT GWENOLE 457-532
GWINWALOE, WINWALOE, ONOLAUS
March 3, June 20 (also April 28)

Trained by Budoc Laveret, and a son of Fracan and Gwen Tierbron, he was the Breton founder of the great monastery of Landevennec in Cornouaille in Brittany. Landewednack on the Lizard Peninsula in Cornwall and the nearby 'Church of the Storms' at Gunwalloe commemorate him. He is patron of the parish of Towednack in West Penwith, and in 1987 a pilgrimage was held in his honour with the abbot and monks from Landevennec participating. His half-brothers were Gwyddno, Majan and possibly Cadfan.

Alphabetical Listing of the Saints of Wales and Religious Events

St Guenole's Chapel in the hamlet of Quellenec, near Quimper in Brittany is one of many dedicated to the saint. Another lies outside Pleyben in Finistere. Some Breton sources say that Gwenole came from Britain, but others say that he was born in Armorica, the son of Fragan and Gwen who had emigrated from Britain in the 5th or 6th century. After St Patrick appeared to him in a dream, Gwenole (Winwaloe) retired from the world with a few monks and built a monastery at Landevennec, 32 miles north of Quimper in Finistere. In 932 the monastery was destroyed by Vikings, but was rebuilt to become an influential spiritual centre until the French revolution. In 1950, Benedictines rebuilt a new monastery there, but the superb old abbey also remains.

Also Locunole, 8 miles north-east of Quimperle is associated with Winwaloe. The turbulent River Elle is dominated by a mass of huge stones, the Devil's Rocks, where the saint built his hermitage. Satan tried to get rid of the saint from this spot, but was tricked into letting the saint stay there. He is also honoured at Tresmere and Tremaine in Cornwall. Other chapels at Roscraddock and St Germans have disappeared since the Reformation. Some experts believe that St Twynell's in Pembroke was also founded by this saint.

He is remembered at Wonastow in Monmouth, where there were two other chapels, and at Llandevenny near Magor, and at Llanwynny. He is also associated with Portlemouth in Devon as well as Landewednack, Towednack, Tresmere and Tremaine in Cornwall. Gunwalloe has a holy well, now choked with sand. In Brittany he was known at Landevennec, Concarneau, Loquenole, Le Croisic, the island of Batz, Plougastel and the Ile de Sein. Probably Gannerew in Monmouth is his foundation. Llanwarw, near Skenfrith in Monmouth, is now called Wonastow and has been given variously to Wonnow, Gwarw or Gwyno, but is Winwaloe's. In the Book of Llandaf it was *'Lann Gungarui on the Trothy Brook'*, which became Wonwarowstoe (using the Saxon *'stow'*, meaning hamlet). The Llandaf entry shows Cynfyr ab Iago buying the church and about 160 acres of land off King Ffernwael ab Ithael. He paid *'a very good horse'* worth 12 cows, a hawk valued at 12 cows, *'a very useful dog'* that worked with the hawk, to the value of 3 cows, and another horse worth 3 cows. The church was then dedicated to Dyfrig, Teilo and Euddogwy, with Trychan, fifth Bishop of Llandaf as witness.

In Norwich, an old weather rhyme remembered David (March 1), Chad (March 2) and Gwenole (March 3):
'First comes David, then comes Chad,
Then comes Winnol, roaring like mad.'

There are villages named St Guenole west of Pont-Abbe, east of Treguier and north of Pleyben with its magnificent calvary. Loc Gwenole is near Pleyben, Locquenole north of Morlaix, and Gwennili is west of Pleyben. St Guenole is north of Pleyben, St Guenolo north-west of Quimper and St Guenolew near Pont l'Abbe. Pleyben is an excellent centre for touring Finistere, and its 'Pleyben biscuits', crepes and ciders must be sampled.

GWENONWY 5th – 6th entury

The daughter of Meurig ap Tewdrig and hence Arthur's sister. She was the mother of the saints Meugant and Henwyn. Bishop Comereg, Ffriog and Idnerth were her other brothers, and her sisters were Anna and Afrella. Her villa, Guennoe, was recorded in the Book of Llandaf. It stood between Pwll Meurig (Pwllmeyrick, the holy spring named after her father), and Mathern where her grandfather, Tewdrig, was buried. Gwenonwy is the name given to the aromatic flower, Lily of the Valley.

GWENRHIW 5th – 6th century
November 1

This was the former name of Kerry in Montgomery, famous for its breed of sheep and the Kerry Hills. She was supposedly a virgin daughter of Brychan. (See Ceri).

GWERFIL 13th century
GWERFEL

There is a holy well of St Beuno in the remote hamlet of Betws Gwerfil Goch (the prayer-house of Gwerfil the Red). This princess was the red-haired grand-daughter of the great Owain Gwynedd, who traditionally founded this place, for pilgrims on the trackway from Holywell to St David's. The doorway is formed from three huge stone slabs, which attests to the antiquity of the site, and it could have been founded by Beuno. There are 15th century carved panels at the altar, unique in Britain, and found by chance in 1840 under rubble. They were part of the rood screen, and the church is one of the most evocative in Wales, with a mediaeval roof and wooden chandelier. A protected colony of bats lives in the church. Ffynnon Werfil holy well was in the Rhydlewis district of Cardigan.

GWERNABUI 6th century

The head of a monastery at Garth Benni, now known as Welsh Bicknor, and a disciple of Dyfrig, he features in a land grant by Arthur.

GWERYDD 4th century?
April 17 was given by the Annals of Tewkesbury as the Feast of St Donat.

Only Iolo Morganwg seems to record this saint, so the story may not be relied upon, in this instance. St Donat's Church (see Dunwyd) was originally called Llanwerydd, dedicated to St Gwerydd, of the line of Magnus Maximus and Elen. Cadfrawd, supposedly Bishop of Caerleon around 314, had a son named Gwerydd who was a saint, so this may be his foundation. Llanwerydd later became Llandunwyd, then St Donat's. There was also supposed to be a chapel to Gwerydd at Emral near Bangor-is-Coed. The hill fort at Caerau outside Cardiff was known as Llanweirydd, and this may be the same saint again (or King Gweirydd).

The Reverend John Montgomery Traherne, a Glamorgan antiquarian, believed that St Donat's church stands on the spot where the gospel was first preached in Wales, and there is a fine 15th century churchyard cross there. Somehow it escaped the Puritan desecration of crosses in the 17th century, despite the fact that Cromwell is said to have visited the castle. There are extremely few mediaeval calvaries still in existence, and it is built of three types of limestone, Sutton, Quarella and Blue Lias. Brackets on it were used for holding palm branches on Palm Sunday, or for illumination during festivals.

Many of the Stradlings of St Donat's Castle (formerly the family was called le Esterling) are buried in the church. The family who built the first castle here, the de Haweyes, also built the first stone church, sometime soon after the 1093 conquest of Glamorgan. The present church dates from 1300, enlarged by the Stradlings, but the original Norman chancel arch can still be seen. The altar dates from around 1407, and the lectern is a mediaeval Breton ambo given in 1913. The castle is said to be on the site of Caractacus' palace, and William Randolph Hearst entertained such luminaries as Clark Gable and Charlie Chaplin here. Some say that Caractacus and Eurgain returned here from Rome, accompanied by Lucius (Sarllog). The nearby Splott farm commemorates the fact that the Knights Hospitallers once owned lands around here.

GWESTLAN see GISTLIANUS

GWETHENOC 6th century
GOUEZNOU
July 24, July 6, November 5 and 7

Gwethenoc and Iago were twins, the younger brothers of Gwenole (Winwaloe), and the sons of Ffracan and Gwen Tierbron, who went to Brittany with their parents. Gwethenoc is remembered at St Enodoc Chapel, which is buried in the sands near Padstowe. St Goueznou near St Brieuc also is probably Gwethenoc's foundation. He is sometimes confused with Gwyddno or Tugdon. (See Iago and Enodoc).

GWILYM

Possibly the founder of Clytha – see Pedr.

GWINEAR sixth century
GUIGNAR
March 23

This Welsh saint features in a 'Life' written eight centuries after his death, which says that he was the leader of a band of 'Irish' missionaries who landed in Cornwall at the mouth of the Hayle river, where he was killed by the local ruler Teudar. Those that escaped founded churches all over Cornwall. With his fellow-Welshman Meriadoc, he seems to have travelled on to be a missionary in Brittany, where St Guignar at Pluvigner commemorates him. St Gwinear's church is near Phillack at Lands End.

GWINWALO d. 432
WINWALOC
August 1

This famous Briton settled in Armorica, and his translation to the Blandin monastery in Ghent is celebrated on August 1.

GWLADYS 6th century
GWLADUS, GWLAWYS
March 29th

This grand-daughter of Brychan married king Gwynlliw Filwr and gave birth to St Cadog. She and her husband lived a holy life on Newport's Stow Hill, until persuaded to separate by Cadog, and Gwaldys moved to Pencannau (Pencarn) near Bassaleg. A mound near Rock Cottages is said to be her grave. The ruined Capel Gwladys at Gelligaer is now hardly visible, but there is a cross there and it is surrounded by Roman training camps. In Tredegar House Park, Newport, the ancestral home of the Morgans, is her holy spring, where she used to bathe naked with Gwynlliw. Now known as Lady's Well (a corruption of Gwladys Well), it had a bath-house erected over it in 1719. A rock on the nearby Ebbw river probably had her chapel on it, as it was known as 'The Chapel' until recently.

Nearby is a statue dedicated to Sir Briggs, a truly remarkable horse that carried Captain Godfrey Morgan, later Viscount Lord Tredegar, to victory at the principal race on Cowbridge race-course at Penllyne Castle. Thousands from all over South Wales attended. This partnership also took part in Crimean War cavalry charges at the battles of Inkerman and The Alma. It possibly goes without saying that the pair returned from the first line of the Light Cavalry Charge at the battle of Balaclava also. If any horse deserved a fitting resting place from a grateful owner, it was this celebrated charger. Sir Briggs died in 1874, aged 28 years.

Ffynnon Wladus is a holy well in Llangynllo parish, Cardigan, and there was a also a Gwladus martyred near Aberffraw at Croes Ladys.

GWLADYS ferch CARADOG see **CLAUDIA**

GWNNOG

Probably Gwynnog, who founded Botwnnog (Bod-tŷ-Wnnog)

GWODLOEW 6th century

The son of Glywys Cerniw, who taught at his uncle St Cadog's monastery at Llancarfan.

GWRAN see **GORAN**

GWRDAF
GWRDA
December 5, November 12

Llanwrda seems to be named after this saint, not Cawrdaf as thought. The day given is Cawrdaf's feast day of December 5, but the wake was held on the 'old' All Saints' Day of November 12.

GWRDDELW 6th century
January 7

A son of Caw, he is said to have had a church at Caerleon, and Capel Gartheli in Llanddewi Brefi was his.

GWRDDOGWY 6th - 7th century
GUORDOCUI

A disciple of Dyfrig, who appears in the titles of land grants made to Dyfrig. He may be the Guordocui was abbot at Llanddewi Dewchurch in Hereford in the early 7th century.

GWRFAN 6th century

Taught by Dyfrig, according to Iolo Morganwg, who made him the patron of Llansanffraid Fawr (St Bride's Major), and also of Drenewydd Ynottais (Newton Nottage), which is now St John's dedication. However, Glywys seems to be the latter's patron. Newton Nottage has a carved figure on its stone pulpit, similar to one found on the nave-wall at Bonvislton (Tresimwn). Orrin believes the Bonvilston carving to be pre-Norman, and is very rare, showing a man with arms bent horizontally across the waist, and with a girdle and high boots. Vine scrolls surround the carving.

GWRFYW 6th century

The son of Pasgen ab Urien Rheged, he had a church dedicated to him in Anglesey, and there was also a chapel of his at Bangor uwch Conwy in Caernarfon. His son was St Nidan.

GWRGON 5th – 6th century

A daughter or grand-daughter of Brychan, married to Cadrod Calchfynydd.

GWRGI 6th century

Gwrgi ab Elifer was the brother of the warrior Peredur and studied at Llanilltud Fawr. He saw the funeral pile of Gwenddolau's forces at Ardderyd, and died in battle in 580. He was said to have founded Penarth and to be buried in the Gower peninsula. His 'Saying of the Wise' was *the lucky person needs but to be born.'* Said to be one of Arthur's knights, with Peredur, and equated by some with Sir Bors.

GWRHAI 6th century

A son of Caw who founded Penystrywaid (Penstrowed) in Arwystli, Montgomeryshire.

GWRHIR 6th century

A bard of Teilo, and the founder of Llysfaen, now named Lisvane in Cardiff. A saint at Bangor Catwg, Llancarfan. His 'Saying of the Wise' is *'he whoso deceives will be deceived.'* He may be buried at Llanarth (see Dewi).

GWRIN 6th - 7th century
November 1, May 1 at Llanwrin

Llanwrin in Montgomery was rededicated to this descendant of Gildas, but was founded by Ust and Dyfnig. There is a *'Field of the Three Saints'* near the church. According to Iolo Morganwg, Gwrin ap Cynddilig ap Nwython ap Gildas also founded Trewrin, Wrinstone near Wenvoe in Glamorgan. Many Roman coins and artefacts have been found at the deserted village and fields around Wrinstone Farm. There was also Gwrin, a *'regulus'* of Merioneth who married Marchell.

William Thomas noted the eagerness in 1767 of the overseer of Wrinston woods to have offenders (male and female) whipped in churchyards for cutting wood. In 1765 Thomas also recorded the use of the *'skymmetry'* or *'skymmington'* at Wrinston. Morgan Daniel's wife had abused him, so she was subjected to *'noise and riots'* in a mock trial, with neighbours acting the traditional roles of Maid Marian and the Sheriff of Nottingham. This little hamlet, just west of Cardiff, still had monoglot Welsh speakers in 1764, as evidenced when Charles Batt of Wrinston married an English girl in Bristol, neither knowing the other's tongue. Thomas's fascinating diary informs us via burial records of the dangers on living in the 18th century – apart from the draconian penal code for trifling offences, we could die of small-pox, quinsy, typhoid fever, typhus, malaria, measles, venereal complaints, consumption, scrofula (TB), worms, dropsy, abscesses or impostumes, gangrene, cancers of the mouth and jaws, other cancers, swellings, stroke, palsy, insanity, ague or heavy drinking.

GWRMAEL 4th – 5th, or 5th – 6th century

Possibly the son of Macsen Wledig and Elen (see Gwerydd), or of Cadfrawd (see Cadfrawd).

GWRNERTH 6th century
April 7

This was the son of St Llywelyn ap Bleiddud of Trallwng (Welshpool). Both Llywelyn and Gwrnerth lived in Trallwng (Welshpool). The tiny flower Speedwell has two names in Welsh, Gwrnerth, and Llysiau Llywelyn (Llywelyn's Herbs). From the latter, it was known as Fluellen in English. (See Llywelyn).

GWRTHEFYR FENDIGAID (the blessed) mid 5th century
KING VORTIMER, son of VORTIGERN

Canonised for patriotism, Gwrthefyr fought against the early Saxon invaders led by Hengist and Horsa. He either died of wounds after the battle of Crayford in Kent in 470, or was poisoned by his step-mother the Saxon Rowena. He wanted his body to be buried at the place where the Saxons first entered Ynys Prydain (the Island of Britain) as a talisman against further invasion. However, his father Vortigern revealed Vortimer's last wish to be buried at Richborough to Rowena. The Saxons thus re-interred him in London, and took over England.

The epithet 'blessed' may have come from Vortimer's blessing by Germanus of Auxerre as a young man. It seems that he was defeated at Crayford (Derguentid), but beat the Saxons at Aylesford (Rithergabail) and Richborough Roman fort (Lapis Tituli) where there was a triumphal arch. Vortigern took over the High-Kingship again after Vortimer's death. In the Triads Gwrthefyr was accounted one of the three canonised kings of Britain. Gwrthefyr Fendigaid had a daughter called Madrun, who married St Ynyr, King of Gwent. His 'Saying of the Wise' was *'a string too tight is easily broken.'*

GWRTHEYRN 5th century
VORTIGERN, GURTHIERN, VICTORINUS? VITALIANUS?

Reviled for being the high king who invited the Saxons to Britain to help defend it against Picts and Scots, Vortigern was the father of the saints Gwrthefyr, Elldeyrn, Aerdeyrn and Edeyrn. (The suffix 'teyrn', mutated to 'deyrn', means 'monarch'). He was a Pelagian, which explains much of the disgust of Gildas with his actions. On the second visit by Garmon of Auxerre to root out the Pelagian Heresy, he failed to root out Vortigern's resistance to Rome's rule, despite assisting in the famous 'Alleluiah' victory against the Irish and Pictish Scots near Mold. When Garmon left, Gwrtheyrn asked raiding Saxon mercenaries to assist him in his efforts against the Irish, who had established themselves in Anglesey and Gwynedd, and against the Scottish Picts. By ceding land to the Saxons in Kent, he opened the way for other German tribes such as the Angles and Jutes to settle in Britain's south-east, where they rapidly destroyed the Roman-British civilisation in that part of Britain. St Gildas wrote between 540 and 544 of *'the general destruction of everything good and the general growth of everything evil throughout the land.'* (There were plagues and crop failures at this time, probably caused by a volcanic explosion – see The Yellow Plague).

The emergence of Ambrosius Aurelianus drove Gwrtheyrn back to the Welsh hills. His fault had been to try to divide his enemies, to protect Britain from the Saxons, Picts and Irish, and he paid with his life. Nennius states that his reign started in 425, as 'Overlord' of Britain, after he had King Constantine (said to be Arthur's grandfather) murdered. After this he killed the king's son Constans and usurped the throne with Pictish help. He abdicated for his son Vortimer to succeed, but Vortimer was possibly poisoned by his step-mother Rowena and Vortigern resumed the kingship. He fled to Wales after the *'treachery of the long knives'*, the slaughter of the British nobles by Hengist on Salisbury Plain. However, Ambrosius caught up with Vortigern at Tre'r Ceiri.

Beuno went to Nant Gwrtheyrn to preach Christianity to the pagans (or followers of Pelagius), but was driven back by the villagers throwing stones. He and his monks laid three curses on the village at the sea's edge. No-one born in the village would ever be buried in consecrated ground. No male and female born there would ever be able to marry each other. Finally, the village would decay and die, to become forever a deserted ruin. The curses came true. The men died at sea or fell off cliffs into the sea. The women were refused burial at Clynnog, the nearest church. Afraid of the curse, all women left the village when old enough to marry, and the men also found wives from outside their valley. Around 300 years ago a village couple resolved to overcome the curse. They exchanged presents on the morning of the wedding, the future groom being given a puppy. The bride-to-be followed local custom of hiding before her wedding and could not be found. The groom's party could not find her to take her to the church. The man searched for years, pacing up and down the shore and valley, with his dog. When the dog died the villagers found it and threw it in the sea. The man also vanished, presumed drowned. Years later a terrible storm split open an old oak, and a skeleton with long silky hair was found in it, clasped as if by a vice. The skeleton was transported by cart along the cliffs to St Beuno's Church at Clynnog, but turned over and the skeleton fell over the cliffs. Nant Gwrtheyrn village became a deserted ruin by 1965, but has now been transformed into an excellent centre and hostel for the learning of Welsh.

From this remarkable centre, there is a footpath up to the triple peaks of Yr Eifl (The Fork, but named in English as 'The Rivals'). From the 1849 foot-high summit, one can descend slightly to the greatest hill-fort in Wales, Tre'r Ceiri (Town of the Giants). It was occupied during the Roman period, and Ambrosius Aurelianus pursued Vortigern here, firing the wooden stockade with arrows. Barber and Pykitt believe that he escaped to fight Ambrosius (and Garmon) at Little Doward hillfort, near Ganarew in Hereford. This site was one of Nennius' 'Twenty-Eight Towns of Sub-Roman Britain', being known as Caer-Guouthigorn (Gwythern's Fort) in the 8th century. The camp ovelooks a bend in the River Wye known as 'The Slaughter', and also the Roman road from Caerleon (Isca Silurum) to Ariconium.

However, Vortigern escaped yet again, making his way to Quimperle in Brittany, where he entered the church and is celebrated as St Gurthiern. His relics were in Quimperle, and he seems to have been helped, in his 11th century 'Life', by King Grallon Mawr of Cornouaille and Count Weroc I of Vannes. The Vitalianus Stone in Nefern Church also has claims to be his burial marker.

Geoffrey of Monmouth wrote of a grim future for *'the people of Britain'*, the Welsh, in the following passage upon Vortigern. He used the metaphor of the Red Dragon of Cadwaldr and Wales against the White Dragon of Wessex and England:
"While Vortigern, King of the Britons, was still sitting on the flank of the pool which had drained of its water, there emerged two dragons, one white, one red. As soon as they were near enough to each other, they fought bitterly, breathing out fire as they panted. The white dragon began to have the upper hand and to force the red one back to the pool. The red dragon bewailed the fact that it was being driven out and then turned upon the white one and forced it backwards in its turn. As they struggled on in this way, the King ordered Ambrosius Merlin to explain just what this battle of the dragons meant. Merlin immediately burst into tears. He went into a prophetic trance and then spoke as follows: 'Alas for the red dragon, for its end is near. Its cavernous den shall be occupied by the white dragon, which stands for the Saxons whom you have invited over. The red dragon represents the people of Britain, who will be overrun by the white one: for Britain's mountains and valleys shall be levelled, and the streams in its valleys shall run with blood'."

GWRTHL 6th century
March 2

Maesllanwrthl in Caio, Carmarthen, and Llanwrthl in Brecon. At the former the famous Paulinus Stone stood. Gwrthl was killed in Cardigan, and was a *'chief elder'* who recognised Arthur as *'supreme king'*. In the churchyard of Llanwrthl is a large Celtic cross-base.

Gwydir Uchaf Chapel.   *CADW: Welsh Historic Monuments. Crown Copyright.*

GWRW
October 21, November 3 (Fenton)

There was a Gwyl Urw Forwy held every year at Eglwyswrw. Also Ffair Meugan was held there on the Monday after Martinmas.

GWRWST 6th century
GWRST
December 1, 2. However, the fair was held on the eve of his festival, November 30, then altered with the 1752 date change to 11 days later on December 11.

Gwrst ap Gwaith Hengaer ab Elffin ab Urien Rheged and Euronwy ferch Clydno Eiddyn is the founder of Llanrwst, where there was a wooden effigy of him until the Reformation. Nearby is the waterfall, Rhaiadr Rwst. He was a signatory, with Deiniol and Trillo, of a grant of land by Maelgwn Gwynedd to Cyndeyrn (Kentigern/Mungo). Ffynnon Newydd in Llanrwst was a healing well within a large building with a dressing room. The Gwydir Chapel at Llanrwst is said to have been designed by that superb Welsh architect, Inigo Jones. The great sarcophagus of Llywelyn the Great lies there, probably removed from Maenan Abbey at the time of Dissolution.

GWRYD end of 12th century
November 1

A friar officially sanctified by the Roman Catholic church, he is supposed to have cured the bard Einion ap Gwalchmai (c. 1170-c. 1220) of a mental illness lasting 7 years.

GWYAR 7th century

A son of Helig Foel. It is faintly possible that Ffynnon Gywer, which was in the centre of the old town of Bala, was dedicated to a church of Gwyar. Someone forgot to replace the stone on it one night, so Llyn Tegid covered the town, and the largest natural lake in Wales was formed. On the shore of the lake is Ffynnon Gower, near Llangower Church, which is dedicated to St Cywair (q.v.). There is a megalith named Llech Gower nearby. Gwalchmai was the son of a female named 'Gwyar', and became Sir Gawain in mediaeval romances (see Govan and Gwawr).

GWYDDALUS 6th century
April 26 Old Style (May 9 New Style) was the fair day

A pupil of Teilo, possibly martyred at Llanwyddalus near Llanerchaeron in Cardigan. He is sometimes confused with Vitalus, who was martyred on April 28 with his wife Valeria and who is venerated at Ravenna. As a result the church at Dihewydd next to Llanwyddelan is now dedicated to Vitalus. (The old name for Dihewydd was Llwynwyddalis). *Gwyl Fidalus a Bidofydd* was held on April 26, but the fair moved to Lampeter when the railway arrived there. Dihewydd village receives its water from Ffynnon Dalis, where there was a small chapel.

GWYDDELAN
August 22

Llanwyddelan in north-east Montgomeryshire, and Dolwyddelan in Caernarfon are his. The former is sometimes attributed to Gwendolina with a date of October 18. Dolwyddelan had a holy well, Ffynnon Elan, with tonic qualities, which steamed slightly in frosty weather. It was regarded as especially efficacious for sickly children and for paralysed limbs. Fenton said that the Roman legionaries *'used to dine'* at this well near the evocative Dolwyddelan Castle. Gwyddelan's holy bell, Cloch Wydddelan, is now at Gwydir Chapel, Llanrwst. However, this saint may well be the same person as Lorcan Wyddel (see entry). Another holy well was on the road from Dolwyddelan to Capel Curig, Ffynnon Offeiriad.

GWYDDFACH d.610
GWYDDFARCH
November 3

A son of prince Amalarus and commemorated with other saints at Meifod. Eglwys Gwyddfarch has now all but disappeared there. It stood just outside the present church of Tyssilio. He was an anchorite, who was said to have died on the rocky bed known as Gwely Gwyddfarch, on the slopes of Gallt (or Moel) yr Ancr (Anchorite's Hill). He was part of a community founded by his spiritual father St Llywelyn at Trallwng (Tre = town, and Llwng = Llywelyn), now Welshpool. This area was part of the 'Eastern Mission', Christian Britons fleeing west into Powys from the sacking of Wroxeter (Cynddylan's Hall, Uriconium) and the Shropshire area.

Meifod was the heart of the later princedom of Powys, and has several holy wells surrounding it. Ffynnon y Groftydd cured cutaneous disorders with its sulphurous waters, Hally Well traditionally had its own chapel, and Holy Well was also in the parish. Ffynnon y Clawdd Llesg, or The Spout Well, was the most famous. In the 19th century people went there on Trinity Sundays to drink sugared water then repaired to a local ale-house, Yr Hen Dafarn, but the custom was stopped by local ministers. Even so, youngsters still went to the well to drink its water and dance on the eighth Sunday after Easter. Only a hundred years ago it was visited to cure nasal polyps, and an inscription read that wounds had to be held under the spout for twenty minutes, three times a day. Ffynnon Darogan had a cupola to protect it, and Gallt y Maen Well was another well frequented by young people who then went to Bryn y Bowliau to indulge in athletics.

GWYDDFAEN

Ffynnon Llandyfaen in Llandyfaen parish Carmarthen, was formerly called Ffynnon Gwyddfaen, with an old ruined chapel. The waters were enclosed, with steps leading to it, and used for curing paralysis and numbness.

GWYDDIN
GWITHIAN, GOTHIAN, GWYDDYN, GWYTHIAN
November 1

A hermit of Llanddwyn in Montgomery, now covered by the reservoir of Lake Vyrnwy. Sarn Wddyn was a causeway over the damp marshes in the flooded valley. Gwely Wddyn is a mound on a nearby hillside. A footpath over the mountain, called Llwybr Wyddin, is the way he used to travel to visit St Melangell in Pennant, five miles away. There are legends of buried treasure at his cell, protected by storms and lightning if anyone dares disturb the ground. His church had been rededicated to John the Baptist, but when it was rebuilt in 1888 after the valley was dammed, it was once again dedicated to its founder Gwyddin, a rare occurrence in ecclesiastical matters in Wales. There was also a Llanwddin in Caernarfonshire.

This may be the Gwythian who is the patron of the ruined chapel of St Gothian in the sands of North Cornwall, associated with Gwenole who settled at nearby Towednack. Nearby Lan-Gwidian has become Lawhitton.

GWYDDLEW 6th century

A son of Gwynlliw Filwr.

GWYDDLOYW 5th – 6th century

The son of Glywys Cernyw and thus the uncle of Cadog, but he may be the same person as the saint Gwyddlew previously noted. Iolo Morganwg stated that he was at Llancarfan then Bishop of Llandaf.

GWYDDNO 6th century
GWETHENOC, GOUEZNOU
October 25

Known as Bishop Goueznou in Britanny. After his mother's death, he left Britain with his father Tugdon, his elder brother Majan and his sister Tugdonia. They probably landed near Brest, as there is a parish called Saint-Houdon (St Toudon) there. Majan settled at Loc Majan in Plougon, and Gwyddno founded Lan-Gouezenou. Conmore of Dumnonia gave Majan and Gwyddno land in 550. A farmer's wife lied to Gwyddno when she said she had no cheese to give him. He therefore transformed her rounds of cheeses into pebbles, which were used as 'cursing-stones' in his church. There are still some of these stones in Breton and Irish churches, where evil could be wished through them onto one's enemies. Gwyddno succeeded Houardon to become Bishop of Leon for twenty-four years. He was killed on October 25 by the fall of a workman's hammer, when visiting the building of a new monastery. He is sometimes confused with Gwethenoc, the son of Gwen Tierbron.

GWYDDNO GARANHIR 6th century
GWYDDNEU

Iolo counts King Gwyddno Garanhir, who lost his lands to the sea at Cantre'r Gwaelod, as a saint, but this is probably wrong. A group of rocks eight miles out from Aberystwyth is called Caer Wyddno (Gwyddno's Castle). The Mabinogion legend of Brân may be a folk memory of being able to cross the Irish Sea by foot, and certainly the water levels have risen overall by 40 feet over the last two millennia. (However, as evidenced by the siting of Harlech Castle, now inland, they have receded again in the last millennium). The Black Book of Carmarthen refers to the sea drowning Maes Gwyddneu. His son Elffin may have been a saint, and is associated with the legend of the birth of Taliesin when he found the infant in a coracle on Gwyddno's weir. This place was known as Porth Wyddno (Gwyddno's Gateway), and is the resort village of Borth on the Cardigan coast. Ffynnon Gwyddno in Llanfachreth, Merioneth is near the church, but is now called Ffynnon y Capel and said to have been formed by St Machreth. Emyr Llydaw possibly had a son named Gwyddno.

When faced with bad news or disaster, and one says not a word, this is still known as:
'Ochenaid Gwyddno Garanhir
Pan droes y don dros ei dir'.
(The sigh of Gwyddno Garanhir,
When the wave rolled over his land)

The 'Caelextus Stone' was used as a footbridge over a stream, then lay on the beach near Kiel Wart Farm in the parish of Llanaber, just north of Barmouth. Over seven foot in length, some lines have been deciphered as *'Hic Iacet CALIXTUS MONEDO REGI'*, which infers that Calixtus, King of the Isle of Man (or Moor or Mountain), was buried under it. Waring's 'Life of

Iolo Morganwg' mentioned several Roman-inscribed stones on the beach at 'Abermo', or Barmouth, but all seem to have been lost. However, John Jones in his 'History of Wales' believed that one inscription read *'Here lies the boatman to King Gwynddo'*, which changes Gwyddno Garanhir's name.

GWYL MABSANT

The Feast of the Patron Saint of a parish, or wake, usually lasted the whole week, and only reduced to three or four days during the Nonconformist revival. By 1860, however, Saints' feasts had just about died out in Wales. Calvinist Methodism, so stringently adopted by the Welsh as their answer to the ills of an oppressive system of government, virtually extirpated the joys of dancing, drinking, sports and singing (except for hymnal dirges). There was usually a great fair associated with the feast day, e.g. Ffair Wyl Deilo at Llandeilo Fawr, formerly held on February 9th and then moved to the 20th following the date changes where Europe *'lost eleven days'*.

GWYN 6th century
All Saints Day, January 7

One of the five saintly quintuplets (Gwyn, Gwyno, Gwynoro, Celynin, Ceitho) of Cynyr Farwyn of Cynwyl Gaio, commemorated at Llanpumsaint in Carmarthenshire. At Cynwyl Gaio, Carreg Pumsaint is a long stone with five hollows where the saints were supposed to lay their heads to sleep. In reality they were mortars where Roman slaves used to crush quartz to extract gold from the nearby mines. On St Peter's Day, hundreds used to gather at Ffynnon Pumsaint by the church. There were also five hollows, or pools, at the well, which cured aching limbs. 'Carreg y Pumsaint', an ancient stone with crosses, has been removed from the churchyard and is now in the church. Ffynnon Gwenno was a healing well here, near the rock called Clochdy Gwenno (Gwenno's Steeple), but gold-mining operations have diverted most of its waters.

RHISIART GWYN
RICHARD WHITE c1537-1584
October 17, 15 (also October 25, 27)

One of the 40 Martyrs of England and Wales, he was born in Llanidloes and educated at Oxford and then St John's College, Cambridge until 1562. A schoolmaster at Overton in Flintshire, he refused to renounce his Catholic faith, and was threatened with imprisonment by the Bishop of Chester if he did not attend the local church. For some time he did this, then repented and moved to Overstock where he opened another school. Recognised in Wrexham, he was arrested as a recusant but escaped in 1579. In 1580 he was rearrested and gaoled in Ruthin Castle. Placed in irons, he was forcibly taken to church in Wrexham, where he rattled his chains so loudly that the service had to be abandoned. The prison was called *'Y Siambar ddu - a vile and fylthy prison.'* He was released, fined for recusancy and fined again until he had no money left, when he was imprisoned and placed in the stocks. (Incidentally, being placed in the stocks could mean death or blindness. The trangressor's hands and ears were pinned with nails, so the face could not be averted or protected to avoid stones and glass being hurled by the crowd.)

From Wrexham Richard Gwynne was sent to Ruthin Gaol, and until his death was regularly transferred between gaols and brought back to Wrexham court for trial. In Denbigh prison he was joined by John Hughes and Robert Morris. From Wrexham gaol he went to Holt prison, and then to Bewdley and Bridgnorth, where he was tortured with Robert Morris, John Bennett, Henry Pugh and John ap Hugh ap Madoc.

Upon his eighth trial in Wrexham, one man was suborned to perjure himself and say that Gwyn had reconciled him to Catholicism. Upon being heavily fined, and asked how he would pay, he smiled and said *'I have something towards it – sixpence'*. The response to this jest was fairly humourless - Gwyn was sentenced to be *'drawn on a hurdle to the place of execution where he shall hang half-dead, and so be cut down alive, his members cast into the fire, his belly ripped open unto the breast, his head cut off, his bowels, liver, lungs, heart thrown likewise into the fire'*. Gwyn responded *'What is all this? Is it any more than one death?'*

On Gwyn's scaffold he acknowledged Elizabeth as his queen, but refused to say that she was *'Supreme Head of the Church'*. After four years of imprisonment and continuous torture, he finally suffered the ghastly ordeal of hanging, drawing and quartering on October 15th, 1584 and was eventually canonised in 1970. *'Gwyn was dragged to the scaffold, hanged and let down almost dead. Then they waited so he could be beheaded according to the judge's order, before they proceeded with the final butchery. But the sheriff of the court affirming that the judge had made a mistake in this respect, ordered that all the other things should be done first, and his head struck off last of all. And so the hangman continued with the other operations following the sheriff's order rather than the judge's sentence. (His genitals having already been cut off) and as he took hold of the knife to pierce his belly, Gwyn valiantly raised himself and would have got up had not the hangman held him down with force. And then when the executioner after violently thrusting in his hand, was about to tear the intestines, the holy martyr of Christ, in the last throes of his suffering twice called out the very sweet name of Christ. Then the sheriff, having pity on the man (as it seemed), calling on the hangman, said "Fool, finish it, seek his heart."* '

Gwynne is regarded by the Church of Rome as the first Catholic martyr in Wales. There is debate on the actual date of his execution, discussed in some detail by D. Aneurin Thomas in 'The Welsh Elizabethan Catholic Martyrs.' An account of his martyrdom, probably by John Bennett, reads:
'And is it any wonder, the people knew his innocency being well acquainted with the good man's conversation (over) ye space of XXtie years together, they knew his cause to be just and honest being directly for religion. They knew ye example to be rare, the like never heard of in Wales since the death of St Winefride, traceing therein the happy steppes of his blessed country man Sant Albano, the first martyr of the ancient Britons and proto martyr of this Island' (quoted in D. Aneurin Thomas).

Waldo Williams also wrote 'Wedi'r Canrifoedd Mudan' ('After the Mute Centuries') about the martyrdom of Richard Gwyn, John Owen and John Roberts:
*'Maent yn un a'r goleuni. Maent wch fy mhen
Lle'r ymasgl, trwy'r ehangder, hedd. Pan noso'r wybren
Mae pob un yn rhwyll I'm llygad yn y llen.'*
(*'They are at one with the light. They are above my head
Where peace prevails in the vastness.
When night darkens the sky each one provides an eyehole,
Through which I can glimpse beyond the veil.'*)

'Y diberfeddu wedi'r glwyd artaith, a chyn
Yr ochenaid lle rhodded ysgol I'w henaid esgyn
I helaeth drannoeth Golgotha eu Harglwydd gwyn.'
('The disembowelling after the torture of the hurdle,
And before the sigh where a ladder was given for their soul
To ascend to tomorrow's broad expanse of their blessed Lord's Golgotha.')

'Concertatio Ecclesiae Catholicae in Anglia' tells us of the suffering endured by John Hughes, Robert Morris and Richard Gwynne in prison. '(John Hughes) *was put in manacles until about 9 o'clock. Now the Manacles are a form of torture in which a person is suspended and racked, with his hands placed into a metal ring with teeth and squeezed very tightly. Such torturing is so painful and intense, that unless a part of the dorsal spine leans against a wall, and the tips of the feet are placed on the floor, then fainting occurs. While John Hughes was hanging in this fashion, the inquisitors again put these questions to him . . . About 3 o'clock the Attorney General returned, bearing with him closer fitting shackles, so that he might afflict the man with still greater torments. These he gladly accepted and having first made the sign of the cross, he raised them to his mouth and kissed them.(This example his companions in suffering later copied in their torments whenever they were tortured). Then he was again raised on the wooden rack and was suspended for two hours in the usual way, those new shackles hurting his hands much more than the old ones, nevertheless by divine help he had much less pain than he had had previously. But the judges and attendants thinking otherwise lowered him on two occasions, believing him to be on the point of death: because engaged in prayer he spoke not to them but to God alone in spirit . . . Having endured that cruel torture for almost five hours he had not lost consciousness during the whole of that time, until now for the first time when they laid him on the ground to remove his shackles.*' The ordeals and inquisitions of Pugh, Bennett, Gwynne and Morris are also recounted.

GWYNAU 5th century
December 13 (with Gwynws)

A son of Brychan.

GWYNDAF HEN 6th century
GWNDA
November 6 (Pembroke), April 21 (Caernarfon)

The son of Emyr Llydaw and brother of Amwn Ddu, he married Gwenonwy, a daughter of Meurig ap Tewdrig. The daughter of Gwyndaf and Gwenonwy, Meugan, was also a saint, as was their son Hywyn. This Breton refugee from Clovis's Frankish invaders (like Amwn and Cadfan) became a confessor at Llanilltud Fawr and then Superior at Dyfrig's college in Caerleon. Like Dyfrig, he retired to Ynys Enlli (Bardsey) to die.

The ancient church of Llanwnda in Pembroke is dedicated to St Gwyndaf, and has no less than six Celtic Christian monuments built into its walls. There are four cross-marked stones, part of a cross-slab and an interesting figural panel which comes from a broken stone cross.
All the carvings were discovered in restoration work in 1881, and appear to be fragments of larger structures. There must be many hundreds of such stones hidden in the soil of Celtic Christian churchyards. One stone suggests a female, or hooded monk, and another features a

carved figure of a cleric with his hand raised in blessing. The church has a 'squint' for the diseased to see the service, and a carving of the face of a tonsured monk on a medieval rafter. Asser, the Welsh counsellor of Alfred the Great, received his early Christian training here. The living was held for some time by Giraldus Cambrensis, and its ancient chalice was said to be stolen by the French during the 1797 invasion, the last foreign invasion of Britain. The church overlooks Strumble Head and Carregwastad, which saw the last invasion of Britain in Napoleonic times. Returning from Fishguard after an argument with St Aidan (Madog), a fish leaped when Gwyndaf was crossing his boundary stream, and Gwyndaf fell and broke his leg. He cursed the stream so that no fish would ever swim in it, but it still springs from the holy well near the church.

Capel Gwnda stood in Troedyraur in Cardiganshire, on the banks of the Ceri where the rectory now stands. A stone in the river shows the marks of the saint's knees as he prayed. Nearby is Cerwyn Gwnda (Gwyndaf's Brewing-Tub), a pool under a waterfall. Also near are Felin Wnda and Capel Wnda, the latter now a farmhouse. Ffynnon Capel Gwnda was famous for curing warts and is in Troedyaur parish, while Capel Gwnda farm is in the neighbouring parish of Penbryn. Parc Ffynnon Wnda is a field name on Penfeidr Farm in the parish of Llanwnda in Pembroke, and Felin Wnda is a working woollen mill near Pont Wnda.

There is another Llanwnda church in Caernarfonshire. From Rhedynog Felen in its parish, just outside Caernarfon, the monastic community moved to Aberconwy in 1192. The new abbey and convent were heavily endowed by the princes of Gwynedd, and Llywelyn the Great and his sons Dafydd and Gruffydd were buried there. Gruffudd's body was allowed by Henry III to be moved from London to Aberconwy after he died trying to escape from the Tower. However, in 1283, after the defeat of Llywelyn the Last, Edward I set up court in Aberconwy and built the great Conwy Castle on the abbey site, forcing the community to set up in Maenan Abbey, six miles away.

Pembroke's Llanwnda has several megaliths in the vicinity. Upon Carn Wnda lies the burial chamber variously known as Carn Wnda and Carreg Samson, and another chamber, Gyllych Dolmen is near Ysgubor Gaer. The seven feet standing stone known as Parc Hen is between Carn Wnda and Hennen School. This site on the headland between Fishguard and Aber Mawr is in line with four burial chambers, four Iron Age forts and two standing stones, all in a distance of three miles across.

GWYNDEG 5th century

The son of Seithenin was said to be a saint at Bangor-is-Coed and the father of Cynyr of Caer Gawch, St David's grandfather.

GWYNELL

The site of Llanwynell in Monmouthshire is not known for certain, but appears to be at, or near, Wolves' Newton. This saint is possibly Gwynhoedl, also known as Gwynhael (q.v.)

GWYNEN
December 3, 13

Llanwnen in Cardigan is hers, and this virgin was associated with Gwenog who had the neighbouring parish of Llanwenog. The fair was held on December 3 both Old Style and New Style dates. (December 13 is the feast date of Lucy of Syracuse.) Some sources say that the church was founded by Gwynen and/or Gwynus, sons of Brychan. Ffynnon Ffair holy well near Llanwnen was possibly Gwynen's well. There is a Lan Guenan north of Dinan, but the link with any Welsh saint is unknown as yet.

GWYNGENAU 6th century

The extinct Capel Gwyngeneu under Holyhead was dedicated to this son of Paulinus (Pawl Hen). He was the brother of Peulin and Gwenfaen.

GWYNHOEDL 5th - 6th century
VENDESETL, GWYNODL, GWYNHAEL
January 1st

A son of Seithenyn, the king who lost his lands at Cantref y Gwaelod to the Irish Sea. His brother was St Tudno. After some time at Bangor-is-Coed, he founded his church at Llangwnnadl (Llangwynoedl) in Caernarfonshire and is remembered on an early inscribed stone 'VENDESETI' at nearby Llannor, which may mark his burial place. He is also mentioned on an inscribed stone ''VENNISETLI FILIUS ERCAGN--' a stone found in the wall of the hilltop church of Llansaint in Carmarthenshire. (Venu = gwyn, or white, and Setli = hoedl, or life). At Llangwnnadl is still Gwynhoedl's sacred bronze bell, hammered from sheet metal, and used by the saint to drive away evil spirits (following the custom of the Egyptian church). The church has been variously rededicated to the Holy Trinity, or Michael and Gwynhoedl. An inscription on a pier in the church reads 'I H S' GWYNHODL IACET HIC'. There is a also nine-feet standing stone at Penybont Farm, Llangwnadl. Another large stone at Llannor is carved *'ICAENALI FILI.'* The Llannor stones were found about a yard underground by a farmer in the 19th century.

Ffynnon Wynhael was documented in the 15th and 16th centuries with regard to St Gwynhael at Wolvesnewton in Monmouthshire (see Gwynell).

GWYNIN 7th century
GWYNNIN
December 31 (Llandygwynin), January 31 (Dwygyfylchi), January 21 (Scotland)

A son of Helig ap Canog, who founded Llandegwning (Llandygwynin) and Dwygyfylchi in Caernarfon. He was said by Sir John Wynn of Gwydir to be buried in Dwygyfylchi with his brother Boda or Brothen (q.v.). This saint may also be the Wynnin commemorated in Caerwinning and Kilwinning in the North of Scotland. Meini Hirion in Dwygyfylchi parish is also known as the Druids' Circle, and is the stone circle with the highest erect stones in Wales. Of the thirty stones remaining, ten are still standing, one up to nine feet high. Traditionally one could not use bad language near the 'Deity Stone', and babies were placed for luck on the 'Stone of Sacrifice'. Chris Barber notes that there are more legends concerning this site than any other stone circle in Wales.

GWYNIO mid-6th century
March 2, May 2

Llanwynio (Llanwinio) in Carmarthen remembers this saint. He was martyred by the Irish, a mile and a half south of his church, at a place still called Cil Sant (Saint's Retreat). The field is still called Parc Ffynnon Winio. Gwynin was then said to have been decapitated at a spot a few hundred yards away, where a spring gushed forth. This is probably Ffynnon Felan. The garage to the farmhouse of Cilsant is on the site of an old chapel demolished in the 1940's. Cilsant (Saint's Retreat) dates back to the 1400's when it was a defended courtyard with its own water supply. Recently for sale, it has been the home of Llwch Lawen Fawr, who in the 11th century killed a particularly fierce wild boar, of Bledri ap Cydifor who interpreted for the Normans during the Welsh rebellion of 1116, and of generations of Phillipses. Lewis Glyn Cothi wrote eulogies to John ap Philip and Philip ap Meredith ap Philip in the 15th century, before the family were legally forced to Anglicise their name to Philips in the 16th century. William Philipps became High Sheriff in 1739, and Owen Philips MP became Lord Kylsant in 1923 but was jailed for a year in 1931 for issuing a false prospectus as chairman for the Royal Mail Steam Packet Company. How many houses in Britain have such a provenance?

In 1867 a Celtic Cross was found when digging the foundations of a new church at Llanwinio. It was moved to Middleton Hall near Llandeilo (the site of the superb new Botanical Garden for Wales). Westwood read the inscription as *'Bivad - Fili Bodibe ve'*, and the Ogham as *'AWWLBODDIB BEWW---'*, which seems to indicate 'Bew, the grandson of Boddibew'. There is a standing stone near Llanwinio of white quartz, about seven feet high. The Book of Llandaf also mentions a church of 'Guinniau' in Pemboke, This could either be Penally (now Teilo's) or St Twinnell's (now St Winnocus'). The curate of Llanwinio appears in an old record as follows: *'We hear by report of ye country he is defamed and scandalised by one Catherine Vychan, a vile and wicked woman and common strumpet, and by report mother of five or six bastard children and regards not to whom she fathers them.'*

GWYNLLEU 5th – 6th century
GWNLLE
November 1

Descended from Cunedda, his father was Cyngar ab Arthog, and Gwynlleu probably founded Llangwnlle (now Nantcwnlle) in Cardigan. His brother was Cyndeyrn. Gwyl Wnlle was a great fair on November 1st. He may have been a cousin of Dewi Sant.

GWYNLLIW FARFOG (the bearded) 5th – 6th century
GWYNLLYW FILWR (Gwynlliw the Warrior), WOOLO, GUNDLEUS, GUNLEUS, GUNLYU
March 29 (also 28th and 27th)

A prince of Gwynlliwg (Wentloog) and son of Glywys ap Tegid ap Cadell. His mother was said to be Gwawr (Gwal) ferch Ceredig ap Cunedda. As the eldest of seven sons, he was acknowledged the superior over the territories passed by 'cyfran' (gavelkind) to his brothers, so was acknowledged as King of Glamorgan and Gwent*. He married Gwladys ferch Brychan. They are the only married couple to share a feast day. The legend is that he took Gwladys by force from the Court of Brychan and Arthur (who also wanted Gwladys) was asked to mediate

Alphabetical Listing of the Saints of Wales and Religious Events

at Fochrhiw. Gwynlliw is also linked with St Tathan, whose cow he stole at Caerwent. The father of Catwg, or Cadog, Gwynlliw has his own 'Life' and is also mentioned in the Life of Cadog. He was known as the 'Prince of the Southern Britons.' Some believe that he was Sir Lancelot, and his son Cadfael (Cadog, the 'battle prince') was Sir Galahad.

According to the Life of Cadog, Cadog's behaviour brings about Gwynlliw's conversion, but in Gwynlliw's Vita, he is a respected man who is converted by an angel, and leaves his wife to pursue a religious life. He was visited on his death bed by St Dyfrig.

Woolos is the Anglicisation of an attempt to say Gwynlliw's Cathedral, which stands on the remains of a Celtic camp on Stow Hill** overlooking Newport. This may have been the site of Gwynlliw's court. It is said that Gwynlliw saw a white ox on the top of the hill, and built his cell there. There is a *'protection curse'* on the site which says anyone who desecrates the church (cathedral) will die. A field on Stow Hill had a moated mound on it, known as Bedd Gwynlliw, but this was probably not his grave but his fort. He was buried by his son Cadog at St Woolos. The district of Pillgwenlli in Newport means Gwynlliw's Creek. Two parishes named after Gwynlliw were once in the parishes of Llanelli and Llanegwad.

Apart from Cadog, his sons included the saints Cammarch, Glywys Cerniw, Bugi, Cyfyw, Cynfyw, Gwyddlew, Cyflewyr and Cammab. His daughter was Maches. Bugi's son was St Beuno and Gwyddlew's son was Cannen. The son of Glywys Cerniw was Gwodloew. However, older sources give as sons of Gwynlliw only Cadog, Bugi and Cemmeu (Cynfyw). Pedrog, who became a Cornish saint, was either a brother or nephew of Gwynlliw.

Near Dryslwyn Castle is a hamlet known as Nantergwynlliw, on the banks of the Towy. Near it was Capel Gwynlliw, in Llanegwad parish, which later became a cowshed. Ffynnon Ddwfach was a holy well in the same parish.

* Note: Lands at this time were were said to be apportioned almost on a Roman pattern of each district under a 'regulus'. It appears rather than be sucked into fratricidal wars for territories, the seven brothers power-shared on the following basis. Gwynlliw was in charge of the area Gwynlliwg, (named after him and later adulterated to Wentloog), the district between the Usk (Newport) and Rumney (Cardiff) rivers. His brother Etelic took the eastern lands of Monmouthshire, and the famous Paul Penychen ruled the Vale of Glamorgan from a base at Penllyn or Pentremeurig. North of Gwyynlliw and Paul, Seru held the lordship of Senghenydd (which later passed down to the famous Welsh hero Ifor Bach). Travelling west across Glamorgan from Paul, Mar had Margam, Guria ruled the Neath area, Cetti took Cydweli and Cornouguill ruled the rest of Carmarthenshire.

** There is a lovely description of Newport's cathedral by Wirt Sikes from 1881:
'On the summit of Stow Hill stands the ancient church of St. Woollos. Its ponderous tower was built by Henry III as a special tribute of esteem to the inhabitants of Newport, whom he further honoured by placing his statue high up in a niche in its front. St Woollos – called in Welsh Gwynlliw, in Latin Gunleus – was a son of a Demetian king in South Wales, who, as he grew old, became convinced that all was vanity, and retiring from the world, led a solitary life, his daily bill of fare being restricted carefully to water and barley bread, "on which he usually strewed ashes". He died towards the end of the fifth century, 800 years before this church was built. It is a queer-looking church. Seen from the street, near its rear, it seems to be three separate edifices, with a little box of a campanile attached to the further one. But passing around into the church-yard in front of the tower its aspect changes, and the church now seems

St Woolo's Cathedral, Newport. © *Wales Tourist Board Photo Library.*

just a ponderous square tower, with some trifling peaked roofs behind it. These roofs cover successively the chapel, the nave, the whole constituting a single edifice of extraordinary length. Stone faces stare at you from all points of the structure; they look out from under the narrow eaves; they peer from the pendants of the window arches; and here and there jutting gargoyles look down on the old graves surrounding the church. Some of the tombstones are sunk almost out of sight in the sward.

High up on the front of the tower stands in the sun the statue of Henry III, with his head broken off – a ghastly object. The effigy was thus beheaded by the rough soldiers of Cromwell after they had taken Newport Castle. The view from the summit is magnificent. In the far distance loom the hills of Somersetshire, across the blue waters of the Bristol Channel, which here is supposed to merge with the Severn, though the point of junction is one which can be discerned by no eye but the map-maker's. I linger long in this steep and antique street which the Newporters call Stow Hill, with its side-walk far above the level of the roadway, like the walk which runs along both sides of the Boulevard Bonne Nouvelle, in Paris . . . '

The 'Saying of the Wise' is:
*'Hast thou heard the saying of Gwynlliw,
In mutual acrimony?
"It avails not to reason with a madman".'*

ROGER GWYNNE (1577 - c.1605)

Hugh Gwynne of Bodvel was investigated as a 'known papist', with his brother-in-law Hugh Owen in exile at Brussels. An MP and sheriff of Caernarfon, his son or younger brother was Roger, a Roman Catholic priest and missioner. When young, Gwynne came under the care of the martyr William Davies (q.v.). In 1591, Roger Gwynne was arrested with Rbert Puw (q.v.) and other aspirants to the priesthood on his way to Ireland. He was imprisoned and tortured for three months at Beaumaris, but refused to recant. On his release, he went to Spain, and entered the seminary at Valladolid in 1596. Ordained in 1602, in 1603 Gwynne returned secretly to Wales as a missionary, but his ship was intercepted. Gwynne was taken to Swansea gaol, interrogated, and then taken to the Tower of London for further interrogation and torture. It was alleged that he had 'confessed' to a plot to kill King James I, which was excelent propaganda for the Hispanophobe faction at James' court, but he was never brought to court for trial. It is known that he was still rotting in the Tower in 1605, and he probably died there. He is not regarded as one of the Catholic martyrs of this time, because the circumstances of his death are (probably deliberately) obscure.

ABBOT GWYNNO b. 487 or 507
GWYNNOG, GYNOG, GWNOG, GWYNO, GENOCUS, GWNNOD, GUINOCHUS
October 26 (22, 23 and 24 with Nwython), April 13 (Scotland), December 26 (Ireland)

One of the three saints after whom Llantrisant in Glamorgan is named, with Illtud and Tyfodwg. The son of Gildas ap Caw, with his brother Nwython (Noethon) he had a chapel in Llangwm Dinmael* in Denbigh (now converted to a mill). Like his brother he trained under Cadog (Catwg), and may be the patron saint of Y Faenor** in Brecon. Llanwynno (Llanwonno), a chapel under Llantrisant is also named after him, with a holy well known as Ffynnon Wyno. (Nearby is St Gwinno's Forest). Llanwnog*** in Montgomery is his dedication. In this church there is a stained glass window in the chancel with the inscription: *'Sanctus Gwinocus, cujus animae propitietur Deus. Amen.'* The Reverend John Parker visited St Gwynog's church here in 1828, and described the chancel screen: *'This gem of Gothic woodwork is as nearly perfect in design as anything that we know of. It would be difficult for us to suggest any alterations that would not be injurious. Never have we met with the variety, lightness, elegance and regularity so successfully combined as in this beautiful screen. It is a remarkably fine specimen of Gothic woodwork in a style very different from that which is met with elsewhere.'*

Llanwynog near Clodock in Hereford, Capel Gwynog in Caerleon, and Capel Gwynog in Llanfachreth, Merioneth have now all but disappeared. Aberhafesp in Montgomery is Gwynnog's but is sometimes ascribed to Llonio of nearby Llandinam. Guto Nyth-Bran

(Griffith Morgan) was the famous runner from Nyth-Bran Farm outside Llanwynno in Glamorgan who was supposed to have won a 12 mile race in 53 minutes in 1737. St Gwinno Forest in mid-Glamorgan is named after Gwynno.

As Genocus he founded Kilglin in Meath, where he is celebrated upon December 26th. After staying with Finnian, he returned to Wales to found Llanwnog near Caersws, at the foot of Allt Wnog. About 540 his father Gildas wrote his condemnation of the Welsh rulers of the day, including Cuneglas of Powys, whom he described as *'a bear, a rider of many, wallowing in the old filth of his wickedness, a tawny butcher.'* This is probably the reason for Gwynno leaving for Rhuys in Brittany where he stayed at Cadog's monastery, and founded Plouhinec. St Guinoux is south of St Malo, St Gueno and St Gwenael are west of Merdrignac, and St Gueno is north-east of Loudeac. In Scotland he is known as Guinochus.

*Ffynon Wnnod near Melysfaen, Llangwm is now named Fron Fach Spring. The church was dedicated to Gwnnod, then Gwnnod and Jerome, but now only Jerome.

**The Vaenor Stone had vanished when Westwood searched for it in 1846. It stood at Y Faenor, a Celtic cross of very unusual form and read *'in nomine dei summi + ilus'*. (See the next entry upon Gwynno).

***The author's grandfather, David Jervis, hailed from Llanwnog, and eventually settled in Trefeglwys after living some time in Llandinam. Repeated here is a fascinating article of his from 1928, showing some of the aspects of farm-work in Wales, including the annual 'hiring' (see Fairs):

'Very briefly I will relate how I became a farm worker. Born in the old-world village of Lanwnog in the year 1896, the only son of a farm bailiff I showed at early age great promise as a scholar and it was decided that I should continue my studies after leaving the elementary school – in fact I was intending to be something better than my father was. How my imagination ran riot; I pictured to myself the rosy future, but already a dark cloud was gathering on the horizon. One day I was called from my studies to learn that my father had but a few hours to live. Then a few days later as I followed behind his bier to the burial ground and saw the coffin lowered into the earth, it seemed that my hopes were being buried with it. Gone were my plans of the future; the castles I had built in the air came tumbling about my head like a pack of cards. I was brought now face to face with the necessity to work; to support my widowed mother. She was not willing to leave her old home and situated as it was in the midst of a farming district I had no alternative under these circumstances but to become a farm worker.

It was now the month of November and a bargain was made with a neighbouring farmer to get into his service as a cowman for the ensuing six months at a salary of one pound per month, with board and lodging, and my new duties started forthwith. The work was very strange at first but I soon adopted myself to my new task. This is what on an average I was required to do. Up in the morning at six o'clock, fodder all the stock which totalled some thirty head of cattle, mix the byres (clean out the hay in the cow stalls), *help to milk, more feeding of the stock, one mixture for feeding cattle, another for milking cows, still another for the store cattle. This would probably take some three hours to perform, it would now be lunch time (bait was the local term) then the stock all required water, with more fodder when they came back into the byre* (cow shed). *Hay and straw had now to be got in from the Dutch Barn and it required a great deal to satisfy all these animals. It would now be dinner time. In the afternoon I did various odd jobs such as chopping firewood, cleaning the farmyard etc.; and preparing for my* own stock such as pulping and mixing it with chaff, getting roots in for the morrow, etc. This it was; day after day, week in week out, with very little difference for the six months. I thought it was rather monotonous.

I will give here a description of the old farmer and his wife as I saw them. He was sixty years of age or somewhere thereabouts with coarse grey black hair, his beard straggly and unkempt. He looked at you out of dull fishy eyes, surmounted by a pair of bushy eyebrows. His clothes generally like the clothes of most farmers were aged, angular and baggy; ill-fitting at the neck and worn at the elbow and knees. Ann, his wife, was thin and shapeless, an umbrella of a woman, always dressed in shabby black with a black bonnet for best wear. You, perhaps, know how it is with some natures, how they fasten themselves like lichens to the stones of circumstances and weather their days to a crumbling conclusion. The big world sounds widely but it has no call for them. The meadow, the cornfield, the pig pen and the chicken run measure the range of their activities. Beyond these and the changes of the weather - the snow, rain and fair days – there are no significant things. All the rest of life is a far-off clamorous phantasmagoria flickering like Northern Lights in the night. Such were the farmer and his wife.

This was too narrow for me so when Maytime came I decided to make a shift. After having a little experience I hired to another farmer for twenty pounds a year. This was a type of farmer so common in this twentieth century; (the 'time is scarce' and 'time is money' type). I afterwards regretted leaving the old couple, where life was easy going, to serve under this new regime; the modern. It occurred that I had jumped out of the frying pan into the fire. But the bulldog tenacity of the Welsh race kept my spirits up and I determined to give a good account of myself. I had no particular task; I was a sort of knockabout ready at everyone's beck and call; to help the waggoner, shepherd, cowman and the 'boss'. It was here that I first made acquaintance with the scythe and I well remember after using it for the first hour, how my wrists ached. It was some time before I mastered the technique of mowing for there is more art in balancing a scythe than any looker-on would believe. The harvesting season brought a host of new tasks; viz. mowing and loading of hay, the cutting and stuckling of corn and with the harvest garnered came ploughing and storing of roots etc. and I managed to survive it all.

The following year the waggoner left us so my master pressed me to take up his work. Having had some experience the previous year I decided to go waggoner. Perhaps there is no task on the farm that requires so much skill as ploughing. It's an art that takes a long time to perfect. To be able to 'line' on an eight acre field as straight as some people can draw lines on paper (with a ruler perhaps) takes some doing. The year passed without anything eventful happening but the ordinary routine of a waggoner's work, but the job didn't suit so when Maytime came around I made up my mind to have a change. I may say here that there were a few farmers around who were anxious to secure my services, so when my 'boss' and myself failed to agree over wages I was at liberty to go where I wished.

I hired to a farmer in the district as a bailiff with a further rise in wages of ten pounds per annum. I looked on this as a sort of promotion – farm bailiff before I was twenty years of age. But I soon found that with promotion usually comes fresh responsibilities. Now I was supposed to know something about the land, the soil, the crops and the animals; to be a microbiologist, a veterinary surgeon and a naturalist – and a good deal of a man. I well remember making the first corn-stack. When about six feet high the corner suddenly collapsed and I was forced to come to the conclusion that the job required some art, and a good deal of confidence in myself. To name the multifarious tasks that a farm bailiff is supposed to be able to perform would be beyond my powers. After harvest comes thatching the various stacks, then hedging and ditching *in winter; only to name the chief. Then with spring comes the various tasks that require my best attention. New arrivals in the pig sty and lambing troubles very often keep me up all night. Sudden snowstorms and floods always give me a good deal of anxiety. But through these stormy days and nights I vision the finer weather that will come with summer when the troubles I have just described have ended. For there is no better time upon the farm than say the months of April, May and June. Just when summer comes tripping after spring across the meadows white with daisies (but I am wandering). I stayed on this farm three years gaining knowledge and experience.*

Then came the Great War and the year 1916 saw me a member of His Majesty's forces. Many a night out on the shell-swept fields of Flanders I thought how nice it would be to be back on the farm, hard though the work may be. I will not dwell upon those two years, they revive bitter memories of nights of suspense, days in an inferno of shot and shell and all the horrors inevitable in warfare. Suffice it to say that when I came home in 1919 my outlook on life had broadened considerably. How things had changed on the farm, wage boards had taken the place of individual bargaining to a great extent. The ten hour day had come into operation; well-meaning middle class persons were endeavouring to brighten village life by some form of recreation or other.

Many farm workers like myself had come back from the Army and they were no longer the tongue-tied countrymen – they had travelled, seen life and it had done them good. About this time another tragedy overtook me, my mother passed away and I was left alone in the world. There are times in our march through life when we stop and look back, a sort of retrospect as it were. It was such a time now with me, a breathing space in the long march of humanity. I seemed but a leaf blown with the wind through the streets of the village. I wanted to come close to someone who would understand the feeling that had taken possession of me after the death of my mother. That is how I married, and another milestone passed on the road we call life. I now moved to the farm upon which my father worked before his demise, and I have tried to be a worthy son of a worthier father, and if I have failed it is not for want of trying.
Now to sum up the life of a farm worker, it's no easy task I know. That the life is hard and exacting I am under no illusion whatsoever, but I'll not deny that it is a varied and healthful life. Even now as I look back over the seventeen-odd years of farm work, I find that a good deal of the irksome character of it is disappearing. Farmhands who possess motorcycles (and a great many of them do) see more of the country than is seen by the majority of town lads, and generally speaking are in better and happier circumstances. Perhaps it is not a great thing to boast about, but I am proud of being a farm worker. We it is who are the backbone of the nation, although abused and looked down upon.

Then consider the fact that the farmer, the farm worker and the countryside have many times been celebrated in poems and novels. Ugliness spreads itself over every page of the industrial novel but when a poet or novelist is tormented by the tragedies of nature there is something majestic and beautiful in what he describes. Life enfolds itself more fully on a farm than anywhere else, and generally speaking, the farm worker absorbs, almost without knowing it, the consciousness of being a **man***. People who complain that the farm worker's life is dull and uneventful, are those who make no means of bettering it. Our lives are what we make them. If it's dull, monotonous and continual drudge, well it's the worker's own fault. Too many of us I'm afraid go through life with closed eyes. They only see the world as through a smoky glass, they go halfway to meet the woes and let the sunshine pass. To a married man like myself, in the spring and summer, there's pottering about in the garden and numerous odd jobs that require doing.*

Despite what people say about the new Summertime Act, I find it very beneficial. It gives one more time after leaving off work to do something for oneself if you have the mind to do it. Then on dark, long winter nights I pass my time studying the daily paper and reading. I should like to see more farm workers purchasing a daily paper not for the sake of reading the murders and divorce cases; but to keep in touch with what goes on in the world of politics, commerce, music and literature. Many will say they can't afford it, that's a very weak excuse. Many see it nothing to spend sixpence on a pint of beer every night or a seal of tobacco, yet a daily paper only costs a fraction of these. I'm not boasting when I say that I read everything that comes my way that's worth reading. **First The Bible**, *the book too much neglected today and looked upon as an ornament. Then I am very familiar with the works of the 'moderns', Shaw, Galsworthy, Bennet, Wells, Hardy, Kipling, to name only a few. But don't think for one instance that I despise the ancient. I know men like Shakespeare, Dickens, Kingsley and Stevenson.*

Now as I pen these lines Autumn is giving place to Winter in the world of nature around me, but it has a deeper significance. It reminds us that we are not to stay here for ever, the autumn of life will come. So whatever our station in life, let us make the most of our opportunity here. I would not change my occupation of a farm worker for a fortune. So as I have lived may I also retire on an old-age pension and a well-earned rest some thirty-five years hence (if I shall live to see it) with those words of Robert Loius Stevenson ringing in my ears:
> *Under the wide and starry sky,*
> *Dig me a grave and let me lie,*
> *Home is the sailor, home from the sea,*
> *And the worker home from the hill.*

David Henry Jervis of Llanwnog went on to have three daughters, and built up a wood-cutting and butcher's business, as well as being the local choir-master and composer. He was prominent in eisteddfodau. Unfortunately with his sudden death in a motor-cycle accident in 1941, his three young daughters were left as orphans. His wife Gladys had died in childbirth in 1938, and another daughter had died of meningitis aged three. David Jervis' precious library of Welsh books, and all his writings and hymns were burnt as the house was cleared. This pattern has been replicated across Wales last century, and there seems to be an increasing disregard for what we can learn from the past. A major purpose of this book is to discover more about the Age of the Saints. This first edition will not be perfect, and there will probably be great mistakes, but the author is willing to keep working on fresh information to help rebuild Welsh heritage.

GWYNNO 6th century
GWYNO
March 3

Only the crumbling tower of St. Gwynno's Church at Vaynor (Y Faenor, Maenor Wyno), just north of Merthyr Tudful, remains. In 1868, the rest of this ancient earth-floored church was demolished to build a new one. Richard Crawshay, the hated ironmaster, is buried here, with his ten ton gravestone slab asking 'GOD FORGIVE ME'. Another epitaph, on a plaque in the west wall tells us of Catherine Morgan, who died aged 106 in 1794:
> *She was born in the third Year*
> *Of the Reign of King James II*
> *And lived under seven Reigns*

Another tombstone commemorates a broken-hearted suitor:
Here lies the body of Gruffydd Shon
Covered here with earth and stone
You may sweep it up or leave it alone
It will just be the same to Gruffydd Shon

It may be that St Gwynno is also one of the five saintly sons of Cynyr, commemorated at Llanpumsaint, and/or the same saint in the previous entry.

GWYNNOG see WINNOC

GWYNNORO 6th century
All Saints Day

One of Cynyr's sons, commemorated at Llanpumsaint in Carmarthen.

GWYNWS 5th century
GWNNWS, GUINNIUS
December 13

A son of Brychan, he founded Llanwnnws, Ystrad Meurig, near Tregaron in Cardigan. Ffynnon Wnnws was famous for curing eye diseases. A nearby farm is still called Penlan Wnws. He is mentioned in the Life of Padarn as being the 'dux' (leader) of a local church. (See Gwynen). There is a Celtic cross-slab in his church with ribbon terminal knots, ring bosses and the letters XPS (Christos). (See Genys.)

The Stone of St Gwnnws in Llanwnnws churchyard is inscribed *'quinque explicaverit hoc nomen det benedixionem pro anima hiroidil filius carotinn,'* and bears Christ's 'xps' monogram. Professor Rhys in 1873 thought that it commemorated the early saint 'Kynydyn ap Bleddid', identical with Canotinn. However, local tradition is that 'Carotinn' was Caradog, with Pwll Caradog waterfall nearby. A farm in north Cardigan is called Nantcaredin, and it may also be the Irish Cairthinn remembered here. Another observation is that 'Hiroidil' may be 'Guoidil the tall', and Guoidil is mentioned in the Book of Llandaf. A final commentary by Dr John Jones is that the inscription commemorates Heraidd ap Caron ap Illtud (see Caron and Illtud). Thus there are four contenders for the provenance of the St Gwnnws Stone.

GWYTHERIN late 6th century

Brother of Baglan and son of Dingad ap Nudd Hael, he founded Gwytherin in Denbigh, where Gwenfrewi retreated and was originally buried. Another source states that the founder was the Elerius who features in the Life of Gwenfrewi. It has been rededicated to James the Apostle. Llanvetherine in Monmouthshire was once *'Ecclesia Gueithirin'*, according to the Book of Llandaf. However, some give a saint Merin as its founder. It is now, like the previous Gwytherin church, rededicated to James the Apostle.

Alphabetical Listing of the Saints of Wales and Religious Events

'The Gwytherin Stone' is one of four upright stones in a row in Gwytherin churchyard. One reads *'VINNEMAGLI FIL SENEMAGL'*. A sculpured stone at Llanvetherine (Llanferin) is almost seven feet long, found about 1730 when a vault was being dug in the chancel. A priest is depicted, and the words *'S. VETTERINUS'* and *'IXCOB PSONA'* could be deciphered. It thus seems to commemorate a priest named Jacobus, rather than St Gwytherin ap Dingad, as was commonly supposed.

GWYTHYR 4th century

This name comes from the Roman 'Victor'. It was the name of the son of Macsen Wledig and Elen, who was killed shortly after his father's death in 388. Iolo Morganwg claims he was the saint of *'Eglwys Wythyr'*, now known as Monington, in Pembroke. However, the church is now dedicated to St Nicholas, and the *'wythyr'* may refer to the *'eight freeholders'* of the parish.

GYNAID

A hermit associated with the earliest days of the saints at Ynys Enlli. He lived in a cave and cured sick islanders.

GYNYR see CYNYR

H

'He that knows about depth knows about God.'

Paul Tillich, 'The Shaking of the Foundations' 1962

HARAN 6th century?

Llanharan lies next to Llanilid in the 'northern' Vale of Glamorgan, and St Haran is noted in many places near Treguier in Brittany, near Illtud foundations - perhaps Haran was a saint who went across from Llanilltud with his abbot.

In his diary, William Thomas noted the marriage of his namesake from Lanharan, aged 93, in Llantrisant in 1794: *(he) had buried his third wife about four weeks before, (and was married) to the niece of late Joe John of Llantrissent, of 19 years of age, and the following Days she absconded from him with £50 he gave her at the day of marriage, and he since have published her in three Market Towns and in the News.'*

HOWELL HARRIS 1714-1773
July 27

Given a Holy Day by the Church in Wales, this religious reformer from Talgarth was refused holy orders because of his 'irregular' preaching, and was told by his friend Griffith Jones to become more moderate. He worked closely with Daniel Rowland (q.v.) and among their earliest converts were Howel Davies and the great William Williams of Pantycelyn (q.v.). In 1742, they formed an Association to parallel the Methodist movement in England, and Harris aligned his followers with the Wesley brothers, against the sterner Calvinistic Welsh supporters of George Whitefield. The reform movement again split in 1750 between the Welsh Methodist supporters of Rowland and those of Harris. In 1752, Harris retired to Trefeca, establishing a 'Family' of his supporters. Much has been written on Harris, and 'The Dictionary of Welsh Biography' aptly summarises his life:
'His greatest contribution to the welfare of the people was his preaching. This was the means of waking the humbler classes of Wales from their torpid slumber and of revealing to them their spiritual endowments. He was, indeed, one of the makers of modern Wales. In spite of his cross-grained and dictatorial temper, his unceasing enthusiasm and his unbounded desire to save souls carried everything before him in the early days of the religious renaissance. The influence which he has had on the life of his people proves that he was the greatest spiritual force in his generation and many believe that he was the greatest Welshman of his age.'

HAWYSTL see TUDGLID

HAWYSTL GLOFF 6th century
The father of saints Deifer and Teyrnog, but probably not a saint himself.

HEILIN 5th – 6th century

A son of Brychan, with a chapel near Llangefni in central Anglesey, and also possibly a church in Cornwall.

HEININ
HERNIN?

In his 'Sayings of the Wise', Iolo Morganwg notes this saint as being in Llanfeithin, just next to Llancarfan:
*'Hast thou heard the saying of Heinin
The Bard, of the choir of Llanveithin?
"The brave will not be cruel".'*

HELEDD 6th – 7th century
HILLEDD

The church of Llanhilleth is now dedicated to Illtud, but in the 16th -17th centuries it was spelt Llanhilledd Vorwyn, Hilledd the Virgin (morwyn). *'Llan Helet'* is also mentioned in the Stanzas of the Graves (Englynion y Beddau), possibly dating from the late 6th century. There was a Hilledd ferch Cyndrwyn, a princess of Powys, and therefore of a saintly family, being the aunt of Aelhaiarn, Cynhaiarn and Llwchaiarn. If so she was the sister of Cynddylan. His death in battle against the Saxons, and the burning of his palace on the great Roman site of Wroxeter, is commemorated in a magnificent saga poem finally written down in the 9th century. Wroxeter had been built on the River Severn crossing of Watling Street, as the base for the Roman invasion of Wales. It became the fourth largest town in Roman Britain, and has been much improved as a visitor centre in the last few years. The most unusual find was the skull of a man, who suffocated while hiding under the floor of one of the hot-air rooms when the city was attacked. He was clutching a bag containing his savings of 132 coins. Some of the lines from 'Cynddylan's Hall' from the 9th century saga 'Canu Heledd' are:

*Dark is Cynddylan's hall tonight
With no fire, no bed.
I will weep awhile, then I will be silent*

*Dark is Cynddylan's hall tonight
With no fire, no candle.
Save for God, who will give me peace?*

*Dark is Cynddylan's hall tonight
With no fire, no light.
Grief for you overwhelms me.'*

Heledd's 'Saying of the Wise' is:
*'Hast thou heard the saying of Heledd,
The daughter of Cyndrwyn, of extensive wealth?
"Prosperity cannot come from pride".'*

According to the Llywarch Hen saga, Cynddylan lies buried in Baschurch.

HELEN see ELEN

HELIG FOEL early 7th century

He owned the land known as Tyno Helig near Beaumaris, which was drowned and became Lafan Sands. The country stretched from Puffin Island on Anglesey to Penmaenmawr in North Wales. Llys Helig (his palace) is said to be 500 yards across, and last century the straight lines of its edges could still be seen. These may be glacial remnants like the 'sarnau' leading into the sea from the Cardiganshire coast. However, estimates are that the sea has risen around 40* feet in the last 1500 years. All the legends of lost lands around Wales and the West Country, enshrined in early verse, means that there were probably settlements offshore (see 'Atlantis' in 'The A-Z of Wales and the Welsh'). Around the same time, the Cantref y Gwaelod of Seithenyn was submerged in Cardigan Bay. Helig turned to religion after the loss of his lands. He was the son of Glanog and the grandson of Gwgan Gleddyf, who fought with Brochwel against the destruction of Bangor-is-Coed. Puffin Island's oldest recorded name was Insula Glannauc, Ynys Glannog, in the 'Annales Cambriae' entry for 629. It seems that it was named after Helig's father. It is now called Ynys Seiriol or Priestholm.

Helig's sons also took up the monastic life in Bangor Deiniol and Bangor Enlli, their names being Aelgyfarch, Boda, Brothen, Bodfan, Bedwas, Celynin, Brenda, Euryn, Gwyar, Gwynnin, Peris and Rhychwyn.

*There are several effects eroding the British coastline. Very, very slowly, the eastern half of Britain is tipping into the sea, and the western half rising. However, global warming may mean higher sea levels. Much Welsh land has been lost by simple erosion of the cliffs and rockfaces, and by inundation of low-lying lands.

HENWG 6th century

Henwg features in the legend of Taliesin's birth. Iolo seems to think that he was at Caerleon, and he may have been the bard, Henwg Fardd associated with Llancarfan. Llanhennock near Caerleon was once known as Llan Henwg and is now dedicated to John the Baptist. (See Taliesin)

ABBOT HENWYN 6th century
HWYN, HYWYN
January 1, 6

This monk was trained at Llanilltud Fawr, and is the patron of Aberdaron on the Llyn peninsula in Gwynedd, where two wakes were held for him in January, on the 1st and 6th. Pilgrims used to visit his church before their pilgrimage to Bardsey Island, where he became abbot. The son of Gwyndaf Hen, Hywyn was said to be confessor to Cadfan. His mother was Anna, or Gwenonwy ap Meurig ap Tewdrig, therefore he was Arthur's cousin. Hywyn's brother was Baglan and his sister Meugant. Another source makes his father Dingad. His 'stone altar', a huge block where pigrims prayed before they made the dangerous crossing, has been unfortunately blasted to make lime, but Ffynnon Saint remains. There are churches dedicated to

'Ewen' in Hereford, Gloucester and Bristol, which may be his, but are more likely to be those of Euny, brother of Ia.

Wales' greatest poets in the English language of the 20th century are Dylan Thomas, David Jones, Idris Davies and the Reverend R.S. Thomas. R.S. was nominated for the Nobel prize, and St Hywyn's was his church until he retired.

GEORGE HERBERT 1593-1633
February 27

Given the Holy Day of his day of death, Herbert was a cleric and poet, the son of Richard and Magdalen Herbert of Montgomery. Educated at Westminster and Trinity College, Cambridge, he was MP for Montgomery in the first Parliament of Charles I in 1625. Herbert was a friend of Nicholas Ferrar, and in this year seems to have had a religious conversion. He then devoted himself to the priesthood from 1626, and wrote 'A Priest in the Temple' and 'The Temple', collections of devout poetry which are superbly sincere, recounting his spiritual struggles. Among his verses are the following:
'He that lives in hope danceth without musick',
'Who aimeth at the sky
Shoots higher much than he that means a tree',
and
'The God of love my Shepherd is,
And he that doth me feed,
While He is mine, and I am His,
What can I want or need?'

HERNIN see ERNIN

Cilhernin, Llanboidy in Carmarthenshire is dedicated to him. Hernin in Llandegwad may be his, but he may be the same saint as Ernin.

HERBOT 5th-6th century
HERBAULT

This Welsh saint went to Brittany in a huge wave of immigrants fleeing the Saxons. Unfortunately his 'Life' was destroyed around 1350 as war swept through Brittany, but his is the most extended of all the cults of the Breton saints. He was stoned by the women of Berrien in Finistere, because their men were listening to him, rather than work in the fields on Sunday. In retaliation he cursed the fields around Berrien to produce nothing but stones. A proverb thus runs: *'There are four things that God cannot do: level Brasparts, clear Plouyé of fern, rid Berrien of stones, and make the girls of Pouallaouen steady.'* The author knows the village of Brasparts, in a hilly area. Plouyé has a single old-fashioned pub, run by a nationalist Welshman, selling traditional dark Coreff ales from Morlaix by hand-pump. Berrien is indeed stony, but research sadly ended before the hamlet of Pouallaouen was approached.

Herbot had cows' tails offered at altars to him, and there is his chapel at Huelgoat, a wonderful vista of tumbling rocks and waterfalls. Huelgoat is one of the great tourist spots of Brittany, with the iron age Camp d'Artus ('Arthur's Camp') overlooking it. With Gildas and Eloi he is the patron of sick horses in Brittany. There are villages named St Herbot outside Huelgoat and south of Lannion.

HIA – see IA

HILARY

St Hilary's Chapel in Denbigh has only a three storey tower remaining. It used to belong to the Welsh foundation of Llanmarchell. This is possibly the same saint as Eilian.

HOEDLOYW 6th century

According to Iolo Morganwg, the brother of Gwynhoedl and son of Seithenin.

THE HOLY GRAIL

Ysrad Fflur Abbey was the centre of pilgrimage for the Holy Grail, and many legends link the grail with Nanteos Mansion nearby (see 'The A-Z of Wales and the Welsh'). A historian named John of Glastonbury made Arthur tenth in descent, by his mother, from Joseph of Arimathea, and claimed that many of his knights seeking the grail were also descendants of Joseph.

The cup used by Jesus Christ at the Last Supper was supposed to have been brought by Joseph of Arimathea to Glastonbury, and from there to Ystrad Fflur (Strata Florida Abbey). Richard Whiting, the last abbot of Glastonbury was hanged, drawn and quartered on Glastonbury Tor on the orders of Henry VIII, possibly because the grail had left there for Ystrad Fflur. When Henry dissolved the monasteries, the last seven monks of Ystrad Fflur are supposed to have taken the cup into the protection of the Powell family at Nanteos near Aberystwyth, the descendants of Edwin ap Gronw, Lord of Tegeingl. A tradition says that the fragment of the wooden bowl remaining inspired Wagner to write 'Parsifal', and visitors are showed to the music room where Wagner worked on the opera. Fiona Mirylees, the last Powell heiress, placed the treasured 'cwpan' in a bank safe in Herefordshire, as the Powell family left Nanteos Mansion in the 1960's. The remaining ancient fragment is about four inches across, made of olive wood. So little is left, because supplicants used to wish to take a tiny splinter home with them. A priest named James Wharton was supposedly cured of severe rheumatism by the Nanteos Cup in 1957.

One of the Thirteen Treasures that Merlin had to guard was the Dysgl of Rhydderch, a sixth century King of Strathclyde. It was a wide platter, where *'whatever food are wished for thereon was instantly obtained'*. This was also a description of the drinking horn of King Brân the Blessed, in which one received *'all the drink and food that one desired'*. Ceridwen's Cauldron contains all knowledge, and she gives birth to Taliesin. The Cauldron of Diwrnach would give the best cut of meat to a hero, but none to a coward. Brân also had a cauldron in which dead men could be revived. The cauldron of the Celts seems to be a precursor of the Grail, or cup of the Last Supper.

Strata Florida Abbey. © *Wales Tourist Board Photo Library.*

HOLY ROOD DAY
September 26

'Ffair Gwyl y Grog' was held on this day in Cardiganshire to mark the beginning of *'amswer gwylad' (the time to keep a vigil)*, i.e. to spend the evenings in the home as the nights grow longer. 'Grog' means holy cross.

RICHARD HOOKER 1554-1600
October 30

Given a holy day by the Church in Wales, he is seen as the *'representative voice of historic Anglicanism,'* by the new Archbishop of Wales, Rowan Williams. Hooker's treatise 'On the Laws of Ecclesiastical Polity' tried to stem the Puritan extremisms of religious opponents like Thomas Cartwright. From Exeter, Hooker studied at Oxford, and became Rector of Bishopsbourne in Kent. He was subject to strong attacks from Calvinists. Izaak Walton wrote Hooker's biography, and he quoted King James I as saying of Hooker's 'Laws': *I observe there is in Mr Hooker no affected language; but a grave, comprehensive, clear manifestation of reason, and that backed with the authority of the Scriptures, the fathers and schoolmen, and with all law both sacred and civil.'*

HUARVE 6th century
HERVE
June 17

The son of the British bard Hoarvian who sang at Childebert's court in Paris. Hoarvian married a Breton, Rivanon and their son Huarve was born blind. The boy grew up to teach in his uncle's monastic school at Plouvien where he became the abbot, before founding a new monastery at Lanhouarneau. Herve is invoked for sore eyes. Villages named St Herve are west of Guincamp, south of St Brieuc and north of Gourin. One of the most popular miracles attributed to Herve is that a wolf ate the donkey which Herve used for ploughing. Herve prayed and the wolf put himself into the harness to help complete the task.

HUNYDD 5th – 6th century

A 'daughter' of Brychan and mother of Cynin (Llangynin, Carmathsnshire). She married Tudwal Befr, and there was a Llystin Hunydd near Cilcain in Flintshire.

HUUI

In a land grant by Caradog ap Rhiwallon around 1060, there were four saints commemorated at Llangwm in Monmouthshire, Huui, Eruen, Cinficc (Cynfig) and Mirgint. Penhow, with its Norman castle, is now dedicated to St John the Baptist, but may also be associated with Huui. The churches at Llangwm Isa and Llangwm Ucha are now dedicated to John and Jerome.

HYCHAN 5th-6th century
August 8, October 1, 12

A son of Brychan and the founder of Llanhychan (Llanychan) in the Vale of Clwyd. He was said to have been martyred by the Irish at Rhandir Hychan (Hychan's District), in a field now adulterated to Cae Henry Fychan. His sister Tybie was also slain here, and the adjoining parish is Llandybie. There was a Llan Hychan in Carmarthen where the fair was October 1 then October 12, but further research is needed to find the present name of this place.

HYDROC
May 5

A Cornish saint remembered at Lanhydroc.

HYGARFAEL ap CYNDRWYN

From Llystinwennan in Caereinion, Montgomery, he was not a saint but his children were the saints Aelhaiarn, Llwchaiarn and Cynhaiarn.

HYWEL 6th century
CUILLUS, HUAIL AP CAW AP GERAINT

This eldest son of Caw was *'a man of great prowess in arms, who, upon the death of his father, succeeded to his kingdom'* (The Life of Gildas). He was killed in civil war or for vengeance by Arthur at Ruthun, possibly before his family moved to Wales from the North country. Another source claims that this warrior saint spent his life fighting for Arthur, before retiring to Llancarfan. There was said to be a church dedicated to him in Ewyas, Hereford, and a holy well exists near Coed Howell in Gwent. There was also Ffynnon Howel near Sutton Wood, and Howell's Well at St Tathan in Glamorgan. It seems that in the run-up to Camlan, which it is generally agreed was fought between Britons, Hywel may have changed sides, possibly to align with Maelgwn Gwynedd against Arthur. Certainly Maelgwn received warmly the family of Caw when they came to North Wales, much as the Breton princes were welcomed by Arthur's family in South-East Wales around the same time. With both noble houses looking for new lands, this may just have been the real cause of Camlan, a battle between Britons, rather than Britons against Saxons or other invaders.

Hywel may have gone to Brittany with his brother Gildas after escaping from the Northern wars in Strathclyde. There are several legends concerning his disagreement with Arthur. One is that he courted a lady friend of Arthur, and wounded Arthur in the leg when challenged to a duel. Arthur told him that his life would be spared as long as Hywel told no-one that Arthur had been hurt. Later, Hywel blamed Arthur's poor dancing on a limp, so Arthur took his vengeance for *'telling the tale.'* This is in the chronicle of Elis Gruffydd, written in the 16th century. Another story, that of 'Culhwch and Olwen', is that Hywel stabbed Gwydre, son of Gwenabwy, the sister of Arthur. For either of these crimes, he was executed on Maen Huail, which still stands in St Peter's Square in front of Exmewe Hall (now Barclays Bank) in Ruthin (Rhuthun).

The famous Llywell Stone was found in 1878 on the road from Trecastle Roman camp in Brecon to Glasfynydd. It was being prepared for use as a gate-post, but the Vicar of Llywell rescued it from a heap of rubble. One of the oddest of Wales' Celtic crosses, it has a St Andrew's cross, and the figure of an owl or a man in a corner. The Ogham marks are indistinct, but it is thought that it was inscribed Mactreni, who is also mentioned on the great stone of Cilgerran (see Llawddog).

The Life of Gildas by Caradog of Llancarfan reads *'Huail the elder brother, an active and most distinguished soldier, submitted to no king, not even to Arthur. He used to harass the latter, and to provoke the greatest anger between them both. He would often swoop down from Scotland, set up conflagrations, and carry off spoils of victory and renown. In consequence the king of All Britain, on hearing that the high-spirited youth had done such things and was doing similar things, pursued the victorious and excellent youth, who, as the inhabitants used to assert and hope, was destined to become king. In the hostile pursuit and council of war held on the Isle of Man, he killed the young plunderer. After that murder the victorious Arthur returned rejoicing greatly that he had overcome his greatest enemy. Gildas the historian, who was staying in Ireland and directing studies at the city of Armagh, heard that his brother had been slain by Arthur. He was grieved with hearing the news, wet with lamentation, as a dear brother for a dear brother.'* The furious Gildas returned to Wales, where *'large numbers from among the clergy and people gathered together to reconcile Arthur for the murder.'*

Giraldus Cambrensis also stated that Arthur killed Hywel, and that Gildas threw all his writings in praise of Arthur into the sea. It seems that Arthur paid blood-money and gave lands to

Gildas, in return for which Gildas gave Arthur *'the kiss of peace.'* The clutch of neighbouring churches of Gildas' family may verify that this happened. Hywel's 'saying of the wise' is *'often a curse will drop out from the bosom.'* In the triads, Hywel is one of the *'three diademed battle-chiefs of the Isle of Britain'*.

HYWEL FARCHOG 6th century
LLYWEL, HOEL MAWR*, RIWAL MAWR
October 31

A son of Emyr Llydaw, and one of the Bretons associated with Arthur, as *'one of the three noble knights of the court.'* He is noted as fighting for Arthur against Lancelot. He seems to be the patron of Llanhywel (near Solva) under Landeloy in Pembrokeshire. There is a painting there called 'The Donation' showing St Teilo, King Aercol and Hywel. Teilo helped bring order to Aercol's riotous court, in return for which Aercol gave Teilo land to build churches. Teilo gave this site, in the 6th century, to Hywel. There is a 6th century burial stone beneath the west window, removed from the church of St Iago at nearby Carnhedryn, and is dedicated to 'Rinacus'. The church is on the 'Saints and Stones pilgrimage trail, and to reach St David's one passes Dowrog Common. This was once known as 'Tir Pererinion', 'Pilgrim's Land', as it was given to the church by Prince Rhys ap Tewdwr around 1080. Also at Llanhowell is a cromlech, recorded in 1911 as having a capstone measuring 15 feet by 11 feet by 4 feet.

Llanllywel in Monmouth is now dedicated to Llywel (q.v.), but was spelt Llanhowel in the 16th century. This knight may be Hywel Fawr, the father of Hywel Fychan, and remembered in Brittany as Hoel le Grand or Hoel Meur. Baring-Gould and Fisher believed that as Hoel Mawr, he was responsible for forcing his father and brothers out of Brittany into Wales, where they married into Arthur's family. His brothers Alan Fyrgan, Owain, Gwyndaf Hen and Amwn Ddu all served Arthur in his battles. One genealogy makes Lancelot a brother. Iolo Morganwg gives as Hywel's children Derfel Gadarn, Tudwal, Dwyfael, Leonore and Armel.

Crickhowell, Crughywel is now dedicated to Edmund, but is at the centre of many interesting cairns. There is a dolmen at Gwernvale, a standing stone called the Turpillian Stone (see Dingad) which vanished in the 20th century, and another large stone near Llangenny. There is a holy well, Ffynnon Howel in Llanrhystud parish, Cardiganshire. Two more holy wells are in Pembroke: Pistyll Howell is in Whitechurch, Cemaes and Parc Ffynnon Howel was near Rhos Howel. Penmark, in the Vale of Glamorgan, was formerly named Penmarch Hywel, and there is a Howell's Well in neighbouring St Tathan. The strange 'Llywel Stone' found in Brecon is in the British Museum, and is described in the Ilid entry, and under Hywel ap Caw.

*Hoel Mawr was a nephew or cousin of Arthur who was said to have landed at Southampton is response to Arthur's request for help against the Saxons. Their joint force won victories at Lincoln, Dubglas, York, Caer-Brithon, Celidon Wood and Badon Hill. They then battled the Scots, Picts and Irish in Moray, and retook York from the Saxon Colgrin, returning the land of Elmet to Loth, Auguselus and Urien. The legend is that Arthur (Armel?) then went to Brittany to take Gaul for Hoel. Hoel's mother was said to be Gwyar, Arthur's sister, in a late Welsh story, and in Breton history he reigned from 510-545. (Gwyar was also identified with Morgan le Fay, who features strongly in Breton legends of Arthur. See Gwawr). He shared the kingship with his father (Emyr Llydaw, Budic II), who died in the same year. The dates and kinship patterns certainly fit with Arthur's time. Hoel is also famous as the father of Iseult of the White Hands, who features in the Tristan legend. He gave land to his cousin, St Briog, to settle in Brittany.

In various genealogies, his children include the kings Tewdwr Mawr, Hoel Fychan (Hoel II of Brittany), Ithel Hael, and the saints Tudwal, Seve, Silun (Sulien), Dwyaraw (Dwywau), Mael (Arthfael) and Llynor. Arthfael has been claimed by some as King Arthur, but this seems too late. There is a 'Saying of the Wise' attributed to Hywel, *'a chieftain powerful in war'*, which reads *'where love exists, it will not be concealed.'*

I

'In a consumer society there are inevitably two kinds of slaves: the prisoners of addiction and the prisoners of envy.'
Ivan Illich, 'Tools for Conviviality', 1973

IA 6th - 7th century
IVES, IVE, HYA
February 3, October 22, 27

This Irish virgin was taught by Baruc, according to Leland who saw her 'Life' (now unfortunately lost) at St Ives. At her parish church near the harbour, there is a beautiful Lady's Chapel, and paintings and wood carvings of the Celtic saints. The Cornish name for St Ives is Porth Ia. Her brothers Elwyn (Euny) and Erth were killed by a local king named Teudar, but Ia escaped. She has a holy well, Ffynnon Ia, at Venton Ia near Porthmeor Beach, but a well and chapel dedicated to her at Troon near Camborne have vanished. Plouyé in Brittany was a centre of her cult (Plou Hya), where she was martyred. A thankfully old-fashioned hostelry in Plouyé is run by a Welsh Nationalist, and serves Morlaix beer (like Brains' Dark) and several traditional Breton ciders and beers.

In 1528 Margaret Hunt was called to the Commissary of London to explain her magical healing. *'First, she ascertained the names of the sick persons. Then she knelt and prayed to the Blessed Trinity to heal them from all their wicked enemies. Then she told them to say for nine consecutive nights five paternosters, three Aves and three Creeds "in the worship of Saint Spirit". At bedtime they were to repeat one Paternoster, one Ave and one Creed in worship of St Ive, to save them from all envy. For the ague she prescribed various herbs. For sores she also recommended herbs, but taken with a little holy water and some prayers. The formulae she had learned from a Welsh woman, Mother Elmet.'* (Thomas, 'Religion and the Decline of Magic')

IAGO 6th century
JAMES
July 24, 6, November 5, 7

The son of Gwen Tierbon and Fracan. With his twin brother Gwethenoc he assisted his father to evangelise Britanny and fight against pagan attacks. It is tempting to ask for further research into the Iago who founded Santiago de Compostela in Celtic Galicia in the 6th century*. Near Denbigh, heading towards Llyn Brenig there is the tiny church of St Iago, with an open-air pulpit built into an aged yew tree. Iago has been given the same feast dates as his twin Gwethenoc.

Caernarfon had three holy wells named Ffynnon Iago. On Ffynnon Iago Farm near Llanybyther his mediaeval chapel was said to stand. The other two were near Cilmaenllwyd, and at Llanllawddog near Bryncroes. Another two are in Glamorgan, south of Maesteg and north of Kenfig Hill. There was also a Ffynnon Iago in Bayvil, Pembroke. St Iago's church at Carnhedryn had a 6th century burial stone (see Hywel Farchog). King Iago of Gwynedd, who

Alphabetical Listing of the Saints of Wales and Religious Events

died at the fateful battle of Chester in the early 7th century, may not have been accounted as a saint.

St James Chapel has been 'rediscovered' in farm outbuildings at Llanquian in the Vale of Glamorgan. It may be surmised that this was a pre-Norman foundation, as the Roman town of Cowbridge was subject to it. Cowbridge's remarkable Holy Cross Church was known for centuries as *'the Llanquian Aisle'*, under the *'capella St Jacobi de Landcoman.'* Remains of a mediaeval village and the ruined de Nerber Castle can still be seen at Llanquian. Visitors to the area must stroll along the architecturally attractive Cowbridge High Street, which is one of the most attractive (and affluent) shopping areas in Wales. One of Cowbridge's mediaeval gate-houses is still intact.

*James the Great, brother of John, was the first apostle to be put to death, by King Herod Agrippa in 44. The shrine at Compostela in Galicia is on the site of an early Christian cemetery, where there is a 'martyrium' attesting to an early saint. There was a bishop of Barcelona named Iago around 360-390. St Mary's Church at Merida possessed early relics of 'Iago' possibly as early as 627, before the Islamic conquest. The cult and relics moved northwards, especially fostered by the Asturian kings Alphonso II and III in the 9th century. Asturia was a Celtic kingdom, like Galicia. The first mention of Iago preaching the gospel in Spain dates from the 7th century. The first record of his burial there is in the 'Martyrology of Usuard' in 865. James the Apostle's bones had been 'discovered' on a Galician hillside in 820, eight centuries after his beheading in Palestine by Herod. Santiago became the most popular pilgrimage shrine in Europe after Rome, with roads being built and the emblems of the pilgrim's hat and scallop shell being associated with the church. In June 1999, around half a million pilgrims came to the church, around 10% by the traditional 'Pilgrim's Route' through the mountains of north-western Spain. The Vatican had declared that pilgrims, who must walk at least 65 miles, will have past sins wiped out if they made the pilgrimage before the year 2000. In mediaeval times, a journey to St David's was equivalent to one to Santiago. By the 1700's the numbers on The Pilgrim's Road dwindled away, when the bones of the saint were hidden to keep them out of the hands of British pirates. They were not found again until 1879, and pilgrimages to the edge of the known Roman world, to Finisterre, restarted to the 11th century church.

Other Galicia-Wales ties are explored with minimal depth in this book, and it would be fascinating to develop a stronger case for the founder of Santiago being a Briton. A test on the bones, which perhaps could find them to be 1400 years old rather than 2000, will probably never be carried out, unlike in the case of St David's.

IANWG

'Each parish church in the Clynnog area had a saint who was held, according to an informant, "in such estimation as that in their extremities they do pray unto him for help . . . when some sudden danger do befall them" – only remembering to couple the name of God after more deliberation, when they say "God and Beuno, God and Ianwg, or God and Mary and Michael help us".' (Thomas, 'Religion and the Decline of Magic').

IARMEN see FEBRIC

IDDO late 6th century

The son of Cawrdaf ap Caradog Freichfras. He features in the 'Dream of Rhonabwy' in the Mabinogion. In the Welsh Triads he was identified, with his brother Modred, as being the Iddog Corn Prydain who fought Arthur at the final Battle of Camlan, but this was Iddawg Cordd Prydain ap Mynio, whose treachery caused Camlan. Iddo's brothers may have been Modred and Cathan.

IDDON AB YNYR GWENT 6th century

This warrior and nobleman later in life devoted himself to religion in the bishopric of Llandaf. He made a land grant of Llanarth, Lantelio Porth-Halawg and Lantilio Crosseny to the church. He also granted 'Lancoyt', and St Teilo was a witness to these gifts (recorded in the Book of Llandaf). His brothers were Ceidio and Cynheiddon, and his sister Tegiwg. Iddon was said to have been converted by Beuno, and became the patron of Llandaf Cathedral. He fought the Saxons at Llantilio, aided by Teilo's prayers. Iddon also raced from Gwent to the court of Aberffraw in Anglesey, to avenge the death of Tegiwg, who was restored to life by Beuno. Llech Eiudon, the Celtic Cross in Carmarthenshire mentioned in the entry on Tyssul, may have marked his burial spot.

IDLOES 6th - 7th century
September 6

This son of Gwyddnai ap Llawfrodedd Farfog Coch (Red-bearded) founded Llanidloes in Montgomery. His daughter was St Meddwid. Iolo calls him a *'knight with Sadwrn'*, so he may have been one of Arthur's followers. The well, Ffynnon Idloes, is in Hafren Street, Llanidloes. Another holy well, Ffynnon Cilyn was used for washing sore eyes.

A 'hiring fair' was held at Llanidloes every May 11th up until the early 1930's, where farm labourers could be hired for the year to come. In Rhayader it was upon May 12th and Machynlleth May 16th. Some labourers renewed their contract every year, but others moved around, such as the author's grandfather David Jervis. They would take a week's holiday before starting work, and then only have Christmas Day off in the whole of the year.

'*A glywaist ti chwedl hen Idloes,*
Gwr gwar hygar ei Einioes,
Goreu cynneddf yw cadw moes'
is his 'Saying of the Wise, and translates as:
'*Hast thou heard the saying of old Idloes,*
A mild man of respected life?
"The best quality is that of maintaining morals".'

IDNERTH d. 720

This last Bishop of Llanbadarn was murdered, but does not seem to be accounted as a saint. The Idnert Stone at Llanddewi Brefi reads '*Hic jacet idnert filius i . . . qui occisus fuit propter p . . . sancti . . .* ' Idnerth ap Cadwgan was put to death '*for violating the sanctuary of St David.*' Idnert was the name of a brother of Arthur ap Meurig.

IDUNET 6th century

Possibly the half-brother of Winwaloe, remembered at the beautiful town of Chateaulin in Finistere, and elsewhere in Brittany.

IESTYN (4th century) see CADFRAWD

IESTYN 6th century
JUST, JUSTANUS, JUSTIN
April 12 and October 10 (Wales), April 19 (Brittany), August 14 (West Country)

The son of King Geraint, he founded Llaniestyn in the Llŷn peninsula, and another Llaniestyn in Anglesey. At the latter a stone was seen in the 18th century stating that he was buried there. There is a beautiful slab in the church commemorating the saint, reading *'Hic jacet sanctus Yestinus cui Gwenllian filia Madoc et Gryffut ap Gwilym optulit in oblacionem istam imaginem pro salute animarum suarum.'* In Penmachno a stone records that it was made *'in the time of Justinus the Consul'*. According to Gwynfor Evans, Justinus was consul in 540, and may be the same person as Iestyn. Near the Anglesey church is Ffynnon Estyn holy well, and its water was used for church baptisms. It then had a reputation as a cursing well, and villagers would not drink from it. The reason probably stemmed from the custom of throwing corpse pennies ('ceiniogau corff') into the well. These were the coins used to cover the eyes of the dead.

In Llaniestyn parish, Caernarfon, was Ffynnon y Filiast holy well which cured female sterility and other women's illnesses, and was also used for sore eyes and depression. Another nearby spring, Ffynnon y Brenin (King Geraint's Well?) cured melancholy and women's sterility. Ffynnon Pistyll y Garn was used to cure stomach and bowel complaints.

Llaniestyn in Caernarfon is now dedicated to his nephew Cybi, and had its fair on October 10. Llaniestyn in Anglesey had fairs upon April 12 and October 10, and a shrine of his relics there vanished during the Reformation. St Just in Roseland and St Just in Penwith are his, but the fairs were August 14, and also Plestin (Plou Iestyn) in Brittany is his foundation. At Venton East was St Just's Well, and Priest Cove there used to be called Por East (St Just's Cove).

IEUAN GWAS PADRIG 6th century
(IEUAN, EVAN, IFAN, IEFAN, IWAN AND IOAN are all Welsh forms of JOHN)
August 29

This saint, a disciple of Patrick, was about to found a new church at Llwyn in Ceinmerch. An angel told him not to build, but to look for a roebuck, which he would find if he travelled south. He found the deer at Cerrig y Drudion, but the church there is now Mary Magdalene and the 'gwyl' was celebrated on her day, July 22. There is a Ffynnon Fair Madlen near the church which could have been Ieuan's, as well as an ancient well in Cae Tudur nearby. This well cured swollen knees, and another well Ffynnon y Brawd (Friar's Well) cured warts. There was a Ffynnon Iwan in Llandysilio Gogo parish in Cardigan. Ffynnon Iwan near Hirnant was famous for curing children's illnesses.

The son of Tudur ab Elidan ab Owain Fychan, he was born near Denbigh at Cinmeirch. Ieuan may be the founder of Llantrisant in Anglesey, with Sannan (June 22) and Afan (December 17).

The 'Saying of the Wise' is:
'Hast though heard the saying of Ifan,
Brother in the Faith to Cattwg of Llancarfan?
"The grain of sand has his portion of the beach".'

IFAN
JOHN, IEFAN, IEUAN, IOAN

Midsummer Day was Gwyl Ifan, the traditional date for sheep-shearing across Wales. Some dedications are to John the Baptist, patron of the Knights Hospitallers, e.g. Ysbyty Ystradmeurig, Ysbyty Cynfyn and Ysbyty Ystwyth in Cardiganshire. (In the Vale of Glamorgan are several farms named Splott, from Ysplottyn, which again signified an ancient place of healing). St John the Apostle is remembered at Betws Ifan in Cardigan, from a date that probably precedes the Normans. There are St John's Wells at Beggar's Bound (Pound) in St Tathan Glamorgan (which has been renovated), and at Newton near Porthcawl. (Newton may have originally been the well of Prince Glywys, and its imposing church was probably originally a fortress of the Knights of the Order of St John of Jerusalem). Bonfires were lit on May Day at these wells. Ffynnon Ifan at Tythegston, Glamorgan, cured King's Evil (scrofula). Llysiau Ioan, John's herb, is St John's Wort, the natural cure for depression favoured over Prozac in Germany. Its older Welsh name is Dail y Fendigaid, which means *'leaves which have been blessed'*. St John's Wort (Common Mugwort) sprigs were placed over doors in Wales on St John's Eve, to purify the house from evil spirits.

St John's Chapel is in Hay on Wye (Y Gelli Gandrell), and was formerly called Eglwys Ifan. The neighbouring parishes are Llanigon and Cusop (St Cewydd), so there may have been a forgotten Welsh saint called Ifan, Ioan or Igon.

IFOR 5th – 6th century
April 24

The son of the saints Tudwal and Nefydd, and brother of St Cynin. He possibly founded a church in England. 'Sir Ifor' features in Arthurian legend. There is a 'Saying of the Wise' which reads:
'Hast thou heard the saying of Ifor
Hael, of the open hall doorways?
"Woe to the aged who shall lose his shelter".'

Alphabetical Listing of the Saints of Wales and Religious Events

IFOR 4th and/or 5th century
YFORUS
April 23

Giraldus Cambrensis tells us of a St Yforus who expelled the rats from Ferns in Ireland, and died upon April 23 around the year 500. It may also be that a British bishop of this name represented York at the Council of Arles in 314.

IGON

Llanigon near Hay-on-Wye is a dediction to St Igon, and St John's Chapel in Hay may also be his. (See EIGION).

ILAN
YLAN
April 30

Eglwysilan in the Vale of Glamorgan was known as Merthyr Ilan in the Book of Llandaf, so it is probably not a dedication to Helen or Eilian. There is an incised figure of a warrior on a Celtic slab there, dating between the 8th and 10th centuries. The man holds a small shield and a long sword is slung from his waist. Just west of St Helen's Church in Eglwysilan is Ffynnon Rhingyll. Trefilan in Cardigan is now St Hilary's church, but was probably an Ilan foundation. There is a Bod Ilan in Merioneth, and a castle named St Ilan just east of Brieuc in Brittany. St Ilan lies outside Lanceaux on the Baie de Saint-Brieuc. Coatilan is near Guerlesquin. (It may also be that Cyngar was the patron of Trefilan at some time.)

Rhys ap Meurig was known as Rice Merrick, Ryce Myryke and Richard Amerike, dying on St David's Day, 1587. The owner of the mansion at Cottrell (now a golf club) near St Nicholas outside Cardiff, he wrote 'Morganiae Archaiographia', which seems to have been copied at Sir Edward Stradling's library in St Donat's Castle around 1670. The only manuscript is in Queen's College, Oxford. He notes *'Eglwys Ylan, a Parish confyning upon Taf, of the Church dedicated to Ylan soe named.*
In time of superstition, upon every May eve, people used to resort to this Church to service, and to offer to the Priest
Believing thereby to ridd their Cattell out of danger of any pestilient or sodaine death.
Within this Parish, neare the River Taf, standeth yet the house of Lln Brenn. Lay downe his History, his Tomb, & Sir William Fleminge's.'
It is notable that the house of the great patriot, Llywelyn Bren remained in situ. Rhys Amerike has been credited with the naming of America, rather than Amerigo Vespucci, as he financed its early exploration from Bristol.

In January 1769, William Thomas recorded the death of Lewis, Eglwys Ilan's sexton, aged 80. *'From a fall he had by going over a gate for cheese, being the custom of the parish to give cheese to the Sexton at Christmas, and he dy'd on the spot he falled.'* Another note by William Thomas is of the death in 1769 of the Rev. Thomas Rogers of Eglwysilan with the chapelry of Caerphilly and Llanvabon. Upon becoming a clergyman he changed his name from Rosser to the more English-sounding Rogers. He died *'from oversurfeiting as some report by eating steaks the night before. But the man was consumptive . . . '* Also in October Thomas described *'the great Northern lights as fire in the elements, to the great surprise of the vulgar'* (i.e. common people). This shows how polluted our atmosphere is in this century, when such a sight is so rare in South Wales.

Thomas also noted the execution in 1791 of Henry James of Eglwys Ilan and his common-law wife, Catherine Howel Griffith of St Fagan's, for stealing silver from Llanilltern Park. She was known as '*Catty Goch*', on account of her red hair, and went to the gallows singing a Welsh lament she had composed. Supposedly she had been seduced by one of the Price family of Llanilltern and the robbery was her revenge. The hanging took place at Wain Ddyfal, which is the busy junction where City Road now meets Crwys Road in Cardiff.

ILAR 6th century
January 13, 14, 15

Llanilar on the river Ystwyth in Cardiganshire was founded by Ilar Bysgotwr (the Fisherman). Ffynon Capel was a holy well on Rhodmad Farm, Llanilar. Some churches now dedicated to St Hilary appear to have been earlier Ilar foundations. Iolo Morganwg believed that Ilar came with Cadfan from Brittany and founded St Hilary in the Vale of Glamorgan (The Bush at St Hilary is one of the few pubs in the Vale still selling real cider). He was also known as Ilar Ferthyr (Martyr) and Ilar Droedwyn (White-footed).

'The Diary of William Thomas' refers to 'St Tillary' in 1763, where was buried *'Thomas Lewis called Thomas of Felynydd, allowed to be the best fiddler in Glamorganshire, the Master of that Vice in St Faggans for every summer this 12 years past and had every summer yearly for £5 to £5 5s. a year.'* William Morgan was the harper at this time, paid the same monies, and *'they had much Joy of their Vanity.'* Y Felyn-Hydd is now known as Howe Mill, near Old Beaupre castle in the Vale of Glamorgan.

ILAR ap NUDD HAEL see ELERI

ILID 1st century
GILEAD? (Galilean?)

A converted Jew, who is supposed to have accompanied Brân, Arwystli and Cyndaf from Rome. Llanilid in the Vale of Glamorgan is Ilid's foundation, but also associated with Prince Ceri and with Ilud (q.v.). There is a healing spring at Llanilid, but also the holy well Ffynnon Ceri lies between the hamlet and Tre-Fran. The Genealogy of Iestyn ap Gwrgant, the last native King of Glamorgan, tells us that Eurgain, the wife of Cadadog (Caractacus) sent for Ilid of Israel to help her convert the Welsh in 36 AD. This Ilid was sometimes identified with Joseph of Arimathea, who supposedly introduced order into Côr Eurgain at Llanilltud Fawr, and was buried at Glastonbury by King Ina or at Ynys Enlli (Avalon). Ilid's 'Saying of the Wise' is: *'there is no madness like extreme anger.'*

Llanilid has always had local fame as the **first church in Britain**, being founded around 61AD. Possibly it was first called Côr Eurgain to honour Bran's grand-daughter. It became known as Llanilid later, as Côr Eurgain seemed to move to the site of the Roman villa just outside Llanilltud Fawr. Nant Ilid is the name of the spring that starts just fifty yards from the church. Tre-Fran farm near Llanilid was traditionally the site of Bran's court. Nearby Caer Caradoc is associated by Barber and Pykitt where Caractacus, the father of Eurgain and son of Brân, lost his last battle against the Romans. There is an earthwork at Llanilid which they believe is Eurgain's original côr. It is not a defensive site as the ditch is on the inside, rather than the outside of the religious circle. North of Llanilid is another Llanilid at Gilfach Goch in Glamorgan, and Capel Ilid in Brecon. At this latter site were found some very early inscribed stones. The famous 'Llywel Stone' from here was sold for £10 to the British Museum in 1852. It depicts a 'walking man' with a crooked staff walking away from a pyramid, and an animal which looks like the Great Sphinx. Another pictogram shows a man crossing the sea.

ILLOG 6th century
ILLOY, ILLOGAN
August 8, October 18, 30

Hirnant in Montgomery has Ffynnon Illog, Carnedd Illog, Gwely Illog and the stream called Aber Illog. Possibly Illogan near Redruth is also Illog's church, where the feast was October 18.

ABBOT ILLTUD c.475-525/537
ILLTYD FARCHOG, ELTUT, ILDUT, HILDUTUS
November 6 and 7, February 7 (Cressy)

He attended Arthur's court and was known as a knight and warrior with Cadog, before he became a saint. One source states that he trained at the monastery of Cassian near Marseilles and was ordained by Germanus of Auxerre. The son of Bicanus ab Emyr Llydaw, and thus of Breton origin, he built a church and later a monastery under the protection of Meirchion prince of Glamorgan. Illtud's wife was Trinihid, who was associated with Llanrhidian in Gower and Llantrithyd near Illtud's great monastery. Llanrhidian Church has 'The Leper Stone', a Celtic slab found embedded in the doorway in the 19th century. Illtud's name Eltut, according to a Norman source, meant *'Ille ab omne crimine tutus'* – *'the one safe from all evil'*.

In the Vita of Cadog, it is stated that Illtud became a monk when fifty soldiers under his command were swallowed up into the earth. As these were probably cavalry, this may have occurred in the swamps and marshes around Llancarfan at the time. No less than seven named streams flow into Llancarfan and the ford is often flooded there. Llanilltud Fawr is on the site of a monastery founded (or refounded) in the late 5th or early 6th century by Illtud, and is mentioned in the 7th century Life of Samson – Samson was taken by his parents Bicanus and Rieingulid to Illtud's famous monastery, and 'magister Eltut' was described as:
'of all the Britons the most accomplished in his knowledge of all the scriptures, both the Old Testament and the New Testament and in every branch of philosophy, poetry and rhetoric, grammar and arithmetic: and he was most sagacious and gifted with the power of foretelling future events.'

His father was a military nobleman and his mother the daughter of Anblaud, Amlawdd Wledig, king of Britain. His aunt was said to be Igerna, Arthur's mother. After serving as one of Arthur's knights, Illtud then served Pawl of Penychen, king of Glamorgan and son of Glywys. Thankful for his deliverance from drowning in the marshes, Illtud went to St Cadog, and left his wife. Illtud, when he turned to religion, was admonished by an angel to send his wife away

into the night and he refused to ever communicate with her again. Leaving Pawl's residence at Penllyn or Pentre Meurig, he slept on the banks of the Naduan (the Dawen, or Thaw), then became a monk on the banks of the next river west, the Hodnant. Named by some as the original Sir Galahad, one of the 'Sayings of the Wise' triads refers to him :
'Hast thou heard the saying of Illtud,
The studious, golden-chained knight:
Whoso doeth evil, evil betide him.'

An important saint, operating mainly in the south-east of Wales, his brother was possibly Sadwrn. His 'Life', written in 1140, is not as important as the references in 'The Life of Samson' written around 650. He founded the monastery at Caldey island, Ynys Pyr, which was formerly called Llan Illtud. His *'bangu'* (holy bell) was recovered from King Edgar's army, and his name was called on to protect the people of North Wales from Marcher Lords in the late 11th century

In 1080 Llanilltud's tithes and advowson were seized by Robert Fitzhamon and conferred onto the new Norman abbey of Tewkesbury, and this was confirmed by 1106 and 1180 charters. The church is unique in Wales, and was once extremely large. John Wesley noted after teaching there on 25th July 1777, *'About eleven I read prayers and preached in Llantwit Major Church to a very numerous congregation. I have not seen so large or handsome a church since I left England. It was sixty yards long but one end of it is now in ruins. I suppose it has been abundantly the most beautiful as well as the most spacious church in Wales.'* Several wall-paintings survive in the church, as well as the famous memorial stones, and the church is well worth visiting.

The church at Llanhamlach in Breconshire is dedicated to St Iltud and St Peter. There is also Capel Illtud (also called Llaniltud) on the Roman road between Brecon and Neath in Defynnog parish. Near Cadoxton-juxta-Neath is Llantwit-juxta-Neath (Llanilltud Nedd), and Ilston in Gower was formerly called Llanilltud Gwyr, shortened to Eltut's Town by Flemish-Norman settlers and hence Ilston. He is also the patron of Oxwich on the Gower, and his holy well is at Llanrhidian on the peninsula. He is the patron of Penbre in Carmarthen. There is a Llanelltud near Dolgellau, and he had a cult in Brittany. Llanelltud in Merionethshire may have started with a cell of one of Illltud's disciples. Villagers rescued a stone from the wreckage of a collapsed cottage near this church. It was then used as a 'washing-stone' for spreading clothes out when washing them. Three feet long, the inscription was transcribed as:
'Vestigiu Reuhic tenetur in capite lapidis et ipsemet antequam p(er)egre profectus est'.
Llantrisant Church in Glamorgan is dedicated to Illtud, Gwynno and Tyfodwg.

According to Ecton, Llanhari, Llantrithyd, Llantwit Fardre, Lantwit under Neath were his in Glamorgan, plus Llanhiledd in Monmouth (with nearby Mynydd Llanhilleth) and Lantwood or Llantwyd in Pembroke. Capel Illtyd under Dyfynog in Brecon and Llanelltyd under Llanfachraith in Merioneth were also his. Ffynnon Illtud remains near the ruined cairn called Ty Illtyd at Llanhamlach. Another Ffynon Illtud can be seen at Llanwonno in Glamorgan, and St Illtyd's Well at Llanrhidian, Gower, was said to have spouted milk in 1185.

Many churches and chapels in Brittany commemorate Illtud, such as Lanildut, Loc-Ildut and St Ideuc. Illtud was the patron saint prayed to for success with poultry. *'Meme les volailles ont leur saint: saint Ildut'* ('even poultry have their saint, Saint Illtud', 'Bretagne, Le Culte des Saints', internet source CyberOuest ©Vannes). Coadout church south of Guincamp, in Treguier diocese has a statue of Ildut. A local tradition is that he used to meet and pray with Briog (St

Brieuc) at a ruined dolmen nearby. A song to Ildut is still sung at his pardon there. Landebaeron is dedicated to St Maudez, but also has a stature of Illtud and a silver reliquary with his skull. Doble notes several other dedications such as Ploerdut's chapel of St 'Iltut'. Aber-Ildut is north-west of Renan. His dedications are all around the ancient dioceses of Vannes, Leon and Treguier.

Some sources state that he taught David, as well as Samson, Maelgwn, Gildas and Pol Aurelian and that he is buried at Bedd Gwyl Illtyd in Brecon. Bedd Gwyl Illtyd means the grave of St Illtyd's Eve. The 'bedd' lies near Llanilltyd Church and Mynydd Illtyd. It was the custom to keep watch there on the night before his feast day. At Llanilltud Fawr, there is a torchlight carnival procession featuring dragons every Bonfire night, the eve of Illtud's day, which by happy coincidence keeps the custom of his celebration alive. The Celtic carved stones in Llanilltud Church are not properly displayed, but are among the most important in Europe.

Illtud was noted in history as having invented a special plough. The fields all around his monastery are full of limestone rock and therefore difficult to till. Before his time it was customary in Wales to cultivate fields by using a mattock and an over-treading plough ('*aradr arsang*'), implements used by the Irish on similar soils for centuries after. Wrmonoc's Breton Vita of Pol Aurelian describes in fabulous terms how Illtud regained lands from the seas to assist his cultivation, and some of the Hodnant valley and land at nearby Aberddawen and Llanfabon-y-Fro (Gileston) was reclaimed at a very early date by earthen banks acting as sea walls.

Illtud's cave on the banks of the Ewenni river can still be seen, where he slept at night. There was also supposed to have been a retreat at Llanhamlach, three miles east of Brecon, recorded by Giraldus Cambrensis. Here, Illtud's '*mare that used to carry his provisions was covered by a stag, and produced an animal of wonderful speed, resembling a horse before and a stag behind.*' It is believed by some that he was born near Brecon. Arthurian legends place Illtud as one of the guardians of the Grail, and as Arthur's cousin. Nennius in his 8th century 'Marvels of Britain' recorded that when Illtud was praying in his cave he saw the body of '*the once and future king*' Arthur, whom Illtud had to bury in a secret place. This story is related to his chapel at Oxwich on the Gower peninsula. Illtud '*was praying in a cave near the sea and a boat came in bearing two men and the body of a holy man, an altar floating above his face. When Illtud went to meet them, they took out of the ship the body of the holy man, the altar still stood suspended and never moved from its position. Then the men in the boat said to Illtud "This man of God charged us to bring him to thee and to bury him with thee, and that thou should not reveal his name to anyone lest men swear by him"*. Arthur did not want anyone to swear vows at his tomb – an eery precursor of the 'lost' king of Wales, Owain Glyndŵr, eight centuries later.

It is a little-known fact that Llanilltud Fawr (Llantwit Major) was ear-marked for the site of the first University of Wales. However, a hotel-building project in Aberystwyth ran into difficulties, and a huge new building was suddenly made available at the right price. The site of Llanilltud monastery and church is near the first century Côr Eurgain (Caer Worgorn), succeeded by the Côr of Tewdws (Theodosius), where foundations can still be seen on the field marked Côr Tewdws in 19th century maps. The Life of Pol de Leon says that Illtud had also a monastery on Ynys Pyr, which appears to be Barri (Ynys Peirio), rather than Caldey Island. A monastery site was marked upon maps of Barri until the railway station was built there, when the island was rejoined to the mainland in the docks construction.

Maen Illtud at Llanhamlach is also known as Ty Illtyd, a dolmen thought to be Illtud's hermitage. There are over 60 inscribed crosses inside the burial chamber, possibly made by a recluse. A standing stone at Llanhamlach stands opposite Peterstone Court (see Pedr). There are several holy wells dedicated to Illtud. Two in Glamorgan could not be located by Francis Jones, but another four are noted, including those at Michaelstone, Llansamlet and Llanwynno.

Llanilltud is one of few Welsh towns or villages to take on a Christian aspect to its Millennium Celebrations. It is also one-and-a-half millennia since Illtud founded **'the earliest seat of learning in Britain'** (Guinness Book of Records). There is a year-long programme of celebrations linking his birthplace in Brittany and Llanilltud Fawr. All the churches inLlantwit major took part in a midnight mass at Christmas, with 1500 candles being lit. Throughout 2000, there are concerts featuring Breton and Welsh choirs, including Cantorian Illtud singing in Dol Cathedral and the Illtud churches of Brittany in May and June. The high-point is the St Illtud's Day service of re-dedication on November 6, 2000, to be attended by the Archbishop of Wales and the Bishop of Llandaf.

NOTE ON LLANILLTUD FAWR. This is such an important site in Welsh history, that it is necessary to add this information in order to try and stimulate fresh research. Hopefully future editions of the book will develop knowledge upon St David's, Llanelwy/St Asaf, Bangor, Meifod, Caerwent, Caerleon, Llandeilo, Llanbadarn and Llandaf. These were the critical centres of Celtic Christianity. Llanilltud Fawr has been chosen for the first detailed treatment simply because of the author's present limited field of knowledge and proximity to the site. The author makes no apology for trying to make history interesting instead of turgid. If we can stimulate interest, even by being wrong, and approach the truth from as many directions as possible, we can build up a body of knowledge before society loses the art of reading for enjoyment. If a book makes the reader interested in finding out more about its subject, it is all that an author can ask for. The following is a mixture of fact, fable and supposition, but how many other villages in the world have so much legend attached to them?

LLANILLTUD FAWR

There seems to be a mystery about the great monastery and religious centre of Llanilltud Fawr, Lantwit Major. It appears that St Illtud, after his vision on the banks of the nearby Dawen (Thaw), founded his monastery on the site of the earliest Christian monastery in Britain, which may even have still been in existence at this time. Further research is needed, but if this is the case, Wales can claim something very special in world history – the oldest educational establishment in the world up until 1100 and the Norman invasion.

The story begins with the great Celtic chief Caradog, Caractacus as he was known to the Romans. A son of Cynfelin, Cymbeline, he led the resistance to the Roman invasion of Britain. His wife, and daughters Eurgain and Gwladys were also captured and taken to Rome with him. Wales was never completely subdued by the Romans. Two of their four British legions were stationed on the borders, at Deva (Chester) and Isca Silurum (Caerleon). Chester controlled the gateway to the Deceangli and Ordovices of North and Mid-Wales. Isca was built, with Venta Silurum (Caerwent) to keep the Silures down. In 78 AD, Tacitus remarked that it was necessary to exterminate almost *'the entire race'* of the Ordovices of mid-Wales and Gwynedd. When the British Catuvellauni tribe of the south-east of England, based around Colchester, were defeated by Aulus Plautius in 43 AD, their leader fled to the Silures of south-east Wales. This was Caradog (the Caractacus of Roman history), the first Celtic hero identified with Wales. Caradog

Celtic Crosses at Llanilltud Fawr Church (Llantwit Major). © *Wales Tourist Board Photo Library.*

led a series of attacks by the Silures against the new Roman provinces in 47 and 48 AD. Tacitus recorded that Scapula received the submission of the Deceangli of north-east Wales on the River Dee in 49AD, enabling him to pressurise the Silures. In the same year a fort was established at Gloucester, with others at Usk and Clyro.

Caradog continued resistance, with a joint alliance of Silures and Ordovices, but was defeated in 51AD, his wife and children captured, and he fled to Queen Cartimandua of the Brigantes in north-east England for support. She chained him and handed him over to the Romans. The site of Caradog's last stand against Rome is still not known, but it appears to have been in the north-east of Wales, near the upper River Severn. Tacitus describes this last battle thus*: 'He chose a spot protected by high, rocky hills, and in the place where the hills were less steep he built a rampart of large stones piled on top of each other; a river flowed through the plain, its fords and shallows of uncertain depth. Ostorius was very surprised by the fearless attitude of the Brythons and the spirit which permeated the whole army. He saw a river to cross, a fence of stakes to throw down, a high slope to climb, and every part defended by a great number, but the Roman soldiers were impatient to attack. The sign was given. The river was crossed without* *much difficulty. The struggle by the fence of stakes was stubborn, but the Brythons had to yield at last and they fled to the tops of the hills. They were followed eagerly by the Romans. The legionaries and the light military pushed their way to the top of the hill after firing a shower of spears. Since the Brythons had neither breastplates not helmets, they could not continue to fight. The legions carried all before them. The victory was decisive.'*

Caradog was marched in chains with his brother, wife and daughters in the triumphal procession for the Emperor Claudius in Rome. Such captives were always publicly executed as enemies of Rome, but Caradog's proud bearing and speech to the Tribunal is again recorded by Tacitus:

'To you the situation is full of glory; to me full of shame. I had arms and soldiers and horses; I had sufficient wealth. Do you wonder that I am reluctant to lose them? Ambitious Rome aims at conquering the world: does the whole human race then have to bend to the yoke? For years I resisted successfully: I am now in your hands. If vengeance is your intention, proceed: the scene of bloodshed will soon be over, and Caradog's name will fall into oblivion. If you spare my life, I shall be an eternal memorial to the mercy of Rome.'

Uniquely, Caradog was pardoned by the Emperor Claudius, and after seven years' captivity is said to have been allowed to return to his base at St. Donat's, near Llanilltud Fawr. It is recorded that his daughter Eurgain married a Roman, as did Gwladys (Claudia). It is thought that Eurgain brought Christianity to Wales, founding a monastic settlement called Côr Eurgain in Llanilltud Fawr (see Llan). Another version is that she stayed in Rome, and the Côr was set up in her honour, first at Llanilid around 60 AD then transferring to Caer Mead* (Côr Eurgain) Roman villa at Llanilltud. One story was that Caractacus came back to St Donats with Eurgain and was buried at Llanilltud. St Paul was said to be a friend of Eurgain and Gwladys, and in legend came to Wales as St Ilid in 61 and 68. Gwladys is mentioned in Epistle 2 Timothy 4-21 as Claudia. (Paul was said to have visited Galicia, which may be Wales rather than the Spanish province). Other versions relate Ilid as Joseph of Arimathea (see Ilid).

Welsh tradition is that Christianity first came to Britain with St Paul who came here with Eurgan (Eurgain). She had married Lucius (Sarlog) in Rome and with him founded the first university at Llanilltud about 68 AD, known as Côr Eurgain, where Illtud's later monastery stood. The church was endowed by King Cyllin whose son had been converted by Eurgain. It was burned by Irish pirates in 322 and rebuilt by St Theodosius, Tewdws or Tewdrig. Then it was known as Côr Tewdws, or the college of Theodosius in Caer Wrgan. It was associated with Emperor Theodosius. (Other sources tell us that Tewdws is an alternative of Tewdrig, the martyred grandfather of Arthur). There is a record that the Irish attacked and destroyed Caer Wrgan in the fifth century. Caer Wrgan is the old name for Caer Mead, the huge Romano-Celtic villa just a mile north of Llanilltud Fawr. Côr is a very early version of Llan, meaning a monastic college. Côr Tewdws is marked on an 18th century map of Llanilltud as being a field north of the monastery site of Illtud.

'Achau y Saint' notes that the College of Caerworgorn was founded by Cystennyn Fendigaid (Constantine the Blessed, q.v.) and soon destroyed by the Irish, at which time its principal was Padrig. This was Padrig Maenwyn, son of Mawon of the Gower peninsula, who was taken into captivity. This tradition is probably fictitious. However, Caer Worgan was just a few hundred yards north of Côr Tewdws. Perhaps after the sacking of the Roman-Celtic villa, a new building was erected, just north of the existing church. Theodosius II, the Great, was a contemporary of Cystennin and supposed to have founded it, but it was more likely to have been named in his honour by a Romano-British principal. Garmon then supposedly restored the foundation in

447, when he appointed Illtud as its principal and Bleiddian as its chief bishop. However, this is far too early for Illtud, who fought with Hywel for Arthur. The Book of Llandaf states that Illtud received the first principalship, of the college that bore his name, from Dyfrig. It would appear that Illtud was included in the Garmon story by mistake, and that Garmon re-consecrated the building as Côr Worgan, if he had any connection at all with it.

It may be that, as well as the monastery (re-founded later by Illtud) the Irish destroyed the fabulous fifteen-room Roman villa at Caer Mead, a mile from Llanilltud. After Macsen Wledig left with the legions in 383, this was taken over by the local prince or king, and there is evidence of over forty Christian burials on the site in the Age of the Saints. It is thought that the kings of Glamorgan and Gwent, from Tewdrig through his son Meurig to his son Arthmael or Arthrwys, may have used it as their palace. Arthmael, the Arthur of legend, has always been associated with being born at nearby Boverton, which claims to the Caput Bovium of the Romans (Cowbridge being Bovium/Bomium). The Caer Mead site covers two acres, and one room (the court?) was a massive 60 by 50 feet. There are mosaics there, and coins pottery and glass were discovered. Excavated in 1888, it has since been covered over and ignored, when it could hold the key to the legend of Arthur. A gold torc was found early in the 19th century, but sold for £100 and melted down. CADW should excavate this priceless site, at present merely humps in the ground, but is severely financially constrained.

King Tewdrig controlled much of south-east Wales, and possibly fought with Constantine the Blessed against the invading Saxons. As mentioned previously, he is said to have refounded the college of Côr Worgan, or Côr Eurgain later to become famous as Llanilltud Fawr. After Constantine's death, Tewdrig allied with Vortigern to keep the peace, and passed on his kingdom to his son Meurig. Tewdrig retired to Tintern, where he was attacked by Saxons. A stone bridge in the nearby Angidy valley is called 'Pont y Saeson', 'Bridge of the Saxons', and this may be where the fight took place. The enemy were driven off, but not before Tewdrig was mortally wounded. His son Meurig arrived and took his father on a cart to a well in Mathern. A plaque there reads *'By tradition at this spring King Tewdrig's wounds were washed after the battle near Tintern about 470AD against the pagan Saxons. He died a short way off and by his wishes a church was built over his grave'*

Tintern was formerly Din Teyrn, the fort (dinas) of the sovereign (teyrn). Mathern is the corruption of 'Merthyr Teyrn', 'the site of martyrdom of the sovereign'. In 822, Nennius described the well as one of 'the marvels of Britain', and also referred to the Well of Meurig. Meurig became known as Uther Pendragon ('Wonderful Head Dragon', leader of the Celtic army), and was the father of Arthmael, the King Arthur of legend.

Illtud became principal of the school at Côr Tewdws, which was then known as Bangor Illtud, and his church, Llan Illtud was the centre of its learning. The son of Biscausius, he was named head of Côr-Wrgan in Caer Wrgan. The saints Patrick, Dyfrig, Samson, Cadog and David were said to have studied here. David was said to have been a student of Paul Hen at Whitland before coming to Llanilltud. St Leonore took 73 monks from Llanilltud to evangelise Brittany. Agriculture was a principal activity of the monks, and the plough in use at the time was called St Illtud's Plough. He died, possibly in Brecon in 537, and was buried at Bedd Gwyl Illtud. A vigil was kept at his grave every November 5th at this place, to commemorate his day of November 6th. In Llanillutud Fawr for centuries the people attended St Illtud's Cross on February 7th, as they believed that this was his date of death and his burial place. At this time they would sing the hymn Bedd Illtyd Fawr. The great festivity of the year was Gwyl Mab Sant, or the Mabsant. Sometimes it lasted for several days, and the whole neighbourhood would celebrate with dancing, cock-fighting, drinking, games and the like. One of the villagers was appointed 'mayor' for this time, and decorated with ribbons, his face blackened, and a cabbage hung around his neck. Free beer was given to the crowd by the local farmers. There was always also an Easter Monday Festival. There is a legend that the Golden Stag of Illtud was stolen by a Welsh prince and buried in the grounds of Ham House. When it is found, Llanilltud will regain its former glory (it had its own charter). Moulds for minting money were found in the Mint Field in the centre of Llanilltud, bearing the inscription 'Iestyn-ap-Gwrgan Tywysog Morganwg'. We can see 'wrgan' coming down through history, as Iestyn was the last prince of Glamorgan, cheated out of his territories by the Normans under Fitzhamon. Tywysog Morganwg means Prince of Glamorgan. The Normans demolished the monasteries and colleges of Llanilltud, but then restored the 'College of St Illtud' in 1111.

Nearby Boverton, the supposed birthplace of Arthur, was formerly called Treberfaidd, Trebefered, Trebeferad or Trebrenin (the place of the king). Trebefered seems to mean '*shining*' or '*brilliant*' place. The older name Treberffaidd may mean perfect place (tref + perffaith). The Normans named it Bovgarton. It was the principal residence of Iestyn ap Gwrgan. At nearby Eglwys Brewis many Roman coins were found in 1798.

In 1801 the Rev. R. Nicholls wrote to the Marquess of Bute explaining his church's structure. He stated that Llantwit Major was one of the most ancient churches in Britain, and that the great pile of buildings was first started in 508. Its tithes supported the church, monastery and seminary until the revenues, emoluments and endowments were transferred by the Normans to Tewkesbury and Gloucester Abbeys. The church had also been attacked by Vikings, Saxons, Irish and Normans and stripped of many precious possessions and records. The Lady, or Gallilee chapel is now in ruins, but built before 1000 on the site of an earlier building. The Old Chapel joins it, and was rebuilt around 1350. It contains the important carved crosses and stones found in the churchyard. The New Chapel is next, built around 1550. The outline of the Tithe Barn measured 128 by 28 feet, and a columbarium with 150 nesting holes still stands.

The story of the stones is an excellent example of how Welsh history is easily lost. Richard Pruden, the village shoemaker from nearby Llanmaes (formerly Llanffagan Fach) told Iolo Morganwg as a child the following story. Many years before that there was a huge stone commemorating two famous Welsh kings of Glamorgan and Gwent, standing against the wall of Llanilltud church. They were venerated by the local population. A youth in the village, known as 'Will the Giant' was 7 feet 7 inches high, and dying from tuberculosis. He wished to be buried near the kings' stone. When his grave was dug, it undermined the stone, which fell into the grave. It was too heavy to move, so was covered with earth and forgotten about. Iolo was a stonemason and working in the churchyard in 1789. Remembering the tale, he asked a local farmer and his hands to help him look for it when he finished work. They found the buried stone, and it took twelve men to move it back to its original position. There it stood until 1793. The stone reads '*In the Name of the Most High God the cross of our Saviour begins......which the King has erected to the memory of Samson the Abbot and to Juthakel and Artmael for the sake of their souls, May the cross protect me.*' **Artmael appears to be King Arthur, who went as Armel to Brittany with Samson and helped Judicael gain the Breton throne**. In 1810 the newly-appointed English rector attempted to destroy the stones, but was prevented by his parishioners. This stone is 9 feet high by 1 foot 7 inches at the top and two feet four inches at the bottom, and called the Pillar, or Cross of Samson. Samson was one of Illtud's pupils who became Bishop of Dol in Brittany.

Alphabetical Listing of the Saints of Wales and Religious Events

The 7 feet high broken cross-shaft at the church is known as the Shaft of Illtud. In 1805, locals called it the 'Druids' Pillar' and folk memory recalled it as being the sepulchral memorial to Illtud. There are interlaced panels with an inscription *of 'Samson placed this cross for his soul'*. The Cross of Huelt (Howel) probably commemorates Hywel ap Rhys, the king of Glamorgan who died in 885. Whether there was another stone to Hywel Dda is not known. Leland stated that Hywel Dda (died 950) was buried at Llanilltud, and part of his tomb could still be seen in the fifteenth century. Other sources believe that Hoel Mawr, the King of Brittany was also buried here. Perhaps television's 'Timeteam' could make a geophysic survey of the graveyard and the site of Côr Tewdws. A hundred years ago the Celtic crosses were brought inside the church as it was restored. At this time the church was described as *'a sepulchre, a charnal . . . The floor unpaved, in the midst are graves . . . an indescribable faint odour oppresses us. A gruesome place indeed.'*

It is stated that a meeting of Welsh princes and holy men occurred at Llanilltud in 560 – at the cross on the south side of the church. The purpose was to ratify a peace treaty between King Morcant and his uncle Trix, in the presence of Oudoceus (Euddogwy, third Bishop of Llandaf), Concen (Concern, Abbot of nearby Llancarfan), Seguleis (Abbot of Llandough outside Cardiff) and Cogen (Abbot of Llanilltud). Morcant later broke the treaty and killed Trix, for which he paid penance to a Synod held at Llancarfan. Morcant may have been Arthur's remaining son Morgan, commemorated in the 'Pompeius Stone' found between Kenfig and Margam, in his territory of Glwysing.

Just as Ynys Enlli was renowned as the birthplace of whisky, Llanilltud was known for a type of 'chartreuse'. The Vita of Samson informs us that *'it was usual to express the juice of certain herbs good for the health, that were cultivated in the monastery garden, and mix this extract with the drink of the monks, by pressing it, by means of a little tube, into the cup of each; so that when they returned from the office of Tierce, they found this tipple ready for them, prepared by the pistor.'* (The famous ode to Owain Glyndŵr also records the availability of Welsh whisky at his court at Sycharth in 1400).

Local names tell the story of the *'magnificent monastery'*, as it was called around 650. Monks' Way still runs from Abbot's Field to Col-huw meadows, and Samson is commemorated in a holy well and two neighbouring fields. When the revenues of the monastery were transferred to Tewkesbury by the Normans, a grange was built on the site now known as 'Monastery' and 'Bishop's Palace' fields. Local tradition placed the monastery where College House and College Terrace now stand, and in the late 19th century builders destroyed an ancient doorway and walls 'half a bow-shot' north-west of the present church. Here was found an 'abbot's girdle key', of which only a drawing now exists. In central Llanilltud is Mintfield, supposedly where the Glamorgan princes issued their own coinage. Llantwit Major used to have many American visitors – its church is one of the finest in Wales, and its history melds legend and fact from the Age of the Saints. However, even many local inhabitants of this fast-growing town do not know the history of their church, a situation replicated across Wales as regards local knowledge. (Because of its rapid growth, and the nearby airbase, it appears than a very large proportion of Llanilltud's population does not have Welsh origins).

The fabulous stones at Llanilltud were ordered to be broken up in 1849 by the church authorities, but all but two survived thanks to the newly-formed Cambrian Archaeological Association. Noted above is a previous attempt to destroy them in 1810. Perhaps Hywel Dda's tomb marker was one of those destroyed. The story of how these stones were wrongly attributed to later dates, and the Hanoverian distortion of British history, is eloquently stated by

Brian Davies ('Archaeology and Ideology, or how Wales was robbed of its early history', 'New Welsh Review' no. 37). British history, as taught in schools, has always started with the *'civilizing'* influence of the Germanic tribes of the Angles and the Saxons upon the British, and anything denying this propaganda for an insecure foreign dynasty had to be destroyed, rubbished or omitted. A recent American doctoral thesis also *'proved'* that the Gospel of St Chad never came from Wales, because its research was based upon the anti-British writings of Bede and following historians (see the article by Patrick Thomas in the same edition of the New Welsh Review, about St Augustine entitled 'Not a Man of God'). According to the American 'doctor' Wales in the 8th century was *'a cultural backwater'*. The purpose of the author's 'A-Z of Wales and the Welsh' and this book is to start the process of disputing the heritage of Wales, which has been sadly disparaged by a neighbouring country which once controlled a third of the world. The American gained his doctorate by basing it upon the rewriting of British history in the 18th century in favour of the tiny German state of Hanover. Interestingly, the Prince of Wales' real surname is Saxe-Coburg-Gotha on his mother's side, and Schleswig-Holstein-Sonderburg-Glucksburg** on his father's side. As one of the old triads states:

'Three things which strengthen a man to stand against the whole world:
Seeing the quality and beauty of truth,
Seeing beneath the cloak of falsehood,
And seeing to what ends truth and falsehood come.'

And as Cicero succinctly wrote:
To know nothing of what happened before you were born is to remain forever a child.'

* It is worth while recalling the description in McAllister's 1936 'Glamorgan, History and Topography' to start a campaign for the excavation of Caer Mead. This possible foundation of Christianity in Britain may rival the palace of Cogidumnus at Fishbourne, and is far better historically documented:

'One mile north-west of the town, adjoining a quiet lane, is a field known as Caermead, wherein is the site of a Roman villa. It is, however, fruitless to visit the spot as no remains are exposed; the site was ony partially excavated in 1888, and was afterwards earthed over and turfed. The villa covered a considerable area, about eight acres big within its defences, the buildings alone occupying two acres, and comprising 20 rooms, one of them being 60 feet by 51 feet, the remaining walls of which rose to a height of nine feet. A smaller room, 39 feet by 27 feet preserved a floor covered with coloured mosaic pavement of rich design, and the plastered walls exhibited vestiges of beautiful paintwork. In this room were discovered 43 human skeletons and bones of three horses, and that and the evidence of burned masonry seem to indicate that the villa was attacked by Irish raiders about the beginning of the 4th century, and the occupants massacred. It is one of the few Roman civil sites in Wales and was probably built before the middle of the 2nd century..... It is to be hoped that this wonderful relic of Roman-British civilisation (unique in Glamorgan) will not be allowed to remain buried indefinitely; **it is a treasure that should be enjoyed.***'* Six decades later, the site is still a series of grassy humps in a forgotten field.

**The Welsh linkage to the Prince of Wales is not even tenuous. James V of Scotland married the French Mary of Lorraine. Their child Mary Queen of Scots married Lord Darnley, a Scots noble, and their son was James VI of Scotland and James I of England. He married Anne of Denmark, and their daughter Elizabeth Stuart married Frederick, King of Bohemia. Their child Sophia married Ernest, Elector of Hanover, and their son George became the first of a German dynasty to rule England since the Saxons. Apart from the Scottish Stuarts and Welsh Tudors, all

England's kings and queens since the Saxons and Danes before this had been mainly French. George I kept the crown in German hands, marrying Sophia of Celle, and their son George II married Caroline of Brandenburg-Ansbach. Their son Frederick married Augusta of Saxe-Gotha and their son became George III. George III married Charlotte of Mecklenburg-Strelitz, and their son Edward married Victoria of Saxe-Coburg-Saalburg. Their daughter Queen Victoria was the fourth pure-bred German to rule as a Hanover, and promptly married yet another German, Albert of Saxe-Coburg and Gotha. Her child Edward VII broke with tradition by marrying Alexandra of Denmark. During the Great War, it was decided to change their name to Windsor because of fears of anti-German hostility. Edward VII's son George V married yet another German, Mary of Teck, and after their feckless son Edward VIII abdicated, George VI reigned. He married the Scot Elizabeth Bowes-Lyon. Their child Elizabeth II married Phillip Schleswig-Holstein-Sunderburg-Glucksburg, a.k.a. Battenburg. Battenburg was changed to Mountbatten. Of the Prince of Wales' thirty direct ancestors listed, we have something like two-thirds from tiny German princedoms, and the remainder from France, Denmark, Greece and Scotland. After 15 royal marriages giving heirs to the throne, the first English person to appear in the list of 'English' royals was Lady Diana Spencer. The Stuart, King Charles I gave the nation a fabulous art collection. The contribution of the Hanovers in the last quarter-millennium to the arts, culture and heritage of the British nation has been less than negligible.

ILUD see JULIOT

ILYR

The only mention of this saint is as a founder of Llanynys in Brecon. Here is one of the most elegant of the early carved stones of Wales, which was found in the wall of a cottage named Neuadd Siarman near Builth. Westwood has illustrated the two sides which could be seen of this 'Llanynys Ornamented Cross'.

INA FERCH CEREDIG
February 1

The sister of Non and the aunt of St David, remembered at Llanina on the coast near St Davids. There is a coastal rock known as Carreg Ina, and a holy well called Ffynnon Feddyg was along the coast from the church. Ina was also a king of Wessex who died at Rome in 727 (commemorated on February 7), to whom Llanina in Cardigan was once said to be dedicated, but this has been discredited. A connection with the St Euny culted at Redruth in Cornwall has been proposed, but it is thought that Euny was a male.

INVASIONS

It may be well to record the pattern of invasions into Britain after the Romans left around 410. From Germany, the east and south coasts of Britain were attacked by the Angles, Saxons and Jutes. The Frisians from the Low Countries invaded the south. The Picts from the far North of the British Isles carried on their raids over the Antonine Wall into what is now southern Scotland and the north of England. The Scots of northern Ireland attacked the Picts, and also the Britons in Strathclyde, Cumbria and Wales. There is a theory that the 'lost' Vandals of

North Africa invaded Wales during Arthur's time. The Irish of southern Ireland constantly attacked Wales and Domnonia (Devon, Somerset and Cornwall). As the Anglo-Saxons consolidated their hold on England, they pressed the Britons back into Wales, eventually taking Cumbria and Domnonia into 'English' ownership. The Britons in Wales were fighting the Saxons, Irish and Scots to hold on to their territories and expel the Irish from North Wales and Anglesey, when the Vikings from Scandinavia became a constant threat. Remnants of the princely families of North Britain and Strathclyde, and those of Brittany (itself under Frankish attack) came to Wales to assist in its defence. Then, of course, the Normans came from France, themselves of Viking stock, conquering England fairly easily but taking hundreds of years to finally subdue Wales. It seems that the non-aggressive nature of most Welshmen may stem from nearly two millennia of being pushed back by invading forces. It has also concentrated a feeling of nationalism, a feeling of 'us against the world', which combined with a sense of ancient Christian heritage, gives an understanding of the 'self-righteousness' of God's 'chosen' people. The feeling of being 'apart' and of being 'the chosen' people has kept on surfacing over the last centuries, with various proponents proclaiming the Welsh to be 'the lost tribe of Israel.'

IOLO MORGANWG 1747-1826
EDWARD WILLIAMS

Born at Pennon, Llancarfan, he was the son of Edward Williams of Gileston and Ann Mathew of Llanmaes, who had married in St Tathan in 1744. From 1756 the family lived in a tiny cottage in Flemingston, and Iolo trained as a stonemason, evenutally moving to Cowbrdge, where a plaque commemorates him.

Professor G.J. Williams wrote the following, which was delivered posthumously on the BBC Welsh Home Service in 1963:
'Iolo was, in his early years, a romantic poet, and throughout his life, a romantic dreamer. Everybody agrees that he was the greatest authority of his day on the subject of Welsh literature and on many aspects of Welsh history. He was also an authority on such subjects as horticulture, agriculture, geology and botany and, in his old age, he was prepared to lecture on metallurgy in the school which his son had opened in the new industrial town of Merthyr Tudful. His manuscripts show that he was a musician who had composed scores of hymn tunes, and that he took great delight in collecting folk-songs. He was a theologian who helped establish the Unitarian denomination in South Wales, and a politician who revelled in the excitement of the early years after the French Revolution.'

Williams was responsible for retrieving much material upon early Welsh history, but has been portrayed as a fraudster by nearly all sources. As a result, the author has been extremely careful in using his material. However, it seems time for a careful study of his life's work – vitriol was heaped upon him for daring to say that British history predated the Germanic invasions. Hanoverian apologists such as Bishop Stubbs hated any church predating the Roman Catholic conversion of the pagan Saxons. A very major reassessment of Iolo is needed, preferably not by professional historians, blinkered in their ways and minds by what they have been taught. A senior administrator at Cardiff University violently disagreed with the author's remark upon the rewriting of history as he was an *'expert in early Welsh history, and it is not what I was taught at university'* (20 years previously). A history graduate, he also scornfully disagreed that William Wallace came of Brythonic Welsh stock, presumably because he did not study Welsh history in its British context. Academics tend to regurgitate what they were taught and what they know, only ever specialising in smaller and smaller areas of esoteric interest, failing to see the wider picture. (At a Conference, I mentioned over dinner to the person sitting next to me that free trade was not necessarily a good thing. This man, a Professor from Cardiff University, responded with a smirk that that *'it's obvious that you never studied economics'*. Actually I took an economics degree at a good university and took a masters at a business school when both qualifications actually meant something. I just refused to accept that Ricardian 200-year-old theories have any place in today's global economy. Theories of comparative advantage, the crux of which is that free trade is necessarily beneficial, rest upon the hypothesis that countries trade for the mutual benefit of each other. In fact, it is companies who trade, and when those companies are stateless, untaxable multinationals, every theory breaks down. Companies now 'own' economies. When the production of any item can be moved easily to cheap labour autocratic regimes that practise institutionalised torture, the only parties who benefit are dictators and transnational corporations. Received wisdom is the worst type of knowledge, but academics have to defend it as the basis for their existence.)

A recent example to justify a re-examination of Iolo Morganwg is that of Oliver Cromwell, alias Williams. This Welsh regicide has been criticised for 350 years for his 'butchery' at Drogheda and Wexford, by historian after historian. A Drogheda amateur historian, Tom Reilly, *'did what all historians should do; he went back to basics and scrutinised the primary sources. In the process, he discovered that the common perception of what Cromwell got up to in Ireland is "historical bunkum" . . . He showed towards non-combatants a rare compassion. Indeed he was so scrupulous, so determined to protect the ordinary citizens of Ireland and so opposed to looting and pillaging that he had two of his own men hanged for stealing hens from an old woman . . . Although professional historians are prone to be stuffy about amateurs, I have always believed that they should be given a special accolade for being in love with their subject for its own sake. At a time when young academics are encouraged to produce yards of garbage rather than inches of value, there is reason to be grateful to people such as Reilly. From simple curiosity about the past, he investigated the history of his home town, took on a cherished myth bravely and doggedly and made it bite the dust . . . Above all, he understands that the past should not be judged by the standards and fashions of the 1990's. Would that we could say that of the majority of those who teach history for a living.'* (Ruth Dudley-Edwards, reviewing 'Cromwell: An Honourable Enemey' by Tom Reilly, in 'The Sunday Times' May 23, 1999).

Iolo Morganwg is a shining beacon of Welsh history. He tried to 'kick-start' the engine of a dying culture, for which the many of the 'crachach' (snobs) of the time hated him. Vitriolic attacks often have a reason that stems not from academic integrity, but from dislike of change. For many academics to change their thinking, to go back to original sources, to approach a problem differently, requires a change in our educational system. Why has no academic looked at the pre-medieval histories of saints and placed them into context with King Arthur? Why has no academic re-visited Iolo's copious writings and analysed them properly?

ISAN mid 6th century

This saint of the college of Illtud was a contemporary of Samson, and founded St Isen's Church in Llanishen, now a suburb of Cardiff, and Llanishen in Monmouthshire. Lann Issan in Pembrokeshire is now St Ishmael's, and was one of the more important of the 'seven bishop-houses of Dyfed' recorded by Hywel Dda.

Upon March 20th, 1773 *'Was buried in Lanishen a young lad of 10 years of age from four days in a severe fever, which turned his body purple black, as the fever do the most and end them in few days, being a sort of putrified fever, called by the vulgar spotted fever.'* (William Thomas). St Denis' Well, Ffynnon Llandenis was situated in Llanishen, in what is now the north of Roath Park, and was used by sufferers of scurvy.

Oliver Cromwell still called himself Oliver Williams as a young man, and Rice Merrick's 1578 'Book of Glamorgan Antiquities' noted his forebears near a hill in a commote called Keuen On (Cefn Onn, now a botanical garden) in Cardiff. *'A. 2. Miles from this Hille by South, and a 2. Miles from Cairdif, be vestigia of a Pile or Maner Place decayed at Eglwys Newith in the Paroch of Landaf. In the South side of this Hille was born Richard William alias Crumwelle yn the Paroche of Llan Isen.'* It is interesting that native Cardiffians, as evidenced by the folk singer Frank Hennessy, still pronounce Cardiff as Care-Diff, much as inhabitants of Newport still refer to Y Gaer, their magnificent hill-fort, as the 'gair', pronounced as 'air' instead of 'ire'.

BISHOP ISMAEL 6th century
ISHMAEL, YSFAEL OSMAIL
June 16, 25

This son of Prince Budic (Buddig) of Cornouaille (Emyr Llydaw, the Count of Brittany) and of a sister of Teilo, was exiled to Dyfed. He returned to Brittany, but later came back with his three sons to Pembroke, where they were trained under David, Dyfrig and Teilo. Ismael was consecrated as Bishop of Menevia after St David's death, by his uncle St Teilo. Euddogwy and Tyfei were his saintly brothers. Several churches in Pembroke, at St Ishmael's (probably founded by Isan), Camrose, Usmaston, Rosemarket and East Haroldston, and St Ishmael's near Cydweli in Carmarthen are dedicated to him.

It is a little-known fact that Henry VIII had an illegitimate son, by Mary Berkeley, whom he then married off to Sir Thomas Perrot of Haroldston. Despite his anti-Catholic stance Sir John Perrot was not executed by Queen Mary, and was one of the four who carried the canopy at his half-sister Elizabeth's coronation. (Further details are forthcoming in 2001, with the publication of 'The Book of Welsh Pirates, Buccaneers, Seafarers and Explorers' by T. D. Breverton). Near St Ishmael's castle mound is a standing stone of laminated sandstone, ten feet high. Also in the parish at Llansaint is Ffynnon Saint holy well.

ISSUI
ISHAW, ISHO
October 30

Issui was martyred at Patrishow (Patricio), a chapel under Llanbedr in Brecon. Fenton described this fascinating church as follows: *'below the church saw the Sainted Well of Isho, being a very scanty oozing of water, to which, however, was formerly attributed great Vertue, as within the building, that encloses it are little Niches to hold the Vessels drank out of and the offerings they left behind.'* This is one of the most famous churches in Wales, with a celebrated 'Doom Figure', a wall painting of a skeleton with an hour-glass and spade. A small 13th century chapel is built over the saint's grave, abutting the Norman nave. The internal furnishings, screens, nave roof, rood staircase, rood loft, dorway and porch all somehow survived the Reformation, making this possibly the most 'complete' of all the old parish churches in Wales. The full name of the church is Merthyr Issui at Patricio.

There is a pre-Norman stone font here with the inscription *'Menhir made me in the time of Genillin'*, possibly referring to Cynddylan's rule of the princedom of Powys before its capital at Pengwern was destroyed in the early 7th century. Cynddylan's death is the subject of one of the greatest of the early Welsh poems, and Pengwern has been placed variously as Shrewsbury and Wroxeter Roman city. However, ther is another candidate for the site of his court, the strangely shaped Iron Age fort at Baschurch, called The Berth. A bronze cauldron was unearthed there, and Cynddylan, after his defeat in *'the battle in the marshes'* was carried to burial at *'Eglwys Basau'*, possibly this Baschurch near Shrewsbury.

ITHEL 5th century

This may have been a son of Ceredig, the 'founder' of Ceredigion, remembered at Bron-Gwyn (Teifiside) in Cardigan, formerly called Betws Ithel. Ffynnon Ithel was a holy well near Llanddulas in Denbigh.

ITHEL HAEL 6th century

A prince of Armorica who left for Wales with the tribe of Emyr Llydaw, to escape the oncoming Franks of Clovis. His children included the saints Llechid, Baglan, Twrog, Tegai, Trillo, Tecwyn, Fflewyn, Tanwg, Gredfyw and Gredifael.

ITHEL AP HYWEL fl. 843

This king of Gwent and Morganwg does not seem to be accounted a saint, but his son King Fferwael gave the land for the church of Llanerddil (Llanarthil) near Raglan, according to the Book of Llandaf. It was then called *'Lann Efrdil in Brehes'*.

J

'Justice is the means by which established injustices are santioned.'

Anatole France (1844-1924), 'Crainquebille'

JAOUA 6th century
March 3

From Glamorgan, this nephew of Peulin (Pol de Leon) succeeded him to the bishopric in 567 after studying at Landevennec. He is remembered at Brasparts, Daoulas and Leon. St Jaoua is near l'Aber Benoit and St Pabu.

JESUS

It is important in a book of conflicting dates like this, to understand the confused nature of early Christianity. Belief in the gospel versions of Jesus is as unthinking as belief in Bishop Stubbs' version of British history. The suppression for decades of the content of many of the Dead Sea Scrolls still shows us that a certain version of history is sacrosanct. As Keith Hopkins remarks, '. . . *the primacy of the canonical scriptures is an illusion created by church power and by our own deeply embedded cultural traditions. Many early Christians believed that Jesus came back to earth for several years, and that Mary Magdalene was his favourite disciple. The true Jesus is not an historical figure, but a sacred hero, constantly reconstructed. Individual believers have always constructed their own Jesus. They still do.'*

Jesus was a Jew born between 4BC (Herod's death) and AD6 (the Roman census of the province of Syria). A combination of Roman rulers and Jewish priests had him killed sometime between AD26 and AD36 when Pontius Pilate was sub-governor of Judaea. After his death, the leader of his followers was his brother James, a committed Jew, who was friendly with the Pharisees and continued worshipping at the temple in Jerusalem.

Early Christian writings tell us that John, the favourite disciple of Jesus, could not bear to see Him suffer on the Cross, so went to a cave in the Mount of Olives, and wept. However, Jesus comes to the cave and tells John that the crowd is ignorant, as another man is being executed. He says *'I am not the man who is on the cross. I was understood to be what I am not. I am not what for the many I am, and what they will say of me is mean and unworthy.'* Later, John laughed when told of the crucifixion as he knew that Jesus was alive. The Gospels of Mark, Luke and Matthew tell us that Simon of Cyrene carried the cross before the crucifixion. Another early Christian account, the Apocalypse of St Peter, has Jesus tell Peter that a substitute (Simon?) was crucified.

The New Testament gospels were written around fifty to sixty years after the death of Jesus, and the canonical New Testament not firmly established until the second half of the second century. Much was rewritten to form a 'reliable' version of the life of Jesus. Mark and John did not mention the story of the virgin birth. Mark was rewritten to include appearances of Jesus after the crucifixion. Several of Paul's letters are not by Paul. The last chapter of John is by a different author. The established church has formed a rigid structure of tenets of belief around the story of Jesus, which is increasingly difficult to sustain. It should drop the pretence, admit to fabricating and destroying evidence over the last two millennia, and concentrate upon spreading the fundamentally socialist teachings of pure Christianity.

DAVID JOHNS 1796-1843

Not a saint, nor given a Holy Day, but this native of Llanina was for seventeen years a missionary in Madagascar. He took a spinning-jenny and a printing press there and helped found over 25 schools with a total attendance of over 2,000. Facing constant persecution and terrible hardship, he helped translate the Bible into Malagasy, translated 'Pilgrim's Progress' and published a Malagasy-English dictionary. He also jointly wrote 'A Narrative of the Persecutions of the Christians in Madagascar'. Forced out of the island in 1839, he stayed in contact with his flock, and managed to return that same year, dying there four years later.

DAVID JONES 1797-1841

He evangelised in Madagascar for 25 years, a contemporary of David Johns and David Griffiths there. From Pen-rhiw in Cardiganshire, he landed on the island in 1818, but was immediately laid low with a fever that killed his young wife and child. He helped David Griffiths (q.v.) and David Johns translate the Bible, and published a 'Hymnary', 'Spelling Book' and 'Catechism'. Expelled from the island, he carried on his evangelical work using Mauritius as a base until his death.

EDWARD JONES d. 1590
May 6

From St Asaf, he was educated with Anthony Middleton of Yorkshire at the Douai College in Reims. As part of the English Mission in Elizabeth I's reign, he followed Middleton in 1588 and was known as a devout and eloquent preacher. They were hunted down and captured with the aid of spies acting as Catholics in 1590. Brutally tortured by Topcliffe, Jones admitted he had been an Anglican and was now a priest. At his trial on May 6th, the judge complimented him on his courageous bearing, but Jones was convicted on high treason and hung, drawn and quartered that same day.

Jones and Middleton were executed before the doors of the houses in Fleet Street and Clerkenwell where they were arrested. Their trial was full of irregularities, and the reaon for their summary justice was *'for treason and foreign invasion.'* After offering their death for the forgiveness of their sins, the spread of true faith, and the conversion of heretics, someone present called out *'Sir, you have spoken well.'* It is noted that they were both disembowelled while still alive.

GRIFFITH JONES (1638-1761)
April 8

Given a Holy Day by the Church in Wales, and born at Penboyr, Carmarthenshire, the son of John ap Griffith and Elinor John. Educated at Carmarthen Grammar School, he became priest at Penbryn in Cardigan in 1708, Penrieth in Pembroke in 1709, and Laugharne in Carmarthenshire in 1709. At Laugharne he was a master of the Society for the Propagation of Christian Knowledge school, and also became rector of Llandeilo-Abercywyn in 1711. He was a superb preacher, which led to Bishop Adam Ottley complaining about his *'going about preaching on week days in Churches, Churchyards, and sometimes on the mountains, to hundreds of auditors.'* Jones was forced to appear several times before Ottley's bishop's court to defend himself against charges of ignoring church laws and customs. Heavily involved with the S.P.C.K., he was appointed rector of Llanddowror in 1716, and in 1718 underwent a preaching tour of Wales, England and Scotland with his patron, Sir John Philipps.

In 1731, Jones proposed a Welsh school in Llanddowror to the S.P.C.K., and then set up a system of 'circulating schools' across Wales. By 1737 there were 37 such schools with 2,400 scholars. He trained schoolmasters, organised the schools, and wrote about 30 books for them. Schools were held for three months a year, usually over winter when there was less farm work, and night schools were available for those who could not attend in the day. Pupils were taught to read the Welsh Bible and to learn the Church Catechism, and by 1761, 3,495 schools had been set up, with 156,000 participating pupils. Of course, these pupils could then teach their own families and relatives to read, and this **gave the Welsh people the highest standard of literacy in Europe, and probably the world** (see the author's 'A-Z of Wales and the Welsh'). In 1764 Catherine II of Russia sent a commissioner to report upon the school system, *which received much opposition from the established church.* It may be that the Bishop of London, Edmund Gibson, was behind the attacks and anonymous pamphlets, because of Jones' friendship with Methodist leaders. Griffith Jones has an honoured place in Welsh history, and died in Laugharne upon April 8th.

JOHN BUCKLEY JONES 1559-1598
July 12 (also October 25)

One of the 'Forty Martyrs'. Born at Clynnog Fawr, Caernarfon, he joined the Franciscans at Pontoise in France. Returning to London in 1592, Jones worked with Henry Garnett (later to be hanged for complicity in the Gunpowder Plot), and was imprisoned for a year in 1597 while evidence that he was a practising minister was collected. He had been captured by the notorious 'priest-hunter' Richard Topcliffe. (A few years later, Topcliffe was torturing the martyr, Edward Jones). His hanging was delayed because the executioner forgot the rope, and Jones asserted that he had never ever thought of treason, but he was killed on July 12th on the Old Kent Road. Jones was canonized by Pope Paul VI in 1970. His brother William was a leading figure in the Benedictine revival at Douai and founder of the order's convent at Cambrai.

ROBERT JONES 1560-1615
August 20

Not regarded as a saint, but born in Oswestry or Chirk, and probably instructed by the martyr Richard Gwyn. In Rheims in 1581, by 1582 he was in the English College in Rome. He became a Jesuit of such renown that he was made professor of philosophy at its Gregorian College in 1590. Returning to Wales, he set up an underground network in Monmouthshire, and bought the Cwm at Llanrothal as the headquarters of the Welsh Jesuit College. The Sheriff of Hereford accused him of political subversion in this same year, and his position was made more difficult with the recommencement of executing Catholic priests from 1608. Jones was made vice-prefect and Superior of the Jesuit mission in England and Wales in 1609, and somehow managed to visit Roger Cadwaladr on the day Cadwaladr was sentenced to death in 1610. Jones' health was deteriorating rapidly under the strain of operating 10 Jesuit missionaries across Wales and 47 in England, and in 1613 he was replaced by Father Walpole. Father Jones died in Wales after falling in a night visit to christen a baby. Walpole wrote *'His career as a missioner had mostly been spent among the Britons, the ancient inhabitants of this island, in Wales a mountainous and not very fertile part of the country. He here led a life full of toil and peril, among a people which still clings to the old religion.'*

JOSEPH OF ARIMATHEA 1st century
March 17 (and 27)

Said to be the apostle of the Britons, and to have died at Glastonbury in 82, after coming to Britain about 63 AD. The rich Jew who asked Pilate for Jesus' body to bury it, he was said to have sailed to Marseilles with the Holy Grail. His companions were Lazarus (mentioned in an old Triad), Mary, Martha, Marcella and Maximin. He was later associated with Glastonbury (Ynys Witrin) and the West Country by William of Malmesbury. Legends give their crossing as from Mont St Michel in France to St Michael's Mount in Cornwall. This route was the same as that of Tristan and Isolde to King Mark in Arthurian legend. This was from Land's End to the Jesus Well near Padstow, hence to the Paradise area (marked on old maps) around the river Brue, then by water to Godney, the port for Glastonbury.

A Cornish legend related how Joseph came there with his relative, the young boy Jesus, whom he taught how to extract tin and extract the wolfram from it. For luck, the Guild of Cornish Tinners at the moment the tin was *'flashed'* shouted *'Joseph was a tinner'*. Both Diodorus Siculus and Herodotus referred to the trade between Cornwall and Phoenicia in this time. In Somerset was the tale that Joseph came with Jesus to Tarshish and stayed in Summerland at 'Paradise'. (Summerland is another name for the county, the exact translation of the Welsh 'Gwlad yr Haf'). Paradise could have been Priddy in Somerset, a hill village where in these times copper and lead mining were carried out, where again there is the story that the two stayed there.

Joseph was also linked with Glastonbury and the Holy Grail legends, and it was said that he was given 12 hides of land there by King Arviragus to build the church. The entry in the Domesday Book would appear to give some credence to this tale; *'The Home of God, the great Monastery of Glastonbury, called the Secret of The Lord. This Glastonbury church possesses its own Villa XII hides of land which has never paid tax.'* (see Ilid and Arwystli).

Arwystli Hen was supposed to have been Britain's first bishop, martyred in 99, following on from Joseph's work. Archbishop Haleca of Saragossa ('Fragmenta') and St Gregory of Tours ('The History of the Franks') both claimed that St Joseph was the first to preach to the Britons. According to Wall, St David's uncle, Maelgwyn of Llandaf wrote around 450 that Joseph was buried in Glastonbury with eleven companions, with *'two silver-white vessels filled with the blood and sweat of the great prophet Jesus'*. Arvigarus was the British king of the Dobuni in this area from c. 45 - 73, with his capital at Cirencester. At Chedworth villa near there were found bricks stamped Arveri, and a stone inscribed Prasiata. Tacitus named Prasutagus as the King of the Iceni and husband of Buddug (Boadicea), and tradition makes him the brother of Arviragus. Two stones with chi-rho symbols were also found there. Glastonbury, with Amesbury and Côr Eurgain (Llanilltud) was one of the three *'perpetual choirs (cors) of the British Church.'* The tradition that Joseph founded the British Church was held all over England and Wales until the Reformation.

JOUVIN (see CIANAN)

JULIAN c.304
JULIUS
July 1 (also June 20 or July 3) (see Aaron, Arfon)

Bede and Gildas referred to his martyrdom at Caerleon, and he is also mentioned with St Aaron in the Book of Llandaf, and by Giraldus Cambrensis. St Julian's farm in Glamorgan and St Julians' in Newport recall his name. Geoffrey of Monmouth says that just before the terrible battle of Camlan, *'Queen Guinevere gave way to despair. She fled to the City of the Legions and there, in the church of Julius the Martyr, she took her vows among the nuns, promising to lead a chaste life.'* The site of this is possibly a mile west of Caerleon, where the mansion of St Julians was demolished in the 1970's. It was reputedly built on the site of monastic buildings. In the centre of Caerleon is the church of Llangattock-juxta-Caerleon. Cadoc sheltered Ligessaw Lawhir at Llancarfan from Arthur, Bedwy and Cai, and met them at a ford on the Usk called Rhyd Gwrthebau (the Ford of Rejoinders) near Trefedinauc (The Town of the Fern, modern Tredunnock).

St Julian's Church on the quay at picturesque Tenby was moved in 1840 from the end of the old stone pier. Waves sometimes broke over the roof of the chapel, and records show that the clergy were paid 'in kind' i.e. with fish and shellfish. The leaflet available at 'the fisherman's chapel' seems to confuse Caerleon's martyr with the mythical St Julian the Hospitaller: *'Mediaeval history informs us that "Saint Julian" was the patron saint of travellers, hospitallers and fishermen and was canonised by Rome just after the "Holy Wars". The late Archdeacon of Newport, Revd. Ivor Phillips, whom I have known all my life, told me he had researched into the history of St Julian mainly because there was a chapel of that name near where the River Wye joined the Severn. The legend referred to the return of Julian from the Wars having been away for many months. He found that his wife was living with another man. He then in a wild rage slew the man only to find that it was his own father who was living there to look after and protect Julian's wife. Julian, filled with grief and remose, went to Rome to seek absolution. As a penance he was sent back to the banks of the Severn to build a hostel and to act as a ferryman bringing travellers across the river to Wales. He named the hostel St Julian's – so much for the origin of St Julians.'*

St Mary's in Tenby is the largest parish church in Wales, with a plaque to Robert Recorde. He not only invented the = sign, but also the + sign and the method for finding square roots.

JULIOT
JULIANA, ILUD
June 16, nearest Sunday to June 29

A daughter of Brychan, who was killed after she was robbed. She has a church and cross at Luxulyan in Cornwall. It is also thought that Tintagel was dedicated to her, but it was later rededicated mistakenly to Julitta of Tarsus. A Celtic monastery site has been found on the headland adjoining Tintagel Castle. The Cornish churches of St Juliot near Boscastle and Lanteglos near Camelford are dedicated to her. Ilud is also given as a son of Brychan and possibly the founder of Llanilid (see Ilid), and of Llanilis and Bodilis in the diocese of Leon in Brittany.

From Capel Ilud, at Cwm Crai, comes the strange Trecastell Stone. In Latin it reads vertically downwards, and Ogham vertically upwards, recording Maccultrenus Salicudunus, and its pictographs show a figure with a crozier or shepherd's crook.

JUSTINIAN early 6th century
STINAN, JESTIN, IESTYN
December 5, August 23

This hermit monk from Brittany settled on Ramsey Island (then called Limeneia) with another monk, Honorius. He asked Hororius to send away his sister and maid-servant. David asked to see Justinian and was so impressed that he gave him houses on the island and mainland. St Justinian was said to have been murdered by his followers on '*Lemeney*', i.e. Ramsey Island. Devils possessed his servants, and when they were told to work harder, they cut off his head. Where it fell a spring gushed forth that cured the sick. St Justinian's Spring soon became famous as a healing well. The murderers contracted leprosy and lived out their days on a crag known as Leper's Rock. Iestyn then walked across the sea carrying his head, coming ashore at St Justinian's Point, where he wished to be buried. This was the origin of St Justinian's Chapel. Because of the fame of the miracles there, his remains were reinterred next to St David's, behind the high altar in the nearby cathedral. Llanstinan Church near Fishguard commemorates him, as does the chapel of St Stinan at Porthstinian in St David's parish. His shrine can be seen in St David's Cathedral. Llanstinan is on the 'Saints and Stones' Pilgrim's Trail, and was situated by the side of a great marsh, with an enclosure of large stones encompassing seven natural springs. The foundations of the preconquest church can still be seen, and it was once the centre of the village of Scleddau, vanished since George Owen's map of 1603. There is a colony of long-eared bats in the rafters.

On St Justinian's Day, December 5, 1664, a ship sank off North Wales and the only survivor of 82 passengers and crew was Hugh Williams. On the same date in 1785, another ship foundered and just one man survived of 62 people. His name was Hugh Williams. A third ship sank in the area in 1860 on the same date, with 25 dead and the sole survivor again being Hugh Williams. The author would be grateful for independent confirmation of these events. In the meantime, any boy born on December 5th should be christened Huw William to keep on the safe side.

JUTHWARA 5th - 6th century
JUTWARA, JUDITH, AUDE, AUDWARA
December 23 (Wales), July 13 (translation), 17 and 18 (Devon) and November 28 (Brittany). January 6 (Roscarrock).

She was a virgin martyred in South Wales according to Cressy, who names her sisters Eadwara, Wilgitha and Sidwella as saints also. Her brother may have been Peulin (Pol de Leon). With her sister, Sidwella of Exeter, she was victimised by a jealous step-mother, who incited her son Bana to murder her, on the pretext that Juthwara was pregnant. She had told Juthwara that the best cure for sore breasts was to cover them with cream cheese. Bana saw her damp breasts, and concluded that she was indeed producing breast milk. Wild with anger, he cut her head off with a single blow of his sword, but Juthwara picked up the head and carried it to the church identified with Lanteglos near Camelford (see Juliot). The sisters are illustrated on the old rood screens in Hennock and Ashton churches in Devon. There is also a statue in Guizeny in Brittany of Juthwara with her head in her hands.

Her religious emblem is two cream cheeses (this is a fact to use for troublesome pub quiz teams). A headless ghost is said to roam around Judith Hill in Halstock. There is a pub called 'The Quiet Woman' there, and its inn-sign depicts Juthwara carrying her head under her arm. This tavern will now be on the hit-list for feminists. (See Peulin)

K

*'**K**ingdoms are clay; our dungy earth alike*
Feeds beast as man; the nobleness of life
Is to do thus; when such a mutual pair
And such a twain can do't.'
William Shakespeare (1564-1616), Antony and Cleopatra

KEA d.c.550
CYNAN, KENAN, CAI HIR (Cai the Tall)
October 3

Probably a cousin of Beuno, he moved from Wales via Dumnonia to Brittany. His father was Lleuddyn Luydog ap Cynfarch, who has given his name to Lothian in Scoland, his mother was Nyfain ferch Brychan, and his brother Urien Rheged. He travelled with Rumon, and Landkey and nearby Romansley near Barnstaple commemorate them. It was said that they met Gildas when he was living on an island in the flooded plains near Street and Glastonbury. At Lantokai (the present Leigh) Kea had a hermitage, with a precious prayer bell given to him by Gildas. St Cynan, or Kea in Cornwall is on the Fal river, and the port of Landegu was once known as Lanty-Kea. Two holy wells are nearby, associated with him, Quenchwell and Holy Well, the latter at which he washed his bloody mouth after Prince Tewdrig had hit him in the face. Kea then went with his disciples from Roseland (Rhos Ynys) to Brittany, with his main foundation at Plouguerneau (Plou-Cernau). The Bretons believe he died at Chinon and is buried at Cleder, but the Welsh tradition is that he rests near Din Lligwy on Anglesey.

Both Kea and Gildas are linked with Arthur, and Kea was supposed to have returned from Brittany to Caerwent to persuade Guinevere (Gwenhwyfar) to enter a nunnery after he attempted to bring peace between Arthur and Medraut (Mordred). However, Mordred and Arthur fought at Camlan in 537. Kea returned to Cleder in Brittany, where he is remembered at St Quay in Treguier, Plogoff and Plougerneau. He had founded the monastery at Cleder near Pol de Leon. In Brittany he is often depicted with a stag and his name was invoked to cure toothache. Les Roches de St Quay lie off St Quay Portrieux near Paimpol, and two other places named St Quay are east of Guincamp and north of Lannion. Cai Hir was the constant companion of Bedwyr and appears in the old poem 'Pa Gur', in 'Culhwch and Olwen' and in 'The Dream of Rhonabwy'. See Cai - this may well be the same saint.

KEBIUS d.370

Cressy states that Kebius was the son of Solomon (Selyf) duke of Cornwall, and he was made a bishop by Solomon on the isle of Anglesey, having been taught by St Hilary of Poitiers. Cressy's date does not fit with Solomon ap Geraint of the 7th century.

JOHN KEBLE 1792-1866
March 29, 30

Given a holy day by the Church in Wales, he was the father with Pusey of the 'Oxford Movement'. His 'The Christian Year' of 1825 helped give the Prayer Book a new appeal, and he helped in the revival of religious orders in the Church of England. His sermon of July 14, 1833, denounced the nation for turning away from God, and was a nationwide sensation, the beginning of the religious revival known as the Tractarian Movement. In 1869, his admirers founded Keble College, Oxford, to commemorate him. Some of his poems were used as hymns, for example:
'Blest are the pure in heart,
For they shall see our God.
The secret of the Lord is theirs;
Their soul is Christ's abode.'

JOHN KEMBLE 1599-1679
October 25, August 22

This Welsh border priest is one of the 40 Martyrs of England and Wales, canonized in 1970. From his brother's house at Pembridge Castle, he set up Jesuit mission centres in Gwent and Hereford, including at the Llwyn, Coedanghred, the Craig and Hilston. After the Popish Plot he was taken to London to face Titus Oates, tried for being a seminary priest, and sentenced to be hung drawn and quartered. On August 22nd the under-sheriff of Hereford came to take the 80-year-old to the scaffold. Kemble asked for time to make a prayer, have a glass of wine and to smoke a pipe, which he shared with the sheriff. The executioner kindly ensured that the venerable old man was dead by hanging before he carried out the disembowelling. Kemble's room in Pembridge can still be seen and his missal and altar are in Monmouth's Roman Catholic church. In Hereford, a 'Kemble Pipe' means to have one last fill of tobacco or a final cigarette. The term is also still used for the last person sitting at a dinner-party or social gathering. His gravestone is in Welsh Newton, near Ross-on-Wye.

KENELM d.819
July 17

The martyred Anglo-Saxon King of Mercia, remembered at Rockfield in Monmouth. He is buried at St Pancras in Winchcombe with his father Coenwulf.

KENEYTHON see CYNHEIDDON

KENTIGERN d. 612
MUNGO, CYNDEYRN, CYNDERYN
January 13 (also January 14)

According to Bonedd y Saint he was the son of King Owain ab Urien Rheged, and Dwynwen ferch Llewddyn Lueddog of Gododdin (Lothian). Late sources state that this Strathclyde prince was driven by persecution from the British stronghold of Cumbria, and founded the monastery at Llanelwy in the seventh year of David's reign as Bishop of Menevia.

Alphabetical Listing of the Saints of Wales and Religious Events

The Red Book of St Asaph states that in 550 he had discovered that *'paganism still lingered in the mountain parts near Carlisle'*, *'fostered by the bards, who recalled the old traditions of the race before they had been Christianised under the Roman dominion'*. His efforts to evangelise led to widespread unrest and he had to flee to St David's. On his travels he had seen a wild boar digging in the earth near the river Elwy, and his monastery there soon attracted 965 monks. He was succeeded by St Asaf as bishop at Llanelwy (now the site of St Asaf's Cathedral), and returned to Glasgow to found the church there, after King Rhederech (the saint Rhydderch Hael) called him to return. Llangyndeyrn in the valley of the Gwendraeth Fach may be another local saint, Cyndeyrn ap Cyngar, rather than Mungo/Kentigern. Mungo was buried in the holy ground of St Ninian, where Glasgow Cathedral now stands. The Glasgow coat of arms features a fish with a ring in its mouth. (see Rhydderch for the reason). Mungo was supposed to have met the 'Scottish' Merlin after the battle of Arthuret (Arderydd)*. There are several churches of St Kentigern in Cumbria.

*There were four British kings in Strathclyde, fighting the Saxons who had invaded the Lothians. North of them was the Scots colony (from Ireland) of Dalriada (Argyll) who were themselves fighting the Northern Picts. There were also Picts in control of the counties of Wigtown and Kirkudbright. Strathclyde, which included Cumbria, was not only warring with the Picts, Scots and Saxons, there were internal problems also. Of the kings, Rhydderch Hael was the most 'Romanised', whereas Morcant and Gwenddoleu represented the old Celtic tribal ways and claimed descent from Coel Hen. In 573, at Arthuret, just 8 miles from Carlisle, the 'pagans' under Gwenddoleu were defeated and Rhydderch Hael became king of the Cumbrian Britons. The other king, Urien Rheged (Sir Urience in Arthurian legend) had died previously fighting in Bernicia, his death being blamed upon Morcant's treachery.

KEURBREIT 5th – 6th century

A son or daughter of Brychan who lived at Casllwchwr, the Roman fort of Leucarum at modern Lloughor, where the church is now dedicated to St Michael. Westwood noted a Roman altar found at Loughor, being used as a step to the rectory. Later incised in Ogham, all that could be deciphered was L?…ASIC, or L?EVIC.

KEW late 5th century
CIWA
February 8

The sister of Cyngar/Docco, who sailed from Gwent and landed in Wadebridge where the village of Kew (formerly called Lan Docco) still carries her name. Her chapel stood next to the church there, until at least the 15th century. Docco would not allow Kew near his hermit's cell until she proved she could master a wild boar (pigs were considered part of the other world by the Celts). When Samson visited Cornwall, he landed at Lan Docco, where he was received by Junavius.

Llangua (Llangiwa) in Monmouth is now dedicated to James. Only the old font and cross base remain after heavy restoration, and the church is one of those transferred from Llandaff to Hereford in 1886.

KEYNE see CENEU

L

*'**L**ike as the arrows in the hand of the giant:
even so are the young children.
Happy is the man that hath his quiver full of them:
They shall not be ashamed when they speak with their enemies at the gate.'*

Prayer Book , 1662

LAMMAS
August 1

Lug was the Celtic god with the Sword of Light, who brought the harvest with the autumn sun. To do this he had to kill his grandfather Baal (Bel), remembered in the great May festival of Beltane. The pre-Christian festival of Lughnasad was replaced by Loaf-Mass, Lammas, the day when the harvesting started. Lammas fairs happened all over Wales until the eighteenth century.

ARCHBISHOP WILLIAM LAUD 1573-1645
January 10

Given a Holy Day by the Church in Wales, he was Archbishop of Canterbury for King Charles I from 1633 to 1645. During his time, the Puritans objected strongly to the use of the surplice (the white over-garment) as it was not mentioned in the Bible, and had been used by Roman Catholics before the Reformation. Sortly before his term in office, a Doctor of Divinity named Alexander Leighton wrote that bishops were the tools of Antichrist, and he was sentenced to be publicly whipped, branded, and his ears cut off. Against this background, Laud punished those who vandalised and attacked the church, upheld the customs of public worship such as the wearing of the surplice, and sought the independence of local clergy away from their financial dependency on local landowners. He proposed to achieve this last end by restoring to the Church some of its lands seized by Henry VIII, now in the hands of landowners.

Laud also attempted to introduce the Book of Common Prayer in Scotland in 1637, which caused widespread rioting. In 1638 Scottish leaders signed the National Covenant, and voted to depose and excommunicate every bishop in Scotland. Discontent, fomented by Puritans and land-owners, spread to England and Laud was arrested in 1640 on a charge of high treason. After four years in the Tower of London, he was tried, aged 71, in 1644 and condemned, not because of proof of guilt, but because the (land-owning) House of Commons had decided that he had to die. On the scaffold he prayed: *'The Lord receive my soul, and have mercy on me, and bless this kingdom with peace and charity, that there may not be this effusion of Christian blood amongst them.'*

LEONORE mid-6th century
LEONARD, LEONORIUS
November 6

He trained at St Illtud's monastery-college, and sailed with seventy-three monks to evangelise Brittany. A very late and obscure 'Life' was written in France. Iolo Morganwg placed him as a son of Hywel ab Emyr Llydaw, along with the saints Derfel, Tudwal, Armel and Dwyfael. Farmer does not make any connection with the St Leonard of the 6th century, whose cult spread rapidly across France in the 11th century. St Leonard, the monastery and shrine, is at Limoges. There are churches across France, Italy and Bavaria, and no less than 177 in England dedicated to Leonard.

LEVAN see SELEVAN

DAVID LEWIS (alias CHARLES BAKER) 1617-1679
October 25, August 27 (executed)

From Monmouthshire, David Lewis went to Abergavenny Gramar School where his father was headmaster, then the Middle Temple to study law. His mother Margaret Pritchard was a practising Roman Catholic, the niece of Father Augustine Baker. He then became a Roman Catholic in Paris, entered the English College in Rome and became a priest in 1642. Under the influence of his uncle, Father John Pritchard (alias Lewis), David Lewis entered the Society of Jesus in 1645.

He became Spiritual Director of the English College in Paris, but 'hiraeth' pulled him and he asked to be allowed to return to Wales in 1648. For the next thirty years he worked from a farmhouse in Cwm in Monmouthshire. For much of this time, Lewis lived with the Morgans of Llantarnam. Frequently denounced, it was not until Titus Oates' *'Popish Plot'*, that Lewis was arrested in a little house at St Michael-Llantarnam. The fanatical MP, John Arnold of Llanfihangel Crucorney, captured Lewis and seven other priests.

After painful interrogation, he was prosecuted for papacy by Arnold, who was closely related to the judge in the trial. He was tried at Usk on the sole count of being a priest in foreign orders and condemned. Lewis wrote an acount of his trial while in prison. His famous library at his college at Cwm was given to Hereford Cathedral. The priest was then sent to London to be confronted with Oates, Bedloe and Lord Shaftesbury to reveal what he knew about the 'plot'. Of course, the poor cleric knew nothing, and he was returned, probably after more torture, to the tender mercies of Arnold. On his execution day, 27th August, the official hangman refused to hang, draw and quarter him, and ran away. A convict was offered his freedom to carry out the sentence, but the crowd threw stones at him, and he likewise refused. A local blacksmith was eventually persuaded to execute Lewis. Before he died, David Lewis spoke to the crowd in Welsh telling them why he was being killed and the reasons for his faith. Lewis had ministered secretly to Catholics in Wales for thirty years, and was known as *'Tad y Tlodion'*, *'Father of the Poor'*.

In 1679 at Usk, Lewis was found guilty, hanged, cut down barely alive, disembowelled, his bowels burned, then his corpse was dismembered and beheaded. He was canonised by the Roman Catholic Church in 1929. The Cwm, in the shadow of Skirrid Mountain, can still be

OWEN LEWIS (LEWIS OWEN) 1553-1595

Not a saint, and born in Llanfeirian, Llangadwaladr, Anglesey, he became bishop of Cassano in southern Italy. Elected a perpetual Fellow at Oxford in 1554, he disliked the new Protestant regime of Elizabeth and fled to Douai around 1558, where he achieved doctorates in law and in divinity. He helped establish the missionary training college at Douai, and impressed Pope Gregory XIII so much on a 1574 visit to Rome, that he was appointed to an influential position at the papal court. He now helped establish the English College at Rome, and suggested Morris Clynnog as its warden. Clynnog and Lewis disputed with the Jesuits here, and Lewis was made vicar-general to Carlo Borromeo, Archbishop of Milan. He tried to get finance for printing papal books in Welsh in 1579, for dissemination back home. From 1580 he worked in Milan with Gruffydd Robert, one of Borromeo's advisors and confessors. After Borromeo's death in 1584, Lewis spent most of the rest of his life at the papal court again. He supported Mary, Queen of Scots from here, but his Hispanophobia led to King Phillip II of Spain asking that Lewis be removed from papal influence. This appears to be the reason for his appointment as bishop of the far-away Cassano in 1588. However, the Pope insisted that Lewis remain in Rome. If the Armada had succeeded, Lewis's supporters thought that he would be the new Archbishop of York, the stepping-stone to the Archbishopric of Canterbury. It appears that he was the favourite of the Pope for the appointment of archbishop in 1595, but he died upon October 14, and was buried within the walls of the English College.

RICHARD LEWIS – DIC PENDERYN 1808-1831
August 13 Dic Penderyn Day

July 2, 1831 saw height of 'The Merthyr Rising', when hungry iron and coal workers took over the town for five days, and paraded under a sheet daubed symbolically with the blood of a lamb and a calf. On its staff was impaled a loaf of bread, showing the needs of the marchers. *This was probably the first time that the 'red flag' of revolution was raised in Britain. (It may the first time anywhere in the world)*. A ten thousand-strong crowd had battled with soldiers at the Castle Inn in June 1831, and up to two dozen men, women and children died in the fighting. Unemployment and reduced wages had fomented the unrest, and the workers burnt Court records and their employers' property. The tyrannical ironmasters Crawshay and Guest were locked up in the Castle Inn, defended by Scottish soldiers, who opened fire on the mob. The Argyll and Sutherland Highlanders were reinforced by the Glamorgan Yeomanry, but the supporting Swansea Yeomanry were forced back to Neath. Major Richards called out the equivalent of the Home Guard, the Llantrisant Cavalry, to rescue the regular soldiers, who sustained no losses.

Lewis Lewis, the truck owner whose loss sparked off the initial revolt, was sentenced to death, commuted to exile for life. A 23-year-old collier, Dic Penderyn (Richard Lewis) was accused of riotous assault and a 'felonious' attack upon Private Donald Black of the 93rd Highland Regiment. Convicted, 11,000 people signed a petition to ask for his reprieve, and the great Quaker philanthropist, Joseph Tregelles Price, appealed personally to Lord Melbourne, the Home Secretary. Dic Penderyn was hung at Cardiff after a two-week respite, his last words being *'Arglwydd, dyma gamwedd'* (*'Oh God, what an injustice'*). He was seen as an example 'pour les autres'. Other defendants were transported to Australia. Forty years later, an immigrant from Merthyr, Ieuan Evans, confessed on his deathbed in the USA that it was he that wounded the soldier. This confession was taken and recorded by the Rev. Evan Evans in 1874. The carter who took Penderyn's body back to Aberafan asked to be, and is, buried next to Dic Penderyn in the churchyard of St. Mary's. It apears that Lewis was born at a cottage named Penderyn, near Pyle. His elder sister married the Rev. Morgan Howells, who addressed the great crowd at the funeral. The procession attracted thousands of followers as it went through the Vale of Glamorgan from Cardiff to St Mary's in Aberafan.

The Merthyr Rising was described by John Davies as **'the most ferocious and bloody event in the history of industrialised Britain.'** Gwyn Williams pointed out that *'these defeats inflicted on regular and militia troops by armed rioters have no parallel in recent British history.'* Publicity was suppressed - after all the starving Welsh working class did not matter in the grand scheme of things. In June 1831 a Mrs Arbuthnot noted in her diary: *'There has been a great riot in Wales and the soldiers have killed twenty-four people. When two or three were killed at Manchester, it was called the Peterloo Massacre and the newspapers for weeks wrote it up as the most outrageous and wicked proceeding ever heard of. But that was in Tory times; now this Welsh riot is scarcely mentioned.'* Gwyn Williams commented that *'bodies were being buried secretly all over north Glamorgan . . . widows did not dare claim poor relief.'* Richard Lewis, Dic Penderyn, was hanged in Cardiff Gaol and his day is commemorated outside Cardiff's Victorian Market. (Extract from the author's 'The A-Z of Wales and the Welsh'). Penderyn has been described as the first martyr of the working classes of Wales.

LILY GWAS DEWI 5th - 6th century
March 3

A servant or disciple of David.

POPE LINUS d.76
September 23

Pope from 64, the first Bishop of Rome according to the records of St Irenaeus, Julius Africanus, St Hippolytus, Eusebius, and the Liberian Catalogue of 364. These all place him as the successor of Peter the Apostle.

St Irenaeus wrote in 174, less than a hundred years after his death: *'After the Holy Apostles (Peter and Paul) had founded and set the Church in order (in Rome) they gave over the exercise of the episcopal office to Linus. The same Linus is mentioned by St Paul in his Epistle to Timothy (St Paul II, Timotheus iv.21). His successor was Anacletus.'* He was buried alongside St Peter at the foot of Vatican Hill. Other authorities place Clement as the first Bishop of Rome, but the 'Catholic Encyclopaedia' firmly refutes this later attribution. Linus was the son of Claudia (q.v.), grandson of Caractacus and nephew of Eurgain, which means that **this first Pope was half-British**. (Adrian Gilbert's 'The Holy Kingdom' explores the links between Linus, Claudia, Aristobulus, Timothy, Paul, Peter and Simon Zelotes. This area is fertile ground for research).

Near Pisa, an 11th century fresco in S. Piro de Grado shows Linus burying St Peter. He was celebrated in the west as a martyr, but there was no known persecution in his 12-year term of office as Pope. The author appends some more information upon the first and second century facts and legends surrounding the earliest Christianity in Europe. It is an area that needs very careful research, as much evidence that did not agree with early theological doctrine was deliberately destroyed. Jowett's 'Drama of the Lost Disciples' is as good a starting-point as any in making a thesis that Britain, and in particular Wales, was more important than Rome in the survival and promulgation of the faith.

LIVES OF THE SAINTS

Many of the early 'Lives' have disappeared or were destroyed, and the only extant pre-Norman works on Welsh saints are Breton. These include the lives of Samson of Dol (written c.610-615), Maclovius (Malo) by Bili (869-870), Gwenole (Winwaloe) by Wrdisten (880), Pol de Leon (Peulin) by Wrmonoc (884), Gildas by Vitalis in the 9th century, Brioc (Briog) and Melanius. The other 'lives' date from after the Norman invasion of England. The best other pre-Norman sources of information in Ireland and Europe are meticulously listed by G. H. Doble. *'Liber Landavensis' (The Book of Llandaf)* was compiled in the 12th century, and contains details on Dyfrig, Samson, Teilo, Euddogwy, etc. A manuscript known as Cotton Vespasian A xiv seems to have come from Brecon or Monmouth priories, and tells us of Cadog, Gwynlliw, Illtud, Dyfrig, David, Clydog, Padarn, Cybi, Tathan, Carannog and Brynach. Other 'Lives' in existence are those of Gwenfrewi, Collen, Beuno and Llawddog. Wade-Evans and Doble have also given us much information upon Cornish saints and their Welsh/Breton links. Ancient place-names are also invaluable for studying British saints.

THE LLANNAU OF WALES see APPENDIX F

LLAWDDOG ap DINGAD 6th century
LLEUDDAD
January 24 (Cenarth), January 15, 21, August 10 (Cilgerran Old Style), then August 19 and 20.

The brother of Baglan, Eleri, Tegwy and Tyfrydog, and probably the patron with Cadfan of Bardsey (Ynys Enlli), rather than Lleuddad ab Alan. Cilgerran in Pembroke, and Cenarth, Penboyr and Llanllawddog under Abergwyli, all in Carmarthen are his, although Cilgerran was rededicated by the Normans to St Lawrence. There were several wells named Ffynnon Llawdog around Ogof Lleuddad at Aberdaron. There is Gerddi Lleuddad on Bardsey (Ynys Enlli) and a walled well, Ffynnon Lleuddad at Carrog near Bryncroes, Caernarfon, which cured diseases in men and animals. Another Ffynnon Llawdog was in a wood on the hill called Bron Llawddog, near Penboyr Church in Carmarthen. Yet another Ffynnon Lawdog near Blaenporth, Cardigan, was visited by the sick until the 20th century. In Bridell, Pembroke was Ffynnon Lawdog. His 'Saying of the Wise' *'for the instruction of a peevish man'* was *'friendless is every loveless person.'* Lleuddad was buried at Ynys Enlli.

In Cenarth, the 'Alehouse by the Church' is the oldest building, dating back to mediaeval times and occupying the original site of Llawddog's monastic community. The holy well by the salmon pool has been beautifully restored with a slate canopy and carved cross motifs. There is a remarkable sarsen stone in the churchyard, and salmon can still be seen leaping the falls in this conservation village. The clear inscription CURCAGNI FILIANDAGELI means 'Caracagnus, son of Andageli'. Locals said that it came from Parc Maen Llwyd, 'the grey stone park' field near the church, but it is known as the Gellidywyll Stone. Another stone inscribed in Ogham and Latin, ANDAGELI FILIUS CAVETI ('Andageli son of Cavetus') was found at Gellidywyll near Llandeilo Llwydiarth. Cenarth church also has a mediaeval font from Llandysilio Gogo. It was thrown out of Llandysilio Church by Puritans who considered it 'Popish' because of the strange faces carved on it. For years it lay in a hedge, and then was used as a flower trough before coming to Cenarth.

Unfortunately (and disgustingly), the 2,500 year-old craft of coracle fishing* is now illegal here. Nine different types of Welsh coracle can be seen in the National Coracle centre and 17th century flour mill at Cenarth Falls. Other coracles can be seen at the Museum of Welsh Life at St Ffagans. At Llanllawdog are three quartz standing stones known as Meini Gwyn in a field called Cae'r Garreg.

*Coracle-fishing is carried out by two men in these little oval boats with a small net between them, which can only take one fish at a time. Often a pool may be 'swept' up to twenty times before a catch is made. A coracle itself cannot safely be handled with two fish of 10 pounds or more in weight. The coracle fishermen never fished the rivers to extinction, as it was their livelihood, but the various water authorities and the Ministry of Agriculture, Fisheries and Food saw them as a threat to the lucrative income from English fly-fishermen for licences. Thus this ancient art has been restricted to just 25 licences in 3 rivers in the tidal estuary waters only. There was a different craft to fishing up-river. One wonders which National Assembly member

Coracle Fisherman, River Teifi at Llechryd.   © *Wales Tourist Board Photo Library.*

might have the courage to try to rescind this penal legislation. The dam for Llyn Brianne Reservoir halved the numbers of salmon on the Tywy, but no action was taken against the water authorities. Coracles took just 220 salmon in 1986 and 1987 – hardly the numbers to hurt the salmon run. Coraclemen must be given licences back upon the Welsh rivers upstream of estuary waters – it will attract tourism and revive a dying tradition. Fishing was legally stopped at Cenarth with the death of the last licence-holder in the 1970's. Each stretch and pool of the Welsh rivers had their names for the coracle fishermen (see 'The Coracle' by J. Geraint Jenkins, published by the National Coracle Centre). There were coracles on all the Welsh rivers in tidal and non-tidal waters, with different shapes, construction methods, paddles and types of net. In the Severn alone there were different types of coracle at Welshpool, Ironbridge and Shrewsbury. A coracle boatman used to retrieve footballs from the Severn during Shrewsbury's matches at Gay Meadow in the 1970's. He received 50 pence a ball, and his highest match reward was £3.50. Coracles were used on the rivers Nevern (at Newport), Loughor, Usk, Conwy, Dyfi, Wye (at Ross), Monmow (at Monmouth), Lower Dee (at Bangor-is-Coed and Overton), Upper Dee (Bala to Ceiriog and Llangollen), Lledr (at Betws-y-Coed) and even on Llangorse Lake.

Coracles are keel-less, bowl-shaped fishing boats made of willow laths, covered by animal skin (now calico). They are almost identical to the Mandan bull-boats made of buffalo-skin and willow by the Mandan Indians of North America, the supposed descendants of Prince Madoc. In 1999 Harry Sitting Bear from the Mandan reservation in North Dakota visited the National Coracle Centre at Cenarth.

LLECHEU 5th – 6th century

A son of Brychan, who lived at Tregaian in Anglesey and is also associated with Llanllecheu in Ewyas, Herefordshire.

LLECHEU 6th century

Possibly the son of Arthur (Arthwys ap Meurig ap Tewdrig) who was slain at Llongborth with Geraint. Talyllechau has become Talley, the beautiful site of the great abbey in Carmarthenshire. There was a Llanlecheu in Hereford, the site of which has been lost, but this may be the previous Llecheu.

LLECHID
December 1, 2, November 1

This daughter of Ithel Hael founded Llanllechid in Caernarfonshire. The nearby Capel Llechid (Yr Hen Eglwys) has disappeared. Ffynnon Llechid, near Cae Ffynnon Farm, cured skin diseases and those who were seriously ill with King's Evil (also called scrofula, which was tuberculosis of the lymph nodes, especially of the neck).

LLEIAN see LLUAN

LLEONFELL
September 25

At Llanlleonfell in Brecon, this date was the night of *'Ffair Capel Coch'*, when everyone returned from the fair and lit a candle to eat supper by its light. In Cardiganshire the following day, Holy Rood Day, saw a similar custom marking the beginning of the nights drawing in.

LLEUCI 5th century
October 21, December 13

Possibly one of the virgin followers of Ursula. Betws Lleici in Cardigan was known as Capel Bettws Leuci. Llanwnen in Cardigan and Abernant in Carmarthen are dedicated to Lucia, but are more likely Lleuci foundations. These was a Ffynnon Leici holy well near Llandygwydd in Cardigan. Ffynnon Leucu in Flint is now named Ffynnon Cilhaul.

LLEUDDAD 6th century
January 13

Lleuddad ab Alan Fyrgan ab Emyr Llydaw was educated at Llanilltud Fawr, and some say that he succeeded Cadfan as abbot of Ynys Enlli. With Cadfan, he is possibly regarded at the patron saint of the 'Isle of 20,000 saints', and his brothers were saints Llonio Lawhir and Llynab. However, see Llawddog.

LLEUDDAD ap DINGAD see LLAWDDOG

LLEUDDAD LLYDAW

Nothing is known of this Breton saint in Wales, and he was probably Lleuddad ab Alan Fyrgan.

LLEURWG MAWR c.137-c.201
LUCIUS, LLEIRWG, LLEUFER MAWR (Great Light)
May 26 or 28 commemorates his baptism, and December 3 his martyrdom

King Lleurwg ap Coel ap Cyllin of the Britons sent two messengers, perhaps Dyfan and Medwy, to Pope Eleutherius in AD180, asking him to send missionaries to baptise him and his people. Dyfan, Medwy, Ffagan and Elfan returned, all Britons. Lleurwg was baptised in 182, upon May 26 or 28, which was celebrated by the Roman church. He was a Silure who converted the kingdom of Britain, according to some sources. In legend, at an old age he became an apostle in Bavaria, and was martyred near Curia in Germany in 201. His martyrdom was commemorated there upon December 3. His grandfather Cyllin was the son of Caractacus and brother of Eurgain.

Two triads say that Lleurwg founded Llandaf, and the old name for St Mellons by Cardiff was Llanlleirwg. He is reputedly buried at St Mary de Lode in Gloucester, but a legend is that he resigned his throne to evangelise Switzerland and was buried at the church of Coire, in the

Grisons. His relics are in the church, with those of his sister Emerita. In the woods above Coire is a rock which was his pulpit, with his fingermarks on it. He preached so loudly from here that he was heard 12 miles away in Lucienstag (The Pass of Lucius). In Coire's Missal, he is said to be *'the son of happy Mother Britain.'* Britain seems to have been recognised as the 'mother-church' of Europe before Rome. Jowett's 'Drama of the Lost Disciples' explores the Lucius legend in some depth.

LLIBIO 6th century
February 28

This son of Seithenin went with Cybi to Aran for four years, and founded the extinct Llanllibio in Anglesey.

LLIDNERTH mid 6th century
June 19

The son of Nudd Hael, and brother of Dingad.

LLONIO LAWHIR 6th century
March 1 (possibly)

The son of Alan Fyrgan, and brother of Abbot Lleuddad, he studied at Llanilltud and became a dean at Llanbadarn Fawr. He founded Llandinam in Montgomeryshire, and Llanio was his chapel in Cardigan. His father Alan led one of the *'three disloyal hosts of the Isle of Britain'* which *'turned back from its lord (Arthur) on the road at night, leaving him and his servants at Camlan, where he was slain.'* Llonio was given land at Llandinam by Gwrai, son of Gildas. Gildas was no friend of Arthur after the death of his brother Hywel. Adjoining land was also given by Maelgwn, another of Arthur's enemies. Llandinam became one of the 'clas' churches of Montgomeryshire, along with those of Meifod, Llangurig and Llanrhaeadr.

Huw Arwystli of Trefeglwys (fl. 1542-1578) received the 'gift of poetry' when sleeping in St Llonio's Church at Llandinam. Llannio is near the Roman station of Loventium, near Llanddewi Brefi. There is a stone inscribed 'VERIONI', and another which reads *'arti(m) ennivs primvs'*. This latter is only a foot long, and was found in a wall in a farm building. Another stone of the Cohors Secunda Augustae was used as a seat in a cow-shed, but only 'COH' can now be read. Another Roman stone high up in a farm house at Llanio reads 'ID/1H/FE/1695'. There is a superb collection of Roman stones in Chester Museum, and another at Caerleon.

JOHN LLOYD 1630-1679
July 22 (October 25)

Brecon-born, Lloyd trained in Valladolid from 1649 and was ordained in 1653. In 1678 he was arrested at Penlline in Glamorgan after the Popish Plot, and charged with giving masses at Llantilio, Penrhos and Trievor. With Philip Evans he was gaoled for five months in Cardiff Castle and tried on May 3rd. Evans was killed first at Gallows Field, Cardiff. After addressing the crowds in Welsh and English, he said *'Adieu Mr Lloyd, though for a little time, for we shall shortly meet again.'* John Lloyd, unnerved by Evans' barbaric execution, made only a short speech, saying *'I never was a good speaker in my life.'* They were hanged, drawn and quartered, *'with particular ferocity'* on July 22nd

LLUAN 6th - 7th century
LLEIAN

The sister of the martyred Tybie, and a grand-daughter of Brychan, possibly remembered at Capel Llanlluan near Llanarthney in Carmarthen. This area is now called Gorslas, and lies next to Llandybie. She married Gafran ap Dwynfal Hen and their son was known as Aidan mac Gabran, but as Aidan Fradog (the Treacherous) in Wales. He was the first independent King of the Scots around 574, and died in 606. He was named as one of the *'three traitors of the Isle of Britain'* because he allied his forces with the Saxons. (The other traitors, who caused the British/Welsh to lose control of Britain, were Medrod and Gwrgi Garwlwyd).

When Aeddan Fradog lost the great battle of Arderydd and fled to the Isle of Man, Lluan settled with him. Capel Llanlleian under Llanarthne in Carmarthen may have been her church, but was more likely the 'chapel of the nun'. Aeddan ap Gafran (Gauran) appears to have succeeded to Conal as King of the British Scots around 572-573, some time after Arderydd.

LLWCHAEARN 6th – 7th century
LLWCHAIARN
January 11, 12

A son of Hygarfael or Caranfael, he is the patron saint of Llanllwchaiarn and Llanmerewig (Llamyrewig, where he is buried) in Montgomery, and of Llanllwchaiarn and Llanychaiarn in Cardigan. His uncle was Cynddylan, whose court at Wroxeter was burnt when his family lost a huge amount of Powys to the Saxons. The court of the Kings of Powys moved west to Mathrafal, and Llwchaiarn and his brothers effectively lost their inheritances and turned to ecclesiastical work (see Aelhaearn). John Parker became the curate at Llanmerewig near Newtown in 1827 and wrote 'A Tour of Wales and its Churches'.

'Newtown' is a terribly unevocative name for this important centre in mid-Wales. In 1279 a charter was granted by Edward I to Roger Mortimer to create a new market to replace that at Dolforwyn Castle, Abermule. He chose a village on a bend in the River Severn, in the district of Cedewain. The place was known as Llanfair-yng-Nghedewain, where Mortimer laid out his mediaeval town after murdering Llywelyn II. Llanfair-yhg-Nghedewain could twin with the other Llanfair's across Wales, and drop the 'Newtown' name.

LLWNI
August 11

Llanllwni in the Teifi Valley, Carmarthen, was founded by this saint, of which nothing as yet is known. A nunnery was supposed to have been established at Maes Nonny Farm, and near a tumulus there called Y Castell is Ffynnon Nonny. A six feet Celtic cross was found near the church entrance.

LLWYDDOG

This saint was possibly martyred at Llanychllwydog in Pembrokeshire, but this could be a Llawddog foundation.

LLWYDIAN
November 19

Hen Eglwys in Anglesey was supposed to be this saint's, but it was formerly called Eglwys Gorbre Sant, so was probably a foundation of St Corbre. Another name for the church, Llan y Saint Llwydion, means Church of the Blessed Saints, so we might assume that there was no saint called Llwydian (see Corbre).

LLYDDGEN

There seems to have been a chapel named Llanllyddgen in Carmarthenshire.

LLYNAB 6th century
LLYFAB

Llynab ab Alan was Lleuddad's brother, and came with Cadfan to Llanilltud Fawr. He retired to Ynys Enlli to die.

LLYR FORWYN
October 21

The virgin founder of Llanllyr, formerly a nunnery in Cardigan. However, 'Forwyn' may come from 'Morwyn', meaning originally 'seafarer' or 'white sea' rather than 'virgin'. A stone was found in the early 19th century, which had been halved to act as two gate-posts. The second and third lines could be deciphered as *'Maclonin'* and *'Llor Filius'*. Gildas referred to Maelgwn Gwynedd as Magloconum. An Irish MS also refers to a 'Mac Lonain' who went on a *'pious journey'*. Llyr was the first century father of Brân and grandfather of Caradog, according to Welsh legends.

LLYR 5th century

Llanyre (formerly Llanllyr yn Rhos), a chapel to Nantmel in Radnor was dedicated to him or the virgin Llyr. Of the line of Coel, Llyr 'Marini' ('from the sea') was the father of Caradog Freichfras in some old genealogies, which gives confusion with Llyr Forwyn. His wife was Gwen, Brychan's grand-daughter. All Saints is now the church's dedication. Llannor may be Llyr's church in Caernarfon. Two ancient hexagonal inscribed stones were found here, on both sides of a grave near a cottage named Beudy-yr-Mynydd. They were discovered when grubbing up a hedge, across which the grave lay at right angles. It contained a man whose height was seven feet. The stones were deciphered as reading *'Icven Rhifidi Eterni Hic Iacet'*, and *'Icaenali fili'*. The second stone was also translated as *'Iovenali'* and on the other side

'Vendesetli'. It is thought to be the grave of Gwynhoedl, and Llangwynoedl is nearby. The stones seem to have vanished since the 1860's, but may have been buried to preserve them. Another Celtic stone is used as a churchyard gate jamb at Llannor, and reads *'Figvlini Fili Locv . . . El Hic Iacit.'*

LLYWARCH HEN d. 634?

The bard patronised by his cousin Urien Rheged is remembered in the name Craig Llywarch, just a mile south of Llanderfel Farm, west of Cwmbran in Gwent. A little north of Llanderfel Farm is Penllan-gwyn. Croes Llywarch is south of Llangybi, also in Gwent. The 9th century 'Canu Llywarch Hen' shows him as besotted with glory, urging his 24 sons into batle until just one, Gwen, is left. Only with Gwen's death in battle does he realise his stupidity and his loss. He was possibly the last king of South Rheged, driven out by Saxons, when he took his family to Penllyn in Powys.

In the wall of the church of Llanfawr near Bala is a Celtic stone with the words *'cavos eniarsii . . . '* inscribed. The field next to the church is called Pabell Llywarch Hen (the camp, or tents of Llywarch Hen.)

His 'Story of an Old Man' was written down in the 9th century, and is a magnificent lamentation, the concluding verses of which are:
This leaf, driven by the wind,
Sad is her fate.
She is old, though this year born

What I loved as a boy is now hateful to me:
A maiden, a stranger, a spirited horse.
They do not suit me now.

Always I hated four things most:
Now they have met in me together.
Coughing, old age, sickness, sorrow.

I am old and alone, mis-shapen, cold.
After an honourable sleep
I am pitiful, I am three times bent.

I am bent and old, perverse and awkward.
I am foolish, I am argumentative.
Those who loved me love me no more.

The girls do not love me; nobody visits me.
I cannot move myself about.
Why does death not come to me?

Sleep and joy do not visit me
Since Llawr and Gwen were slain.
I am an irritable corpse. I am old.

Sad was the fate that was meant for Llywarch
Since the night he was born.
Long hardship without release.

His greatest poems include the lament of his son Cynddylan of Pengwern (see Heledd), and that of his kinsman Urien Rheged. He was present at the assassination of Urien near Lindisfarne, and had to recover his head for burial. A fragment of his elegy for Geraint ab Erbin is included in the Geraint entry.

LLYWEL ap CAW see HYWEL

LLYWEL mid 6th century
LUHIL, LOUGUIL

A disciple of Dyfrig, then a companion (with Fidelis, Cynmur, Gurmaet, Lunapeius, and Toulidauc) of Teilo on his return from Armorica. He was sent by Teilo with Fidelis to the court of Aircol Lawhir in Dyfed, to prevent the king being poisoned. He witnessed a grant of land to Teilo marking Aircol's gratitude. Aircol was noted by Gildas as one of the 'tyrants' of Britain, and his gravestone still exists, as does that of Vortipor, another prince listed.

The village of Llywel in Breconshire is named after him, and the church dedicated to Llywel, with later David and Teilo being added. His companion Gurmaet also had a church nearby at Llandeilo'r Fan. Llanllowel (Llanllywel) near Usk in Monmouth is also his dedication. Llywel could well the same person as Hywel ab Emyr Llydaw, the saint known as Hywel Farchog (q.v.).

LLYWELYN 6th century
April 7 (with Gwrnerth)

This son of Bleuddan ap Meirion founded a religious house at Trallwng (Welshpool). His brothers were the saints Mabon, Cynfelyn and Cynudyn. He was known as Llywelyn Trallwng, and with his son Gwrnerth is its patron saint. The original name of Welshpool was Trallwng Coch ym Mhowys (The Town of Llywelyn in the Red Marsh in Powys). An English name for Speedwell is Fluellen, which comes (in a Shakespearian manner) from the Welsh 'Llysiau Llywelyn'. Speedwell is also known as 'Gwrnerth'. It appears that his brother Cynfelin ap Bleuddad founded Welshpool before Llywelyn.

There was a Ffynnon Llywelyn near Llangybi, Caernarfon, said to cure King's Evil, and a Ffynnon Lewelin in Landysul, Cardigan. Trellewelyn Well in Manorowen, Pembroke cured sore eyes, and there was a Ffynnon Llywelyn near Mathry in the same county. The author remembers the conical Iron Age burial mound, Twyn Llywelyn (also known as Llywelyn Twt), which has been buried under millions of tons of fly ash (and other waste) at Aberthaw Power Station, as was Marsh House (the last castle built in Wales), a 15th century customs-house known as The Booth, a beautiful harbour, hotel and 18-hole golf-course.

LLYWELYN 9th century

Llywelyn ab Einion ap Bleuddud ap Tegonwy ap Teon died at Ynys Enlli. Probaby some generations are missing from this genealogy. His mother was the daughter of Rhodri Mawr, and he fought for him. '*Llywelyn sant was the captain of Rhodri's bodyguard (teulu).*' Rhodri was killed by Mercians in Anglesey in 877.

LLYWES 6th century

Llowes in Radnor is dedicated to the saints Meilig (Maelog) and Llywes, and the Life of Gildas mentions that Meilig joined Llywes there.

LLYWYN
LLYWEN 6th century

One of Cadfan's companions from Brittany who died in Wales.

LONGINUS 1st century

Only noted here because of a curious story at Chepstow Castle noted by Wirt Sikes in 1881:
'*From the tower of Marten we walk out through a caseless doorway in the third story, or what was once the third story, on to the top of the castle wall, which has a sunken pathway below the battlements, now overgrown with ivy and with grass. It is a delightful stroll along this wall; and by-and-by we come to a very elegant room, called the chapel, concerning which there is a legend that it was erected by the Jew soldier Longinus, who pierced the side of Christ, and who was condemned to visit Britain, and built a Christian edifice there. That he selected Chepstow as the place at which to do this penance, was a matter of considerable advantage to the resident priesthood for many generations.*'

LORCAN WYDDEL 6th – 7th century
August 22

Lorcan the Irishman was martyred at Llanllugan in Montgomery, although this church is now ascribed to St Tyssilio (see Cynddelw's poem in the Tyssilio entry). After 1170 the church became a convent under Strata Marcella (Ystrad Marchell). Lorcan was one of six people variously raised from the dead by Beuno, and he may also have founded Llanwyddelan nearby, which is ascribed to Gwyddelan. Gwyddelan means 'little Irishman', so nearby Gwyddelan may be his, rather than a saint named Gwyddelan, in which case we can take the wake celebrated at Gwyddelan on August 22 as Lorcan's feast. He features in the Arthurian triads.

LUMAN

According to Cressy, a British companion of St Patrick, who founded Trim in Ireland.

M

'**M**y opinion is, that power should always be distrusted, in whatever hands it is placed.'

Sir William Jones, Letter to Lord Althorpe, 1782

MABLI
MABLE

The Norman church at Llanvapley in Monmouthshire is this virgin's sole invocation, but she is also possibly remembered at Cefn Mably on the Monmouth-Glamorgan border.

MABON 6th century
September 21

According to Iolo, Mabon ab Usyllt (Enlleu) was the brother of Teilo, also called Mabon Wyn. His mother was Anavaud. Llanfabon in the parish of Eglwys Ilan near Cardiff commemorated him. In Llandeilo Fawr, there were ancient manors named Maenor Deilo and Maenor Fabon (Manoravon). Gileston Parish Church was dedicated to St Mabon, and the Welsh name for the parish was Llanfabon-y-Fro, not Silstwn as the local road sign states. The name of Gileston came from the Norman family that held the lands around 1350. In Welsh Celtic mythology, Mabon was a divine youth, who was also a hunter, the equivalent of the Gallic Maponos, a healer associated with springs. There is a 'Saying of the Wise':
'Hast thou heard the saying of Mabon,
When giving instruction to his sons?
"Except for God there is no searcher of the heart".'

Mabon has also been named as one of Arthur's followers, the son of 'Modron' and a servant of Uther Pendragon, in the 'Black Book of Carmarthen'. As Arthur is linked with Boverton, just 2 miles west of Llanfabon-y-Fro, and Uther (Meurig) at Pentre Meurig, about 5 miles north, then this may well be the case.

William Thomas records flatly a notable case of marriage when the Revd. Willis, the Rector of Gileston (Llanfabon-y-Fro) died in 1780 aged 80 . . . *'he married four wives and the fourth buried him, whom he married these few years past, being but a child from he, for he was near 60 years older than she, without nothing. The other three, he gained from them, and from one of them Gileston came to him. But he left her at his death a very rich widow.'*

Rhyd-y-Gloch (Ford of the Bell) is on the River Taf near Pontypridd, the boundary of the parishes of Llanfabon and Llanwynno. The men of Llanfabon went to steal the 'silver-tongued' bell from St Gwynno's church. They wrapped the bell in straw to stop it pealing, and were crossing the ford when a full moon appeared from behind the clouds. They dropped the bell in surprise, its sound woke the villagers of Llanwynno, and the Llanfabon men fled without the bell. In the locality, the full moon was known as *'haul Llanfabon' (the sun of Llanfabon)*. 'The Changeling of Llanfabon' is one of the most beautiful Welsh fairy tales, based at the farmhouse of Berth Gron in the parish. A widow consults the sage of Castell-y-Nos to rescue her three year-old son Pryderi from the fairies.

MABON 6th century

A son of Bleiddyd (Bleuddyn) ap Meirion and the brother of saints Llywelyn, Cynfelin and Cynudyn. He is said to have founded Rhiwfabon in Denbigh, which became Ruabon.

MABON HEN

Only mentioned by Iolo Morganwg, this is a mythical character, it seems. 'Mabon' however was the chosen 'eisteddfodwr' name of William Abraham (1842-1922) when he entered singing contests. The first President of the South Wales Miners' Federation, his miners would not work the first Monday of every month in the 1890's, to limit production and hold wages at a living level. The day was called *'Mabon's Monday.'* Known universally in Wales as 'Mabon' he became a Radical, then Labour MP from 1885. In 1892, a proselytizer of the Welsh language, he appears to have been the first person to speak in Welsh in the House of Commons. Some members started laughing. When he finished, he calmly informed the House that he had been reciting The Lord's Prayer.

MABSANT

The festival associated with a local saint often lasted a week, when people would return to their home parishes to take part. These patronal festivals withered after the Reformation (unlike in Britttany) but fairs carried on as normal. Many fairs kept to the old dates after the 1752 date change, so if communities wish to revive their 'mabsantau' with games, singing, dancing, competitions and festivals, they have a choice of convenient date. *'Mabsantau'* was the colloquial name given to church ales brewed to celebrate October 1st and 2nd across Glamorganshire up until the early 19th century.

Stan Awberry wrote about the Lanilltud Fawr festivities thus:
When the method of travelling from village to village was by horseback or foot only, the villagers had to make their own entertainment except that occasionally they joined with a neighbouring village in some great festival. The annual rally was called the "Mabsant" or the "Gwyl Mab Sant". It was the principal amusement of any day of the year. It was the local Saint's day and sometimes lasted for several days. The whole village usually turned out for games, cock-fighting and drinking. One of the active villagers was made Mayor for the period and was decorated with ribbons, his face blackened and a cabbage hung around his neck. The crowd, during the festival, marched around the village and to the principal farmhouses where beer was humorously demanded and always given. A spirit of fun and merriment prevailed among all.' (Farms used to brew their own beer, mead (metheglin) and cider for their workers, especially near harvest-time).

Another lovely description of the Llantwit (Llanilltud) mabsant occurs in Redwood's descriptions of the Vale of Glamorgan in 1839:
'*Aye, it was with my nephew Davy that I last visited the happy assembly. "It is," said he, "the second night of Lantwit mabsant, and there will be many pretty girls there: come, uncle, let us go and see it." And even so, I was fain to accompany him.*
The Mabsant is the celebration of the holiday of the tutelary Saint of the village, after whom the church and the place are generally called, and is an occasion of great gaiety in the villages of our neighbourhood. Profuse is the finery then displayed by the country maidens, and many

the arts they practise to captivate the affections of the rustics. The chief amusement is dancing; but it is, beside, a time of great carousing, - of ball-playing, and sometimes fights and uproar.

We reached Lantwit early in the evening: and after winding our way through a few narrow lanes, came into the full sound of music. It was the harper, in attendance for the dance, at a public-house hard by, who was playing the old Welsh air, "Ar Hyd y Nos." The windows of the room where he was, were crowded with gay folk; and a host of children surrounded the door. Two old women, who, knitting as they went, had been taking a stroll, to see how things were going on, sate on a stone bench opposite the house, and now relinquished their knitting for a few pinches of "high-dry". The old snuff-taking dames listened with much complacency, shaking their aged heads, in unison with the tune. "Aye, aye; Ally Howell;" said one of them, "you and I may never hear the like again." "No" replied the other crone; "when the worm and the clay are in our ears, Wil Howe's harp will sound in vain."

It being too early for the dance, which we were told would not begin for yet a little while, we strolled about the old place, during the time we had to wait.

There was something very agreeable in the look of relaxation from all care, and of a disposition to be nothing else but happy, which appeared on every face we met. The children, dressed out in their Sunday clothes, were playing about the streets; the men were flocking in groups to the jolly taverns; and every now and then a gaily dressed damsel would issue out of a cottage, and be followed, maybe, to the door, by her admiring mother, who would there stand, with arms a-kimbo, contemplating, with great satisfaction, the girl's flaunting and gay appearance.

Thus we sauntered about, making our observations upon all we met, and not ourselves unheeded of by the blithe folks; until night closed in, and the dance began, when we repaired to that grave and aged building, the "church-loft,", which, in the times of the Lords Marchers, was a place for holding courts of law.

And there, in the dingy old loft, lighted with candles stuck against the walls, were the gay revellers disporting it, with quick music and the spritely dance. It was like a nose-gay of spring flowers smiling in the button-hole of a dusky Methodist.

The harper had a seat on a part of the floor slightly elevated above that where the company danced. Every thing proceeded with order and decorum; for indeed some of the "better degree" were there, and the dancing of both the young men and women was good and sprightly. One could not help remarking the exactness with which these rustic folks observed the mazy figures of their dances, and kept time with the music; as well as the manly vigour of the young men, and the bloom and neatness of the girls.

When the dancing had been kept up for some time, they retired to benches along the walls, and there sate to rest themselves, the young men generally taking their partners on their knees. Beer was provided; and they did not omit in the first place to regale the harper; and then, when the girls tasted any, it was always out of the mug or cup of their partners.

Worthy too of all remembrance were a couple of old women who had baskets of gingerbread and cakes there for sale. These wily crones passed along from one to the other of them as they sate on the benches, complimenting the vain girls on the prettiness of their dress, or of their persons, and the young men on their good dancing; and thus coaxed the simple-hearted creatures into a purchase of sweet-meats. Great was the delight of the rustic lovers at treating their sweethearts to a pennyworth of gingerbread!'

Alphabetical Listing of the Saints of Wales and Religious Events

MABYN 6th century
MABENA, MABENE
November 18, February 15

A daughter of Brychan who founded the church of St Mabyn in Cornwall. She is also depicted in a stained glass window at St Neot.

MACHES 6th century
MACHUTA

This daughter of Gwynlliw and sister of Cadog was martyred at Llanfaches (formerly called Merthyr Maches) in Monmouth. The 'Cambrian Biography' states that '*she gave alms to all who asked; and a pagan Saxon, who appeared before her as a mendicant, stabbed her with a knife.*' It appears that Machuta is the saint mentioned in the Life of Tathan, and that Llanfaches was formerly called Llandathan. It appears that Tathan raised a church in her honour, and buried her in the floor of Caerwent church.

Wirt Sikes, in his 'Rambles' noted the antiquity of Caldecot and the '*decayed Roman city*' of Caerwent. He related an interesting legend of nearby Porthskewitt, with its Roman camp, '*where Harold before he was king had a palace, in which he entertained Edward the Confessor with great splendour. This palace was set up here on the border of the land which Harold had lately conquered from Gruffydd, Prince of South Wales, and Harold's elder brother Tosteg was very jealous of the younger's successes. One day at Windsor, burning with envy of the favour in which Harold was held by King Edward, Tosteg struck Harold as he was in the act of reaching the cup to the king; and they rolled on the floor at the king's feet, fighting like wild beasts, for the elder brother had dragged the other to the ground by the hair of his head. The weak and superstitious Edward mildly rebuked Tosteg for his bad manners, and forbade him the court. So away rides the furious Tosteg, bursting with rage, to Harold's palace, where a host of servants were preparing an entertainment for the king, and setting upon the unfortunate retainers, cuts off a lot of their heads, legs, and arms, and throws them into the wine butts; after which he charges those whom he has left alive to tell their master there is plenty of fresh meat for the king's feast, pickling in wine. Such conduct as this was really too much for good nature, and this time the king sentenced the obstreperous Tosteg to perpetual banishment. He shook the dust of Porthskewitt from his feet, and came back no more. But soon after his departure the palace was fallen upon by revenge-seeking Welshmen, from whom the domain had been taken, and they killed all who were under its roof, and after having stripped it of the rare and costly ornaments which helped to furnish it, defaced its walls and marched away.*

After defeating Gruffudd ap Llywelyn, Harold Godwinsson married Gruffudd's Saxon wife, Ealdgyth (the swan-necked). He was then faced by the threat of William the Bastard's invasion force gathering on the Somme estuary. Harold had been elected, in the Saxon way, by his fellow nobles as King upon the death of Edward the Confessor. William insisted that he had been promised the throne, but his Norman invasion force was held back by prevailing winds. Harold gathered an army and set off for Sandwich in Kent, as he did not know where William would land, and there were also reports of Tosteg, Harold's brother, landing in the Isle of Wight. With no sign of any enemy, and provisions running low, Harold disbanded his army and returned to London. However, he heard immediately that Tosteg and Harold Hardrada had landed in Yorkshire, so gathered another army from his nobles. He was too late to stop

Scarborough and York being ravaged, but killed Tosteg and Harald at the battle of Stamford Bridge on September 25.

The news reached him there of the Norman landing at Pevensey Bay on September 29. Harold led his exhausted army on another forced march, from Yorkshire to Hastings, and was busy fortifying Senlac Hill when the Normans attacked. With great fortune, the Normans just won this 'Battle of Hastings' on October 14, 1066. Ealdgyth retrieved Harold's body and was allowed to bury it in Westminster Cathedral. Harold's mother Gytha had fled with the ladies of the court to Flat Holm island, and had offered Harold's weight in gold to be allowed to bury the body. William refused, knowing that a burial place outside his control would be a focus of dissent. Thus the festering dispute of two Saxon brothers led to the total French control of England. William was of Viking blood but one of his 'legitimate' claims to the throne of England was that he was descended from the family of King Arthur in Brittany - could this have been Armel?

MACHRAETH 6th century
MACHRETH
January 1

Llanfachraith in Merioneth, and in Anglesey. There was a Cell Machraith near her Merioneth church, in Cwm yr Eglwys. Gwynnog visited her there, and caused a spring of healing waters to rise, over which he built Capel Gwynnog, where the well is still called Ffynnon y Capel. Used for sore eyes, this well is attributed by Francis Jones to Gwyddno. There is a well of witchcraft and sorcery ('swyngyfared') nearby, named Ffynnon Llawr Dolyseler ('the well of the floor of the cellar of the ailment', or 'the well of the floor of the cellar of the image').

MACSEN WLEDIG d. 388
MAGNUS MAXIMUS

Not a saint, but so important in the very early history of Wales that this Roman emperor must be included. Gildas, the first British historian, was bitter in his invective against Macsen, because his departure with the legions left Britain open to attack by the pagan Picts, Irish and Germanic tribes:
'The island retained the Roman name, but not the morals and law, no, rather than casting a shoot forth of its own planting, it sends out Maximus to the two Gauls, accompanied by a great crowd of followers, with an Emperor's ensigns in addition, which he never bore worthily nor legitimately, but as one elected after the manner of a tyrant and amid a turbulent soldiery. This man, through cunning art rather than by valour, first attaches to his guilty rule certain neighbouring countries or provinces against the Roman power, by nets of perjury and falsehood, he then extends one wing to Spain, the other to Italy, fixing the throne of his ubiquitous empire at Treves, and raged with such madness against his lords that he drove two legitimate emperors, the one from Rome, the other from a most pious life. Though fortified by hazardous deed of so dangerous a character, it was not long before he lost his accursed head at Aquila: he who had, in a way, cut off the crowned heads of the empire of the whole world.' –
'Lamentation Concerning the Ruin of Britain', written about 540. Macsen had left around 383, and just three decades later the rest of the legions left, leaving England and Wales in a desperate situation against attacks from all sides – from the Scots, Irish and Germans.

Magnus may have been Galician, and as commander of the legions in Britain he made a treaty with the Votadini for them to hold the lands north of Hadrian's Wall as a buffer kingdom. His wife Elen's brothers Cynan and Gadeon helped him take Rome, according to the 'Dream of Macsen Wledig' in the Mabinogion. The story also relates that they were given land, to become the first Britons to settle in Brittany (see Elen)

MADOC ap JUDICAEL see WINNOC

MADOG 6th century
MADOC, AIDAN?
November 12

Madog ap Gildas was a saint of the college of Cenydd, his brother, at Llangenydd on the Gower peninsula. He founded the church at nearby Llanmadog, where there is a crude Celtic stone cross. Madog seemed to have also been associated with David, with two churches on St Brides Bay. Haroldston West and Nolton were his foundations, or those of Aidan of Ferns. There is also a Llanfadog in Brecon and an extinct Llanfadog (Capel Madoc) in Radnorshire's Elan valley. It is so difficult to differentiate between Madog and Aidan that they may have been the same person. Any further information would be welcomed by the author.

Gwyl Mabsant at Llanmadoc was November 12th, where pies were made of chopped mutton and currants. Farmers tried to sow their wheat before this Mabsant in order to let it lie in the ground 40 days before sprouting. Besides the Roman road from Coelbren to Brecon Gaer is the eleven feet high memorial stone known as Maen Madog (the Stone of Madoc). Its inscription reads 'DERVACI FILIUS/IUSTI IC IACIT' (Dervacus son of Justus lies here). In Cardigan are two holy wells named Ffynnon Fadog and Pistyll Madoc, in Penbryn and Llanilar parishes respectively. Ffynnon Madoc is a spring of great repute for healing in Llanfair Caereinion, Montgomery. Another Ffynnon Fadog was at Llanddoged in Denbigh. St Madoc's Well is outside St Michael's Church at Rudbaxton, Pembroke, so it was possibly Madoc's foundation. There is also a St Madoc's Park field near Trerhos in Hayscastle. This is one of the reasons it is so important to hold onto the names of fields – they are all numbered now, according to EU dictat, but a named field map of Wales would tell us more about the unknown past than any book such as the forthcoming Welsh Encyclopaedia, sponsored by the indirect taxation of lottery monies.

At Llanmadoc west of Gower, an inscribed stone was found by Westwood, being used as a quoin-stone in the repair of the parsonage. It seemed to read 'VECTI FILIVS GVAN HIC IACIT'. There is a 'Victi' noted on the cat-stone at Edinburgh, and 'Guan' seems to be St Govan (q.v.). A small Celtic hand-bell was found in a field near Llanmadoc, and removed to Penrice castle.

MADOG ap SAWYL 6th century

Aidan of Ferns, Madog ap Gildas and Madog ap Meurig are often confused together. Some sources make Madog ap Sawyl the same saint as Madog Morfryn, while others believe that Madog Morfryn was the son of Meurig ap Tewdrig and the brother of Arthur. Perhaps the matter can be cleared up in a future edition of this book.

MADOG MORFRYN early 6th century
April 25

A teacher at Illtud's college, of the lineage of Coel, and father of the bard Myrddin Wyllt. This may also be the Madoc remembered at Llanbadock, now part of the town of Usk (Brynbuga). At a bridge near here, 300 of the captives from the attack on Gruffydd ab Owain Glyndŵr were beheaded in 1405. Gruffydd was executed, and the abbot of Llantarnam was also killed fighting for Glyndŵr. According to Williams' 'Eminent Welshmen', Madog was one of the three Gwynfebydd, Holy Teachers, of the Isle of Britain, along with Deiniol and Cattwg. The church came to belong to the Priory of Usk, and has a superb Elizabethan communion cup made of silver. Gilbert makes Madog Morfryn a son of Meurig ap Tewdrig and the brother of Arthur. There may also have been a Madoc ab Emyr Llydaw, and there was a British Bishop Madoc of Galicia in 596 (see Galicia).

MADRON 6th century
MATRONUS,
May 21 (and 17)

His well at Madron near Penzance told the number of years remaining in one's life, and cured lunatics and sickly children. He may have been a disciple of Tudwal, who died with him in Brittany. May 17 was the day when Noah entered the Ark, in Welsh tradition.

MADRUN 5th century
MATERIANA, MADRYN
June 9, April 9, October 19

The mother of Ceidio and the wife of Ynyr Gwent, prince of the Silurian region around Caerwent, she was the daughter of Vortimer (Gwrthefyr Fendigaid). Nennius says that she fled with her infant son Ceidio when her father was killed, to Carn Madryn and then to Cornwall. A church at Minster near Boscastle is dedicated to her, as is one at Tintagel. It is said that she is buried in the chancel at Minster. With her hand-maiden Anhun, she founded the church at Trawsfynydd in Merioneth. They had stopped to sleep, and had identical dreams instructing them to found a nunnery on the site. She also possibly married Gwgon Gwri, by whom she bore St Cedwyn. Trawsfynydd in Merioneth is her foundation, where her wake was June 9th. Hedd Wynn, the poet remembered at the 'Black Eisteddfod' was the subject of an Oscar-nominated film. His Bardic Chair was empty at the prizegiving as he had been killed in the First World War. Materiana was remembered in Cornwall at Tintagel on October 19th and at Minster with Ceidio on April 9th. Madrun died at Minster.

In days past, poets could change people's opinions and moods. It is a pity that Hedd Wynn's talents could not have been directed agains the monstrous Trawsfynydd Nuclear Power Station. Forced upon one of the most lovely areas in Europe, it stopped generating electricity in 1991 because of concerns about the integrity of its reactor pressure vessels. This 'Welsh Chernobyl' receives no national publicity, and is being 'covered' by another eyesore, postponing final site clearance until 2136. Not one decision to build a nuclear power station has taken into account the cost of decommissioning, which is many times the building cost. Nuclear reactors cannot make economic sense. Lord Marshall admitted that the power industry always underestimated the construction costs. Because of the time taken to build, when the site goes over budget, it is too late for the government of the day to stop construction. The decommissioning problem has always been ignored as it costs too much, and happens when the decision-makers are safely retired or dead. The nuclear power industry proposes 'entombment' of Trawsfynydd for 136 years, relinquishing control of the contents of the reactors. In the meantime, the proposed nuclear waste 'safestore' option ignores site, design, structural integrity, safety and biological issues. The Welsh National Assembly must act to get the British Government to take action now. The geology of Trawsfynydd is very complex and the basement rock underneath the reactor is fractured down to 80 metres. Far more Intermediate Level Waste has 'backed up' at Trawsfynydd than at any coastal nuclear power station. Radioactivity already leaks into the ground, will continue to do so, and affect water supplies for hundreds of years. Trawsfynydd also lies 19 miles from the epicentre of Britain's strongest earthquake in July 1984. (There were also 1903 and 1940 earthquakes in the area.)

To some, this note may seem out of place in a book upon Celtic Christianity, but the author also cares about Wales and its future. Much of its land has been taken by a London government for military purposes, more covered with alien pine forests and some forcibly taken to build reservoirs for English towns. None of this has happened with any consent of any form from the Welsh people. The nuclear industry wants to delay dismantling the reactors to save money, an approach described by the Radioactive Waste Management Advisory Committee to the Government as *'ethically wrong'*. If something is ethically wrong, as well as deadly dangerous, it is time to ask politicians to do something to earn their salaries. The present government, elected as a 'socialist' party, could be sued for misleading advertising if 'social justice' is a prerequisite of socialism.

MAEDDOG, MAEDOC OF FERNS see Aidan

MAEL 6th century
ARTHMAEL
May 13 (with Sulien)

Son of Hywel Mawr, and a follower of Cadfan from Brittany, Cwm church in north Flintshire is dedicated to him and Sulien. Ffynnon Fael a Sulien was a famous holy well there, useful for curing eye ailments. They are also joint patrons of Corwen (formerly called Llansilien) in Merioneth (see Sulien). Llandrillo Church near Corwen was possibly also dedicated to Mael, but now is St Trillo's.

Built into Corwen's entrance porch is a prehistoric standing stone, *'Carreg y big yn y fach rhewllyd'*, *'the pointed stone in the icy corner'*, and the preaching cross in the churchyard may date from the 9th century. Another ancient stone forms the lintel of the south door, incised with a dagger-like cross. It was supposedly cut by the weapon of Owain Glyndŵr, flung from his 'seat' on Pen-y-Pigyn hill behind the church. His statue is in the market square. Corwen has always been an important place in Welsh history, on the Roman road from London to Holyhead where the route from Bala to Chester crosses it. Nearby, Owain Glyndŵr's Mound was where one of his mansions was sited, and where he was proclaimed Prince of Wales on September 16th, 1400, beginning the great rising against the English.

MAELDUBH

A Celtic saint who founded the religious community at Malmesbury.

MAELGWN GWYNEDD d. 547
MAGLOCUNOS, 'THE ISLAND DRAGON', MAELGWN HIR (The Tall)

Not a saint, but King of North Wales around the time that Arthur ruled the south of Wales and the West Country. Like Arthur, he features in many of the legends of the saints, and famously argued with St Curig. He called all the northern chiefs to Ynys Las, near the beach still called Traeth Maelgwn on the Dyfi Estuary. Maelgwn *'the Ambitious'* asked them to join him in a contest to sit on their thrones on the sands as the tide rolled in. The longest to remain seated would be overlord of North Wales. Maeldaf Hen had constructed a huge chair, coated with waxed feathers, which floated on the incoming water. The chieftains recognized his ingenuity, and Maelgwn became their overlord. **This story is five-hundred years earlier than that of Canute** who died in 1035. The Canute story first surfaced in 1130, told by Henry of Huntingdon, and was probably based upon Maelgwn's legend.

After the death of Einion Yrth, the kingship of Gwynedd passed to his sons Cadwallon Lawhir and Owain Ddantgwyn. After Cadwallon's death, his son Maelgwyn had Owain assassinated. (Owain was equated by some historians with Arthur, because of his friction with Maelgwn). Portrayed as ruthless, Maelgwn was a descendant of Cunedda, and once retired to a monastery (Llanilltud?) for some time before returning to his court at Deganwy to resume his rule. There is a Bryn Maelgwn near Deganwy. Taliesin (q.v.) prophesied his death at the hands of the *'Yellow Beast'*, and the Yellow Plague (*'Fad Felyn'*) spread northwards through Britain from Europe. In 547, Maelgwn shut himself in his palace of Llys Rhos forbidding anyone to come in or out. However, he looked through the keyhole when he heard his name called, and recoiled, dying in agony saying *'The Yellow Beast'*. This high king, Brenhin Pennaf, was left in the palace by his fleeing courtiers, and his body was left for weeks before anyone dared recover it for burial. This is remembered in the saying *'Hir hun y Faelgwn yn Llys Rhos'* – *'the long sleep of Maelgwn in the palace of Rhos'*. The ruins of a mediaeval hall, Llys Euryn, can still be seen on the spot where Maelgwn perished near Rhos-on Sea. Maelgwn is associated by some as Lancelot, who had an affair with Gwenhwyfar and eventually fought against Arthur. He argued with Tydecho, the Breton who moved into his lands, and also with Padarn. It seems likely that there was a power struggle between Arthur and Maelgwn. Maelgwn's daughter married Elidr ap Cynfarch, King of Rheged, and Elidr appears to have been killed around 560 by Rhun ap Maelgwn. Urien ap Cynfarch, who took over Rheged from his brother, is associated with fighting for Arthur as 'Sir Urience'.

Maelgwn is said to have founded the monastic college at Caergybi, the priory at Penmon, and also endowed Bangor, making it a bishopric. The Brut states that in 546 he was elected nominal sovereign (Gwledig) over the Britons, adding six islands (Ireland, Iceland, Gothland, Orkney, Llychlyn [Norway] and Denmark) to British possessions. Gildas hated Maelgwn, possibly because of his Pelagian leanings, but called him *'Maglocunus, draig yr ynys'* (Maelgwn, dragon of the island), probably meaning that he became Pendragon soon after Camlan (c. 539). Could Camlan have been a battle of a force of Saxons and Pelagian Celts against the 'Romanised' Silures of Glamorgan/Gwent and their Domnonian allies? After Arthur's disappearance from Camlan, Maelgwn is referred to as 'High-King' and asked for tribute from Gwynlliwg (Arthur's territory in south-east Wales). His men captured the daughter of the warrior-saint Cadog's steward at Llancarfan and full-scale war almost broke out. Maelgwn's son Rhun also led a warband that burned Cadog's monastery, showing the antagonism between the houses of North and South Wales. Gildas states that Maelgwn killed his own wife, then murdered his nephew and married the widow. It is important to note that Gildas was writing in the lifetime of Maelgwn*. A poem, *'Ymddiddan Myrddin a Thaliesin'* in 'The Black Book of Carmarthen,' records an attack by Maelgwn Gwynedd on Dyfed.

Aberffraw on Anglesey seems to have been first used as a palace by Cunedda, whose grandson Cadwallon finally drove the Irish out of North Wales. It became a royal court of the King of Gwynedd in the time of Maelgwn ap Cadwallon, and later the great Rhodri Mawr (844-878) ruled over most of Wales from there. It was attacked by Vikings in 968, but was the court of Llywelyn the Great and the palace remained intact until 1316 when its timbers were used to carry out repairs to Caernarfon Castle. Once an important port, it has now silted up.

*Of all the British kings, Maelgwn was the most despised by Gildas:
'. . . And likewise oh thou dragon of the island who hast deprived many tyrants as well of their kingdoms as of their lives and though the last mentioned in my writing, the first in mischief, exceeding many in power and also in malice, more liberal than others in giving, more licentious in sinning, strong in arms but stronger in working thy own soul's destruction, Maglocune . . . Thy sensual mind . . . hot and prone runneth forward with irrecoverable fury through the intended fields of crime . . . The former marriage of thy first wife was now despised by thee . . . and another woman; the wife of the man then living, and he no stranger but thine own brother's son, enjoyed thy affections . . . That stiff neck of thine is now burdened with two monstrous murders - the one of thy aforesaid nephew, the other of her who was once thy wedded wife . . . Afterwards also didst thou publicly marry the widow . . . and take her lawfully as the flattering tongues of thy parasites with false words pronounced it, but as we say most wickedly . . .'

MAELGWN THE MONK 5th - 6th century

The uncle of Curig, with a cell at Llangurig. Maelgwn Gwynedd is recorded as giving him land.

MAELOG 6th century
MAILOCUS, MEILIG, MEILIG
November 12, 13, 14, December 31, January 30

A son of Caw, who studied at Llancarfan under Cadog. 'The Life of Gildas' tells us that *'Mailocus who was destined by his father to the study of sacred literature, in which he was well instructed . . . left his father, and bidding adieu to his paternal estate, came to Lyuhes (Llowes) in the district of Elmain (Elfael, Radnorshire), where he built a monastery, in which, after serving God incessantly with hymns and orations, with watchings and fastings, he rested in peace, illustrious for his virtues and miracles.'* Maelog founded Llandyfaelog Tref-y-Graig and Llandyfaelog in Brecon, and Llandyfaelog in Carmarthen. Some sources say that Llowes in Radnorshire was the foundation of his brother Meilig, there being both a Meilig and a Maelog. The Book of Llandaf calls Llowes *'Lann Meilic ha Lygues'*. From Llowes, Maelog went to Munster. There is a Ffynnon Faelog for the relief of rheumatism at Llanfaelog. In St Meilog's Church, Llowes, not far from Hay-on-Wye, is St Meilog's Cross. It originally stood at the place still called Croes Feilig on the Begwns (the nearby hills), but was moved around 1200 to the churchyard. A later, 11th century cross can also be seen there.

The Cross of Einion, Margam Stones Museum.
CADW: Welsh Historic Monuments. Crown Copyright.

Maelog is mentioned in 'Culhwch and Olwen', and this brother of Gildas joined Cybi at Aran. It is surmised that his move to Llowes in Radnor was to take some land, given as blood-money by Arthur for Huail ap Caw's execution. Capel Maelog also existed near Llanbister. Llyswen, on the Wye between Llandyfaelog and Llowes, was also his church, with his festival there on November 13, but on November 14 at Llowes. At Llanarth in Cardigan, offerings were made *'for Meilicke sake'* in 1592. This is now David's church, but the wake was Maelog's Day, held on November 12th there.

Mailoc, Bishop of Bretona in Galicia, attended the Second Council of Arles in Braga in 572 – intriguingly, this could be the same person. Much research is needed into early Galician links with Wales (see Galicia). The 'Saying of the Wise' of this *'knight of far-extending sight'* was *'the good will not make friendship with the wicked.'*

Capel Maelog, at Llandrindod Wells, was covered by a housing estate in the 1980's. Built on a previous Christian burial site, it used blocks of Roman masonry taken from the old fort of Castell Collen, just a mile away. A huge nearby standing stone has vanished – it was supposed to have gone every dawn to take a drink at a nearby stream. Water was sacred to the ancient Celts, and there are many similar tales throughout Wales of sacred stones moving to drink holy water, and then returning. Standing stones were often associated with wells. Llanfaelog has many ancient burial sites. The Bodfeddan Stone near Llainwen has a Latin inscription, and there is a dolmen named Pentre Traeth on the side of the Afon Crugyll. Ty Newydd burial chamber has a huge coverstone, and 110 pieces of white quartz were found inside the chamber. Similar pieces were found at Newgrange in Ireland, and it appears that they may have been used to 'face' the chamber entrance.

Ffynnon Maelog is a holy well near Maelog Lake, Rhosneigr, Anglesey. Used for curing rheumatism, it was said to have the purest water in North Wales. In Cwm Maelog at Margam is a holy well with a vaulted baptistry and a sunken bath. The ruined Hen Eglwys (Old Church) lies nearby, re-dedicated at some stage to Mary, with another holy well. Hen Eglwys looks over the Cistercian Abbey at Margam, which was founded in 1147. The Margam Stones Museum here has been recently renovated to better display its Celtic Christian monuments, the finest collection in Wales. Margam Park, with its 18th century orangery, the largest in the world, is also well worth visiting. About 500 years west of Margam Village is another holy well, Ffynnon Bedr, but it does not rival Maelog's spring.

MAELRHYS 6th century
MAELRYS, MAELERW
January 1

The son of Gwyddno ab Emyr Llydaw and brother of Meilyr. Maelrhys lived on Ynys Enlli and founded Llanfaelrys, a chapel under Aberdaron on the nearby mainland. Aberdaron had his cousin Hywyn's church. A nearby upright stone is called Lladron Maelrys, Maelrys' Robber. The saint is supposed to have turned a thief into stone here. There are similar stones, such as Lleidr Tyfrydog (St Tyfrydog's Thieves), on Anglesey.

MAETHLU 6th century
AMAETHLU
December 26

The brother of Cawdraf, Tangwn and Cadfarch, and the founder of Llandyfalle in Brecon. At Llanfaethlu in Anglesey is a magnificent quartz standing stone, near Fadog-Fach.

ABBOT MAGLORIUS d.575-586
October 22, 24, July 24

This son of Umbrafel (the brother of Amwn Ddu) and Afrella (a daughter of Meurig ap Tewdrig) was trained at Llanilltud Fawr under Illtud, and went to Brittany with Samson to found monasteries (under the protection of King Childebert). This nephew of Arthur must have gone at the same time as Armel. Maglorius had been brought up with his cousin Samson (the son of Amwn Ddu and Anna ferch Meurig ap Tewdrig) at St Illtud's great college, and

The Cross of Ilquici, Margam Stones Museum.
CADW: Welsh Historic Monuments. Crown Copyright.

succeeded him as Archbishop of Dol. Maglorius did not like administration, and quickly handed the office on to Budoc. He retired to, and died in, Sark, where he founded another monastery. His relics were transferred to a church near Dinan, then to the superb Church of St. Jacques in Paris (which must be visited). He is remembered at Lehon, Mahalon, Plomodiern and Trelivan.

MAGNUS 6th century

Rhygyfarch's Life of David says that on his way to the great synod of Llanddewi Brefi, David raised the boy Magnus from the dead. Magnus stayed with David for years, living a holy life.

Alphabetical Listing of the Saints of Wales and Religious Events

MAIR see MARY

MAJAN 6th century

The son of Tugdon, and brother of Gwyddno, who founded Loc Majan at Plougon in Brittany (see Gwyddno).

MALLTEG
November 1

At Llanfallteg, wakes were held on All Saints' Day.

BISHOP MALO Cressy states that he died in 564, which is too early. 525-621?
MACHUTUS, MACLOVIUS, MACHU, MECHELL
November 15 (and 14)

Either from Caerwent, or from near Llancarfan in south-east Wales, he was the son of Caradog ab Ynyr Gwent and Derwela (Dervel, Amwn Ddu's sister). His Life tells us that he was born in Llancarfan monastery in the vigil of Easter, and baptised by the abbot, who was named as Brendan. The cousin of Samson, Malo became a missionary, after training at St Illtud's college or at Llancarfan. His parents wished him to leave the monastic life, but it appears that he became bishop at Llancarfan. He left Wales with Illtud and other clerics to escape the Yellow Plague in 547. Malo sailed to an island on the estuary of the river Rance in Brittany, or to Saint-Servan (Aleth, Aletha), the present Saint-Malo. He settled at Saintes, and died at Archingeay. Saint-Malo, the ferry port 37 miles north of Rennes, has its own character, epitomised in the town motto:
'Malouin first and foremost, Breton perhaps, French only if there's anything left.'

Malo had great problems with the usurper-king Conmore until Conmore was killed in 555 on the Monts d'Aree. Malo was rewarded for his resistance by the new king Judual, with land grants. Malo was a kinsman of Arthur, who may be the Armel who also fought against the usurper Conmore. St Malo de Beignon lies south of Arthur's Foret de Paimpont, Loc Malo is near Josselin and Tre Malo is outside Pont-Aven. St Malo-de-Phily is near St Senoux and Bain-de-Bretagne. Nicholas Crane summed up St Malo in a recent article in 'The Independent': (September 18th, 1999):
'Once at Portsmouth, the traveller passes a pampered night on a luxury ferry, waking within range of St Malo's warm boulangeries. Over the bows, Flaubert's "crown of stone" rises from an islet on the ragged coast. Behind Vauban's military bulwarks, the tall stone houses stand shoulder-to-shoulder around St Vincent's spire. St Malo, the Dubrovnik of La Manche, is the most romantic landfall in northern France.'

It appears that St Maughan's in Monmouth is Malo's church rather than Maughan's. Bishops of Winchester encouraged the following of his cult, possibly because the Latin name for Caerwent (Caer-Guent) is similar to that of Winchester (Caer-Wint). Llanfeinor in Monmouthshire and Llanfechell in Anglesey are also his (however, see Mechyll). In Penrhos Llugwy churchyard in Anglesey is a stone with the inscription *'HIC IACIT MACCV DECCETI.'* Rowland, in 'Mona Antiqua', observed that *'Mechell or Macutus, as in the Roman Calendar, was the son of*

Eccwyd, the son of Gwyn, who was grandson of Gloyw-gwlodlydan, Lord of Gloucester, in the time of the Saxon massacre at Stonehenge. (The so-called 'Treachery of the Long Knives'). *He was made Bishop of St Maloe's in Little Britain. His church or cloister was called from his name Llanvechell. He died in what seems like the Isle of Anglesea, and was buried, not at his own church, but at a neighbouring church called Penrhos Lligwy, in whose churchyard there is an old-fashioned gravestone with an inscription which, by the form of letters, seems to be genuine.'*

MARCELLINUS 2nd century
MARCELLUS
September 4

In Cressy's saints, a Briton who became Bishop of Trier, and the first British martyr in 166. Martletwy in Pembroke is associated with Marcellus.

MARCELLUS AND MARCELLINUS 4th century
September 25 Gwyl Mabsant of the parish

Llanddeusant in Anglesey is dedicated to Marcellus and Marcellinus, possibly the popes who were martyred in the early 4th century, and whose feast days were January 16 and April 26. It may be that Marcellus of the 2nd century had something to do with the original foundation of this church, because of the September feast date.

MARCHAN 6th century
May 21

There was a pilgrimage chapel called Llanmarchan in Pembroke for this saint, who had a vision of the dying Brioc being carried away by angels.

MARCHELL 7th century
MARCELLA

The daughter of Arwystl Gloff and Twyanwedd ferch Amlawdd Wledig, she was the foundress of Ystrad Marchell in Montgomery. The abbey built on the site was called Strata Marcella. Capel Marchell under Llanrwst is also dedicated to her. Her brothers were the saints Teyrnog, Diefer and Tudur. She was the patron of Eglwys Wen, now Whitchurch in Shropshire.

The parish church at Denbigh, then Denbigh itself, was called Llanfarchell until the 15th century. St Marcella's Church in Denbigh is the finest of the county's churches, and was also known as Eglwys Wen. Her hermitage was next to her holy well. The present parish church was rebuilt in the 15th century, and the effigy of Humphrey Llwyd, the 'Father of Modern Geography' dates from 1568. There are impressive Myddelton and Salesbury memorials also. Denbigh itself, with its castle and history, is well worth visiting, and excellently situated for touring between St Asaf and Rhuthun. Ffynnon Farchell was a few hundred yards from Denbigh Church, in which coins were thrown, but little remains.

MARCHELL 5th century
MARCELLA

The daughter of Tewdrig ap Teithfallt of Garthmadrun, and the mother of Brychan Brycheiniog, the half-Irish founder of Brecon and progenitor of over two dozen saints. At Tewdrig's request, she is said to have gone to Ireland to marry Amlech (Anlach mac Coronac) from Llanfais (Breconshire) via Llansefin (Glansefin near Llangadog in the Tywi valley) and Meidrim in Carmarthenshire, to sail from Porth Mawr near St David's. Her only child, before Amlech died, was Brychan. It was so cold, that 300 of her attendants were said to have died on the journey. Brychan succeeded to Tewdrig's lands in Brecon, Garthmadrun was renamed Brycheiniog after him, and his many descendants became one of the three tribes of the saints of Wales, alongside those of Caw and Cunedda. As Meurig's sister, Marchell was Arthur's aunt, and Brecon acted as a buffer-state for his homeland of Glamorgan and Gwent. One wonders whether the diaspora of the sons and daughters of Brychan from Brecon was due to pressure from Maelgwn in North Wales. His son Rhun attacked South Wales. After Camlan there seems to have been a power vacuum that Maelgwn filled, as Arthur's son Morgan was too young to succeed. All of Arthur's other sons had died in battle.

MARCHELL 6th – 7th century

A grand-daughter of Marchell ferch Arwystli, she married Gwrin, the *'regulus'* of Meirionydd (Merioneth).

MARGARET
MARGED
July 13

This was Marina of Antioch, who was a very popular Norman dedication following the Crusades, and was the patroness of childbirth. There are a few Welsh churches which were rededicated to her in the Middle Ages, and her cult was suppressed by the Vatican in 1969. As she was a fictional character, Pope Gelasius declared her legend apocryphal in 494, but over 200 English churches were dedicated to her. Her famous well at 'Coed Ffranc' near Skewen was possibly one of the 'lost' wells of Illtud in Glamorgan.

Between the valley of Dulas Brook and Hereford's Golden Valley is the Norman church of St Margaret's, with a fabulous Tudor rood-screen and rood loft. A local saying runs:
'Turnips and carrots,
Say the bells of St Margot's.'

Nearby is Craswall Priory, a rare example of the community of the Grandmont Order of monks, and also St Michael's Church in Michaelchurch Escley. A 1500 wall painting here depicts 'Christ of the Trades'. This shows Christ with long arms surrounded by all the working tools of the age - wheel and flail, axe, shears, spade, plough, adze, L-square and dividers, etc. Its purpose was to remind worshippers that to work on the Sabbath would re-open the Blessed Wounds of Christ.

MARK
April 25

In many parts of Wales, farming work was prohibited on his day.

MARTIN (316-397)
MORTHIN
November 11, 12, July 4

Not a Welsh saint, but commemorated in some churches, and St Martin's on the Welsh border is dedicated to him. He was used to replace the great drinking and orgiastic festival of Bacchus, the Greek and Roman god of alcoholic debauchery. His name was invoked at Martinmas to cure drunkards. To be *'Martin Drunk'* was to have drunk oneself sober. This date is the start of *'St Martin's Summer'*, a traditionally mild period also called the November Halcyon Days. Martin was said to have given his coat to a beggar, and God rewarded him with fine weather. In many places a bull, the Mart, was ritually killed on this day – it was the time of salting meat for the winter months ahead. Martinmas was also the *'servant's hiring day'* when hiring fairs were held across Britain (see Fairs). This century, many Martinmas customs disappeared with the commemoration of Armistice Day, the moving period of remembrance for the bloody pointless slaughter of The First World War, when the Armistice was signed on the 11th hour of the 11th day of the 11th month.

Llanborthin in Cardigan is possibly Martin's rather than an unknown Welsh saint named Morthin. If it is, it is the only medieval chapel dedicated to him in Wales. In France there are 500 villages and 4000 parish churches dedicated to Martin, and in 1800 there were 173 old British churches called St Martin's. This 'Saying of the Wise' seems to be Martin's:
'Hast thou heard the saying of Marthin,
The exalted saint, to the public?
"Except for God there is no sovereign".'

St Martin's Church at Cwmyoy, just south of the evocative Llanthony Abbey, leans crazily in all directions. A visit here can take in Llanthony, Capel-y-Ffin (where Eric Gill and David Jones worked) and the marvellous Patrishow Church (see Issui).

Martin of Tours is important in that he is linked to Magnus Maximus (Macsen Wledig) and Elen. In the *'Dialogues'* of Sulpicius Severus, Macsen is seen as a very close friend of Martin, and Doble believes that Martin's *'dynamic, militant monasticism'*... *'no doubt reached Wales through Maximus's widow Helena, and her sons Constantine and Peblig. Victricius of Rouen, a disciple of Martin, had visited Britain about 397.'*

HENRY MARTYN 1781-1812
October 19

Born in Cornwall, and given a Holy Day by the Church in Wales, he was converted at Cambridge in 1800. He was a Fellow of St John's College, and curate at Holy Trinity under Charles Simeon (q.v.) who was vicar there for many years. In 1805 Martyn left for India as chaplain to the East India Company. A brilliant linguist, in under five years he translated the New Testament into Urdu and Persian (Farsi), and supervised its translation into Arabic. He

Llanthony Priory. © *Wales Tourist Board Photo Library.*

died tragically in Armenia, aged just 31. The Henry Martyn Trust in Cambridge was set up in 1881, the 100th anniversary of his birth, and still promotes missionary work.

MARY 1st century
MAIR FADLEN
August 15 (the Assumption) was the most important feast date of Mary. The patron saint of around fifty old Welsh churches including Nefyn, her fairs were held upon April 4, August 25 and September 18, the feasts of her Annunciation, Assumption and Nativity.

The early Norman settlements in Pembroke from 1100 obliterated the traces of many Welsh dedications. As a result there were in the early 19th century 23 dedications to Mary in

Llanthony Priory, Distant View.   *CADW: Welsh Historic Monuments. Crown Copyright.*

Pembrokeshire. In Glamorgan there were 18, as it was colonised from 1090. In Gwynedd there were only 6, plus 2 chapels. In Anglesey, there was only one, with 9 chapels. The number of dedications correlates with the date of Norman influence. One of the objectives of this book is to find, for future editions, the original Welsh dedications of many of the churches attributed to Mary, Michael, John and the like. For instance, Cydweli was probably dedicated to Catwg (Cadog) before William de Londres built his castle there in 1094.

Llanfair-ar-y-Bryn in Carmarthenshire has a church that stands on a Roman fort, which became the monastic cell of an as yet unknown Welsh saint. The church was rebuilt in the 13th century and dedicated to Mary. This is where William Williams Pantycelyn was buried in 1791. He is Wales' most famous hymn-writer, known for hundreds of works including *'Guide me, O Thou Great Jehovah.'* At Llanbryn-mair there was the saying *'dillad cig rhost'* – *'clothes for roast meat'*, indicating one's *'Sunday-best'* clothes worn for the only roast-meat day of the week. (Most Welsh daily food was *'spoon-food'* based upon soups, dairy products, cereals and bread. Meat was a luxury reserved for Sundays.)

There are intriguing remains at Llanfair Cilgoed near Skenfrith (originally Ynys Cynfraith, the isle, or land near water of Cynfraith). *'Cil'* is the equivalent of the English *'cell'* and of the Irish/Scottish *'kil'*, meaning retreat. This *'retreat in the wood'* was associated with Catholic recusancy, holding illegal weddings and services in the 17th century. A nearby public house was called until the 19th century *'Porth-y-Widdon'* – *'The Witch's Gate'*.

Ffynnon y Santes Fair is in the gardens of the 17th century Bodrhyddan Hall near Rhuddlan. The holy well was enclosed in 1612, possibly by Inigo Jones, in an octagonal well-house, and was once favoured for illegal marriages. The house and grounds are open on Summer afternoons, and the well-pool and well-house are still in good condition. Nearby Rhuddlan, with its original grid-pattern of streets laid out in 1277 when Edward I built the first of his 'Iron Ring' of concentric fortresses, and its parish church of St Mary, must be visited.

There are more wells dedicated to Mary than St David in Wales, usually on sites founded by the Celtic Christian Church. Followed by Michael and Arthur, she has the highest number of holy wells in Wales. The sadly dilapidated Ffynnon Fair Penrhys in Glamorgan was a centre for South Wales Catholics, with a famous effigy and well-chapel. The statue was removed secretly by William Herbert on Thomas Cromwell's instructions in 1538, for fear of provoking a local uprising. It was taken to London and burnt on September 26. The image of the Virgin and her child was described by Bishop Latimer as *'the Devyll's instrument to brynge many (I feere) to eternal fyre'*. He threw a similar effigy out of a window of St Paul's Cathedral.

Still used for centuries as a healing well, Penrhys was restored and a pilgrimage of 4,000 Roman Catholics took the waters and prayed on September 12, 1947. 'The Cambrian Journal' in 1862 noted *'the spring, which is entered by stone steps, is arched over, and at the back, above the spring, there stands a niche, in which it is evident that there originally stood an image of the Virgin, to whom the monastery was dedicated . . . When I visited Pen Rhys about twenty years ago, some portions of the monastery existed, though incorporated into modern erections, and difficult to identify. The present farmhouse of Pen Rhys has been erected on the site of the ancient monastery . . . The barn, which stands in a field near the house, called to this day "Y Fynwant", or the churchyard, was formed, to a considerable extent, out of portions of the ancient monastic buildings . . . '* According to Iolo Morganwg, the monastery was suppressed in 1415 for the favour that it had shown to Owain Glyndŵr against Henry V.

It is not good enough to let such sites decay, upon the excuse that vandalism makes their restoration unnecessary. Other, more remote, wells could also be restored by farmers and local councils. Welsh farmers are desperate for further sources of income. How many farms in the world can boast holy wells from the Dark Ages? They could help sell bed and breakfast breaks or farm holidays, which is a small price to pay for a possible gate left open. Self-closing gates can help alleviate this perennial problem for farmers, anyway. (At the time of writing, calves and lambs are literally worth nothing, and it costs farmers to keep them alive, so they are being slaughtered. However, the consumer pays £10 for a leg of lamb. The average farmer's income has dropped to around £4500 p.a. Farmers and clerics cannot rely upon politicians to keep their communities surviving - they both have to begin working to revive sources of income. The Common Agricultural Policy costs each British family £1000 a year, and membership of the European Union costs Britain billions of pounds a year. When the Eastern European nations join the EU, they will have first call upon any support funds [such as Objective 1], and food subsidies will be diverted there. Answers need to be found now to the Welsh rural problem. The slavish devotion of political parties to control by a parasitic, un-democratic bureaucracy, in Brussels and Strasbourg, can only be explained by the fact that there is 'something in it' for politicians. As usual, the people of the British regions outside the south-east of England suffer in silence, swamped by layers of unaccountable politicians, councils, quangoes and civil servants, and the Welsh people suffer the most economically.)

St Mary's Church at Maenclochog in Pembroke dates to at least the 10th century, so was probably the foundation of another saint such as Teilo or Brynach. There was once a monthly fair at Maenclochog, which means 'ringing stones' referring to two large stones which used to stand next to Ffynnon Fair. The well and its stones seem to have disappeared. The church was saved from dereliction by the success of Edward Cropper's Maenclochog Railway. His widow gave generously to the church in 1881, as did Barrington Price of Bwlch-y-Clawdd, which is situated next to St Teilo's ruined church at Llandeilo Llwydarth (the holy place of Teilo at the Grey Bear). In 1291 the church belonged to St Dogmael's Abbey, and has a mediaeval font. It is worth quoting from the church 'pilgrim's trail' leaflet: '... *its later history was troubled: one Vicar, John Griffiths was in danger of being dismissed by his Bishop in July 1670 and his parishioners begged that he should be kept on for the winter rather than turned out into the cold, while in 1743 a subsequent generation of churchwardens and parishioners wrote again to the Bishop, humbly requesting that William Crowther be discharged on eleven counts of negligence, drunkenness and lewd behaviour. Major hardship and social unrest hit the village at the end of the 18th century: in 1779 Lloyd of Bronwydd, Lord of Cemais tried to remove the rights of turf cutters on the common, who were usually the poorest families from all the local parishes. Then there were bread riots in 1795 in which the then vicar intervened with the magistrates on behalf of the parish; in 1820 enclosures threatened the livelihoods of those who had grazing rights on the common. So it was not surprising that when the toll gate charges for their produce became outrageous in 1839, men from Maenclochog were prepared to join the protest in what became known as the Rebecca Riots.'*

The ancient Roman site of Caerhun probably had a Celtic dedication before Mary. It is the centre of some superb megalithic remains. Near Caerhun, in the mountain pass known as Bwlch y Ddeufaen is a standing stone, but Porth-Llwyd Dolmen nearby seems to have vanished. Picell Arthur is a 7 foot pointed standing stone, a 'spear' that Arthur hurled at his dog from Tal-y-Fan. Cerrig Pryffaid Stone Circle (The Stones of the Flies) has 14 stones, and nearby is Maen y Bard dolmen and Barcoliad-y-Gawres dolmen.

In the introduction to this book, the duty of the 'authorities' to restore our heritage was mentioned. St Mary's Church in Caerau, in western Cardiff, is a 13th century building upon a Celtic 'llan', and within the ruins of an ancient monument, a hill fort. Near it was a Celtic holy well known as Ffynnon y Saint. Until the 1960's it was in continuous use as a church, but the Church in Wales abandoned it and it was deconsecrated in 1973. It was handed over to South Glamorgan County Council, as houses could not be built on the site of an ancient monument. The council gave it to Cardiff City Council, which is proposing to demolish the Grade II listed building. To raze the church will cost £30,000, but the Society for the Protection of Ancient Buildings, describing the decision as one of the worst it has seen, states that it will only cost £25,000 to make the building safe and secure. Councils are not subject to the same rules as private owners, who could be forced to make repairs. CADW, the guardian of Welsh architecture (the equivalent of English Heritage), is ominously silent on the affair. There are Roman remains here, and Caerau (Llanweirydd) may have been founded by a 9th century King of Glamorgan, or much earlier. The ancient encampment has been identified with the Jupupana of Ptolemy, in Welsh Tref-iwbiwb, *'the town of wailing'*.

Such sites simply have to be preserved – they cannot be re-created. Too many have gone already. No other Northern European country would be as cavalier with its past. One day hopefully there will be a back-lash against Disney-Land, Crystal Mazes, Alton Towers, Pokemon, MacDonalds, Lara Croft and other symptoms of decaying intelligence in the modern world. Society needs to keep hold of what is important for our children's children. CADW's funding dropped from £3.8m in 1995-96 to £3.1m in 1997-98. It was thus only able to make grants to 97 of Wales' 22,300 listed properties. By the year 2005, it is estimated that there will be 35,000 listed buildings in Wales, and there must be more funding made available. CADW recently was refused Heritage Lottery monies to restore Dolbedr, the home of Henry Salesbury, who wrote the first English-Welsh grammar. The new Welsh Assembly must propose a Welsh National Lottery to help restore Welsh heritage. To apply a new rugby law to our heritage, we have to 'use it or lose it.'

Mary's name has been associated with many Welsh flowers, for example Chwys Mair means Mary's perspiration, and is the Welsh name for buttercup. Briallu Mair is the cowslip (Mary's Primrose); Dagreu Mair (Mary's Tears) is also the cowslip; Celyn Mair (Mary's Holly) is the shrub known as butcher's broom or 'knee holly'; Mantell Fair is lady's mantle; Llysiau St Mair (St Mary's vegetables or herbs) is rosebay willow herb; Clustog Fair (Mary's Cushion) is sea thrift; Llaith Bron Mair (Mary's Damp Breast, possibly so named as it cured congestion) is lungwort; Ysgol Fair (Mary's school) is centaury; Ysnoden Fair (Mary's Ribbon) is Galingale; Tapr Fair (Mary's Candle) is yellow mullein; Rhos Mair (Mary's Roses) is rosemary; Rhedyn Mair is Mary's fern; Gwyldd Melyn Mair (Mary's Yellow Chickweed) is yellow pimpernel; Meigen Mair (Mary's Little Retreat) is black brony; Miaren Mair (Mary's Thorns) is sweet briar and Melyn Mair (Yellow Mary) is marigold. Allweddau Mair (Mair's [musical] keys) is ashkeys and Cribau Mair (Mary's combs) or Ysgallen Fair (Mary's thistle) is ladies' thistle; Eirin Fair (Mary's Plums) are gooseberries and Ffiled Fair (Mary's fillet) is London Ribbon. Mantell Fair (Mary's cloak) is ground ivy; Mintys Mair is spearmint; Rhedyn Mair is the male fern and Ysgaw Mair is dwarf elder.

The foxglove is Menig Mair (Mary's Gloves) but better known as Menig y Tylwyth Teg (Fairies' Gloves). Other local names are Bysedd Ellyllon (elves' fingers), Menyg Ellyllon (elves' gloves), Bysedd Cochion (red fingers) and Bysedd y Cwn (dog's fingers). Llysiau Mair Fadlen, the 'herbs of Mary Magdalen' is colmary or sweet maudlin, and Mari Waedlyd (Bleeding Mary) is love-lies-bleeding. However, the most attractive name of all Welsh herbs and flowers is Croeso Haf, the wild hyacinth or bluebell. It means 'Summer's Welcome'.

Golwg Crist (Christ's Sight) or Llygad Crist (Christ's Eyes) is eyebright, Llysiau Crist (Christ's Tears) is milkwort, Sawdl Crist (Christ's Heel) is ribwort and Ysgol Crist (Christ's School) is another name for St John's Wort.

MATHAIARN 5th century
MARCHAI

Mathafarn in Cyfeiliog, Mongomery, commemorated him.

MATHRY

This church of the Holy Martyrs stands on an ancient hilltop site in Pembroke, is on the Menter Preseli 'Pilgrim's Trail', and is the fifth church to occupy the site. It may be dedicated to the six brothers rescued from drowning by St Teilo. The Book of Llandaf records them as settling at 'Mathru.' There is also a legend of 'seven' martyr saints of Mathry. Two Celtic inscribed stones can be found in the west wall of the churchyard. One was found in the wall of Rhoslanog farmyard, where there is an ancient burial ground. Another was found being used as a gatepost at Tregidreg farm. Both have simple crosses within a circle. Inside the church is a 5th-6th century stone reading *'mac cudicci filius cartic uus'*, *'Maccuoicci, son of Caticuus lies here.'* It was recorded by Edward Lhuyd in 1689, then lost, then rediscovered in 1937 head-down, being used as a church gate-post. Some of it, bearing Ogham inscriptions, is missing.

MAWAN 1st century
MEUGANT, MEIGENT, MAUGHAN

Supposed to be the son of Cyndaf, he was said to have accompanied Bran, Arwystli, Ilid and his father from Rome to evangelise Britain.

MAWAN 6th century
MEUGAN, MAUGHAN
June 18

In Gwent, St Maughan's Green may have been founded by Malo. However, Sir Joseph Bradney ('The Hundred of Skenfrith') notes that the parish was called Llanfocha, and in the Liber Landavensis (Book of Llandaf) it appears as Llanmocha. Bradney writes about Meugan:
'This saint was originally a member of the College of Illtyd at Llantwit Major, and afterwards at Dyfrig's College at Caerlleon. He lived in the 6th century, and was buried on Bardsey Island. Llanfocha was given by Brittwn and Ilinc to Llandaff for the salvation of their souls in the time of Dyfrig, the first bishop of Llandaff, and was confirmed to the see by Brithgon Hael in the time of Bishop Gracielis in the eighth century.'

Mawan may well have been the son of the prince Cyngen ap Cadell, and brother of Brochwel the Fanged. The village is about half a mile from the church, and was called the Maypole. The green is now enclosed, but the base and stump of an ancient cross-shaft can still be seen there. There was also a St Maughan's holy well in the parish. Iolo Morganwg also gives us a Maewan who was a principal at Bangor Illtud, and whose son Padrig was captured and carried away to Ireland (see Padrig). St Maugan is just south of the Arthurian district of the Paimpont Forest.

The 15th century church of St Meugan at Llanrhudd is said to be dedicated to *'a hermit-saint from Caerleon in Gwent'*, and has a beautiful 15th century rood screen and rare 17th century altar table. This was the original mother church of the settlement that became Ruthin (Rhuthun), where Arthur executed Hywel. In the graveyard is the decorated nine-foot shaft of a mediaeval preaching cross. Cilfeigan is a hamlet in the Llanbadoc parish west of Usk, which may give credence to his Caerleon origins. Usk was the Roman fort Burrium, in constant contact with Caerleon further down the valley of the Usk.

MAWES 5th century
MAUDEZ, MAGUDITH, MAUDITH, MODEZ
November 18

Associated with Budoc (Beuzec), this Welsh missionary is commemorated in Cornwall (St Mawes) and Brittany, where he is known as Maudez. He settled with followers on the Ile Modez near Leon, and his relics are claimed by churches at Quimper, Treguier, Lesneven, Bourges and elsewhere among the chapels and churches in Brittany dedicated to him. His name was invoked to cure snake-bites, worms and headaches. There are over sixty chapels dedicated to St Modez in Brittany, including Locmaudez in Plestin, Locmaudez in Clohars-Carnouet and Lan Modez. St Maudez is outside Guerlesquin, and another St Maudez is east of Gourin. The Ile Maudez is north of Paimpol and there is a hamlet of Maudez north-west of Guincamp. As noted earlier, his Cornish foundation is opposite that of Budoc's, and their monasteries in Brittany were also near each other.

MAY DAY
May 1

The great festivals for the Irish Celts were the first days of November (Samhain), February (Imbolc), May (Beltane) and August (Bron Trogain, or Lughnasadh). Samhain, which marked the beginning of the year, was the most important date for the Irish, but in Wales Calan Mai and its Eve were by far the most important days of the year. In the tale of Pwyll, a demon stole new-born children and animals on May Eve. In the tale of Lludd and Llefelys, dragons fought and terrorised people on this day. In the Brecon Beacons, a doorway into fairyland opened each May Day at Llyn Cwm Llwch. The festival features strongly in old Welsh literature, and the first reference to a maypole in British literature seems to have been in a 14th century poem by Gruffyd ab Adda ap Dafydd. The May Day Festival at Padstow in Cornwall could date back to pre-Christian times.

The bard Nefydd (William Roberts) in 1852 wrote *'Crefydd yr Oesoedd Tywyll'*, an account of Welsh traditions such as *'Codi'r Fedwen'* (raising the birch), which was accompanied by the *'dawns y fedwen'* (the dance of the birch). The maypole was painted in various colours and *'then the leader of the dance would come and place his circle of ribbon about the pole, and each in his turn after him, until the May-pole was all ribbons from one end to the other. Then it was raised into position and the dance begun.'* Sometimes, for example in Tenby, several poles were set up close to each other, being used as stopping places for a round-dance of the town. An 1858 record tells us that *'May-poles were reared up in different parts of the town, decorated with flowers, coloured papers, and bunches of variegated ribbon. On May-day, the young men and maidens would, joining hand-in-hand, dance round the May-poles and "thread the needle" . . . A group from 50 to 100 persons would wend their way from one pole to another, till they had traversed the town.'* In the Vale of Glamorgan, similar poles were erected to mark Midsummer. *'Y fedwen haf'* (the summer birch) was erected on June 24th, St John's Day, and garlanded before the dancing started.

MEBWYN
MEBWEN, EBWEN

Ffynnon Mebwyn was documented as a holy well is the parishes of Lampeter and Llanfihangel Ystrad. There is also a Rhyd Nebwen in Trelech ar Betws, Carmarthen. There was a Tŷ Capel Ffynnon Ebwen at Lampeter, but nothing much is known of this Cardiganshire saint.

MECHAIN

In the Cain valley near each other are Llansanffraid ym Mechain and Llanfechain (Montgomeryshire).

MECHELL 6th century?
MECHYLL, MALO?

The son of Echwydd ap Gwyn Gohoyw, he founded Llanfechell in Anglesey according to some sources, but others say that it is Malo's church. He was buried at the nearby Penrhos Llugwy churchyard, where a stone was found reading 'HIC IACIT MACCVQ ECCETI.' There is a cromlech at Foel Fawr, Llanfechell, and a tall standing stone near Carrog. Another standing stone near Maes Mawr was named Maen Arthur, and Meini Hirion is a triangle of 6 foot stones on Cromlech Farm. (See MALO).

MECHELL 5th century

Possibly the eldest of Brychan's daughters, who married Cynyr of Caergawch near St Davids.

MECHNYD late 6th century

The son of Sandde Bryd Angel ap Llywarch Hen. Llywarch was the famous 6th century bard, and Sandde was one of Arthur's knights. Llywarch had a 'Saying of the Wise' – *'though not yet intimate, yet offer greeting.'*

MEDDWID 7th century
MEDDVYTH ferch IDLOES, FODDHYD
August 27

Clocaenog in Denbigh was dedicated to this virgin, and there is now St Foddhyd's Church. It was previously attributed to Caenog and Trillo, but Caenog Mawr was possibly not a saint. It stands on a hill (Clocaenog means 'mossy hill') above the village, and has several mediaeval features. There is a massive dug-out chest, hewn from a single piece of wood, a 1538 rood screen and a 1725 wooden chandelier in the church. Most rood screens were destroyed in Tudor times as being 'idolatrous' because their purpose was to display 'roods' or crucifixes.

MEDROD late 6th century
MODRED, MEDRAUT

The brother of Cathan ap Cawrdaf, confused in the early Triads with the Modred, Medraut, who fought Arthur. There may be a germ of truth in this, however, as the final Battle of Camlan appears to have been fought between the kingdoms of North and South Wales, and the Arthur involved in this campaign had uncertain relations with the church. (The author's forthcoming book upon the series of 'Arthur's' who actually existed is exploring this link.)
Modred's son was St Dyfnog. The early poets made Modred a standard of bravery, and not until Geoffrey of Monmouth do we see him as a 'betrayer' of Arthur.

One of the *'three unrestrained ravagings of the Isle of Britain'* was Modred's sacking of Arthur's court at Wentloog near Cardiff, when he dragged Gwenhwyfar from her chair and slapped her. Arthur retaliated by devastating Modred's court. (Another ravaging was that of Rhydderch Hael's court at Dumbarton by Aeddan Fradog.)

Alphabetical Listing of the Saints of Wales and Religious Events

MEDWY 2nd century
MEDWIN, MEDWYR
January 1

Medwy was said to be one of the very early British saints, with Ffagan, Dyfan and Elfan, sent by Rome to Christianise the Welsh in 180. Michaelston-y-Fedw was formerly Llanfedwy, and the church was burnt in the wars of the 11th century and never rebuilt. There is a ten feet standing stone upon private property at Druidstone House in St Mellons, Michaelstone-y-Fedw. It is one of the many Welsh megaliths that frequently goes down to a river for a drink in the evening.

MEIGAN 6th century
MEIGANT, MEUGAN

The daughter of Gwyndaf Hen who may have founded Cilfeigan near Usk and another chapel in Gwent. See Meugan, as the details or this saint or saints are very difficult to untangle with any certainty. Other sources state that this was a son of Gwyndaf Hen ab Emyr Llydaw and Gwenonwy ferch Meurig ap Tewdrig. He was a member of Illtud's college, and moved to Dyfrig's foundation at Caerleon, over which his father presided. He retired to Ynys Enlli to die.

MEIGYR and MEILYR late 5th century

The brothers of King Caswallon and sons of Gwron ap Cunedda. They fought with Caswallon to expel the Irish and Picts from Anglesey and Gwynedd. Llys-y-Fran in Pembroke may be Meilir's church, but some attribute it to Maglorius.

MEILIG 6th century

Some say that this was the brother of Maelog ap Caw who founded Llowes, but it may be the same saint.

MEILYR 6th century
MYLOR
October 1

A son of Gwyddno ab Emyr Llydaw, the brother of Maelrys and cousin of Cadfan. He was a disinherited prince, as his father's lands were lost under Cardigan Bay. According to local legend, his uncle Rivoldus had murdered Gwyddno and wanted to kill Mylor. Bishops agreed to a compromise whereby Mylor's right hand was replaced by one of silver, and his left foot by one of bronze. This did not stop Rivoldus from chopping off Mylor's head, but he himself sickened and died within three days.

Mylor was commemorated upon October 1 at Mylor, Merther Myle and Linkinhorn in Cornwall, and his relics were acquired by Amesbury Abbey in Wiltshire. It is claimed that Gwenhyfar (Guinevere) founded Amesbury Church, and she retired there and died after her affair with Medraut or Maelgwn (Lancelot).

MEIRION 6th century
MEIRIAN, MEIRCHION
February 3, 4

Like Seiriol, a brother of Cynlas and Einion Frenhin. The chapel of ease of Llanfeirion, near Llangadwaladr in Anglesey, was named after him. He was the son of the murdered Owain Ddantgwyn, and Criccieth was once Merthyr Meirion, but now St Catherine's is its church.

MEL d.488
February 6

A Briton who was a disciple of Patrick and became Bishop of Ardagh after evangelising the area. Two other Britons went with him to Ireland to aid Patrick, namely Melchu and Muinis, for whom have lately been claimed Irish genealogies. The rewriting of history never ceases. To a great extent, this book is thankfully 'un-rewriting' history. Because of the destruction of sources and the author's deficiencies, there will be errors of omission and errors of substance, but in essence the history of the Celtic church has shaped the Wales of today. This book is seen by the author as a 'starting-point' to stimulate interest and discussion, in order to publish a definitive early history within the next ten years. Mel may have been the son of Daererca (Monenna), said to be Patrick's Welsh sister. There is a Plomel north of the marvellous prehistoric site of Carnac, near St Cado. The Life of Brigid states that he had no fixed see, which makes Mel a missionary, and Patrick was said to have given his church at Ardagh to his nephew, Mel.

MELCH see MEL

MELAINE d.c.535
November 6

A Briton and the patron of Mullion and St Mellyan in Cornwall. He became Bishop of Rennes and advised King Clovis. The great Abbey of St Melaine at Rennes celebrates him, and some letters survive.

ABBESS MELANGELL d.641
MONACELLA
January 31, May 27 or 28 (and May 4 according to Edwards)
Patroness of hares and the natural environment

The daughter of King Cufwlch and Ethni (Eddni) Wyddeles (the Irishwoman), Melangell fled to Wales to escape a forced marriage, and settled at Pennant. Another source states that she was the daughter of Tudwal (Tugdual) and descended from Macsen Wledig, the sister or neice of Rhydderch Hael, King of Strathclyde. In 604 Prince Brochwael Ysgythrog of Powys was hunting a hare with his hounds. She protected it by hiding the animal in the sleeve of her gown. When it peeped out to look at the dogs, they fled, and Brochwael acknowledged the presence of this holy woman, giving her the land across which he had hunted. She lived here, at Pennant Melangell, for another 37 years, and no animal was killed in her sanctuary. Hares were known as *'wyn bach Melangell'* or Melangell's little lambs, and to kill a hare in her parish was regarded as an act of sacrilege. To call after a hunted hare *'God and Melangell go with thee'* was thought to save it from a pack of hounds.

Llanfihangel-y-Pennant near Llangynog is probably Melangell's foundation, then became one of the ubiquitous Norman rededications to Michael. Hares can be seen on its mediaeval rood screen, and her 12th century shrine survives there, until recently in a 17th century room, Cell-y-Bedd in the east end of the church. The coffin-shrine, supported on pillars, is a unique survival in Britain (-'unique' here is used as per its dictionary definition). Ffynnon y Cythraul in the parish was used for eye complaints and to cure warts in both humans and animals. Another well, Ffynnon Lewyn cured rheumatism and skin disorders.

At nearby Bryn-Crug is an inscription at the chapel reading
'In Memory of MARY JONES Who in the Year 1800, At the age of 16, Walked from Llanfihangel-y-Pennant to Bala to procure a copy of a Welsh Bible from Rev Thomas Charles, BA. This incident led to the formation of the British and Foreign Bible Society.'
This barefoot journey took Mary over the rocky paths of Cader Idris and back, with the three shillings and sixpence that she had saved from the ages of ten to sixteen.

MELERI 5th – 6th century

The daughter of Brychan who married King Ceredig, so was the mother of Sant and the grandmother of David.

BISHOP MELLON 257-311
MALLONUS, MELANIUS, MELONINUS
October 10, 22

From Llanllewrig (Llanlleurwg) on the eastern outskirts of Cardiff, now St Mellons, he was traditionally the first Bishop of Rouen after visiting Rome. He was bishop for 55 years. The Wentloog area around St Mellons was an extremely important centre at this time. There is a farm there called Pont Mellon.

MELORUS d.411
August 28

This martyr was the son of Melianus, duke of Cornwall.

MELYD
May 9

Meliden in Flint was called Gallt Melyd, and Ffynnon Felid was also there. Just between Dyserth and Prestatyn is Meliden, with its small mediaeval church of St Melyd, attractively restored in Victorian times.

The Book of Welsh Saints

MERCHWYN VESANUS 6th century
MARCIANUS, MARK

Not a saint but the son of Glywys, king of Gorfynedd (east of Gower), with his palace at Llanilltud. He may be remembered in the name Penmarc nearby. Merchwyn had several conflicts with Illtud, once forcing the saint to hide in a cave at Ewenni, despite the fact that he had granted church lands to Illtud.

BISHOP MERIADOC 6th century
MERIASEK
June 7 (also 3 and 9)

A fellow missionary of St Gwinear who travelled from Wales via Cornwall to Brittany, where he became Bishop of Vannes. There is a church in Camborne, Cornwall, dedicated to him where he was also said to be bishop. His feast is celebrated in several areas of Brittany.The marvellous *'Bewnans (Beunaus) Meryasek' ('Life of Meriasek')* is a medieval Cornish play in the vernacular about the saint, transcribed into Cornish in 1504 by a local priest. It was revived in Redruth in 1924, and related to his search for drinking water in Cornwall.

He has holy wells in Cornwall and Brittany. The patron saint of tin miners, even around 1900 it was common to see his clay image at the entrace to workings. At the start of each shift, the miners would cross themselves and say *'Saint Meriasek, we pray to thee'* to invoke his protection through the images. If they met a snail going to work, they would give it some lantern wax for good luck. Meriadec lies between Vannes and Auray in Brittany.

MERIN
MERRIN
January 6, April 4

St Merin's Church Gwynedd, and Llanferin (Lanfetherin) in Monmouth remember this son of Seithenyn. However, another source makes Gwytherin the founder of Llanvetherin. Bodferin, a chapel under Llaniestin in Caernarfon, seems to have been where he lived for most of his life. In Brittany a feast is celebrated on April 4 at Lanmerin south of Perros Guirec, and at Plomelin nearby. He may also be the St Merryn of Cornwall, whose feast day was April 4 at Padstow.

MERWALLT 6th century
MERGUADUS

The first abbot of Llandeilo Ferwallt (Bishopston in Gower), which had been founded by Cynfor.

MEUGAN 6th century
MAWGAN, MEIGANT? MEIGAN?
September 24, 25, 26, February 14, April 24, November 15

He seems to have been the Abbot of Demetia, or Dyfed, who is remembered in the Isles of Scilly and two Cornish churches. He crossed to the West Country in the company of Brioc.

Four miles from Helston in Cornwall is Mawgan-in-Meneage, and near Newquay, Cornwall, the Vale of Mawgan still bears his name. In this valley, the church of Mawgan-in-Prydar is said to stand on the site of a Celtic monastery. In Cadog's Vita, the holy man Moucan or Maucan intervenes to resolve the dispute between Maelgwn Gwynedd and Cadog, and is possibly St Mawgan.

One of the 'peregrini' associated with Cadoc's foundations, Meugan is remembered at Llanfeugan in Cemais, the centre of his cult, and at nearby Llanfoygan, Pant y Deri, Capel Meugan in Bridell parish, and at St Meugan's chapel and holy well in the parish of Llanfair Nant-Gwyn. There is also Trevigan in Llanrhian near St David's, Capel Meugan near Cilhernin, Llanboidy (Carmarthenshire), and his cult was followed at Ruthin.

According to Iolo, this son of Goronw studied under Beuno at Clynnog Fawr. However, Bradney's 'The Hundred of Usk' refers to Cilfeigan near Usk as the *'retreat of Meigan'* . . . *This refers probably to Meigan, a member of the college of Illtuyd in the 6th century, who removed with his father Gwyndaf Hen to the college of Dyfrig at Caerlleon.'* Bradney may have confused Meigan with Meugan, whom he places at nearby St Maughans. This is an area which may be made more explicit in future editions of this book. However, entries have been made for Meigan and Mawan earlier in this book. There may indeed be three or four Meigans or Meugans, and assistance would be welcomed from readers in this respect.

Llanrhydd under Ruthin in Denbigh was his. There were many dedications in Pembroke. Meugan's Chapel at Pistyll Meugan Farm *'in Kemes'* (Cemaes) was demolished, with its holy well, in 1592 to stop *'offrings and superstitious pilgymages'* being made there. The Church Commissioners also forbade any rebuilding of the church. Meugan's Well, 'Pistyll Meugan' was a fast-flowing spring near Eglwyswrw in Pembroke. There were said to be three types of healing water there that did not mix: one for eyes; one for warts; and one for heart ailments, rheumatism and lameness. Ffair Feugan (Meugan's fair) was held here on Ascension Day, upon the Thursday after Trinity Sunday and the first Monday after Martin's Day. The well building was destroyed, but the well still flows. At Eglwyswrw, Ffair Feugan was held on the Monday after Martinmas, and there was another fair at St Dogmael's.

Llanfeugan (Llanfigan) in Brecon is thought to be his foundation, and there are chapels consecrated to him at St Maughan's under Llangattwg Feibion Afel in Monmouth, and at Capel Meugan under Llandegfan in Anglesey. There are two poems attributed to him in the Myvyrian Archaiology. The Welsh took great pride in being buried within the church rather than the churchyard, which led to graves being covered with very little earth. Archbishop Payne recorded a complaint in the late 18th century from the curate of Llanfeugan. This vicar stated that he often had to leave the church in the middle of a service, *'being quite overcome with the stench from putrid carcases.'* Payne mentioned approvingly the example of a Reverend Skinner who left instructions to be buried in the churchyard – *'Yr eglwys i'r bobl, y fynwent i'r meirw.'* (*'The church for the people, the churchyard for the dead.'*) This earth from the bare church floors, mixed with the remains of the dead, was thought to be particularly potent, and in Dolwyddelan was used as an ointment to cure rashes. The usual covering for floors was rushes, changed just a few times in the course of a year.

His 'Saying of the Wise', *'when parting from his foes'* was *'the children of the wicked are evil spoken of.'*

MEURIG AP TEWDRIG AP TEITHFALLT, KING OF MORGANWG 5th – 6th century

King Tewdrig was martyred at Tintern in 470, but Meurig had taken over his kingdom prior to this date, and is thought to have been Uther Pendragon, the Dux Bellorum or leader in battle of the British against the Saxon and Pict invaders. Pendragon was an honorific title, and Uther's children included Arthur and Anna. Meurig was the father of King Arthur, and was excommunicated for breaking an oath and killing a rival, but canonised after his death for founding many churches. He married Onbrawst ferch Gwrgant Mawr, to reunite Glwyssing and Gwent with Ergyng. (Glamorgan, Gwent and Hereford/Worcester had been the heartland of the Silures).

His children included Arthwys (Athrwys/Arthmael/Arthur), whose son was Morgan Mwynfawr, whose son was Eunydd. Eunydd's descendants ruled Glamorgan until the Norman Conquest. Meurig's daughter Anna married Amwn Ddu ab Emyr Llydaw, the dispossessed Breton prince. Amwn became a saint, and friend of Illtud and Dyfrig. Amwn's children were the important saints Tydecho, Tathan and Samson, who returned to Brittany. Another of Meurig's daughters was Afrella, who married Umbrafael ab Emyr Llydaw. Meurig's third daughter was Gwenonwy who married Gwyndaf Hen ab Emyr Llydaw, King of Brittany. Their children were Meugan (Meigant) and Hywyn. Hywyn was a confessor at the monastery on Ynys Enlli, where Arthur went to recover after Camlan. *The marriage of three daughters of Meurig to the three sons of Emyr Llydaw (Budic II of Brittany) gives credence to the claim that Arthur fought with his kinsmen in Brittany.* It appears that after the Bretons supported Arthur, he helped Hywel Mawr and Budic II regain their lands, and then overcame Conmore for Iuthael to gain the Breton throne.

Meurig gave lands to the church around where his father Tewdrig was buried, as recorded by Godwin, Bishop of Llandaf in 1615. Under Meurig's protection Llandaf and Llancarfan were founded, and he gave lands to both. It appears that he controlled most of Hereford, all of Monmouth and most of Glamorgan, i.e. the ancient kingdom of Siluria, and he seems to have ruled from Caerleon. After Meurig treacherously slew Cynvetu, Euddogwy summoned the bishops of Llancarfan, Llandough and Llanilltud to excommunicate him, but he was pardoned for giving lands to Llandaf, where he is buried. He may have founded the monastery at Llanfair Misgyn, Miskin. King 'Mouric ap Teudiric' is recorded as granting Roath in Cardiff (Reathr) to Gourcinnim for a sword with a gilded hilt valued at 25 cows. A smithy of this time has been recorded at nearby Dinas Powys in the Dark Age fort. Meurig's kingdom of Glwysing may have included Brychan's Brecon as a vassal kingdom. There is a 13th century church at Alltmawr in Brecon dedicated to Mauritius, which may be his foundation.

Pwll Meurig, a mile or so from Chepstow, was his holy well, and famous for miracles. It ebbed and flowed with the tide like many Welsh coastal wells. The legend is that people used to stand on a magical log in the well to wash their faces. The well was flooded by the River Severn and the log floated out to sea, but always returned on the fourth day. Meurig's father Tewdrig also had a famous holy well. Barber and Pykitt believe that Meurig is buried on Mynydd y Gaer in Glamorgan, possibly on a site near Arthur's grave.

Alphabetical Listing of the Saints of Wales and Religious Events

MEUTHI 6th century

This was said to be an Irish hermit who founded Llanfeuthin (Llanfeithin) near Llancarfan, but was in fact St Tathan, of whom 'Meuthi' was a familiar form of address.

ABBOT MEWAN d.611
MEEN, MEVENNIUS, MEIN, CONAID
June 15 and 21

From South Wales, possibly Ergyng, Mewan followed his uncle St Samson to Brittany, and operated (with St Austell) around the Brocielande region associated with the Arthurian and Merlin romances. He may have fled from the sacking of Caer Loew (Gloucester) where his brother Eldad was martyred in 577. Mewan may have been a member of the royal house of Powys, centred at Pengwern, the Roman city of Wroxeter. He founded, near Paimpont, the superb monastery known as Saint Meen-le-Grand, where pilgrims came from all over France.
There is an exhibition there of images of famous Breton saints and their banners, which includes all the Welsh 'founder-saints' of Brittany. The surrounding Brocielande Forest is associated with Arthurian and Merlin's legends, and there are fascinating walks, cromlechs and relics in this area.

Saint Mewan and Mevagissey in Cornwall commemorate him, and Glastonbury holds some relics. He was a friend and relative of King Judicael of Domnonia*, in Brittany. He is commemorated at St Meen near Lesneven and St Meen south of Guer. Prayers are still given to Meen for *'les troubles de l'esprit'*. There is another St Meen north of Carnac, and a Petit St Meen south of Plancoet.

*Note that this name parallels Domnonia or Dumnonia, which was the kingdom of Devon, Somerset, Cornwall and part of Wiltshire. 'Cornuaille' is also the name today for a large part of Brittany.

MICHAEL
MIHANGEL
May 8, September 29 Michaelmas, October 10 (Hay Old Style)

Many Welsh churches were rededicated to Michael by the Normans, so there are many places called Llanfihangel* in Wales. However, there were several Celtic churches dedicated previously to Mihangel in the 10th and 11th centuries, probably because of his association in the Book of Revelation with being the principal fighter of the dragon. It is difficult to know how many were original dedications. In Cornwall and Devon many churches and place names commemorate Michael, e.g. St Michael's Mount. Sen Myghal is the patron saint of Cornwall, and appeared to some fishermen standing on a western promontory of St Michael's Mount, known as Cadar Myghal or St Michael's Chair. This occurred on May 8, 498, and this date is still used by Helston for its famous Floral Day.

The Chronicle of the Princes, 'Brut y Tywysogion', seems to refer to the first dedication to Michael in Wales between 710 and 720, and the Anglo-Saxon Chronicle gives the date for a Llanfihangel as 719. Four of the Cardiganshire dedications alone point to an earlier origin than the Normans, at Genau'r Glyn, Penbryn, Ystrad and Y Creuddyn.

Michaelmas Eve on September 28th often saw a lamb being slaughtered, and Michaelmas itself was usually a time of great fairs. At Kidderminster, in the county of Hereford and Worcester, the fair had a *'lawless hour'* called *'Kellums'*. This was the period between when the old bailiff stepped down at 3 p.m. and the new bailiff was elected at 4 p.m. In this hour there were pitched vegetable fights, with much of the ammunition directed at the incoming bailiff.

The church of St Michael at Llanfihangel-yng-Ngwyfa contains the grave of Ann Griffiths, the greatest female hymn-writer in Wales, who died in 1805, aged only 29. Her house, Dolwar Fach near Pontrobert, has a visitor's book and one can find further information on this spiritual poetess.

The saddest entry in the diary of William Thomas is for July 10th, 1794:
This Night about 11 a clock, William, my beloved and Blessed son expired, after he had been half a year in a pityful condition from the King's Evil, which on his right side and back broke, and at last turned to a Dropsey and swollen his Legs, with Bitter Coughing all the while, and turned him to his bed for five weeks nearly. O my Blessed son, in whom was the fear of God, and God had given him knowledge very far in the Mathematicks and Botany above many Thrice his age, that he knew more plants than the most men. My greatest loss since my Birth on Earth. Of 14 years five months and ten days old and was buried the 12th Instant at the Church yard of Michaelstone super Eley, against the Chancel's wall in a new grave. A man in Knowledge and a Child in age, willing to die and willing to live, Beloved of all sober people for his Sense and Knowledge. It is surely a clergyman's most difficult task to console parents who outlive their children. Thomas often refers to his son in his later diary notes, as in the entry for October 25th, 1794: *This morning dreamed as if my dear son called upon me sharply "Daida", which caused grief to me afterwards to think of him.'*

Of the many places named and renamed Michael, Llanfihangel Ystern Llewern near Skenfrith means *'the church of Michael in the place of the burning Will 'o the Wisp'*. It was in later centuries also known locally as Llantafarn Bach after a little inn there. The legend is that King Ynyr of Gwent was travelling along the Trothy valley when he saw a light ahead at dusk. He rode towards the 'will-o'the-wisp', thinking it to be a house light, but was caught up in bogland and only just managed to escape. He then built the church in thanks for his survival, dedicating it to Michael. The nearby manor known as the Pant was an inportant place of refuge for Quakers, and its owner Walter Jenkins was committed to Cardiff Gaol in 1661, where he died.

The Menter Powys leaflet following St Michael's churches in Radnorshire notes D. Parry-Jones in 'A Country Parson' (Batsford 1975) as stating: *'There is a local legend that the last Welsh Dragon lies asleep deep in Radnor Forest and that long ago the people of this area built four churches in a circle around the forest. These were dedicated to St Michael, the conqueror of the dragon, to make sure he does not escape. Many believe that if any one of these churches is destroyed the dragon will awaken and ravage the countryside once more. The churches are at Llanfihangel Cefnllys in this parish, Llanfihangel Rhydithon, Lanfihangel Nantmelan and Llanfihangel Cascob.'* The church trail is marked by a logo depicting the yellow Radnorshire Lily, a species only found in the area and not discovered until 1974. At Nant Melan is *'Water-break-its-neck'* where Llywelyn the Last hid from his English pursuers under a waterfall. The church only dates from 1846, following the demolition of its mediaeval precursor, but there was a Celtic church on the site, which has a circle of yews, one with a roughly shaped stone in its trunk. There is a 'sacrificial' stone at nearby Llanerch Farm, and a Bronze Age tumulus and four stones at Rhiwiau Farm. The next church, at Cascob, is 13th century, with a Radnorshire 'tie-beam' roof and a 17th century 'abracadabra charm' used for exorcism. St Michael's at Beguildy is 14th century, with a 15th century rood screen and 13th century dug-out chest (used for keeping church treasures). John Dee (Black Jack) was born in Beguildy in 1527, and was Elizabeth I's favourite polymath – an astronomer, mathematician, alchemist, geographer, scientist and ambassador to Poland. There is a short and disjointed book by Gwyn Alf Williams about him, and he deserves a new biography.

The church of St Michael at Kerry may have been founded by Ceri, and the Menter Powys leaflet is worth quoting here: *'Archdeacon warns Bishop "not to thrust his sickle into another man's corn." Bishop threatens Archdeacon with excommunication. Bishop excommunicates Archdeacon. Archdeacon then excommunicates Bishop, with bells and candles. Bishop gallops off pursued by the sticks, stones and clods of earth of the Kerry villagers ! This colourful scenario took place in 1176 following the rebuilding of the earlier church, when Bishop Adam of St Asaph tried in vain to bring Kerry into his diocese before Giraldus Cambrensis could re-redicate the new church. Read the full account in Noel Jerman's Guidebook "Kerry, the Church and Village." . . . Visitors marvel at the thickness of the walls in the Tower and the pillars of the North aisle. The oldest bell dates from c.1400 and the clock, hopefully to be restored for display, from c.1720. The 15th century font with its inset panels depicts instruments of the passion, the Welsh Chained Bible is c.1690 and the parish chest from 1759. Those who worship here will be thankful to know that the "Ting-Tang Bell" is no longer rung to rouse sleeping members of the congregation during the service !"* The churches of St Michael at Llanfihangel Rhydithon, Llanfihangel Helygen and Cefnllys are also worth visiting on the Menter Powys 'Where the Dragon Sleeps' trail. Cefnllys has a Celtic circular churchyard with its boundary marked by yew trees over 1000 years old.

Francis Kilvert's diary entry for October 9, 1870, reads: *It is an old custom in these parts for the poor people to go about the farm-houses to beg and gather milk between and about the two Michaelmasses, that they may be able to make some puddings and pancakes against Bryngwyn and Clyro feasts, which are on the same day, next Sunday, the Sunday after Old Michaelmas Day of Hay Fair, October 10th. The custom is still kept up in Bryngwyn and at some hill farms in Clyro.'*

*Lanfihangel Crucorney claims to have the oldest pub in Wales, and the Skirrid Inn has been there since at least 1170. It was used as a court-house by 'Hanging' Judge Jeffries after the failure of the Monmouth Rebellion in 1685. (The Duke of Monmouth's mother was the Welsh courtesan, Lucy Walters). Scorch-marks from the rope used can still be seen on a beam above the stairwell. The inn is haunted by a one-legged rebel who stabbed himself to escape the noose here. The other ghost is of the 'Lady of the Ring', Eleanor Thomas, who appears from the waters of Llanfihangel Pool to warn of an imminent death. Slightly mad, she was regarded as a witch, and forced to wear of hoop of iron around her waist to prevent her casting spells on the villagers. Perhaps this iron band led to her drowning in the pool. The ruin of St Michael's Church, probably on the site of an older foundation, sits atop the Skirrid Mountain (Ysgryd Fawr) above the beautiful Gafenni Valley. Farmers used to take soil from the top of this mountain as it had been brought there from the Holy Land, or by St Patrick. These hills were associated with the Apostles, Peter and Paul. They scattered this 'holy' soil on their lands to ensure a good harvest. The earth was also placed within coffins prior to burial. Catholics are said to have celebrated Mass here, prior to the last service around 1680, and the remains of the church are in the enclosure of an Iron Age hill-fort.

MILBURG mid-7th century
February 23

An Anglo-Saxon virgin abbess of Wenlock in Shropshire, commemorated in Llanfilo in Radnor, although some think that the church was founded by Milo.

MILO
MEILW?

Possibly a saint (see Milburg). Plas Milo in Anglesey is now called Plas Meilw, and has two large standing stones named Meini Hirion.

MINVER 6th century
MENEFREDA, (MWYNWEN possibly)
February 23 (and 24), November 24

A grand-daughter of Brychan and also possibly a daughter of Brynach, it appears she was at Minwear, near Slebech in Pembroke, then a nun at Tredesick near Padstow, where the church and well survive at St Minver. The Devil was said to have fled to nearby Lundy Hole, as she threw her comb at him, when he tempted her at the well. There was also a Seynts Well in Minwear parish.

MIRGIN

Llangwm in Monmouth, see Huui.

MOR AP PASGEN AB URIEN RHEGED 6th century

Buried at Ynys Enlli

MOR AP CENEU AP COEL

An early saint, who possibly founded Llanynys in Denbigh before Saeran's association with it. Llanfor Deiniol may also be his, but Llannor is a corruption of *lann fawr, great church*. However, Mike Salter states that this remote church near the River Irfon is dedicated to St Llyr.

MORDEYRN 5th – 6th century
July 25

Mordeyn's chapel was in Nantglyn, Denbigh, and the church of Nantglyn celebrated this son of Edeyrn ap Cunedda. James the Apostle has replaced him. Rhyd Saint was a holy well just outside his chapel ruins. There was also a Ffynnon Mordeyrn near the church, but this may be the same well as Rhyd Saint.

WILLIAM MORGAN c.1545 - 1604
September 10

This bishop has been given the same Holy Day as William Salesbury, in recognition of their wonderful service in the translation of the Bibly into Welsh, and thereby being the 'saviours' of the Welsh language. His house at Tŷ Mawr, near Penmachno, can still be visited. He was the son of John ap Morgan ap Llywelyn, and of Lowri ferch William ap John ap Madog. After studying at Cambridge, he became deacon at Ely in 1568, then was successively vicar of Llanbadarn-fawr, Welshpool, Llanrhaeadr-ym-Mochnant and Llanarmon, parson of Pennant Melangell and rector of Llanfyllin. His Bible translation was probably started at Cambridge, and printing began in 1587. He also became Bishop of Llandaf, and then of St Asaf. According to 'The Dictionary of Welsh Biography', *'his work marks the real beginnings of the literature and Protestantism of modern Wales.'*

MORHAEARN
MORHAIARN

November 1

Trewalchmai, under Heneglwys in Anglesey.

MORWENNA see MWYNEN

MOSES
February 7

A British apostle to the Saracens, according to Cressy.

MUINIS 5th century
December 18

A Briton who went with Mel and Melchu to Ardagh to help evangelise Ireland.

MWCHWDW

This was the name of an old chapel south of Parys mountain in Anglesey, where ancient tombstones were found.

MWROG 6th or 7th century?
January 6, 15, 16 or 24

The church at Llanfwrog in Denbighshire is dedicated to St Mwrog and St Mary. There is another Llanfwrog in Anglesey, where this virgin was feasted on January 6, compared to January 16 in Denbigh. The mediaeval church is in typical 'double-naved' Clwydian style, and there are superb views from the circular 'Celtic' churchyard. There was a mutilated Celtic stone over the north entrance in the 19th century, but the inscription was illegible. His old chapel was in a field named Monwent Mwrog, but no trace remains. Nearby, in the wooded Clywedog valley, is the lovely mediaeval church of St Mary in Cyffylliog.

MWYNEN 6th century
MORWENNA
July 5, August 12, 14

A descendant of Brychan, Morwenstow in North Cornwall is dedicated to her. She was carrying a stone from the cliff to build her church, when she laid it down to rest. A spring gushed forth on the spot, and it was decided to build the church on this new site, where the holy well was venerated. Exactly the same story is told for her founding of Marhamchurch in Cornwall. On the Monday after August 12, Marhamchurch (outside Bude) celebrates at the site of Morwenna's cell outside the church. A Queen of the Revel, selected by local children, is crowned by 'Father Time', whose identity is always a secret. Confusingly, there was a Ffynnon Mwynwen holy well at Merthyr Dyfan Church in Barri, Glamorgan. Marhamchurch also celebrated Nectan (q.v.), Brychan's eldest son, so he was possibly its founder.

Morwenstow saw the first ever *'Harvest Thanksgiving'* in 1843 – the tradition of praying and offering blessings for the crop, and giving produce to the needy, started here. It was also the time for the making of *'corn dollies'* in Wales and the West Country. The figure made from the last straw of the harvest was known as the *'wrach'* ('gwrach means 'witch' or 'hag') in Wales.

MYDAN late 6th century

A son of Pasgen ab Urien Rhegen, who studied at Llancarfan.

MYFOR
May 9

According to the book of Llandaf, Merthyr Mawr was commemorated to St Myfor, which seems to have become Mouor, then Mawr. However, it may have been a saint called Mor, prefixed with the honorary title, My, equivalent to our Reverend. Iolo Morganwg tries to make a case of St Gofor being the founder of Llanover, but this was probably Myfor (see Gofor).

MYGNACH 6th century

The son of Mydno, and from Caer Seiont (Caernarfon), he was the principal of St Cybi's college at Holyhead.

MYLLIN d.696
MOLING
June 17, 28

Remembered as the first saint in Britain to baptise by immersion, thought to be an Irish monk. Llanfyllin lies in the Cain Valley in northern Montgomery. *'Ffest y pen'* ('the end of harvest feast') was recorded in Llanfyllin where *'cwrw cyfeddach'* (strong 'carousal beer') was brewed for the festivities. Friends and neighbours were invited into houses, the harp was played and penillion were sung. In Caernarfonshire this custom was known as *'boddi'r cynhaeaf'* ('drowning the harvest'). The custom survived until the arrival of the steam-driven thresher in the late 19th century. There was also recorded the *'ceffyl pren'* dialogue used in Llanfyllin district to stop a man and wife quarrelling openly. The wooden horse was paraded in a noisy procession to the couple's door, and this question and answer rhyme was recited:

'Am bwy 'r wyt ti' marchogaeth?'
'Am ddeuddyn o'r gymdogaeth.'
'Pwy yw'r rheiny, Gymro?'
'Wil ac Ali Beuno.'
'A ydyw Ali'n curo'n arw?'
'Mae hi bron a'I ladd e'n farw,
Ry ferch a hithau
Mae'r gwr yn las o'I gleisiau!'
(For whom are you riding?
For two people from the district.
Which two people, Welshman?
Wil and Ali Beuno.
Does Ali hit hard?
She has nearly killed Wil.
Between the daughter and her,
The husband is blue with bruises.)

Ffynnon Fyllin (Ffynnon Coed Lan) rag well is near his church, where he baptised converts. On Trinity Sunday females made sugared well water for the local men, who responded by taking them for cakes and beer at Tynllan ale-house. His fairs were held on June 28 after the date change to New Style.

To celebrate the night's *'plygain'* at Christmas, special thick candles known as *'canhwyllau plygain'* were made to withstand the gusts of wind in the procession to church. The 'George de la Tour' effect, of the brilliant light that they give off, is sometimes seen in Breton 'fest noz' festivals today. Also hundreds of candles in the church were fixed right next to each other to illuminate the building. Plygain, or plygaint, seems to have derived from the Latin *'pulli cantus'* or cock's crow, and the Manx festival of Oiel Verrey paralleled it. Some academics believe that the custom survived because it replaced the Christmas Mass when it was suppressed. It was even taken up by the Nonconformist chapels and churches. Until the Victorian period the custom across Wales was for whole families to make treacle toffee, then celebrate plygain, then visit each other's houses while the traditional goose was cooking. People would go hunting, play football or bando. In Victorian times families turned 'inwards' and increasingly celebrated Christmas as family units in their own homes. The beautiful Plygain service could easily be revived across all Wales, and local customs resurrected, as many only died out in the twentieth century.

From Llanfyllin one can take the wonderful trail known as Glyndŵr's Way with its gold dragon symbol. Leaving the footpath, one can follow the Ann Griffiths Walk to Dolwar Fach, the home of famous hymn-writer, then go to her memorial chapel at Dolanog before returning along the beautiful River Vyrnwy (Afon Efyrnwy), past Plas Dolanog, the mansion built in 1664 for the Watkin Williams Wynne family.

MYNNO

Moylegrove, formerly Tre Wyddel (Irish Place), was dedicated to this Irish saint, but is now the church of St Andrew.

N

'Ni edrych angau pwy decaf ei dalcen'
Death considers not the fairest forehead

Old Welsh Proverb

NECTAN 5th - 6th century
NEITHON, NIGHTON
June 17, February 14 (also May 18)

This oldest and 'most illustrious' of Brychan's 24 children, he was killed by thieves at his hermitage at Hartland, the most north-westerly point in Devon. This occurred at New Stoke on June 17th. He was said to have picked up his head and carried it back to the well near his hut. He laid it on a stone, where red streaks signifying his blood can still be seen. One robber went mad and died there and then, and the other was almost blinded, but he buried Nectan's body inside the small hut. There are five churches dedicated to Nectan, including Barnstaple, and Marhamchurch in Cornwall, and another two in Brittany. His feast is still celebrated at Nectan Fair in Launceston, in Wells and Exeter, and St Winnow Fair was held in his honour. Lan-Neizant and Ker-Neizan commemorate him in Brittany. He has a Holy Well at Poundstock, and is remembered at Ashcombe and St Winnow's Chapel. One of his bones was a relic at Waltham Abbey.

At St Nectan's Well, Hartland Point, there is an annual mass on his day, preceded by a procession of children bearing foxgloves. When he was killed, he carried his head half a mile, and foxgloves grew where drops of blood fell. The other story about his death takes place at St Nectan's Glen at Trevethyn, near Tintagel in Cornwall. His cell was above the Trevillit river, where his waterfall, St Nectan's Kieve emerges from the rock-face. On his deathbed he ordered his silver bell to be thrown into the waters, to prevent unbelievers hearing it. If anyone now hears the bell, it is a portent of bad luck. On his death two unknown ladies appeared and diverted the river, and buried him underneath the waterfall, before letting the river flow over him again.

NEFFEI 6th century
DEDYU

Supposed to have been a son of Clydwyn ap Brychan, who went to Spain with Pabiali and Pasgen ap Dingad, possibly to Galicia. Baring-Gould calls him a son of Brychan by his third wife, Proistri of Spain, who went to Spain with his brothers to become saints and principals. Neffei has also been thought to be the same person as Dedyu ap Clydwyn ap Brychan, and in the early 18th century Hugh Thomas stated that he was King of Brecon with a son named Tudor. Thomas again repeated the Spanish sainthood story, saying that he emigrated with Pabien/Pabiel and Pasgen ap Dingad.

NEFYDD early 6th century
HUNYDD

One of Brychan's descendants, the son of the martyred Nefydd Ail ap Rhun Dremrudd, he founded Llanefydd. There was also a daughter of Brychan by this name who may have founded it. Llanefydd, like many other churches in Denbigh and Flint, has a blocked door in the north wall of the church. The door was opened during a baptismal service just as the curate entered, so that the devil could escape. Ffynnon Nefydd was about 300 yards from the church.

NEFYDD AIL 5th – 6th century
September 8

The son of Rhun ap Brychan, and brother of St Andras. His son was also called Nefydd (see above). He may have put to flight the Saxons who killed his father Rhun, and become a bishop in the North of Britain (Llechgelyddon?), where he was himself killed by Picts or Saxons. Llanefydd in Denbigh may be his, or his son's dedication, and it is now dedicated to the Virgin Mary, with her feast date of September 8. Tradition says that it was called St Effydd's, but Edward Lhuyd in 1699 thought it was dedicated to St Ffrymden or St Frymder, as the locals referred to Bedd Frymder as the saint's grave in the churchyard. Ffynnon Ufyod there was used in the 17th century, where one could be cured of an illness by bathing upon three successive Fridays. It was reconstructed in 1604, but is now dilapidated.

NEFYDD 5th century
GOLEUDDYDD

The wife of St Tudwal Befr and daughter of Brychan. Her sons Ifor and Cynin (Llangynin) were saints, and Llannefydd in Denbigh was attributed to her. It may be impossible to resolve whether Llannefydd is hers or belongs to Nefydd ap Rhun or Nefydd ap Nefydd. A place named Llanhesgin in Monmouth was also recorded as being her foundation.

NENNIUS fl. c.800

The author of the early Latin work known as the 'Historia Brittonum', the account of the time from the invasion of Julius Caesar until the end of the 8th century. In his preface, he states that he is a disciple of Elfoddw (Elvodugus), who died in 809, *'the chief bishop in the land of Gwynedd.'* From internal evidence, it seems that he was a native of south-east Wales, and he is mentioned in the 9th century Irish 'Psalter of Cashel'. His sources included Gildas, Eusebius, Jerome, Isidore and Prosper.

NEOT 9th century?
July 31

Regarded as a Cornish Celtic saint, possibly the 9th century illegitimate son of Ethelwulf, remembered at St Neot's.

WILLIAM NICHOL d. 1558

Burned at the stake in his home town of Haverfordwest, he was one of the three Protestant martyrs executed in Wales during Mary Tudor's reign.

NICHOLAS 4th century
December 6
Patron of perfumiers, pawnbrokers, children and Christmas

Not a Welsh saint, but the bishop of Myra (modern Mugla) in Lycia (south-west Turkey). He replaced many Welsh dedications, for example Baruc in Barri, and he became popular in Europe in the 10th century when Pope Urban II arranged for a new church to house his relics in Bari, Italy, an area with a strong Norman influence. Nicholas was said to have given three bags of gold to three virgin sisters to prevent their becoming prostitutes, and it is claimed that this is the origin of Christmas stockings to hold gifts. This was also said to be the origin of the three '*gold*' balls that served as the sign of a pawnbroker. He was the patron of perfumiers, as a strong smell of myrrh came from his shrine. His patronage of children came from his reviving three boys slain by a butcher and pickled in a brine tub. Dutch settlers took this '*Sinter Klaas*' to New Amsterdam, where the legend linked to Nordic folklore of a magician giving presents only to '*good*' children. Hey Presto ! Santa Claus, the fir tree and Christmas came together to give us our modern festival of radical over-indulgence (see Christmas).

It is worth mentioning the church of St Nicholas, on the pilgrim's trail in Pembroke, between the churches of Rhian and Gwyndaf. The real name of the hamlet of St Nicholas is Tremarchog, the 'town of the knights'. However, the church was called 'Ecclesia de Villa Camerarii' in 1287, the church of 'The Chamberlain's Town'. It is a pre-Norman foundation, and its parish contains Trefasser, said to be the birthplace of Asser (Asserius Menevensis) who was the biographer of King Alfred the Great. On the chancel wall is a Celtic stone inscribed *'tunccetace vxsor daari hic iacit' (here lies Tunccetace, wife of Darius)*. Two 'pillar stones', which were found being used as gateposts at Llandruidion Farm are also in the church. One is inscribed '+ *pann*', and the other, now illegible, was noted in the 18th century to be inscribed '*valavitivi.*'

NIDAN 6th century
IDAN
September 30, November 3 in Scotland

The son of Gwrfyw ap Pasgen ab Urien Rheged, he studied in the college of Seiriol at Penmon. Like Ffinnan, he was said to have been a disciple of St Cyndeyrn (Mungo) in North Wales, and he founded Llanidan on the Menai Straits. This Anglesey church was built over a spring, so there was an ever-filling stoup in the now-ruined church. Two hundred yards away, in the grounds of Plas Llanis is Ffynnon Idan, and Nidan was said to have lived at Cadair Idan. The church was replaced by a new one at Bryn Siencyn. He was also said to have accompanied Cyndern (Mungo/Kentigern) to Strathclyde to evangelise the North, where Midmar was founded by him.

Llanidan Church was later dedicated to St Aiden of Lindisfarne, who was possibly misplaced as founder by the Normans. The church contained 'Maen Morddwydd' (the Thigh Stone), possibly a small Bronze Age carved pillar which always returned to its original spot if taken away. Earl Hugh ('the Fat') of Shrewsbury reputedly chained it to a larger rock and dropped it into the sea, but it came back to the church. Gerald of Wales informs us that the Earl then decreed that no-one should be allowed to move the stone, and a protective wall was built around it. Llanidan had Tre'r Dryw Bach stone circle, with twelve stones recorded in 1772. In 1872, there were just two left, one measuring 18 feet high, by 10 feet wide and 2 feet thick. The site can still be seen at Castell Bryn Gwyn. Perthi Cromlech is near Brynsiencyn and a giant is supposed to be buried there. Also just outside Llanidan is Bodowyr Dolmen with a capstone that measured eight feet by six feet.

NINIAN d.432
August 26

A Welsh-speaking Briton from Cumbria, Ninianus became the first bishop of the southern Picts. St Ninian's was a district of Glasgow, and it seems Ninian used as his base the *candida casa*, (white house) at Whithorn, Wigtownshire. This was still part of Celtic Cumbria, and he then may have evangelised the Stirling area. St Ninian's Cave on the Mull of Galloway still has wishes written on paper inserted into its cracks, and small crosses made of driftwood are left there.

NINNOC 6th century
GWENGUSTLE, NINOCHA, CANDIDA, GWENGU, VENGU
June 4, first Sunday in August, second Sunday in May

One of Brychan's children who is said to have became a nun and abbess in Brittany. At Ploemeur she founded the Priory of St Ninnoc. (Ninnoc means 'little nun'). There was a statue of her as an abbess with a stag at her feet, and she was invoked to cure illnesses in children. Ninocha Gwengastel was a Welsh abbess who was remembered at Scaer in Finistere as St Candida, or Gwen, where her feast is the first Sunday in August. At Plouermeur her pardon is the second Sunday in May. Gwengustle became Gwengu, then Vengu, in Brittany. She may be the same saint as Gwen of Cornwall (q.v.). Gilbert gives St Ninocha as the wife of Gwrgan Mawr of Gwent and the mother of Caradog Freichfras and Onbrawst, who married Meurig and was the mother of Arthur.

NOE 6th century?
NOGU, NWY, NEWLYN, NOALA, NOUALEN, NOYAL
April 27, July 6, November 8

She had a chapel, bridge and holy well in Skenfrith in Monmouthshire. This is possibly the same female saint Newlyn (Newelina), who had a holy well at Newlyn in Cornwall, who in turn may be the Breton saint Noyola, killed by a king. The Welsh feast day was April 27, in Newlyn November 8, and the Breton Pardon at Pontivy near Vannes was July 6. Her Breton legend is a replica of Gwenfrewi's, and she may have been the sister of Cybi. There is a Noyal south-west of Vannes, Noyal outside Lamballe and Noyal-Muzillac east of Vannes.

Alphabetical Listing of the Saints of Wales and Religious Events

NON 5th – 6th century
NONNA, NONNITA
Feast day March 3 (also March 2, March 5) June 15 and 25th at Altarnon and Tavistock, and July 3 at Launceston.

Some sources say that she was a noblewoman, the daughter of Gynyr (Cynyr) of Caer Gawch and his wife Anna ferch Gwrthefyr Fendigaid. Rhygyfarch's Life of David states that Non was a nun at Ty Gwyn monastery at Maucan, near Whitesand Bay in Pembrokeshire, who was seduced or raped by Prince Sant (Sandde) and gave birth to St David. Sant ap Ceredig ap Cunedda was the former king of Ceredigion who had possibly become a monk. Other records state that she and Sant were married, but he was never sanctified.

Non seems to have the attributes of the Celtic goddess Anna, Nonna or Dana, mother of the gods and ancestress of Celtic nobility. The cult of St Anne is still strong in Brittany. In the Northern Tradition, she is Nanna, mother of the slain god Balder, and in the Roman deology she is Annona, goddess of the Harvest. This ancient Celtic goddess became St Anne, the mother of Our Lady and the grandmother of Jesus, during the general conversion to Christianity across Europe.

Gildas was said to have lost the power of speech, being overwhelmed with the presence of her unborn baby David. Non left the monastic school when pregnant to live among standing stones

St Non's Chapel, St David's Head.   *CADW: Welsh Historic Monuments. Crown Copyright.*

417

on the cliffs behind Bryn y Garn. The birth was accompanied by thunder and lightning, and the stone upon which she lay was split apart by the force of the birth, leaving the imprint of her hands on it. Part of the stone was later used as the altar slab in her chapel. St Non's Chapel is on the coast of St Bride's Bay, and is where she gave birth to St David. A slab with a ring cross in the ruins has been dated from AD 600-800. David was supposed to have been born dead, but St Ailbe resuscitated him and fostered him.

St Non's Well, near the chapel, sprang from the ground during St David's birth, and the holy waters were said to cure rheumatism, eye illnesses and headaches. George Owen wrote during the reign of Elizabeth I that every St Non's Day people offered pins, stones and the like to the well. In 1811 Fenton wrote *'the fame this consecrated spring had obtained is incredible, and still it is resorted to for many complaints. In my infancy . . . I was often dipped into it, and offerings, however trifling, even of a farthing or a pin, were made after each ablution, and the bottom of the well shone with votive brass. The spring . . . is of a most excellent quality, is reported to ebb and flow, and to be of wondrous efficacy in complaints of the eye.'* To cure a lunatic, he had to be persuaded to stand upon the well wall, then be knocked down into the water. He was then tossed up and down in the water until his strength was sapped, a procedure known as *'bowsenning'*. The madman was then taken to the nearby church for Mass. If he was not cured, the bowsenning was repeated, and so on. The well was restored by the Roman Catholic Church in 1951, re-dedicated, and a pilgrimage made to it.

It appears that Non became a nun after the death of Sant, and moved to Altarnon in Corwall around 527 at the request of her sister St Gwen, where there is also a chapel and well named after her. There is a Celtic cross of this period by the churchyard gate. The insane were also *'precipitated'* into this Altarnon well to cure them. There are also dedications in Pelynt in Cornwall and Bradstone in Devon. Llannerch Aeron and Llansanffraid on Cardigan Bay are dedicated to Non, with the latter formerly being known as Llan Non. There is also a Llan-Non in both Carmarthen and Radnorshire. Carmarthen's Llannon has a fifteen feet high pillar stone known as Bryn Maen, and a holy well Ffynnon Non where the saint drew water. At Ilston in Gower and Eglwys Newydd near Margam Abbey in Glamorgan are two more dedications.

Her tomb survives in Dirinon in Finistere. Her statue is in a niche behind her holy well there. A mystery play, *'Buhez Santes Nonn'* was performed for centuries at Non's pardon in Dirinon. (See Pardon). Within a mile of Dirinon are holy wells dedicated to David and Non. In Brittany Nonna is regarded as a male companion of St David, rather than his mother. In the Irish tradition, Non is the mother of St Mor, the mother of St Eltin, and her other daughter was Magna, the mother of St Setna.

She came to be regarded as the mother of the church in Wales, and as a peace-maker and healer – she is attributed to have said that *'There is nothing more stupid than argument.'* A 1717 'Survey of St David's' recorded that for the first three days of March, dedicated to David, Non and Lily *'if any of the people had been known to work upon any of these Days, it would have been esteemed a very heinous Offence.'*

NONCONFORMIST REVIVAL

Nothing destroyed two thousand years of Welsh culture so much as this semi-Calvinistic phenomenon, which was thoroughly adopted by the Welsh people as the light at the end of their dark tunnel of enslavement and poverty. Folk dance, alcohol, non-religious singing, consorting

Alphabetical Listing of the Saints of Wales and Religious Events

with the opposite sex, etc., etc., were all frowned upon and/or banned. Many customs died out entirely. Whisky production ceased, without which *'Welsh'* rather than *'Scotch'* would be famed all over the world. Nothing sums up this time so much as the fact that the wildly popular John Wesley believed that contagious laughter was the work of the Devil.

Feast days suffered under this semi-Calvinistic dogma - they had been almost wiped out two-hundred years earlier with Henry VIII's break with Rome, and then under Cromwell's Puritan Inter-regnum. Puritans called the Prayer Book *'witchcraft'* and called church services *'witchery, conjuration and sorcery'*. Gerrard Winstanley, the leader of the *'Diggers'*, wanted a *'utopia'* where anyone who professed the trade of preaching and prayer was to be put to death *'as a witch'*. Later, Howel Harris and his cohorts almost killed the remains of Welsh culture with their preaching of enjoyment as a sin. The best response to the doom-laden muscular Christianity which evolved in Wales has been by Wales' most under-rated poet, Idris Davies, in his satirical poem 'Capel Calvin', probably written in the 1920's:

> *'There's holy, holy people*
> *They are in capel bach –*
> *They don't like surpliced choirs,*
> *They don't like Sospan Fach.*
>
> *They don't like Sunday concerts,*
> *Or women playing ball,*
> *They don't like Williams Parry much*
> *Or Shakespeare at all.*
>
> *They don't like beer or bishops,*
> *Or pictures without texts,*
> *They don't like any other*
> *Of the nonconformist sects.*
>
> *And when they go to Heaven*
> *They won't like that too well,*
> *For the music will be sweeter*
> *Than the music played in Hell.*

The cumulative speed with which Nonconformism spread through Wales is amazing. In 1649, a Puritan church was organised at Llanfaches, near Newport, Monmouthshire. In 1659 the first Baptist chapel was at Ilston on the Gower peninsula. The movement grew quietly, and two of the earliest chapels to survive are Llanwenarth Baptist at Govilon, Monmouthshire (1695) and Maesyronnen Independent in Powys (1696). The movement accelerated in the 18th century, and the first Calvinistic Methodist chapel opened in 1742 near Caerphilly, Capel Groes Wen. A fine example from the Teifi Valley, Capel Pen-rhiw, has been re-erected at the Museum of Welsh Life, Cardiff. By the end of the 18th century, there were over a hundred chapels in Wales. However, the 19th century saw Nonconformism outstrip the Anglican church in Wales. A census in 1851 showed 2,784 chapels compared to 1,176 Anglican churches, making Wales probably the country with the most places of Christian worship per head of population in the world. By 1905, there were at least another 2000 chapels in Wales, with well over 5,000 buildings by the start of World War I. However, with the retreat of religion, many have disappeared or are derelict. In the little street the author where spent his childhood in Cadoxton, two chapels have disappeared in the 20th century. Cadw has published an excellent free booklet with suggestions upon keeping these remarkable buildings in use: 'Chapels in Wales: Conservation and Conversion', by John Hilling.

In the 1851 Census, there were over two-thirds of the population of Wales were attending 3,883 places of worship, giving 898,442 seats for a population of only 1,188,914. At this time, Nonconformity had still not spread to places like Merthyr Tydfil. It appears that Independent denominations and Baptists were the favoured chapels in South Wales, while Calvinistic and Wesleyan Methodism were far more popular in North Wales. The author's feeling, as evidenced from the tenor of this book is that religion should not be a grim, severe affair. This drives youngsters away forever. I recently attended a funeral in Barri for a friend's mother I had known for forty-five years. The clergyman informed a packed church that if we did not go to his church we would burn in the flames of hell. The author was trapped for several weeks in Iran after Ayatollah Khomeini ousted the Shah, and feels that fundamentalism has always been the regressive gene in the DNA of any religion. A note from 'The Dictionary of Welsh National Biography' referring to the Calvinistic Methodist,Thomas John (1816-1862) informs us that *'He was a celebrated preacher in his day. His bony, emaciated body, his pallid countenance, and his dramatic and bodeful manner when preaching inspired his congregations with something akin to terror.'* Churches must be joyful places, where one wants to attend and be rejuvenated and refreshed, not frightened.

It must be noted that we have lost hundreds of churches in the last three–hundred years, which is a reason for trying to save the chapels. The sad record of Erasmus Saunders, describing the condition of church buildings in 1721, should act as a warning: *'The desolate appearance of most of these (churches) that are yet standing, speak how difficultly they subsist, and how miserably they are neglected. In some, not only the Bells are taken away, but the Towers are demolished, and in many others there are scarce any Seats, excepting here and there a few ill contriv'd and broken stools and Benches; their little Windows are without Glass, and darken'd with Boards, Matts, or Lettices (lattices); their Roofs decaying, tottering, and leaky; their Walls green, mouldy, and nauseous and very often without Wash or Plaister; and their Floors ridg'd up with noisome Graves without any Pavement and only cover'd with a few Rushes.' ('A View of the State of Religion in the Diocese of St David's').*

A footnote to history is that the spate of chapel-building carried on until the slaughter of the First World War and the terrible Great Depression that followed. What the author did not realise was the untiring attempt of the new churches in Wales to try to keep the Welsh language alive. With the massive immigration into the Welsh steel and coal industries, English was pushing the native language back into the furthest recesses of Wales. In holding on to Welsh services, for all the right reasons, the Church unfortunately lost its grip upon many of the people. It was only by reading this extract by R. Tudur Jones, reprinted in 'Sacred Place, Chosen People' that the author understood the dilemma faced by ministers – it was almost like the times of the Welsh refusing to evangelise the heathen Saxons back in the time of Augustine . . . *Between 1890 and 1911 . . . The majority of the population ceased to speak Welsh. As a result of losing their language, people lost the connection with their own past. And this was not only a matter of losing connection with the religious past. It meant also losing a sense of national identity. For those who knew Welsh, religious services and Sunday school and concerts were a link between them and their national and Christian past. The Christian churches were increasingly forced to bear the responsibility for safeguarding the national tradition and culture . . . Complicity with the state of affairs which considered Welsh a holy language, the language of poets, and English the language of all else was a fatal path for the churches.'*

Alphabetical Listing of the Saints of Wales and Religious Events

'The A-Z of Wales and the Welsh' outlined the problems caused by English 'placemen' in Welsh churches, and Janet Davies has recently reinforced the case that the huge push in numbers attending Methodist and other churches in the 19th century, had been due to the feeling that they were more willing to meet the needs of Welsh-speakers than the Church of England. *'By the late 18th century the upper reaches of the Church of England in Wales had become thoroughly Anglicised.* **No native Welshman was appointed bishop in Wales from the accession of the Hanoverian dynasty in 1714 until 1870**, *and Welsh-speaking clerics, viewed by their superiors as rustics, rarely received a position beyond that of parish clergyman.'* The curate Evan Evans angrily denounced the *'unfit shepherds'* who were driving their flocks into the arms of the Methodists. Davies repeats the tale of Thomas Bowles, a septuagenarian monoglot English appointee to two parishes in Anglesey where only 5 of the 500 parishioners spoke English. When moves were made to oust him, his attorney stated that as *'Wales is a conquered country . . . it is the duty of bishops to promote the English in order to introduce the language.'*

NORTH

'The Old North' used to belong to the Britons, and roughly described the area from a line between Stirling and Loch Lomond, south to include Cumbria, and most of Lancashire and Yorkshire as far as the Humber estuary. This was 'Combrogi', or 'Cumbria', and its lands merged with Wales until the Battle of Chester. Its language was very similar to Welsh, and its kingdoms were Gododdin (the buffer state of the Votadini safeguarding the territories above Hadrian's Wall), Strathclyde (north-west of the Clyde and Stirling) and Rheged (the Brigantes area centred on Yorkshire and Northumberland.) Elmet was a princedom centred on York, and subject to Rheged. Strathclyde was ruled from Dumbarton, with its ecclesiastical centre at Glasgow. Rheged was ruled from Carlisle and included Galloway, Cumbria and Catterick (Cattraeth) in Yorkshire. Gododdin was centred on Edinburgh, controlling the east of Scotland south of the Firth of Forth. From north-west Gododdin (Manaw Gododdin) came Cunedda and his dynasty to Wales. A Gododdin force was annihilated by the Angles at Cattraeth in 600, and with the loss of Edinburgh in 638 the kingdom disappeared. Rheged was subsumed by marriage into Oswiu's Northumbria in 635.

Strathclyde kept its independence for centuries, leading King David 'the Lion' of Scotland to address its people as his **'Welsh subjects'** around 1140. From this area William Wallace (Braveheart) was known as William Wallensis, William the Welshman. Hung, drawn and quartered in 1305, his death was due to lack of support by the Scots nobles led by Robert the Bruce. They did not want a leader from the lower nobility. Wallace's rebellion had been caused by the murder of his wife Marion and his father and brother by the Franco-English, and he became guardian of Scotland following King Edward I deposing John Balliol. According to the *Irish Annals*, 15,000 Strathclyde Welshmen supported King John (Balliol) in 1296. Despite Wallace's great victory at Stirling Bridge (1297), he was defeated by Norman levies of Welsh longbowmen at Falkirk (1298) and betrayed. Robert the Bruce, with a Scots-Norman father and a Welsh mother, is remembered for Bannockburn in 1314 but is a far less attractive 'hero' than Wallace. Again, many of the Strathclyde Welsh fought at Bannockburn for Bruce. The cowardly Edward II fled the field at Bannockburn, and was no warrior like his father. Bruce had actually served the King of England from 1302, after initially supporting Wallace, and he connived in the death of Wallace in 1305. In 1306 Bruce murdered Balliol's nephew and rightful heir to the throne, John Comyn. For this he was excommunicated until 1320. Wallace had never sought the Scottish crown from the Balliols.

NOTOLIUS 5th century

Llanddeusant in northern Carmarthenshire is dedicated to Notolius, and Potolius, the brothers of St Peulin (Peulinus).

NUDD 6th century

A king and saint who studied at Llaniltud Fawr is supposed to have founded Llysfronydd, now known as Llysworney, in the Vale of Glamorgan, which is now dedicated to Tudful. Iolo Morganwg mentions two persons by this name. Nudd ap Ceidio ab Arthwys, the brother of Gwenddoleu and Cof, is said to have died at the battle of Arderydd in 573. Nudd Hael ap Senyllt died in the North, and a 6th century stone in Selkirk with the names Nudus and Liberalis may commemorate him. Llysworney seems to be a corruption of Llys y Bro Nudd, the Court of the Vale of Nudd. Iolo says that Nudd Hael had his court here. However the author has seen a different derivation of Llyswrinydd, the Court (Llys) of the cantref of Gwrinydd. (See Gwrin).

NWYTHEN 6th century
NOETHON
October 22, 23, 24 (with his brother Gwynog)

This son of Gildas was a monk at Llancarfan and Llanilltud Fawr, and the father of Cynddilig, Teilo Ferwallt and Rhun. There was a chapel at Llangwm Deiniol in Denbigh to Nwythen and Gwynog. He is mentioned in the tale of Culhwch and Olwen. His brothers were the saints Cenydd, Aidan (Maidoc), Dolgan and Gwynno (Gwynog). According to Geoffrey of Monmouth, Nwython's brothers Rhun and Cynddilig were summoned by Arthur to his coronation at Caerleon. Some sources also say that Nwythen was a son of Dunawd Fawr and therefore the brother of Deiniol. (The brother of Deiniol was also said to be the 'Black Knight' of Arthurian romances, Sir Breunor). One of Arthur's knights was 'Nwython'.

The Welsh term for the *'Pipes of Pan'* is *'Pibau Bugeilior'*, or *'pipes of the shepherd'*. However, an old phrase used was *'pibau Nwython'*.

NYFAIN 5th – 6th century
NEFYN, NYVEN, NUVIEN
August 13, 14, 15 and March 24

Possibly a daughter of Brychan, the wife of Cynfarch Gul ap Meirchion (or Cynfarch Oer) and mother of Urien Rheged by Caradog Freichfras. Nefyn is possibly not her dedication, however. There was a festival there upon August 15, and fairs at Llanfair yn Nefyn on August 13 - 15 and March 24. (Could she also be Nefydd?)

At Crick, just a mile east of the Roman town of Caerwent (Venta Silurum), is a private barn with a medieval window, in the yard of Crick Manor. This used to be a chapel dedicated to St Nyven, which later came under the jurisdiction of Llandaf Cathedral. In Crick manor house King Charles I dined after his defeat at Naseby, before moving on to Raglan Castle. A record that it is in 'Mamouric', i.e. Meurig's place, dates the chapel to the time of Meurig ap Tewdrig.

O

> '*Our revels now are ended. These our actors,*
> *As I foretold you, were all spirits and*
> *Are melted into air, into thin air:*
> *And, like the baseless fabric of this vision,*
> *The cloud-capp'd towers, the gorgeous palaces,*
> *The solemn temples, the great globe itself,*
> *Yea, all which it inherit, shall dissolve*
> *And, like this insubstantial pageant faded,*
> *Leave not a rack behind. We are such stuff*
> *As dreams are made on, and our little life*
> *Is rounded with sleep.'*
>
> **William Shakespeare, 'The Tempest'**

ONBRIT

Merthyr Onbrit has been placed around Fairwater and Llandaf in modern Cardiff – nothing else is known of this saint.

ORDERS OF WELSH SAINTS

The First Order of holy men are the bishops, some of the earliest Celtic saints, who seemed to have a roving comission to evangelise in their areas of Wales. David and Dyfrig can be included in this class. The Second Order were the men in charge of the great monastic houses, where monks were trained. Cadog, Teilo, Padarn, Seiriol, Cybi, Tathan and Illtud can be included here. The Third Order were the 'peregrini' such as Pedrog, the wandering holy men who roamed across Corwall, Wales, Ireland, Scotland, Brittany and possibly Galicia, spreading Celtic Christianity and often seeking a lonely site to set up a hermitage.

OSWALD 604-642
OSWALLT
August 5

The Anglian King of Northumbria was martyred at Oswestry (Croes-Oswallt) and is remembered there, just over the present border in Shropshire but under the see of St Asaf. The church is only smaller than Ludlow of all the old 'Border' parish churches. In 634 King Oswald had defeated the Celtic King Cadwallan at Heavenfield near Hadrian's Wall. At the age of 38 he was killed at Masefield in present-day Shropshire by the Mercian army of Penda, avenging his ally Cadwallan. Oswald's body was dismembered, but his brother Oswy later retrieved the head and hands which he took back to Lindisfarne and Bamburgh castle respectively. An eagle took one of his arms and where it dropped King Oswald's Well bubbled forth, a place of pilgrimage renowned for healing. St Aidan, when he had originally blessed Oswald, said '*may this hand never wither with age.*' One arm was '*uncorrupted*' for almost a millennium until it was destroyed in the Reformation. A wooden hand in Oswald's church at Lower Peover near Knutsford in Cheshire is a medieval *'glove'* used to indicate that a free-trading fair was under way. Ffynnon Oswallt was a famous healing well in Whitford, Flintshire. It was situated in a field known as Aelod Oswald (Oswald's Limb), the name commemorating the king's dismemberment.

At Grasmere in Cumbria, the famous August 5 *'rushbearing'* ceremony takes place. Children assemble at 3 p.m. carrying hand-made bearings woven from wild flowers and rushes, including Oswald's 'hand', a serpent on a pole, and a 'Moses-in-a-basket'. After a parade, open-air service and church service, the children are given 20p and a ginger-bread biscuit marked St Oswald. These special biscuits with a secret recipe replace the former 'payment' of strong beer. Rushbearing was an ancient tradition whereby parishioners used to strew hay in churches when they had no floor-boards, with just packed earth or clay floors over the recently interred. Oswald is also commemorated in Jeffreyston, Pembrokeshire. Other Anglo-Saxon saints, to whom churches have been dedicated in Wales, are Edward, Edith, Edmund, Ina, Kenelm, Milburg, Tecla and Tetta.

Wilfred Owen's father was the station-master at Oswestry, and it is an excellent place from which to ancient hill camps, and Offa's Dyke and Wat's Dyke. The large church is well worth visiting, and has a monument to one of the Welsh Yale family which founded Yale Universtiy in America. At the church gates is the 'Coach and Dogs' restaurant. This beautiful 17th century building belong to the last Lloyd of Llanforda who travelled in a light carriage which was pulled by four dogs. Worcester Cathedral used stone from St Oswald's Benedictine priory in the town, for building in 961, and records show a Bishop of Worcester back in 680.

OUDOCEUS see EUDDOGWY

OWAIN AP BELI AP NWYTHON fl. 624

Probably not a saint, but a poem interpolated in the 'Gododdin' refers to the Battle of Strathclyde in 624, where he defeated the Goidel King Dyfnwal Frych:
'I saw an array, they came from the headland,
And splendidly they bore themselves around the great fire.
I saw two war-bands, which came swiftly from their town,
Having arisen on the orders of the grandson of Nwython.
I saw great strong men, they came with the dawn;
And the head of Dyfnwal Frych, ravens gnawed on it.'

OWAIN FINDDU ap MACSEN WLEDIG 4th – 5th century

Not regarded as a saint, but there is a St Owen's in Gloucester. Owain's great grand-parents were Macsen Wledig and Elen Lluyddog, he was the father of St Madog, and his brothers were Ednyfed, Cystennin and Peblig. Some say that he stayed in Britain with his mother when the legions left. The Triads state that Britain was restored under him after the Romans, and that he is buried at Bedd Owain at Dinas Ffaraon (Dinas Emrys) near Beddgelert. It seems that Owain took control of Cernyw (east Glamorgan and west Monmouth). He was killed by a giant Goidel (Irishman) whom Owain also slew in the combat.

A 'Song of the Graves' tells us that that this sub-king of Glwysywg lies in Llanhilleth (Llanheledd), Illtud's church:
*'Having worn robes of red, brown and white colour,
And ridden fine and handsome steeds,
Owain has his own grave in Llanheledd.'*
It may be that red is the warrior's colour, white that of the druid/lawmaker, and brown that of the Christian monk's robe.

Another Welsh 'prince', Owain ap Cyllin, was supposed to have been taken captive by the Romans, but was brought back home to be buried and supposedly regarded as a saint. The provenance of this latter Owain is unknown to the author at present (see Cyllin).

OWAIN ab URIEN RHEGED 6th century

Owain was king of North Rheged and a warrior who was said to have founded Aberllychwr (modern Loughor, where the Romans had a camp). He is supposed to be buried there, when it was known by its other name of Llanmorfael. Brân Fendigaid is supposed to have founded that church (thus linking mythology again with the Romans). Owain was the father of Cyndeyrn (Kentigern) according to the 'Bonedd y Sant'. Not regarded as a saint, but St Owen's in Gloucester* could have been his foundation, or that of Euny (Ewin), Hewyn (Henwyn) or Owen (Owini).

William Newport, vicar of St Owen's in Gloucester, practised divination of a guilty party by *'key and book'* in 1551. He inserted a key into a Bible, along with a list of the names of suspects for a theft. He then invoked invoked the Father, Son and Holy Ghost, bidding the key to turn when he reached the name of the thief. It turned when he pronounced *'Margaret Greenhill'*, whence the participants left the church to search her belongings and bedstraw for the stolen property. Different methods of *'divination by key and book'* were practised in rural areas of Wales and its border country up to the 19th century.

In Pembrokeshire were three holy wells known as Ffynnon Owen, in the parishes of Llandysul, Llanerchaeron and Tremain. There was also St Owen's Well in Narberth, and Ffynnon Owen in Llysfaen, Caernarfon. A mile north of Gorslas in Glamorgan is Llyn Llech Owain. The pool covers the site of a magic well, which would never run dry as long as the stone slab cover was replaced after water had been drawn. Owain, one of Arthur's knights, fell asleep after drinking, and awoke to find the well overflowing and the countryside flooding. He leapt onto his charger, and rode around the edge of the flood waters, which stopped encroaching when they touched the hooves of his horse. Owain is said to have been so ashamed at what he had done that he rode off with his men to a cave at Craig y Ddinas near Llandybie. They are sleeping there until Wales needs them again. Llyn Llech Owain park, lake and peat bog are a SSSI, with Bogbean, Snipe, Dabchick and Green Woodpecker to be seen. Cerrig Meibion Owen ('the stones of the sons of Owen') are two prehistoric stones on the Preseli mountains.

Owain was said to be a giant at Arthur's court, the son of Sir Urience. His great rivalry with Arthur is shown in the Dream of Rhonabwy where they played Gwyddbyll (a form of Celtic chess). Chretien de Troyes' 'Yvain' is based upon Owain. He killed King Theodoric Flamddwyn (Flame-bearer) of Bernicia at Argoed Llwyfain (Leeming Lane in Yorkshire). After Urien Rheged's assassination, Owain only held Rheged for a short time against the forces of Gwallawg, Dunaut and Morcant, the latter who planned Urien's death. Owain fell at Cattraeth

(Catterick) and Northumbria was lost forever by the British. It is said that Owain is buried either at Llan-Forfael (Loughor) or Lan-Heledd (Llanhilleth).

*Hereford has St Peter's Church, from where the Marcher Lord Walter de Lacy fell to his death from the battlements when inspecting his church in 1085. The wonderful cathedral has the tomb of St Thomas of Hereford (1218 - 1282), and the wonderful Chained Library of 1444 books, the largest such library in the world. Of course the 1289 Mappa Mundi must be seen, but also it contains the superb 14th century illustrated manuscript, the 'Decretals of Gratian'. From Castle Green in Hereford, one can walk past the duck pool that once was a part of the castle moat, through St Ethelbert Street to St Owen Street. It may be that the cathedral is on the site of St Owen's Celtic foundation. Where St Owen's Gate used to stand in the city walls is an old pub called The Barrels. Across its courtyard, in the former stables, the excellent Wye Valley Brewery produces reasonably priced real ales. One can also drink real ciders in the pub.

Many of the small cider-makers on the Welsh borders use old variety apples from ancient Welsh orchards. Local cider, beer and mead manufacture can help stimulate the Welsh economy in agricultural areas in the long term. The Cwm Deri Vineyard at Martletwy, Pembrokeshire, and Maesmor Meadery at Corwen near Llangollen produce ranges of flavoured meads. The author has recently made mead ale (honey beer) using local honey and discovered a list of a hundred 17th century recipes by the Elizabethan courtier Sir Kenelm Digby. One of the most attractive recipes was a 'light mead' made for the Queen Mother in 1699: *'Take 18 quarts of spring water, and one quart of honey. When the water is warm put the honey into it. When it boils, skim well and keep skimming any scum that rises. Then put in a thinly sliced root of ginger, four cloves and a small sprig of rosemary and boil for an hour. When the mead liquor cools to blood temperature, put in a spoonful of ale-yeast, and put in a suitably-sized vessel to ferment. After two or three days bottle and drink it after six weeks to two months.'* There must be a market for organically produced drinks like this, made from Welsh ingredients.

A writer in 1911 noted that *'it is a great blessing . . . that this trade has disappeared and we hope that the day is not too far removed when the business will be but history in all our towns and villages'*, regarding the closure of a cider brewery in Sennybridge. However, even in the 1930's a Methodist minister at Trefeca took as his sermon's theme *'Brecknockshire - the cider-besotten county.'* J. Geraint Jenkins describes the Brecon method of making cider in his excellent book on rural Wales. He notes the travelling cider makers (still in existence in Brittany) who would crush the apples, a method employed by the New Inn at Talgarth, near Brecon *'the last Welsh public house at which cider was made.'* Monmouth, Radnor and Brecon farmers could plant new orchards of the old varieties of apple and pear as an alternative source of income in these difficult times.

OWAIN ap MORGAN HEN 10th century
August 14

This prince built the chapel and castle at Ystrad Owen outside Cowbridge. The church there is dedicated to him, with a parish feast day of August 14.

NICHOLAS OWEN d.1606
February 2, October 25, March 22 or 2 (Catholic Online Saints)

The eldest son of a Welsh Catholic family in Oxford. A lay brother in 1580, and then a full member of the Jesuits from 1590, from 1587 he was the principal maker of priest-holes in England to save the lives of priests and laymen. In 1594 he was arrested with Father John Gerard, but under prolonged torture revealed no names of Catholic colleagues. His release was procured by a ransom from a wealthy Catholic supporter. Often captured and tortured, he never revealed anything, and engineered the great escape of Father Gerard from the Tower of London in 1597. Owen was known as 'Little John' because of his large stature. In 1606, in the aftermath of the Gunpowder Plot, he gave himself up after four days in hiding at Hinlip Hall, to draw away the search from Fathers Garnet and Oldcorne, and Brother Ashley. The searchers had already discovered no less than eleven priest-holes in the property, but no priests. However, County Sheriff Sir Henry Bromley persisted, and four days later discovered the other priests.

Owen was ruptured during his final torture, which legally should have exempted him from further punishment, but the torturers fitted him into an iron girdle before continuing. He still revealed nothing, and *'his bowels burst out'*. His death in the Tower of London was reported as 'suicide' by the Council. His life is an absolutely fascinating story of a pure and brave man – he also served Father Campion – and deserves a good biographer. Of his three brothers, two also became priests, and one a Catholic printer. Fine examples of his work can be seen in Broadoaks (Essex), Hinlip Hall and Huddington Court (Hereford and Worcester), Harrowden (Northants) and Sawston Hall (Cambridge). For 26 years he had built these priest-holes in secret, at night, with muffled tools so as not to alert household members, who might inform the authorities. One installation involved a revolving floor as well as hidden doors. He was canonized in 1970.

P

*'Progress, far from consisting in change, depends on retentiveness. . .
Those who cannot remember the past are condemned to fulfil it.'*
George Santayana, 'Life of Reason', 1906

PABAI 5th – 6th century
PABIAN, PABIEL

A son of Brychan who went to Spain (Galicia?), also known as Papai, Pianno, Pivalus and Pabiali (see Neffei).

PABO POST PRYDAIN d. 530
November 9

This King Pabo 'Pillar of the Britons' was a king in Cumbria who fought a rearguard action against the invading Picts on one side and Saxons on the other. When eventually defeated, he fled to Wales and became a monk on the holy island of Anglesey, where Llanbabo was his foundation. Cyngen ap Cadell had received him and also given him and his family lands in Powys. His father was Arthwys ap Mar ap Ceneu ap Coel. His sons by Gwenaseth were the saints Sawyl Penuchel, Cerwydd and Dunawd Fawr. At Llanbabo a sculptured slab, said to show his effigy, reads
HIC JACET PABO POST PRUD CORPORS . . . TE . . . PRIMA.

The stone was found by a gravedigger in the reign of Charles II, six feet down in the earth. (When recounting the fortuitous discovery of the stones at Llanilltud Fawr also, it must be worthwhile making a non-intrusive electronic survey of all the ancient church grounds in Wales.) There is a similarly designed stone in the church of Llaniestyn, dating from the 5th or 6th century. There is a tradition is that Pabo and his queen were buried at nearby Llanerchymedd. Near Bodeiniol Farm, Llanbabo is an eight-foot standing stone. There are places named Lambabu, St Pabu, Pabu and Kerbabu in Brittany, but it is not yet known whether they are linked to Pabo. Lan pabo in Brittany is dedicated to Tudwal.

PACIFISM

In five years of writing 'The A-Z of Wales and the Welsh', the author came to realise the Christian socialist-pacifist nature of the Welsh people, and how this process developed over 1900 years. In researching this book, there are two quotations which must be included to demonstrate how important pacifism is to the concept of Welsh nationhood, and to show why an abhorrent festering situation like that in Ireland has never happened in Wales in the last century. Christianity of the purest kind intertwines socialism, community, justice, nationhood, language and pacifism in Wales, like a strand of DNA in the genetic make-up of its people. Wales is not a violent nation, even when alcohol is involved, compared to many places on earth. Many communities still leave their doors unlocked. It has always voted away from right-wing parties, much to the detriment of its economic health. The Laws of Hywel Dda of over a millennium ago were the most enlightened in the world until the present day. Women were treated as equals, and if someone stole because he was hungry, it was no crime. Wales has kept the oldest language in Europe alive and thriving by co-operation rather than aggression. There is a groundswell of nationalism in Wales now, at the turn of the millennium, but it is of the 'at last' variety, rather than 'we want it now.' Wales has accepted its fate, and its place in the natural order of affairs. There is a life-cycle to every organism, and the organism of Welsh nationhood is emerging, after being buried as a chrysalis since the success of Henry Tudor in attaining the crown of England. Its time seems to have come, as Welsh people realise that their problems have grown immensely over the past two decades.

Emrys ap Iwan (1851-1906) was a 'founding-father' of Welsh nationalism, and his sermon 'The Old and New Teachings' is instructive.
'Remember that God who made men also ordained nations; to destroy a nation is only one grade less of a disaster than to destroy the whole of mankind, and to destroy the language of a nation one grade less of a disaster than to destroy the nation itself . . . It pleased God to reveal that he made people as nations . . . Remember that you are people of the same blood as the English and the Boers and the Kaffirs and the Chinese. Be therefore ready to render them all the rights that you would wish for yourselves. Remember also that you are a nation, through God's ordinance. Do therefore all you can to maintain the nation as a nation, by maintaining its language, and all other valuable things that may pertain to it. If you are not faithful to your country and your language and your nation, how can you expect to be faithful to God and humanity? Do not be ashamed of those things which distinguish you from other nations; and if you wish to imitate the nation next to you, imitate her in those things in which she excels, but not in her pride, her arrogance, her boastfulness, her love of war, her frivolity, her narrowness of thought and her lack of sympathy with other nations.'

And the former leader of Plaid Cymru, Gwynfor Evans, commented:
'The fact is that the character of nationalism varies from country to country, and that there are two different kinds of nationalism competing for the commitment of the Welsh people, namely Welsh nationalism and the nationalism of the British political parties, (nationalisms which are) respectively pacifistic, moderate and non-violent, anti-militaristic and anti-imperialist, and that of nations of great military power, militaristic and imperialist . . . The campaign for freedom and justice for Wales is part of the campaign for world peace which is so important for humanity, and it is all part of the campaign for the Kingdom of God. The Welsh Christian's place is in the pacifist movement.' (1972, 'Gwinllan a Roddwyd' ed. D. E. Davies).

BISHOP PADARN 5th-6th century
PATERNUS, PATERN
April 15, 16, 17, 20, May 15 (also June 20, September 23 and November 1)

From south-east Wales, he studied at Llancarfan and founded Llanbadarn Fawr near Aberystwyth where he was abbot and bishop for twenty years. Some sources say that he was a Breton, the son of Pedrwn ab Emyr Lydaw, and studied at Llanilltud Fawr from 516. Most of his churches are on the tracks of the old Roman roads. His brothers were Amwn Ddu and Umbrafael and his sister Gwen Tierbron. Local tradition is that he was the brother of St Samson, which makes him a son rather than grandson of Emyr Llydaw. The late 'Vita' tells us he was a Letavian, from Llydaw, or Brittany. Trefeglwys in Cardiganshire was formerly called Llanbadarn Fach. At Trefeglwys Llanbadarn (Cardigan), the *'ceffyl pren'* approached an offender in 1834. He drew his knife on the procession, and was consequently beaten up so badly that he died.

Padarn's churches are also at Pencarreg, Y Creuddyn, Llanbadarn Odwyn (or Odin) near Llangeithio, Llanbadarn Fynydd under Llanbister in central Radnorshire and Llanbadarn y Garreg under Creguna in south Radnorshire. Ffynnon Badarn near Aberllwyenfi in Montgomery is his. In his church at Llanbadarn Fawr is an impressive freestanding cross, brought in from the churchyard in the 1890's. It once stood around eight feet above ground level, and has Celtic ribbon decoration and a key-and-fret pattern wheelhead, with portraits of Christ and Mary. It was hewn from solid rock on the Llŷn Peninsula, and somehow transported to Aberystwyth in Cardiganshire around 1300 years ago. It is called Carreg Samson, and the legend is that Samson threw it from Pen Dinas. Another Celtic cross can also be seen here. At Llanbadarn Fynydd is Banc Du Stone Circle, sixty feet across, but only 5 out of 19 stones remain.

The very important monastery at Llanbadarn was ransacked by Saxons in 720 (along with St David's and Llandaf), after which there is little record of the great centre of learning, and the diocese was eventually annexed by St David's. Previously Llanbadarn had absorbed the see of Llanafan. Sulien wrote that Padarn ruled the see of Llanbadarn for 21 years. Like many Welsh saints of this period, Padarn argued with Maelgwn Gwynedd, and also with Arthur. The legend concerning Maelgwn was that the king sent two servants with sacks of treasure for safekeeping at Llanbadarn Fawr. Later, the servants came to take them back to Maelgwn, but the king found them full of rubble and moss. Padarn decided to submit with the servants to a test of boiling water. All three submerged their hands and the servants were badly scalded, proving Padarn's innocence. Maelgwn was struck blind, after he confessed that he had wanted an excuse to plunder church lands. Padarn gave him back his sight in return for all the lands between the Rheidol and the Clarach rivers.

Sarn Badarn stretches out into the Irish Sea, and there was a chapel near the lake at Dolbadarn. The evocative castle at Dolbadarn features strongly in Welsh history. It was here that Llywelyn the Last imprisoned his elder brother Owain ap Gruffud (Owain Goch) for twenty years. This castle of the Welsh princes was later stripped of its woodwork by King Edward for Caernarfon, the grandest of his *'Iron Ring'* of castles built to strangle Gwynedd. (It was fitting that the investiture of a foreign 'prince' Charles, with no Welsh [or English] bloodline of any significance, should be crowned 'Prince of Wales' in a castle built to repress the Welsh). Later, that greatest of all Welsh heroes, Owain Glyndŵr, imprisoned the disgusting Reginald de Gray of Ruthin at Dolbadarn, while awaiting his ransom.

Padarn is said to have moved to Brittany to become Bishop of Vannes, but he argued with the Armorican bishops and retired to live with the Franks. He is recorded as having attended the Council of Paris in 557, towards the end of his life. Around this time Padarn was commended as an abbot and bishop by Venantius Fortunatus, his contemporary. He died on April 20, was consecrated Bishop of Vannes on June 20, and November 1 marks his reconciliation with the Armorican bishops, which explains his three recorded remembrance days. His 'Saying of the Wise' is *'what man does, God will judge.'*

The sixth century monastery that Padarn founded *'would be made up of a dozen or so monks under the supervision of an Abbot. . . . All the monks took a vow of perfection, which included humility, obedience, almsgiving and charity. They lived in individual beehive-shaped cells and not in a single building. In addition to the monks' cells there was a little wooden, wattle and daub church, a special cell for the Abbot, a hospice or lodgings for visitors, and a kiln for drying corn before it was sent to the mill.'* (Euros Bowen, 'History of Llanbadarn Fawr'). There would also have probably been some sort of distillery and a brewing area.

There is a tradition that Dafydd ap Gwilym, one of the greatest mediaeval poets in Europe, was baptised in the church font at Llanbadarn. A plaque on the floor in the choir commemorates the great Lewis Morris (1701-1765), *'the prime mover in the classical revival of Welsh learning and writing during the 18th century' ('Oxford Companion to the Literature of Wales')*. There were two holy wells named Ffynnon Badarn in Cardigan. One was in a field named Pistyll Padarn next to Llanbadarn Road, Aberystwyth, and the other near Penuwch in Llangeitho parish. Another was at Mynydd Ffynnon Badarn in Merioneth.

PADOG

There may be a saint of this name remembered at Llanbadock near Usk, but the church is dedicated to Madog.

PADRIG ab ALFRYD late 6th century
March 17

This son of Alfryd ap Goronwy ap Gwdion was a saint at Cybi's monastery in Anglesey, and founded Llanbadrig on the island. He was wrecked at Little Mouse Island, Ynys Padrig, on his return from visiting Iona, and built the church there to commemorate his escape. Ffynnon Badrig is near the cliffs – his niche can still be seen. The spring was medicinal, especially for children's illnesses. Local place-names include Dinas Badrig, Rhos Badrig, Porth Badrig, Pen Padrig as well as Ynys Badrig. His brothers were the saints Meigan, Cyfyllog and Garmon. At Llanbadrig, the Gwylmabsant took the form of a fair that replaced the traditional football game in the late 18th century. Ffynnon Badrog in Llanenddwyn cured children's ailments, and its waters were used in the fonts at Llanenddwyn and Llanwywe. His story, like his feast date, is interlinked with that of Padrig of Ireland.

PADRIG c.390-461
PATRICK
March 17

Born in Bannaviem Tabarniae*, Bannventa, possibly modern Banwen near Neath, (near the village of 'Enon') he was the grandson of a priest named Potitus, and the son of a deacon and decurio (town councillor) called Calpurnius. Padrig was captured as a 16-year-old by Irish pirates organised by the (pagan) High King of Ireland. He was treated as a slave by a Pict in Antrim for six years. Padrig either escaped or was freed, returned to Wales, received some training as a priest, and returned to Ireland around 430-433. From his Armagh base, he wrote the first literature identified with the early British church, following the simple Welsh monastic life and attempting to abolish paganism and sun-worship.

Another version is that Saint Patrick was born in Pembrokeshire in 389, and was carried off by Irish raiders in 406, becoming Bishop of Armagh in 432, being consecrated by St Garmon at Auxerre. Recent evidence seems to point to his birth in Banwen. In St. Patrick's 'Confessio' he states he was born at Banaven Taberiar, a small-holding near a Roman fort, which could be Tafarn-y-Banwen, a farm near an old Roman stronghold. This is also on the strategically important Sarn Helen, once a major Roman road through Wales. Local tradition says that Patrick came from Banwen, and there are placenames such as *'Hafod Gwyddelig' ('Irish Summerhouse')* and a *'Nant Gwyddelig' ('Irish Stream')*. George Brinley Evans also points to the nearby Hirfynydd Stone, the extremely rare early Christian carving of a man in prayer, surrounded by Irish symbolic patterns. (Note that *'Gwyddelig'*, the Welsh for *'Irish'*, is identical to *'Goidelic'*). The Welsh were the Brythonic Celts, and the Irish were the Goidelic Celts). Cressy states that Patrick was born in Glyn Rosina, the valley of St Davids, in 361, and died at Glastonbury in 472, aged 111. (Iolo Morganwg also names a Padrig as the son of Maewan, Principal of the monastery at Bangor Illtud, who was carried away by Irish pirates.) Evans, in his 'History of Glamorgan', tells us:

'. . . other writers doubt the existence of Eurgain, but all agree that a college was founded by the Roman General Theodosius (called by the Welsh, Tewdws) some time between the years 368 and 395 AD. The principal and chief teacher of this college (Llanilltud), now called Côr Tewdws, was one Balerius, a learned Roman Christian. He was succeeded by Patrick, a native of Glamorgan, and a former student of the college. The college prospered exceedingly until it was attacked, despoiled, and destroyed by some Irish pirates, who, when they retired, carried Patrick with them a prisoner. Patrick continued his good work in Ireland, preaching the Gospel boldly, and he is still loved by the Irish as their Patron Saint.'

Eisteddfa Padrig is a chair-like rock in the sea cliffs of Pembrokeshire near St David's cathedral, where God showed Padrig the view of Ireland and told him that it was now all in Padrig's care (see Dewi). An angel had told Padrig that he could not settle at Glyn Rhosyn, as that place was reserved for David's birth in thirty years' time. Under the sandy shoreline of Whitesands Bay lies the sixth century St Patrick's Chapel, which itself lies upon an older burial ground. A rectangular mound now stands in the field called Parc-y-Capel near the shore. Excavated in 1924, it is a single cell chapel with human remains below the west wall. There is a nearby rock called Carn Patrick. There was also a Paterchurch, or Patrickchurch, in Monkton, Pembrokeshire. One of the gates to St David's Cathedral is still known as Porth Padrig. Cefn Padrig is a ridge of coastline between Burry Port and Llanelli.

Pawl Hen traditionally founded the great monastery at Whitland in Carmarthen, variously known as Alba, Rosnat or Tŷ Gwyn (being whitewashed), but some say that it was founded by Padrig before he went to Ireland. Perhaps Pawl Hen founded the famous school there in Patrick's monastery, which would explain the large numbers of Irish monks said to have studied there.

*In preparing a book upon St Tathan, the author discovered another link with Wales, recorded by Marie Trevelyan in 1910. Padrig was known as Maenwyn (Holy Rock) and educated at Caerworgan (Llanilltud), where the Latin honorary name of Patricius was given to him. A very old folk lament was remembered by two people who lived far apart. The lament was sung at 'Mal (sic) Santau' and was familiar at the firesides of Penmark, St Tathan and Llanilltud Fawr in the 19th century. A boy named Maenwyn was born at Nant-y-Tirion, Treberfaydd (Boverton), who was caught in a nearby bog when the Goidels (Irish Picts) burned Caerworgan. Another antiquarian states that Maenwyn was born at the village of Pedr Onen (Peter's Ash), now called Broadway, near Bonafon (Cowbridge).

PALLADIUS see BELERIUS

PARDON

In Brittany the *'Lann'* was the mother-church, corresponding with the ancient holy site, or *'llan'*, in Wales. Subject to a lann were *'treves'* (compare the Welsh *'tref'*, or small town), each with its own chapel, but served by the mother church. With Viking attacks and civil wars, many of the old lanns were renamed simply after their founder, or replaced with the term *'plou'* (the centre of a tribal settlement). Thus Lann Arthmael became Ploermel. However, many Breton names are still prefixed *'loc'*, which was the place of retreat for Lent, or hermitage, associated with a saint. Each chapel in a parish or plou had a story associated with a saint. Although some were only used once or twice a year, a festivity (*'fest noz'*, evening festival) was associated with all of them, usually on the local saint's feast day. This was the feast of the patron saint, or Pardon, often centred on some magnificent crosses or monumental calvaries.

From the Cyber © Ouest Vannes internet site, the author has translated the following explanation:

*'**Pardons** – a remarkable expression of Breton folk lore. From the 15th century, with the construction of churches, the 'fest noz' is celebrated by the selling of crepes and cider, by dance and folk groups, and by processions of local people in the costume of the area. The wonderful high lace bonnets vary from town to town.*

Principal pardons are celebrated as follows:
S Yves at Treguier – 3rd Sunday in May
S Pierre and S Paul at Plouguerneau – last Sunday in June
Ste Barbe at Le Faouet – last Sunday in June
Notre Dame de Bon Secours at Guincamp – 1st Sunday in July
Notre Dame du Roc at Montautour – 1st Sunday in July
Petite Tromenie at Locronan – 2nd Sunday in July
Ste Anne d'Auray at Sainte-Anne d'Auray – 26th July
S Guenole (St Gwenole) at Batz-sur-Mer – 1st Sunday in August
Querrien at Loudeac – 15th August
Notre Dame de la Joie at Penmarc'h – 15th August
Tromenie de Haute-Bretagne at Becherel – 15th August
Pardon de la Vierge at Mont-Dol – 15th August
Pardon de la Mer at St-Suliac – 15th August
Notre Dame de Quelven at Guern – 15th August
Notre Dame de la Tronchaye at Rochefort-en-Terre – 3rd Sunday in August
Ste-Anne-la-Palud at Plonevez-Porzay – last Sunday in August
Pardon de La Baule – last Sunday in August
Notre Dame de Folgoet at Foelgoet – 1st Sunday in September
Notre Dame du Roncier at Josselin – 7th and 8th September
Notre Dame de Grand Puissance at Lamballe – 8th September
Pelerinage de Notre Dame de La Peiniere at Saint-Didier – first ''of September
Notre Dame du Voeu at Hennebont – 3rd Sunday in September
Notre Dame des Marais at Fougeres – 1st weekend in October

There are literally hundreds of other, less splendid, pardons and festivities associated with local saints, and the custom could easily be replicated in Wales. One problem is that some local churchmen in Wales are not too proactive in arresting the decline of the Christian faith and its social and moral values. To reactivate feast days, feast weeks and pride in the local community needs deep dedication, hard work and leadership. Some clerics prefer to rely on the word of the

Bible to speak for itself, and passively watch the concept of communal society decline. Churches should not be dotted about with a few grey-haired widows, using it as an insurance policy to go to Heaven, but must become thriving centres of community for all ages. Clerics could lead in activating local fairs and festivities, as outlined in Chapter 4 of this book. Some, like Patrick Thomas of St Teilo's Church in Brechfa, are leading by example. Wales has to help itself to reinvigorate the economy and offer tourists something to see all the year round. If the church takes no lead, it will be left further behind, drowning in the wake of society's direction. It is not enough to spend one's time upon administration and contemplation when traditional Christianity is dying. Evangelism - telling people what they should be doing - is no answer when society has moved on from blind acceptance of one's superiors. The church has to compete with all that is on offer for people's precious time today. A start would be for the church to be accepted as a necessary part of the community, helping the community to develop socially. Too many people retreat into their homes these days, and rely upon the electronic media for too much of their leisure time.

There has rightly been much debate about the lack of a Christian focus in the British government's obscene expenditure on the Millennium Dome*. Most people are not able to afford to travel to, and stay in London overnight, let alone enter the Dome, which was originally supposed to be celebrating two millennia of Christ's ministry. The author's point is that, unless the church in Wales commits itself to help Wales, there will probably be no debate in another Millennium – Christianity will be dead in Wales, the country where it has existed without interruption for longer than any other place in Europe. Perhaps this does not matter to church leaders who believe they are going to Heaven. However, if they wish to resuscitate ethics, morals and family values across Wales to last for another Millennium, they must act now, and not by forming committees to address problems. Committees kill responsibilities – it is the duty of every Welsh churchman, whether he be Catholic or Protestant, to lead all his local community, not to minister to 3% of it.

*Apart from the well-documented fiasco of the opening of the Dome on New Year's Eve, 1999, we can see that the general public is actively shunning it, and that its operations are being taken over by the Alton Towers operators. The Dome sucked in almost half of the £2 billion that the Millennium Commission paid out. It broke the rules by taking £399 million more in public funding than could be matched by industry (creative accounting made this look 'better' than £400,000,000. Another £40 million had to be 'loaned' before it opened, and a few weeks later, in January 2000, another £60 million was 'found' for yet another loan. Money will constantly be diverted to this white mammoth at the expense of hospitals and education.

PASGEN 5th century

With Neffai and Pabiali (Papai, Pianno, Pivannus) he was supposed to have been a son of Brychan by a Spanish (Galician?) woman, and they went to Spain to become saints and legislators. He may however have been the son of Dingad ap Brychan, and a stone existed, now lost, in the churchyard at Tywyn inscribed PASCENT. Gwendydd, a daughter of Brychan, is a saint of Tywyn, so it may have been Pasgen's burial stone. There was also a Pascent, son of Vortigern who was said to have killed Ambrosius Aurelianus. The son of this latter Pascent could have been Bishop Rioc (Riagath).

Alphabetical Listing of the Saints of Wales and Religious Events

PAUL d. 65
June 25, 29, 30, January 25

Paul keeps on appearing in connection with the legend of Caractacus (Caradog) and his family at Rome. The following notes are taken from a website called 'A Changed Rome' at iwc.net/levi/Rome and pull together several legends of this time. Amazingly, the unknown author claims that the bishops in charge of the first 1000 years of Christian conferences were British. It is not known whether this can be confirmed by research, but if so the claim that Britain has the oldest Christian community must be taken very seriously:

Two years after Constantine was accepted by the Romans as their new Emperor, he created an international Christian council of churches. ***At the first meeting, of the 318 Bishops present, only ten were Latin-speaking. At this council and at the future councils, the Bishops were seated according to the time that their church was established. In all the council meetings after this, for more than a thousand years, Britain has always had the first chair.***

The Apostle Paul ordained Linus (Caradoc's son) the first Bishop of Rome and in AD 56, Linus established the first church of Rome. Therefore, the roots of the Church of Rome came from the Culdee Church of Britain, established between AD 39-41 from Joseph of Arimathea . . . In AD 593, Gregory the Great established the doctrine of Purgatory and seven years later, imposed that Latin be the language of prayer and worship . . . In the early stages of Christianity, the church leader of the community was a Bishop. The Bishop was basically the organizer and representative of the congregation. Bishops were not above the people spiritually, ***all Christians were and are intended to be at the same level****; with Christ as the Head of the Church . . . The first Bishop given the title of Pope (Universal Bishop or the Bishop of Bishops) was in AD 610 by Emperor Phocas. The emperor did this because of the Bishop of Constantinople, Bishop Ciriacus, who had justifiably excommunicated him for causing the assassination of his predecessor, Emperor Mauritius. Gregory I was then Bishop of Rome and had refused the title but Boniface III, who came to be the Bishop of Rome after Gregory I, accepted the title . . .*

By AD 788, what originally started in Babylon, then spread to Egypt, Phoenicia, Greece and then in Rome, was clearly beginning to show itself with Pope Hadrian I, who first introduced into the Roman Church Council, the worship of images and relics. It was not until the eleventh century when the Roman Church introduced the Mass as an obligatory attendance, and the weekly ritual of Communion or the Eucharist was practised. The Eucharist . . . was in commemoration of the goddess Ceres or Demeter, the goddess of corn. In Egypt, it was practised in the same way for Isis. The shape of the little round wafers was to symbolise their sun-god Baal and the image upon the wafer was their Queen of Heaven. Dionysius or Bacchus was the god of wine and Demeter or Ceres was the goddess of corn. With Dionysius came the blood sacrifice - wine; with Demeter came the bloodless sacrifice - the wafer. The Passover meal of the Hebrews was once a year, not every week.

The Apostle Paul

St Paul's mission was supported financially in part by Caradoc's other daughter, the Princess Eurgain. Eurgain was much like Constantine's mother Helen. The two women used much of their royal resources to build and establish Christian churches, schools and libraries throughout Western Europe. They also funded missions for the cause of Christ. Eurgain met Paul when she was held by the Romans with other captive members of Caradoc's family.

There is a piece of ancient writing which is believed to be a record of St Paul continuing his final mission to the British Isles. It is called the "Lost Acts of the Apostles" or the 29th chapter of Acts. The book of Acts in today's Bible only has 28 chapters.

"And Paul, full of the blessings of Christ, and abounding in the spirit, departed out of Rome, determining to go to Spain, for he had a long time proposed to journey thitherward, and was minded also to go from thence to Britain. For he had heard in Phoenicia that certain of the children of Israel, about the time of the Assyrian captivity, had escaped by sea to The Isles afar off as spoken by the Prophet (Esdra) and called by the Romans - Britain" (29:1-2) . . . The document was translated by C.S. Sonnoni from the original Greek manuscript found in the Archives at Constantinople . . . "And on the morrow he came and stood upon Mount Lud" (Ludgate Hill and Broadway where St Paul's Cathedral stands in London, England) "and the people thronged at the gate, and assembled in the Broadway, and he preached Christ unto them, and they believed the Word and the testimony of Jesus." (29:9). The author goes on to state that the Druids who approached Paul informed him that they were descended from the house of Ephraim, Judahites who escaped from the Assyrians as 'the lost sheep' from the north of Israel. If this document exists and is genuine, then St Paul preached on the site of St Paul's.

There are several legends linking Peter and Paul with the area around Dyfrig's later base of the Wye Valley. Between Hay-on-Wye and the Vale of Ewyas, one can pass through Bwlch-yr-Efengl' (Pass of the Evangelist) where Peter and Paul are said to have preached. They had been blown off course on their way to Spain, and came to Wales. Lower down the Vale of Ewyas is Llanthony Abbey, where St David is said to have built a chapel. Peterchurch is the centre of the parallel Golden Valley. The Norman church was erected on the site of the great Saxon church of 786, itself built on the order of King Offa of Mercia when Offa's Dyke was being constructed. Tradition states that Peter and Paul parted company at the Gospel Pass above Capel-y-Ffin near Llanthony, and Peter made his way to the more hospitable Golden Valley. At Peterchurch the Apostle consecrated a well, conferring baptismal status on its waters by dropping in a massive carp with a gold chain around its neck, which he had caught in the River Dore. For centuries a fish was kept in many Welsh wells used for baptisms. Abbey Dore has the poignant remains of a Cistercian monastery. Incidentally, the Golden Valley, just inside Herefordshire takes its name from the French *'d'or'*, I.e. 'of gold', or 'golden'. The Normans probably derived its name from the native Welsh *'dwr'* (water). At Dorstone at the head of Golden Valley are the remains of Arthur's Stone, a 5000 year-old long barrow with a 20 feet capstone. Not far from this area, the soil at the top of the Skirrid Mountain was thought to have come from the Holy Land, which may be a folk-memory of foreign evangelists (see Michael).

Paul is believed to have died with Peter, so June 29th is their joint feast. Interestingly, there are 43 churches devoted to Paul in England, but 283 to Peter and Paul together.

PAULINUS, PAWL HEN see PEULIN

PAWL PENYCHEN 6th century

He inherited from his father Gwynlliw Filwr the kingdom of Penychen, based on Penllyn or Cowbridge, and was the patron of Cadog to whom he gave land at Llancarfan. Illtud was one of Pawl's soldiers before Cadog converted him. At Merthyr Mawr, south-west of Penllyn, a broken 6th century stone was found on the site of Teilo's church, with only the name 'PAUL' remaining.

Alphabetical Listing of the Saints of Wales and Religious Events

ABBOT PEBLIG 4th - 5th century
PUBLICIUS, BIBLIG, PEBLIQ
July 3

The son of Macsen Wledig and St Elen, and brother of Cystennin (Constantine), Llanbeblig in Caernarfonshire commemorates him. His other brothers were St Ednyfed and Owain. St Helen's chapel, which used to exist in Caernarfon's Roman ruins, was subject to Llanbeblig. Nennius noted the inscription on a tomb at Segontium (Caernarfon) denoting his brother Constantine the Blessed. King Edward I in 1283, after the death of Llywelyn the Last, ordered that 'the Emperor Constantine' be transferred into Llanbeblig Church (see Cystennin).

PEDIC

Kilpeck in Hereford, now David's, was originally the 'cil' (cell) of Pedic or Pedoric. The Book of Llandaf records that *'Kilpeck Church with all its lands around'* was given to the diocese around 650. One of the most fascinating Saxon-Norman churches in Britain, a sculpture known as the 'Welsh Warriors' on a column shows costumes unknown elsewhere in 12th century sculpture.

PEDITA 5th century

The sister of the martyred Clydog and grand-daughter of Brychan.

PEDR 5th - 6th century
June 29, 6 (externalised from the saints Peter and Paul)

A cousin of St David, many churches may have been founded by him, but have been subsumed by Peter the Apostle. He was the brother of Tyssul, Pedrwn, Carannog and Tyrnog, and the son of Corun ap Ceredig of the line of Cunedda. More research is needed into the twenty or so places named Llanbedr* in Wales to find their founder, as another Pedr was a son of Emyr Llydaw. Lampeter (Llanbedr-pont-Steffan) is probably his, replaced by Peter the Apostle in more recent times. Just half a mile away, the Pont Faen Stone was found in 1878, half being used in a wall, and the other half in a house. It came from the nearby holy Peter Well. Llanbedr outside Langstone (Newport), and Llanbedr Gwynllwg (Peterstone Wentlooge) outside Cardiff may have had memorial stones. Gwynlliwg is the land reclaimed from the sea, known as the *'levels'* between Newport and Cardiff, in the area known as Cernyw (e.g. Coedkernew, Coedcernyw). There has been much confusion about this area in Arthurian legend because the Celtic-Welsh for Cornwall is Cerniw.

The church at Bryngwyn, near Raglan, was said to have been founded by Aeddan ap Gwaethfoed, Lord of Grosmont and Clytha, as a consequence of the visit by Archbishop Baldwin and Giraldus Cambrensis. Just 300 yards south-east is Ffynnon Pedr. Bettws Newydd nearby was also founded by Aeddan in 1188, and formerly known as Bettws Aeddan. Aeddan also built the church at Clytha, now ruined and near Chapel Farm. Aeddan took the cross to crusade from Archbishop Baldwin. It may be that Clytha was built on a spot dedicated to a saint named Gwilym, as Llan-Wilym Lane leads to it, past some springs marked Ffynnonnau.

Peterswell is now a district of Penarth. There were other wells dedicated to Peter in Glamorgan at Llanilltud Fawr, Bishopston, Cibbwr Castle, Caer Worgan (near Llanilltud), Barri and Margam Abbey. There was a Ffynnon Bedr in Ferwig, Cardigan, and another on a farm called Fron Bedr near Peterwell, Lampeter. A king of Gwent was Pedr ap Glywys, who may have retired to a monastic life, and who may have been responsible for many of the south-east Wales dedications. Perhaps Pedr ap Corun founded churches to the north and west.

Only two standing stones remain at Llanbedr near Harlech, with the tallest being ten feet high. There is also a stone circle in the parish of Llanbedr near Tal-y-ffynnonau in Clwyd, made up of at least 14 smallish boulders. Llanbedr-y-Cenin churchyard has a standing stone with an incised spiral. Ffynnon Bedr there once had a well-building where sickly children were bathed. Opposite Llanhamlach Church in Brecon is a Maen Hir (standing stone) next to Peterstone Court. Legend says that this is where St Peter preached. Simeon Metaphrastes, writing around 900, says that Peter the Apostle visited Britain, and Theodoret wrote around 423 that Paul had taught in far off islands. St Simon Zelotes was crucified in Britain, according to Bishop Dorotheus of Tyre writing in the 3rd century. Philip the Apostle is said to have preached to the Galicians, from which his word spread to Britain. The disciple Aristobulus is stated by Dorotheus to have been Bishop of Britain (see Arwystli Hen), and there is a strong tradition that Joseph of Arimathea came to Britain (see Joseph, Ilid and Eurgain). The history of the very earliest Christian Church in Britain has rightly been compared to a *'rope of sand'*.

St Peter ad Vincula church at Pennal is reputed to be on the site of Owain Glyndŵr's first parliament, called in 1406 after he defeated Henry IV's army. From here he wrote his famous letter appealing to the French for help against the English. The letter is being returned on loan to Wales from the Paris archives, with diplomatic pressure from the new Welsh Assembly.

St Peter's Church at Llanbad, Llanbedr-ar-Fynydd, is a desolate ruin on Mynydd y Gaer near the Ridgeway Walk. Barber and Pykitt believe that Arthur and his father Meurig are buried here, just north-west of Llanharan, and the area is covered with tumuli and encampments. St David's Day was the occasion of a great Gwyl Mabsant held here, until Methodist preachers prevailed against such festivities. Also in 1731, Cowbridge tradesmen were fined for selling ale, gingerbread and cakes on a Sunday near the church.

In a strange marriage of St Peter and the Welsh national symbols, 'Cenhinen Bedr' means 'Peter's Leek', but is the Welsh name for daffodil.

*Llanbedr had an eccentric clergyman referred to by Francis Kilvert as an 'anchorite' - *'if the Solitary had lived a thousand years ago he would have been revered as a hermit and perhaps canonized as a saint.'* At St Peter's Church on the B4594, one can find the grave of the Reverend John Price, vicar of Llanbedr from 1859 - 1895. His impoverished parish had no grand rectory, and from his arrival there he resorted to living in three dilapidated bathing machines in a valley above the church. Kilvert recorded first finding him on July 3, 1872: *'a sunny little green cwm (valley) it was secluded among the steep green hills, and until you came close to it you would not be expecting the existence of the place . . . What was my relief when I knocked upon the door to hear a strange deep voice from within saying "Ho! Ho!" . . . A strange figure came out, dressed in a seedy faded greasy suit of black, a dress coat and a large untidy white cravat, or a cravat that had once been white, lashed around his neck with a loose knot and flying ends. Upon his feet he wore broken low shoes and in his hand he carried a tall hat. There was something in the whole appearance of the Solitary, singularly dilapidated and forlorn, and he had a distant absent look and a preoccupied air as if the soul were entirely* *unconscious of the rags in which the body was clothed.'* Kilvert went on to describe the interior of the clergyman's hut: *'wild confusion of litter and rubbish almost choking and filing up all available space . . . broken bread and meat, crumbs, dirty knives and forks, glasses, plates, cups and saucers in squalid hugger-mugger confusion . . . the hearth foul with cold peat ashes, broken sticks and dust, under the great wide open chimney through which stole down a faint, ghastly, sickly light. The squalor, the dirt, the dust, the foulness and wretchedness of the place were indescribable, almost inconceivable.'* So much for cleanliness being next to Godliness.

PEDR ap GLYWYS see PEDR ap CORUN

PEDROG 6th century c.504-c590 (d.564 according to Cressy)
ABBOT PETROC, PETROX, PETROCUS
June 4 (also October 1, September 14 and May 23)
Emblem – a wolf
Patron saint of skinners and glovers in Bodmin

From South Wales, he studied there and then in Ireland before he founded a monastery at Lanwthinoc, which was then renamed Petroc's Stow, the modern Padstow. (Could Gwethenoc have been its founder?) A Celtic wheel-cross and another old stone may still be seen there. He also founded a monastery at Little Petheric (Nanceventon) and later retired to live as a hermit in a beehive hut on Bodmin Moor. One can still see it near Fernacre Stone Circle, and it has been described as *'one of the oldest Christian holy places in England'* (The Downside Review LXVI 1948). He died at Treravel, was buried at Padstow, but later his relics, shrine, staff and bell were removed to Bodmin. The relics were stolen and taken to St Meen in 1170, but with Henry II's intervention were returned. A beautiful Islamic ivory casket contains the saint's skull, one of the finest reliquaries in Britain. His dedications are near those of Cadoc, which led later writers to place him as Cadoc's uncle. 'Catholic Online Saints' seems to place Petroc as the son of a Welsh king, so the Cadog link may be correct.

According to the 'Lives of British Saints', Pedrog wanted to see Samson, but Samson was extremely reluctant to talk to him until Pedrog kissed him and he relaxed. Petroc is an excellent example of one of the 'peregrini', setting up foundations at Timberstone near Watchet, and Anstey West in Somerset, seventeen in Devon and six more in Cornwall, at Llanbedrog* on the Llŷn Peninsula, at Y Ferwig (Verwig) near the Teifi estuary, and at St Petrox in Pembrokeshire. St Petrox Well can still be seen near the latter church. Ffynnon Grog** in Mwnt, Ferwig parish, is probably a corruption of Ffynnon Pedrog. Mwnt's church was called Eglwys y Grog, although 'grog' means holy cross in Welsh. The litle church at Mwnt is too easily seen from the sea to have been a very early foundation. According to Dafydd Nannor in the 15th century, this Pedrog Paladrddellt (Pedrog of the Splintered Spear) was one of the seven*** knights who survived Camlan, and became a clifftop hermit in Pembroke, dying at Y Ferwig a mile from Mwnt. He was known as *'one of the three just knights'* of Arthur's Court.

There were miraculous cures at Ffynnon Bedrog on Bryn Ddu in Llanbedrog, especially for gangrene. Also a mysterious dark stone full of pins was found at the bottom of the well. A victim of a theft used to throw a piece of bread into the well and read out a list of suspects. The bread sank when the real thief's name was called out. The well has been renamed Mary's Well. There was also a holy Ffynnon Dduw (God's Well) near the village, possibly formerly Engan's Well.

The Harold Stone at St Petroc's in Pembroke is said to be the second of the three 'Devil's Quoits' aligned with Angle's 'quoit'. Along with Sampson's Cross at Sampson's Farm, these menhirs are supposed to meet at the waterfront and dance at Stackpole Elidir, returning to their individual sites when they tire. At Llanbedrog in Caernarfon is Mynydd Tir Cwmmwd Cromlech, and on the slopes of nearby Moel Mawr, Ffynnon Fair was a healing well also used to detect thieves.

In Brittany there are another eight churches and chapels. Buried at Bodmin, some consider he established a bishopric there. This most noted saint of the West Country was possibly the brother of Gwynlliw Filwr ap Glywys, and in Brittany is remembered at Perreuz and Tregon. (However, most sources do not note him as Gwynlliw's brother). It may also be that the patron saint of Cornwall was Petroc ap Clemen ap Bledric (see Geraint), a later 7th century prince.

*Llanbedrog now has a third of its houses as 'holiday homes' for English people, who come into the village for a few weeks a year. A December 1999 survey showed the average detached house price in London as £252,000, compared to £72,000 in Wales. (A further problem is that many English people realise their gains upon their houses upon retirement and move to Wales, placing a strain upon medical services.) In the past, people came to Wales to work, and were assimilated into Welsh life, their children growing up 'Welsh'. With TV, home entertainment, and many neighbours from Essex, Surrey and the like, there is no need for many new 'incomers' to bother with the Welsh language or contribute to a vibrant community. Some incomers truly believe that Wales is 'lucky' to have them to put money into the local community. The local answer is that Welsh youngsters cannot afford local houses and their prices are artificially inflated. There are two elements here that need addressing. Holiday-homers who spend money for a few weeks a year in local shops are not any answer to a community's needs. The other element, those who come to retire, are helping toll the death-knell of the Welsh language and adding to the burden on local services while putting nothing back in. They usually contribute as much to the community and its heritage as the gin-swilling monoglot expatriates who retire to the Costa del Sol. As most politicians in power have two or four homes, there is no way that they will place a prohibitive tax upon second home ownership. Instead more estates are built to blight our fields.

**The Welsh name for paeony is rhosyn y grog, or rose of the Holy Cross.

***The four who survived Camlan, above the traditional three, were Pedrog, Cynfelin, Cedyn and Derfel, all who became saints. In Peniarth MS 127, we read:
'Three Just Knights were in Arthur's Court: Blaes son of the Earl of Llychlyn, and Cadog son of Gwynlliw the Bearded, and Pedrog Splintered Spear, son of Clement Prince of Cornwall. The peculiarities of those were that whoever might do wrong to the weak, they contended against him who did him wrong in the cause of justice; and whoever might do wrong they slew, however strong he might be. For those three had dedicated themselves to preserve justice by every Law; Blaes by earthly Law, Cadog by the Law of the Church, and Pedrog by the law of Arms. And those were called Just Knights.' 'Gwawe Pedrok' (Pedrog's spear) was recorded as being preserved as a relic in Llanbedrog Church in 1535.

PEDRWN 6th century

Pedrwn ab Emyr Llydaw was Pedr's brother and the father of St Padarn. He was a saint at Côr Illtud, a brother of Amwn Ddu, and went with his son Padarn to Llanbadarn and Ireland.

PEDYR LANUAUR 6th century
PEILLAN

A saintly daughter of King Caw.

PEIRIO 6th century
PEIRO

This son of Caw founded Rhosbeirio under Llanelian, or Boderwyd, in Anglesey. He succeeded Illtud as head of Llanilltud Fawr on Illtud's death, but only survived a day before being succeeded by Samson ap Amwn Ddu. He may have been the son of Gildas ap Caw. Llanfair y Mynydd, now called St Mary's Hill, near Bridgend is his foundation. He is possibly buried at Llanilltud, and Barri Island, Ynys Peiro, was named after him prior to Baruc's death there. The 'Insular of Peiros' (Ynys Peiros) had a monastery where Samson was taught*, and it seems that the monks joined those at Llanilltud. A monastery was marked on old maps of the island before the docks were built at the entrance to a tunnel by the present railway station. There was also an 'abbey church' on the island where St 'Doeninas' settled from Somerset, before moving on to Llandough. The church at Llandough, with its fabulous Irbic's Cross, was said to be commemorated to Doeninas as well as Cyngar (Dochwy). There was a chapel on the island a hundred yards west of Friar's Point House on Barri Island, but it has now been swept into the sea. A 'Roman' kitchen was also excavated upon the island, and a Roman port building can be seen above the adjoining Cold Knap beach.

*From various sources it seems that *'Insular Pironis'* was Barri Island rather than Caldey island, where Samson stayed. He also stayed in *'Eltut's magnificent monastery'*, according to the *'Vita Samsonis'*. G. H. Doble mentions that M. Fawtier ('La Vie de St Samson', 1912) queries the attribution of Caldey (Ynys Byr), but states that *'no other site has yet been suggested.'* In the Vita Samsonis, Samson left Llanilltud monastery for *'a certain island lately founded by a certain holy presbyter called Piro.'* Dyfrig was also supposed to have spent Lent regularly on the island and met Samson there. With both these saints based in south-east Wales, and a monastery being marked on old maps of Barri Island with its 'Friars' Point' headland, the case seems substantial. The author would also like to use this book to note that the ancient 'Roman Well', certainly at least mediaeval and used as a holy well, on Barri Island has recently been built over. St Baruch's Well on the island has also been built over in the latter part of the 20th century.

PEITHIEN 6th century
PETEONA

A virgin daughter of King Caw, she is associated with her brothers Eigrad and Gallgo in evangelising Anglesey. The old chapel at Llugwy was possibly her foundation, near those of her brothers at Llanallgo and Llaneigrad. Another brother was Gildas, and her sisters were Cywyllog and Gwenabwy, who also had oratories named after them in Anglesey.

PELAGIUS (MORGAN) c.352-c.430's

Morgan (*'from the sea'*) was traditionally born in Bangor-is-Coed, the site of the famous monastery and was said to be a lay monk there. If this is the case, Dunawd Fawr's 6th century foundation was on an existing monastic site. In Montgomeryshire, however, he was said to be a native of Llanrhaeadr, who first preached his *'heretical'* ideas in the churchyard at Castle Caereinion. Some say that he was not British, but St Augustine, Prosper, Gennadius, Orosius and Mercador wrote that he was. A respected religious teacher in Rome in the 380's, he was forced to escape from the oncoming Goths, who eventually sacked Rome in 410. He was then living in Carthage, but the church leaders combined to get his ideas dismissed as heretical. Leaving another Briton, Caelestius (see Celestine), Pelagius went to Palestine, and was supported by Bishop John of Jerusalem.

Pelagius was not a saint, but his vision of Christianity was far closer to the principles of humanitarian morals and ethics than the evolving Roman church of his times. In the early fifth century this Celtic monk denied the concept of *'original sin'*, the teaching that Adam's sin corrupted all of his descendants. This was a practical denial of the need for the established church to grant grace and salvation to mankind. He believed that men could by themselves, and by their own Christian works be taken to Heaven. He was condemned by Pope Innocent I and Zosimus, but his teachings affected European history down to Luther, Calvin and the Cathars. 'Paying for salvation' was not the way to heaven. 'Following a leader' was not the way to Heaven. Following the example of Christ was the only way for Pelagius. Salvation mainly lies with the person, who by acts of will and self-control could make himself or herself better, more acceptable to God and mankind in general. The doctrine was initially accepted by Jerome. Also, in the 4th century John of Cassian had accepted it in his thirteenth conference. The Roman church later expunged this manuscript from John's writings. The supremacy of the human will over the grace of God, as decided by the power of the church, could simply not be accepted. As Augustine stated in his *'Sermons'*, *'Roma locutus est; causa finita est'* – *'Rome has spoken; the case is finished.'*

Pelagius had followed Origen's doctrine of 'free will', and in 401 settled in Rome lecturing upon mankind's natural dignity and the absurdity of 'original sin' as preached by Augustine. Thus priests who could absolve sins were unnecessary. A true believer could reach Heaven by his acts alone. *'Everything good and everything evil, for which we are either praised or blamed, is not born with us, but done by us'*, he wrote. When Alaric and his Visigoths invaded, Pelagius escaped to North Africa, where he met Augustine. Augustine later condemned Celestine (Celestius), the British follower of Pelagius, for heretical teachings. Pelagius now went to Palestine, where his teachings found favour, but Augustine persuaded the Church of Rome to condemn him in 417, which the Council of Carthage confirmed in 418. Many Italian bishops supported Pelagius, and they were banished alongside him. In 429 the bishops Germanus (Garmon) and Lupus (Bleiddian) were sent to Britain because of its adherence to Pelagianism, *'that noxious and abominable teaching that men had no need of God's grace.'* Pelagianism was formally pronounced heretical in 431. It was obvious that Pelagianism threatened the very core of the money-making authority of Rome. The British had already threatened Rome's civil power with the cavalry of Macsen Wledig (Maximus) and Cystennin (Constantine) across Gaul, and Morgan (Pelagius) had to be stopped in his tracks.

Basically, Pelagianism took money away from the Roman Church, and thence economic and political power. Men were basically good, and the church was not needed for them to go to heaven. Mankind is God's masterpiece of creation, because it has the capacity to reason between what is a good and what is an evil act. If mankind freely chooses good, it deserves salvation. If mankind chooses evil, it breaks the contract that binds it to God. For these ideas, Pelagius was accused by Prosper of Aquitaine of denying the concept of Original Sin, and of claiming that man can avoid sin by the power of *'free-will without the aid of Divine Grace'*. It was therefore heresy to the Italian church that infants who die unbaptised are not necessarily banned from heaven. The Roman church as a *'command and control'* system replicated that of any army, and Pope Celestine (d.432) saw the Pelagian Heresy as the greatest menace to the unity of the church in the West, with Britain as its stronghold. Prosper said that Pope Celestine called the Pelagians *'Enemies of Grace'* (of course, a state of grace could only be achieved by submitting to, and paying, the Roman Church). Prospero also declared that Agricola, son of the Pelagian Bishop Severianus, was corrupting the churches of Britain around 429. Pope Celestine thus sent Germanus, Bishop of Auxerre, to the Isle of Britain, to try to extirpate the teaching, and a Briton, Palladius, to Ireland.

The ascetic Pelagius wrote two tracts and several letters that have survived. In one he states that *'It is not much to set an example to pagans; what is much better is to set such an example that even the saints can learn from you.'* His truth that all people, rich and poor, are created equal by God, never gained favour with the mainstream church, which preferred the North African theology of St Augustine. Augustine (354-430) said *'Salus extra ecclesiam non est'* – *'There is no salvation outside the church'* a doctrine still followed by many 'Christian' sects, which thus condemns those born in countries outside the ecclesiastical authority of the Christian church. As a result there is no Saint Morgan, but there should be. His ideas, based on Druidic and Stoic thought, were so widespread in Britain that in 429 Germanus of Auxerre had been asked to suppress them, as mentioned above. Germanus returned in the 440's to try again, in the reign of Vortigern, a Pelagian Christian. This seems to have been the time of the famous *'Alleluiah'* victory at Maes Armon, near Mold in Flint. Vortigern kept Britain independent until 442, but has been pilloried throughout history, partially because of the Germanic bias of academics since the Hanovers took the English throne, but mainly because the early chroniclers of the history of Britain were anti-Pelagians. Anti-Pelagianism gave us the terrible deeds of the Inquisition, Simon de Montfort's dreadful *'crusade'* against the Cathar *'perfecti'* in France, and led indirectly to the strict Calvinism that almost destroyed two thousand years of Welsh society and culture.

It is instructive to note that Pelagianism would have destroyed the Roman Catholic church by starving it of funding and power. The Roman system of confessions and the selling of indulgences and pardons produced a steady income stream and lands from those in power. Thus Norman barons could steal Welsh land, blind and torture children and women, but be forgiven by God and go to Heaven in exchange for money and endowments of land. Much of church land was taken by bloody means in Wales, via Normans and Angevins, from its original owners. The author is not a theologist, but it seems that Pelagius is nearer to Christ's teachings than the established church, and his acceptance would have led to a far more peaceful 1500 years of history across the globe.

The following extracts are taken from 'The Catholic Encyclopaedia' of 1913, and are added without comment. *'As all his ideas were chiefly rooted in the old, pagan philosophy, especially in the popular system of the Stoics, rather than in Christianity, he regarded the moral strength of man's will, when steeled by asceticism, as sufficient in itself to desire and to attain the loftiest ideal of virtue. The value of Christ's redemption was, in his opinion, limited mainly to instruction and example, which the Saviour threw into the balance as a counterweight against Satan's wicked example, so that the nature retains the ability to conquer sin and to gain eternal life even without the aid of grace. By justification we are indeed cleansed of our personal sins through faith alone but this pardon implies no interior renovation of sanctification of the soul. How far the sola-fides doctrine "had no stouter champion before Luther than Pelagius" and whether, in particular, the Protestant conception of fiducial faith dawned upon him many centuries before Luther probably needs more careful investigation. . . . To explain psychologically Pelagius's whole line of thought, it does not suffice to go back to the ideal of the wise man, which he fashioned after the ethical principles of the Stoics and upon which his vision was centred. We must also take into account that his intimacy with the Greeks developed in him, though unknown to himself, a one-sidedness, which at first sight appears pardonable.* **The gravest error into which he and the rest of the Pelagians fell, was that they did not submit to the doctrinal decisions of the Church.**'

The article goes on to comment on the *'last traces of Pelagianism'* which held on in Celtic Britain: *'After the Council of Ephesus (431), Pelagianism no more disturbed the Greek Church, so that the Greek historians of the 5th century do not even mention the controversy or the names of the heresiarchs. But the heresy continued to smoulder in the West and died out very slowly. The main centres were Gaul and Britain. About Gaul we are told that a synod, held probably at Troyes in 429, was compelled to take steps agains the Pelagians. It also sent Bishops Germanus of Auxerre and Lupus of Troyes to Britain to fight the rampant heresy, which received powerful support from two pupils of Pelagius, Agricola and Fastidius. Almost a century later, Wales was the centre of Pelagian intrigues. For the saintly Archbishop David of Menevia participated in 519 in the Synod of Brefy, which directed its attacks against the Pelagians residing there, and after he was made Primate of Cambria, he himself convened a synod against them. In Ireland also Pelagius's "Commentary of St Paul" was in use long afterwards, as is proved by many Irish quotations from it.'* (The Synod of Brefi was in 545, not 519, which makes Wales the last stronghold of Pelagianism.

JOHN PENRY 1563-1593
JOHN PENRI
May 29 (Execution)

The first Welsh Puritan martyr was the Presbyterian John Penry from Breconshire, executed in 1593. He was born at Cefnbrith near Llangammarch, and educated at Cambridge and Oxford. In 1587 he presented a treatise to parliament lamenting the lack of preaching ministers in Wales ('A Treatise containing the Aequity of an Humble Supplication'). He was arrested but released. Penry's second book was secretly printed in 1588, the year of the Armada. It was called *'An Exhortation unto the Governors, and people of His Majesties countrie of Wales.'* In it, he appealed to Parliament in it for Welsh-speaking preachers in *'my poor countrie of Wales'*. He described the Welsh bishops of the established Church of England as *'excrements of Romish vomits'*, and pleaded for the sovereignty of the individual conscience (see Religion). A third book by Penry was published in in 1588, and the the search for the secret press intensified because of its association with the first of the Marprelate tracts. The press produced more Marprelate material at this time.

Penry had fled after the publication of the 1589 book 'Supplication unto the High Court of Parliament', as its printer John Hodgkin was arrested. In Scotland he published three more pamphlets, but was later betrayed and seized in London in 1592. He was thought by the bishops to be 'Martin Marprelate', which accounted for their venomous hatred of him. (The real Marprelate was probably Job Throckmorton, MP for Warwickshire). Penry was indicted under the Act of Uniformity, which did not provide for a death penalty, but nevertheless he was executed at St Thomas a Watering, London. He had a personal interview with Lord Burghley, Elizabeth I's Welsh Secretary of State, but it did not save him. Penry had been betrayed by the Vicar of Stepney, but in prison (The Poultry Compter) managed to write *'Declaration of Faith and Allegiance.'* Because of his pure preaching voice, Penry was nick-named 'Telyn Cymru', the 'Welsh Harp'. He left a widow and four young daughters.

PEREDUR
PRYDERI AP DOLAR

The origin of the Grail and Arthurian character of Percival, Iolo Morganwg states that he and Gwrgi were the sons of Elifer Gosgorddfawr and were Welsh saints, but they were probably Northern Celtic warriors of Deira and Bernicia. Peredur is mentioned in the Arthurian Traids (see Dwyfael), and his sons were said to be the saints Gwrgi and Dwyfael. However, Iolo Morganwg placed Peredur as Gwrgi's brother.

PERIS 7th century
July 26 (also December 11)

One of the many saintly sons of Helig Foel, he founded Llanberis in Caernarfon. Llangian chapel under Llanbedrog in Caernarfon was dedicated to him, along with Cian, his servant, who was feasted on December 11. He is called *'Cardinal of Rome'* in the old bonedds. Ffynnon Beris is in front of the cottage known as Tynyffynnon where a 'priestess' lived. Bathing in the well cured rheumatism, scrofula and children with rickets. Two sacred fish were always kept in the well, and two new trout were placed there in 1896. In 1828 Cathrall had noted *'a poor woman, who lives in a cottage near the spring, has a few pence given to her by strangers for showing one or two large trout which she feeds in the well'*. Large numbers came here until the 19th century, and 'Cyff Peris' can still be seen in the church. If a fish appeared when drinking, or bathing in the water, a cure was certain. If one of the fish died, it was not replaced, as it was thought that the survivor would not co-exist with a new fish, and soon die. The average life span was said to be 50 years for a fish in the holy well. The remaining fish that died in 1896 measured 17 inches, and was buried in a nearby garden.

Nearby are Llyn Peris, Nant Peris and Gorphwysfa Peris (the saint's resting-place). Edward Lhuyd wrote in 1699 that he had *'seen a fellow march nine times around Gorphwysfa Peris at Carnedh under Snowdon Hill, repeating ye Lord's Prayer, and casting in a stone at every turn: when I am apt to imagine ye St Peris or some one lies buried here, tho' their tradition be only that he was used constantly to rest after he came up ye steep hill below it.'*

PERWAS

Bettws Perwas under Llanrhuddlad in Anglesey was known as Llan Berwas, and Leland called him a *'swete servant.'* There may be a link between this saint and Eglwys Brewis (see Brice, Brewys). The 13th century Eglwys Brewis Church is to the north of the airfield and is possibly the 'crudest and smallest' in use in the Vale of Glamorgan, being only 35 feet by 19. There is a Norman font, and a 1643 tombstone in the floor dedicated to the 12-year-old Mary, daughter of Miles Bassett. The de Braose family held lands in Llanmaes, and may have been its founders.

William de Braose was Bishop of Llandaf from 1266-1287. In 1254 the church was valued at £2, and in 1535 at £4-0s-2d. Known as 'Eglis Priwes' in the Taxatio of Norwich in 1254, its first recorded cleric was Ricardus de Egluspirwys in 1443. No-one yet seems to have made the link between Perwas and *Egluspirwys*. (Eglwys is the Welsh for church, from the Latin Ecclesia). There are wall-paintings in the church, and its structure, save for some remodelling of the nave in the 15th century, is essentially as it was in the 13th century.

PETROC see PEDROG

Roman Milestone of Maximinus Daia, reused as Memorial to Cantusus.
CADW: Welsh Historic Monuments. Crown Copyright.

PEULAN 6th century
November 1 or 2, with Wakes at Llanbeulin on March 17

A son of Pawl Hen, and the founder of Llanbeulan in Anglesey. His sister was Gwenfaen, patroness of Rhoscolyn, and her brother was Gwyngenau, patron of the extinct Capel Gwyngeneu near Holyhead. Peulan was a disciple of Cybi.

BISHOP PEULIN d.c.550
POLIN ESGOB, PAUL, PAWL HEN, PAULINUS, POL AURELIAN, POL DE LEON
March 12 (Farmer informs us that the March 12 feast was overshadowed by the October 10 subsidiary feast, through a confusion with Paulinus of York)

Possibly a Briton of Cumbria, he seems to have resided in the Isle of Man before coming to Caerworgorn (Lanilltud Fawr) to study at Illtud's great college. Another source makes him the son of Perpius ap Pawl Penychen of Glamorgan, and the brother of Sidwella and Juthwara. He was said to be descended from Macsen Wledig and the son of Nudd Hael, and his wife was Tonwy ferch Llewddyn Luydog. He and his eight brothers lived at 'Brehant Dincat', which Doble places as Llandingat, i.e. Llandovery.

Peulin later lived as a hermit near Llandovery and founded the monastery at Llanddeusant.
In Llanddingad parish in northern Carmarthenshire are two of Peulin's chapels, Capel Peulin and Nant-y-Bai, and the holy well, Ffynnon Beulin. A few miles away, Llanddeusant is dedicated to Peulin's brothers, Potolius and Notolius. He also has a church of St Peulin at Llangors in Breconshire. One chapel there is dedicated to Peulin and the other to Llan y Deuddeg Sant ('the llan of the twelve saints'). At this Llangors, near Talgarth, a Celtic stone was found when the old chancel-arch was pulled down. The inscriptions appear to read '+ gurci' and 'bledru?s'. Bledrws ap Bleidyd was one of Hywel Dda's advisors, and Gurci (also Gwrgi and Gurcu) was another common Welsh name.

Wrmonoc says that Peulin took twelve presbyters from Llanddeusant to King Mark's court in Cornwall, and then moved on to Brittany. Paulus Aurelianus was said to have been born around 480, in Penychen Glamorgan, which may signify that he was of the family of Pawl Penychen, or merely confused with this local king. Nennius stated that Peulin's family lived in *'a cave in the region of Gwent, having wind constantly blowing out of it.'* This would have been Glamorgan's Barri Island, with the *'wonder of Wales'* 'blowing' cave noted by Giraldus Cambrensis. Barri Island was also known as Ynys Peirio, and it may be here rather than Ynys Pyr that Peulin was sent by Illtud. As a contemporary of David, Samson and Gildas under Illtud at Llanilltud, perhaps he assisted in building the dykes around Col-huw, Aberthaw and Gileston to form arable lands.

Peulin later landed at Ushant, built the monastery at Ploudalmezau, and was made bishop, Pol de Leon. He was still living in 545 as he seems to have attended the Synod of Brefi back in Wales. Saint-Pol-de-Leon in Finistere is 10 miles north-west of Morlaix, with a superb cathedral. Lamballe, 24m east of Dinan, on the Cotes-d'Armor, was founded by St Pol, and was formerly called Lan Pol. Paulinus was patron of Paul in Cornwall, and there are a few Welsh dedications also, such as Llan-gors in Brecon. He was very closely associated with the children of Brychan as they evangelised Cornwall and Brittany.

PEULIN late 5th century
PAULINUS
November 22

Rhygyfarch tells us that St David was instructed by Paulinus, at Tŷ-Gwyn in Whitland, after a period under Giustilianus at Hen Fynyw. Peulin made Gredifael and Fflewyn superiors of classes in the monastery, and his children were the saints Peulan, Gwenfaen and Gwyngenau. In a field still known Pant-y-Polion, on Maes Llanwrthwl Farm in Caio, Carmarthen there were found three pieces of a 6th century monument, now in the Carmarthen Museum. The inscription reads

SERVATUS FIDAEI
PATRI ( ) EQ ( ) SEMPER
AMATOR HIC PAULIN
US IACIT CUL ( ) VLTOR PIENT ( )
SIM ( ) VS AEQVL

Late 17th century records have the full inscription of *'Preserver of the Faith, constant lover of his country, here lies Paulinus, the devoted champion of righteousness'*. This is the famous 'Cynwyl Caeo Stone', on the border of the parish of Llanddewi Brefi where this or the previous Peulin attended the Synod where David renounced Pelagianism.

There is a great deal of confusion with the noble Paul of Penychen in Glamorgan. A monk called Wrmonoc wrote the Vita of Paul about 880 in Brittany, and seems to have mixed up the various Welshmen with this name. Paulinus had a monastery at Llanddeusaint in Carmarthen, and may be the same as Pol de Leon, but Paul of Penychen is more difficult to reconcile with the legends. 'Paulinus' was also found on a pillar-stone in Llantrisant, Anglesey, and may be his. Capel Peulin and Nant-y-bai chapels in Llandingat were both dedicated to Paulinus, but more research is needed to definitely attribute these foundations to either Peulin. Dedications to Peulinus were found at Caio, but also at Port Talbot and Merthyr Mawr. The stone at Merthyr Mawr was discovered by accident when the new church was erected around 1800, and reads PAVLI FILI M . . . The father's name seems to begin MA, and similarly, 'NUS' has been broken off Paulinus.

A stone was found on the Roman road from Nidum (Neath) to southern Bovium or Bomium, which has been variously identified as Ewenni or Boverton. (Bovium being Cowbridge, and Boverton being directly south of Cowbridge and the home of the Romanised Kings of Glamorgan, the author believes Boverton may also have a claim as a Roman site). Westwood found the stone in the harbour-master's office at Port Talbot, broken into six pieces, and bearing a Roman inscription in capitals:

IMPC
FLAVA
?DMAXI
MINO
INVIC
TOAV
GVS

For various reasons as explained by Westwood, this has been translated as the Emperor Caius Flavius Valerius. On the other side of the stone is a later inscription, reading: *'Hic IACIT CANTUSUS PATER PAVLINUS'*, *'Here lies Cantusus, the father of Paulinus.'* However, it may also indicate that the father of Cantusus was Paulinus. Another stone found on the same road is a Roman military stone, now in Swansea Museum. It reads:

Alphabetical Listing of the Saints of Wales and Religious Events

IMP
MCPIA
VONIO
VICTOR
INOAVG

This was probably erected in the time of the usurpation of Victorinus in Gaul, 265 AD, and coins bearing his name were also found at Gwindy, near Llansamlet in 1835. Another Victorinus-inscribed stone was discovered at Scethrog between Llanhamwlch and Llansantffraid in Brecon. Formerly on the roadside, it was discovered being used as a garden-roller, being over 40" long, and cylindrical. Westwood deciphered it as *'Nemnivus Filius Victorini'*.

PINNOCK (see CYNOG)

PIRAN early 6th century
PERRAN, CIARAN (Irish)
March 5, November 18 (Launceston Church Calendar)

This Welsh monk gave his name to Perranporth, and pilgrimages were made to his shrine, but in the early middle ages his oratory and hermitage near Perran-zabuloe in Cornwall were covered by sands. In 1835 an excavation found three headless skeletons and three heads on the site. There is a tall Celtic Cross marking his hermitage. Piran is the patron saint of Cornish tinners. Piran dolls or engravings were left at the entrance of caves to invoke his blessing. In 1760 it was noted that an allowance of one shilling for men and six pence for boys was given at the mine near Breage for celebrating his feast at 'Perran-tide.' Canon Doble recorded that at that time a *'man of unsteady step and festive appearance'* was known as a *'Perraner.'*

Giraldus Cambrensis mentions a chapel of St Piran at Cardiff Castle, where Henry II celebrated Mass when he returned from Ireland. It is said that Piran founded a church at Caer-Teim (Cardiff) as a young man after being trained in Llancarfan, where he met Finnian. In Brittany, St Piran's Bed is a flat stone and shrine between St Pol-de-Leon and Lesneven, where indentations are supposed to be where he knelt in prayer. St Peran is north of Plelan-le-Grand on the outskirts of the Arthurian Foret de Paimpont. Perran-ar-Worthal, Perranzabuloe (with the remains of a 7th century oratory) and Perranuthnoe parishes in Cornwall recall his name. In Arthurian tradition, Piran became Archbishop of York but did not take up the see.

PLOU

The Brythonic Welsh Lan, or Llan, generally denotes an ancient holy foundation in Wales, Brittany and Cornwall, much the same as the prefix Cil or Kil does in the Goidelic Celtic Ireland and Scotland. In addition, the word *'plou'* is associated in Brittany with such sites. M. de la Borderie's 1896 'Histoire de Bretagne' explains the significance of *'plou'* or *'plo'* as a prefix in Brittany:
'The word exists with slight variations in all the Breton dialects. In Welsh and Cornish it is a parish in the ecclesiastical sense but means rather the body of parishioners in the parish territory. With the Bretons it has a special significance. The 'plou' means the small colony formed by British immigrants, settling by leaving its boats somewhere is a corner of the desert

of Armorica (Brittany), under the direction of a brave warrior, secular chief or pious monk, the spiritual leader of a little society formed in the land of exile, by community of misfortune. On this soil, the plou replaces the clan or tribe. In the terrible storm that broke over Britain the clan was for the most part dissolved by the disaster of invasion, and dispersed by the opportunity of emigration. The plou is derived from it, an image, a modification, a reconstruction on a new basis, linked not by ties of blood, but by those, no less strong, of common suffering, or peril and exile faced and endured in common.

The civil institution of the plou still subsisted and was full of life in the ninth century . . . the functions of its chief, or 'mactiern', possessed a hereditary dignity, special to Brittany and of a highly original character. His first and principal privilege was that of exercising judicial authority throughout the plou, over all its inhabitants. The chief possessed beside certain rights, dues, subventions, and certain lands forming the domain that sustained his dignity. All the members of the plou owed to him their chief fidelity and assistance, as to a hereditary lord. He could claim their military help if attacked in his person or his goods, and, in case of need, to enforce his judgements. The plou must be considered as the elementary social and political unit, as the distinctive and original feature of the British community on the Continent. It represents the little colony originally settled on the Armorican soil by the immigrants. And the word remains fixed to the present day, incorporated into the names of some 200 Breton parishes.'

The reasons for the Welsh and Devon/Somerset/Cornwall emigration, which gave Brittany its language, lay not only in flight from Saxon and pagan Goidelic invasions, or from the Yellow Plague, but also because the Welsh laws of cyfran (gavelkind) meant that no person could build up land. Inheritances were constantly being shared evenly, with even illegitimate children taking an equal share. Armorica/Brittany represented a land of opportunity for many settlers, much like the West did in the United States of America. Evangelical work was another pull in the movement of Welsh and Cornish families to France. They followed, and reinforced, the remains of the British forces of Magnus Maximus in Brittany, which then retained its independence from France until the sixteenth century. About the same time as the Welsh Tudor dynasty was taking over the throne of England, the Duchess of Brittany consented to a marriage to join France and her country together.

POTOLIUS 5th century

Llanddeusant in northern Carmarthenshire is dedicated to Potolius, and Notolius, the brothers of Peulin (Peulinus).

EDWARD POWELL 1478? - 1540

This Catholic theologian was born in Wales and educated at Oxford, later holding livings in Bleadon (Somerset), Salisbury, Carlton-cum-Thurlby, Lyme Regis, Bedminster, Bristol and Sutton le Marsh. He preached at Henry VIII's court, but declared himself opposed to Lutheranism and attacked it in a dissertation, *'Propugnaculum summi Sacerdotii Evangelici.'* He then allied himself with Catherine of Aragon, constantly preaching against the Protestant Movement, to try to prevent Henry marrying Anne Boleyn. Powell obviously lost favour at court, and his refusal to acknowledge Boleyn as Queen led to his being accused of high treason. With five others he was executed in July, 1540.

Alphabetical Listing of the Saints of Wales and Religious Events

PHILIP POWELL 1594 - 1646
June 30

Born at Trallwng Cynfyn, Breconshire, the son of Roger ap Rosser Powell, he attended Abergavenny Grammar School, whose Catholic headmaster Morgan Lewis recommended Powell to Father Augustine Baker. Baker supervised his law studies, then paid for Powell to attend university at Louvain from 1614-1619. Becoming a priest, Powell went to Douai and then came to Britain as part of the English Mission in 1622. After a year in London, he spent the next twenty years as a chaplain to various families in Devon and Somerset. In the Civil War he was a chaplain to Royalist troops, and tried to cross the Bristol Channel to Monmouthshire in 1646. However, he was intercepted off the Mumbles, kept for two months in Penarth Roads on Captain Crowther's ship, and then taken by sea to London. On June 16th, he was condemned at Westminster Hall for being a priest, and executed at Tyburn on June 30th.

PRAXEDES and PUDENTIANA 1st - 2nd century
July 21, September 21, and May 19, 21 respectively

Daughters of Claudia and Pudens, and therefore half-British, these Roman virgin martyrs have adjoining graves in the catacomb known as Potentiana, in the cemetery of Priscilla on the Salarian Way. The church of S Prassede was built on the site of Praxedes' house. Praxedes was said to have been converted by St Peter the Apostle. The Catholic Church suppressed their feasts in 1969. Catholic Online Saints states that the sisters sheltered and sustained Christians during the persecution of Marcus Antoninus. Praxedes could stand their suffering no longer, and asked God if she might give up her life in alleviation of their pain. On July 21 she was called to heaven to reward her goodness. Her body was laid to rest next to those of Pudens and Pudentiana by the priest Hermas Pastor. At first she was venerated as a martyr in the Ecclesia Pudentiana, but later a separate church was built in her honour. When this church was rebuilt by Pope Paschal I as the present Santa Prassede, her relics were taken there.

RHYS PRICHARD 1579-1644
January 11

A poet and clergyman from Llandovery, who went to Jesus College, Oxford. Rice Rees gives his father as Dafydd ap Richard ap Dafydd ap Rhys ap Dafydd. He became curate of Llandovery, and was appointed by the king as rector of Llanedy. He was made chaplain to Robert, Earl of Essex, then Chancellor and Canon of St David's Cathedral in 1726. The living of Lawhaden was attached to this position. Commonly known as *Yr Hen Ficer (The Old Vicar)*, his 1681 Canwyll y Cymru is perhaps the Welsh equivalent of 'A Pilgrim's Progress'. He is buried in St David's churchyard.

PROTESTANTISM

Henry VIII's Protestant Refomation and dissolution of the monasteries cut deep into local traditions in Wales. The annual feast of the parish church was compulsorily moved to the first Sunday in October, and **thus many of the original saints' days have been lost**. The old Rogation ceremonies, held on 'cross days' to bless the crops, were halted. All 'Plough Monday' processions were banned in 1548, and the saints' days associated with local trades and professions prohibited a year earlier. The Protestants made the case that holy water originated in the Roman *'aqua lustralis'*, that the wakes were the equivalent of the *Bacchanalia,* rogation processions were the *ambarvalia,* Shrove Tuesday festivities were the *Saturnalia*, and so on. The Maypole, Summer Birch, Rush-bearing processions, Morris dancing, Whitsun ales, remaining holy days, Sunday dancing and the like were all repudiated in the 16th century (and again by Cromwell's puritans a century later). The crwth and pibgorn (fiddle and pipes) could not be used to accompany the bridal couple to the church, and the throwing of corn in churchyards (from whence comes modern confetti) was made punishable by fines.

Tolling bells at funerals, funeral customs, the use of mourning garments and the distribution of alms to the poor were also sanctioned against, as being superstitious. The practice of giving gifts at New Year's Eve was rejected, and the drinking of toasts was seen as a throwback to heathen days. It is a great wonder that any traditions survived this legislative assault of Henry VIII and then Oliver Cromwell's bishops. (Henry VIII was of the Welsh Tudor dynasty, and Cromwell's name as a young man was Williams. His grandparents came from Llanishen in modern Cardiff). In Elizabeth Tudor's reign, Bishop Richard Davies reminded the Welsh people that *'superstition, charms and incantations'* formed the religion of Popish times, and a manifesto of the time called the Church of Rome the source of *'all wicked sorcery'*.

EDMWND PRYS 1544-1623
May 15

Given the Holy Day of May 15th (the same as John Davies), this archdeacon of Merioneth was possibly born at Llanfor in the same county. After St Asaf's Cathedral School, he went to St John's College, Cambridge, and in 1572 was given the living of Ffestiniog and Maentwrog. In 1576 he was appointed rector of Ludlow, and that same year made archdeacon. From 1576 until his death he lived at Tyddyn-ddu, Maentwrog. Llandenddwyn was given him in 1580, and he was made canon of St Asaf in 1602. Prys assisted William Morgan in his translation of the Bible, and published a book of psalms in 1621, *'the first Welsh book in which music was printed.'* He also wrote 'contemplative' poetry. His first wife was Elin ferch John ap Lewis of Pengwern, and his second wife was her cousin, Gwen ferch Morgan ap Lewis of Pengwern. 'The Dictionary of Welsh Biography' notes the distinguished children of the marriages.

PUDENTIANA see PRAXEDES

PYR, PIRO 6th century

A contemporary of Illtud, his name is from the Latin Porius. This abbot of the monastery of Caldey Island is one of the few Welsh saints who shows human weakness. He took over the island (then called Llan Illtud after the monastery's founder, and now called Ynys Pyr) but did not control the monks well. Strong mead was extremely popular amongst monastic communities, and there may also have been whiskey distilled, as on Bardsey Island. His successor, the ascetic Samson*, resigned because of the lax behaviour of the monks there. Fittingly, the drunken Pyr had fallen into a well on the island and was dead when he was hauled out by his fellow monks.

On Caldey Island was an early stone inscribed in Ogham 'MAGL DUBR', which possibly means 'the tonsured servant of Dubricius (Dyfrig)'. Maenor Pyr opposite Caldey, now called Manorbier Castle, was the birthplace of Giraldus Cambrensis. King's Quoit outside Manorbier has a capstone of 14 feet by 8 feet.

*This story appears to relate to Barri Island - see Peirio.

R

'Riches are a good handmaid, but the worst mistress.'

Francis Bacon (1561-1626), 'De Dignitate et Augmentis Scientarum'

REDEDICATIONS

We may never be able to find the original Celtic dedications of some churches and wells, and it is hoped that readers will send any relevant information to the author at the address given in this book's introduction. Back in 1903, Baring-Gould and Fisher noted:

'In Wales, whenever the Norman prelates could, they displaced the Celtic patrons from their churches, and rededicated them to saints whose names were to be found in the Roman Calendar. The native saints were supplanted principally by the Blessed Virgin, but in a number of dioceses by St Peter. To take a few instances, from one diocese only, that of St Asaph. Llanfwrog (St Mwrog), Llannefydd (St Nefydd), and Whitford (St Beuno), have been transferred to St Mary; Northop (St Eurgain) and Llandrinio (St Trinio) to St Peter; Guilsfield (St Aelhaiarn), and Llangynyw (St Cynyw) to All Saints. The two southern cathedrals have received rededications, St David's to St Andrew, and Llandaff to St Peter. Bangor was rededicated to St Mary, but St Asaph has escaped.

In Cornwall, Altarnon has been taken from St Non and given to St Mary, St Neot's at Menhenniot to St Anthony, St Finnbar at Fowy has been supplanted by St Nicholas, St Merryn by St Thomas a Becket. At Mawnan, St Stephen was coupled with the patron when the church was rededicated. St Dunstan, on a like occasion, was linked with St Manaccus at Lanlivery and Lanreath. St Elwyn had to make way for St Catherine, and St Ruan for the apocryphal St Christopher. The same process was going on in Brittany . . .'

RHAIN DREMRUDD (Red-Eyed) 5th century
RHUN

Like Clydwyn, a son of Brychan who became a soldier. He took over Eastern Brecon and was buried at Llandefaelog Fach outside Brecon. He may have been Brychan's second son. His sons were the saints Nefydd and Andras. He had a church at Mara, near Llangors Lake in Brecon. Rhain was martyred at Pont-y-Rhun near Troedyrhiw south of Merthyr Tudful, by Saxons. Nefydd then forced the Saxons and Gwyddyl Fichti to flee. Tudful was possibly martyred at the same time by the this marauding warband.

RHAWIN 5th century
RHWFAN

A son of Brychan who established a church on the Isle of Man. On his return from Man, he died with his brother Rhun Dremrudd on a bridge called Penrhun (Pont-y-Rhun) at Merthyr Tudfil, defending it from Saxons around 480.

RHEDYW
RHEDIW
November 11

Llanllyfni in Caernarfon seems to have been Gredfyw's foundation, but Gwyl Redyw was celebrated there on November 11, and the church is dedicated to Rhedyw. Ffynnon Rhedyw near the church was used for baptisms. A megalith called Eisteddfa Rhedyw is on Mynydd Llanllyfni. Possibly Rhedyw is the same saint as Gredfyw.

RHEITHIAN

Llanrheithian under Llanrhian in Pembroke. However, the church was dedicated to Caron, according to George Owen in the 16th century.

RHIAN 5th – 6th century
RAYN, RIANUS
March 8

Llanrhian, in the Deanery of Dewisland in Pembroke is his foundation. He is said to have been one of St David's followers, who founded a place of worship here in the 5th – 6th century. The church would have been a wattle and daub hut behind an earth wall. It is on the Menter Preseli 'Pilgrim's Trail', and the present building dates from the 13th century. There is an indecipherable Ogham stone, and an 8th century stone built into the tower bears a Celtic cross. The decagonal font is said to have been brought back from Jerusalem by Sir Rhys ap Thomas, one of Henry VII's greatest captains in the Battle of Bosworth Field, and bears his coat of arms. In Llanrhian parish, not far from Tregynon, is Llain y Sibedau (Place of Whispers), a ruined stone circle. Fenton described it in 1603 as Stonehenge in miniature, just 60 feet across with many white quartz stones.

RHIDIAN 5th - 6th century

Llanrhidian in Glamorgan celebrates this saint from the college of Cenydd at Llangenydd in Gower. Llanrhidian and its well are now dedicated to Illtud. Said to be a contemporary of Macsen Wledig, and to have converted Brynach Wyddel. Nearby, the Greyhound Inn Stone is made of white quartz. There is also Pitton Cross Standing Stone near here, and the nine feet Samson's Jack which stands on Llanrhidian's village green. It was being used as part of a field bank in the 1950's then moved to its present position. How many other stones can be found in field banks across Wales?

RHIENGAR 5th-6th century
A daughter or grand-daughter of Brychan, commemorated in Llech in Maelienydd, Radnor, and the mother of St Cynidr.

RHUDDLAD
September 4

She founded Llanrhuddlad, at the foot of Moel Rhyddlad in Anglesey, and was the daughter of a king of Leinster, according to Rowland's 'Mona Antiqua'.

RHUN AP MAELGWN GWYNEDD fl. 550

Not a saint, but he succeeded his father as King of Gwynedd, and is listed as one of the *'three fair princes of the Isle of Britain.'* He either killed Elidyr or revenged his death, and Caerhun in the Conwy Valley may have been his fortress. He attacked Cadog's settlement at Llancarfan after Camlan.

RHUN ab URIEN RHEGED 6th – 7th century

Possibly not a saint, but Owain's brother who became a priest. He was at the court of King Iago of Gwynedd before Iago was killed at Chester. Rhun is recorded as baptising the young King Edwin of Deira, before Edwin was reconverted by St Paulinus.

RHWYDRYS
November 1, or First Sunday in November

A son of Rhwydrim, king of Connacht, he founded Llanrhwydrys, under Llanfairynghornwy in Anglesey. There is a nearby standing stone at Cemlyn Bay, and a taller one near Pen-yr-Orsedd.

RHYCHWYN 7th century
June 10, Founders Day, the first Sunday after June 21, June 12

Possibly one of the dispossessed sons of Helig, he founded the remote Rhychwyn under Trefriw in Caernarfon, still called 'Llywelyn's Old Church'. However, Llywelyn ab Iorwerth then built Trefriw for easier access, where there is a 16th century glass window depicting Rhychwyn and David.

RHYDDERCH HAEL d. 612 (the same year as Kentigern)
RHYDDERCH HEN

A descendant of Macsen Wledig, who won the battle of Arderydd (on the Esk, near Carlisle) in 573. This was a critical victory for the Romano-Christian Cumbrians against the British who melded the old ways of Druidism with Christianity. Urien and Rhydderch beat the 'reactionary' forces of Gwenddoleu and Morcant. Cyndeyrn had fled to Wales to escape Morcant's persecution, but Rhydderch asked Cyndeyrn (Kentigern) to come to his kingdom of Strathclyde, from Llanelwy, to help convert the 'pagans'. Rhydderch saw a ring he had given to his wife on the hand of one of his nobles, who was asleep. Enraged at her infidelity, he pulled the ring off and hurled it into the river Clyde. He then summoned Queen Langueth, and asked for the ring back on pain of death. Distressed, she consulted Mungo (Kentigern), who prayed and discovered it was in the stomach of a salmon. The fish was caught, served to the queen, she found the ring and was saved from execution. Rhydderch is supposed to be buried at Abererch in Caernarfon. His 'Stanza of the Wise' says *'frequent is seen extreme hatred after extreme love.'*

Bohn placed Rhydderch as a vassal of Maelgwn Gwynedd, and also states that Rhydderch took part in the Battle of Arderydd in 573. There seems to be some evidence that Maelgwn of North Wales and the Men of the North (Cumbria and Strathclyde) were in conflict with Arthur of South Wales, who led his vassal princes of the West Country and kinsmen of Brittany. Rhydderch is mentioned in the 7th century Life of St Columba, who died in 597. In the Triads Rhydderch is one of the *'Three Generous Men of the Isle of Britain.'*

RHYSTUD 6th century
RESTITUTUS
Tuesday before Christmas

Possibly a son of Hywel ab Emyr Llydaw and brother of Cristiolus, Sulien, Derfel Gadarn and Dwywau. He was said to have been a bishop at Dyfrig's foundation at Caerleon. Llanrhystyd in Cardigan is dedicated to him, where Ffynnon Ffyn was a healing well. Other records place his father Hywel Fychan as the son of Hywel Farchog.

BISHOP RICHARD OF CHICHESTER 1197-1253
April 3

Given a holy day by the Church in Wales, Richard de Wych was born in Droitwich and studied at Oxford, Paris and Bologna. In 1235 he became chancellor at Oxford. He shared the exile of Archbishop Edmund Rich of Canterbury in 1240, and became a priest, studying with the Dominicans at Orleans. Henry III opposed, but Pope Innocent IV consecrated Richard as Bishop of Lyons in 1245. He returned to Chichester and was canonized in 1262. Its cathedral became a centre of pilgrimage to his shrine. Somehow, he became over the years the patron of the coachmen's guild in Milan.

RIOC fl.450-460
RIGAT, RIOCATUS
June 21

A British bishop who visited Lerins and met St Faustus around 450. Faustus gave him some anti-Arian writings fron southern Gaul to return to Britain, and he is known as Rigat or Riocatus at Trefiagat in Cornouaille, Brittany. He may be Riagath ap Pascent ap Vortigern.

RIOC 6th century
February 6, August 1

A Briton who was the son of Conis and Darerca (Padrig's sister), who helped Padrig evangelise Ireland. Commemorated at Lough Ree, and St Rock's, Kilkenny.

JOHN ROBERTS 1576-1610
December 10 (also October 25)

Born at Trawsfynydd, Merioneth, Roberts was taught at St John's Oxford and at the Inns of Court. His father was Robert ap Ellis ap William ap Gruffydd of Rhiw-goch. He then joined the Church of Notre Dame in Paris and entered the English College in Valladolid in 1598. He studied at Salamanca, became a Benedictine monk and returned to Britain in 1602 to minister to the sick in plague-ridden London. He was arrested four times in seven years, banished twice and escaped from prison once. In 1605 he was accused of implication in the Gunpowder Plot. During this period, London was ravaged by plague, and a contemporary wrote of Roberts: *'Among all the religious who have worked in that island this man may almost be reckoned the chief, both as regards labour and fruitfulness of teaching.'* In one of his periods of exile, he helped found St Gregory's College at Douai, 1606-7, intended to train priests for the English Mission, and he was one of the pioneers of the revival of the Order of St Benedict in Britain.

Arrested for a fifth time in 1610 for saying Mass in Holborn, he was hanged, drawn and quartered at Tyburn on December 10. In his trial he was accused of being a *'seducer of the people.'* His reply was *'If I am, then our ancestors were deceived by St Augustine, the apostle of the English, who was sent here by the pope of Rome, St Gregory the Great . . . I am sent here by the same Apostolic See that sent him before me.'* On the evening of his execution, a Spanish lady named Luisa de Carvajal paid for a huge feast to be held in his honour at Newgate prison. He was canonized in 1970.

ROMANS

The major reason that Wales became Christian was the Roman presence in Wales, attracted by its mineral wealth. As well as Welsh silver heading towards the Imperial Mint at Lyons, Dolaucothi Gold Mine was probably the most advanced mining site in the world at this time (see 'The A-Z of Wales and the Welsh'). The Romans used slaves to mine lead in Flint, Shropshire, Monmouth and Pumlumon, and exploited Parys on Anglesey for copper. Copper was also taken from Great Orme's Head, Llandudno, and Llanymynech Hill near Oswestry. Iron was also mined in the Forest of Dean. Julius Caesar made little headway in Britain in 55 BC and was forced to retreat to Gaul, despite the bravado he displays in his 'De Bello Gallico'. Another invasion in 54 BC led to partial gains up to the Thames before he was forced by Caswallon to leave Britain. Almost a hundred years passed until Claudius came across in 43 AD with 40,000 troops, leading to a Roman presence of around 350 years in Britain. However, in the 'Annals of Tacitus' we read *'In Britain, after the captivity of Caradoc, the Romans were repeatedly defeated and put to rout by the single state of the Silures alone.'* (12:38.38). Not until Caerleon was built did the Silures settle to a grudging accommodation with Rome.

Tertullian noted in 208 that *'places in Britain . . . though inaccessible to the Romans, have yielded to Christ'*, and the statement of Origen (c.240) also refers to the presence of Christianity in Britain. There seems to have been a wave of martyrdoms in Britain between 250 and 260. Three British bishops attended the Conference of Arles in 314 and the Synod of Rimini in 359. Athanasius, Patriarch of Alexandria, and Hilary of Poitiers both recorded the British as resisting Arianism in the 4th century, but it was at the centre of Pelagianism in the 5th century (see Pelagius). While the Lucius legend states that Wales was Christian in the 2nd century, and the Eurgain story has Christianity in Wales in the 1st century, we can certainly say

Caerleon Roman Amphitheatre. © *Wales Tourist Board Photo Library.*

that Christianity was well-established in Britain by the 3rd century, so there are at least 1800 unbroken years of traditional worship in Wales.*

Hanning commented that during Gildas' time *'Rome was more of a memory and less of a political heritage there than anywhere else in Europe.'* Gildas' 'De Excidio' was an attempt to make theological sense of the waves of Northern Picts, Scots (Irish) and Germanic tribes attacking and settling in his country. Around 540 he fixed upon the notion of the religious laxity of his leaders and churchmen as being the root cause of the 'punishment', which probably explains his contempt of Vortigern and his admiration for 'the last Roman', Ambrosius Aurelianus. Early Welsh history, as evidenced in triads, poems and the Mabinogion, truly 'romanticised' the era of Roman occupation of Britain. The Silures were a strong tribe, far enough away from the troubled Eastern coast of England, living in a fertile area, which embraced Roman ways at Caerleon and Caerwent. This area was the place of birth of at least two 'pendragons', pro-Roman faction warlords fighting the pagans, Meurig and his son Arthur.

*From the 'Timelines' Appendix, we can see the following evidence of British and Welsh Christianity:
209 Tertullian's testimony
239 Origen's testimony
250 Sabellius' testimony
314 Council of Arles

315 Eusebius' testimony
347 Council of Sardica
358 Hilary's testimony
359 Council of Rimini
400 Jerome's testimony
403 Victicius' visit
423 Theodoret's testimony
429 Garmon and Lupus visit
446 Appeal to Aetius
447 Garmon's second visit
461 Council of Tours
465 Council of Vannes
511 Council of Orleans
540 Gildas' 'De Excidio'
580 Vanantius' testimony
603 Augustine meets Welsh bishops
664 Synod of Whitby

Sabellius wrote around 250 that *'Christianity was privately confessed elsewhere, but the first nation that proclaimed it as their religion and called it Christian, after the name of Christ, was Britain.'* Gildas also proclaimed *'We certainly know that Christ, the True Son, afforded His light, the knowledge of His precepts to our Island in the last year of Tiberius Caesar.'* Tiberius died in March 37, while the traditional date for Joseph of Arimathea's arrival was 36. Claudius and the Romans did not invade until 43.

Martin of Louvain wrote in 1517 that: *'Three times the antiquity of the British Church was affirmed in Ecclesiastical Council. The Council of Pisa, 1417; The Council of Constance, 1419; The Council of Sienna, 1423. It was stated that the British Church took precedence over all other churches, being founded by Joseph of Arimathea, immediately after the Passion of Christ.'* This was an immensely important statement.

ROMAN STONES

Wales possesses a preponderance of Roman milestones and gravestones, and more are to be found in hedgerows and walls. Some were re-used for Celtic Christian burials. As with the Celtic stones, a complete and updatable dossier should be compiled upon these links with the past. Caerleon and Chester Museums are the best places to see collections of such stones. Among the hundreds of Roman inscriptions, one of the best was dug up in 1877 at Battle in Brecon. The best reading of the inscription is:

DIS.MAN(ibus) C.JULI
CANDIDI.TANCI
NI FILI EQ(uitis) ALAI
HISP(anorum) VETTON(um) C(ivium) R(omanorum) IFL(ius)
CLEMENS DOMIT(ius) VALENS H(eredes) F(eceunt)
ANNORUM XX STIPENDIORUM III H(ic) S(itvs) E(st)

This was found near a Roman encampment, and dates from the late 1st or early 2nd century.

Dolaucothi Roman Goldmines at Pumsaint. © *Wales Tourist Board Photo Library.*

DANIEL ROWLAND 1713-1790
October 16

Given a Holy Day by the Church in Wales, his father was the rector of Nantcwnlle and Llangeitho in Cardiganshire. Ordained a priest in 1735, he worked as a curate for his brother John, who now held his father's former livings. Griffith Jones' preachings brought about a change in Rowland's character, and he began to evangelise across the country, meeting and allying with Howel Harris (q.v.). After his acrimonious split with Harris, Llangeitho became the Mecca for Welsh Methodists. Rowland wrote a number of hymns, and many of his sermons have been published. He died at Newport, Pembrokeshire on October 16th, 1790, and is buried at Llangeitho.

RUTHIN

It seems strange that the superb town of Rhuthun (Ruthin) is not associated with its own saint, but there is a St Ruthin celebrated at Longden in Shropshire. Further research is needed upon this saint.

RYDOCH see CADOG ap BRYCHAN

S

'Sweet are the uses of adversity,
Which like the toad, ugly and venomous,
Wears yet a precious jewel in his head:
And this our life, exempt from public haunt,
Finds tongue in trees, books in the running brooks,
Sermons in stones, and good in everything.'

William Shakespeare, 'As You Like It'

SADWRN 6th century
SATURNINUS
November 29

Sadwrn Farchog (the Warrior) ap Bicanus Farchog, said to be the brother of St Illtud and grandson or nephew of Emyr Llydaw, is remembered at Llansadwrn in Anglesey and on an inscribed stone dug up there in 1742. His carved head had also been found. The stone is inscribed

> *'hic beatus*
> *satvrninus se*
> *acit. Et sua sa*
> *conivx. Pa'*

The fragmented remains possibly once read:
'Hic beatus vir saturninus sepsemit iacit, et su sancta conuix. Paterna cui sit terra levis.'
Also Llansadyrnin, or Llansadwrn in Carmarthenshire, a chapel under Cynwyl Gaio, recalls his name. Maen Cilau is a huge monolith over nine feet high at Abermorlais Park, Llansadwrn. Also near here are Cremlyn Dolmen and another cromlech near Hendrefor. In Henllan parish, Carmarthen, is Ffynnon Sadwrn.

Sadwrn was an old man when he accompanied Cadfan on his flight from Brittany, and was married to Canna ferch Tewdwr. The effigies of a warrior and his wife in nearby Beaumaris church, removed from Penmon Priory at the Dissolution, may be those of Sadwrn and Canna. Ffynnon Sadwrn is near Llandudno. There is a Pont Sadwrn (Sadwrn's Bridge) just outside the Roman town of Caerleon.

SADWRN 7th century

Sadwrn is mentioned in the legend of Gwenfrewi, and is considered the patron saint of Henllan in Denbigh. After her beheading she went to the hermit, Deifer, at Bodfari, who sent her on to the *'venerable'* Sadwrn to advise her. He in turn passed her on to St Elerius at Gwytherin after a night's prayer. Henllan Church has an unusual detached tower, built on a rocky outcrop above the steeply sloping churchyard, ostensibly because the bells could be heard further in a parish which stretches for 16 miles. Next to the church is the Llindir Inn (named after the llin, flax, that used to be grown in the area), and said to be haunted by the murdered wife of a landlord.

SADWRN 8th century
SATURN

There seems to have been an abbot of Llandough and Llanilltud with this name, mentioned in the Book of Llandaf, and Tref Saturn was mentioned as a boundary of Merthyr Mawr.

SADYRNIN d.832
November 29

A Bishop of St David's, one of the few Welshmen officially sanctified by the Roman church. Attempts have been made to link him with Llansadyrnin, which was an older foundation. The day of the Welsh 'Sadwrns' is the same as that of Saturninus, the 3rd century bishop and martyr of Toulouse.

It is tempting to place this cleric as a signatory in the 'Gospels of Teilo' (now the Book of St Chad), which was written in the early 8th century. A land grant in the margins, referring to Brechfa (the district around Llandeilo) was mutilated by a bookbinder at some time, but we can read:
'This writing sheweth that Rhys and Hirv . . . Brechva as far as Hirvaen Gwyddog, from the desert of Gelli Irlath as far as Camddwr. Its rent payment is sixty loaves, and a wether sheep, and a quantity of butter. Almighty God is witness; Sadwrnwydd the Priest, witness; Nywys, witness, Gwrgi, witness; Cwdhwlf, witness; of the laity, Cynwern, witness; Collwyn, witness; Cyhorged, witness; Erbin, witness. Whoever will keep it shall be blessed; whoever will break it shall be accursed.'

SAERAN mid 6th century
January 13

Of Irish origin, the son of Geraint Saer, he was buried at Llanynys in Denbigh's Vale of Clwyd, which was formerly called Lann Saeran. Bishop Usher wrote that he founded the Bishopric of Cloyne in Ireland between 520 and 550. The tiny 13th century church of St Michael and All Angels in Efenechtyd has a circular Celtic churchyard, and is thought to have been founded by monks from Saeran's community at Llanynys. Efenechtyd may mean 'place of the monks'. There is a rare mediaeval wooden font in this twenty feet wide building. The rounded stone by the font is the 'Maen Camp', formerly used at the local 'campau' or sports, on September 29th, St Michael's Day. The object was to lift it and throw it backwards over one's head, as far as possible.

Ffynnon Saeran is now called Ffynnon Sarah, and stands by the ancient pilgrim trackway above Derwen. The Pilgrim's Track runs from Holywell to St David's. The well was restored in 1972 by the Rector of Derwen. A spring fills a tree-shaded stone bath, overflowing into the stream known as Nant Mynian. It cured rheumatism and cancer, and 'gifts' of pins were dropped in before descending three steps to bathe in the well-tank. Cure-seekers came until at least Victorian times. Derwen's church is now dedicated to St Mary, but was probably a Celtic foundation originally. The 15th century preaching cross there is of national importance with a carved octagonal shaft. The church has its beautiful rood screen and rood loft still intact.

St Saeran's Church at Llanynys was once the mother-church of southern Duffryn Clwyd. There is a 13th century west doorway, and yew trees lead to an imposing Tudor porch. There is a hammer-beamed roof, but St Saeran's greatest glory is a massive 15th century wall painting of St Christopher, rediscovered under plaster in 1967. A stone figure of a mitred bishop in the church may have come from a 14th century shrine to Saeran in the graveyard. One can also see telescopic dog-tongs, used to seize and expel unruly hounds from the church and its grounds. Ffynnon Saeran was a holy well at Llanynys.

An annual memorial service in Llanynys Church for the murder of Llywelyn II was addressed by Dafydd Iwan, Kenneth Griffith and Richard Livesey MP in December 1999. In the afternoon a brief service was held at Llywelyn's Cave at Aberedw, and the annual memorial lecture delivered at Abbey Cwm Hir.

SAINTS DAYS

A notable fact is that the Welsh held their saints' days and village fairs 11 days after the time given in the Gregorian Calendar. After 1800 it increased to 12 days. This makes calculations somewhat problematical for the celebration of festivities. In 1752, the 'New Style' calendar was adopted on September 2, following on from August 21. The dates August 22 to September 1 had no existence in 1752. A proclamation was made in Henry VIII's reign prohibiting almanacs which transmitted the belief that saints rule the weather.

WILLIAM SALESBURY 1520? - 1584?
September 10

Given the same Holy Day as Bishop William Morgan, this scholar was the first translator of the New Testament into Welsh. Born at Llansannan, the son of Ffwg ap Robert ap Thomas Salbri Hen, he spent most of his life at Plas Isa, Llanrwst. It was at Oxford that he probably left the Catholic faith and became Protestant. He and Bishop Richard Davies of St David's translated the Prayer Book and New Testament between 1563 and 1567, when they were published. He and Davies argued in their translation of the Old Testament and stopped work, allegedly disagreeing over the meaning of just one word, and it was left to William Morgan to complete this task in 1588. Salesbury also wrote a dictionary, perhaps the first book to be printed in Welsh, and was a brilliant linguist, the greatest Welsh scholar and man of letters of his age.

SAMLED

Llansamlet in Glamorgan.

SAMSON 6th century

The son of Caw, who studied at Llanilltud Fawr, and had a church at York (Caerefrog).

Alphabetical Listing of the Saints of Wales and Religious Events

BISHOP SAMSON OF DOL 485-565 (Cressy states d.599)
July 28 [died May 28]

His father Amon (Amwn) Ddu was from Brittany and his mother from Gwent, Anna ferch Meurig ap Tewdrig. The cousin of Malo, Samson was born in Glamorgan and trained under Illtud at Llaniltud Fawr. Samson's Well at Llanilltud seems to have been transmuted to 'Nancy's Well' over the centuries. He left to go to Caldey Island, Ynys Byr*, where he became abbot. However, he soon left, as he was disgusted by the drinking and poor behaviour of the monks who had not been controlled by Abbot Pyr. After reforming an Irish monastery, he again retired as a hermit near the river Severn. In Cornwall he then led Austell, Mewan and Winnow in evangelising the area, and also visited the Scilly Isles and Channel Isles. He then founded the monastery at Dol in Brittany and another at Pental in Normandy.

There are many dedications to Samson in Brittany, such as villages named St Samson north-west of St Renan and north of Dinan. Kersamson is near Armel's foundation of Ploermel, and Armel may be his kinsman Arthur. There are churches bearing his name at Bally Samson in Wexford, and at Ballygriffin near Dublin.

Samson is associated with many standing stones. In Cornwall, he incised a cross on a pagan stone in the district of Tricurius, and there are three stones in Glamorgan named after him, Carreg Samson (Samson's Stone), Samson's Jack and Ffust Samson (Samson's Flail). There are other Carreg Samsons spread throughout Wales. There are two groups of cromlechs in north Pembrokeshire, a stone at Llanddewi Brefi, and a stone cross in the churchyard at Lanbadarn Fawr. At Dol, Samson's Mitre stands, and there is another Samson stone at Penvern, Cote-du-Nord, next to his chapel.

The tiny, ruined St Roque's Chapel at Merthyr Mawr is only seventeen feet by twenty-two feet. It is set within a iron age hill-fort, near a huge pot-hole. There are two early Christian burial stones in the chapel, the larger being the seven feet tall wheel cross known as the 'Goblin Stone'. A goblin was supposed to have grabbed passers-by and forced their hands and feet through the four holes in the wheel-cross. The smaller stone at Merthyr Mawr is surmounted by an eleventh century cross, and reads '*Conbelan* (Cunobelinus, or Cymbeline) *placed this cross for his soul (and the souls) of St Glywys, of Nertat, and of his brother and father. Prepared by me + Sciloc*'. In the life of St Samson of Dol, Samson left his abbey at Caldey Island and came to a 'desert'. He set up a church inside an ancient 'castle', near a cave where St. Samson made a spring by driving his staff into the ground. Only Stackpole in Wales can rival the possibility that this is the site of Samson's church. Both have 'deserts' of sand-dunes, the highest in Europe being those at Merthyr Mawr.

St Samson founded a monastery in Dol-de-Bretagne, fifteen miles south-east of St Malo, and soon became the most famous saint in Brittany. His church conferred a special dignity on the town, and Nominoe was proclaimed Duke of Brittany here in 848. (Brittany was totally independent of France until the fifteenth century). Nominoe then raised the bishops of Dol to the status of Archbishop and Primate of all Brittany. The great St Samson's Cathedral there has 13th century stained glass windows and no less than eighty 14th century oak choir stalls.

Samson's mother Anna was the daughter of Meurig ap Tewdrig, so Samson's brothers were the saints Tydecho and Tathan. Importantly, his uncle was Arthwys ap Meurig, the King Arthur of history, and his cousin Morgan became king of Glamorgan. (Some historians place Samson as Arthur's cousin). Welsh accounts state that he returned from Brittany to Wales to die at Illtud's college. In the church at Llanilltud are three stones, the first has inscriptions that it is the cross of Iltutus and Samuel, that it was the cross that Samson erected for his soul, and that Samson was the sculptor. Another stone states that it was prepared for Samson's soul, and for the souls of Juthael the king, and Arthmael. Arthmael may be the Arthur of history, which some modern sources also claim to be the warrior-saint Armel. Armel collaborated with Samson to overthrow Conmire in Brittany and restore Iudael to the crown. It seems clear that this stone commemorates this event. If it is true, history has to be rewritten. After Conmire's defeat, Samson visited King Childebert in Paris to attend the episcopal diet of the Franks, and signed the resolutions as *'Samson peccator episcopus.'* This was the Third Council of Paris in 557.

Samson is traditionally said to be buried at Llanilltud Fawr, but this was possibly a Bishop of Llanilltud. There is a cave of Samson's at Stackpole in Pembroke, and he founded Marcross near Llanilltud, now dedicated to the Holy Trinity. There is a Ffynnon Samson at Llangolman and at Llandeloy in Pembroke. Pistyll Samson, another holy well, is near Bedd Samson (Samson's Grave) at Newport, Pembroke. His foundation at Coleborne, Gloucester, is now that of James. There is another hardly-known Shropshire foundation of Samson's in Cressage. It is now called Christ Church.

Marcross Well inspired the following local rhyme:
'For the itch and the stitch,
Rheumatic and the gout,
If the devil isn't in you
The well will take them out.'
Intriguingly, it appears to be the only holy well in Wales which could restore hair. International revenues from its botled water could solve Wales' economic problems overnight if the remedy proved efficacious.

*The author believes that this was Barri, rather than Caldey Island, being far nearer to Llanilltud. (See Peirio).

SANCTAN AP SAWYL 5th – 6th century
May 7, 9

The brother of Madog, he followed him to Ireland, and founded Kilnasantan near Dublin, now dedicated to Anne. He, not Sannan, may have founded Llansannan in Denbigh, as its fair was held on May 7. May 9 was the traditional date for calving in Wales, and Gerald of Wales noted a Norman knight called Gilbert Hagurnell giving birth to a calf, *'the punishment for some unnatural vice.'* Around this time the wild cherry flowered in Wales, and Francis Kilvert noted in his diary upon May 9, 1870: *'Now the various tints of green mount over one another in the hanging woods of Penllan above the dingle . . . The grass was jewelled with cowslips and orchises. The dingle was lighted here and there with wild cherry, bird cherry, the Welsh name of which being interpreted as "the tree on which the devil hung his mother".'*

SANNAN 488-544 or 568
SENANUS, SENEN, SENY
March 1 (June 30 Ireland, March 6 Brittany, March 8 Wales – date of burial, June 13 also in Wales, and April 29 according to Cressy and Catholic Online Saints, December 17 Baring-Gould at Llantrisant)

Alphabetical Listing of the Saints of Wales and Religious Events

A great friend of St David who possibly founded Llansannan in Denbigh. Bedwellty in Monmouth is his foundation. He was known as Seny in Brittany. An Irish deacon, but possibly the brother of Patrick, which makes him Welsh. Sannan's son was a saint called Patrick, and said to be St Patrick's nephew. This Patrick is often confused with his uncle. Sannan died on the same day, but possibly not the same year as St David.

Gwyl Mabsant at Llansannan was in the middle of June, near June 13, with another fair on May 7 (possibly Sanctan's). Bedwellty celebrated on March 8, and Ffynnon Sant Sannan was near the church. He is also celebrated at Llantrisant on Anglesey on June 13, with the co-patrons Afan on December 17 and Iefan (John the Baptist) on August 29. A field near Llansannan is called Tyddyn Sannan, near Pant yr Eglwys where a ruin was supposed to have been his church. The hill of Foel Sanan stands nearby. St Sennen at Land's End in Cornwall also commemorated him. The stone of St Sannan is mentioned in the Tudno entry.

The website Catholic Online Saints refers to two saints called Senan, one being a 7th century Welsh hermit who laboured in North Wales, and whose feast day is April 29. The other Senan is celebrated on March 8, and was said to have been born in Munster. After serving as a soldier, he became a monk under Abbot Cassidus, who sent him to Abbot Natalis at Kilmanagh in Ossory. Senan then met St David in Pembroke after returning from a pilgrimage to Rome, before settling on Scattery Island. It is difficult to disentangle these two saints, and it may be the same person.

SANT 5th century

This father of St David was possibly not venerated as a saint, but Lesant in Cornwall was formerly Lan-Sant, and its nearness to Landue (Dewi) and Bradstone (Non) makes it a strong candidate for his foundation.

SARLLOG 1st - 2nd century

In some accounts, Eurgain ferch Caradog (Caractacus) married Sarllog, Lord of Caer Sarllog (Old Sarum). Iolo Morganwg also mentions a Côr Sarllog in Llandaf with 30 saints and Sarllog as its penrhaith (principal). This may be a fabrication. Other accounts have Eurgain marrying a Roman noble, Lucius, who returned with her to St Donat's. This is supposed to be the same person as Sarllog.

SAWEL 6th century
SAWYL
January 15

Sawyl Felyn ap Bledri Hir is the patron saint of Llansawel, a chapel under Cynwyl Gaio in Carmarthen. There is a nearby Ffynnon Sawyl which now supplies the village, which was once known as Pistyllsawil. Briton Ferry in Glamorgan used to be known as Llanisawel, and is now dedicated to Mary. Carreg Hir standing stone at Briton Ferry is in the school playground opposite Giant's Grave. Some sources give Sawyl Benuchel as the founder of these places.

In 1881, Wirt Sikes noted a unique 'friendly society' like the Oddfellows, Foresters, Buffaloes, Shepherds and Ivorites . . . The Friendly Sisters of Briton Ferry. After noting the unusual tradition of female equality for over a millennium in Wales, he wrote: *'Briton Ferry is one of the oldest villages in Wales. It is packed full of dissenters. Its people are chiefly workers in copper and coal. The poets Gray and Mason were both in their day much at home in Briton Ferry . . . The planting of graves (is) specially favoured in the old churchyard here. I found the Friendly Sisters to be a society whose members were exclusively women, but which employed a masculine slave as a secretary - a worthy man, who served in the same capacity for the Briton Ferry Oddfellows and Foresters, but who feelingly confessed to me that he had more trouble with his "sisters" than with all the brethren of the other two societies combined. There were something like 100 sisters, with a lodge-room at the Cross Keys Inn, a hostelrie appropriately presided over by a landlady. Here they met weekly, and here on a pleasant September evening they celebrated their eighth anniversary in friendly fashion, by sitting down to tea. After tea the sisters repaired to the ball-room, and danced till a late hour to the music of the harp. This event, however, was but a light incident in the life of the society, whose serious purpose was to raise funds, by entrance fees, subscriptions, fines, donations, and interest on capital, for payment of the funeral expenses of members or members' husbands. Members paid one shilling a month, and an additional shilling whenever there was a death of a member or member's husband. In return they received ten pounds when the death was their own, besides getting a guinea out of the treasury at a "division" fixed to take place every three years. "Indeed," said their much-enduring secretary, "the last division was done in two years, and I can't impress upon them how wrong it is to do so. I am very soon placed aside in these matters by their facile tongues; I have no chance in arguing with them, whether I am right or wrong. They are rather an unmanageable society." With £100 in the bank, and ninety members, how can it be, the women ask, that it is unwise to distribute the funds?'* Sikes goes on to mention some rules, such as a fine of twopence for not behaving properly in meetings.

SAWYL BENUCHEL early 6th century
SAWYL BENISEL

The father of St Asaf, and possibly of Sanctan, Madog and Pyr. The son of Pabo Post Prydain and brother of Dunawd and Cerwydd, and described as *'an overbearing prince'*. He appears to have lost territories in the South Pennines to the Saxons and retired to live at Dunawd's college at Bangor-is-Coed. Possibly he did not retire but went to Tegeingl (Flint), then Glamorgan, holding court at Allt Cynnadda near Cydweli.

There is a story that Cadog's provisions were stolen by this warlord at Llangadog. Sawyl is said to be buried in a mound called Banc Benuchel near where Cadog enticed his men into a bog. It is said that his body was found here in 1850, covered by a hexagonal stone imitiating his war-shield. There is a Ffynnon Sul outside Cydweli Castle, where traditionally a prince named Benisel was slain. This may be another tenuous link to support the theory of territorial dispute between Arthur's men of South Wales and Domnonia, against those of North Wales and the North of England.

SEGIN WYDDEL

Obviously of Irish origins, said to have studied at Llanilltud Fawr and to have founded nearby Llanfihangel, now dedicated to Michael. The Holy Well at Llanfihangel had water spouting from stone breasts, and was destroyed in the Reformation. Sigingston (Tresigin) is a pretty hamlet nearby, possibly named after Sigin, and Sigin's Well was one of the six wells of nearby Llanilltud Fawr.

ABBOT SEIRIOL 6th century
February 1 (also 3, 11 and 15)

St Seiriol, the brother of Einion Frenhin and Meirion, was a relation of Maelgwn Gwynedd, whose court was at Deganwy. His father was Owain Danwyn ab Einion Yrth ap Cunedda Wledig. His brother, King Einion, established Penmon College, with Seiriol as its first principal. Ynys Seiriol, the Island of Seiriol, was also known as Priestholm to the invading Vikings, and now is called Puffin Island. Another old name was Glanach. Before Seiriol it was known as Ynys Llannog, giving the island no less than five distinct names. (See Helig Foel). Seiriol had his cell here, and also built a church on neighbouring Anglesey at Penmon. No women were allowed to come onto the island. There are still remarkable remains at Penmon, and it is said to have been a considerable druidic holy site.

Next to Penmon Priory remains is a massive mediaeval dovecot. Through a stone doorway takes one to St Seiriol's Well, which he used to baptise Norse settlers on Anglesey. His cell foundations are just a few yards away. Just a ten minute walk from here was a stone cross over a thousand years old, with worn carvings said to denote the Temptation of St Anthony. The Penmon Cross has been moved into the Priory Church for safety. Another pre-Norman high cross and stone slab can also be seen in Penmon Church. If one walks in the opposite direction from the well to the Pilot House Restaurant at Black Point, one can see Ynys Seiriol and its tower (which is supposed to stand on the site of Seiriol's hermitage) and also Penmaenmawr on the mainland.

Sir John of Gwydir wrote in the 16th century in his 'Caernarvonshire Antiquities' that *'Seiriol also hadd a hermytage at Penmaen Mawr, and there hadd a chapell where hee did bestowe much of his tyme in prayers, the place being then an uncouth desert and unfrequented rock and unaccessible both in regard to the steepness of the rock and also of the desertedness of the wilderness.'* Penmaenmawr is on the coast of Conwy Bay, upon the Welsh mainland, five miles from Puffin Island. It seems that at this time it was possible at low tide to walk between the two churches on a track of seamarsh and sand. The record continues:
'(Seiriol) made from Priestholm to Penmaen Mawr a pavement whereupon he might walk drye from his church at Priestholm to his chappell at Penmaen Mawr, the vale beynge very lowe grownde and wette, which pavement may bee discerned from Penmaen Mawr to Priestholm when the sea is cleere, if a man liste to goe in a bote to see itt.' Excavations at Barri Docks at the end of the 19th century seemed to confirm that sea levels have risen about forty feet since the times of 'The Age of the Saints'.

With his friend St Cybi, he is one of Anglesey's principal saints. He was said to be one of the 'seven Cousins' who went on pilgrimage to Rome. He met Cybi often at their holy wells at Clorach in Llandyfrydog parish in the centre of Anglesey. Seiriol walked east to west in the morning to meet him, and went to east in the afternoon, so always had his back to the sun. Cybi, travelling in the opposite direction, always was walking into the sun. Thus they were known at Seiriol Wyn (Bright, or White) and Cybi Felyn (Yellow, Tanned or Dark).

There were three holy wells dedicated to Seiriol on Anglesey. One, with the remains of a cell is less than 100 yards from his church at Penmon, another is three miles away in Llaniestyn parish and the other Ffynnon Seiriol is at Llanerchymedd. This last well was visited at midnight and its water taken away for the use of ailing people. There is also a Ffynnon Seiriol at Penmaenmawr in Caernarfon.

SEITHENYN 5th-6th century

This king shared with Gwyddno the lost lands of Cantref y Gwaelod, which was flooded on the Cardigan coast around 520 (see the author's A-Z of wales, and the entry on Atlantis). His children included the saints Gwynodl, Merin, Senwyr, Tuglyd, Tudno, Tyneio and Arwystli Gloff. All except the last studied at Dunawd's college at Bangor Is Coed, today's Bangor-on-Dee, which was destroyed by barbarians.

SELYF 5th – 6th century
SALOMON, SALMON, SELEVAN, SOLOMANUS, LEVAN
February 1, June 25 (Catholic Online Saints)

A king killed by rebels and made a saint. Selyf's father, Geraint ab Erbyn was King of Dumnonia (Wiltshire, Devon, Somerset and Cornwall) and died fighting for Arthur at Llongborth. St Salmon's Well was the name of a field near Steynton, Pembroke.

Selyf was called Solomon, Duke of Cornwall, but there are no churches in Wales associated with him. It is said that he placed his son Kebius as a bishop in Anglesey. He married Gwen ferch Cynyr, Non's sister. His mother was Gwyar ferch Amlawdd Wledig, his brothers were Cyngar, Iestyn (Just), Caw and Cado, and his sister Breage. His hermitage-chapel and well at East Levan in Cornwall survive. St Salomon is west of Pontivy. St Manacca, a Cornish abbess who gave her name to Manaccan, may be his sister and her feast date is October 14th.

His church at Lansalos in Cornwall is next to those of Dulo (Cybi's) and Pelynt (Non's). At nearby Morval is a church dedicated to his wife, Gwen (Wenn). His holy well was at Lansalos. St Levan has a huge pre-Christian boulder in its churchyard. Selyf split it with a blow from his fist and said:
'When, with panniers astride,
A pack-horse, one can ride,
Through St Levan's Stone,
The world will be done.'

SELYF AP CYNAN GARWYN d. 603, 607 or 613
February 1?

This grandson of Brochwel of Powys was called by Iolo Morganwg a saint, and known as Selyf 'Sarfgaddau', *'the serpent of battles'*. In the Triads he was also known as *'one of the three grave-slaughterers of Britain'*, as his death at Chester was avenged after his death, that is from the grave. He was the father of St Dona.

Alphabetical Listing of the Saints of Wales and Religious Events

Either Selyf ap Cynan, Selyf ap Geraint, or Selevan noted earlier may be associated with Usk, which stands on the Roman township of Burrium. I am indebted to Wirt Sikes for the following. He describes the ancient castle, where he believed Richard III was born, and gives details of the church and Leland's description of the priory. He continues:

There is a inscription in the church, on a brass plate, which is celebrated throughout Wales for the amount of botheration it has afforded antiquaries:-

Nole clode yr ethrode yar adnorade llawn hade
Ilnndeyn Abarnourbede breynt amle tynebaioty hanab
Seliff suunoier sinn a seadam yske eval kuske
Deke kuwmode doctor Kymmeu Ileua i llawn a leue

Many be they who have racked their brains over this puzzler, and fantastical enough are some of the interpretations which have been offered. The inscription is doubtless Welsh of an ancient and corrupt dialect of Gwent, and sings the praises of an illustrious man whose ashes lie beneath. "Noted also as an astrologer, Seliff lies in silken slumbers here in Usk.'

SENAN d.660
April 29

With Beuno, an instructor of Gwenfrewi

SEN PATRICK d.493

Born on the Gower Peninsula near Swansea, he is closely associated with St Patrick, and is said to have been told by that they should go to heaven together.

SENWYR
SENEFYR
September 1

Llansannor Parish Church is dedicated to St Senwyr, an obscure saint mentioned in the 12th century Bonedd y Saint. This is possibly Senewyr or Senfyr ap Seithenyn, from Cardiganshire, the brother of Tudno. Like his brothers Gwynodl, Merin, Tudno, Tudglyd and Tyneio, he studied at Bangor-is-Coed. The mediaeval chapel of '*St Senwer de la Thawe*' is recorded in The Book of Landaf, but Senwer/Sannor is not recorded anywhere else.

In 1570, Gwenllian ferch Harry of Llansannor (formerly Llansanwyr) was hanged for stealing 40 shillings from the mill of John Nicholl at St Hilary. Intriguingly Llansanwyr was also known as St Dawen. The Dawen is the river (Thaw) which emerges into the Bristol Channel at Aberddawen (Aberthaw).

SERIGI WYDDEL 5th century

This Irish chief is accounted a martyr, who was killed in Anglesey by Cadwallon Lawhir ab Einion Yrth by his own hand, at Cerrig y Gwyddyl near Malldraeth. Serigi had a fort at Dinas Ffaraon (Dinas Emrys) near Beddgelert. Eglwys y Bedd where he died became a shrine to

SETNA 5th – 6th century
SITHNEY
September 19 (Brittany), August 3, 4 (Cornwall)

His mother was David's sister, Magna, and he was a disciple of Sannan. Remembered at Sithney in Cornwall, and buried at Kinsale.

THE SICILIAN BRITON fl. 410

An unknown Briton and radical follower of Pelagius. After the Goths took Rome in 410, he wrote 'De Divitiis'. This strongly socialist tract has the recurring message *'Tolle divitem' (Down with the rich man).*

SIDWELLA 5th - 6th century
August 2 (August 1, July 31)

The sister of Juthwara (q.v.), remembered at Exeter, where there was a healing well mentioned by Leland and William of Worcester. She was killed at Exeter when her pagan step-mother incited the reapers of the harvest to cut off her head. August 1st marks the start of Lammas, so Sidwella may have been replacing a corn goddess revered in pre-Christian times. She is depicted with a scythe and a well in stained glass at Exeter Cathedral. She was possibly the sister of Peulin, Pol de Leon, who also had a church dedication in Exeter. St Sidwell's holy well was at Llaneast in Cornwall.

SILYN 6th century
SILIN [SSILIN=GILES]
January 27, September 1

An Irish monk who had a hermitage near the River Clydach in Brechfa Forest*. His healing well near the village of Gwernogle (the place of the adders) is where he saved a stag from hunters. It was destroyed when the well chamber was filled in by a farmer, to prevent his animals from harming themselves. The Church of St Giles in Wrexham celebrates on September 1, but Giles may have replaced a Denbighshire Silin. Capel San Silin at Llanfihangel Ystrad in Cardigan commemorated Silin, who may have been Giles of Saint-Gilles in Provence, who was extermely popular after the Crusades. It may also have been Julian, bishop of Le Mans, whose cult spread to Britain before the Normans.

George Owen noted a Capel Silin and Capel Cawey as pilgrimage chapels at Mynachlog-ddu in Pembroke, but neither survives, only the church attributed to Dogmael. There was a Ffynnon Shan Shilin at Letterston Pembroke which may have been Silin's, and the church is now dedicated to Giles. Well water was sold at one shilling a bottle in the early 20th century, which was an extremely high price.

Alphabetical Listing of the Saints of Wales and Religious Events

* A narrow lane, in places banked by six-feet high ditches, with six feet high hedges above them, winds through the outskirts of Brechfa Forest between St Teilo's church at Brechfa and the beautifully sited church at Llanllawddog. Upon August 8, 1999, the author saw a puma leap at least ten feet from the middle of the lane over the hedge. The distance was not possible for a normal cat or dog. Upon August 17, the Western Mail carried reports of a family of three or four pumas living in the Brechfa Forest.

SIMAUS d.550
SIVIAU, SIEU, CIEUX

Lancieux, on the Cote-d'Armor, 12 miles north west of Dinan, is named after Simaus who came after Brieuc (Briog) to convert the Bretons to Christianity. The stoup in the church is carved out of a 4th century Roman milestone. He had been a monk under Briog at 'Landa Magna' in Cardigan, and a dream told him to follow Briog to Armorica. Just before his arrival in Brittany, Briog died, and Simaus founded the church now known as St Cieux.

CHARLES SIMEON 1756-1836
November 13

Given a Holy Day by the Church in Wales, he was an eccentric don at Cambridge, who trained hundreds of students and established a standard for setting up major service organisations. He served Holy Trinity parish for 54 years until his death. The non-profit Simeon Institute at Cambridge carries on his work, *'creating unique alliances internationally to build community crisis management capacity through project-based syatems.'*

SIMON ZELOTES 1st century
SIMWN
October 28 (West), July 1 (East)

Bishop Dorotheus of Tyre, writing in the 3rd century, believed that Simon was crucified in Britain. The Eastern Church states that this Canaanite died in Egypt, but the Western Church tradition from the 6th century is that Simon left Egypt and was martyred in Persia with Jude. Simon and Jude are depicted in East Anglian screens with a boat, which may be a folk memory of the legend of their arrival in Britain. Tresimwn is the former name of Bonvilston in the Vale of Glamorgan.

SOCRATES see STEPHANUS

STEFFAN see YSTYFFAN

STEPHANUS and SOCRATES d.c.303
September 17

According to Cressy, two disciples of St Amphibalus, these *'two noble British Christians'* were martyred during the Diocletian prosecution in Britain around 303. They possibly came from the Monmouth area. A stone with an inscription to Diocletian and also Giordanus was found in a carpenter's work-shop in Aberavon, with inscriptions on three sides. It probably came from the ancient burial ground at Yr Hen Eglwys. The stone was used as ballast in a pilot boat journey from Aberafan to Swansea, and set up on the lawn of the rector's house. Inscriptions read: 'DAEC MAGOR DIANUS AVG; IMM CAE NO L F A G; and IMPCC DIO CLETTI ANO MARC VRE OA.' The Giordanus inscription is twice as big as the one to Diocletian. The Emperor Giordanus was treacherously put to death in 244 after six years' rule.

STINAN see JUSTINIAN

SUL Y BLODYN
SUNDAY OF THE FLOWERS, PALM SUNDAY

Dressing graves in preparation for Easter coincided with the wearing of new clothes after the time of Winter and Lent. It seems to be a pre-15th century tradition which became associated with Easter, especially in South Wales. Charles Redwood, in his 1839 book 'The Vale of Glamorgan: Scenes and Tales among the Welsh', notes the following:

'On our return, I was surprised, as we came to the churchyard, to find it the scene of extraordinary employment, until I recollected that this was Easter Eve. All the village were there, engaged, after the old custom, in trimming and adorning the graves of their deceased relatives. Some were raising the sides with fresh turf, and putting fresh earth upon the surface; and others whitewashed the stones at the ends; while the women planted rosemary and rue, and the girls brought baskets of spring flowers, crocuses, daffodils, and primroses, which were placed in somewhat fantastic figures upon all the graves.'

Iolo Morganwg said that the custom was carried out a month after the burial, and every Christmas, Easter and Whitsun. The Easter Sunday custom was eventally superseded by the Palm Sunday tradition in many parts of Wales. Marie Trevelyan, that remarkable writer from Llanilltud Fawr, recorded in 1909 the continuation of a pre-Reformation tradition in the Vale of Glamorgan: *'The image of a donkey is made of wood. On this a stuffed effigy was placed, and these were glued fast to a platform, which was set upon wheels. The donkey and the effigy were decorated with flowers and bundles of evergreens. When brought to the church door by the procession, each member carried a sprig of evergreen, seasonable flowers, or herbs, box-wood predominating. The people were met by the clergyman, who blessed the procession and the evergreens and flowers. The sprigs were carefully preserved for the year as a charm to keep away evil spirits and witches, and a protection against mishaps.'*

SULFED

Llandysulfed church in Llandysul parish in Cardigan may note a saint named Sulfed, with the endearment 'tŷ', or meaning 'the house of' Sulfed.

SULFYW 5th - 6th century

Llancillo, subject to Rowleston in Hereford, was mentioned in The Book of Llandaf as *'Sulbio Lann Sulbiu'*, in the time of Meurig ap Tewdrig.

SULIEN 6th – 7th century
SILIAN

King Gorwg ap Meirchion of Glamorgan called his court Tresilian, after a martyred saint. This small cwm (valley) leading to the sea is near St Donat's Castle. At this cove the noted Breton pirate Colyn Dolphyn was buried up to his neck to await the oncoming tide. The largest cave in the cliffs, known as Reynard's or Cathedral Cave, extends 40m, and is 12m wide and 8m high. It is spanned by an internal bridge of rock. Couples visited the cave, and if the girl managed to throw a pebble over the bridge at her first attempt, she would marry within the year. A marriage was solemnised here, in what was intended to be a practical joke. The 'pretend parson' was in fact the rector of Llandow in disguise, which validated the 'marriage'. The 'lucky couple' were the parents of the heroic general Sir Thomas Picton, who died at Waterloo in 1815. There was a Ffynnon Silian in Merioneth, near Rug Chapel. At Silian in Cardigan was found an ornamental Celtic stone which is indecipherable. Other stones appear to have been 'lost' in this area.

SULIEN 1011-1091
SILIN
September 1

The father of Rhygyfarch, who wrote the Life of St David, and also of Ieuan, who wrote a famous poem about Sulien. Sulien the Wise was associated with Llanbadarn, and Ieuan's poem shows that the great monastery there had either been ravaged or had declined from greatness by this early time.

Sulien's sons were Arthen, Rhigyfarch, Deiniol and Ieuan (d.1137). A Welsh chronicler records his death *'And then Sulien, bishop of Menevia, the most learned of the Britons and eminent for his pious life, after the most praiseworthy instruction of his disciples and the keenest teaching of his parishes, died, in the eightieth year of his life and the twentieth but one from his consecration, on the eve of the Calends of January.'* Letterston in Pembroke may be his foundation.

A variety of plantain (psyllium), Fleabane Wort, known as Llysiau Silin (Silyn's Herb) is named after him.

SULIEN 6th century
SILIN
September 2, October 1, May 13 (jointly with Mael), December 17 (Cornwall)

Sulien ap Hywel ab Emyr Llydaw settled at Bardsey with his cousin Cadfan. Sulien shares a joint dedication with St Mael at Corwen parish church (formerly known as Llansilien), Llandrillo near Corwen and at Cwm near the coast of northern Flintshire. There was a Ffynnon Sulien a mile away from Corwen church, and the water used for its baptisms. The great fair there was held on May 13. Ffynnon Fael a Sulien was near his Flint foundation.

Wall Painting at Rug Chapel. CADW: Welsh Historic Monuments. Crown Copyright.

Llansilin in Denbigh celebrated on October 1, and has a nearby Ffynnon Silin, surely not related to the Norman St Giles. Until the 19th century at Llansilin, the last tuft of corn cut, the *'harvest mare'* was mixed with the seed corn for the following year *'to teach it to grow'*. The ashes from the *'yule-log'* were also used, mixed with the 'mare' and seed. This harvest mare custom evolved into the *'corn dolly'* we see in souvenir shops today. (See 'The A-Z of Wales and the Welsh', and Trefor Owen's 'Pocket Guide to the Customs and Traditions of Wales'.) George Borrow in his 'Wild Wales' describes going to Llansilin to find the grave of the poet Huw Morris, whom he called *'the greatest songster of the 17th century.'*

Sulien founded Wrexham in Denbighshire (one of the 'Seven Wonders of Wales' and now dedicated to Giles/Silin), and Llansilin in the same county. There was a ruined chapel at Capel Silin near Wrexham and another ruin at Capel Sant Silin, in the parish of Llanfihangel Ystrad in Cardigan. His brothers were saints Rhystud, Derfel Gadarn, Dwywau and Cristiolus. He is culted in Brittany, at St Sullien, Sulice, St Suliac, Lan-Sulien and Plou-Sulien. At his foundation at Luxulyan in Cornwall, upon December 17th, the Saturnalia of the Romans, there was a huge tinners' feast.

Gileston in the Vale of Glamorgan has wrongly been renamed Silstwn, by presupposing that the original foundation had something to do with Giles or Silin. It was founded by Mabon, and was formerly called Llanfabon-y-Fro. Silin may have rededicated or refounded the church however. He was known in the Gower Peninsula in South Wales at Rhossili, formerly called Rosulgen (Rhos Sulien) acording to the Book of Llandaf. He was said to have been trained at Llancarfan and Llanilltud Fawr, and may have been the 'Sulgen' of Llancarfan who became abbot at Llandough-juxta-Cardiff in the time of Bishop Euddogwy. Tresilian was named by Gorwg ab Eirchion after the martyrdom of a saint there, which may be another Sulien. Silian in Cardigan celebrates on September 2. At Silian Church, two miles north of Lampeter, there is a rectangular Celtic slab with interlinked knots and a squared fret motif, very similar in its sculpture to one in Llanilar church. This stone in Llanilar, near Aberystwyth, originally came from Cribyn earthworks, near Silian. There was a Capel Sulien under Llaniestyn in Carmarthen.

T

'Two nations; between whom there is no intercourse and no sympathy; who are as ignorant of each other's habits, thoughts, and feelings, as if they were dwellers in different zones, or inhabitants of different planets; who are formed by a different breeding, are fed by a different food, are ordered by different manners, and are not governed by the same laws.'
'You speak of - ', said Egrememont hesitatingly.
'THE RICH AND THE POOR.'

Benjamin Disraeli, 'Lothair', 1870

TALHAEARN 5th-6th century
TALHAIARN

This descendant of Coel and son of Garthwys was claimed by Iolo Morganwg to be a bard and saint of Cadog's congregation. According to the same source, he was the domestic chaplain of Emrys Wledig, Aurelius Ambrosianus at Caerleon. His ancient prayer reads:
'God, impart strength;
And in that strength, reason;
And in reason, knowledge;
And in knowledge, justice;
And in justice, the love of it;
And in that love, love of everything;
And in the love of everything,
The love of God'

After Emrys was killed, Talhaearn lived as a hermit at Llanfair Talhaiarn in Denbigh, where his church is also dedicated to Mary. He was linked with King Arthur, and was the father of St Tangwn. The 'Saying of the Wise' was:
'Hast thou heard the saying of Talhaiarn,
To Arthur of the splintered lance?
"Except God there is none strong".'

TALIESIN 6th century

Said to be the son of St Henwg of Caerleon, he erected the church of Llanhenwg there, and is named as *'one of the three baptismal bards of the Isle of Britain'*. He may have been educated at Llanfeithyn under Cadog or Tathan, and have died at Bangor Teifi in Cardigan. The legend of his birth is as follows.

At Llanfair Caereinion, Ceridwen, mother of Afagddu, concocted a brew of 'Science and Inspiration' to give to her son to compensate for his ugliness. Gwion Bach was instructed to stir the cauldron for a year and a day, but three drops of the magic potion fell onto his fingers which he licked clean. Being now able to foresee the future, Gwion fled in fear. He knew that Ceridwen would kill him. Ceridwen followed him, so he turned himself into a hare, whereupon she changed into a greyhound. Gwion became a fish, and Ceridwen an otter, then he flew as a bird but Ceridwen was a hawk. Despairing, Gwion tried to hide by becoming a grain of wheat, but Ceridwen became a hen and swallowed him. She bore him for nine months and delivered him as a beautiful baby, so could not bring herself to kill him. Thus Ceridwen tied the baby in a leather bag and threw him into the sea.

The legend continues in that King Gwyddno, after losing his lands off the Cardigan coast, took to fishing in the Leri's estuary at Borth (Porth Wyddno). May 1st was traditionally the best day's fishing in the year, so he allowed his son St Elffin to take over his fish-weir for the day. However, there were no fish that day, just a leather bag with a baby inside it. The baby had such a beautiful head that he was named Taliesin (Radiant Brow). Being taken home in Elffin's saddlebags, the boy started singing in regular bardic metres, and grew to be Wales most famous bard. Bedd Taliesin, a 3000 year-old Bronze Age cairn near Llyn Geirionydd above the Conwy Valley, was supposed to mark his grave. It was opened in 1847 in the presence of the Deans of Hereford and Bangor. However, traditionally he is also said to have been buried above the estuary where he was found by Elffin.

Taliesin prophesied the death of Maelgwn Gwynedd:
'A wondrous beast shall come up from Morfa Rhianedd,
The Sea Marsh of the Maidens,
To avenge the iniquities of Maelgwn.
Its hair and teeth and its eyes shall all be yellow,
And this beast shall be the end of Maelgwn Gwynedd!'
In 547 (or possibly later), Maelgwn died of the Yellow Plague.

He is more famously remembered for his prophecy concerning the future of the British nation:
'Their Lord they shall praise,
Their language they shall keep,
Their land they shall lose –
Except wild Wales'.

His 'Saying of the Wise', *'while conversing with Merlin'*, was *'excessive laughter is customary with the fool'*. The herb brooklime is known as Llysiau Taliesin.

Wirt Sikes noted the link between Taliesin and Llanhenog in Monmouthshire:
'The distance from Usk to Caerleon may be transversed by rail, but he who likes, as I do, to trudge along the hedge-embowered roads by the riverside, will pass through many a quaint and pleasant village: Llangibby, with its castle of Trergreg, "communely called Llankibby", says Leland, "bycawse yt is in the paroche of Kibby", Llanhenog, whose church was built by Taliesin, and in whose "great house" died Sir Digby Mackworth. You may sup at the "Mackworth Arms" in many a Welsh town, for the motto thereof was a right sturdy one, and more popular in Wales than "Ich Dien": "Gwell angau na cywilydd" – Rather death than shame!'

This 6th century bard sang the praises of Urien Rheged, and some of his lines read:
'I am Taliesin, I sing perfect metre
My original country is the Land of the Summer Stars
I was with my Lord in the highest sphere
When Lucifer fell to the depths of Hell
I have borne a standard before Alexander
I know the names of the stars from north to south

I have been a blue salmon
A dog, a stag, a buck on the mountain
A stock, a spade, an axe in the hand
A stallion, a bull, a roebuck
A grain which grew on the hill
I was reaped and cast in an oven
I have been dead, I have been alive
I am Taliesin.'

Incidentally, Taliesin wrote *'Christ, the word from the beginning, was from the first our teacher, and we never lost His teachings. Christianity was a new thing in Asia, but there never was a time when the Druids of Britain held not its doctrines.'* For more information upon the earliest Christianity, see Appendix I. Gildas in the 6th century commented *'We certainly know that Christ, the True Son, afforded His Light, the knowledge of His precepts to our Island in the time of Tiberius Caesar.'* The last year of Tiberius' reign was 37 or 38, which is in line with the version of events in which Christianity came to Britain within five years of the Passion.

TANGWN mid 6th century
December 15

The brother of Cawrdraf, Cadfarch and Maethlu, and with Cawrdaf the saint to whom Llangoed in Anglesey is dedicated. His father was Caradog Freichfras, and mother Tegau Eurfron.

TANGWN early 6th century
TANGUSIUS?

The son of Talhaiarn ap Garthwys, he founded a church in Somerset (then part of the kingdom of Dumnonia) called Tangynton. This may be the same person as Tangusius who succeeded Tathan as second abbot of Caerwent.

TANGWSTL see TUDGLID

TANWG 6th century
TANNWG
October 10

Tanwg ab Ithael Hael, a Breton prince who escaped from Armorica at the same time as the sons of Emyr Llydaw. He studied at the Bangor of Ynys Enlli. Tanwg founded Llandanwg in Merioneth, and his brothers were Gredifael and Fflewyn. The churches at Llanbedr and Harlech, dedicated now to St Peter and Mary Magdalen, were chapels to Llandanwg.
The superb late medieval church dedicated to St Tanwg in Llandanwg, Merioneth, is slowly being buried beneath shifting sands, so the interior cannot now be entered.

Nothing is known of this saint, but the church contains two very early inscribed stones. One fifth century stone is built into the east window of the chancel as a lintel. The other has Roman capitals dating from the sixth century, and is now in the south window of the chancel. Llandanwg was used as a chapel of rest for corpses going to Bardsey for burial, a 'trade' mentioned as late as 1710. A local saying was *'God and Tanwg help us.'* The remains of Arthur's Quoit dolmen can be seen at Llandawg, between the great castle of Harlech and the beach. At nearby Llanbedr on a hill was a spirally-marked Ogham stone, standing between two pillar stones, the remains of a stone circle.

TATHAL 5th century?
TATHALIUS

An early saint, remembered in the name Caer Dathal in Arfon, who may be the father of, or the same person as Tathan.

TATHAN 5th-6th century
TATHEUS, TATHAI, TATHAR, ATHEUS, MEUTHI
December 26, 30

Legends place Tathan as the son of an Irish king, or of Tathalius, a Goidel from North Wales. He came to Portskewett in Gwent by boat, and a stag stood on the mooring rope to keep the boat fast while Tathan evangelised the area. (Tathan's, Cadoc's, and Tewdrig's encounters with stags also seem to have symbolised the defeat of the pagan fertility symbol Cernunnos, who had cloven feet and horns). However, this warrior saint is more likely to have been the son of Amwn Ddu and Anna, the daughter of Meurig, the king of Glamorgan and Gwent. This would make him King Arthur's brother-in-law, the brother of Samson and nephew of Illtud. He was trained at Llanilltud and founded a church at nearby Llandathan (Sain Tathan) in the 6th century, then went to Caerwent to found a monastic school, Côr Tathan, where he became known as the *'Father of Gwent'* and renowned for miracles. His great influence almost certainly indicates that he was from royal stock.

He was said to have taught Abbot Catwg (Cadog), who founded Llancarfan, and encountered problems with Gwynlliw Filwr, Catwg's father, before Gwynlliw's late conversion. The very early ruined Christian church at Caerwent is built on the Roman bath site. It has many features in common with the church built on the Roman site of Silchester in the Thames Valley. While at Caerwent, he became the confessor to Ynyr Gwent according to some sources, but is more likely to have been the confessor of Caradog ab Ynyr Gwent. There seems to have also been a female hermit saint called Tathana, who lived in a cave in woods near the River Thaw at Sain Tathan. (Llandathan is named in maps and road signs as Saint Athan, as is its huge RAF base, but there was never any saint called Athan). There are several wells in the parish of St Athan, including St John's Well, Rills Well, Howell's Well and Ffynnon y Green. The latter cured sore eyes if they were bathed before the dawn.

His original côr at Caerwent, where the church is dedicated to Stephen (d. 35)*, is supposed to be where the present vicarage stands. In 1911 there were found on this site a dozen skeletons oriented east to west. It was thought that a coffin of stone slabs was his, and it was removed to the local parish church. He is also said to be buried at Llandathan, but this may be Tathana. His 'Saying of the Wise' *'after losing the whole'* was that *'God will not portion out unjustly.'* Llanfair Discoed just above Caerwent had two stone circles on its south side, overlooking the

Bristol Channel. One appears to have been destroyed in the 1870's but is still marked on some maps. The other is a small circle, just over 30 feet in diameter with thirteen stones remaining.

The 'Life of Cadoc' refers to Tathan as 'Meuthi' or 'Meithin'. This is interesting, as it clears up the problem of the founder of Llanfeithyn, just a mile from Catwg's Llancarfan, near Dyfrig's Well. There is also a Trevethin (Trefeithin) just outside Pontypool, and a Trefethin in Monmouth. ('The Dictionary of Welsh Biography' notes of Tathan and Meuthi, *the names are identical, the variant forms being due to the honorific prefixes of "mo" and "to" and the endearing suffix "an"*) The parish of Advent in Cornwall was originally dedicated to Tathan, and was called St Tawthen in 1559 and Tathen alias Advent in 1572.

The ghost and legend of 'Y Lady Wenn' at St Tathan is mentioned at length here as an example of the stories attaching to just one little village, which has only grown in size since the 1930's building of the RAF base by the War Office. These legends can be built into themes for the new celebrations of feast days across Wales. There are hundreds of ghosts reported across Wales in its castles, ruined mansions and priories. On the old Llanmaes road leading out of the village, before it is cut off by the airfield, is the 'Humpty Dumpty field', with the few remains of West Orchard Castle (a corruption of West Norchete). It is believed that it was slighted in the Glyndŵr rebellion in the early fifteenth century. A couple of miles due east is the less ruined manor that is known as East Orchard Castle.

Sir Jasper Berkerolles of West Orchard married Lady de Clare, daughter of the Lord of Glamorgan, then went off to the Holy Land, fighting the Second Crusade in 1148, returning several years later. On his return, he accused his wife of adultery with Sir Gilbert d'Umfreville of East Orchard Castle. She denied it, but overcome with jealousy, this noble Norman buried her up to her neck by the side of the old road near Bats Lays Farm (– now called Batslays). This was obviously a torture he had learned on Crusade. He forbade anyone to go near her to give her food or drink, but her sister implored him that she might visit Lady Berkerolles. He made her promise not to take any drink or water. The sister made visits early every morning when the dew lay heavy on the grass, and walked up to her sister so she could suck the hem of her long white gown. She provided enough moisture for the poor woman to stay alive for ten terrible days.

After her death, Sir Jasper found out that he had been wrong, and went mad. Marie Trevelyan, née Emma Thomas from nearby Llanilltud Fawr, wrote in 1909 that *'up to 1863 women who went sheep-milking in the early morning declared they often saw a beautiful lady dressed in white "going round and round" a certain spot in the field, but they could not make out why.'* (The spot where she was buried was off an ancient road which was known as Rogers Lane, which led to the old Chapel at Eglwys Brewis, before the RAF camp flattened the landscape. Arthur Hammett, the ninety-four year-old farmer who farmed West Orchard Farm, remembered his mother, who died aged ninety-seven, talking about the *'ghost of the white lady'* who tried to keep her sister alive). Several people in the village living today have seen the ghost at dawn, and the appearances are now on the site of the RAF camp.

Another version of 'Y Ladi Wen', 'The White Lady of Bats Leys', is that Sir William Berkerolles responded to Archbishop Baldwin's tour of Wales in 1188 (with Giraldus Cambrensis), recruiting people to go on the Third Crusade (1189-1192). When he returned, a Norman lord told him that his wife had been unfaithful. Sir William locked her in a room in East Orchard Castle, but her servants smuggled food into her. Sir William determined to bury her up to her neck on the boundary of St. Tathan and Llanilltud Fawr, and she survived for ten days

Caerwent Romano-Celtic Temple. CADW: Welsh Historic Monuments. Crown Copyright.

protesting her innocence, and blessed her husband as she died. It turned out that the knight who informed Sir William that she had been unfaithful had in fact been spurned by her, in his many advances. A relative of his at nearby Penmark Castle told Sir William the truth, and he turned to drink. Yet another version says that Sir Lawrence Berkerolles was the lord who buried his wife, who was the beautiful daughter of Sir Thomas Despenser, Lord of Glamorgan. Whether it was the evil Sir Jasper, Sir William or Sir Lawrence, there certainly seems some truth in the story.

Finally, in Thomas Hopkin's Coychurch record of 'The Royal Lineage of Coetty':

'Sir Laurence Berkrolles, who succeeded next to the Lordship of Coetty. His wife was Matilda, the daughter of Sir Thomas Despencer, who lived at the castle of Ffili (Caerphilly). She poisoned her husband, Sir Laurence Berkrolles, so that he died; whereupon she was buried alive, agreeably to the sentence pronounced on her by the country and the Lord Sir Richard Began, who was Lord of Glamorgan.'

As well as the 'White Lady', there is a *'Black Lady'* who haunted nearby Boverton Castle. Hadwisa, daughter of the Earl of Gloucester, was married to Prince John. When John succeeded to the throne on the death of his brother Richard I, he divorced her to marry Isabella of Angouleme. The grieving Hadwisa was sent to live at Boverton Castle, where it is said that she hid King John from his barons at one time. 'The Black Lady of Boverton' was last seen by workmen dismantling the ruins in the nineteenth century, and was well known to locals as 'Old Wissy'.

Caerwent Roman Town, South Wall. CADW: Welsh Historic Monuments. Crown Copyright.

The two castles in Sain Tathan have an interesting history, only a couple of miles apart, and near the castles at Penmarc, Castleton, Flemingston and Fonmon. There were two royal orchards in St. Tathan. West Orchard Castle was first destroyed by 'Ifor Bach', Ifor ap Meurig, Lord of Senghenydd, probably around the time he captured the great Earl William of Gloucester from Cardiff Castle in 1158. It seems to have been rebuilt by the Norman Berkerolles family in the thirteenth century, and was destroyed again in the Llywelyn Bren revolt of 1318. It was probably slighted yet again in the great Owain Glyndŵr rebellion between 1401 and 1410. It then passed to the Stradlings of St Donat's Castle when one married the heiress of Sir Lawrence Berkerolles in 1411. The Stradlings then again rebuilt the castle there to rival that at East Orchard. Iron shot from the Second Civil War has been found on the site, plus a cannon ball, and it appears that the castle was almost destroyed after the Battle of St. Fagans in 1648. Experts can still detect the remains of a chapel there, but much of the masonry has been used for local building since the seventeenth century. Some arches can still be seen in the old West Orchard Farm, and its converted barn, Porth Glyndŵr, opposite.

East Orchard Castle, overlooking the River Thaw (Dawen), was built in the same year that Earl Gilbert de Clare built St. Quintin's Castle at Llanbleddian, and Robert St. Quintin put the protective walls around Cowbridge. It appears that St. Quintin's was never completed, as De Clare died, aged only twenty-three, at the Battle of Bannockburn in 1314. This places East Orchard as an younger castle than West Orchard. Half-hidden by woodland, it overlooks the marshy valley of the Thaw, and has its own chapel, barn and dovecote. The columbarium, or dovecote, is twenty feet square, with two hundred recesses. The hall was forty feet by twenty-five, the outside kitchen twenty-eight feet by twenty-five, and the chapel forty-four feet by nineteen. In 1350, an octagonal bellcote was added, and it was taken to Fonmon Castle's stable block around 1850. The thatched Castle Mill is in ruins on the main road nearby, but was working until the early twentieth century. There is a legend of buried treasure at the castle, and the law of libel prevents the author at the present time noting the activities of any person 'guarding' the site.

Hugh Despenser appointed Pain Turberville of Coity Castle to be Custodian of Glamorgan. Sir William Berkerolles of East Orchard was Despenser's sub-lord, given full powers over the estates of Llywelyn Bren. This was done to evict Bren from his rightful possessions across Glamorgan. The Normans had found it far easier to subdue these flatter and richer southern parts of Wales, where reinforcements from the sea were available during their slow and uneven conquest. (The Normans only took four years to conquer England, but three-hundred and fifty to completely subdue all of Wales).

However, Berkerolles owed Llywelyn Bren his life, as Llywelyn had previously protected him in a Welsh attack, where thirteen Norman soldiers on Berkerolle's bodyguard were killed. Bren's estates had been taken while he and his two sons were imprisoned in the Tower of London. Llywelyn appeared before the King and barons at Lincoln Parliament on 28th January, 1316 because he had tried to restore Glamorgan to the Welsh. He received a full pardon on June 17, 1317 and came back to Wales to lawfully recover his lands, which had been taken over by the local Norman lords.

He returned to his base of Castell Coch, which the Normans had taken, and they refused to hand it over. Gathering around a thousand supporters, he scaled the castle walls and started a revolt that lasted nine weeks. He destroyed the castles at Sully, Barry, Old Beaupre, Kenfig, Flemingston, West Orchard and East Orchard. He besieged the mighty Caerphilly Castle, but was eventually surrounded by two English armies. Llywelyn surrendered in order that his followers would not be killed. Llywelyn Bren was slowly and barbarously executed at Cardiff Castle by the order of Despenser to Berkerolles, whose life Bren had previously saved.

He was hung drawn and quartered, according to Despenser on the orders of King Edward II, but Despenser had received no such authority from the King. He wanted Bren out of the way, to take his lands, and had made Berkerolles execute him to distance himself from the disgusting event. Thus Despenser was executed himself near the Black Tower of Cardiff Castle, and was said to be buried in the adjoining Greyfriars Monastery ruins, alongside Llywelyn Bren. The full charge against Despenser reads ' *That he did wrongfully adjudge Llywelyn Bren, causing him to be beheaded, drawn and quartered to the discredit of the King and contrary to the laws and dignity of the Crown*'. Bren's grieving widow attacked the castles of Cardiff, Caerphilly and St. Quintin's.

Berkerolles was judged innocent in the tragic affair, and kept his castle at East Orchard. Both royal orchards had been built by the Berkerolles who had received lands from Robert Fitzhamon after the conquest of much of South Glamorgan in 1091. The orchards flourished for centuries. It is said that Henry II (1154 – 1189) passed by in 1171 and was so impressed that he ordered all further fruit for his table to come from them. The orchards were possibly managed by Flemish cultivators (from nearby Flemingston) who were settled in the Vale of Glamorgan by the Normans. An ancient fig tree was reported to be still bearing fruit back in 1823. King John, whose divorced wife Hadwisa is said to have haunted Boverton Castle, is said to have favoured apples from St. Tathan.

There is a local legend linking Wales' greatest hero with the Berkrolles family. Edmund, Lord Mortimer, had been imprisoned by Owain Glyndŵr after the great victory at Pilleth**, and married Owain's daughter Jane in 1402. He died fighting to hold Harlech for Glyndŵr in 1409, so the following story comes from between 1402 and 1409. Glyndŵr was travelling alone with Earl Mortimer, and it was customary for travellers in these troubled times to ride from castle to castle, or abbey to abbey, rest free and move on. It seems that Glyndŵr pretended he was a harpist, and stayed with Sir Lawrence Berkerolles at East Orchard Castle. The blind Sir Lawrence told the couple that they might get the chance to see the great Glyndŵr, as he had been sighted in the Vale, and his men were out searching for him. Upon leaving after staying for four nights, Glyndŵr announced that he and his travelling companion had to be on their way, and thanked the Norman knight for his hospitality. Sir Lawrence implored him to stay, as it was only a matter of time before his raiding parties would capture Glyndŵr. Then Glyndŵr introduced himself to the Norman knight, jumped on his horse and rode away. Berkerolles is said to have been struck dumb, and lost his speech for ever.

In the Church of Sain Tathan are two beautiful painted tombs of the Berkerolles. Sir Roger Berkerolles died in 1351, and lies with the effigy of his wife, Katherine Turberville of Coity Castle. At the end of his tomb is the coat of arms of Iestyn ap Gwrgant, the last native Welsh Prince of Glamorgan (Morganwg). Sir William Berkerolles, who died in 1327, is nearby with his wife Phelice de Vere. He was the son of another Sir Roger, and the grandson of another Sir William Berkerolles and his wife Lettice de Nerber from Castleton.

Every little village in 'Bro Morganwg' (The Vale of Glamorgan) teems with such history and tradition – there are abandoned chapels, castles, manor houses interspersed with tumuli and cromlechs. Llancarfan and Llanilltud Fawr (Llantwit Major) were centres of world Christianity when it was all but extinguished, except on a couple of Irish rocks out in the Atlantic. It is beautiful countryside with thatched pubs, and used to be frequented by American tourists, yet no-one knows about it, not even many of its inhabitants. There is a great need to publish the patchwork of fable and fact for every village and locality in Wales (only now is a History of Gwent being mooted). With a knowledge of local and surrounding history, the Welsh people can begin to see the bigger picture of what Wales actually is. History teaches us to be better people.

* Several sources mention that Arthur was married at St Stephen's Church in Camelot. Chretien de Troyes mentions that Arthur moved his court from Caerleon (the fort) to Camelot, which is probably Caerwent, the Roman town near Caerleon rather than Winchester. Thomas Malory places Camelot as *'that which in English is called Winchester'*, **i.e. Caer-Went**. In the introduction to Malory's 'Faery Queene', the printer Caxton confirms that Camelot was indeed in Wales. After Arthur's demise, Caradog Freich-Fras had his court at Caerwent also. Overlooking Caerwent is Llanmelin, the chief hill-fort of the Silures who were Arthur's ancestors.

**On June 22, 1402, Glyndŵr was blamed for burning the old church at Pilleth. The Church of Our Lady was a place of pilgrimage to a statue of the Virgin. Some still seek at her holy well, by the north wall, a cure for eye problems. Pilleth was one of the few places in Wales to be mentioned in the Domesday Book. Behind the church four fir trees mark a mound where the dead of Pilleth were buried. Edmund Mortimer, Lord of Wigmore, was captured, and in captivity married Glyndŵr's sister. Mortimer died of starvation in Harlech Castle, fighting for Owain Glyndŵr against the Franco-English.

TATHAN THE YOUNGER 6th century

Possibly Tathan's son, noted on a panel in St Tathan church.

TATHANA 6th century
BRAUST

In local histories, Tathana is posited by some as the founder of St Tathan, not Tathan, and the author fortunately came across 'The Welsh Outlook', November 1924, which gives the legend of the saint, in an article by Augusta F. Jenkins (the wife of the rector of St Tathan). If any readers know of other information upon Welsh saints, kindly write to the author and it will be included in future editions. An intriguing part of the legend places the court of Meurig ap Tewdrig at 'Treberfaidd' (Boverton, wrongly named Trebeferad in recent years. The meaning seems be 'sparkling', 'perfect' or 'beaver' town). As local legends constantly place Boverton as the birthplace of Arthur, and Athrwys ap Meurig ap Tewdrig was the real Arthur of history, perhaps the ruins of Boverton Castle should attract tourism into the area. There is a 'World of Camelot' opening in the west of England, but while Dumnonia was a subject princedom under Arthur, Boverton in the Vale of Glamorgan seems to have been his home. Penllin, just five miles north, was the palace of Pawl Penychen, prince of Glamorgan, and Llanilltud Fawr is just a mile away from Boverton. Half a mile from Penllin is Pentre Meurig.

According to Jenkins, when Meurig was dying in Boverton, his sons and daughters gathered around him, including his daughter Anna, and her children St Samson and princess Braust. Braust, because of her kinship with Illtud the Knight had been dedicated to the Lord, and was destined to rule as abbess at Amesbury. However, Meurig feared for her safety, and his dying wish was that she was sent for protection to her great-grandfather Gwgan, who ruled the West Country from his court at Bath. She sailed from the old port of Aberddawen (Aberthaw) to Caer Brito (Bristol), then travelled the Roman road to Bath. There she fell in love with a pagan Irish slave, Diarmait, cup-bearer to Gwgan. Gwgan was seeking a peace between the invading Saxons from the east, and the Irish threat from the west, and arranged for Braust to marry a Saxon prince. The wedding turned into a riot as the Irish slaves, led by Diarmait, revolted and Braust and Diairmait escaped in the confusion. Diairmait soon abandoned his now pregnant wife, and returned to Ireland, leaving only a bronze armlet. Braust named the child Conan, and noticed a strange mark on his shoulder which Diarmait also had possessed. He had told her that it was the sign of kingship.

After many adventures, Braust and Conan crossed the Severn (Hafren) to Caerwent (Bangor Tathan) and stayed near Tathan's tomb. Tathan appeared to her in a vision that night, telling Braust to live a holy life, succouring the poor and pilgrims. On her journey the Archbishop at Caerleon blessed her, and she followed the Via Julia Maritima from Caerwent. (The Roman road that leads through Cardiff to Neath and Carmarthen). She turned south at Cowbridge (Bovium) to go through Llanfeithyn and Llandathan, both dedicated to Tathan, tutor of the great St Cadog. She thus returned to Treberfaidd, where she was met by her uncle Prince Ffrioc, Arthur's brother. Ffrioc granted her the villa of Eurgain in Llanilltud Fawr (Eurgain ferch Caradog had built a villa in the Roman style, which is now called Caer Mead, excavated over a century ago, with Christian burials there). This is marked as Caer Worgan on all old maps, and only seems to have been renamed Caer Mead in the 19th century. She stayed here for 16 years helping the poor and weak, and was now called Tathana in honour of her vision, while her son Conan grew up into a lawless man. He consorted with the Irish slaves at

Llanilltud's great abbey, and he stole the keys to the great gate to allow Irish pirates to sack and pillage Llanilltud Fawr. He cut off his mother's hands to take her rings and bracelets before escaping with the pirates to Ireland. Her villa burnt, Tathana's slaves built her a hut of mud and reeds at Pont Newydd, where there was a well of pure water. This is near where the ruined East Orchard Castle mill stands on the River Thaw on the Barry-Llanilltud road today.

To truncate the story, Conan killed his father Diarmait, who had become king, in trial by combat. Famine struck Ireland, and Conan led a force that was repulsed by the men of Glwyssing (Glamorgan) at Aberddawen (Aberthaw). Conan's disillusioned pirates tied him to a stake near the tidal river Thaw, next to Tathana's hut, and left him to drown. His cries for help alerted Tathana, who took her coracle out to him. Conan asked her to take his dagger and cut his cords, and the water swirled around his waist, but then he saw that she only had stumps instead of arms. At the same time she saw that he was wearing Diairmait's bronze armlet and had his father's mark on his shoulder. Tathana forgave her son, and the wave that covered his face also overturned her coracle so that they died together. Her body was found on the Leys (the local beach), and she was taken by villagers and buried in the church of Tathan *'which they called after her name from that day, but the village after the old abbot, as it is to this day. Thus was the sin washed out in tears and the waters of the Ddawen, which had begun in fire and blood at the burning of the Church of Bath.'* It is entirely regrettable that the village of Llandathan has come to be known as St Athan, with a Welsh alternative of Sain Tathan, upon road-signs and maps. The illiterate local authorities responsible for such misinterpretations are helping to destroy Welsh culture. There are many such instances in the Vale of Glamorgan. Nearby Llanfabon-y-Fro was renamed Gileston by the Normans, and now has an alternative of Silstwn instead of Llanfabon. To rename the 'Holy Place of St Mabon in the Vale' with a Welsh translation of Giles' Town is nonsense. The author is tempted to place her chapel in 'Chapel Field'*, where there are ruins on the moors between Flemingstone and Castleton just outside St Tathan. The sea still sometimes floods these moors, and in her time would have come to here upon each tide.

* Note: As this book goes to print, the author has discovered a medieval chapel, previously unrecorded, below Chapel Field. See the author's "The Secret Vale of Glamorgan" for further details, and the Addenda in this book.

BISHOP JEREMY TAYLOR 1613 - 1667
August 13

Given a Holy Day, he was born in Cambridge, ordained in 1633, and from then until 1645 was chaplain to Archbishop Laud and King Charles I. From 1645, under Puritan rule, he was imprisoned three times, and forced into retirement as a family chaplain in Wales. After the Restoration of the Monarchy, he was Bishop of Down and Connor in Ireland. He wrote many books on moral, theological and devotional subjects, arguing for freedom of conscience and freedom of speech in a religious context. Some quotations from his works include:
'Men are apt to prefer a prosperous error to an afflicted truth';
'Whatsoever we beg of God, let us also work for it';
'Meditation is the tongue of the soul and the language of our spirit'; and
'Knowledge comes by eyes always open and working hands, and there is no knowledge that is not power.'

TEGAI 6th century
TYGAI

Tegai ab Ithel Hael founded Llandegai in Caernarfonshire, formerly called Maes Llanglassawg. There is a nearby henge. His brothers were Trillo and Llechid, and Llanllechid adjoins his parish. Tegai traditionally lived at Maes y Llan near the present church, where portions of his coffin and cross (destroyed in the Inter-Regnum) are preserved. Cors Dygai, near Llangristiolus, is the marsh where he had his cell, on a small portion of firmer ground in its centre.

At Landegai the remains of a small rectangular timber structure were found over a levelled Neolithic cursus. It contained a single, central, oriented grave with signs of later disturbance. On the north side of the building an inhumation cemetery of oriented rows of graves was also found. It seems that the bones of Tegai were exhumed to be removed to the 14th century stone chapel of St Tegai, just 600m away. At Ffynnon Bach Farm, Llandegai, is a burial chamber known as Yr Hen Allor Dolmen.

TEGAN

In Llanwnda parish, Pembroke is the site of Capel Degan and a holy well named Ffynnon Degan which runs a half mile into the sea. Cnwc Sant Degan was a nearby tumulus where local people went on holidays and Sundays, and there is still a field there called Park y Capel. Fenton noted the well's fame, and that of the saint, and Francis Jones notes that the unusual surname Tegan survives in north-west Pembrokeshire.

TEGAU EURFRON 6th century

The wife of Llyr Merini and mother of Caradog Freichfras. Mediaeval poets used her as the ideal of chastity. In tradition she saved her lover from a poisonous snake, which then bit her on the breast. The breast had to be removed and replaced with a golden one. Her magical cloak would not fit any woman who had forsaken her wedding vows.

TEGFAN 6th century
Easter Monday

The son of Carcludwys, and the brother of Gallgu Rhieddog. He was the uncle of St Elian and a confessor at Bangor Gybi, and is sometimes confused with Degeman. Tegfan of Anglesey's grandfather was Cadrod Calch Fynydd (Chalk Hill – from Dover?). Tegfan stayed for several years with St Dogfael at Llandudoch (St Dogmael's), and was also associated with Cybi. The site of Tegfan's Chapel and oratory in north Pembroke lies near the little cove of Porth Sychan. He is the founder of Llandegfan Church, west of Beaumaris on Anglesey, formerly known as Merthyr Tegfan, where the Gwyl Mabsant was always Easter Monday. His son may have been the Gwynedd warrior Cynfelin mentioned in The Book of Aneirin. There is a tall standing stone near Llandegfan Church, at Plas Cadnant (the Palace, or Place, of the Valley of Battle).

TEGFEDD FERCH AMWN DDU 6th century
December 18

The virgin sister of Tydecho, she settled near him in the Mawddwy district of Merioneth, and resisted the attentions of a local chieftain called Cynon. To appease Tydecho's wrath, Cynon gave Garthbeibio to him. In 1856 a broken Celtic cross was found in Maes Llymystyn at Garthbeibio.

TEGFEDD FERCH TEGID FOEL 6th century
TEGWEDD

The martyred wife of Cedig ap Ceredig, and mother of the saint Afan Buallt, she was killed by Saxons at Llandegfedd near Caerleon. This was the 'Merthyr Tecmed' given by Catwg (Cadog) to Teilo for settling Catwg's dispute with Arthur. She was born at Tegid's court at Penllin, where a castle still stands. She also features in some records as the wife of Enlleu ap Hydwyn Dwn ap Ceredig ap Cunedda, so may have married twice. Tegfedd is said to be the mother of the great saint, Teilo, with Enlleu as his father.

One version of her death is that she was martyred upon Craig-y-Saeson (Saxon Rock) two miles away from Llandegfedd. The church guide however says that she was so generous to the poor that she was stoned to death for being a witch. Laurence Main has a third account of her demise ('Western Mail, April 13th, 1999): *Did Derfel Gadarn ride this way when he brought the Holy Grail to his pregnant lover Tegfedd in December 537? Derfel was one of the party of knights escorting the Holy Grail from Glastonbury to Strata Florida and safety from the Saxon menace after the Battle of Camlan. Derfel returned after this mission to find Tegfedd had been murdered – but not by Saxons. "St" Illtyd had arranged for the vicious death of the woman who held secret the location of Arthur's tomb.'* The author is unsure of the derivation of this last legend. Illtud was a kinsman and knight of Arthur's, however.

TEGIWG 6th century
TIGWG, THUMETE (Brittany)

St Beuno restored the severed head of this princess where her holy well, Ffynnon Digiwg, rose at Pennarth in Clynnog. This parallels his restoration of Gwenfrewi's head. Tegiwg was the daughter of Ynyr Gwent and Madrun ferch Gwrthefyr (Vortimer the Blessed). Her humble betrothed felt that he was not worthy of marriage to her, so he cut off her head. Her brother King Iddon searched for the killer to avenge her decapitation, and found him at the palace at Aberffraw. He cut off his head, which Beuno again restored. She then travelled with her father Ynyr Gwent to Brittany where she was known as Thumete.

Francis Jones relates that strange creatures like spineless hedgehogs could be seen in the bottom of Ffynnon Digwg, that pins and eggs were offered there, and that its waters cured warts.

Valle Crucis Abbey. CADW: Welsh Historic Monuments. Crown Copyright.

TEGLA d.790
TECLA, THECLA
June 1, October 15 was Llandegla Fair (later October 26), September 23 also? (see next entry)

Tegla allegedly became abbess of the monastery of Ochanfort in Germany. She had been sent to help St Boniface, by Abbess Tetta of Wimborne in Dorset. Her shrine at Kintzingen was destroyed during the Peasants' War of the 16th century. Tegla produced two stars in her hand to cure Leffius, a man blind from birth, when she placed them in his empty eye-sockets. She cured Lord Cynan of headaches when he promised to release some prisoners. She was one of the most invoked saints for healing and the alleviation of suffering. Her shrines, at Llandegley in Radnorshire, and Llandegla in Denbighshire were famous for curing epilepsy. Ffynnon Degla, on Gwern Degla was especially famous, and epilepsy in an old Welsh dictionary was known as 'Clwyf Tegla', Tegla's sickness. Llandegla church has a brass chandelier said to have come from Valle Crucis Abbey at the time of Dissolution (as also has the neighbouring Llanarmon church).

In 1699 Edward Lhuyd recounted:

'At St Tegla's Well near Ruthin, epileptic men had to carry a cockerel, and women a hen. Hands and feet were washed in the water, the chicken pricked with a pin, and the pin thrown into the well. A groat (four pennies) was given to the clerk of the well, the Lord's Prayer was said three times, and the sufferer walked three times around the church holding the bird. The epileptic then slept under the altar of Llandegla church on a Friday, with a Bible for a pillow and the chicken as a hot-water bottle. Next morning, the patient blew down the chicken's beak, transferring his or her epilepsy. The foul was left in the church, while the patient did another three trips around the church and well, gave the clerk another groat, then put another groat in the Poor Box. The cure would only work if the chicken died in the church, but it could not be killed by foul means. As a result, the church was sometimes more full of chickens than a congregation. A man kept a cock with him under the altar, a woman a hen, a boy a cockerel (young cock) and a girl a pullet. The disease was passed on to the chickens in the forms of black marks on their skin.'

Similar practices were carried on until at least 1813, with a chicken being pricked with a pin, the pin then being thrown into the well. As late as 1855, old people remembered *'birds staggering about from the effects of the fits which had been transferred to them.'* On the other hand, the well at Llandegley was a sulphur spring with miraculous healing properties of a more general nature than Llandegla's 'epileptic' spring. There was a Croes Degla between Llangollen and Llandegla. Llandegla Fair was famous for the Welsh Black cattle sold there.

St Tegla's Well is still annually honoured on her September feast day (see next entry). The spring has never been known to run dry, even in times of severest drought, and 1935 excavations produced many pins and coins. Llandegla Well, on the river Cymaron in Radnor, has now dried up. Here, small pieces of white quartz and calcite were found, which relate to grave goods rituals of Celtic times. Pennant noted a Celtic stone next to the well, but only a few letters could be deciphered.

St Tecla's Chapel ruins lie on a small island, accessible at low tide from Beachley Point, at the Chepstow end of the first Severn Bridge. In AD 602 St Augustine had his famous meeting with the Celtic bishops here. They despised his arrogance and left the meeting without agreeing to his many demands to Romanise their natural and socialist form of Christianity (very different from the 'socialite' form of Christianity practised by today's governments). Also near this ancient site Gruffudd ap Llywelyn met Edward the Confessor as equals, and overcome with respect for the Saxon's humility, was said to have carried the king across the shallow seas to their conference. (Also see Tegla below).

TEGLA 1st century
THECLA
September 23, 24, 25, 27, 28

A 'British' follower of St Paul, she was a virgin whom the Romans tried to burn, but the bonfire blew out. She then was put in the amphitheatre but none of the lions would attack her. Released, she spent 70 years in a cave. Could Tecla have been one of Caradog's relatives, or another daughter along with Gwladys Claudia and Eurgain in Rome? It is not known whether the 'Acts of Paul and Thecla' are apocryphal. The legend that Eurgain ferch Caradog financed Paul's evangelist journeys may link Tecla with Paul. A 'Life and Miracles of Thecla' in Lambeth Palace ms. 94 tells us of miracles connected to Thecla at Llandegley Church.

TEGONWY 5th century

Teon's son (see Teon).

TEGWEL (see DOGMAEL)

TEGWEN 5th century

The sister of Meurig and Marchell. Marchell was the mother of Brychan. Only Iolo Morganwg seems to denote her as a saint.

TEGWYN 6th century
TECWYN
September 14, or the first Sunday after Holy Cross Day

He came with Cadfan and Emyr Llydaw from Brittany, the son of Ithel Hael, and founded Llandecwyn under Llanfihangel y Traethau in Merioneth. A monument there was translated as *'(the cross of) St Tegwyn priest, to the honour of God and the most illustrious servant of God; Heli, deacon, made me.'* It was found when the old church was pulled down in 1879 to build the existing church. In 1699 Edward Lhuyd mentioned *'Ffynnon Dekwyn by Plas Decyn near the church, now called Ffynnon y Foel.'* A memorial stone, Maen Tecwyn, in Cae Maen Tecwyn close by, was destroyed to build a cowhouse. Nearby are the lakes Llyn Tecwyn Ucha and Llyn Tecwyn Isa, and a common called Gwyllt Tecwyn. The solitary house at Llandecwyn is called Ty'n Llan.

BISHOP TEILO OF LLANDAF CATHEDRAL d. 580
ELIDIUS, ELIUD, TEILIAU, TELIAUS, THELIAU, ISSELL, DUB
February 9 (then February 20 Ffair Wyl Deilo at Llandaf and Llandeilo Fawr), November 26, June 11
Patron Saint of horses and apple trees in Brittany

Widely venerated in Wales and Brittany, an influential religious leader who founded the monastery at Llandeilo Fawr in Carmarthenshire. Born near Penally (Eccluis Gunnian), he was the son of Ensic (Enlleu) and Guenhaf*. His first name was Elios, the Welsh name for Helios, the pagan sun-god. He was descended from Cunedda Wledig and supposed to have accompanied Dewi and Padarn on their trip to Jerusalem, caused by the wars against the Irish invaders. At Jerusalem, the Patriarch was said to have given Teilo a magical bell, which was kept at his shrine at Llandaf with his mitre and ritual comb. On his return to Britain, he went first to Cornwall and became Geraint's confessor, but left to avoid the Yellow Plague in 547. He went to Samson's monastery at Dol, founded in 544. Geoffrey of Monmouth believed that Teilo succeeded Samson as abbot there.

Another source states that Teilo was the son of Enlleu (Usyllt) ap Hydwyn Dwn ap Ceredig ap Cunedda, and Tegfedd ferch Tegid Foel of Penllyn. His sister married Emyr Llydaw (see Ismael). Teilo's half-brother was Afan, bishop of Llanbadarn. He was taught by Dyfrig, and founded the college of Llandaf which was called Bangor Deilo. Teilo was also said to have

Llandaf Cathedral, Epstein's 'Christ in Majesty'. © *Wales Tourist Board Photo Library.*

been taught by Dyfrig and Paulinus. He then went to Tŷ Gwyn, where he came into contact with David, and followed David to the new monastery at Glyn Rhosyn, the present site of St David's Cathedral. During the Yellow Plague he went and stayed with St Samson in Brittany for seven years and seven months, planting the great orchard that stretched three miles from Dol to Cai. Teilo was said to have helped King Budic (Emyr Llydaw) battle a great serpent there. He located a holy spring at Kerfeuntain, and is associated with the stag in Brittany. When Teilo returned, Cadog asked seven 'fundamental questions' to the seven wise men of his college at Llancarfan. Teilo was asked what was the greatest wisdom in a man. Teilo responded *'to refrain from injuring another when he has the power to do so'.*

In 577 the Angles won the great battle of Deorham near Bath, cutting off the Welsh from their fellows in Dumnonia. The victorious army crossed the Wye to chase the defeated Welsh. Prince Iddon, son of King Ynyr of Gwent, asked Teilo as the family priest to lead his army spiritually. Teilo led the prayers on a hill near the battle site, and when Iddon's troops were victorious he gave Teilo the hill for a church, which he founded at Llantilio Crosseny. The White Castle stands where Teilo prayed. Early in the 20th century this important church between Monmouth and Abergavenny was still pronounced Llandeilo. Croesenni is the Anglicisation of Croes Ynyr, the Cross of Ynyr. The battle took place along the meadows between the church and Tre Adam, and the large field there is still known as Maes-y-Groes, after the cross which Iddon probably raised for his father after the battle. The present church dates from the 14th century.

Teilo died at Llandeilo Fawr, from whence came the fabulous Chartulary which was later appropriated from Llandaf by Lichfield Cathedral. It is now known as the Book of St Chad. Teilo was supposed to have been the second Bishop of Llandaf, and Euddogwy (Oudoceus) was his nephew. Llandeilo, Penally and Llandaf all claimed his body, which miraculously mutiplied into three. In 1850 his tomb was opened in Llandaf cathedral and his staff and pewter 'crotcher' discovered.

Thirty-seven churches are associated with Teilo in south and mid-Wales. The roofless Llandeilo Abercywyn church, outside Carmarthen, stands where the little river Cywyn joins the Taff. A nearby ancient farm building is known as *'The Pilgrim's Rest'*, and there are mediaeval *'Pilgrims' Graves'* in the facing church of Llanfihangel Abercywyn. They may be the resting places of the Lords of Llanfihangel castle, or the tombs of pilgrims on their way to St David's Cathedral. The Llandeilo Cross was found in pieces at Llandeilo Fawr when digging the foundations for the present church (surely a non-intrusive survey would find dozens more of these crosses). Westwood describes the remains, but the inscription appears to have been lost.

St Teilo's Church at Llandeilo Llwydarth, near Maenchlochog in the Preseli Mountains, is now totally ruined. Burial stones from the fifth or early sixth century, inscribed to Andagellus and Coimagnus, sons of Cavetus, have been moved to Maenchlochog Church. A third slab, dedicated to Curcagnus, son of Andagellus, was moved to Cenarth. (There was also a stone to Curcagnus, now lost, at Llandeilo). The last entry in the Baptismal Register was in 1897, and the church ruins lie in a much larger, defended complex which also enclosed the farms of Prisk (Prysg means wood, or bush) and Temple Druid (formerly called Bwlch y Clawdd, Gap in the Embankment). A few hundred yards from the church is St Teilo's Well, once called the Oxen Well, which became a centre of pilgrimage to Teilo in the Middle Ages. In his church at Llandeilo, Carmarthenshire, are two ornately carved stone wheelheads, all that remains of the high crosses that marked his early 'clas'.

Rice Rees gave the following existing churches dedicated to Teilo:
Llandeilo Fawr – 3 chapels at Taliaris, Capel yr Ywen and Llandyfaen in Carmarthenshire;
Brechfa in Carmarthen;
Llandeilo Abercywyn in Carmarthen;
Capel Bettws in Trelech a'r Bettws;
Llanddowror in Carmarthen;
Cilrhedin – Capel Ifan;
Llandeilo near Maenchlochog in Pembroke;
Llandeilo – the chapel of St Hywel in Pembroke;
Llandeilo Graban in Radnor;
Llandeilo Fan in Brecon;
Llandeilo Talybont in Glamorgan;
Llandeilo Ferwallt (Bishopston) and Caswel in Glamorgan;
Llandaf Cathedral and Whitchurch in Cardiff;
Merthyr Dyfan in Glamorgan;

Merthyr Mawr** – St Roque's Chapel in Glamorgan;
Llanarth in Monmouth;
Llandeilo Bertloeu i.e Llantilio Pertholey (Porth-halawg) in Monmouth;
Llandeilo Rwnnus in Llanegwad near Talley Abbey;
Llwyngraddan near Llanddewi Velfrey;
Trefgarn in Pembroke;
Penally near Tenby;
Manorbier (Maenor Byr);
Lanion near Pembroke;
Llandeilo Llwydiarth near Cemaes;
Brechfa in Brecon;
Penclecir in Castle Martin, Pembroke;
Talgarth, Brecon:
Elfael in Radnor;
Llowes in Radnor

One of Teilo's holy wells, north-east of the church at Llandeilo Llwydarth, now is built into a pump-house to supply water to the neighbouring farm. Even up to this century, it was used to cure tuberculosis, whooping coughs and other chest illnesses. In World War I local people dropped pins into the well, hoping to end the slaughter. The water had to be drunk early in the morning out of part of **St Teilo's skull, 'penglog Teilo'**. From around 1057 the Mathews family were recognised as the hereditary guardians of Teilo's Llandaf shrine, saving it from vandalism and desecration. In recognition of this devotion, in the 15th century they were given his skull, which they brought to Pembroke. In 1658 it was inherited by the Melchiors, owners of Llandeilo farm, and it became the focus for the healing waters of Teilo's holy well. This relic became shiny through constant use over the centuries, and was handed to pilgrims by the senior member of the Melchior family. It was bought back by the Mathews family in 1927 for £27. These hereditary keepers of the ancient relic were 'conned' into selling it in the 1950's by two people posing as museum officials, and Penglog Teilo vanished. It reappeared in 1994 in Hong Kong and has now been installed in its own niche in Teilo's chapel in Llandaf.

St Margaret's Church in Marloes, Pembrokeshire, was originally a Teilo dedication. Cilrhedyn Church on the borders of Pembroke and Carmarthen is also dedicated to Teilo. Teilo's Well by the Bishop's Palace in Llandaf came to be known as the Dairy Well, and in its wall was found the remains of a Celtic cross with knotwork, which has now been removed to the south aisle of the cathedral. If visiting Llandaf Cathedral, one can walk a couple of miles south through parkland, following the river Taf, past Cardiff Castle, to go to the National Museum of Wales. It has a room dedicated to casts of all the major Welsh Celtic crosses, and some original stone carvings.

Near Waungron, between Gorseinon and Pontardulais, were the remains of St Teilo's Church, Llandeilo Tal-y-Bont. They were moved to the Museum of Welsh Life at St Ffagans. Known locally as *'the church in the marsh'*, it lies near the first crossing point of the river Loughor upstream from the old Roman fort of Leucarum (Loughor). Normans built two castles on either side of the river here, for it was an important strategic site for their slow and relentless conquest of South Wales. The church was superseded by one at Pontardulais in 1852, but annual services were still held until 1973. However, upon deconsecration vandals moved in removing the slate roof, and the church fell into decay in the 1980's. Fortunately a survey discovered mediaeval wall-paintings under the layers of whitewash and they have been moved for conservation prior to replacement in the re-erected church.

His church at Talgarth is in an area full of megaliths. Unfortunately Croes Llechan was destroyed, sometime in the late 19th century, but Maen Llwyd on Pen Cader and Ty Isaf dolmen can still be seen. There is also a nearby stone circle, sometimes called Gader Arthur, on Pen Cader in the Black Mountains.

Teilo's churches are mainly clustered in south-west Wales, in eastern Pembrokeshire and western Carmarthenshire. However, he has dedications in Llannarth, Llandeilo Gresynni and Llandeilo Porth Haelog in Monmouthshire, Llandeilo'r Fan in Brecom and Llandeilo Graban in Radnorshire, and two in Gower among his thirty-five or so churches. Teilo was 'claimed' by Llandaf as a saint because of his glory, and somehow the illuminated missal from Llandeilo Fawr was taken there before 850. However, at some time it was stolen and resurfaced in Lichfield Cathedral as the Book of St Chad – possibly the greatest treasure of Wales, comparable with the Book of Kells and the Lindisfarne Gospels. It may have been taken in the time of Wynsi, Bishop of Lichfield from 974-992, but another authority believes that it was taken in the 16th century. More research is needed here to make a serious claim for its return. The Trinity College exhibition of the Book of Kells and the Book of Durrow in Dublin shows how great a tourist attraction it could be for Wales. Nearly everything else of Welsh heritage has been stripped out or melted down during eight-hundred years of legalised looting. A monk named Ysgolan in the 13th century was responsible for burning those libraries of Welsh princes which had escaped Irish, Viking and Norman depredations. Not only did the writings show pre-Roman influence, but they could have been dangerously tainted with Pelagianism. More valuable early Welsh books were lost in the Civil War, such as the great library of the Herberts at Raglan Castle. It is little known that the Second Civil War was mainly a Welsh affair.

This Gospel contains the **earliest known written Welsh**, except for that carved on stone. Llandeilo, as recorded in the Gospel, was a bishopric, and its remaining two stone cross-heads attest to its importance. When the cult of Teilo was transferred to Llandaf, Llandeilo became a church within the diocese of St David's. Arglwydd Rhys, The Lord Rhys, founded Talley Abbey in the 12th century and passed on much of Llandeilo's wealth to it. This community of Praemonstratensian canons was based on the French model, and Normanised the Welsh 'clas' pattern of churches in the area. All Llandeilo's records have been destroyed or lost except the Gospel.

The boundary dispute between Llandaf and St David's for the premier bishopric in Wales lasted for a few hundred years, with both claiming Teilo. Teilo was far more associated with David, however, and may have travelled with him to Brittany and Cornwall. In Brittany Teilo is the patron saint of apple trees and horses. Chateauneuf du Faou and Lennon, both near Pleyben may be his foundations.

Throughout the Middle Ages, oaths were taken on Teilo's tomb. When it was first opened in 1736, the remains of his staff and chalice were found. An old Glamorgan proverb is that if no snow falls before Teilo's Day (February 9), then any that falls after will clear quickly from the ground. His 'Saying of the Wise', *'while doing penance'* was *'it is not wise to contend with God.'*

There were four fairs a year in the churchyard at Llandeilo Fawr, about which the churchwardens were *'reticent in telling their Bishop'*. The following notes are from that church's excellent parish magazine 'Y Groesfaen'. *'Archdeacon Tenison tells us about these: "On the fair-days" he reported, "Horses, sheep and lambs, & casks of Ale are brought into the Churchyard and sold there." The main fair was held on St Barnabas' Day (June 11th), and indeed was the only official fair recognised by the manor court, as the court record stated in 1710: "We present no fair or markett should be kept in the church yard except Barnaby faire." It was a fair with a long history, first being mentioned in 1324, when the Black Book of St David's recorded of Llandeilo that "The Lord (of the manor) has a fair once a year, namely, on the feast of St Barnabas the apostle, and it lasts for three days".'*

From 'Teulu Teilo', the church magazine of Brechfa (written by Bob Lenny and the Reverend Patrick Thomas), the author notes the following commemorative services:
Sul y Blodau (Palm Sunday) young people carry the cross to Maes-y-Groes Farm, where there is an open air service, before returning to the church for Hot Cross Buns. Sul y Pasg (Easter Sunday) begins with the 8 am service and lighting of the Paschal Candle, then at 11 am the Easter garden is blessed and Easter eggs and butterflies given to the children. On Sul y Drindod (Trinity Sunday) there is a joint Cymanfa Ganu (singing festival) with the parishes of Abergorlech, Caio, Talley, Llansawel and Llanfihangel Rhos-y-Corn. A recent addition is the Gwyl Sant Teilo a'r Afallennau (The Feast of St Teilo and the Apple Trees) on the third Sunday in September, following the Breton custom. Lessons are read in Breton, French, Welsh and English and the church is decorated with apple branches. (This is the type of innovation based upon tradition that the author would like to see spreading across Wales). Y Cyrddau

Margam Stones Museum.   *CADW: Welsh Historic Monuments. Crown Copyright.*

Diolchgarwch am y Cynhaeaf (Harvest Thangsgiving Services) are bilingual, in mid-October. Patrick Thomas writes on Welsh saints in that excellent magazine 'Cambria', and gives free Welsh classes in his parish.

Apart from the holy wells mentioned, in Carmarthen they were also at Llandeilo Fawr, and near Cydweli, the latter being good for curing rheumatism and sprains and next to Capel Teilo. In Pembroke, Ffynnon Deilo was near Crinow Church, Lampeter Velfrey.

* Although 'Guenhaf' is given as his mother, this may be another name (White, or Holy Summer) for Tegwedd ferch Tegid Foel.

**'*Sancti Teiliaui de Merthir Myuor*' has a lovely footpath leading across the River Ogwr to Ogmore Castle. The ancient stepping stones are known as '*Stepsau Teilo*'.

TEITHFALLT 5th century
TUDFWLCH

Arthur ap Meurig ap Tewdrig ap Teithfallt was the great-grandson of this king. According to Gilbert, he was a monk at the peace conference in 466 when '*The Treachery of the Long Knives*' wiped out the cream of the British nobility. Teithfallt ap Teithrin escaped and with his royal family killed, had to take up the kingship of Glamorgan. At the Margam Abbey Museum is a stone inscribed 'ThIThELL', which some believe is Teithfallt's memorial stone.

TELOI

Llandeloy in Pembrokeshire. Llanddinog Well and chapel were at Llanddinog Farm here, and Llandeloy Church Well had an eel and was enclosed by carved masonry. Ffynnon Wen was another holy well in the parish, near Hendre Cross. Could Teloi have been the 6th century Eloi who went to Brittany with Gildas, and Llandeloi have come from Llan Tŷ Eloi?

TENENEN 6th century
TININOR, TENENAN
July 16

This Briton crossed to Brittany, becoming Bishop of Leon and dying at Ploabennec, where his forest hermitage became a place of pilgrimage. Said to have been a disciple of Caradoc, he is remembered at Landerneau, Ploabennec, Lannilis, and at the village of Brittany's greatest hero, Bertrand de Guerlescin. (In Guerlescin's time, he was the most famous knight and war-lord in Europe. Second in fame only to Bertrand, was Owain Lawgoch, the last of the House of Gwynedd, who was assassinated by the orders of the English crown in France.) Catholic Online Saints states that Tenenen became Bishop of Leon in Spain, rather than Leon in Britanny.

TENNI

Llandenny in Monmouth, Hendredenny in Eglwysilan, Glamorgan.

TENOI 5th – 6th century

The abbess at Gwytherin in Denbigh, a 'dual' abbey, where her son Eleri was abbot, and where Gwenfrewi went from Holywell. Now extinct, there was a chapel named Llandenoi, under Llanrheithan in Pembroke.

BISHOP TEON 5th - 6th century

This Welsh chieftain, and his son Tegonwy were saints who studied at Llanilltud (when it was Côr Tewdus). His grandson was Llywelyn. Tegonwy's son Iorwerth Hirflawdd married one of Brychan's daughters. Teon was born in Guilsfield (Cegidfa) near Welshpool. The wonderful Stiperstones range of hills in Shropshire were known as Carneddi Teon, when they were Welsh territory.

The legend is that Teon went from Llanilltud to become Bishop of Gloucester then London in 542, but was driven out by the Saxons at the same time as they attacked Caerleon and York. All three British bishops then escaped to Brittany or Wales. He died in Wales in 586, according to this tale, but most sources believe that Teon existed in the 5th century – there were thus possibly two Britons with this name.

TETTA d.750

The Anglo-Saxon abbess of Winburn in Wessex, remembered at her 14th century church at Llanddetty in Brecon. There is a tall 9th century inscribed pillar stone here. She sent St Tegla to Germany.

TEULYDDOG 6th century
TOULIDAUC, THELAUCUS

A disciple of Dyfrig, who went to Brittany with Teilo to escape the Yellow Plague. He is regarded as the original patron saint of Carmarthen, where Lan Toulidac was situated inside the walls of the Roman 'caer' of Maridunum, according to the Book of Llandaf. The land at Llandeulydog was given to Llandaf by Rhydderch ap Iestin. The church became the Priory of St John the Evangelist and St Theulacus, then the Normans dedicated the church entirely to St John. (This Thelaucus is sometimes confused with Teilo). Lann Deulydawc was mentioned in the Laws of Hywel Dda as 'one of the seven bishop-houses of Dyfed', and stipulated that *'the abbot of Teulyddog should be graduated in literary degrees.'* (It may be noted here that the Saxons were thought to be illiterate by the British, but they were surpassed by the Normans, of whom William the Bastard [William the Conqueror of England] could only sign his name as a cross).

The Black Book of Carmarthen (Llyfr Du Caerfyrddin) is the oldest manuscript collection of poetry in the Welsh language, and appears to have been copied and written over many years by a member of the Priory of St John and St Teulyddog.

Alphabetical Listing of the Saints of Wales and Religious Events

Tintern Abbey. *CADW: Welsh Historic Monuments. Crown Copyright.*

KING TEWDRIC 5th century
TEWDRIG, THEODORIC, TEWDREC
April 1, January 3

One of the *'three canonised Kings'*, with Cadwaladr and Gwrthefyr (Vortimer). Tewdrig ap Teithfallt ap Nynio's descendants controlled Glamorgan until the Normans defeated by treachery Iestyn Gwrgant in the eleventh century. In old age Tewdric gave his kingdom of Glamorgan and Gwent to his son Meurig and retired to a cell near *'Dindeyrn'* (Tintern)* according to the Book of Llandaf. 'Dindeyrn' translates at 'Fortress of the Sovereign'.

King Tewdrig had controlled much of south-east Wales, and fought with Constantine the Blessed against the invading Saxons. After Constantine's death, he allied with Vortigern to keep the peace, and passed on his kingdom to his son Meurig. Tewdrig retired to Tintern as a monk or hermit, where he was attacked by Saxons. A stone bridge in the nearby Angidy valley is called *'Pont y Saeson'*, *'Bridge of the Saxons'*, and this may be where the fight took place. The enemy were driven off, but not before Tewdrig was mortally wounded by a sword cut to the head. His son Meurig arrived and took his father on a cart to a well in Merthyr Tewdrig, modern Mathern. A plaque there reads *'By tradition at this spring King Tewdrig's wounds were washed after the battle near Tintern about 470AD against the pagan Saxons. He died a short way off and by his wishes a church was built over his grave.'* The well is near Mathern House, and his son Meurig's holy well is also near this place.

Tewdrig had wanted to be buried upon Flat Holm**, Ynys Echni, but a wagon drawn by two stags appeared. His body was placed on it, and the stags pulled it south to Mathern on the banks of the Severn, where he was buried. Mathern is the corruption of *'Merthyr Tewdrig'* then *'Merthyr Teyrn'*, *'the site of martyrdom of the sovereign'*. In 822, Nennius described the well as one of *'the marvels of Britain'*, and also referred to the nearby Well of Meurig. Meurig seemed to become known as Uther Pendragon (*'Wonderful Head Dragon'*, leader of the Celtic army), and was the father of Arthmael, the King Arthur of legend.

Tewdrig founded the churches of Llandow in the Vale of Glamorgan, Bedwas and Merthyr Tydfil. There is a ruined church and well near the present village of Llandow. He also had a hermitage near the mouth of the Afan river, and was said to have re-founded Côr Eurgain after it was wiped out by Saxons, for Illtud to take over. Bangor Illtud later became Llanilltud Fawr, but the site is marked on old maps at Côr Tewdws. (However, Tewdws probably refers to Theodosius). Gilbert repeats the claims of Wilson and Blackett that the 'Einnion Stone' at Margam Abbey Museum is dedicated to Tewdrig. It reads 'THUORTHOREC', i.e. Theodoric.

Bishop Godwin of Llandaf opened the saint's stone coffin in Mathern Church in the early 17th century. He found a skeleton with a badly fractured skull, and observed that Tewdric's bones were *'not in the smallest degree changed . . . the skull retaining the aperture of a large wound, which appeared as if it had been recently inflicted.'* (Cox's Monmouthshire, 1610).

Tewdrig's Day of April 1 is now 'All Fools Day' or 'April Fools' Day' and was referred to by Mark Twain in 'Pudd'nhead Wilson's Calendar' as *'the day upon which we are reminded of what we are on the other three hundred and sixty-four.'*

*Wordsworth visited Cistercian Tintern Abbey ruins in 1793 and 1798, and the area inspired him to one of the greatest poems in the English language. 'Lines Composed a Few Miles Above Tintern Abbey', a verse of which is as follows:

*'I have learned
To look on nature, not as in the hour
Of thoughtless youth; but hearing often-times
The still, sad music of humanity,
Nor harsh nor grating; though of ample power
To chasten and subdue. And I have felt
A presence that disturbs me with the joy
Of elevated thoughts; a sense sublime
Of something far more deeply interfused,
Whose dwelling is the light of setting suns,
And the round ocean and the living air,
And the blue sky, and in the mind of man.'*

**Tewdrig may have actually been buried on Flat Holm (Echni), a place sacred to the Welsh and the site of Cadog's hermitage. His dying request was to be taken *'hence to that desirable place where I wish to lie after death . . . to the Island of Echni.'* According to this version, his body was taken to the shore on a wagon drawn by stags, then carried across the Severn and interred on the island. A fragment of stone slab dating back to the 6th or 7th century was found on the island, bearing an incised cross.

TEWDWR BRYCHEINIOG 6th century

The son of Nefydd ap Nefydd Ail ap Rhun ap Brychan, therefore one of Brychan Brycheiniog's tribe. Only Iolo Morganwg appears to note this saint.

TEWDWR late 6th century
TEWDWR, TUDOR, TUDYR
October 15 (also its eve and morrow), and March 13

The son of Arwystli Gloff and brother of Marchell, he founded Darowain (Darowen) in Montgomery, where he is said to be buried. At Darowain there was a curious custom called *'Curo Tudur'*, where the most unpopular boy in the village was carried around on the back of another and beaten with sticks. Later, an effigy of the saint was used, and the practice was not discontinued until 1830. There is a Ffynnon Dudur at Darowen, plus others at Llanelidan in Denbigh and at Drefelyn near Llangeler in Cardigan. Ffynnon Deudir is at Penbryn in Cardigan. Edward Lhuyd mentioned an *'Eglwys Dydyr'* in Llanlluwchllyn, Merioneth. He also notes a holy well in Cae Tydyr, near Cerrigydrudion Church in Denbighshire.

TEYRNOG 6th century
TYRNOG, TWRNOG
April 4 (also September 25)

Llandyrnog in Denbighshire is the foundation of this son of Arwystli (Hawystl) Gloff. His mother was Tywanwedd ferch Amlawdd Wledig, and her brothers were Tyfrydog, Diefer and Tewdwr. His sister was Marchell. Diefer's foundation at Bodfari adjoined Llandyrnog, and Denbigh itself was known as Llanfarchell. For some time he had been a monk at Bangor-is-Coed. There is a 'Saying of the Wise' for *'Diyrnig, the wise and distinguished warrior'*, *'God will provide comfort for the lonely.'*

There is mediaeval stained glass from the 1490's in the double-naved church of St Tyrnog, plus a remarkable dug-out oak chest, and the church was restored in 1876-78 by Nesfield. His unusual but attractive style rendered the church pink, with flowered roundels on the timbered porch and choir stalls.

Ternegacus Standing Stone stood near Brithdir Chapel, outside the Roman camp of Gelligaer, but is now in the National Museum of Wales at Cardiff. Nine feet high, it was called Maen Teyrnog. According to Evans ('The History of Glamorgan') this marked the place of burial of the *'founder of Tintern Church'*. Westwood notes an inscription *'TEGERNA CUS FILI US MARII HIC IA CIT'*, *'Teyrnoc, son of Marius lies here.'* Another standing stone at Gelligaer, known as the Cefn Gellligaer Stone, leans precariously and had an inscription that had been defaced. Fochrhiw is small dolmen nearby.

In 1830, an inscribed stone *'CATACUS hic jecet filius Tegernacus'* (here lies Cattoc, the son of *Teyrnoc)* was built into the south wall of Llanfihangel-cwm-du church in Brecon. It was moved from a field called Tir Gwenlli, about a mile from St Michael's Church, but formerly seems to have been at the Gaer Roman fort. It is supposed to be the burial stone of Cadog, but Cadog's father was Gywnlliw Filwr. The field Tir Gwenlli may be relevant in this aspect. Cadog's name also appeared on a stone forming the threshold to Llandyfaelog Church, another claimant to his burial place, but the stone appears to have vanished in the eighteenth century. The Rev. Price of St Michael's possessed a rubbing in the early 19th century of another stone. It was found at Faenor, three miles from Merthyr Tydful, and was accidentally destroyed on its way to Swansea Museum. It read *'Tir . . . (fil)ius Catiri* . Yet another ruined cross lies in Llanfihangel-cwm-du churchyard, but only 'hic iacet' could be deciphered. One wonders if technology could recover the original markings upon weathered stones, by tracing the compressed crystalline structure of the rock in the layers under the blows of the sculptor's tools?

THEGONNEC 6th century
September 8-14

A British disciple of Pol-de-Leon who went with him to Armorica and founded St Thegonnec and Loc-Eguiner-St Thegonnec, both south-west of Morlaix. South of Morlaix is Le Cloitre St Thegonnec.

THOMAS the APOSTLE 1st century
December 21

'Yta' or *'Thomasing'* took place on his day, when Welshwomen went to houses to collect corn and flour to make cakes and loaves for Christmas.

TILULL

A ninth century charter in the Book of Llandaff mentions a grant by Aguod ap Ieuaf of the *'vill of Penn Onn'* and its church of *'Lann Tilull'* to Bishop Cerennyr. Lann Tilull is St-y-Nyll, which became in mediaeval times a dependent chapel in the parish of St Bride's-super-Ely near Cardif.

TIMOTHEUS d. 140
March 24 (but since 1969, March 26, and March 22 in the East)

A disciple of Paul, born in Rome and the reputed son of Claudia (the daughter of Caractacus) and Pudens. He was called the *'apostle to the Britons'*, and martyred by stones and clubs in Rome during the pagan festival of Katagogia. Roman sources make him a native of Lystra with a Gentile father and Jewish mother named Eunice, which seems to confuse two men of this name. The Acts of Timothy tell us of his martyrdom by pagans, and his relics supposedly went to Constantinople in 356, but this was the Apostle Timothy who died in 97, a family friend after whom Timotheus, this son of Pudens was named. See Appendix I.

TONSURE

The tonsure was originally a pagan and druidic habit of shaving the head. It was used by the Christian church to distinguish its holy men. The Greek *'tonsure of St Paul'* involved shaving the whole head. In the Roman *'tonsure of St Peter'*, we see just the top of the head shaved, with a ring of hair around it, much like Friar Tuck is depicted in films. However, the tonsure of the Britons and Scots consisted in shaving all of the front of the head from ear to ear. The *'Rule of St Benedict'* laid strict conditions for the type of tonsure, and the Britons refused to adopt the Roman method. Along with the different date of Easter, this enraged St Augustine, but the British clergy still would not change their ancient ways.

TRIADS

The Welsh triads followed the oral tradition of remembrance by grouping people or events in threes, and seem to date from the 6th - 7th century, although only mediaeval collections survive. Sources include the Peniarth Manuscript, Llyfr Gwyn Rhydderch (The White Book of Rhydderch), the Red Book of Hergest and the Black Book of Carmarthen. Many of the Welsh saints feature in them, especially as 'warrior-knights'. Peniarth 16 is worth recording for its references to Arthur:

'Three Tribal Thrones of the Island of Britain:
Arthur as Chief Prince in Mynyw (St David's), and Dewi as Chief Bishop, and Maelgwn Gwynedd as Chief Elder;
Arthur as Chief Prince in Celliwig in Cerniw, and Bishop Bedwyn as Chief Bishop, and Caradog Freich-Fras as Chief Elder;
Arthur as Chief Prince in Pen Rhionydd in the North, and Gerthmwl Wledig as Chief Elder, and Cyndeyrn Garthwys (Kentigern) as Chief Bishop.'

'Celliwig in Cerniw' is not Cornwall, but Wentloog area near Cardiff, Bedwyn's bishopric probably being Caerleon. Bedwyn features as Sir Baudwin, and Caradog as Caradoc Bris-Bras in Arthurian legend.

TRIDIAN
RHIDIAN?

There is Llanrhidian and Ffynnon Rhidian in St Nicholas parish, Pembroke, and a farm called Llanridion outside St David's. Possibly he also founded Llanrhidian in the Gower Peninsula, where there is a St Illtud's Well. There is also an Aberthridian in Eglwysilan, Glamorgan that stems from Rhidian or Tridian.

TRILLO 5th – 6th century
June 15 and 16 (also 24, 25, 26)

There are churches dedicated to St Trillo at Llandrygarn in Anglesey and at Llandrillo yn Edernion near Corwen in Merioneth, which had an associated holy well for curing rheumatism. This latter church seems at one time to have been dedicated to Mael and Sulien, also followers of Cadfan. In the mid-19th century a farmer refused access to the well, whereupon it mysteriously stopped flowing, only to resurface in a neighbouring field with free access. In 1699 Edward Lhuyd mentioned the grave of Trillo's wife on the banks of Cadwed brook. There is an ancient yew and an early Celtic circular churchyard, and a very rare 'hooded' tomb can be seen in the graveyard. (There is also a St Trillac near Lamballe in France, which may be this saint).

The old oratory at Llandrillo-yn-Rhos on the Denbighshire coast was used for baptism, and built over a spring. He founded this small chapel when he saw a Celtic cross of light appear above the waters there. Even today, supplicants write requests to God for healing on scraps of paper, and leave them on the altar. Capel Trillo on the shore was built over a perpetual spring, and tithes were taken from a weir there. Prayers were said three times a day in the chapel in the salmon season. A notice reads:

Parish of Llandrillo-yn-Rhos
All reverence is due to this sacred spot
This ancient chapel
Is built over the holy well of Saint Trillo
A Celtic saint of the sixth century
Pilgrim turn in and offer prayer
The Lord be with you

Intriguingly, nearby in a private garden is a brass plaque to the Welshman who is said to have discovered America 300 years before Columbus, reading:

Prince Madoc sailed from here
Aber-Kerrik-Gwynan, 1170 AD
And landed at Mobile, Alabama
With his ships
Gorn Gwynant and Pedr Sant.

There was also a Ffynnon Drillo in Llansannan, Denbighshire, and Clocaenog has sometimes been attributed to Trillo. The feast date changed from June 15 at the great Fair of Drillo at Bangor, to the eve, day and morrow of June 25. Trillo ab Ithel Hael witnessed the grant of land by Maelgwn Gwynedd to Cyndeyrn (Mungo), in the presence of Deiniol, Gwrst and Rhun ap Maelgwn. His brothers were Tegai, Llechid, Dygwel, Ffflewyn and Gredifael.

There is an interesting letter from a bishop in 1316 which notes the continuing use of his church as a sanctuary, a legal protection that had been confirmed by the Statute of Rhuddlan in 1284:

'Dafydd, Bishop of St Asaph, complains to King Edward that when Ieuan ap Madog of Edeyrnon, on account of a charge of homicide, had taken sanctuary in the church of Llandrillo, in the diocese of St Asaph, certain of Ieuan's enemies came to the church, and in defiance of ecclesiastical immunity, violently took him from the said church, and led him over to the castle of Hartleigh (Harlech), in the diocese of Bangor, and handed him over to the Justice of North Wales to be imprisoned in the King's prison, where he still remains, to the prejudice of ecclesiastical liberty. Although we have asked the Justice to restore Ieuan to the aforesaid church, the Justice has refused to restore him. We therefore pray the King for the restoration of the aforesaid Ieuan to sanctuary.'

Sanctuary was enshrined in the Laws of Hywel Dda, and Gerald of Wales in 1188 described its operation in Wales:

'Around the churches the cattle graze so peacefully, not only in the churchyards, but outside, too, within fences and ditches marked out and set by bishops to fix the sanctuary limits. The more important churches, hallowed by their greater antiquity, offer sanctuary as far as the cattle go to feed in the morning and can return at evening. If a man has incurred the hatred of his prince and is in danger of death, he may apply to the church for sanctuary and it will be freely granted to him and his family. Many people abuse this immunity.'

TRINIHID 6th century

The wife of Illtud, sometimes associated with Llanrhidian on the Gower peninsula, and Llantrithyd near Bonvilston in the Vale of Glamorgan. The evocative ruin of Llantrithyd House, next to the church, was the home of the family of the famous essayist and diarist John Aubrey (1626-1697). Aubrey was also a great antiquarian, recognising the significance of Avebury before anyone else, and he named the 'Heel Stone' at Stonehenge. He also noted the 56 holes at Stonehenge which had held timber uprights, which are today known as the Aubrey Holes. The church is dedicated to Illtud, and contains fine effigies and memorials to the Aubrey, Basset and Mansel families.

TRINIO 6th century
June 29 (also its eve and morrow celebrated at Llandrinio Fair)

Trinio ap Difwng ab Emyr Llydaw emigrated with Cadfan from Brittany to Ynys Enlli, and founded Llandrinio in Montgomeryshire. He was also commemorated in the chapels of Llandyssilio and Melverly.

TRYDDID 6th century

Iolo Morganwg thought that this may have been Illtud's wife, and the founder of Llantrithyd in Glamorgan, but it is more likely to have been Trinihid.

TRYGARN

'The Parish Churches of North Wales' by Mike Salter notes the 13th century Llandrygarn Church on Anglesey as belonging to this saint.

TUDCLYD 6th century
TUCLYD, TYDDUD
May 30

The son of Seithenin Frenin, who founded Llandudclyd in Caernarfon, which is now known as Penmachno. He studied at Bangor-is-Coed. Rice Rees thought that Tyddud founded Penmachno, but it seems to be the same person as Tudclyd. The church at Penmachno was known as that of Enclydwen, i.e. Tudclyd Wyn (Tudclyd the White, or Blessed). The holy wells Ffynnon Dyclid and Ffynnon y Drewi were in Llanwrtyd Wells, Brecon. When the old church at Penmachno was taken down, several Celtic stones were discovered. One reads *'Oria ic iacit.'* Also the famous Carausius Stone bears the legend *'CARAUSIUS HIC JACIT IN HOC CONGERIES LAPIDUM.'* It is not thought that the individual buried under this 'mound of stones' is Marcus Aurelius Valerius Carausius, the Roman ruler of Britain. He was killed by the British prince Allectus at York in 297, although his body may have come to Wales in triumph. Another Penmachno stone seems to have gone to Voelas Hall, and was marked *'Cantorius Hic Iacit Venedotis Cive Fuit Consobrino, Ma . . . Fili Magistrati.'*

TUDFUL d. 480
TYDFYL, TYDFIL
August 23 was Mabsant Merthyr; September 24 was the 'Apple and Pear Fair'

This daughter of Brychan was said to have been assassinated by Saxons, with her brother Rhun, by a band of Saxons and Irish Picts. Rhun's son Nefydd put the warband to flight. Merthyr means shrine as well as place of martyrdom, so she may not have been martyred. Llysworney Church in the Vale of Glamorgan is dedicated to this female saint, as was a chapel of Llanilltud Fawr until it was given to the Abbey of Tewkesbury. Ffynnon Dudful seems to have disappeared.

From William ab Ieuan ap Morgan of Llysworney came the Williams family of Llanishen, Cardiff, from whom Oliver Williams was descended. This Williams changed his surname as a young man to that of Cromwell, after Thomas Cromwell, his father's benefactor. Thus **the only two successful insurrections by the British people since the Norman Conquest were headed by the Welshmen Henry Tudor and Oliver Cromwell**. However, Llysworney seems to have been called Llysyronen, and Tudful may not have been associated with it. It is more likely that St Dial's under Llanfihangel Llantarnam near Caerleon may have been her church, as it seems to be the place called Llandudful mentioned in the Book of Llandaf (However, see Tylull).

The great Saturday market of Merthyr Tudful was lovingly described by the US consul, Wirt Sikes in 1881, and is notable for its description both of Welsh costume (including the tall beaver-skin hats) and the 'spoon-food' tradition:
'But women reign at most of the stalls. Here is a brisk Welshwoman selling lace caps to a crowd of elderly Welsh dames, who gravely remove their bonnets, untie their old caps, and try on the new with religious care; and a lively trade drives the cap-seller, for here every woman

wears a cap of lace or muslin under her bonnet or hat. There is a noticeable change, too, in the costumes of the market-women. The peasants of Wales, like those of most lands, cling less strenuously to their distinctive costume in these latter days than they were wont to do. Formerly a farmer's wife or daughter who should make her appearance at market or church (or on any like occasion which calls for the donning of one's best) without wearing a tall hat, would have been deemed careless of her personal appearance, or peculiar in her tastes; so that twenty years ago these were seen in every direction in Merthyr market, as well as the distinctive long cloaks of bright colours, and the occasional scuttle-shaped bonnets. Nowadays this custom is so greatly relaxed that we see but few of these in Merthyr market. The head-coverings of the women are chiefly mushroom hats of dark straw, or close-fitting bonnets of black crepe, always with a lace or muslin cap underneath.

There are, however, some specimens still to be seen of the Welsh peasant costume as it has been for generations past; notably a comely young woman behind a vegetable stall, who wears the full costume in all its glory. She is a pink of neatness, and her beaver is superb. I at once christen her the Pride of the Market, and if ever I go to live in Merthyr Tydfil, I shall buy my vegetable marrows off none but her. Her hat is prodigiously tall, and shines with a gloss that betokens careful brushing; it has a broad rim, and a peaked crown, and is adorned about the base of its chimney with a twist of some pinky stuff. Underneath it is seen a muslin cap of snowy whiteness, with blue ribbons, and the woman's hair is drawn back smoothly from her shining forehead. A short semi-coat of red flannel reaches to her knee, and over her shoulders is pinned a gay green kerchief, striped with yellow. A blue chequered apron hangs from her waist, and a dark stuff gown reaches to her ankles, clearing the ground by some inches, and showing her stout shoes tied with a bit of ribbon. All these stuffs were home-made, I judged. The hat looked as if it were new, just out of the shop, but she told me that she had had it some years. Such a hat will last the wearer a life-time, with care, but it is likely to grow wrinkly at its peak as the burden of years grows heavy on it. Later in the day, while rambling about in the neighbourhood of Merthyr, I came upon two elderly dames before a cottage door; whose hats were as old as themselves, to all appearance; one of the beavers indeed awakened the suspicion that it had been sat on in some dark hour of its existence . . . '

'At a stall near the great entrance a buxom Welsh dame in the forties presided over a display of eatables. In pursuit at once of information, experience, and luncheon, I sat on the wooden settle behind the bench on which the viands were spread, and surveyed the board. A bouquet of flowers in a pot-bellied white pitcher, with blue rings around it, stood surrounded by pies and tarts of various sorts; a huge rice pudding in a deep dish, a bowl of eggs, square cuts of German-looking pastry, and certain round boulders of black plum pudding. A pile of what I took to be sausages were steaming furiously over a brazier of burning coals on one end of the bench, with a teapot leaning lazily against it and thinking aloud. Choosing what seemed to be the least formidable specimen of the food before me, I pointed to the brazier and said, but in a tone so low I was not heard, "I will take a sausage." Obeying my gesture, the woman served me a saucer-full of the black balls, swimming in hot gravy, and gave me a pewter spoon with which to eat it, instead of the knife and fork which might have been expected with meat. The balls proved to be not unpalatable eating, and were, according to my best judgement, made of liver. What they were actually made of, however, is a question upon which I subsequently learned to entertain doubts; they are a savoury compound locally called "faggits" or fagots. (Query, fag-ends?)

My hostess addressed me in the Welsh language this question: "Will you have some bread?" This being the first Welsh I had heard spoken out of doors in Wales afforded me profound *satisfaction; and thinking perhaps my hostess could not speak English, I made bold to ask for cwrw da, which means good ale. She had no ale, but proceeded to mention other beverages with Welsh names to an extent that threw me into a perspiration. I concluded that I would conduct the remainder of the conversation in English, if possible. The good woman knew English well enough, it appeared, but uttered it in a fashion I could hardly understand better than her Welsh; she recommended me, for instance, to have a bottle of "pup" which I should certainly have never taken to mean ginger-pop, had I not gathered the fact from her showing a bottle. I took a cup of tea. In my cup was a curious little spoon of brass, worn thin like the old silver teaspoons which come down to us from our grand-mothers, and stamped on its handle with a sheaf of wheat. Concluding my feast with rice pudding, what was my surprise at seeing the woman cut it from the dish with a knife, serve it on a plate instead of a saucer, and give me with it an iron-pronged fork instead of a spoon? A fork to eat rice-pudding; a spoon to eat liver balls? Why this revolution in one's notions respecting table-ware? I asked myself. It was not due to any carelessness or poverty of outfit; the woman was scrupulously attentive of my comfort, and had an abundance of utensils. The luncheon cost me sixpence, and was very filling at the price.*

At the adjoining stall I saw several glasses standing on a neat slab, containing drinkables, some of which were white, and some bright red. Inferring that the white liquid was "pup", and the red lemonade (such as the Germans sell, colouring it with some harmless essence), I put a glass of the red liquid to my lips. It tasted like some nasty medicinal draught; I set it down again, but drew my purse; whereupon the girl in attendance plumped a teaspoonful of white powder (more medicine, thought I) into the red liquid, causing it to fizz and bubble in a surprising manner. Price a ha'p'ny. I did not drink it; it seemed too eccentric in its habits. Subsequent better acquaintance again enlightened me regarding this beverage, which is a favourite of the poorer classes at fairs and the like.'

There is a wonderful verse in 'Gwalia Deserta' by Idris Davies that describes Merthyr Tydful after the ravages of industrialisation:

'Ride you into Merthyr Tydfil
Where the fountains have run dry,
And gaze upon the sands of fortune
But pray not to the sky.

If you will to Merthyr Tydfil,
Ride unarmed of dreams;
No manna falls on Merthyr Tydfil,
And there flow no streams.

Pints of pity give no healing,
Eyes go blind that will not see,
Ride you into Merthyr Tydfil
With salt of charity.'

In one of the angles of Merthyr Tydful Church, high above the ground, is a stone inscribed with a cross and the words ARTBEU. A paper given at the Meeting of the Cambrian Archaeological Association in 1853 by a Mr Stephens posited the stone as being dedicated to Arthen (Artgen), a son of Brychan and therefore Tudfyl's brother.

TUDGLID fl. 600
TANGLWST, TANGWYSTL, TUDGLYD, GWTFIL,
May 9

The wife of Cyngen ap Cadell Deyrnllug and mother of Brochwel Ysgythrog, who was the leader of the defence of the monks of Bangor-is-Coed. She was a daughter or grand-daughter of Brychan, so may be the same saint as Hawystl mentioned earlier, and/or Tudwystl mentioned later in the text. She lived at Caer Hawystl, possibly modern-day Aust (Awst) near the present Welsh border in Gloucestershire. There was also a Llan Awstl near Machen in Monmouth.

Tudglid married Cyngen, Prince of Powys, and was the mother of Cadell, Mawen, Brochwel and others. Llanwrtyd in Brecon is now dedicated to David, but was hers, and Edward Lhuyd mentioned her feast-day, Dy-Gwyl Dyclid there, plus a holy well called Ffynnon Dyclid. Llanwrtyd Wells is probably the only locality in Wales at present that understands the needs of tourists and how to implement a schedule to make the area attractive all the year round. (See the author's 'The A-Z of Wales and the Welsh' under its 'Marketing' section). Hafod Tanglws Ucha is a farmhouse near Merthyr Tydfil, where Tudfil was supposed to have been visiting Tanglwst at the time Tudful was martyred.

Tanglwst (meaning 'the hostage of peace') was still in use as a name at Peterstone outside Cardiff in 1789. Welsh was still the main language around the capital until the 19th century. In Sully, just along the coast from Cardiff, characters at this time were known as Nan y Gof Gwyllt (Mad Nancy, *'a wild, swearing, bitter tongued sort of woman'* according to William Thomas), and Howel yr Aur (Howel the Gold).

TUDNO 6th century
June 5, November 31

Tudno ap Seithenyn studied at Bangor-is-Coed and is known as the patron of Pant-yr-Eglwys on the cliffs overlooking Llandudno. This church of St Tudno dates in part from the twelfth century but is probably on the site of his cell. Ffynnon Tudno is just a hundred yards from the church. Ogof Llech on the shore below is supposed to be the cave he used as a cell or retreat. There was a rocking stone here (which unfortunately no longer moves) called Cryd Dudno ('Tudno's crib'). Tudno Tudclyd is one of the *'Thirteen Treasures'*, a whetstone that sharpens the sword of heroes and blunts those of cowards. However, this is more likely to be named after Tudwal Tudclyd, the father of Rhydderch Hael. On the Great Orme's slopes at Llandudno is Llety'r Filiast Dolmen, where Ceridwen the mother of Taliesin is said to be buried.

A Celtic stone stood in a cottage wall at Llandudno, probably inscribed *'Santagnus Filius Sacerdoti.'* This appears to be Sannan (Senanus), and Llansannan is nearby.

TUDUR AB HYWEL 6th century
October 7

The church of Mynydd Islwyn in Monmouth is probably this saint's foundation, because of the differing date from Tewdwr ap Hawystl Gloff.

The Book of Welsh Saints

TUDWAL BEFR 5th century
TUGDUAL
June 3

A saint and bishop descended from Cynan Meriadog. He was married to Nefydd, one of Brychan's daughters, and their son Ifor was also a saint. The ruins on St Tudwal's island have been attributed to him, as well as to the later Tudwal. The sea lane between the Llŷn peninsula and the St Tudwal's Islands is known as St Tudwal's Roads. A church on the nearby mainland was called Tydweiliog. Llanstadwell in Pembroke is a derivation of Llan-Sant-Tudwal, and it was formerly known as Llanystudwal and also Llan-ynys-Tudwal. Ffynnon Dudwal in Llanengan (near Penrhyn) was drained by lead-mining, but was once resorted to for illness and healing wounds. Merthyr Tudful has been spelt Tutuil and Tudeuel in the past, so the churches at Llysworney and Merthyr may also be Tudwal's.

BISHOP TUDWAL 6th century
TUGDUAL, TUAL, TUDY, TUDEC, PABU (One of the Breton Founding Saints)
December 1(also November 30 and December 2), September 3

St Tudwal (or the Tudwal noted above) is supposed to have founded a sixth century ecclesiastical settlement on St Tudwal's Island East, off the Sarn Peninsula in Llŷn. Celtic monks inhabited the island for centuries, but in the fifteenth century administration was handed over to the Augustinians. There is a large complex of mediaeval buildings here, rotting gently since the 1536 Reformation, and much archaeological work needs to be done on this historic site. It was mentioned in the 'Taxatio' of 1291 as *'Ecclesia Prioris de Enys Tudwal'*, but by Leland's time had been converted into a barn.

Tudwal landed in Brittany with his family and followers, at Leon, and built a monastery at Lan Pabu, on lands belonging to his cousin but confirmed by King Childebert I. The king insisted that Tudwal became a bishop. St Tugdual's Cathedral is one of the most beautiful Gothic buildings in France, in Treguier, 19 miles north of Guincamp. (The tomb of the patron saint of lawyers is in this cathedral – St Yves was allegedly incorruptible, and his shrine is surrounded by hundreds of burning candles lit by those who want real justice.) Tudwal's relics are claimed by Treguier, Laval and Chartres, and he is depicted like Armel holding a dragon. Renan wrote *'Treguier, my native town, is a city wholly ecclesiastical, foreign to commerce and industry, one vast monastery indeed, penetrated by no rumours from the outer world, where other men pursue what is called vanity, and where what laymen call chimaeras are held to be the sole realities of existence.'* (A chimaera is a wild, or impossible idea, which comes from the Greek fire-breathing monster, with the head of a lion, the body of a goat and the tail of a serpent. A modern example of a chimaera might be the 'Millennium Experience' whereby politicians feel that people will travel for the best part of a day, and spend hundreds of pounds upon their families experiencing something too amorphous to be advertised.)

The Iolo mss. seem to be correct in placing Tudwal as the son of Hywel Mawr, and the brother of Derfel Gadarn, Armel, Dwyfael and Leonore. He was known as *Pabu* to the Bretons, where his cousin Deroc was King of Domnonia, according to the Catholic Online Saints website. This also states that Tudwal founded 'Lan Paku' at Leon in northern Spain. St Tugdual is near Le Faouet and St Tual is south of Dinan. There are several places named Lanbabu or Lambabu in Brittany.

TUDWEN 6th century
October 21 or 27

Llandudwen, under Ceidio in Caernarfon, was founded by this daughter of Brychan. Ffynnon Dudwen, which cured poor eyes, epilepsy, numbness and rheumatism, was a pin and coin well, but has disappeared. According to Francis Jones secret marriages were solemnized at the well.

TUDWG 6th century
May 9

Tudwg ap Tyfodwg was taught in St Cenydd's foundation, and founded Llandudwg, now called Tythegston in the Vale of Glamorgan. He is also commemorated along the Cotes du Nord and at Plessala in Brittany. Westwood notes a small Celtic cross which was found in the 19th century in the Tythegston churchyard. An Ogham stone was found in the parish of Llandugwd, Cardigan, known as the Troed-rhiw-fergam stone, so there may also have been a saint named Tugwd.

TUDWYSTL 5th – 6th century

A daughter of Brychan (who may be the same person as Tudglid). There was a Capel Tudyst near Llandeilo Fawr, where she was martyred. Her sisters Tybie and Lluan had adjoining foundations at Llandybie and Llanlluan. (See Tudglid).

TUDY 5th century
TEGWIN, TUDINUS
May 11 (May 9 then May 20 at St Tudy)

It used to be thought that this saint was Tudwal, but he seems to have been a disciple of St Briog who became abbot at Landevennec. His parish of St Tudy lies next to St Breoke in Cornwall. He moved on to Brittany operating from Ile-Tudy near Quimper. Port-Tudy is on the Ile de Groix, and Ile-Tudy and Loctudy are north of Benodet.

TUGDON 6th century
HOUDON

The father of the saints Gwyddno, Winwaloe (Gwenole) and Majan (see Gwyddno), who founded Saint-Houdon in Brittany.

TUGWD see TUDWG

TWROG 6th – 7th century
June 26 (also August 15)

Twrog ab Ithael Hael founded Llandwrog in Caernarfonshire and is the patron of Maentwrog in Merioneth, a chapel under Ffestiniog. Bodwrog in Anglesey is also his. The stones that comprised Bedd Twrog have now disappeared from Llandwrog. At Maentwrog, a huge stone different to local rocks (possibly a glacial boulder) is attached to the angle of the church, and is known as Maen Twrog. It was supposed to have been thrown by Twrog from the top of the mountain of Moelwyn. Maen Llwyd is a standing stone in Glynllifon Park near Maentwrog. Ffynnon Fair, just a hundred yards from Maentwrog Church, was possibly Twrog's holy well rather than Mary's.

TWYD

Nothing is known of this saint, noted by Mike Salter as patron of Llantwyd in Pembroke.

TYBIE 5th century
January 30 (but her Gwyl Mabsant was held upon December 26)

Killed by pagans at Llandybie in Carmarthen, she was a daughter of Brychan. There was a popular holy well, Ffynon Dybie there, and a field nearby where she had her cell is still called Cell Tybie. Neighbouring Llanlluan is dedicated to her sister Lluan, who used to stay with Tybie. A nearby Neolithic stone circle at Capel Hendre is called Y Naw Carreg (The Nine Stones) and is sixty feet in diameter. Near Drysgol in Llandybie parish is Ffynnon y Pentre, which cured sore eyes. West of Dinan in Brittany is Landebia parish, with a St David's Well. Catholic Online Saints confuses this virgin with St Tudy.

The Rev. Gomer Roberts wrote in 1863 about Capel Hendre in Llandybie district:
'Dances were held on Banc y Naw Carreg and in another place called Pan-teg. The dance was to begin on St John's Day and to continue, if the weather were favourable, for nine days. There were one or two harpists, and the assembly, both males and females, used to dance. They used to set a birch tree in the earth and decorate its branches with wreaths of flowers. The prettiest wreaths were placed on the highest branches. This custom was kept up until 1725.'

TYDDUD see TUDCLYD

TYDECHO 6th century
December 17

He was the cousin of the saints Padarn and Cadfan, the men who led an influx of Bretons into Wales around 515. The son of Amwn Ddu and Anna ferch Meurig, and brother of St Tathan and St Samson of Dol, he lived in Mawddwy with his sister Tegfedd, and was an ascetic persecuted by Maelgwn Gwynedd. Arthur was his uncle. He stayed with Dogfael and Tegfan for some time at St Dogmael's. Llanymawddwy (formerly Llandudech) church in Merioneth was founded by him, and there is a ruined chapel in the hills there. One of Cadfan's disciples, he had cells in Merioneth at Cemmaes and in Montgomery at Mallwyd.

Alphabetical Listing of the Saints of Wales and Religious Events

The church at Garthbeibio is dedicated to him, and his holy pin well was much visited for the cure of rheumatism. There was a carving of his head here, which has disappeared. A chapel was consecrated to him at Llandegfan in Anglesey. At Ffynnon Dydecho near Garthbeibio was his carved effigy, and there was his pin well there which cured rheumatism. He was celebrated in Llanymawddwy (where he was buried) on the first Sunday after Lammas, in Cemmaes on the Sunday after Michaelmas day, and in Mallwyd on Easter Monday. His most noted miracle was to turn a stretch of the Dyfi into milk for the poor, and this part of the river, near its source, is still called Llaethnant (Milk stream).

TYDIEU 5th – 6th century

A virgin daughter of Brychan who seems to have founded the extinct Capel Ogwr near St Bride's Major.

TYDIWG 5th – 6th century

Llandidiwg in Monmouth is the *'Henlan Titiuc'* mentioned in the Book of Llandaf. Tydiwg was the son of Corun and brother of Carannog and Tyssul. Llandidwg is now named Dixton, with a former name of Dukes-Town, and has been rededicated by the Normans to St Peter.

Bishop's Palace, Llamphey, from the South. © *Wales Tourist Board Photo Library.*

Bishop's Palace, Lamphey, aerial view. © *Wales Tourist Board Photo Library.*

TYFAELOG
March 1, February 26

His festival was on March 1 in Llandyfaelog just north of Brecon, and on February 26 in other dedications. At Llandyfaelog Fach there is a seven feet high cross-slab with ornate carvings above a central warrior figure and the inscription + BRIAMAIL FLOU – could this be Brochwel (Brocmael) Ysgyrthog? The depiction is of a bearded man in a tunic, with a short sword ('seax') in one hand and a club or mace in the other. This is a very rare example of a representation of a British warrior. It leads Westwood to surmise that the sculptor was influenced by the nearby Maen y Morwynion, the 'Maidens' Stone' found on the Roman road from Brecon to Aberscyr. This reads *'Alancina Civis et Conjuni Eius H S Est'*, and shows two full-length figures of a Roman soldier and his wife. In Llandyfaelog parish, Carmarthen is Pistyll Gwyn, a healing well for sore eyes, and another healing well called Ffynnon Ddwfach.

TYFAEN

There was a chapel near Llandeilo Fawr named Llandyfaen, with a spring used for the holy treatment of paralysis. There were nine steps down to the bathing area, but it was drained in 1897 to supply Llandeilo with water. However, the origin may be llan-tŷ-faen - the holy place of the house of stone.

TYFAI ap BUDIC 6th century
TYFEI, TYFIL, TYMOI?
March 27 and October 6

Ismael's brother and Teilo's nephew, he was accidentally killed as a child by Tyrtuc, and was sainted as a martyr. The local tradition is that he was killed by a farmer, while trying to protect a swineherd, whose pigs had damaged crops. This happened in the woods of the banks of the Tywy, beneath the hill where Dinefwr castle stands. Tyfei was buried at Penally in Pembroke, also said to be his birthplace. He is the patron saint of Lamphey, then known as Llandyfei, where the ruins of the palace of the bishops of St Davids still attract visitors.

There was a church near Llandeilo Fawr called Llandyfeisant, in Dinefwr Park, which also commemorated this only child saint culted in Wales. Llandyfeisant Well was said to be an 'ebb and flow' well. Foy, on the Wye, was formerly called Llan Timoi, and is now rededicated to St Faith, whose day is October 5. The extinct chapel at Lampha in the Vale of Glamorgan was also dedicated to Tyfei, and there may be monastic remains there.

TYFALLE

Llandyfalle in Brecon? (or the holy place of the house of Malle?)

TYFANOG
DYFANOG
November 25

Ramsey Island was known as Ynys Dyfanog, where there was a Capel Dyfanog near Capel Stinan. There is an Anglo-Saxon inscription on a stone which probably comes from an early Christian burial site on Ramsey Island. It reads S(.)TURNBIV, and seems to relate to Saturnbiu Hael, a Bishop of St David's who died in 831.

TYFODWG 6th century
June 25

Tyfodwg ap Gwilfyw ap Marchan was associated with Cadfan, and founded Llandyfodwg in Glamorgan. One of the three saints, with Illtud and Gwyno, after whom Llantrisant in Glamorgan is named. There was also a chapel named Ystrad Tyfodwg under Llantrisant. His son Tudwg founded Tythegston. Trained at Llanilltud Fawr, his 'Saying of the Wise' is that *'no good will come of wantonness.'* His memorial stone is is on the floor of the church in Llandyfodwg, and Gilbert claims that the saint was actually Teithfallt, the grandfather of

Meurig ap Tewdrig, and this church is the final resting place of Emrys Wledig. (See Teithfallt, Emrys Wledig, Tewdrig and Meurig). This thesis states that the 'peace conference massacre' happened just a mile away at Mynwent y Milwyr (Soldiers' Monument) and the survivor Teithfallt (Tdufwlch/Tyfodwg) built a church in the memory of the slain British nobles.

William Thomas records that on February 21, 1763 *'was buried in Lantrissent, old Catherine of Court Llantrissent, from a lingring disease. Aged 113 years, the oldest I believe in our County. She was one of the Black Army of Lantrissent.'* Cardiff's Great Sessions of April 7, 1789 sentenced to death John Edward of Porth of Ystrad Tyfodwg for sheep stealing. His accomplices were two other small farmers, David Water of 'Lantrissent' and Lewis Thomas of Eglwys Ilan. The first two were hung at Wain Ddyfal upon April 29th, but Thomas was reprieved and transported. (Wain Ddyfal on Crwys Road Cardiff had four gallows-fields around it. One was known as Cae-Budr, 'the putrid close', and another as Cut-Throats field.) Upon April 30th, William Thomas reported that David Water's eight-year-old daughter died of a broken heart, and also John Edward's wife died suddenly.

Thomas' diary is a splendid insight into the 'real' 18th century, and he ascribes anyone with 'base' children, (i.e. bastards) as slovenly, sluttish, drunken etc., unless he is describing the gentry. When he notes the death in Llantrisant of William Bassett junr. Esqr. In 1769, he is regarded as *'A very knowing man in the Law, a Justice of the Peace for the Hundred of Miskin, a Treasurer of the Turnpikes, and a Captain of the Militia of the County of Glamorgan. Much regretted of all his Neighbours, being the flower of your Gentlemen all in the law, in having the same justly performed and what he says in Sessions etc. should be done, being he was very eloquent and ready in discourse, and a favourer of Justice. He had married these few years past an English lady and a great fortune, but had from her no child, but having three Base children, a son and two daughters.'* Even in these private diaries, the moral high ground could not be taken against one's natural 'superiors'. The hypocrisy of the class system is a barrier to true Christian beliefs of equality to this day.

Near Llantrisant, a 34-foot standing stone was found in road excavations for the M4. It appears to have been left in situ, but would have been the tallest recorded standing stone in Wales if re-erected. Instead money is spent upon meaningless modern metal sculptures which rot in months, not millennia. The 'Fish Stone' is the tallest in Wales at 18 feet, with another 9 feet below the surface.

TYFRIOG ap BRYCHAN see BRIOC

TYFRIOG AP NUDD HAEL 6th century
May 1

The brother of Tygwy, who founded the nearby Llandyfriog. However, Brioc may have founded this church (see Brioc).

TYFRYDOG late 6th century
January 1

The son of Arwystli Gloff ap Seithenin and Tywynwedd ferch Amlawdd Wledig, he founded Llandyfrydog in Anglesey. The Robber's Stone, Carreg Lleidr, nearby, is said to be the petrified remains of a man who stole a Bible from the church. Every Christmas Eve, as the clock strikes midnight, the stone circumnavigates the field three times. This red sandstone Maen Hir (Long Stone, the origin of Menhir) used to be called Lleidr Tyfrydog and is on Clorach Farm near the holy wells of Cybi and Seiriol. The remains of Maen Chwyf, or Maen Chwyt dolmen is at nearby Bryndyfrydog. One source says that it used to be a Maen Sigl (rocking stone) known as Arthur's Quoit.

Gerald of Wales described Earl Hugh of Shrewsbury kennelling his dogs in Llandyfrydog church in 1098, and they were found mad next morning. Hugh was killed a month later, which was ascribed to the 'vindictive' nature of the saint.

TYGWY late 6th century
TEGWY, TYGWYDD
January 18 (and 13)

The son of Dingad ap Nudd Hael, he founded Llandygwy (Llandygwydd) near Cenarth Falls in Cardigan. North at Neuadd Cross, Ffynnon Gripil seems to have been resorted to by cripples. Ffynnon Ddewi near there may have originally Tygwy's. Capel Tygwydd is a few miles away.

TŶ GWYN

We must mention the description of Mrs Dawson in 'Archaeologia Cambrensis' in 1898...
'Tŷ Gwyn is situated above Porth Mawr, and about two miles from St David's. It stands on the south slopes of Carn Lidi, the purple rocks above it springing out of the heath, with here and there a gorse bush, like a puff of flame breaking out of the crannies of the rock. Below it, near the sea, are the foundations of St Patrick's Chapel, in the site of his embarkation. The foundations of the church of Tŷ Gwyn, **the cradle of Christianity among the Southern Irish,** *are trodden underfoot by sheep and oxen, that wander over the wide cemetery where lie thick, in narrow coffins of unshaped stones, the bodies of the first inmates of that* **earliest Mission College in Britain.** *When we visited the spot in 1898, the farmer had torn up the grave slabs of the tombs in the cattle-yard, and the drainage of his cow stalls and pig styes soaked into the places where the bodies of the ancient fathers of the British and Irish churches had crumbled to dust.'*

Candida Casa, at Whithorn in Wigtownshire, followed the pattern set by Tŷ Gwyn. When someone can write a book about the Irish saving Christianity in the Western world and not mention the fact that without Wales, Ireland would have remained pagan like England and Scotland, it is time to rethink how Wales can publicise its contribution to civilization.

TYLULL

Given by some sources as the saint responsible for St Dial's in Llantarnam. The chapel ruins were taken to repair farm buildings in the 19th century.

TYNEIO 6th century.

A son of Seithenyn. Deinio (now Pwllheli), a chapel under Llanfor in Caernarfonshire, was named after him.

TYRNOG 6th century
TEYRNOG, TERNOC
July 2 Ireland, October 3 Brittany

The brother of Carannog and Tyssul, but no churches are known to be dedicated to this son of Corun ap Ceredig. This relative of David probably went to Ireland with Carannog, and seems to be the saint known there as Ternoc of Clonmore. In Brittany he was visited by David at Leon, and he founded Landerneau (known as Lan-Ternoc). He also seems to have become Bishop of Tregantarec, and had a holy well at Ploudaniel.

ABBOT TYSILIO d. 640
TYSSILIO, SULIA, SULLAC (Breton)
November 8 (also 12, and in Brittany October 1)

The grandson of Pabo Post Prydain, he fled from Wales after the great defeat of the Welsh at Chester by the Saxons. His father was Brochwel Ysgythrog ap Cyngen ap Cadell, prince of Powys, and his mother was Arddun ferch Pabo. A brother was Cynan Garwyn, and among his cousins were Asaf and Deiniol. The family fled from Pengwern after the battle around 613. Born at Pengwern (Shrewsbury), he wished to become a monk but his father did not want this. He fled to Abbot Gwyddfarch's monastery at Meifod, then went to an island in the Menai Straits but returned to the mainland after seven years, and studied under his old teacher Gwyddfarch. Tysilio had moved away from his home to escape the desires of a female, and his work was centred around Meifod in Powys. He refused to take his father's crown. Tysilio was possibly one of the delegation of British bishops who consulted a hermit on how to deal with St Augustine around 600. They could not accept his unsufferable arrogance, and the British (Welsh) church refused to accept Roman rulings on the new date of Easter and the type of tonsure. They refused to participate in the Christian conversion of the hated Saxons, who by now had conquered most of England except Cumbria and the West Country.

In Montgomery there is a Llandysilio where the rivers Tanad and Cain join. His cell was close to the Roman road at Llandysilio, and there are dedications to him at Anglesey's Llandysilio on the banks of the Menai Straits, Llandysilio-yn-Ial in Clwyd, Bryn Eglwys in Denbighshire (where there was Ffynnon Dyssilio) and in Cardiganshire, Pembrokeshire and Carmarthenshire. There is also a St Tysilio (Suliau) in Brittany, which was probably this wandering evangelist. The great bard Cynddelw recorded his founding of churches in the following verse:

> 'A church he raised with his fostering hand,
> The church of Llugryn,
> With a chancel for Mass;
> The church beyond the floods –
> By the glassy streams;
> The church filled to overflowing,
> By the palace of Dinorben;
> The church of Llydaw,
> Through the influence of his liberality;
> The church of Pengwern (Shrewsbury), chiefest in the land;
> The church of Powys, paradise most fair;
> The church of Cammarch (Llangammarch),
> With a hand of respect for the owner.'

> 'Llan a wnaeth a'I lawfaeth loflen,
> Llanllugryn, llogawd offeren;
> Llan tra llyr, tra lliant wyrdrien;
> Llan drallanw, dra llys Dinorben;
> Llan Lyydaw gan llydwed wohen;
> Llan Bengwern, beenaf daearen;
> Llan Bywys, Baradwys burwen;
> Llangammarch, llaw barch ei berchen.'

The churches and chapels which claim him as a patron saint are Meifod and Llandyssilio in Montgomery, Llandyssilio and Bryn Eglwys in Denbigh, Llandyssilio a chapel under Llanfairpwllgwyngyll in Anglesey, Llandyssilio yn Nyfed in Carmarthen, Llandyssilio Gogo in Cardigan, and chapels in Hereford at Pencoed, Marstow, Kings Chapel, Llansilio and Sellack. Meifod is extermely interesting in that this ancient churchyard site once contained three churches, *'trefod y triseaint'* – abode of three saints – with the oldest dedicated to Gwyddfarch, the next to Tyssilio and the third, consecrated in 1155, to St Mary. Tyssilio is also associated with Llangammarch.

Chirk was probably also Tyssilio's church, from a 1467 record, as were Guilsfield and Welshpool, where wakes were held. (Near Welshpool was the famous St Tyssilio's Spout holy well). Meifod was the pre-eminent mother-church, clas, in Montgomery with daughter churches at Pool, Alberbury, Llanfair Caereinion and Guilsfield. Lhuyd mentions Ffynnon Nant Tyssilio near Oswestry where wakes were held on the first Sunday after Lammas. At Llantysilio outside Llangollen, the 15th century church has a mediaeval roof and a rare mediaeval oak lectern. It is kept open on some summer afternoons with financial assistance from Andrew Lloyd Webber's 'Open Churches Trust.' Tysilio's church at Bryneglwys is flanked by old yew trees, with a chapel built in 1575 by one of the Yale family, an ancestor of Elihu Yale who founded the great university. Meifod Church Is now dedicated to Mary and Tysilio, and has a large Celtic slab-cross with a figure of the crucified Christ. Some authorities think it may be later, however, the coverstone of the tomb of Prince Madoc ap Maredudd who died in 1160.

Cynddelw Brydydd Mawr (Cynddelw the Great Poet) sang the praises of Meifod church:
'Stately is the holy place by candleshine,
Gracious its men with their long drinking horns of flashing blue.'

The Book of Welsh Saints

However, he was better known as the bard of Madog ap Maredudd *'the roof timber of Powys, the mighty dragon of dragons'*, and for his superb battle poetry:
'I have seen bitter battles and rigid red corpses
That the wolves of the forest were free to bury.
I have seen them left with their arms a-lacking
Beneath birds' talons, men mighty in war.
I have seen their sore trouble, three hundred corpses;
I have seen after battle their bowels on thorns.'

One legend about Tysilio is that his former mentor Gwyddfarch began to take tuition from his pupil. Gwyddfarch asked Tysilio if he could make the great pilgrimage to Rome, but Tysilio walked the old man over the Snowdonia mountains instead. Exhausted, Gwyddfarch lay down and dreamed of the great churches instead of wrecking his health by visiting them.

On Anglesey, the famous railway station name of Llanfairpwllgwyngyllgogerychwyrndrobwllantysiliogogogoch means *'St Mary's Church in the Hollow of the White Hazel near a rapid Whirlpool and the Church of St Tysilio near the Red Cave'*. This is a fabricated name to bring in tourists, but Tysilio's cell can still be seen on a nearby island. In Llanfair P.G. there is a statue over 90 feet high to the Marquis of Anglesey. He was mounted next to Wellington at Waterloo, when a cannonball knocked his leg off. He turned to the Iron Duke and remarked *'By God sir, I've lost me leg !'* Wellington phlegmatically replied *'By God sir, so you have !'* before returning to his perusal of the slaughter. The Marquis survived to own the first articulated artificial limb in history.

After the great battle of Chester, the court of Powys moved from Pengwern to Mathrafal near Meifod. When Tyssilio once again refused to take up the kingship of Powys, he fled from persecution from his own family to Brittany around 617, where he settled near Malo's foundation on the estuary of the Rance. One legend is that he fled to escape the relentless attention of his brother's widow, and another that he wished to avoid his father's demands that he leave the church. A statue above the altar at Rance remembers him. St Suliac and Sizun near Quimper are his. He has a chapel in Pleyben and is remembered at Plomodiern. He died at St Suliac in 640 after he had sent his crozier and gospel back to Wales.

At Llandyssilio East there is was a stone circle called Buarth Arthur or Meini Gwyn, but only two of the seventeen stones remain. Edward Lhuyd counted 15 in 1695. There is also a nearby burial chamber known as Dolwilim Dolmen. At Llandyssilio is the 'Clutorigus Stone', which reads *'Lutorici Fil. Paulini Marinilatio.'* Some authorities believe that Paulinus may be Pawl Hen. Another stone at Llandyssilio reads *'Evolencus Fil- Litogeni Hic Iacit'* , and there is a third Celtic Cross there.

TYSOI 6th century
SOY

This seems to be St Soy, who was a witness to a grant of Llancarfan in the time of Abbot Paul. Soy lived in the time of Bishop Berthwyn, was a pupil of Dyfrig, and Landesoy in Monmouth probably stems from Llan-Tŷ-Soy.

Alphabetical Listing of the Saints of Wales and Religious Events

TYSSUL 6th century
TYSUL
January 31, February 3 – however, the fair was celebrated on February 11

Founder of Llandysul in the counties of Cardigan and in Montgomery, and of the royal line of Cunedda, the son of Corun ap Ceredig.

At Llandysul in Cardigan, the 'Hen Galan', 'Old New Year' is celebrated in a church service, with the local *'pwnc'* chanting. The only other place in Wales that seems to keep to the pre-1752 date changes is the strange Gwaun Valley, bear Fishguard. There are records of the *'ffest y bugeiliaid'* (shepherds' feast) being held on August 12 in Llandysul. Ffynnon Dysul was at the north end of Llandysul village. Another Ffynnon Dyssul was near Llanfynydd in Carmarthen. Llech Eiudon was found on the farm of Glan Sannan at Llanfynydd, and taken to the Earl of Cawdor's mansion at Golden Grove. Over six feet tall, local tradition was that it commemorated a Roman soldier who fell in battle on the site. It may, however, commemorate the saint Iddon ab Ynyr Gwent. In Llandysul parish, Ffynnon Ffeiriad was a haunted well, and Ffynnon Pwllfelin pin well has vanished into the river Clettwr. The 'Llandyssil Stone' near Newcastle Emlyn reads *'Velvor Filia Broho'*.

In Llandysul in Cardiganshire, until just before the First World War, 'Poten Ben Fedi' was made to celebrate the harvest. Potatoes were boiled in a cauldron, a handful of wheat flour sprinkled over and then mashed in. Pieces of boiled bacon and salted beef were added, with chopped onion and the mixture put in a pot on a peat fire. The covered pot was left alone until the fire had burnt itself out, and the person who cut the last tuft of corn had the place of honour at the table. This last tuft was called 'Y Caseg Ben Fedi' (the end-of-the-reaping mare) and was plaited by the reapers. They then withdrew to a distance of ten to twenty yards and threw sickles in turn at it. When it had been cut down to a manageable size, one of the reapers hid it under his clothes to carry it to the kitchen table of the farmhouse. The servant girls would be waiting with buckets of water, trying to wet the 'harvest mare' on its way. If it was soaked, it could not be taken into the house for hanging up until the next year, and the carrier did not take the place of honour at the table. These customs across Wales are brilliantly described by T. Gwynn Jones.

U

> '*Unless the Lord has built the house, its builders have laboured in vain. Unless the Lord guards the city, it's no use its guard staying awake.*'
>
> **The Bible, Revelations 126.1**

BISHOP UFELWY 6th century
UFELWYN, UBILWINUS
November 20

The grandson of Caw, and son of the crippled Cenydd ap Gildas, he was a hermit in Gower, probably near Llangennith. It seems he had been a disciple and suffragan bishop to Euddogwy (St Oudoceus, Bishop of Llandaf) whom he succeeded. Ufelwy was honoured in Cornwall as St Eval, and churches at St Eval and Withiel are his. The latter is now dedicated to Clement. The brother of Ffili, he went as a youth to Brittany. St George's-super-Ely was formerly Llanufelwyn, and he is commemorated at Llandaf, Bolgros (Belley-Moor in Madley, Hereford), and Lancillo, also in Hereford.

ULCHED see YCHLED

ULO
IULO (JULIUS?)

Capel Ulo near Holyhead is now a farm, and there was a Ffynnon Ulo or Iulo near it. Dwygyfylchi near Penmaenmawr was also known as Capel Iulo.

UMBRAFAEL 6th century

The Life of Maglorius states that Umbrafel ab Emyr, like his Breton refugee brothers Amwn and Gwyndaf Hen, married a daughter of Meurig ap Tewdrig, Afrella. The Book of Llandaf states that he was ordained a priest in Wales, and was appointed abbot of an Irish monastery (possibly at Ballysamson or Ballygriffin) by his nephew St Samson. It seems that the sisters of Arthwys ap Meurig ap Tewdrig married King Amwn Ddu of the Graweg region of Brittany and his two brothers. Latest research that Arthur did not die after Camlan, but recovered to fight in Brittany, may mean that he was trying to reclaim lands for his new kinsmen. Maglorius was the son of Umbrafel.

URIEN RHEGED fl. 500-542

It is sometimes claimed that this son of Caradog Freichfras*, who expelled the Picts and Irish from Carmarthenshire and west Glamorgan, was a saint in the congregation of Cadog. He was a patron of the bards Llywarch Hen and Taliesin, and met his death by treachery while besieging Deoric, son of Ida, at Lindisfarne in Bernicia. Morgan, one of the four kings of the North, killed him. This Morgan (Morcaunt) was also an enemy of Kentigern. Urien is known as Sir Urience in Arthurian mythology. His 'saying of the Wise' is *'God can make the afflicted cheerful.'*

Y Gaer Roman Fortress, Brecon. © *Wales Tourist Board Photo Library.*

King of Cumbria, he had courts at Carlisle and possibly Stranraer and Moray. (Chester was at the limit of South Rheged, and also may have been a court. He once captured Selyf Sarfgaddau, king of Powys which bordered Rheged at Chester.) In legend he married Modron ferch Afallach (Ynys Afallach is Bardsey Island, Enlli), who may be the basis for the story of Morgan le Fay, who tended Arthur on Avalon after Camlan. She was said to have been Arthur's half-sister. Traditionally Arthur visited Urien's court whenever he was in the North, and Urien and his son Owain fought for Arthur.

At the end of a long rule, Urien led a coalition of the British kings Rhydderch Hael (Strathclyde), Gwallawg of Elmet and Morcant of Bryneich. They fought together at Gwen Ystrad and the 'Cells of Berwyn'. Berwyn may have been the Roman fort at High Rochester (Bremenium), Arthur's eleventh battle of Bregouin. Urien's son Owain (q.v.) killed Theodoric Fflamddwyn (Firebrand) of Bernicia in battle in Yorkshire, and Urien then pushed Hussa's Bernicians back to besiege them at Lindisfarne. However, Urien was assassinated at Ross Low (Aber Lleu) by Llofan at the instigation of Morcant, who was jealous of his victories and the hegemony of the house of Rheged. This internecine strife among the British kingdoms soon led to the fall of the British in the North of England, as the kings turned their malign attention to Owain ab Urien.

* Some genealogies place Urien as the son of Cynfarch Oer.

URSULA d. 453
October 21, November 1

The story is that she was the virgin daughter of a British Christian king, Dionatus of Cornwall, and betrothed to a pagan prince. She asked for a three year delay and sailed with four, seven or ten virgin companions, being blown into the mouth of the Rhine, from where they sailed to Cologne, the site of the massacre of Maurice and the Theban Legion in 287. They were martyred by the Huns for her refusal to marry their chief. A stone carved around 400 records that Clematius restored the ruined church of St Ursula at Cologne in the memory of local virgin-martyrs. Her cult was widespread on the continent and her feast day was celebrated by Catholics until the reform of the church calendar in 1969.

Her fair at Llanybydder was October 21 old style and then November 1, and was called Ffair y Santesau on November 1 and its eve. It developed into the huge monthly horse fairs at Llanybydder, famous across Europe. There was also a Capel Santesau near Llanwenog, and also in Cardigan, a chapel called Llangwyryfon (The Church of the Virgins). Tradition says that she with eleven hundred virgins came to this latter place from Brittany with St Padarn, and *'rid the country of the many wolves who devastated it.'* A crossed Celtic stone was found at Llanwgwyryfon being used as a gate-post, but was formerly in the churchyard.

UST 6th century
JUSTUS
May 1

A Breton who accompanied Cadfan to Britain, and with Dyfnig founded Llanwrin in Montgomeryshire. It was later rededicated to Gwrin, a descendant of Gildas. Cae y Tri Sant is near the church. Llanust was an extinct chapel outside Fishguard. Gwrin's Day was November 1, and Llanwrin Wake May 1. Maen Madoc stone on the Roman road near Y Gaer, Brecon, reads *'Dervacus, son of Justus, lies here'*.

USTEG early 7th century
USTIG

The son of Geraint ap Carannog, and a confessor of Garmon at Llancarfan, his brother was Eldad.

USTIG AP CAW 6th century

This seems to be the Iustic mentioned in 'Culhwch and Olwen'.

USYLLT 6th century
AUXILIUS, ENLLEU, YSYLLT

The father of Teilo and son of Hyddwyn Ddu ap Ceredig ap Cunedda Wledig, he married Gwenhaf by whom he had Teilo. Usyllt then married Anaufed, and their child was St Mabon. After Usyllt's death, it appears that Anaufed married Prince Budic (Emyr Llydaw), and their children were Euddogwy, Ismael and Tyfai. St Issell's was next to Penally, where Teilo was born, and it used to be known as Llan Usyllt, one of the seven bishop-houses of Dyfed in 'The Laws of Hywel Dda'. (See Guenhaf - Llan Geneu, Eglwys Unniau and Eglwys Guinia were all former names of Penally.)

V

*'Vanity of vanities, saith the Preacher, vanity of vanities; all is vanity.
What profit hath a man of all his labour which he taketh under the sun?
One generation passeth away, and another generation cometh.'*
The Bible, Ecclesiastes 1.2

VIKINGS

As well as the vicissitudes of attacks by the Irish, Picts and Anglo-Saxons from 850, the hard-pressed British in Wales were subject to raids by the Vikings, variously known as the Black Gentiles, the Black Host and the Black Pagans. Anglesey was ravaged in 853. They looted St David's on at least eleven occasions, and destroyed Llanilltud Fawr in 988. Attacks on monastic churches included St Dogmael's (Llandudoch) in 907, Caergybi (Holyhead) in 961, Tywyn in 963, Penmon in 971, Clynnog Fawr in 978, Llanbadarn Fawr in 988 and Bangor in 1073. Slaves were taken to their markets in Dublin and Scandinavia, gold and silver melted down and precious deeds, parchments and gospels burned. Many of Wales' islands now have Norse names or suffixes, such as Flat Holm and Anglesey. From 1000 to 1150 contact became more trade-oriented as the Vikings came under Christian influence. However, their depredations were substituted by those of the Normans (themselves of Danish stock) from 1080. After they had conquered England in a couple of years, they spent the next 350 trying to conquer Wales. Not until after Glyndŵr's rebellion, in the early 15th century did Wales acquiesce to English rule, but by 1485 a Welsh invasion force had put Henry Tudor on the throne of England.

VORTIPOR 6th century
GWRTHEBYR, VOTEPORIUS

King of the Demetae (the Celtic tribe of Dyfed), and one of the five Welsh kings who enraged Gildas in 'De Excidio'. He is noted here because it appears that his gravestone may be in Castell Dwyran Church, Carmarthenshire. It reads in Ogam '*VOTECORIGAS*' and in Latin '*MEMORIA VOTEPORIGIS PROTICTOR*', and its joint inscription enabled scholars to decode Ogam (Ogham) inscriptions across Wales and Ireland. The stone is now in Carmarthen museum.

W

> '*Wild animals never kill for sport. Man is the only one to whom the torture and death of his fellow-creatures is amusing in itself.*'
>
> **J. A. Froude, 'Oceans', 1886**

WATER

Water was sacred to the Celts, which explains the association of the early saints with springs and wells. As we have seen, pins and ornaments were thrown into holy wells, which related to the Celtic practice of throwing a dead warrior's sword into water. In Llyn Fawr, Glamorgan, there were found axes, sickles, cauldrons (also sacred to the Celts) and harnesses dating from 600BC. Swords were usually bent or broken before being thrown into a lake. The most important sacred lake in Britain was Llyn Cerrig Bach in Anglesey. From a low cliff were thrown over 150 weapons and aristocratic ornaments with a few other items such as slave shackles. This took place between 200BC and 43AD, and represented more than the wealth of local rulers. The Romans looked upon Anglesey as the centre of druidism across Gaul as well as Britain.

WDDYN

Llanwddyn in Montgomery. This is traditionally a giant, or an anchorite who visited Melangell on the other side of the mountain.

WELLS

Apart from curative and blessing purposes, wells were important from pre-Christian times as a source of water for villagers. In Sain Tathan, Glamorgan, Beggar's Pound seems to have been named because of its proximity to St John's Well. All local inhabitants would have to go to the well during the course of the day, and it was there that the crippled, lame and ill would gather to beg for food. The well was in fact the hub of activity for local inhabitants, and with water being sacred to the Celts, it is not surprising that the first Christians used such sites for their churches.

Apart from the famous shrine at Holywell, some Welsh wells are still used today to pray for cures, for example the rag well at Trellech in Monmouthshire. Sir John Rhys made the valid point that:
It is curious to observe that, while Christian missionaries appear to have made comparatively short work of the greater Celtic gods of Aryan origin, the Church fulminated in vain against the humble worship of wells and sticks and stones. The cult required no well-defined and costly priesthood which could be overturned once for all, and, a little modified, it thrives in some Celtic lands to this day. All that the Church could do was to ignore it for a time, and ultimately to assimilate it: to effect its annihilation has always been beyond her power. ('The Growth of Religion as illustrated by Celtic Heathendom', Hibbert Lectures, 1886).

Alphabetical Listing of the Saints of Wales and Religious Events

St Seiriol's Well.   © *Wales Tourist Board Photo Library.*

The pagan worship of trees and wells by the British is shown today in many Welsh placenames. Early missionaries to England and Scotland were told to purify and adapt the heathen Celtic temples rather than destroying them, in order to 'take over' the beliefs of holiness surrounding such sites. In 567 the Council of Tours denounced the worship of fountains, but especially in Brittany and Wales little notice was taken. A cleric wrote as late as 1102 *'Let no-one attribute reverence or sanctity to a dead body or a fountain without the bishop's authority'* and during the Reformation pilgrimages to wells were forbidden (however, see Gwenfrewi).

Etheridge also notes the use of such springs for cleaning the feet before entering church:
"Shoes were expensive items, much valued and cared for. The Welsh girl going to chapel or dressed for some special occasion would sometimes carry her shoes in a little box and put them on when she reached the main road, placing her clogs in the box and hiding it in the hedge. He quotes James White in 1805 "I have heard in common with some other old parish churches – Pembrey for one – that there was a spring of clean water at the entrance of the churchyard primarily used by ones who came to church with bare feet. They were obliged to wash them before entering the church. My mother informs me she had seen it every Sunday when she was a child."

There is a wonderful book, 'The Holy Wells of Wales' which has recently been reprinted. Now almost 50 years old, it needs updating by a researcher to bring attention to these sites and encourage restoration before those remaining vanish.

WEONARD 6th century
GWENNARTH, WANNER, WANNARD

Possibly an associate of Dyfrig, this early Celtic saint founded St Weonard's near Hereford and Llanwennarth in Gwent. A lost window in St Weonard's church showed an old man with an axe and a book, described as St Wenardus Heremyta.

RAWLINS WHITE c. 1485? – 1555
March 30

An old, illiterate fisherman of Cardiff who had learned passages of the Bible by heart. His son had read them to him, and White had become a Protestant. With Ferrar and Nichol he was one of the three Marian martyrs of Wales, and was burnt at the stake in Cardiff. He had land where Womanby Street meets Westgate Street in Cardiff, where the Taff used to flow, and was licensed to have five 'hang-nets'. The bishop of Llandaff, Anthony Kitchin, desperately tried to make White recant his opinions. Fox's Book of Martyrs says that White was confined in the Coquemarel, the ancient prison in Cardiff, with its damp dungeon below the level of the moat. This seems to be the Cock's Tower which was on Cardiff's east wall.

WHITSUN

As mentioned, Whit Monday was the one great holiday in Wales for centuries. In late May, Whitsunday recalls the descent of the Holy Spirit upon the assembled disciples in the form of tongues of fire. It is a movable feast, occuring 50 days after Easter, and is called *'Sulgwyn'* in Welsh. In 1602, Carew wrote of the Welsh and Cornish custom in his 'Description of Cornwall': *'For the Whitsun church-ale two young men of the parish are yerely chosen to be warders, who make a collection among the parishioners of whatsoever it pleaseth them voluntarily to bestow. This they employ in brewing, baking and other acts against Whitsunday; upon which holidays the neighbours meet at the church house and merrily feed on their own victuals . . . which, by many smalls, groweth to a meetly greatness.'*

P. Roberts, in 'The Cambrian Popular Antiquities', describes Whit merriment in 1815: *'The dancers are all men; their dress is ornamented with ribbands, and small bells are attached to the knees. The dance is somewhat like that of the Country Bumpkin; and in the course of it, some of the more active exhibits a king of somerset (somersault) with the aid of two others. They are attended by Jack and Gill, or as they are called in Wales, the Fool and Megen. The fool is the same as the clown of the old comedy; the megen, a man dressed in women's clothes, with the face smutted to represent a hag. Both entertain the mob by ridiculous tricks, the megen generally solicits contributions from the spectators, and keeps off the crowd by dread blows of her ladle.'*

ISAAC WILLIAMS 1802-1865
January 11 Holy Day

He was a native of Llangorwen in Cardiganshire. Educated at Trinity College, Oxford, he became a curate at Bisley in Oxford, and wrote some notable religious poetry. Williams became one of the Oxford Movement's most notable leaders. He was expected to receive the poetry chair at Oxford on the retirement of his friend John Keble, but was disappointed and retired from public life. He died on May 1, at Stinchcombe near Dursley where he was curate.

MORRIS WILLIAMS 1809-1874
NICANDER
January 3 Holy Day

Poet and hymn-writer. Born in Caernarfon and schooled in Llangybi, Caernarfonshire, he went to Jesus College Oxford, and became curate of Holywell, then Bangor and finally Llanrhuddlad in Anglesey. Under the pseudonym Nicander, he won the Chair at Aberffraw Eistedfod in 1849, and also won prizes in 1858, 1860 and 1862. He has more hymns in the Anglican church hymnal than any other person except William Williams (Pantycelyn). He is buried at Llanrhuddlad and there is a memorial marble pulpit in Bangor Cathedral. His Holy Day is the date of his death.

WILLIAM WILLIAMS 1717-1791
January 11 Holy Day

Often referred to as Williams Pantycelyn, or merely Pantycelyn, he is a mighty figure in Welsh literature. From Cefn-coed at Llanfair-ar-y-bryn in Carmarthenshire, his mother was from Pantycelyn, a neighbouring farm. He was brought up at Pantycelyn when his mother was widowed. Taught by Vavasor Griffiths and converted by Howel Harris at Talgarth, he became a curate at Llanwrtyd, Llanfihangel Abergwesyn and Llanddewi Abergwesyn in Brecon. In 1743, he was not allowed to become a priest because of his Methodist activities, and became an itinerant Methodist minister. He wrote over ninety books of devotional prose, religious poetry and hymns. **He is Wales' most important hymn-writer** and for many its most important poet. Saunders Lewis placed him as a major author, profound thinker, and as *'the earliest exponent of Romanticism in European literature'*.

WINEFRIDE (see GWENFREWI)

WINNOC d.717
GWYNNOG, WINOCUS
November 6th

He was the son of Judicael, King of the Bretons, and with his brothers Madoc, Ingenoc and Kadanoc was a monk of the monastery of St Sithin (now St-Omer) under St Bertin. He fled to Cerniw as a youth, and possibly founded St Winnow in Cornwall, then moved to the monastery of Saint-Omer. He finally founded the monastery of St Winoc at Wormhout near Dunkirk, where he also built a church and hospital. His brother Judoc who flourished around 650 is also noted as a saint by Cressy. Winnoc's relics rest in Bergues-Saint-Winnoc.

WINNOW 6th century
GUINNIUS
October 25 (also May 31)

A disciple of Padarn and Samson, possibly remembered at St Winnow Chuch near Samson's church at Fowey, and who was known as St Guinou in Brittany. He is possibly the founder of St Twinnell's in Pembroke. The website Catholic Online Saints makes Winnow, Mancus and Mybrad Irish saints who evangelised Cornwall, feasted on May 31. Mancus or Manaccus is celebrated on August 3rd at Lanreath in Cornwall. Mybard, or Meubred, had a shrine at Cardyngham Church, Cornwall, and was celebrated on the Thursday before Whitsun.

WINWALOE see GWENOLE

WITCHES

Unlike England, there seem to be no records of witches being hung, burned, disembowelled or otherwise harmed in Wales. In 1872 at Penrhos Bradwn farm in Anglesey, workmen unearthed a black pot sealed with a piece of slate. On the slate was written 'Nanny Roberts', and inside the pot was a dried frog pierced with 40 pins. This was a favoured form of protection against local harmful witches, a sort of 'self-help' anti-witching device. Belief in witches predated Christianity, and to some extent the early saints replaced 'white witches' and druids for the population.

WULVELLA 7th – 8th century
November 12

The sister of Jutwara and Sidwella/Sativola, remembered at Gulval in Cornwall, where she there was a holy well.

Y

'Ye have sown much, and bring in little; ye eat but ye have not enough . . . and he that earneth wages, earneth wages to put it into a bag with holes.'

The Bible, Haggai 1.6

YCHLED
UCHLED
May 9 or January 6

The parish of Llechychled in Anglesey

THE YELLOW PLAGUE – 'PLA FELYN' 547 - 550
Y DYLYT MELEN, CHRON CHONAILL, THE YELLOW DEATH

A seminal event in the Age of the Saints, forcing many Welsh nobles and clerics to flee to Brittany and causing the death of Maelgwn Gwynedd. This seems to encompass the 'wasteland' period of Arthurian legend, although it was a few years after the battle of Camlan. Around this time a huge asteroid hit South America and there was a massive volcanic eruption at Krakatoa in south-east Asia in 535*, destabilising the world climate, and triggering the world's first known outbreak of the Bubonic Plague. Roger of Wendover reported seeing a huge flaming comet in 540 or 541, and tree ring studies at the University of Belfast seem to confirm a freezing winter with constant cloud cover and crop failures leading to plague. This wiped out a huge proportion of the population of Europe as it spread. David Keys ('Catastrophe: An Investigation into the Origins of the Modern World') surmises that this population deficit allowed the Celts to be pushed out of the Cotswolds and West Midlands further west by the Anglo-Saxons. Maelgwn Gwynedd died of the plague in 547, and the epidemic where a local king is suffering from recurring bleeding in the groin is mentioned in Arthurian legend. A symptom of plague was such bleeding from large pustules in the armpits and groin. There is still debate about airborne diseases being carried by asteroids, but the vacuum of these 'Dark Ages' certainly seems to fit with the bubonic plague theory.

According to Keys ('Secrets of the Dead', S4C, August 16, 1999), Krakatoa was the biggest blast in the last 1500 years, throwing up so much ash that summer turned to winter, with years of crop failures and millions dying. The amount of power generated in the Sunda Straits, between Java and Sumatra, was the equivalent of 2000 million Hiroshima-sized nuclear bombs. Using a computer simulation he demonstrates that there was a second massive eruption when the molten rock fountain hit the sea-water, and a tower of ash thirty miles high fell up to a thousand miles away. It was a nuclear winter - temperatures dropped, the atmosphere became drier and droughts led to famine and plague. The Holy Roman Empire, under Justinian in Constantinople, was brought to its knees. A 'grey fever' hit the city in 542. Outbreaks of plague are linked to changes in climate, as the temperature affects how plague bacteria are formed in a rat's gut. Cooler conditions caused the disease, which originated in Ethiopia and spread by the trade routes into Alexandria in Egypt and hence to Rome. It was brought into Rome by the insatiable demand for hundreds of tons of ivory each year.

There seem to be two waves of the plague, with the *'Blefed'* of 543 being followed by the *'Chron Chonaill'* (*'Yellow Death'*) in 547. Mark Horton, Reader in Archaeology at Bristol University, believes that the plague was carried by rats from Unguja Ukuu port in Zanzibar, after excavating there. Ships brought ivory for the Romans into Europe, and the disease spread rapidly from 541 from the Mediterranean into Northern Europe. In Constantinople, up to 16,000 people a day died, and officials stopped counting when they reached 250,000. Carried by Black Rats in ships, the plague reached Ireland, Wales and Domnonia in the 540's. Some sources date the Yellow Plague at 557, a decade later, lasting until 562. The mediaeval 'Black Death' was said to have killed two-thirds of the Welsh population, and the Yellow Plague probably had the same effect. In 1348 it seems to have come in with rats to the little port of Melcombe Regis, now part of Weymouth, Dorset. Within weeks it had entered Bristol, Cardiff and Exeter, and in early 1349 ravaged London. Pneumonic plague attacked the lungs, usually causing death within forty-eight hours. The other main form of plague, the bubonic variety, was more painful, with stinking yellow boils and pustules erupting from putrefying flesh, but some survived it. There has been a outbreak in Russia in late 1999, but it is cured easily if caught in the early stages.

Geoffrey of Monmouth described the plague thus: *'It was called the Yellow Pestilence, because it made everyone it attacked yellow and bloodless. It appeared to men in the form of a column, consisting of a watery cloud passing over the whole region. Everything living that it touched with its pestilential breath either died straightway or became sick unto death.'* Wales, which included much of the English Midlands at this time, turned into the *'wasteland'* of Arthurian legend, with possibly half its people dying. Keys seems to think that the Saxons were not as badly affected, but for the Welsh there was depopulation, with little corn, few fish and dying animals. Perhaps the 'wasteland' of Welsh tradition was the folk-memory of this time. The plague came into Wales and the West via the Cornish ports trading with Rome. There was little contact at this time, except in battle, between the Romanised native Celtic Britons and the East Angles and Saxons from Germany. The latter traded with Germany and Scandinavia. The Celtic West of Britain suffered a huge depopulation, and the Saxons moved into the vacuum, creating the modern England.

There is an interesting charter in the Book of Llandaf granting Lann Cingualan, Lann Arthbodu, Lann Congur and Lann Penreic in Gower. The llannau were disputed between Biuon, Bishop of Llanilltud Fawr and Oudoceus (Euddogwy) Bishop of Llandaf *'from the time of mortality, that is, Y Dylyt Melen, up to the time of Arthruis son of Mouric'*. The dispute was settled with the property being given to Llandaff in perpetuity, but it shows the confustion at this time between the loss of Arthur around 539 and the onslaught of the Plague in 547. Buion was one of Illtud's 'family', and Jacob, abbot of Cadog's Llancarfan witnessed the charter.

*This Indonesian volcanic explosion blocked out the sun for 18 months, according to David Keys, triggering the first known outbreak of Bubonic Plague. There are two interesting entries in 'The Anglo-Saxon Chronicle'. In 538 *'the sun darkened on February 16th from dawn until nine in the morning.'* For 540, it reads *'The sun darkened on June 20th, and the stars showed fully nearly half an hour past nine in the morning.'* This could indicate that the asteroid hit and the most violent volcanic eruption in recorded history almost coincided.

Alphabetical Listing of the Saints of Wales and Religious Events

YNYR GWENT 5th – 6th century
HONORIUS, ENEURE
May 4

King of the old territory of the Silures, and like Gwynlliw he founded a dynasty of saints. His wife was Madrun, ferch Gwrthefyr Fendigaid (St Vortimer the Blessed). Ynyr claimed the Gwentish throne by marrying Madrun, and their dynasty lasted until the Norman Conquest. He was the son of Dyfnwal Hen, and the great-grandson of Macsen Wledig and Elen. His children were the saints Caradog Freichfras (possibly), Iddon, Ceidio, Cynheiddion, and Tegiwg. He was sanctified probably because he founded Tathan's college at Caerwent, where he held his court in the ruins of the Roman city. He founded the churches of Abergavenny and Machen.

King Ynyr went in 547 to Brittany to escape the Yellow Plague, where he was known variously as St Eneure, Iner or Tiner. He founded the following churches, all since rededicated, at Plouneour-trez, Plouneour-menez and Plonouer Lanven (the plou, or llan of Eneur on the shore, mountain and alder-grove, respectively). It also seems that Penclawdd was his, as its former name was Llanyrnewydd, but on John Speed's 1610 map it is Llannyenwere (=Llanenoure). The name Enouri was found on an inscribed stone now in Goodrich Court chapel, in Herefordshire. It is probable that his daughter Tegiwg was with him in Brittany, where she was known as St Thumete. Ynyr appears to be Ynwyl of Caer-Teim (Cardiff) in the Mabinogion story of Gereint and Enid.

YSGIN AB ERBYN early 6th century
YSGWN

The brother of Geraint, and son of Erbyn, possibly the founder of Llanhesgin in Monmouth. Another record places him as the son of Cystennin and brother of Digain and Erbyn.

YSGWN AP LLYWARCH HEN 6th century

The father of St Buan

YSTYFFAN 6th century
STEFFAN, STEPHEN

Ystyffan ap Mawan ap Cyngen ap Cadell was the founder of Llansteffan in Carmarthen, and Llanstephan in Radnor, both next to Teilo dedications. There was a Ffynnon Styffan in Carmarthenshire, a healing well, and he was claimed to be the second bishop of Glamorgan. Based at Margam, the 'Saying of the Wise' of this *'bard of Teilo'* was that *'Man desires, God confers'*. Cadog supposedly asked him what was the greatest folly in man, to which he responded *'to wish evil on another without the power of inflicting it'* – an early example of Celtic pragmatism.

The Lord Rhys held Llansteffan castle in 1189, as did Owain Glyndŵr and Jasper Tudor in the 15th century. Walking from St Ystyffan's Church past the castle one comes to the well-preserved Ffynnon Antwn Sant, St Anthony's Well, which was previously Ystyffan's wishing well. It is to be hoped that more local authorities become interested in well conservation, as has been the case here. Anthony (the 'desert monk') was honoured in Wales elsewhere with crosses dedicated to him at Nash Manor in Glamorgan and Penmon in Anglesey. His ascetic life of solitude was copied by many Welsh holy men. Another St Stephen's Well was at Llan-y-bri, Carmarthen.

In Denbigh's Bodfari, St Stephen's Church is on the site of Deifer's holy well. Apart from Llansteffan in Carmarthen he founded Llanstyffan (Llanstephan) in Radnor, both next to churches of Teilo (Llandeilo Abercywyn and Llandeilo Graban). Carmarthen's Llansteffan, apart from a notable castle, has many Neolithic stones. Near Pilgrim's Rest is a standing stone in the marsh called Pant yr Athro Maen Llwyd, there are two other five feet standing stones called Maenau Llwydion, and Maen Melyn and Maen Llwyd are also near. Fron Uch Dolmen has a capstone over nine feet long. At Llanstephan in Radnorshire is an eight foot standing stone near Rhydnest. The plant, enchanter's nightshade, is called Llysiau Steffan.

The Peniarth manuscript details the belief in murder by a ghost at Llansteffan:
'The mother of Tomas ap Llywelyn ap Ywain, lord of Iscoed, was Annas, daughter of Tomas ap Robinod, constable of Llanstephan Castle. This Robinod came, with 21 knights on white steeds, to invade Korrws . . . On the way . . . He was met by the ghost of Gruffudd ap R. ap Phylip Fychan . . . who was nicknamed Gruffudd Corr y Gryngair, and his ghost killed Robinod on the road.'

Chapter 6

FEAST DAYS OF THE SAINTS

'States, like men, have their growth, their manhood, their decrepitude, their decay.'
                    Walter Savage Landor (1775-1864), 'Pollio and Calvos

Some saints obviously have more than one feast day, and these are referred to in the alphabetical listing of saints. Also added are the dates of Celtic festivals, 'fixed' anniversaries and festivals across Britain, and the 'quarterdays' which vary between England/Wales and Scotland. The 'movable' dates are Ash Wednesday, Good Friday and Easter Day, Ascension, Pentecost, Trinity Sunday and Advent Sunday. These are not included in the following feast days. Some Holy Days are in the Calendar of the Church of Wales e.g. Rhys Prichard on January 11, but entries upon these individuals are not included in the A-Z listing of saints.

JANUARY	Associated Places
1	
CIRCUMCISION	
THE NAMING OF JESUS	
GWYNHOEDL 6th century	Llangwnadl, Llannor
MACHRAETH 6th century	Llanfachraith
MAELRHYS 6th century	Llanfaelrhys
MEDWYN 1st century	Michaelstone-y-Fedw
TYFRYDOG 6th century	Llandyfrydog
HENWYN (see January 6)	
2	
BODFAN 7th century (also June 2)	Abergwyngeryn
3	
Holy Day of Morriss Williams, priest and poet 1874	
GWENNOG (Her fair was held on January 14)	Llanwenog
TEWDRIC (see April 1)	
4	
5	
CYNWYL 6th century (also January 8, April 30, November 21)	Cynwyl Elfed, Penrhos, Bangor-is Coed (Cynwyl Gaio and Aperporth Fairs were other days)
EDWARD (see October 13)	
6	
EPIPHANY (GWYLL YSTYLL)	
OLD CHRISTMAS DAY	St Ffagans, Gwaun Valley and elsewhere
JESUS born according to the Eastern Orthodox Church.	
EDERN 7th century (also December 2)	Bodedern, Edern
ABBOT HENWYN (also January 1)	St Hywyn's at Aberdaron
MERIN (April 4 in Brittany)	St Merin's, Llanferin, Bodferin, Lanmerin
YLCHED	Llanulched
LLAWDDOG (see 15)	

JUTHWARA (see December 23)
EUGRAD (see June 8)

7

CHRISTMAS DAY in RUSSIA
BRANNOC 6th century — Braunton
CELYNIN, CEITHO, GWYN, GWYNORO GWYNO 7th century (also All Saints Day) — Llanpumsaint - Gwyl Pumsaint was a huge fair held this day to celebrate these quintuplets
CYWYLLOG 6th century — Llangywyllog
GWRDDELW 6th century — Capel Gartheli, Caerleon

8

CYNWYL (see January 5) — Cynwyl Gaio

9

10

Holy Day of Bishop William Laud (1645)
TATHAN (New Style, see Dec. 30)

11

Holy Day of the poet-priests RHYS PRICHARD (1644), WILLIAM WILLIAMS (1791) and ISAAC WILLIAMS (1875)
LLUWCHAIARN

12

HEN GALAN
The 'Old New Year's Day' is still celebrated in the Gwaun Valley with a 'noson lawen' — *At Llandysul Church there is a Hen Galans ervice, with 'pwnc' chanting, a local style of singing*
LLWCHAIARN 6th - 7th century (also 11) — Llanllwchaiarn, Llanmerewig, Llanychaiarn

13

ANE (ANGAWD) 6th century — Llanelian
ERBIN 5th - 6th century (also May 29) — St Ervan, Erbistock
LLAWDDOG 6th century (also January 15, 20, August 10, 19, 20) — Ynys Enlli's patron saint, Cenarth, Cilgerran, Penboyr, Llanllawddog
SAERAN 6th century — Llanynys, Efenechtyd
KENTIGERN (see 14)
FAUSTUS (see 16)

14

KENTIGERN d.612 (also January 13) — Llanelwy/St Asaf, Glasgow
EILIAN 6th century (also January 13) — Llanelian
GWENNOG (see 3)
FFINNAN (see September 14)

15

LLAWDDOG (see 13) — Llanllawddog, Cenarth, Penboir, Cilgerran
SAWYL 6th century? — Llansawyl
ILAR 6th century (also 13 and 14) — Llanilar, St Hilary
MWROG (see 24)

16

FAUSTUS 5th century (also 13, September 28) — Riez, St Faustus
MWROG (see 24)

17

CYNFELIN (6th century) — Llangynfelin, Trallwng (Welshpool)
BERWYN (see February 2)

18

CYNIN 5th century (also January 7 and November 24) — Llangynin
TYGWY 6th century (also January 13) — Llandygwy

19

BERWYN (see February 2)

Feast Days of the Saints

20
  BERWYN (see February 2)   Berwyn Hills

21
  LLAWDDOG (see 15)
  GWYNIN (see January 31)

22
  Eastern Feast of TIMOTHY 1st century
  (see 26)

23
  ELLI (see August 12)

24
  CADOCUS d.490   Beneventum?
  MWROG (also January 6, 15, 16)   Llanfwrog
  Western Feast of TIMOTHY 1st century
  (see 26)
  LLAWDDOG (see 15)   Cenarth
  CYNOG (see October 9)

25
  CONVERSION OF ST PAUL (also June
  25, 29, 30)
  DWYNWEN   Llanddwynwen, Porthddwynwen. On Dwynwen's day,
                                       love tokens were traditionally exchanged, sometimes in
                                       the form of love spoons from the male, and in Wales this
                                       is replacing Valentine's Day

26
  TIMOTHEUS 1st century (since 1969,   Ephesus, Rome
  with TITUS - see Claudia)

27
  SILYN 6th century (also September 1)   Capel Sant Silin

28
  GILDAS c.498-c.570 (also January 29)   Brittany, Ireland, Flat Holm, Wick, Rhuys in Morbihan

29
  GILDAS (see 28)

30
  MAELOG (see November 13)
  TYBIE 5th century (also December 26)   Llandybie

31
  AIDAN (MAEDOC) d.626   Llawhaden, Nolton, Haroldston West, Solfach, St
                                       Bride's Bay
  EWRYD 5th century   Bodewryd
  GWYNIN 7th century   Llandygwynin, Dwygyfylchi
  (also 21, December 31)
  TYSSUL 6th century (February 11 New   Llandysul, Llanfynydd, St Ives, Vihan,
  Style) (also February 3, November 11)   Lan-Zul
  MELANGELL (see May 28)

FEBRUARY

1
  THE CELTIC FEAST OF IMBOLC Also   The start of the lambing season for the Celts
  known as Ogronius, 'The Time of Ice'
  ELLDEYRN 5th century   Capel Llanilltern
  FFRAID c450-c525 (also March 24)   Diserth, St Brides, Llansantffraid
  INA 5th century   Llanina
  SELYF 5th - 6th century (also June 25)   Lansalos, St Levan
  SEIRIOL (see 15)

2
  PURIFICATION   The Catholic Feast of the Purification, now
  CANDLEMAS   called The Presentation of Our Lord

BERWYN (GERWYN, BRANWALADR, BRELADE) 5th-6th century (Also January 17, 20, February 9, May 16, June 6, July 5)
St Brelade, Milton, St Broladre

NICHOLAS OWEN d.1606
Hung, drawn and quartered in the Tower of London

3

IA 6th - 7th century (also October 22, 27)
St Ives, Venton Ia, Plouye

MEIRION 6th century (also 4)
Llanfeirion, Criciech

TYSSUL (see January 31)

SEIRIOL (see 15)

4

BISHOP ELDAD (ALDATE) d.577
Churches in Gloucester and Oxford. Martyred at the battle of Dyrham near Bath

MEIRION (see 3)

DILWAR

5

DWYNWEN (New Style, see January 25)

6

MEL d.488
Ardagh

RIOC 6th century (also August 1)
Lough Ree, St Rock's, Kilkenny

7

AUGULUS d.305

ILLTUD d.c. 537 (also November 6, 7)
Caldey Island, Llanilltud Fawr, Llantrithyd, Llanhamlach, Ilston, Lantwit-juxta-Neath, Llanhilleth, Lantwood, Lanhari, Llantwit Fardre, Brittany

MOSES
A British Apostle to the Saracens

8

KEW (CIWA) 5th century
Llangiwa, Kew

9

EINION 6th century (also February 10 and 11, August 5)
Llanengyn, Ynys Enlli, Penmon

TEILO d.566 or 580 (also November 26)
Llandeilo, Penally, Llantilio Crosseny, Marloes, Brechfa, Merthyr Mawr, Trefgarn, Penally, Manorbier, Lanion, Talgarth, Llowes

10

FFAGAN d.c. 193 (also August 8 and May 24, 26)
St Ffagans, Llanmaes

11

CYNOG (see October 9)

SEIRIOL (see 15)

TYSSUL (see January 31)

12

FFILI 6th century
Rhosilli, Lamphil, Kervili, Caerffili

13

DYFYNOG 7th century
Llanrhaiadr, Ddyfynog

14

VALENTINE

NECTAN 6th century (also May 18 and June 17)
Hartland, Launceston, St Nectan's, Wells, Exeter, Lan-Neizant, Poundstock

MEUGAN (see September 24)

15

ABBOT SEIRIOL 6th century (also February 1, 3 and 11)
Penmon, Puffin Island (Ynys Seiriol), Clorach

MABYN (see November 18)

16

LEONORE 6th century (also July 1,3 and October 13
Aleth, Limoges

17
CURIG (see June 16)
18
AUGULUS (New Style, see 7)
19
Holy Day of Thomas Burgess, Bishop
and Teacher (1837)
20
EINION and TEILO (New Style, see 9)   Teilo's fairs at Llandaf and Llandeilo Fawr
21
CWRDA   Jordanston
22
CANOC (New Style, see 11)
23
FFINIAN d.549 (also December 12)   Clonard
MILBURG 7th century   Llanfilo in Radnor, Wenlock
MINVER 6th century (also February 24,   Minwear, Tredesick, St Minver
November 23, 24)
24
CADOG c450-510 (also September 25)   Cadoxton, Llancarfan, Llangattock, Pendeulwyn,
   Llanmaes, Portheinon, Trefethin, Ile de Cado,
   Ploucadeuc

MINVER (see 23)
25
CIANAN 6th century   Plouguerneau
NECTAN (New Style see 11)
26
TYFAELOG (also March 1)   Llandyfaelog
27
Holy Day of George Herbert, priest (1633)
AILBE (see Sept 12)
28
CANDLEMAS QUARTERDAY in
SCOTLAND
LLIBIO 6th century   Llanllibio
29
LEAP DAY, BACHELOR'S DAY   Women could propose to men in some areas, the men
   paying a forfeit if they refused to wed. Traditionally the
   luckiest day of any year.

MARCH
1
DAVID, DEWI SANT 5th - 6th century   St David's, Glascwm, Llanddewi Brefi,
(July 1 in Brittany)   Brechfa, Raglan, Kilpeck, Little Dewchurch, Much
   Dewchurch, Whitchurch, Llanychaer, Bridell,
   Llanddewi, Hubberston, Abergwili, Meidrim, West
   Country
LLONIO 6th century (also March 17)   Llandinam
SANNAN d.544 (also June 13, April 29,   Llansannan, Bedwellty
March 6, 8, December 17)
CYFELACH d. 927   Llangyfelach
TYFEILIOG (see February 26)
2
BISHOP CHAD 7th century   Lichfield
GWRTHL 6th century   Maesllanwrthl, Llanwrthl
JAOUA   Daoulas, Brasparts, Leon
GWYNIO (see May 2)

3
NON 5th – 6th century (also March 2 and 5, June 15 and 25, July 3) — St Non's, Llannon, Dirinon, Altarnon and many others
GWENOLE 6th century (also April 28, June 20) — Landevennec, Gunwalloe, Locunole, Landewednack, Wonastow, Ganarew
GWYNNO 6th century — St Gwynno's at Vaynor, Llanpumsaint
LILY GWAS DEWI 5th - 6th century
JAOUA — Brasparts, Leon, Daoulas, St Jaoua

4
GISTLIANUS (GWESTLAN) 5th century (also 2) — Hen Fynyw

5
CARON 7th century? (also 15-17 of — Tregaron Fair was held on the 15th-17th March
PIRAN d.480 (also November 18) — Perranporth, Cardiff Castle

6
MILBURG (New Style see February 23)
SANNAN (see 1) — Brittany

7
DIER d.664 (also March 8) — Bodfari
ENODOC (see July 13)
CYNGAR (see November 7) — Llangefni Wake

8
RHIAN 5th - 6th century — Llanrhian
DIER (see 7)
SANNAN (see 1)

9
KING CONSTANTINE 6th century (also March 11, 13) — St Merryn, Dunsford, Illogan

10
AILBE (New Style see September 16)

11
LLIBIO (New Style see February 28)
CONSTANTINE (see 9) — Scotland
DYFRIG (see May 29) — Whitchurch near Monmouth

12
OLD ST DAVID'S DAY
PEULIN 6th century (also October 10, November 22) — Pol de Leon, Founder Saint of Brittany, Llanddeusant, Ploudalmezau, Lamballe, Llangors

13
TEWDWR 6th century (also October 14 and 15) — Darowain
CONSTANTINE (see 9)

14
BISHOP CYNOG d. 606 — Llangynog
CARON (see 5)

15
ARWYSTL HEN (ARISTOBULUS) d.99 (also 17) — Glastonbury or Ynys Enlli
TEWDWR (see October 15)

16
CARON (see 5) — Glastonbury or Ynys Enlli

17
JOSEPH OF ARIMATHEA 1st century (also July 31, March 17, 27) — Glastonbury, Llanilid
PADRIG (PATRICK) c. 390-461 — Banwen, Armagh
PEULIN AP PAWL HEN 6th century (also November 1, 2) — Llanbeulan
LLONIO (see 1)

Feast Days of the Saints

    PADRIG ab ALFRYD 6th century   Llanbadrig
18
    FINAN 6th century   Llanffinan
19
    JOSEPH 1st century
    CYNBRYD 5th century   Llandulas
20
    RHIAN (see 8)
21
    ALBAN EILER DAY   In the Celtic calendar, when the days begin to become
                                                   longer than the nights
    ENDA (see 31)
22
    ELFODD d. 809   Bangor
    TIMOTHEUS (see 24)
    NICHOLAS OWEN
23
    GWINEAR 6th century   St Gwinear's, St Guignar
24
    TIMOTHEUS d.140 (also 22, August 22)   Martyred in Rome
    FFRAID (see February 1)
    NYFAIN (see August 15)
25
    ANNUNCIATION   The Feast of the Annunciation
    OUR LADY QUARTERDAY (also   (Old Lady Day was April 6 when
    December 8 Conception and August 15   new agricultural appointments
    Assumption are dedicated to Our Lady)   were taken up.)
26
    GOVAN (see June 20)
    TIMOTHY (see 24)
27
    GWYNLLIW 5th-6th century   St Woolos Cathedral
    (also March 28, 29)
    TYFAI 6th century Wales' only child saint   Llandyfeisant, Penally, Lamphey, Foy,
    (also October 6)   Lampha
    JOSEPH of ARIMATHEA (see 17)
28
    TRADITIONAL DATE OF THE BIRTH
    OF JESUS also April 18 and May 29 (see
    Christmas)
    GWYNLLIW (see 27)
29
    GWLADYS 5th-6th century (with her   Pencannau, Capel Gwladys
    husband GWYNLLIW)
30
    Holy Day of John Keble, priest and
    teacher (1886)
    ROBERT FERRAR d. 1555   Executed at Carmarthen
31
    ENDA d.530 (also 21)   Aranmore

APRIL
    EASTER   Of all the festivals in Wales at Easter,   Mabsant Tudful
                                                   was probably the Greatest

1
    TEGFAN 6th century (Easter Monday)   Llandegfan
    KING TEWDRIG d.470 (also January 3)   Mathern, Llandow, Bedwas, Merthyr Tudfil

2
3
Holy Day of Bishop Richard (1253) — Chichester
4
CYNIDR AP GWYNLLIW 6th century (also December 8) — Aberysgir, Llangynidr, Glasbury, Kenderchurch
TEYRNOG 6th century (also September 25) — Llandyrnog
MERIN (see January 6)
GONERI (see July 18)
5
DERFEL GADARN 6th century — Llanderfel
BRYCHAN c. 390 - c. 450 (also 6)
6
OLD LADY DAY
BRYCHAN (see 5)
7
BRYNACH d570 — Cwm-yr-Eglwys, Nevern, Penllin, Llanfyrnach, Llanfernach, Henry's Moat, Llanboidy, Pontfaen, Lavernock
KING DOGED 6th century (also 22, and July 23, 27) — Llandoged
GORAN 5th century? — Goran, Bodmin
GWRNERTH 6th century — Welshpool (Trallwng)
LLYWELYN 6th century — Welshpool
GONERI (see July 18)
8
Holy Day of Griffith Jones, priest and teacher (1761)
DYFAN 2nd century (also May 24 with Ffagan) — Merthyr Dyfan
9
MADRUN & ANHUN 5th century (also June 9, October 19) — Minster, Trawsfynydd
10
ENDA (see April 30)
11
DEATH OF LLYWELYN FAWR — In 1240, Llywelyn the Great, Prince of Aberffraw and Lord of Eryri, died peacefully as a monk in Aberconwy, aged 67.
12
Holy Day of Bishop George Augustus Selwyn, missionary (1878)
IESTYN 6th century (also October 10, April 19, August 14) — Llaniestyn, Brittany
13
CARADOG OF LLANCARFAN (d.1124) (also April 14) — Lawrenny, Haroldston East
GWYNNO (see October 26) — Scotland
14
CARADOG (see 13)
15
BISHOP PADARN 5th-6th century (also 16, 17, 20, May 15, June 20, September 23, November 1) — Paternus, Founder Saint of Brittany; Llanbadarn, Trefeglwys, Vannes
16
PADARN (see 15)

Feast Days of the Saints

17
  DUNWYD (see August 17)
  GWERYDD 4th century?   St Donat's (Llanwerydd)
18
  TRADITIONAL DATE OF BIRTH OF
  JESUS (also March 28 and May 29)
  (see Christmas)
  NECTAN (see February 14)
19
  IESTYN (see April 12)   Brittany
20
  TRADITIONAL ALL SAINTS DAY   Before the 9th century, this was the traditional date. Not until the 12th century did it move to November 1st in Wales

  BEUNO d.642 (also 21)   Aberffraw, Llanfeuno, Dolbenmaen, Clynnog Fawr, Llanycil, Gwyddelwern, Betws, Berriew

  CALLWEN 6th century (also July 6)   Cellan
  PADARN (see 15)
21
  BEUNO (see 20)
  DYFNAN 5th century (also April 22, 23, 24)   Llandyfnan
  GWYNDAF HEN (see November 6)
22
  DYFNAN (see 21)
  DOGED (see April 17)
23
  GEORGE d. c. 300   The Lebanese patron saint of England
  IFOR 4th or 5th century   Ferns?
24
  MEUGAN (see September 24)
  DYFNAN (see 21)
25
  MADOG MORFRYN 6th century   Łeitrim
  MARK 1st century   Farming work was prohibited on this day
26
  GWYDDALUS (May 9 New Style)   Llanwyddalus
27
  CYNIDR AP RHIEGAR 6th century   Maelienydd
  NOE (NWY) 6th century? (also July 6,   Newlyn, Skenfrith, Pontivy
  November 8)
28
  GWENOLE (WINWALOE) (see March 3)
29
  ENDELLION 5th-6th century   St Endellion's, Lundy Island, Tregony
  SENAN d. 660
  SANNAN (see March 1)
30
  BELTANE EVE With the Feast of Oimelc,   The death of the Celtic Goddess of
  the greatest night for drinking for the Celts   Winter. In Germany Walpurgis Night
  – in other words, a Spring New Year's Eve   when witches ride on broomsticks and he-goats
  AMWN DDU c. 480-540   Llanilltud Fawr
  BRIOC c. 440-530 (Also May 1)   Llandyfriog, Founder Saint of Brittany
  CYNWYL (see January 5)
  ILAN   Eglwysilan, St Ilan, Trefilan

MAY

1

ASCENSION DAY (now moveable)

BELTANE To the Celts, the First Day of Summer.

The busiest time of the year for Fairies *hundreds of May day traditions still extant. Maypole Raiding was extremely popular in Wales*
DIPPING DAY

The Chief festival for well-worship, a practice outlawed by Henry VIII
Cattle were driven from shelter to grass.
Twin bonfires were lit for the cattle to pass between, to protect them from evil.
At Puck's dale near Crickhowell a door leads and spirits to affect us. There are into the fairy kingdom. In Somerset, dew will cure freckles
In Cornwall, 'Dippy day was when people were sprinkled with dew water to bring them luck

PHILIP AND JAMES 1st century
ASAF (ASAPH, ASA) 6th-7th century — St Asaph's, Llanasa
(Also 5 and 11) Feast from April 30-May 2
BAGLAN AB ITHEL HAEL 6th century — Baglan
(also 2, 3)
TYFRIOG 6th century — Llandyfriog, Little Lidney
CORENTIN (see November 2)
UST and DYFNIG 6th century — Llanwrin (before Gwrin)
GWRIN 6th century (also November 1) — Llanwrin, Wrinstone
BRIOC (see April 30)

2

GWYNIO 6th century (also March 2) — Llanwynio
GENYS 6th century? (also 3, and July 19) — Launceston, Trigg Minor

3

CROUCHMAS DAY — A festival where people bowed (crouched) to the Holy Cross

CARADOG FREICHFRAS 6th century — Porthskewett, Caerwent
GLYWYS 6th century — Merthyr Mawr, St Gluvias, Coedkernew, Newton Nottage

GENYS (see 2)
BAGLAN (see 1)

4

ALLGO 5th - 6th century (first Sunday in May, see Nov 27) — Llanallgo
KING YNYR GWENT 5th - 6th century — Abergavenny, Caerwent
MELANGELL (see 28)

5

ASAF (see April 1)
HYDROC 6th century — Lanhydrock
BRITO — Trier

6

GLYWYS (1st Sunday in May, see May 3)
EDWARD JONES — London, St Asaf

7

SANCTAN 6th century (also 9) — Llansannan, Kilnasantan

8

WORLD RED CROSS DAY
MIHANGEL/MICHAEL
(September 29 is Michaelmas)
FURRY DAY

Many Welsh churches were renamed by the Normans, but some were original Mihangel dedications.
Helston, Cornwall, celebrates the 'feriae', or festival. (This may stem from the Welsh 'fory' or tomorrow, signifying that the dance is carried on until the morrow)

546

Feast Days of the Saints

9
EUROPE DAY
SANCTAN (see 7)
TUDGLID 6th - 7th century — Llanwrtyd Wells
TUDWG 6th century — Llandudwg (Tythegston), Plessala
MELYD — Melidan
MYFOR — Possibly Merthyr Mawr, Llan
GWYDDALUS (see April 23)

10

11
TUDY (also 9 and 20) — St Tudy, Loc Tudy
ASAF (see May 1)

12
CYNGAR (see November 7) — Brittany

13
MAEL & SULIEN 6th century — Cwm, Corwen

14
MATTHIAS 1st century
ENDDWYN — Llanenddwyn

15
Holy Day of Edmwnd Prys, priest, poet and translator (1624)
Holy Day of John Davies, priest and translator (1644)
CENEU 5th century — Llangenneu under Llangattock
PADARN (see April 15)

16
BRENDAN c.486-575 — Llancarfan, Clonfert
GEREINT 6th century — Magor, Cilgerran
CARANNOG (see 27)
CARADOG (see April 13)

17
CATHAN late 6th century — Llangathen
MADRUN 6th century (also May 21) — Madron

18
NECTAN (see February 14)

19
PUDENTIANA 1st - 2nd century — Rome

20
AMO (ANNO) — Llananno, Newborough
TUDY (see May 11)

21
COLLEN 7th century (also May 31) — Llangollen, Brittany
CONSTANTINE the GREAT d. 337 — Rome
ELEN (with son Constantine) (see August 18) — Rome
MARCHAN 6th century — Llan Marchan
MADRUN (see 17)

22
ELEN LLUYDDOG 4th century (also August 25) — Llanelen, Bletherston, Caernarfo (Segontium)

23
ABBOT PEDROG d.590 (also June 4, September 14, October 1) — Padstow, Y Ferwig, Mwnt, Llanbedrog, St Petrox, Bodmin

24
DYFAN AND FFAGAN 2nd century (Dyfan also April 8) — Merthyr Dyfan, St Ffagan's, Llanmaes

25
MAEL and SULIEN (see 13)
26
LLEURWG MAWR c.120-c.190   St Mellons was called Llanlleurog
(martyred on December 3)
FFAGAN (see February 10)
RUFUS PUDENS   Rome, the martyred husband of Gwladys Claudia ferch Caradog

27
CARANNOG 6th century (also May 16)   Llangrannog, Crantock, Llandudoch, Chernach, Carantec
ELEN (see August 18)
MELANGELL (see 28)
GARMON of MAN (see July 1)
28
WHITSUNDAY QUARTERDAY in SCOTLAND
The Birth of Owain Gyndŵr in 1349
ABBESS MELANGELL d.641 (also   Pennant Melangell
May 27 and January 31)
GARMON of MAN (see July 1)
SAMSON (died, see July 28)
29
TRADITIONAL DATE OF BIRTH OF
JESUS (also March 28 and April 18)
(see Christmas)
DYFRIG c.485-c.546 (also November   Mochras, Moccas, Archenfield, Hentland,
4 and 14, March 11)   Whitchurch, Madley, Caldey Island
ERBIN (see January 13)
JOHN PENRY executed 1593   Llangammarch Wells
30
CADOG 7th century   Centule
TUDCLYD   Penmachno
31
WINNOW (see October 25)
COLLEN (also 21)

JUNE
1
GWEN TIERBRON 5th - 6th century   Whitchurch Canicorum
EUDDOGWY (see July 2)
TEGLA (see October 15)
2
BODFAN (see January 2)
3
CWYFAN 6th century (also 7)   Llangwyfan, Dyserth, Glendalough
TUDWAL BEFR 5th century   Llanstadwel, St Tudwal's Island, Tudweiliog
MERIADOC (see 7)
4
NINNOC 6th century   Ploemur, Scaer
PEDROG (see May 23)
GUDWAL (see 6)
5
TUDNO 6th century (also November 31)   Llandudno
6
GUDWAL d. 603 (also 4, 7)   Finstall, Worcester, Gulval, Finistere, Ghent, St Malo
GURWAL (see 12)
PEDR (see 29)

Feast Days of the Saints

7
BISHOP MERIADOC 6th century   Camborne, Vannes
(also June 3 and 9)
CWYFAN (see 3)
GUDWAL (see 6)
COLMAN (see November 20)

8
EUGRAD 6th century (also January 6)   Llaneugrad, Treouergat

9
ANNUN (ANHUN) with MADRUN   Trawsfynydd
5th century (also October 19, April 9)
MERIADOC (see 7)

10
RHYCHWYN (also June 12 and first   Llanrhychwyn
Sunday after June 21)

11
BARNABAS 1st century
TEILO (see February 9)

12
GURWAL 6th century (also 6)   Guer
RHYCHWYN (see 10)

13
ELERI 6th century   Gwytherin
SANNAN (see March 1)
ARMEL (see Aug 16)

14
TEGWEL (see DOGMAEL, October 31)

15
CENEU 5th century   Llangeneu
MEWAN d.c.590 (also June 21)   Saint Meen-le-Grand, St Mewan, Megavissey
TRILLO 5th-6th century (also June   Llandrillo, Llandrygarn
16, 24, 25, 26)
NON (see March 3)

16
CURIG 6th century (also February 17)   Llangurig, Capel Curig, Porthkerry, Llanilid, Newport, Locquirec
ELIDON (see September 1)
JULIOT (ILUD) (also nearest Sunday   Luxulyan, Tintagel, St Juliot, Lanteglos
to June 29)
ISMAEL 7th century (also 25)   St Ismael's

17
BRIAVEL   St Briavels
MYLLIN d. 696   Llanfyllin - Thought to have introduced baptism by immersion
HUARVE 6th century   St Herve
NECTAN (see February 14)

18
MAWAN 6th century   St Maughan's, St Meugan

19
LLIDNERTH 6th century

20
MIDSUMMER EVE   Celebrated by the Celts
ALBAN 3rd century (also June 17, 22   Caerleon, St Alban's
and July 22)
GOVAN 6th century (also March 26)   St Govan's
ARFON and JULIUS (see July 1)
PADARN (see April 15)

549

The Book of Welsh Saints

GWENOLE (see March 3)
NOVATUS (see Appendix I) — Rome

21
THE LONGEST DAY — *Villagers stayed up all night to see the spirits*
Celebrated by the Celts — *of those to die in the year to come.*
CIWG 6th century — Llangiwg
RIOC fl. 450 — Trefiagat, Rigat
CERI 1st - 2nd century — Porthkerry, Fontygari, Kerry?
MEWAN (see 15)

22
AARON (AIHRAN) early 6th century — Pleumeur-Gautier, St Malo
CELER 7th century? (also 21 - 29) — Beddgelert, Llangelert
GWENFREWI martyred (see September 19)

23
CELER (see 22)
RHYCHWYN (see 10)

24
ST JOHN THE BAPTIST 1st century — Some Celtic rites like jumping fire embers
MIDSUMMER QUARTERDAY — were transferred to the Eve and Night of St John
TRILLO (see 15)
CELER (see 22)

25
AMPHIBALUS d. 287 — Caerleon
ISMAEL (see 16)
TYFODWG 6th century — Llantrisant, Llandyfodwg
NON (see March 3)
PAUL (see 30)
SELYF (see February 1)

26
TWROG 6th century (also August 15) — Llandwrog, Maentwrog
SIMAUS d.550 — St Cieux
CEITHO, CELYNEN, GWYN, — Llanpumsaint
GWYNNORO, GWYNOG 6th century

27
CENYDD (see July 5)
CELER (see 22)

28
AUSTOL (AUSTELL) d. 627 — St Austell, St Meen
CELER (see 22)
MYLLIN (see 17)

29
EURGAIN 6th century — Llaneurgain (Northop)
TRINIO 6th century (also 28 and 30) — Llandrinio, Melverley, Llandyssilio
PEDR 5th - 6th century — Llanbedr
CIWG 6th century — Llangiwg

30
JULIOT (ILLUDIANA) Nearest Sunday to 29, see June 16)
PAUL d. 65 (also 25, 29 and January 24)

Feast Days of the Saints

JULY

1
  ARFON (AARON) d.287   Caerleon, Newport, Llanharan
  (also June 20, July 3)
  JULIAN (JULIUS) d. 287   Caerleon, Newport, Llanharan, St Julians
  (also June 20, July 3)
  DAVID (see March 1)   Brittany
  CEWYDD (see 15)
  SIMON ZELOTES (see October 28)
  GOULVEN (see 8)

2
  EUDDOGWY (OUDOCEUS) 545-616   Llandaf, Llandogo
  TYRNOG 6th century (also October 3)   Clonmore, Tregantarec, Ploudaniel
  AMPHIBALUS (see June 25)

3
  THOMAS 1st century
  PEBLIG 4th-5th century   Llanbeblic
  AARON and JULIUS (see 1)
  GARMON of MAN (see July 31)   Isle of Man (Manaw)
  NON (see March 3)

4
  ILUD (see JULIOT, June 16)
  MARTIN (see November 11)

5
  CENYDD 6th century (also August 1   Llangennith, Senghenydd, Caerphilly,
  and June 27)   Brittany
  MWYNEN (MORWENNA) see August 14

6
  DARERCA d. 518   Killeavy
  ERFYL 6th century?   Llanerfyl
  GREDFYW 6th century   Llanllyfni
  (also November 11)
  CALLWEN 5th - 6th century (also April 20,   Cellan
  November 1)
  GWENFYL 5th - 6th century   Gwynfil
  (also November 1)
  NOE (NOYALE) see April 27
  IAGO (see 24)
  GWETHENOC (see 24)

7
  EFRDDYL (see August 6)
  GOULVEN (see 8)
  DOGED (see April 7)

8
  GOULVEN 6th century (also 1 and 8)   Goulven, Goulien

9
  CEWYDD (see 15)

10
  CEWYDD (see 15)

11
  CYWAIR   Llangywair

12
  JOHN BUCKLEY JONES d. 1598   Clynnog Fawr - Hung, drawn and quartered on the Old
                                                Kent Road

13
  ENODOC (also March 7)   St Minver
  MARGARET (cult brought back by   A few Welsh churches are dedicated to this
  Norman crusaders)   'Marina of Antioch'

DOGFAN (see 23)
JUTHWARA (see December 23)
GWETHENOC (see 24)

14
WELL DAY *The Celts believed that wishes made at holy wells would come true on this day*

ALLIANCE BETWEEN WALES AND FRANCE — *A signed treaty in 1402 with Owain Glyndŵr*
ELLYW 5th - 6th century (also July 17) — Llanelieu

15
CEWYDD 6th century (also July 1, 2 and second week in July) — Llangewydd, Aberedw, Dyserth, Monknash?

16
CYNLLO 5th century (also July 17 and August 8) — Rhayader, Llanbister, Llangynllo, Llangoedmor, Nantmel
BISHOP ISMAEL 6th century — St Ishmael's, Rosemarket, Camrose, Uzmaston
TENENEN (TININOR) 6th century — Leon, Ploabennec

17
CYNLLO (see 16)
KENELM d. 819 — Rockfield, Winchcombe
JUTHWARA (see December 23) — Devon

18
GONERI 6th century (also 19, and April 4, 7) — Gonery, Plougescent, Langoat, Plougras, Ploezal, Locarn
JUTHWARA (see December 23) — Devon

19
GENYS (also May 2, 3) — Trigg Minor
CYBI (last Sunday before July 25, see November 9) 19

20
ARILD 6th century (also October 30) — Oldbury, Gloucester

21
Holy Day of Howell Harris, preacher (1773) — Trefeca
PRAXEDES 1st - 2nd century (also 22) — Rome

22
PHILIP EVANS executed 1679 (feast day October 25) — Monmouth, captured at Sker House, Porthcawl
JOHN LLOYD d.1679 — Penrhos - Evans and Lloyd were hung, Drawn and quartered at Cardiff

MAIR FADLEN 1st century — (Mary Magdalene)
ALBAN (see June 20)
PRAXEDES (see 21)

23
DOGFAN 5th-6th century (also July 13, 24) — Llanrhaiadr-ym-Mochnant
DOGED (see April 7)

24
IAGO 6th century — St Iago
GWETHENOC 6th century (then July 13 New Style, also July 6, November 5 and 7) — St Enodoc, St Goueznou
MAELOG (see October 24)

25
JAMES 1st century
CYNDEYRN 6th century (also August 5 and 6) — Llangyndeyrn
MORDEYRN 5th - 6th century — Nantglyn

Feast Days of the Saints

26
ANNE 1st century
ANNA 5th - 6th century
PERIS 7th century (also December 11)

Llanfihangel, Malvern Wells, Trelech, Buxton
Whitstone (Cornwall), Oxenhall (Glos)
Llanberis, Llangian

27
WILLIAM DAVIES d. 1593
ARMEL (see August 16)

Llandrillo, martyred at Beaumaris

28
SAMSON d.565 (also May 28)

Samson of Dol, Founder Saint of Brittany
Llanilltud Fawr

29
BLEIDDIAN (LUPUS) 4th-5th century

Llanbleidian Fawr (Llanblethian), Llanbleiddian Fach (St Lythan's)

30

31
LUGHNASADHA - This celebrated the ripening of the crops. This Irish Celtic god was known in Wales as Lleu Llaw Gyffes (The Bright One of the Skilful Hand)
GARMON OF MAN c.410-475 (also May 27, 28, July 13, 14, October 1 and 12)
GARMON of AUXERRE (see August 1)
NEOT 9th century

In the Celtic Calendar, this was a great festivity for the gods, when women could choose husbands, sometimes for trial marriages.

Capel Garmon, Llanarmon, Llanfechain, St Harmon's, Pleyben, Castell Caereinion
Plougastell
St Neots

AUGUST
1
LAMMAS

GULE OF AUGUST

ALMEDHA (EILIWEDD) 5th - 6th century (also 12, March 17, October 9)
GARMON OF AUXERRE d.448 (also July 31)
GWINWALO d.432
ELLI (see August 12)
RIOC (see February 6)
CENYDD (see July 5)

The pagan festival of LUG, Christianised into the Harvest Festival of 'Loaf Mass'.
An old phrase across Britain, probably from the Welsh 'gwyl' meaning festival.

Auxerre, Llaniarmon yn Ial

Ghent

2
SIDWELLA 5th - 6th century (also 1, July 31)

Exeter Cathedral, Llaneast

3
SETNA 5th - 6th century (also August 4 and September 19)

Sithney, Kinsale

4
BUAN late 6th century
SETNA (see 3)

Bodfuan

5
CEITHO (also January 7)

STINAN 6th century (also August 23)
KING OSWALD d.642
CYNDEYRN (see July 25)

Llanpumsaint (with his four brothers on January 7), Llangeitho
Llanstinan, Porthstinian, St David's Cathedral
Oswestry

6
TRANSFIGURATION
EFRDDYL 5th century (also July 7)
CYNDEYRN (see July 25)

Madley (Lann Ebrdil)

7
TYDECHO (see December 17) 1st
Sunday after Lammas

8
CLAUDIA (GWLADYS) 1st-2nd century	Rome
CRALLO 6th century	Llangrallo (Coychurch)
ELID	St Helen's (Scillies)
HYCHAN 5th-6th century (also October 1, 12)	Llanhychan
ILLOG (also October 18, 30)	Hirnant
CYNLLO (see July 16)	
FFAGAN (see February 10)	

9
Holy Day of Augustine Baker, priest (1641)

10
LLAWDDOG (see January 15)	Cilgerran (Old Style)

11
LLWNI (also September 16)	Llanllwni

12
Holy Day of Ann Griffiths, poet (1805)

ELLI 6th century (also August 1 and January 23)	Llanelli

13
DIC PENDERYN DAY – execution of Richard Lewis in 1831	Remembered outside Cardiff market, the place of his wrongful hanging after the Merthyr Riots

Holy Day of Bishop Jeremy Taylor (1667)

14
MWYNEN/MORWENNA 6th century (also July 5)	Morwenstow, Marhamchurch
OWAIN 10th century	Ystradowen
NYFAIN (see 15)	
IESTYN (see April 12)	West Country

15
FEAST OF THE ASSUMPTION	The Catholic feast of the Virgin Mary's reception into heaven
NYFAIN 5th - 6th century (also 13, 14 and March 24)	Nefyn, Crick, Llanfair yn Nefyn
TWROG (see June 26)	

16
ARMEL (ARTHMAEL) d.570 (also 14,15,17, June 13, July 27)	St Armel, Plouermel, Stratton and St Erme (Cornwall), Westminster

17
DUNWYD d. 876 (also 22, April 17)	St Donat's, Welsh St Donat's

18
DOCHDWY
ELEN d. c. 330 (also May 21 with Constantine)	Rome

19
CLEER 5th - 6th century (also October 23, November 3 and 4)	St Clear's, Clether
KING CLYDOG (CLINTANC) 5th century (also November 3)	Brecon, Clodock
LLAWDDOG (see January 15)	

20
LLAWDDOG (see January 15)

Feast Days of the Saints

21
22
GWYDDELAN/LORCAN — Llanwyddelan, Dolwyddelan, Llanllugan
JOHN KEMBLE d.1679 — Pembridge Castle, Llwyn - Hung, drawn and quartered at Hereford

DUNWYD (see 17)
23
EURYN 6th-7th century — Ynys Enlli
TUDFUL d.480 (also Mabsant at Easter, and Fair on September 24) — Merthyr Tydfil, Llysworney
JUSTINIAN (see December 5)
24
BARTHOLOMEW 1st century
25
MARY (MAIR) 1st century (Assumption date, her Annunciation is April 4 and her Nativity September 18) — Nefyn – her dedications are mainly in Pembroke, as the Normans rededicated many Welsh churches as Llanfair
ELEN LLUYDDOG (see May 22)
26
NINIAN d. 432 — Whithorn
27
DEGEMAN 7th-8th century (also 30) — Llandegeman, Rhoscrowther, Watchet
DAVID LEWIS d.1679 — Cwm in Monmouth -Hung, drawn and Quartered in Usk

MEDDWID 6th century — Clocaenog
CAENOG 6th century — Clocaenog
ROGER CADWALADR d.1610 — Executed at Leominster
28
LAMMAS QUARTERDAY in SCOTLAND
MELORUS d.411
29
IEUAN GWAS PADRIG — Cinmeirch, Cerrig-y-Druidion, Llantrisant (Anglesey)
30
DEGEMAN (see 27) — Norwich, Cornwall
31
Holy Day of Bishop Aidan (651)
GARMON of MAN (see July 31) — Caernarfonshire

SEPTEMBER

1
ELIDON (also June 16) — St Lythan's
SULIEN d.1091 — Llanbadarn, Letterston
SENWYR — Llansannor
2
SULIEN 6th century (also October 1, May 13, December 17) — Gwernogle, Llansilin, Corwen, Wrexham, Silian, Luxulyan
3
TUDWAL (see December 1)
GWYDDELAN (see August 22)
4
MARCELLINUS d.166 — Trier, Martletwy
RHUDDLAD — Rhuddlad
5
MARCHELL (also October 7) — Llanfarchell
CORENTIN (see November 2)
6
DUNAWD FAWR 6th century — Bangor-is-Coed (Bangor-on-Dee) - He founded this great monastery, destroyed by pagans

7
IDLOES 6th - 7th century — Llanidloes
NINIAN (see August 26)
GARMON of MAN (see July 31, first Sunday after August 31 in Caernarfonshire)

8
NATIVITY OF THE VIRGIN MARY — Llanfair
CYNFARCH 6th century — Duffryn, Clwyd
NEFYDD 5th - 6th century — Lanefydd

9
AELRHIW 6th century — Rhiw
THEGONNEC (see 11)

10
BARLOC — Chester
Holy Day of William Salesbury, translator (1584) and Bishop William Morgan, translator (1604)
DEINIOL WYN 6th century (also September 11, 21, 22, November 21, December 10) — Bangor, Marchwiel, Llanwchllyn, Llanfair, Itton, St Deiniol's Ash, Llanddeiniol, Hawarden, Worthenbury, St Daniel's, Brittany

11
DEINIOL (see 10)
THEGONNEC 6th century (all through September 8-14) — St Thegonnec

12
AILBE (ELFYW) d.527 or 531 (also 13, Feb 27) — St Elvis, Emly
THEGONNEC (see 11)

13
AILBE (see 12)

14
HOLY CROSS DAY — *When the Holy Cross appeared to Constantine*
DWYWAU 6th century — Llanddwywau
FFINAN 6th century (also possibly January 14) — Llanffinan, Lumphanan, Llancarfan

15
TEGWYN 6th century — Llandecwyn
(1st Sunday after Holy Cross Day, see September 14)

16
Glyndŵr Day - It is celebrated at the site of his mansion at Glyndwrfydwy — *Owain Glyndŵr was invested as Prince of Wales by the nobility in 1400*

17
SOCRATES AND STEPHANUS d. c. 603 — Monmouth

18
THE NATIVITY OF MAIR see August 21

19
GWENFREWI (WINIFRED) 7th century (also September 20, November 3 and 4, June 22) — Holywell, Shrewsbury, St Winifred's Well, Gwytherin
SETNA (see August 3) — Brittany

20
Glyndŵr died, 1415 — *Monnington Court*
EIGION (1st Sunday after September 20) — Llaneigion
GWENFREWI (see 19)

Feast Days of the Saints

21
The Nights Grow Longer than the days   *A significant date in the Celtic Calendar*
MATTHEW 1st century
MABON 6th century   Llanfabon, Gileston

22
DEINIOL (see September 10)

23
POPE LINUS d. 76 (also November 26)   Rome
TEGLA 1st century (also 24, 25, 27, 28)   Rome, Llandegley?
PADARN (see April 15)

24
MEUGAN 6th century (also 25, 26,   Mawgan, Llanfeugan, Capel Meugan,
February 14, April 24, November 15)   Ruthin, Trevigan, St Maughan's, Llanrhydd
TUDFUL (see August 23)   Apple and Pear Fair at Merthyr Tydfil

25
CAIAN 5th-6th century (also November 1, 15)   Tregaian
MARCELLUS 4th century   Llanddeusant
LLEONFELL   Llanlleonfel
CADOG (see February 24)
MEUGAN (see 24)
Teyrnog (see April 4)

26
HOLY ROOD DAY   *Ffair Gwyl y Grog, Cardigan*
Holy Day of Bishop Lancelot Andrewes
BARUC (BARRI) 6th century   Barri, Penmark, Bedwas
(also 27, November 29)
ELFAN 2nd century   Glastonbury, Aberdare
MEUGAN (see 24)

27
BARUC (see 26)

28
CYNWYD 6th century (also October 15)   Llangynwyd Fawr - At Christmas and New Year, the Celtic custom of the 'Mari Llwyd' and wassail has still not died out in this village

FAUSTUS (see January 13)

29
MIHANGEL, MICHAEL
MICHAELMAS QUARTERDAY   Traditionally the luckiest day of the year, only bettered by February 29

30
NIDAN 6th century (November 3 in Scotland)   Llanidan, Bryn Siencyn

OCTOBER

1
MEILYR 6th century   Mylor, Amesbury Abbey
SULIEN (see September 2)
HYCHAN (see August 8)
TYSILIO (see November 8)
GARMON of MAN (see July 31)

2
ANDRAS (also October 1)   St Andrews. Mabsantau held also at St Fagans, Whitchurch, Fairwater, Michaelstone

3
KEA (CYNAN) d.c.550 (also November 5)   Landkey, Kea, St Quay, Cleder

FFRACAN 5th - 6th century   St Fragan, Ploufragan
TYRNOG (see July 2)
4
5
TUDUR 6th century (also 7)   Mynydd Islwyn
CYNHAFAL (7th century)   Llangunhafal
6
TYFAI (TYFEI) (see March 27)
7
CAIN (CEINWEN, KEYNE) 5th century   Llangain, St Keyne's Well, Llangeinor,
(also October 8)   Runston (St Kenya's)
TUDUR (see 5)
CYNOG (see 9)
MARCHELL (see September 5)
8
CAMMARCH 6th century   Llangammarch
CEINWEN 5th - 6th century   Llangeinwen, Cerrig Ceinwen
CAIN (see 7)
CYNOG (see 9)
9
CADWALADR FENDIGAID d.664   Llangadwaladr, Magor, Michaelston-y-Fedw
(also November 12)
ALMEDHA (see August 1)
CYNOG AP BRYCHAN d. 492 (also   Defynog, Ystradgynlais, Battle, Penderyn,
7, 8, 10, 11, Sunday after second   Llangynog, Padstow, Merthyr Cynog,
Thursday in October, February 11,   Llangunnock, Pinnick
January 24 in Padstow)
10
PEULIN (see March 12)
MELLON c. 257 - c. 311 (also 22)   St Mellons, Rouen
TANWG 6th century   Llandanwg
IESTYN (see April 12)
11
CENNECH (CANICE) c. 525-600   Llangennech, St Kenox, Llancarfan, Glasnevin
LEVAN 6th century   St Levan
12
HYCHAN (see August 8)
GARMON of MAN (see July 12)
13
EDWARD THE CONFESSOR d. 1066   Knighton
(also January 5)
LEONORE (see February 16)
14
BROTHEN 6th - 7th century (also 15   Llanfrothen, Dwygyfylchi
and 18)
SELEVAN 6th century   East Levan, Brittany
TEWDWR (see 15)
15
RHISIART GWYN, RICHARD WHITE   Overton, Overstock -One of the 'Forty
c.1536-1584 (see 17, also October 25)   Saints', he was hung, drawn and
    quartered at Wrexham

SELEVAN (see 14)
TEGLA d.750 (also 26, June 1)   Llandegley, Llandegla, St Tegla's Well,
    Ochanfort
TEWDWR 6th century (also 14, 16,   Darowain
March 13)
CYNWYD (see September 28)

Feast Days of the Saints

16
Holy Day of Daniel Rowland, priest
and preacher (1790)
TEWDWR (see 15)

17
ABBOT CYNOG (Sunday after 2nd
Thursday of October, see 9)
RHISIART GWYN (alternative date
for his execution)

18
LUKE 1st century
CADWALADR 6th century   St Segal near Chateaulin
GWEN OF CORNWALL d. 544   St Wenn, Gwennap
GWEN (GWENLLIAN) d. 492   Talgarth, Llanwensan
ILLOG (see August 8)

19
Holy Day of Henry Martyn, pastor,
translator and missionary
MADRUN (with Anhun) (see April 9)   Trawsfynydd (with Anhun), Tintagel, Minster
ETHBIN 6th century

20
CAMMARCH (see 8)

21
LLEUCI 5th century (also December 13)   Bettws Leici, Abernant
LLYR FORWYN 5th century?   Llanyre, Llanllyr
URSULA d.453   Cologne
GWRW (also November 3)   Eglwyswrw
TUDWEN (see 27)

22
THE EARTH'S BIRTHDAY   In Jewish folklore, God created the Earth on this day in
                                4004 BC

CORDULA 5th century
MELLON (see 11)
MAELOG (see 22)
IA (see February 3)
GWYNNO and NOETHON (see 23)

23
GWYNNO and NOETHON 6th century   Llancarfan
(also October 22, 24)
CLEER (see August 19)

24
UNITED NATIONS DAY
CADFARCH mid 6th century   Penegos, Abererch
MAGLORIUS d. 575 (also 22, July 24)   Dol, Sark, Dinan, St Jacques in Paris
GWYNNO and NOETHON (NWYTHON)
(see 23)

25
THE FORTY MARTYRS OF ENGLAND   These were Catholics, executed between
AND WALES including PHILIP EVANS 1535 and 1679, canonised by the Pope
(July 22, 1679), RICHARD GWYN   in 1970
(October 15, 1584), JOHN JONES
(July 12, 1598, JOHN KEMBLE
(August 22, 1679), DAVID LEWIS
(August 27, 1679), NICHOLAS OWEN
(February 2, 1606) and JOHN ROBERTS
(December 10, 1610).
CANNA 6th century   Llangan
GWYDDNO 6th century   Leon, Lan-Gouezenou, Saint Houdon

559

WINNOW 6th century (also May 31) — St Winnow, St Twinnell's?
SADWRN (see November 29)
Holy Day of Bishop Lewis Bayley, writer

26
GWYNNO b. 487 or 507 (also 22,23,24, April 13, December 26) — Llanwnog, Llanwynno, Llantrisant, St Gwynno's Forest
ANEIRIN GWAWDRYDD 6th century

27
TUDWEN 6th century (also 21) — Llandudwen
LLYR FORWYN (see 21)
IA (see February 3)

28
SIMON ZELOTES 1st century (also July 1)

29

30
Holy Day of Richard Hooker, priest and teacher
ISSUI — Patrishow
ILLOG 6th century (see August 8)
ARILD (see July 20)

31
EVE OF SAMHAIN, OMEN EVE, HALLOWE'EN — *For the Celts, the spirits of the dead roamed the night. This was the Celtic 'Old Year Night'*
VIGIL OF ALL SAINTS
DOGMAEL 5th-6th century (also June 14 as TEGWEL) — St Dogmael's, Dogwel, Brittany
HYWEL FARCHOG 6th century — Llanhowell, Llanllywel, Crickhowell
ERTH 6th century — Slane

NOVEMBER

1
NEW YEAR'S DAY IN THE CELTIC CALENDAR — *The Celtic First Day of Winter - The Goddess Cailleach made the ground Hard by hitting it with a hammer*

ALL SAINTS DAY – Also known as All Hallows Day — For centuries this was the date of Caernarfon's famous hiring fair
AELHAIARN 6th-7th century — Llanaelhaiarn, Guilsfield (Cegidfa)
BIGAL (BIGEL) — Llanfigel, Ynys Bigel (West Mouse Island), Begelly
CADFAN 5th century — Llangadfan, Tywyn, Ynys Enlli
CAFFO 6th century — Llangaffo
CALLWEN 5th century — Capel Callwen, Cellan
CEDOL — Llangedol
CLYDAU 5th century — Clydai
CLYDWYN 5th century — Llanglydwyn
CYNFELIN 6th century — Llangynfelin, Trallwng (Welshpool)
DWNA 6th - 7th century — Llanddona
GWENFYL 5th century (also 2, July 6 with Callwen) — Defynog, Gwynfil
GWENRHIW 5th - 6th century — Kerry (Gwenrhiw)
GWYNLLEU 5th - 6th century — Nantgwnlle
GWRIN 6th century (see May 1) — Llanwrin
GWRYD 11th - 12th century — A Welsh friar canonised by the Catholic church
GWYDDIN — Gwythian
GWYNNORO 6th century — Llanpumsaint
MORHAEARN — Trewalchmai
RHWYDRYS — Llanrhwydrys

Feast Days of the Saints

2
ALL SOULS — Souling Day involved Souling Songs And Soul-Caking

CORENTIN 5th century (also May 1, September 5, December 11, 12) — Founder Saint of Brittany, Quimper, Cury
ERNIN 6th century — Locarn
LLECHID 6th - 7th century (also December 1) — Llanllechid
CELYNIN 7th century (also 20) — Llangelynin, Caernarfon
GWENFYL (see November 1)

3
CAEMEN 6th - 7th century — Eglwys Gymmun, Antrim
CRISTIOLUS 6th century — Eglwyswrw, Penrydd, Llangristiolus
GWENFOE — Wenvoe
GWYDDFACH d. 610 — near Meifod
GWENFREWI (Feast of her Death, see September 19) — Holywell
GWRW (see November 3)
CLYDOG (see August 19)

4
DYFRIG (see May 29)
CLEER (see August 19)
CLYDOG (see August 19)
GWENFAEN (see 5)
RHWYDRYS (1st Sunday in November) — Llanrhwydrys
GWENFREWI (see September 19)

5
CYBI 6th century (also November 6, 7 and 8) — Llangybi, Holy Island (Ynys Gybi), Llangibby, Tredunnock, Cornwall
GWENFAEN (also 4) — Rhoscolyn
KEA (see October 3)
IAGO (see July 24)
GWETHENOC (see July 24)

6
CEIDIO AB YNYR GWENT 6th century (also November 3) — Ceidio
EDWEN 7th century — Llanedwen, Eglwys Fach
GWYNDAF HEN 6th century (also April 21) — Llanwnda (Pembs), Llanwnda (Caerns)
MELAINE d.c.535 — Mullion, St Mellyan, Rennes
WINNOC d.717 — St Winnow, St Winoc
ILLTUD (see February 7)
LEONORE 6th century — Limoges, France, Italy, Bavaria

7
Holy Day of Bishop Richard Davies, translator
CYNGAR (DOCHAU) 5th century (also November 27, March 7, May 12) — Llangefni, Langar, Llanwngar, Llandough-juxta-Cardiff, Llandough-juxta-Cowbridge
IAGO (see July 24)
ILLTUD (see February 7)

8
HOLY DAY OF THE SAINTS OF WALES
EDI — Llanedy?
TYSILIO d. 640 (also November 12, and October 1 in Brittany) — Meifod, Llandysilio, Llanfair P.G., Bryn Eglwys, Cammarch, Shrewsbury, Chirk, Llanllugan, Guilsfield, Welshpool, Pleyben, Plomodiern, Sizun
CYBI d. c. 554 (also 5, 6, 7, August 13, last Sunday before July 25) — Holy Island, Holyhead, Llangyby, Llangibby

NOE (see April 27)

9
CYNON 6th century — Capel Cynon, Tregynon, Llangynwyd
PABO d. 530 — Llanbabo, Llanerchymedd

10
CYNFARWY (also November 7, 8 and 11) — Llechgynfarwy
ELAITH 6th century — Amlwch

11
MARTINMAS
St Martin's Day replaced the day of the Graeco-Roman god of wine and parties, Bacchus — An invitation to Martin was said to cure drunkards. To be 'Martin drunk' was to have drunk oneself (relatively) sober. At Martinmas Fairs, servants were hired.
CYNDDILIG 6th century (also November 1) — Llanrhystud
EDEYRN 5th-6th century (also November 23) — Llanedeyrn
MARTIN 4th century (also 12, July 4) — St Martin's
RHEDYW (GREDFYW) see July 6 — Llanllyfni

12
OLD ALL SAINTS DAY
CYNFRAN 6th century (also November 11) — Llysfaen
FFRAID LEIAN 6th century — Llansanffraid Glyn Conwy, St David's
MADOG AP GILDAS 6th century — Llanmadog, Nolton
WULVELLA 7th - 8th century — Gulval
KING CADWALADR (see October 9)
GWRDAF (see December 5)
MARTIN (see 11)

13
Holy Day of Charles Simeon, priest and teacher (1836)
BRICE — Eglwys Brewys
MAELOG (also 12, 14)
GREDIFAEL (see 30)

14
DYFRIG (see May 29)
MALO d. c. 621 (also November 15) — St Malo, Saintes, Archingeay – One of the Seven Founders of the Breton Church
MAELOG (see 13)

15
CAIAN (see September 25)
CYNFAB — Capel Cynfab
MALO (see 14)
MEUGAN (see September 24)

16
AFAN BUALLT fl.500-542 (also November 17, December 16, 17) — Llantrisant in Anglesey, Llanafan Fawr, Llanafan Trawsgoed, Lanavan

17
AFAN see November 16

18
CEIDIO AP CAW 6th century — Rhodwydd Geidio
MABYN 6th century (also February 15) — St Mabyn
MAWES 5th century — St Mawes, Ile Modez, Quimper, Treguier, Lesneven, St Modez

PIRAN (see March 5)

19
LLWYDIAN

Feast Days of the Saints

CORBRE (see 22)

20
COLMAN 7th century (also June 7) — Fishguard, Llangolman, Capel Golman, Dromore
EDMUND IRONSIDE 9th century — Crickhowell
UFELWY 6th century — St George-super-Ely (Lanufelwyn), St Eval, Withiel, Lancillo, Bolgros

CELYNIN (see 2) — Llangelynin (Merioneth), Trywerin, Capel Celyn

21
KING DIGAIN 5th century — Llangernyw
CYNWYL (see January 5) — Aberporth
DEINIOL (see September 10)

22
CORBRE 6th century — Hen Eglwys
(also November 19)
PEULIN (see March 12)
GREDIFAL (see 30)
DEINIOLEN (see 22)

23
CLEMENT 1st century — Tenby
DEINIOLEN 6th century — Bangor, Llanddeiniolen Fab
(also November 22)
MINVER (see February 23)
EDEYRN (see November 11)

24
BUDOC d. 560 — Beuzy, Castanec
CLEMENT d. 100 (see 23)
MINVER (see February 23)
CYNGAR (see November 7)
CYNIN (see January 18)

25
CATHERINE 4th century — *Worcester*
TYFANOG — Ramsey Island (Ynys Dyfanog)

26
EDREN — St Edren's
TEILO (see February 9)
POPE LINUS (see September 23)

27
ALLGO 6th century — Llanallgo
(also 1st Sunday in May)
CYNGAR (see 7)

28
MARTINMAS QUARTERDAY in
SCOTLAND
JUTHWARA (see December 23)

29
SADWRN 6th century (also October 25) — Llansadwrn, Henllan
SADYRNIN d. 832 — St David's
BARUC (see September 26)

30
ANDREW 1st century
GREDIFAL 6th century (also November — Penymynydd
13, 14 and 22)
GWENLLWYFO — Llanllwyfo
TUDNO 6th century (see June 5)
GWRST (see December 1)

563

DECEMBER

1
Holy Day of Nicholas Ferrar, deacon (1637)
GWRST 6th century (his fair was on November 30, later December 11 and 12) — Llanrwst
BISHOP TUDWAL 5th-6th century (also November 30, December 2, September 3) — St Tudwal's Island, St Tugdual's cathedral in Treguier, Chartres, Laval – One of the Breton Founding Saints

LLECHID (see 2)

2
LLECHID 6th century (also 1) — Llanllechid
TUDWAL (see 1)
GWRST (see 1)
EDERN (see January 6)

3
LLEURWG (see May 26)
GWYNEN (see 13)

4
EMERITA 2nd century

5
CAWRDAF 6th century (also November 12) — Abererch, Llangoed under Llaniestin, Miskin
JUSTINIAN 6th century (also August 23) — Ramsey Island, Llanstinan, St Stinan

GWRDAF (also November 12) — Llanwrda (possibly the same saint as Cawrdaf)

6
BISHOP NICHOLAS 6th century — A Turkish saint, favoured by the Normans, who is now associated with Christmas

7
EDREN (see November 26)

8
BUDOC d. 600 (also December 9) — St Budeaux, Budoc, Steynton, Plourin
CYNIDR 6th century (see April 4)

9
BUDOC (see December 8)

10
JOHN ROBERTS d. 1610 — Trawsfynydd – Hung, drawn and quartered in London

DEINIOL (see September 10)

11
CIAN 7th century — Llangian
GWRST (see December 1) — Llanrwst
PERIS (see July 26)
FFLEWYN (see 12)
CORENTIN (see November 2)

12
LLYWELYN II KILLED BY TREACHERY
At Cilmeri or Aberedw, near Builth Wells, 1282 — *The Welsh army was slaughtered in cold blood at nearby Llanganten*
FFLEWYN and GREDIFAEL 6th century (also 11) — Llanfflewyn, Whitland
FFINIAN c475-550 — Clonard, Llancarfan
GWRST (see 1)

13
MEMORIAL SERVICE FOR LLYWELYN II — 'Ein Lliw Olaf' is commemorated in the Ruins of Abbey Cwmhir
COLUMB 6th century — St Columb Major

Feast Days of the Saints

GWYNEN 6th century (also December 3) — Llanwnen
GWYNAU & GWYNWS 5th - 6th century — Llanwnws

14

15
TANGWN 6th century — Llangoed

16
ISAN 6th century — Llanishen, Rhoose?
AFAN (see November 16)

17
SATURNALIA This Roman Feast of — *Saturn was the god of vegetation and*
7 days was the precursor of Christmas, — *crops, which explains the need for*
and slaves became master for the day — *greenery in Christmas tree decorations*
It was also the time of giving gifts..
BRIAC d. 570 — Bourbriac
TYDECHO 6th century — Llanymawddwy, Garthbeibio, Cemaes
SANNAN (see March 1)

18
THE CELTIC FEAST OF EPONA — The Celtic goddess of Horses
TEGFEDD ferch AMWN DDU 6th century — Llanymawddwy, Garthbeibio
MUINIS 5th century — Ardagh

19
RHYSTUD 6th century — Llanrhystud
(the Tuesday before Christmas)

20

21
THOMAS 1st century
IN THE CELTIC CALENDAR,
THE LONGEST NIGHT
GWYNIN (see December 31)

22

23
JUTHWARA 5th - 6th century — Lanteglos, Guizeny, Halstock
(also July 1 3, 17 and 18),
January 6 and November 28

24
CHRISTMAS EVE

25
CHRISTMAS QUARTERDAY

26
BOXING DAY, ST STEPHEN'S DAY — *Traditionally when church alms boxes were*
 — *opened and distributed to the local poor*
MAETHLU 6th century — Llandyfalle
TATHAN (see 30)
GWYNNO (see October 26)
TYBIE (see January 30)

27
ST JOHN THE EVANGELIST 1st century

28
CHILDERMAS DAY, — When Herod killed the children of
HOLY INNOCENTS DAY — Bethlehem

29

30
TATHAN 5th-6th century — Caerwent, St. Tathan, Advent
(also December 26)

31
THE CELTIC FEAST OF OIMELC — The 'Winter Hag', the goddess Cailleach,
The true origin of the New Year's — sends a dragon to kill the lamb of Ffraid of
Eve festivities — Spring. The lamb always wins.

565

THE MARI LLWYD

GWYNIN 7th century
(also January 21, 31)
MAELOG (see November 13)

Llangynwyd, Glamorgan. The 'Grey Mare' is the horse's skull taken round by a party of singers, the Welsh form of 'Wassail'
Llangwynin, Dwygyfylchi

Appendix A

DERIVATIONS of CURRENT WELSH PLACE-NAMES

Many names have been corrupted into 'English', e.g. Y Clas-ar-Wy into Glasbury. We also have the comical case of Oystermouth, derived from Ystumllwynarth. More problematical is the case of Gileston. The roadside Welsh alternative is Silstwn, but the original name was Llanfabon-y-Fro, one of the oldest foundations in Wales, near Llandathan (Sain Tathan, but Saint Athan on the maps today), Caer Eurgain (later Llanilltud Fawr and Llantwit Major) and Nant Carban (later Llancarfan). Some examples are shown below. Any additions to this list would be extremely helpful in compiling a map of Wales as it was in the sixth and seventh centuries. The author would sincerely appreciate local authorities restoring the proper names to Welsh villages to show their heritage, and has approached the local council, the county council, local MP and MEP, and Welsh Office with regard to St Tathan (there was no saint called Athan) and Gileston.

Abererch – Llangawrda
Aberthaw - Aberddawen
Anglesey – Ynys Mon
Bardsey Isle – Ynys Enlli
Barri Island – Ynys Peirio
Bishopston – Llandeilo Ferwallt
Bishton – Trefesgob
Boverton – Trebefered, Trebeferad previously Treberfaidd and possibly Caput Bovium
Brawdy – Breudeth (dedicated to Ffraid)
Bristol Channel – Mor Hafren (Severn Sea)
Briton Ferry - Llansawel
Builth Wells - Llanfair-ym-Muallt (the holy place of Mary in the oxen pasture)
Caldey Isle – Ynys Byr
Canton – Treganna (near Pontcanna in Cardiff)
Chirk – Y Waun
Church Village - Gartholwg
Coychurch – Llangrallo
Crickhowell – Crugywel
Denbigh – Llanfarchell
Devil's Bridge - Pontarfynach
Fairbourne – Y Friog
Flat Holm – Ynys Hafren – previously Ynys Echni
Flemingston - Llanelwan
Gileston – Llanfabon-y-Fro (not Silstwn as on the roadsign)
Goodwick – Wdig
Grassholm Island - Gwales
Guilsfield – Cegidfa
Hawarden - Pennarlag
Holyhead – Caergybi
Holy Island – Ynys Gybi

Holywell – Treffynnon
Hope – Llangyngar
Ilston - Llanilltud
Knighton - Trefyclo
Lampeter – Lanbedr Pont Steffan
Landow – Llanandras
Laugharne - Talacharn
Llandough – Llandochau
Llandovery – Llanymddyfri
Llan-gors Lake – Llyn Syfaddan
Llanmaes – Llanffagan Fach
Llanthony – Llanddewi Nant Hodni
Llantilio Crosseny – Llandeilo Gresynni (Llan Teilo plus Croes Ynyr)
Llantilio Pertholey – Llandeilo Bertholau
Llantwit Major – Llanilltud Fawr, Llanelltut Fawr from the fourth century, previously Caer Wrgan and Caer Eurgain
Llanfapley – Llanfable
Llawhaden - Llanhuadain
Loughor - Casllwchwr
Manorbier – Maenor Byr (the manor of Pyr, the saint and abbot of Caldey)
Middle Mouse Island – Ynys Padrig (East Mouse is Ynys Amlwch)
Mold – Yr Wyddgrug
Monmouth - Mynwy
Montgomery - Trefaldwyn
Nevern – Nanhyfer, Nyfer
Newborough – Rhosyr-yn-Mon – but previously Llanamo
Newbridge - Trecelyn
Northop – Llaneurgain
Oystermouth - Ystumllwynarth
Painscastle – Llanbedr Castell-paen
Pass of the Cross – Bwlch-y-Groes
Penllyne – Penllin – previously Llanfrynach
Penymynydd, Anglesey – Llangredifael
Penterry - Llanbedeui
Peterston Wentloog – Llanbedr Gwynllwg
Presteigne – Llanandras
Puffin Island, Priestholm – Ynys Seiriol, Glanach, Ynys Llanog
Ramsey Island – Ynys Dewi
Radnor – Maesyfed
Rhoose – Y Rhws
Ruabon – Rhiwfabon
Rumney – Tredelerch
St Andrews Major - Llanandras
St Asaph – Llanelwy
St Athan – Sain Tathan, but previously Llandathan
St Clears – Sancler
St David's – Ty Dewi or Mynyw
St George's - Llanufelwyn
St Dogmael's – Llandudoch
St Donat's – Sain Dunwyd, but previously Llanwerydd

Appendix

St Lythans – Llwyneliddon, also Llanbleiddian Fach
St Mellons - Llaneirwg
The Skerries – Ynysoedd y Moelrhoniaid
South Stack Island – Ynys Lawd
Steep Holm - Ronech
Strata Florida – Ystrad-fflur
Strata Marcella – Ystrad Marchell
Tythegston - Llandudwg
Welshpool – Y Trallwng
Wentloog – Gwynllwg
West Mouse Island – Ynys Bigel
Whitland – Hendy-gwyn
Wick – Y Wig Fawr – previously Llanildas

Appendix B

ROMAN SITES

The following places are the Roman sites associated with earliest saints, followed by their English, then Welsh names. Often, the local princes took over the sites of the Roman occupation, and their families were associated with the first churches.

Alabum – Llandovery – Llanmyddyfri
Blestium – Monmouth - Trefynwy
Bomium/Bovium – Cowbridge – Y Bontfaen
Bovium – Holt in Clwyd
Bremia – Llanio near Tregaron
Burrium – Usk - Brynbuga
Caput Bovium/Bomium – Boverton (Treberfaidd, not Trebeferad as on the road sign)
Cicutio – near Brecon – Y Gaer
Conovium – Caerhun near Conway
Gobannium – Abergavenny – Y Fenni
Isca Silurum – Caerleon - Caerllion
Lavobrinta – Forden Gaer in Powys
Leucarium – Loughor – Casllwchwr
Luentinium - Dolaucothi
Mediomanum - Caersws
Moridunum – Carmarthen – Caerfyrddin
Nidum – Neath – Castell-nedd
Segontium – Caernarfon
Varae – probably St Asaph - Llanelwy
Venta Silurum – Caerwent

Appendix C

TIMELINES OF THE AGE OF SAINTS

It is instructive to attempt to place dates to Britain's 'Dark Ages', in order to see not only how the church evolved in Wales, but how the Welsh nation came into being in the period of the Romans and Saxons. All dates are approximate. Several recent books point to there being two chieftains named Arthur. The warlord who fought at Camlan against Medrod seems certainly to have been Arthur ap Meurig ap Tewdrig. It is hoped to firm up conflicting dates in the 5th and 6th centuries with a future book upon King Arthur by this author and Breton colleagues.

* Notes external sources confirming Christianity in British England/Wales in the Dark Ages.

DATE	EVENT
30	Crucifixion
51	Caradog, Eurgain, Gwladys and Bran taken to Rome for Claudian Triumph
61	Bran Fendigaid and Arwystli return to Britain
63	Joseph of Arimathea brings Holy Grail to Britain (see Ilid). Possible foundation of Côr Eurgain and Llanilid
64-76	First Pope Linus is half-British
70	Work begins on the Colosseum
99	Bishop Arwystli (Aristobulus) martyred in Britain
100	The Roman Empire reaches its greatest extent
101	Gwladys Claudia dies in Rome
177	Leurwg Mawr (Lucius) sends to Rome for missionaries
184	Lucius Artorius Castus leads a detachment of troops from Britain to Gaul to subdue a rebellion. Some authors place him as the original 'Arthur'
208*	Tertullian's Testimony to Christianity in Britain, outside the rule of Rome
239*	Origen's Testimony to Christianity in Britain
250*	Sabellius wrote that Christianity was first in Britain
256	Mel, a Briton, Bishop of Rouen
293	Christian monument to Carausius at Penmachno
303	Diocletian Persecution. Constantius tests loyalty of Christian troops
304	Possible martyrdom of Alban, Amphibalus, Julius and Aaron in Britain
312	Constantine marches against Maxentius
313	Edict of Milan allowing Christians public worship in the Roman Empire
314*	Council of Arles with British Bishops
315*	Eusebius stated that disciples had been to Britain
325*	Council of Nicaea with British bishops
326	Elen, Constantine's (British?) mother, finds the Holy Cross
343	Irish pagan raids on Britain
347*	Council of Sardica (Sophia, Bulgaria) with British bishops
358*	Declaration by Hilary of Poitiers that Britain is free from heresy
359*	Council of Rimini with British bishops
363	Pagan Picts and Irish take over North of British Isles for ten years
367*	Chryostom witnesses Christianity in Britain

369	Theodosius organises British defence against the Irish, possibly Côr Eurgain renamed Côr Tewdws at Llanilltud in his honour
380	Constantine I declares Christianity to be the state religion in Rome
383	Macsen Wledig is proclaimed Emperor in Britain, and conquers Gaul, Spain and Italy. His British wife Elen is in contact with Martin of Tours
388	Macsen (featured in the Mabinogion) is executed by Theodosius at Aquila in July. Many of his British troops settle in Armorica (Brittany – the 'first migration'). The Isle of Britain now has fewer defensive forces
395	Theodosius, the last emperor before division into east and west, dies. His son Arcadius becomes eastern emperor, and the younger son Honorius takes the west
396	Stilicho, regent of the western empire, reorganises British defences, beginning to replace Roman commanders with local British chieftains
397	Death of Martin of Tours
399	Stilicho visits Britain to repel attacks by Picts, Irish and Saxons
400*	Jerome attests to orthodoxy of Britons. Pelagius goes to Rome
402	One of the two British legions is recalled by Stilicho to defend Italy against Alaric and the Visigoths. The VI Victrix legion was the one which was stationed in the north to keep out the Picts (Irish) and Scots
403*	Victicius, Bishop of Rouen, visits Britain to strengthen the case against the Pelagian Heresy
405	The VI legion never returns to Britain, as it is used to fight Radagaisus' barbarians in Italy. Only II Legion remains, in Wales.
407	With the assassination of Marcus, Gratian becomes emperor, but is soon displaced by Constantine III. He was elected by the remaining troops in Britain, the II Legion stationed along Wales' borders and throughout Wales. Nennius called this *'the end of the Roman Empire in Britain'*
408	Increasing attacks from German tribes, led by the Saxons, and by the Irish and Scots
409	The British expel the remaining Roman officials and take up the defence of Britain by themselves
410	Alaric's Goths sack Rome, and Britain is independent. British pilgrims in Jerusalem
418	Pelagianism outlawed in Rome, but favoured by the Celtic tribes in Britain
423*	Theodoret attests to Christianity in Britain. Pelagius meets Celestius in Rome
429*	Palladius asks Pope Celestine 1 to send help to combat Pelagianism. He sends Germanus of Auxerre and Lupus of Troyes. Garmon (Germanus) leads Britons to 'Hallelujah' victory near Wrecsam. The 'Rule' of St Benedict established in mainland Europe
432	Padrig lands in Ireland. Palladius, consecrated by Pope Celestine in 431, flees Ireland
438	Birth of Ambrosius Aurelianus, the Romano-Briton (Teithfallt?)
440-450	Civil war and famine in Britain. It seems that the pro-Roman citizens moved west. Constant attacks by the Picts and Saxons. Some migration to Brittany from Britain
441	Gallic Chronicle records that *'Britain, abandoned by the Romans, passed into the power of the Saxons'*. It is worth noting that the Saxons never took over Wales
445	Vortigern becomes 'overlord' of Britain. His periods of rule may be 440-456 and 470-472 446 * Pro-Roman Britons appeal to Aetius, Governor of Gaul, for

Appendix

	help against the Picts and Irish, but no aid comes, because Attila the Hun is pressing him back
447	Germanus (with Severus of Trier) revisits Britain. The Irish Picts, and the 'Scots' of Ireland were heavily defeated.
448	Civil war and plague
450	Hengist and his Saxons are welcomed by Vortigern, the 'adventus Saxonum.'
451	Aetius drives back Attila at Chalons-sur-Marne 452 Saxons are raiding across Britain
456	*'Treachery of the Long Knives'* where the flower of British nobility is killed at peace talks. Vortimer takes over the High Kingship from his father Vortigern
457	Ambrosius, with Vortigern's sons Vortimer and Cateyrn, defeats Hengist at Aylesford in Kent
458	Hengist recovers and takes over all of south-east Britain
458-460	Riothamus leads emigration of British nobles to Brittany (the second migration)
460-470	Ambrosius Aurelianus (Tewdrig?), son of Ambrosius leads pro-Roman Britons in constant warfare against the Saxons. Vortimer may still be High King, or he may be identified with Riothamus
461*	Council of Tours with British bishops
465*	Council of Vannes with British bishops
466	Huge battle of Wippedesfleot, where Saxons win, but severity of slaughter stops hostilities for some years
469	Riothamus leads large British army to help emperor Anthemius against the Euric's Visigoths, and is heavily defeated
470	Battle of Wallop in Hampshire where Ambrosius defeats Vitalinus, leader of the pro-Pelagian Britons. Ambrosius (Meurig?) assumes high kingship of Britain. His father Tewdrig martyred
473	Another push by Hengist against Ambrosius. Vortigern is deposed around this time
476	Eclipse of Western Roman Empire after 100 years of decline. Romulus Augustus is deposed by Odoacer, the first barbarian king of Italy. Christianity has been the state religion for less than 100 years in Rome
477	Aelle brings more Saxons into Britain and takes Sussex. In 486 fights bloody and indecisive battle at Mercredesburne
482	Posited birth of Arthur, the son of Meurig
485-496	Period of Arthur's '12 Great Battles' – either these are mis-dated or there are two 'Arthurs' - it may also be that Meurig fought these campaigns rather than Arthur
490	Hengist dies and is succeeded by his son Aesc, who reigns for 34 years
495	Cerdic and his son Cynric land and invade Hampshire and Dorset
497	Ambrosius nominates Arthur as his successor, with Meurig and Gereint as 'pendragons' - it may be that Meurig passed on the duties of 'wledig' to his son Arthur to avoid conflict between his sons on his death.
500-537	Approximate rule of Arthur ap Meurig ap Tewdrig, ended with the Battle of Camlan, possibly against Maelgwn Gwynedd
501	Jutes and Gewissei pillage Portchester
508	Arthur fights at Llongborth, where Geraint ap Erbyn is killed
510	Cerdic defeats British king Natanleod at Netley near Southampton. Pendragon (possibly Meurig) killed, and Arthur assumes battle command.
511*	Council of Orleans with British bishops. Death of Clovis, who has almost united Gaul.

517	Badon Hill – Saxon advance stopped by Arthur
519	Cerdic founds kingdom of West Saxons – Wessex. Fights indecisive battle against British
522	Dyfrig retires to Ynys Enlli
524	Riwal Mawr of Brittany (Hywel, Arthur's nephew) dies
528	Saxons capture Verulam (St Albans)
530-540	Mass emigration of British monks to Brittany – the 'third migration'. Armel (Arthur?) appears in Brittany at this time. Maelgwn takes over Gwynedd in 530.
537	Battle of Camlan – Arthur, wounded, goes to Avalon (Ynys Enlli). Maelgwn may have become 'High King'
534	Cynric rules Wessex on Cerdic's death
c.540*	Gildas writes 'De Excidio', claiming the church has existed since Joseph of Arimathea came to Britain. The tradition that Arthur was 'unmanned' by his wound may have turned him to a religious way of life
544	St David dies, aged 82
547	'Yellow Plague' decimates British territories and Ireland, and possibly kills Maelgwn. It seems not to affect the Saxons. Ida the Angle invades Yorkshire. More British monks leave for Brittany, possibly including Armel (Arthur), the warrior-saint
550	Evangelical mission to Ireland by David, Gildas and Cadoc
554	Armel argues with Conmire and sees King Childebert in Paris
555	An army under Armel, Samson and Judwal defeats Conmire, and Armel is given land by Judwal. The three victors are recorded on the Llanilldud Fawr cross.
562	Death of Armel
565	Death of Samson
569	Synod of Llanddewi Brefi where David refutes Pelagianism. A British see is already founded in Spain
570	Death of Gildas
572	A British suffragan to Archbishop of Braga in Spain
573	Battle of Arderydd – Rhydderch Hael consolidates control of British Cumbria and Strathclyde, fighting other British princes. Kentigern in Strathclyde. Death of Paul Aurelian.
577	Battle of Dyrham near Bath, Wales cut off from Domnonia (West Country)
580*	Vanantius Fortunatus attests to orthodoxy of Britons
586	Theonus, last British Bishop of London, forced to flee from Saxons; Thadioc, last British Bishop of York, forced to flee from Angles
597	Augustine lands in Kent to convert Saxons, and is consecrated bishop
600	Aneirin writes 'Y Gododdin' about the battle of Cattraeth, referring to Arthur
601	Augustine becomes first Archbishop of Canterbury. Canterbury is a much later foundation than the Welsh bishoprics of St David's, St Asaf, Bangor and Llandaf
603	Augustine meets the British bishops but his arrogance drives them away
600-700	Welsh triads composed, but only mediaeval collections survive
610 or 613	Battle of Chester, Selyf killed, Wales cut off from Cumbria, effectively creating the Welsh nation of today. 'Massacre of the Saints' at Bangor-is-Coed
616	Bishop Mellitus expelled from London, London pagan from 616-654
626	Angles spread over midlands of England, fighting the princes of Powys
633	Cadwallon of Gwynedd kills Edwin

St Dogmael's Abbey Church. *CADW: Welsh Historic Monuments. Crown Copyright.*

635	Cadwallon killed in battle
653	Glastonbury taken by the Saxons
664*	Synod of Whitby – refusal of Celtic church to accept Rome. Easter eggs first used by Christians.
732	Bede's 'Ecclesiastical History of the English People' established a church-inspired notion of national identity for the English.
850?	Nennius compiles 'History of the Britons'
890	Anglo-Saxon Chronicles compiled
1019	Breton legend of St Goeznovius written, referring to Arthur as King of the Britons
1090	Lives of saints Gildas, Padarn, Cadog, Illtud etc. written
1138	Geofrey of Monmouth's 'History of the Kings of Britain' is published and becomes a best-seller across the continent
1409, 1417, 1424, 1434*	Councils of Pisa, Constance, Sienna and Basle, where the British bishops held precedence over French and Spanish prelates because of the tradition of the founding of the British Church by Joseph of Arimathea in 63 AD
1450	Sir Thomas Malory's Le Morte d'Arthur, one of Caxton's earliest books, revives the traditions of Arthur

Appendix D

A NOTE UPON WELSH LANGUAGE MUTATIONS

The modern words mum and dad seem to come from the Welsh 'mam' and 'tad', where the 'tad' is soft-mutated to 'dad'. This is a major area of difficulty in learning the Welsh language - sometimes initial consonants change, for instance Cardiff is 'Caerdydd' in Welsh, and 'in' is 'yn'. However, 'in Cardiff' becomes 'yng Nghaerdydd'. 'To Cardiff' in Welsh is not ' i Caerdydd ' but 'i Gaerdydd'. 'And Cardiff' is 'a Chaerdydd'. Only some initial consonants change, for instance the initial letters c, p and t are subject to soft, nasal and spirate/aspirate mutations, whereas b, d and g are subject to just soft and nasal mutations, and the consonants of ll, m and rh only soft mutate.

For anyone learning Welsh, usually locals will correct you, although you can get by without knowing the rules for mutating words. The table below explains better how the initial letters of saints are often altered in place-names associated with them:

Consonant	Word	Soft	Nasal	Spirant
C	Caerdydd Cardiff	Gaerdydd	Nghaerdydd	Chaerdydd
P	pen head	Ben	mhen	Phen
T	tad father	Dad	nhad	Thad
B	bach small	Fach	mach	
D	dyn man	Ddyn	nyn	
G	glas blue/green	Las	nglas	
Ll	llawen merry	Lawen		
M	mam mother	Fam		
Rh	rhyd ford	Ryd		

Appendix E

AN URGENT WARNING TO THE WELSH

'The Guardian' on November 8th, 1995, carried the following question from Toby Alcock of Sydenham in London:
'Is it true that, according to an unrepealed ancient statute, it is legal to shoot any Welshman who crosses into England on a Friday?'
The answer is as follows:
'It is true. Deriving from the Act of Union, the Recognition of Borders Act 1772 dealt with the growing influx of Welsh goods and trade to the Welsh border which passed through the weekend markets untaxed. The law permits a Welshman to be killed crossing the border with supplies attempting to attend a weekend market. In Shrewsbury in 1776, seven Welshmen were killed, three by musket, three by sword and one was bludgeoned to death with his own crops. The Borders Act has never been repealed and the situation was resolved by mutual English/Welsh subsequent taxation laws.'

Appendix F

THE LLANNAU OF WALES

Hundreds of Welsh place-names have retained the prefix 'llan', and it most cases it denotes that there is a church connected with a Celtic saint of the fifth or sixth century. These were called 'The Dark Ages' by the historians of Hanoverian times, attempting to wipe out British history and replace it with a Germano-Saxon version. However, this period after the Roman legions left Wales in 383 under Magnus Maximus, Macsen Wledig, is known in Wales as 'The Age of Saints'. The Welsh of Brittany, Cornwall and Wales kept the light of Christianity flickering as barbarians over-ran the rest of Europe.

'Llan' meant an 'enclosure', and it is seen in the Welsh words for sheep-pen, orchard and vineyard, 'corlan', 'perllan' and 'gwinllan'. In Brittany and Cornwall, the place-name prefix of 'lam' or 'lan' serves the same purpose as the Welsh 'llan'. The llan was a piece of land consecrated or associated with a saint. Llandeilo will thus be associated with St Teilo, Llangybi with St Cybi and so on. (Often the first letters of saints' names will be 'mutated' after a prefix – a list of Welsh mutations appears in Appendix D). One problem, however, is that many ancient Welsh churches were rebuilt and rededicated, as the Normans pressed through Wales. Many of the Llanfihangels and Llanfairs dedicated to Michael (Mihangel) and Mary (Mair) were sites associated with earlier Celtic saints. For instance, St Mary's Church at Kilpeck, Herefordshire (a Welsh-speaking area until the seventeenth century) was earlier St David's Church, and before that St Pedic's. Also St Mary's at Rhiwabon was formerly St Collen's. If any reader can add to other examples shown throughout this book, the author would be most grateful.

Dr Euros Bowen has found over 600 dedications to Celtic saints in Wales and in its borders with England, most on lower valley-slopes and valley floors, and close to the sea and tidal waters. However, many ancient names and attributions need to be recovered. My mother and aunt, with a combined age of 160, could not remember the name of their childhood church in Trefeglwys, Montgomery – to them, it was just known as the 'llan'. It is now 'St Michael's', but was possibly an earlier foundation to Cedwyn. Francis Jones has noted over 400 holy wells attributed to saints in Wales, and often by linking these with field names we can reconstruct the past of 1500 years ago.

It must be remembered that, apart from the llanau based in original Roman stone buildings, such as at Caerwent, Caerleon, Caer Worgan at Llanilltud, Caernarfon, Carmarthen and so on, most llannau were very simple affairs. The monastic settlement was a circular enclosure, with earthen walls or banks, and a church of sawn oak with a rush roof. (Thus sites with circular churchyards are almost always Celtic). Sometimes the site was a Druidic religious centre or Roman villa or fort. The church was normally surrounded by small 'beehive' cells, such as those still seen in Ireland, some in stone, but most of wattle and mud. The llanau, as pointed out by eminent scholars, were nearly always positioned out of site of the coast (and its pagan invaders), and possessed a plentiful supply of fresh water for baptisms. An echo of these beehive cells may be the twenty or so remaining beehive pigsties in Glamorgan, constructed without mortar. One can be seen at the Museum of Welsh Life at St Ffagans.

Appendix G

THE TWENTY-EIGHT TOWNS OF SUB-ROMAN BRITAIN

Nennius, in his 8th century 'History of the Britons', shows how important Wales and the West were in these times. No less than 15 of his list of 28 cities are from this area of civilization, leaving 13 spread across the massive area of the rest of England and Scotland. The words 'Caer' or 'Y Gaer' normally means a camp or fortress in Welsh, and usually denotes a Roman camp ('castra') much as the suffix 'caster', 'cester' or 'chester' does in the English langauge. The Welsh word 'Dinas' or 'din' meaning 'fort' is often attached to hill-camps that precede the Roman invasions. The British/Welsh bases are as follows:

Caer-Caratauc, which is Cary Craddock in the parish of Sellack, Hereford. This hillfort in Ergyng was said to be a palace of Caradog Freichfras, son of King Ynyr of Gwent.
Caer-Costoeint - an unknown site in Dumnonia
Caer-Ddraiton is Din-Draithou in the Life of St Cadog, and is Dunster in Somerset. Cado entertained Arthur here, and another name was Din-Torre, the fort on the river Torre.
Caer-Guent is Caer Gwent or Caerwent, the Venta Silurum of the Romans. The walled Roman city became the capital of Gwent, replacing the Silures' hill-fort of Llanmelin nearby. Coin hoards from around 425 and burials denote continuing occupation throughout the 'Dark Ages'. Caerwent was 'given' by Caradog Freichfras to Tathan when he moved his main court to the more easily defended camp at Portskewett nearby. The Roman walls are remarkable at Caerwent, but it is by-passed by most visitors to Caerleon and Wales. The site covers 20 hectares and the walls once stood 20 feet high. They are around 12 feet wide at the base. The main road to South Wales ran through the East and West gates.
Caer-Guiragon is Worcester.
Caer-Guouthigorn is Little Doward hillfort at Ganarew, Hereford, supposedly the site of Vortigern's last stand, although he may have escaped to Brittany.
Caer-Guricon is Viroconium, Wroxeter, the capital of Powys under Vortigern but later sacked by the Anglo-Saxons, forcing the princes of Powys back to Mathrafal. The Roman remains here are excellent.
Caer-Legeion-guar-Uisc is Isca, Caerleon on the River Usk outside Newport, with some of the best Roman features in Europe.
Caer-Legion is Deva, Chester, where Arthur possibly fought. With Caerleon, this was the second great fortress on the Welsh borders as the Romans pushed out from Gloucester and Wroxeter. In 603 Augustine held his second conference with the British bishops here, and around 610 or 613 the British lost the great battle when Bangor-is-Coed was destroyed.
Caer-Meguaidd is Meifod at Mathrafal, the court of Powys.
Caer-Pensa-uel-Coyt is South Cadbury hillfort.
Cae-Peris appears to be Caer Beris just outside Builth Wells.
Caer-Segeint is the great fort at Segontium, Caernarfon the old capital of the princes of Gwynedd before they moved to Aberffraw, and forever linked with Macsen Wledig and Elen. The river Arfon flows to the sea at Caernarfon, which means 'fort on the Arfon/
Caer-(D)Urnac appears to be Dorchester
Caer-Luit-Coyt is Wall, outside Lichfield, retaken from the Saxons by Prince Morfael of Pengwern around 650.

The thirteen other towns listed by Nennius were Dumbarton, Canterbury, Colchester, Doncaster, York, Grantchester, Leicester, Carlisle, London, Manchester, St Albans, Ilchester and Silchester.

Other towns at this time included Caer-Baddan or Aquae Sulia, Bath. King Ffernfael had his court here, and it was lost to the Saxons at the fateful battle at nearby Dyrham in 573. Ffernfael died, as did King Cyndyddan who had his capital at Caer-Ceri (Cirencester). Cirencester was the capital of the province of Britannia Prima, and Wales was Brittania Secunda to the Romans. The third British king to die at Dyrham was Cynfael of Caer-Gloui (Gloucester). Caer-Teim was Tamium, Cardiff, where king Ynwyl was mentioned in Gereint and Enid as living in the ruined palace (the Roman fort), while the new kings of Glywyssing settled themselves at Dinas Powys hillfort just west of the city.

Appendix H

THE DEMOCRATIC DEFICIT IN PARLIAMENTARY REPRESENTATION IN WALES

'Silence is the virtue of fools.'
    Francis Bacon (1561-1626), 'De Dignitate et Augmentis Scientiarum'

Throughout this book, we have noted decisions taken by a London-based House of Commons and House of Lords which have not been helpful to Wales as a nation. The rapid relative decline of Wales in the last twenty years has been because the Conservative party, with large majorities, has seen no political benefit in putting resources into Wales. The Labour Party, until recently assured of strong Welsh support, has likewise seen no reason to woo its voters. The behaviour of many Labour-controlled councils has further alienated the Welsh people who vote in fewer numbers at every election. The first vote for a National Assembly demonstrated that the people saw no need for a toothless talking-shop full of place-men. The second vote which narrowly approved a National Assembly was seen as a step in the right direction – something, anything, was preferable to the current situation across the Welsh nation. However, even this grudging step was tainted by the 'placing' of the anonymously grey favourite of Mr Blair, Alan Michael as First Secretary, above the 'people's choice', Rhodri Morgan.

We should, however, examine why the Scottish Parliament has been given real political and economic power compared to Wales. The author checked the backgrounds of the members of the British Cabinet when the devolution decision was made. All the top four responsible jobs are taken by Scots. Another four Scots are in the 22-man Cabinet, compared to just 3 members from the populous South-East, and only one from Wales. Of these 22 men running the business of the country, only one has any business experience, at a minimal and low level. Of their 68 unelected 'political advisors' (paid for by the tax-payer), only 3 have any business experience. They cost the taxpayer almost £4,000,000 a year (over double what the Conservative Party paid for such 'support', and one is allocated to the Prime Minister's wife, Cherie Blair. (Mrs Blair complains about the cost of high-fashion clothing to accompany the Prime Minister on his overseas trips. One does not remember her being on the electoral roll to be chosen to represent this country). The Americanisation of British politics continues. Surrounded by a coterie of advisers, the court of the elected leader fawns him with the knowledge that all is well with the world. In the Camelot of Westminster, the court of Blair sees its houses and salaries rising in value by the minute. Any messengers with bad news from the provinces are quickly put to the sword before they approach the throne. Top people take advice off top advisors, but no-one consults the people. In America, the tallest candidate with the fullest head of hair always wins. Façades of glamour and style, under a rich gloss coat of spin-doctors and speech-writers, rather than intelligence, real-life experience and endurance beget power in today's democracy.

Non-qualified people running the British economy is bad news for the electorate. For Wales it is disastrous, as politicians with no knowledge of how multinational business works, acquiesce meekly to free market doctrines. (Incidentally, the Welsh National Assembly also displays an utter ignorance of business in the make-up of the majority of its members). When their time is up as politicians, they join the boards of companies, for instance Mrs Thatcher is now personally worth over £40 million (approximately the same as her son Mark). The largest tobacco company in the world employed her as a 'consultant' on hundreds of thousands of pounds a year, and paid over a million pounds for her two 70th birthday parties. There is little difference between parties. When Mrs Blair pays over £5000 for her personal hairdresser to accompany her on a state visit to China, and another £2000 a few months later on another overseas junket, one knows that top politicians have lost touch with the reality of balancing a family budget for the vast majority of the over-taxed population. Nothing demonstrates their utter uselessness more than the Dome fiasco. Even more worrying is that a 'socialist' government (which could be sued under the Trades Descriptions Act) with a firmly Christian Premier has been suborned by the arms industry into allocating £16 billion into new fighter aircraft (at £60 million a plane) and £36 billion on Trident nuclear submarines. Can they not understand that Britain is not the world's peace-maker, but a little country, amongst the poorest in Western Europe, nearing the end of its life-cycle of global influence?

Wales is desperate for Objective 1 funding, as acquired by all the other poorer areas across Europe, but money has been thrown at weapons industries and a tacky temporary carbuncle in London. A problem for Wales is that its own Assembly members have an identical profile of not knowing how to run a chip-shop, let alone an economy. Their civil servants will be of the same (no decision is a good decision) mode, as are the great and good who lead many of the non-elected Welsh quangos. Some may feel that these comments are out of place in a book on Welsh saints, but **the purpose of this book is to inspire action, not to regurgitate legends.** My point is that action has to begin at the local level, despite the dead hand of bureaucracy. The only way forward for the Welsh people is if it helps itself and does not rely upon political support. The alternative is to try and change the political system by electing people from outside the public service sector, and to lobby for members of quangos to be elected or quangos abolished. It is not just farmers on £4,500 p.a. who suffer hardship from political ineptitude - they are only the tip of an iceberg.

The British Government only spends 0.11% of the national income upon culture and heritage, much of that directed towards preserving London ballet and opera to subsidise the rich. There is a huge opportunity as shown in this book, for Wales to present itself to the world as the home of Christianity and of the most potent legends in the Western world, those of Arthur. Wales needs to uncover the Roman villa outside Llanilltud Fawr, to show that it cares about its past. Wales needs to delve deeper into early Christian writings, including those suppressed by the church, to explore the original links with Israel and Rome. Wales needs to reinvigorate itself with feast weeks. Wales needs a localised food-processing industry. The budget for the Department of Health, as a proportion of national income, has dropped from 4.67% to 4.46% in the last five years. The budget for the Department of Education and Employment has dropped from 2.12% to 1.74% in the same period (-'The Times', August 31, 1999). Wales has some of the worst health statistics in Europe, and its education at all levels is in desperate need of investment, not cuts. The country has to generate its own income to address its problems, as history has shown that neither the WDA inward investment programme nor any Governmental assistance has halted its relative decline. At the moment of writing, there is a 'feel-good' factor across the nation, inspired by Welsh actors, rock groups, the partial (but temporary) success of the rugby team and its new stadium. Cardiff is one of the greatest capital cities in the world, and inspires pride. However, outside Cardiff, with perhaps the exception of Swansea, the economic outlook is grim.

Appendix

The following list should be instructive for all those who proclaim the British parliamentary system as being the 'best in the world'. Leaving aside the anachronistic House of Lords, one could imagine the outcry if Neil Kinnock had been elected Prime Minister and appointed another seven Welshmen (including some arrogant adulterers), four controlling the most powerful government posts. The English media would simply not have allowed it to happen. The full Cabinet make-up in 1999 when Wales was 'granted' its own Assembly was as follows:

Name	Position	Origin	Educated	Business Experience
Blair	Prime Minister	Scots	Fettes Edinburgh public school. Edinburgh Univ.	0
Brown	Chancellor of Exchequer	Scots	Kirkcaldy. Edinburgh Univ.	0
Cook	Foreign Secretary	Scots	Aberdeen. Edinburgh Univ.	0
Lord Irvine	Lord Chancellor	Scots	Inverness. Glasgow Univ.	0
Robertson	Defence	Scots	Dunoon. Dundee Univ.	0
Smith	Culture	Scots	Gordon Watson College Edinburgh. Cambridge Univ.	Housing Association
Darling	Social Security	Scots	Loretto public school. Aberdeen Univ.	0
Dewar	Scotland	Scots	Glasgow. Glasgow Univ.	0
Prescott	Environment, Transport	English (North)	Ellesmere Port, Hull Univ.,	Ship's steward 1957-63
Dobson	Health	English (North)	York, LSE	CEGB HQ (nationalised industry)
Taylor	Chief Whip	English (North)	Bolton. Bradford Univ. Sheffield Univ.	Housing Corporation
Byers	Trade and Industry	English (North)	Chester. Liverpool Poly.	0
Milburn	Treasury	English (North)	Newcastle. Lancaster Univ.	0
Blunkett	Education	English (North)	Sheffield. Sheffield Univ.	0
Cunningham	Duchy of Lancaster	English (North)	Jarrow. Durham Univ.	0
Straw	Home Secretary	English (South)	Brentwood. Leeds Univ.	0
Baroness Jay	Leader House of Lords, Women	English (South)	Blackheath. Oxford Univ.	0
Brown	Agric. Fish	English (South)	Tunbridge Wells. Manchester Univ.	Minimal, in advertising
Short	Int. Dev.	English (Midlands)	Birmingham. Keele Univ. Leeds Univ.	0
Mowlam	N. Ireland	English (Midlands)	Coventry. Durham Univ.	0
Beckett	Leader House of Commons	English (East)	Norwich. Manchester Poly.	0
Michael	Wales	Welsh (North)	Colwyn Bay. Keele Univ.	0

Appendix I

A NOTE ON THE EARLY BRITISH CHURCH

'Operationally, God is beginning to resemble not a ruler but the last fading smile of a cosmic Cheshire cat.'
Julian Huxley, Director-General of UNESCO, 1957

There does seem a need for research in this area, as proved by Jowett's 'The Drama of the Lost Disciples.' Unfortunately, this author has not the time to carry out such a huge project. Perhaps the Department of Theology at Lampeter could resource this type of work. Recent books and web-sites have carried Jowett's findings, but most are reporting his work rather than investigating and adding to it. The hypothesis is that Britain, and specifically Siluria, was the home of early Christianity in Europe. Thus Glamorgan, Monmouth, Brecon, Hereford, Worcester, Gloucester and Somerset were incredibly important in the history of Christianity, possibly more so than Rome. Linked with this is the fact that the family of Caradog in 1st century Rome was the catalyst for the early church there, and that the first Bishop of Rome, Linus was half-British. The two that followed were Britons. There are further possible links with Elen, the mother of Constantine* who made Christianity an accepted religion in the Roman Empire in 312. (This latter part of Jowett's analysis is omitted from what follows, in the interests of brevity and clarity).There seem to be far too many early sources and coincidences to dismiss Jowett's work. The author has discovered some of the more recent sources for Jowett. The Rev. W. Morgan seems to have been the catalyst for most of the work. His 1869 'St Paul in Britain' seems an excellent analysis, but the author has thus far only been able to source the 1984 abridged version. Morgan's work, and Taylor's 1906 'The Coming of the Saints' were used extensively used by the Rev. Lionel Smithett Lewis of Glastonbury in 1953, for 'Joseph of Arimathea in Glastonbury.' Lewis worked for most of his life upon the links between the disciples and Britain. Jowett's book is an overview of a fascinating and badly neglected area of study.

Unfortunately, academics are taught to criticise and deconstruct, rather than to build up empirical evidence and push barriers forward. They also tend to research using other people's previous researches, research by accretion rather than stripping away the layers and returning to original sources. Early British history has, for the last 200 years, been replaced by a Germanic version of events in Britain, where nothing happened before the coming of the pagan Saxons, Jutes, Angles and Danes. The following is an abridgement of Jowett's work, supplemented by internet and other sources. If any reader wishes to contact the author and add to this body of knowledge, perhaps a new book upon this period could be published by Glyndŵr Publishing. Many of the books referred to in Jowett's bibliography are difficult to source by inter-library loan. An interesting aspect is that Marie Trevelyan's 1910 book upon Llantwit Major notes many of these traditions, and is dedicated to St Eurgain as well as St Illtud. Iolo Morganwg has been denigrated for repeating and transcribing many legends of this time, but we can see that the original church sources, written in the 1st to 5th centuries, seem to back up the twin

Appendix

coexisting threads of the British Christian Church in Rome and Britain. (A point that many critics of Iolo miss is that he did not claim Arthur for Wales. If Iolo was such a shameless propagandist for Glamorgan and Wales, surely the legend of Arthur would have been embroidered by him).

Jowett tells us that Joseph of Arimathea** controlled the world tin and lead trade, including the most important tin mining sites in Cornwall. His ships transported the ingots to the Mediterranean. He was a *'nobilis decurio'*, a high Roman administrator, and for a Jew to hold such a high position is surprising. Joseph of Arimathea was the uncle of Jesus, a rich and influential man whom the Sadducees did not dare oppose. He claimed Jesus' body from Pilate, removed the body from the cross, wrapped it in clean linens and took it to a private tomb. Under Jewish law, when Jesus' father died, the next male kin of the family became the legal guardian of the family. Cornish traditions are that Joseph and his nephew Jesus came to visit the tin mines in Cornwall. St Augustine wrote to the Pope that Jesus had built a wattle church at Glastonbury. Herodotus in 450BC and Aristotle in 350BC had referred to Britain as the *'Tin Islands'*.

According to Acts, on Jesus' death in 36, the Church of Jerusalem was scattered abroad, with even the Apostles fleeing. (The Roman persecution of Jews and Christians lasted for centuries, with Augustus, Tiberius and Claudius, up to Diocletian in 320 all making Christianity a capital offence. Diocletian's co-ruler Maximian slaughtered his own Christian Gaulish legion in cold blood. Writers believe that only the Christians and Druids were exterminated for their faith under centuries of Roman rule - is there any current authority who can verify this assertion?) Cardinal Baronius, the most outstanding historian of the Catholic Church, and Curator of the Vatican Library, wrote of AD 36:
'In that year the party mentioned was exposed to the sea in a vessel without sails or oars. The vessel drifted finally to Marseilles and they were saved. From Marseilles Joseph and his company passed into Britain and after preaching the Gospel there, died.'

It seems that the early arrivals in Marseilles included Mary Magdalene, Martha, the handmaiden Marcella, Lazarus, Maximin (whose sight Jesus restored), Philip, James, Mary the wife of Cleopas, and Mary the mother of Jesus. St Philip is documented as 'The Apostle of Gaul', and Lazarus also appears to have evangelised there. Philip was crucified in Hierapolis, Phrygia, and Lazarus was said to have died in Cyprus. (However, Marseilles claims Lazarus' relics, and church records at Lyons say that Lazarus returned from Britain to Marseilles to become its first Bishop, dying in 44 or 45. His relics are also claimed at St Maximin, Lyons, Aix and La Sainte Baume in France). French gypsies were reported in the London Morning Post in 1923 as making their annual May 28th pilgrimage, to relics in the church of St Maries de la Mer at the mouth of the Rhone, This was where they believed that Lazarus first came to Gaul, on May 28th, with St Mary Salome, St Mary Jacobus (Mary Cleopas?) and Sara, a black servant. This may denote the arrival of Lazarus with his sisters Mary and Martha (with Marcella their handmaiden) from Britain. (Mary Magdalene and Mary of Bethany are regarded as the same saint in France). Maximin joined Mary Magdalene at Aix, where he became Bishop. Parmena, a disciple of Joseph, became Bishop of Avignon. Another disciple, Drennalus, went to Morlaix with Joseph and then became first Bishop of Treguier. Philip was said to have guided the Judaeans from Britain to different parts of France to establish Christianity. Eutropius became first bishop of Aquitaine, and Archbishop Rabanus of Mayence wrote of the saints of the British mission to France around 830. The saints Clean, Sidonis and Saturninus are also recorded preaching in Gaul, and Joseph was said to have founded the churches at Morlaix and Limoges. St Martial was the only one of Joseph's band who remained in Britain, where he was joined by his parents Marcellus and Elizabeth, and St Zacchaeus. Marcellus was said to have taught Linus, the son of Caradog, and first Bishop of Rome. Another Marcellus, a Silurian prince, left Glastonbury some time after Joseph's death, to become first Bishop of Tongres and first Archbishop of Treves (Trier) in France before his martyrdom in 166. The Archbishops of Rheims and Treves were for centuries supplied by Glastonbury. Cadfael left Glastonbury to found the church of Tarento in Italy in 170, and he has been confused with the later Cadog (Cadfael) of the 6th century.

Suetonius, a Briton from Glastonbury/Avalon, was baptised by St Barnabas, brother of Aristobulus, and went to Helvetia (Switzerland). Known there as St Beatus from Unterseen on Lake Thun he evangelised the country, dying in 96. Mansuetus*** was baptised by Joseph in 40AD, and was a friend of Clement and Peter in Britain, founding the mother church of France at Toul in Lotharingia, and the church of Lorraine. Mansuetus stayed at the Palatium Brittanicum in Rome, befriending Linus, and succeeding Clement as the third Bishop of Rome. He was martyred in 110. He had gone to Rome with Clement. **Thus of the first three Bishops of Rome, Linus was half-British, and the second two came from Britain**. Luke was said to have been a visitor to Avalon in Professor Smith's 'Dictionary of Christian Biography'. To the list of Disciples said to have been associated with Britain - Joseph of Arimathea, Lazarus, Barnabas, Simon, Paul, James, Luke, Zacchaeus and Peter, we can also add James the brother of Jesus. Cressy stated that he visited Britain and Gaul after leaving Spain in 41AD. Other records state that he was also present at the death of the Virgin Mary at Avalon in 48. Only three of the Disciples, Stephen, James the brother of John and Judas are not associated with the kingdom of the Silures.

Jowett notes many early sources concerning Philip's mission to Gaul, and notes Joseph of Arimathea as Philip's *'dearest friend.'* Joseph had been invited to Britain by the Silurian prince Arviragus, the cousin of Caradog in 36AD. According to Cardinal Baronius, the following crossed with Joseph to Cornwall:
St Mary of Bethany (wife of Cleopas), St Martha of Bethany (the sister of Lazarus and Mary), St Lazarus, St Eutropius, St Salome, St Clean, St Saturninus (Sadwrn), St Mary Magdalene, St Maximin, St Martial, St Trophimus, St Sidonius (Restitutus), and Marcella, the maid to the Bethany sisters. St Willibald, Bishop of Eichstatt (d. 786) wrote that he visited the tomb of Mary Magdalene in England. It may be that the Virgin Mary also accompanied the party and was buried on the site of St Mary's Church in Glastonbury. (This appears to be the only dedication in Britain to the Virgin dating before the 12th century. The Catholic church made her a saint in 600, but this was never accepted by the Celtic Church.) Arviragus gave Joseph's mission 12 hides of land (1,920 acres) at Glastonbury, free of tax in perpetuity. This was later used by British sovereigns to refute papal authority, and the British claim of superiority in the early church was affirmed by papal statement as late as 1936. A wattle church of 38 AD survived the Norman Conquest, until a great fire accidentally burned the church and St Mary's Abbey in 1184. The little church had been encased in lead by St Paulinus in AD 630, when he erected St Mary's chapel. The saints Lazarus and the Bethany sisters, Trophimus, Maximin, Eutrophius and Parmena were sent by Joseph from Britain to evangelise Gaul. Trophimus joined Martha at Arles****, where he became Bishop.

Perhaps Christianity was accepted by the Britons so easily as it paralleled their Druidic beliefs. In his ill-fated invasion of 54BC, Julius Caesar wrote *'They make the immortality of the soul the basis of all their teaching, holding it to be the principal incentive and reason for a virtuous life. Believing in the immortality of the soul they were careless of death.'* (Incidentally, from 55BC it seems that British citizens were the only people allowed to walk the streets of Rome as

Appendix

freemen. Was this because British lead and tin were so important? Lead was needed for water systems. The important property of tin, a soft metal, is that when alloyed with copper, another soft metal, it forms bronze, a hard metal). Lucanus and Mela, writing in 38AD and 41AD respectively, also ascribed the bravery of the British warrior to this religious doctrine.

Arviragus seemed to rule southern Britain, while Caradog had Wales. Jowett calls Arviragus *'the most famous Christian warrior in history, not excepting his illustrious descendant, the Emperor Constantine.'* Arviragus ruled as Pendragon, while Caradog was in Roman captivity, and Juvenal stated that the Romans feared him greatly . . . *'Hath our great enemy Arviragus, the chariot borne British King, dropped from his battle throne?'*. According to Jowett, he was the first king of any country to fight with the cross as his battle flag. St Clement (30-100), the second Pope after Linus, refers to the disciples in Britain in 'The Epistle to the Corinthians', as did Eusebius of Caesarea. Bishop Ussher noted that in AD 48 the King of Ulster, Conor Macnessa sent his priests to Joseph's mission to commit to Christian law and teachings.

In 42AD, the Emperor Claudius sent the largest army in the history of Rome, to subdue the Silures and Christian Britain. It was led by Aulus Plautius, the most brilliant commander of his day, who made his headquarters in Colchester in 43. The elder brother of Arviragus, Guiderius, was king of the Silures, but was killed in the second battle against the invaders, and then his cousin Caradog took over battle command as Pendragon. The first battle had been won by Arviragus and Guiderius in 43. The series of battles was so intense that Agricola wrote that it would be no disgrace to fall in battle against so brave a people. According to Jowett, the British battle cry was 'Y Gwir erbyn y Byd', 'The Truth against the World'. The Claudian campaign lasted nine years, with one brief interlude, during which Tacitus said *'the fierce ardour of the British increased.'*

In 45, after the Silurian-Roman battle at Brandon Camp, there was a six-month armistice when Caradog and Arviragus were invited to Rome to discuss peace. Claudius offered Arviragus his daughter Venus Julia as his wife. At the same time Caradog's sister Gwladys married the Roman commander Aulus Plautius in Britain. Gwladys, with Arviragus, Guiderius and Caradog's daughter Eurgain had been converted by Joseph of Arimathea. Tacitus recorded the marriage of Gwladys, when she took the name Pomponia, the clan name of Aulus Plautius. She was henceforth known as Pomponia Graecina Plautius. In 47, Plautius and his British wife were recalled to Rome. It seems that Claudius did not trust the conduct of the war when his commander was related to Rome's greatest enemies. The new Roman leader was Ostorius Scapula, and the wars continued until Caradog lost a great battle at 'Clune' (Clunbury Hill?) in Shropshire in 52. Scapula was reinforced by Geta, the conqueror of Mauretania, who brought with him the II and XIV legions from Gaul. Vespasian, a future Roman Emperor was another general on the field, with his brother, and son Titus (who later burned Jerusalem and scattered the Jews). Caradog's entire family was taken captive, and Caradog handed over in chains by the queen of the Brigantes, to whom he had fled for assistance. In the 'Roman Records' of Eutropius, he states that in nine years, 32 pitched battles were fought, with victory swaying from one side to the other. 'The British Annals' give 39 battles, and still Rome had not conquered Britain. The British Triads state that Caradog was betrayed at the battle, when the Coranaid (Coritani) tribe, in the secret pay of the Romans, attacked his rear.

Tacitus records that three million people watched the triumphal procession leading Caradog and his family to his trial. He records also that Caradog's daughter Gwladys never left his side, although it was against the law for a woman to enter the Senate. After Caradog's speech (noted in the Caradog entry), the Senate applauded, and Queen Agrippina congratulated Caradog and

The Book of Welsh Saints

his daughter. The only restriction imposed was that the British royal family was exiled in Rome for 7 years, and were never to bear arms against Rome again. When Caradog returned home, possibly to Dunraven or St Donat's in 59, he kept out of the war still being fought by Arviragus and Galgacus. Jowett believes that he returned to Abergwerydd, St Donat's. In Rome, Caradog had lived in the Palatium Brittanicum, with his sons, Cyllin and Cynon. The eldest son, Cyllin, was allowed to return to Britain to act as regent for his father in Wales. According to Iolo, he was a saint. Cynon took a religious life, and seems to have been renamed Linus in Rome. Caradog's grandfather Llyr had died shortly after arriving in Rome, and Bran, Caradog's father, offered to replace him as a hostage. Bran's seat was at Trefran, in the parish of Llanilid, Glamorgan. Llanilid has the reputation as the oldest church in Britain. Bran returned from Rome in 58, a year before Caradog, with Eurgain, Aristobulus, Manaw the son of Aristobulus, Brennus, Ilid and Cyndaf, the latter two being Judaeans. Eurgain, married to the Roman Salog, Lord of Salisbury, founded Côr Eurgain at Llanilltud Fawr, the oldest Christian monastery in the world.

In 44 Peter first went to Rome, eight years after Joseph came to Britain, and in 56 Paul arrived in Rome. Baronius states that Peter was received in the Palatium Brittanicum, later Pudens' house, on Viminalis Hill in 44. The Bible refers to two churches in Rome, the Jewish Church for the circumcised, and the Gentile Church controlled by Hermas Pastor. The first group met secretly at the house of Aquila and Priscilla. St Paul backed the Gentile church of the Britons, which gradually absorbed the Jewish church. Aulus Plautius and Venus Julia, or Venissa, from 45 were back in Rome, both now Christians, Venissa being related to Caradog. Caradog had two daughters with him in Rome, the eldest Eurgain and the youngest Gwladys born in 36AD (Gwladys means 'princess'). Eurgain returned to Britain and devoted her life to missionary work in South Wales. The Emperor Claudius, impressed by Gwladys, adopted her, and she was then known as Claudia. The Christian Claudia (baptised by Joseph) in 53 married Rufus Pudens Pudentius, a former aide-de-camp of Aulus Plautius, in a service performed by Hermas Pastor. Pudens had served in the Claudian campaign in Britain, and owned vast estates in Umbria, but stayed with Claudia in the Palatium Britannicum, which Caradog had given them as a dowry. (The Chichester Stone records Pudens' stay in Britain, when he was still a pagan). The Roman Martyrology states that Pudens brought 400 servants from his Umbrian estates to serve him at the British Palace.

Claudia and Pudens had four children. Next to the Palace were the two largest baths in Rome, called after two of their children Thermae Timotheus and Thermae Novatianae. Timothy was the eldest son. In his will he left his estates and palace to the First Christian Church at Rome, the only properties owned in Rome by the church up to the time of the Emperor Constantine. Hermas Pastor regarded the palace as the home of hospitality for Christians, a sanctuary, where no Roman soldier dared to enter to arrest any member, or guest, of the Pudens household. Martial was a constant visitor from his coming to Rome in 65, who extolled the beauty of the British-born Claudia Rufina, who had won the hearts of the Roman people, and whose scholarship even surpassed her famous aunt, Pomponia. Martial also wrote poems about Claudia's marriage and the birth of her daughter Pudentiana. From the age of marriage at 17, to the age of 21, Claudia bore Timotheus and Pudentiana. Her daughter Praxedes and son Novatus were born some time later. Timotheus was named after a frequent visitor to the Pudens household, the Apostle St Timothy, Bishop of Ephesus. According to Baronius, the martyr Justin was staying at this time in the Pudens home. (However, his dates of 100-165 mean that he stayed at the Titulus Pudentis much later). St John and St Paul were closely associated with St Timothy, and Jowett makes a case for Paul being the brother of Pudens. Thus Claudia was sister-in-law to the Apostle to the Gentiles, and Paul stayed at the Pudens household in his few

Appendix

years in Rome. Paul's mother, Priscilla, was also staying in the Palatium Brittanicum. In the Roman Martyrologies we read that from 56AD *'the children of Claudia were brought up at the feet of St Paul.'*

The Palatium Britannicum was later variously known as the Titulus Pudentis and the Hospitium Apostolorum before it became the Ecclesia Pudentiana, the church of the martyred daughter of Claudia, by which name it is still known. Smithett Lewis believed that the building, upon Viminalis Hill, was where Praxedes hid martyrs, and then it became a hospice for pilgrims from the East, before Pope Evaristus (AD100-109) built a church named Pastor's after Pastor Hermas. 'The Apostolic Constitutions' refer to Linus: *'Concerning those Bishops who have been ordained in our lifetime, we make known to you that they are these; of Antioch, Eudius, ordained by me, Peter, Of the Church of Rome, Linus, brother of Claudia, was first ordained by Paul and after Linus's death, Clemens, the second ordained by me, Peter.'* Peter also confirmed that Linus was the princely son of a British king. Clement stated that Linus was British, and the brother of Claudia. Clemenus Romanus (Clement), the second Pope, had been one of Joseph of Arimathea's followers in Britain, according to Jowett. Clement also affirmed that St Paul lived in the Palatium Britannicum and instructed Linus, that **the First Church of Rome was founded by the British royal family and that St Paul had preached in Britain.**

In the meantime, the Christian Arviragus had escaped from Clune and carried on the fight against Rome, now as Pendragon. Titus fought 30 battles against him, from Anglesey to the Isle of Wight, without any major gains. In 53, the year after the battle of Clunbury Hill, where Caradog was defeated, Ostorius Scapula was very badly defeated at 'Caerfelin', Llanmelin hillfort, the Silurian tribal capital near Caerwent and Caerleon. A crack Roman legion was wiped out here. In 57 Scapula, broken by ten years of campaigning, petitioned Nero to be allowed to return to Rome. Nero accepted his resignation and sent Aulus Didius, also known as Didius Gallus. (It may be that the Roman fort at Cardiff, Caerdydd, is named after him). Didius lost several more skirmishes against Arviragus and was shortly replaced by Veranius, who was besieged by the Silurian chief at Verulam (St Albans). Nero sent more reinforcements under Suetonius Paulinus to Britain. The crack Second Augusta Legion, and the IX, XIX and XX legions now tried to finally subdue Britain, but again were repulsed time and time again. Tacitus complained that Rome was sending their most capable generals and finest legions to this extremity of the Empire, and stated *'in Britain, after the capture of Caractacus, the Romans were repeatedly defeated and put to rout by the single tribe of the Silures alone . . . the race of the Silures are not to be changed by clemency or severity.'* Suetonius Paulinus now followed a scorched-earth policy from 59-62, with the centre for European druidism, Anglesey, being targeted first. In 60 Buddug (Boadicea) led an uprising of the eastern Iceni tribe, after her daughters had been raped and her tribe attacked, while on peaceful terms with Rome.

This massive uprising from a previously quiescent tribe took the weight off the attacks on the Silures, and the Roman legions raced back from Wales to deal with the revolt. Venusius, the Pendragon of the Iceni, came to Arviragus, offering him joint command of the Iceni and Coronaid tribes. We do not know Arviragus' response, but he possibly refused because the Coronaid had betrayed his cousin Caradog. Boadicea's chariots crossed the Grimsdyke, crushing a small Roman force near Newmarket, on her way to vengeance at Colchester. The IX Legion under Petilius Cerealis was slaughtered at Coggeshall after marching from Lincoln. Cerealis escaped on horse, and Colchester was now destroyed. The Trinobantes, who had fought against Julius Caesar a century before, had also joined the Iceni. Next the 40,000 Roman defenders of London were killed and the city razed to the ground. Verulam, St Albans was next to feel the force of Boadicea's army, and the city was levelled. According to Dion

Cassius, from 60-61 many battles were fought, *'with the heavy balance of disaster borne by the Romans.'* Not until 62 was the revolt ended, at Newmarket in Flintshire. The battle swayed one way then the other, until at dusk Boadicea was cut off with a small section of her army. Believing she was trapped and fearing capture, she committed suicide and the fighting stopped. The Romans quickly came to peace terms with the Iceni leaders, restoring the illegally-confiscated wealth of their nobility and people. Welsh place-names at Newmarket have survived through the years as 'Cop Paulinus', 'Hill of Arrows', 'Hollow of Execution', 'Field of the Tribunal', 'Knoll of the Skirmish', 'Hollow of No Quarter', 'Hill of Carnage' and 'Hollow of Woe'. 'The Stone of Lamentation' is supposed to mark the spot where Boadicea took her life, and on the road to Caerwys was 'The Stone of Buddug's Grave', since moved to Downing (see Cwyfan). After the battle, Arviragus and Venusius, with a new Pendragon, Galgacus, carried on the battles against Rome in the West and North.

Against this background of war, Ussher believes that Joseph of Arimathea left Glastonbury to go to Gaul and bring back more recruits to the work of God in Britain, including Simon Zelotes. Baronius believes that Simon first came to Britain in 44 during the Claudian War (when Claudius expelled Christians from Rome), and this was his second stay. Nicephorus, Patriarch of Constantinople (758-829), wrote:
'Simon born in Cana in Galilee who for his fervent affection for his Master and great zeal that he showed by all means to the Gospel, was surnamed Zelotes, having received the Holy Ghost from above, travelled through Egypt, and Africa, then through Mauretania and all Libya, preaching the Gospel. And the same doctrine he taught to the Occidental Sea, and the Isles called Britanniae.' Simon was arrested under the orders of Caius Decianus and crucified by the Romans at Caistor in Lincolnshire on May 10, 61. In 300, Dorotheus, Bishop of Tyre wrote that Simon was crucified in Britain.

In 58 or 59, Aristobulus had been martyred, making him the first martyr in Britain, and Simon Zelotes was therefore the second. Aristobulus may have been the brother of Barnabas and the father-in-law of St Peter. (Barnabas introduced Paul to the other Apostles. Jowett places Aritobulus, Arwystli Hen, as the son of King Herod). Hippolytus, around 200AD wrote that Aristobulus was *'Bishop of the Britons'*. The 'Martyrologies of the Greek Church' state that Aristobulus was chosen by Paul to be a missionary bishop to Britain, and *'was there martyred after he had built churches and ordained deacons and priests for the island.'* Dorotheus in 303 and Ado around 850 also confirmed Aristobulus in Britain as bishop and martyr. 'Achau Sant Prydain' tells us *'these came with Bran the Blessed from Rome to Britain - Arwystli Hen (Aristobulus the Ages), Ilid (Joseph of Arimathea), Cyndaf (chief) man of Israel, Mawan son of Cyndaf, Josephes (Joseph of Arimathea's son).'* The region of Arwyslti in Montgomery is supposed to be named after this first martyr, and his church was at Llanilid in the northern Vale of Glamorgan.

Twenty years after Joseph's arrival in Britain, direct from Jerusalem, Caradog's family in Rome were responsible, with St Paul, for this mission of Aristobulus to Britain. Gwladys (Pomponia) from 47AD had used her home as a meeting place for the Apostles Peter and Paul, as she had known Joseph, Lazarus and Mary Magdalene in Britain. Gwladys (Claudia) and Pudens used their house as the first above-ground centre of Christian worship in Rome, with Hermas Pastor leading the services. After 7 years of this Christian tradition in Rome, Paul arrived at the refuge of the Palatium Brittanicum and established the Church of Rome. Hermas wrote that the Apostles taught all four children of Claudia Britannica. Caradog still had three years left of exile to complete in Rome. Paul personally confirmed Caradog and his father Bran, and chose Claudia's brother Linus to be the First Bishop of the Christian Church in Rome. Paul addressed

Appendix

Linus in the Epistles, and St Peter stated: *'The First Christian Church above ground in Rome, was the palace of the British. The First Christian Bishop, was a Briton, Linus, son of a Royal King, personally appointed by St Paul, A.D. 58.'* Paul and Linus are together engraved in two contemporary glass paterae in the Vatican Museum. While under house arrest for two years at the British Palace, Paul wrote the four 'captivity epistles.' Paul was also connected to the British virgin-saint Thecla, or Tegla, and Baronius (created Vatican Librarian in 1596) disagreed with Jerome that the 'Acts of Paul and Thecla' were apocryphal. In 61, after his friend Aristobulus had left for Britain, Paul was freed from house arrest and travelled to Spain.

Paul may then have landed in Sandwich, Kent, at the port of 'Raphinus' or at 'Bonefon', Sandown in the Isle of Wight. At the former Roman port was an ancient house until Saxon times known as 'The House of the Apostles'. From the latter Roman harbour Paul was said to have crossed to the mainland at Aber Deo, God's Port (the modern Gosport) near Paulsgrove. St Paul's Cathedral and St Paul's Cross are supposed to be where Paul preached to the inhabitants of London, and Paul is the patron saint of the English capital city. London was destroyed in 62. The abbots of Bangor in North Wales regarded themselves as the successors of St Paul, and there are traditions of him preaching there and in Gloucester and Monmouthshire. Capellus, in his 'History of the Apostles' noted *'I know of scarcely one author from the time of the Fathers downwards who does not maintain that St Paul, after his liberation, preached in every country of the West, in Europe, Britain included.'* Paul's visit to Britain is attested by Irenaeus (125-189), Tertullian (122-166), Origen (185-254), Mello (256), Eusebius (315), Athanasius (353) and Theodoret in the 4th century and Ventanius in the 6th century.

Jowett asserts that St Peter preached from Avalon in the wars of Caractacus and Arviragus against Claudius, and was known to the Silurian royal families. Eusebius in 308 said that Peter had been in Britain as well as Rome. Jowett also notes an ancient stone found at Candida Casa in Whithorn, Galloway stating *'Locvs Sancti Petri Apvstoli'* (the Place of St Peter the Apostle). A vision of Peter's death was supposed to have occurred to him at Lambedr, the old church of St Peter's, where St Peter's Abbey, Westminster, now stands. Peter's daughter Petronilla was celebrated on May 31 in Britain, and was mentioned by Bede and in the Anglo-Saxon Chronicles. Her tomb was found in 1910 on the site of the Basilica of Nereus and Achilleus in Rome. The martyred Petronilla is depicted in churches in Bury St Edmunds and Ipswich.

In 64 (or 68?), Peter was crucified in the persecution of Nero, and Bishop Linus buried him. The event is recounted in a fresco at St Piero a Grado near Pisa, probably based upon lost paintings from St Peter's in Rome. In 65 or 66, Claudia Britannica Pudens and her family rescued the martyred body of St Paul and interred it on their Roman estate. Before his execution Paul had sent a message from prison to his sister-in-law, Claudia, Pudens his brother, his beloved Linus, to Eubulus the cousin of Claudia, and to the *'household of Aristobulus'* (Arwystli Hen). Eubulus may well have been the same person as Aristobulus, and the cousin of St Barnabas. (Another source postulates Caradog as Eubulus. Eubulus is supposed to be the same word as 'Helbulus', meaning 'one full of perplexity.') Pope Linus was said to have been martyred in 80, as was his brother-in-law Rufus Pudens Pudentius in 96. Claudia died in 97 in Samnium. Pudentiana was martyred in 107, and her brother Novatus in 137, while his brother Timotheus was in Britain, baptising his nephew, Lleurwg Mawr, the grandson of Arviragus. According to Cressy, *'our ancient histories report that Timotheus the eldest son of Rufus came into Britanny where he converted many to the faith, and at least disposed King Lucius to his succeeding conversion.'* On his return to Rome, Timotheus was martyred with Marcus. Also in 140 Praxedes, the remaining child of Pudens and Claudia was martyred. They were all interred alongside St Paul in the Via Ostiensis. Priscilla, the mother of Pudens and Paul, is in the nearby catacomb of St Priscilla on the Salarian Way. According to Farmer, the church of St Prassede is on the site of Praxedes' house, and she is buried in the cemetery of Priscilla. Praxedes and Pudentiana had been taught by St Peter.

The grandson of Arviragus, Lucius the Great (Lleuwrg Mawr) was baptised by his uncle St Timothy at Caerwent or Winchester (Morgan - 'St Paul in Britain'). According to Ussher, and the *Augustinicio Mission* of 597, Lucius proclaimed Christianity as the national church of Britain in 156. The Roman Catholic hierarchy was not created until c.350.

In 180, Irenaus wrote *'The Apostles having founded and built up the church at Rome, committed the ministry of its supervision to Linus. This is the Linus mentioned by Paul in his Epistles to Timothy . . .'*

Tertullian of Carthage, writing in 208, noted that Christianity flourished in Britain, in parts 'inaccessible to the Romans'. In 250, Sabellus wrote: *'The word Christian was spoken for the first time in Britain, by those who first received The Word, from the Disciples of Christ . . . Christianity was privately confessed elsewhere, but the first nation that proclaimed it as their religion and called it Christian, after the name of Christ, was Britain.'* Also in the 3rd century Origen wrote that *'the power of the Lord is with those who in Britain are separated from our coasts.'* In 306 Simon Metaphrastes stated that St Peter had been in Britain as well as Rome. (Winchester Cathedral was known as St Peter's of Cornhill). St Jerome wrote in 378 that Britain was Christian. In 402, Chrystosom, Patriarch of Constantinople, further added to the weight of evidence:
'The British Isles which are beyond the sea, and which lie in the ocean, have received virtue of the Word. Churches are there found and altars erected . . . Though thou shouldst go to the ocean, to the British isles, there thou shouldst hear all men everywhere discoursing matters out of the Scriptures, with another voice indeed, but not another faith, with a different tongue, but the same judgement.'

The title of Pope was officially given to the Bishop of Rome in 610 by Emperor Phocas. He had assassinated the Emperor Mauritius, for which he was excommunicated by Bishop Ciriacus of Constantinople. In retaliation the new Western emperor offered the title of Pope, and head of the Western church to Gregory I, Bishop of Rome. He refused, but his successor Boniface III accepted the title and began to accrue power towards Rome from the rest of Europe. The British Church refused to accept the authority of this new Pope in Western Europe, denying the worship of the Virgin Mary or the use of the term 'Mother of God' proclaimed in 431 by the Roman Church at the Council of Ephesus. It also did not accept the doctrine of Purgatory, established by Gregory the Great in 593. (The Mass was not adopted until the 11th century as part of church procedure). The British Church saw Rome as a later, sister church, and Rome acknowledged its precedence until the 19th century. The Council of Whitby confirmed the split between the established church of Britain and that of Rome.

During the Reformation, the Roman Catholic divine Polydore Virgil stated that *'Britain partly through Joseph of Arimathea, partly through Fugatus and Damianus* (Ffagan and Dyfan), *was of all kingdoms the first to receive the Gospel.* In 1571, Theodore Martin of Louvain wrote:
'Three times the antiquity of the British Church was affirmed in Ecclesiastical Council. 1. The Council of Pisa, A.D. 1417; 2. Council of Constance, A.D. 1419; 3. Council of Siena, A.D. 1423. It was stated that the British Church took precedence over all other churches, being founded by Joseph of Arimathea, immediately after the Passion of Christ.' This was over 160 years before Rome accepted Christianity, according to Bishop Ussher.

Appendix

In 1931 Pope Pius XI received British Catholics at the Vatican and told them that St Paul, not St Gregory, first introduced Christianity into Britain, and the Morning Post reported upon March 27th, 1931:

'The Pope spoke the truth; in fact St Paul was authoritatively the first to deliver the Message from Rome, though actually his appointed representative, Aristobulus, preceded him. The important point to remember here is that St Joseph did not go to Britain from Rome. He went direct from Palestine, via Marseilles, and preceded St Paul in Britain by twenty years. At the Ecclesiastical Councils of the Roman Catholic Church the religious representatives of each country were accorded honour of place at the Council, in the order that each had received Christianity. Due to the bitter envy some of the countries bore towards the British they vigorously sought to dispute Britain's precedence in priority but on each occasion Britain's position was defended by Vatican authority.' (It may be however that the Marseilles connection is an 11th century fabrication).

Cardinal Baronius***** in the 'Annales Ecclesias' wrote:
'It is delivered to us by the firm tradition of our forefathers that the house Pudens was the first that entertained St Peter at Rome, and that of all our churches the oldest is that which is called after the name Pudens.' The Jesuit Robert Parsons noted in 'The Three Conversions of England' *'Claudia was the first hostess or harbourer both of St Peter and St Paul at the time of their coming to Rome.'*

Thus the house of the British royal family succoured the infant Christian church in Rome at the same time as Britain was the only Christian country in the world. Jowett finally noyes the Natal Days celebrated for Pudens (May 17), Pudentiana (May 17 and 19), Novatus (June 20), Timotheus (August 22), Linus (September 23 and November 26) and Praxedes (July 21 and September 21). Joseph of Arimathea was celebrated upon July 31 in the East and March 17 in the West. Priscilla, or Prisca, the wife of Aquila, was feasted upon January 18, and there was a church on Rome's Aventine Hill from the 4th century. Where there are two dates for the saints, both those in Farmer's 'Oxford Dictionary of Saints' and those given by Jowett have been used.

A final, interesting twist to the legend is that Constantius of Lyons, who saved the city of Clermont from the ravages of Euric the Goth in 473-492, took the remains of all the apostles and martyrs of Gaul to the sacred island of Britain, and put them in a special tomb at St Albans. The Virgin Mary is said to be buried at Glastonbury, and Joseph of Arimathea, Aristobulus and Simon Zelotes are also supposed to be buried in Britain. St Peter's and St Paul's bodies are not in their empty tombs in Rome. Pudens had buried the body of Paul on his estate of the Via Ostensia, and the remains were disinterred by Constantine. He placed the bones in a stone coffin, and built a new church, St Paul's Without-the-Walls. The present building dates from 1824 after a great fire, and there is a Benedictine priest who stands guard over a grill in the floor near the high altar. Underneath is a crude slabstone inscribed *'Pavli'* but there are no remains. Pope Vitalian in 656 wrote to King Oswy, as noted by Bede:
'However, we have ordered the blessed gifts of the holy martyrs, that is, the relics of the blessed apostles Peter and Paul, and of the holy martyrs Laurentius, John, and Paul, and Gregory, and Pancratius (Pancras), to be delivered to the bearers of these our letters, to be by them delivered to you.' Canterbury Cathedral received the remains, but the record of their location was destroyed during the Civil War. It is believed by some Roman Catholics that Paul actually lies under the high altar of St Paul's.

*Authorites which state that Constantine (the emperor who established Christianity in Rome in 312) was British, include: Cardinal Baronius, 'The Panegyrics of the Emperors', Polydore Virgil, Sozomen, Pope Urban and Hewin.

**The Rev. Smithett Lewis noted that Maelgwyn (Melchinus) of Avalon had written in 450 that Joseph was buried with his disciples at Glastonbury, and his tomb was found in 1345. The sarcophagus was re-enshrined in St Katherine's Chapel by Lewis in 1928. The Holy Grail was supposed to have been taken from Glastonbury to Strata Florida Abbey in Wales during the Reformation, to hide it from Henry VIII, for which crime Abbot Whiting of Glastonbury was hung, drawn and quartered. An ancient stone was also found at St Mary's Church, Glastonbury, inscribed *'Jesus - Maria'*.

***Mansuetus is an intriguing figure. The Independent newspaper ran an article headed *'Cloning saves oldest tree in Europe, where Pilate played as a boy.'* (February 24th, 2000). In the tiny churchyard at Fortingall (the fort of 'strangers') in Perth is an 8000 year-old yew tree. Yards away are the remains of a Roman camp, where Pontius Pilate was said to have been born. His father was a Roman envoy for Augustus Caesar, about 10BC, who visited the court of a Caledonian tribe whose ruler was Metallanus. During the negotiations, a local woman gave birth to the Roman's son, and the envoy took the child back to Samnium. The boy was made a free man when he grew up, and given a 'pilateus', the felt cap worn by a freed slave. Meanwhile, Metallanus sent his son or nephew, Mansuetus, to Rome in 25AD, where he converted to Christianity, returning home in 52AD. Mansuetus would therefore have been in Rome during the trial of Pontius Pilate, the disgraced Governor of Judaea. Pilate was banished, and it is speculated that he returned to his mother's family at Fortingall, where he converted to Christianity.

****Arles in 314 was the site of the first Christian Church Council, since the one recorded by St James in the Acts of the Apostles. The second great council was at Nicaea in 325, with the Emperor Constantine presiding. (At this council of 318 bishops, only 10 spoke Latin). The third event was at Constantinople (Byzantium) in 337. The Bishop of Constantinople presided although the Bishop of Rome was present. At each of these councils, and for the next thousand years, representatives took their seats in the order in which their lands had received Christianity. Every time, British bishops took the first seats. In the 14th century, Spain and Italy challenged the British right, which was confirmed by the Pope, as Britain was the first Christian country. At the church council of Pisa in 1409, the presiding bishops were Hallam of Salisbury, Chicele and Chillenden of Canterbury, with Hallam as leader of the council. At Constance in 1417, the senior bishops were Bubwith of Bath and Wells, and Beaufort of Winchester. Bishop Hallam also led the council at Sienna in 1424. In 1434, Frome of Glastonbury was chief of all the delegates of the European and North African churches at Basle.

*****Cardinal Baronius was notable in that he bravely supported Galileo, writing *'(The Bible teaches) how one goes to Heaven, not how the heavens go.'* Born at Sora in the Kingdom of Naples in 1538, he died in Rome in 1607. His name was known across Europe as a synonym for unprecedented historical research at the Vatican, of which he was Librarian from 1597. The 1907 'Catholic Encylolpaedia' has full details on the Venerable Baronius.

Footnote: a recent book by Graham Phillips, 'The Marian Conspiracy', claims the mother of Jesus was buried in Llanerchymedd, Anglesey. Phillips believes that Augustine's letter about seeing Mary's tomb, in an island of the west, coast refers to Anglesey.

Appendix J

THE LANGUAGE PROBLEM

In the text has been noted the problems of retirement homes and holiday homes in Wales destroying local language and heritage. Flint adjoins Cheshire and Lancashire, so is a border environment, and has the highest rate of people born outside Wales. Denbigh again has similar problems adjoining the former Welsh territory of Shropshire. However, the third placed Welsh area, Conwy, was formerly a stronghold of the Welsh language. Again, the attractive and massive county of Powys, across mid-Wales, has almost 40% of its people born outside Wales. Fifth is the border county of Monmouth, but worryingly the far West county of Cardigan is in 6th position. In seventh place is the holy island of Anglesey, with Gwynedd a former stronghold of the Welsh language. 8th is another extremity of Wales, Pembroke, and yet another extremity, the Welsh-speaking Gwynedd is 9th. This is not a nationalist, but a cultural problem.

The following analysis is from statistics upon local government in Wales supplied in 'The Wales Yearbook 2000.' It also demonstrates the extent to which the Conservative party is very much a minority force in Wales, with a reasonable showing in only two administrative areas (Monmouth and the Vale of Glamorgan) out of twenty. Its performance in the Vale has been greatly assisted by scandals involving former Labour council leaders in Barri. The Labour Party is losing its grip upon Wales, as the Blair government is seen to be a London-centred continuation of the Thatcher-Major years. The Welsh economy has suffered for decades compared to the rest of Britain, and the controversy which raged over Blair's undemocratic 'placing' of Alan Michael as leader of the National Assembly has also helped swell the feeling of disappointment across the land. The only jobs coming to Wales are 'call-centres', low-paid, high-pressure and unskilled. The greatest warning for Labour is in the constituencies of their former strongholds of Rhondda-Cynon-Taff and Caerffili. These areas have moved massively towards Plaid Cymru, giving the party its first toe-hold in the heavily-populated south-east of Wales.

(* = overall majority. C = Coastal constituencies. B = 'Border' constituencies. Non Welsh-born citizens have moved towards the most attractive coastal areas of Wales. The % speaking Welsh is people over 3 years old, and is a very imperfect measure which overstates reality. The ability to speak a little 'school-Welsh' and the propensity to use the language in every-day conversation are two very different things. The Welsh Language Board uses this measure, as it reflects that it seems to be an effective body. However, the Welsh Language Society, unlike the former subsidised quango, believes that only where Wales is a 'living' language should be reflected in these tables. The % should be based upon those who use Welsh as their first language in everyday life, in which case the proportions would be miniscule. The danger to the survival of the Welsh language cannot be over-stated. The author is learning Welsh.)

The Book of Welsh Saints

	AREA	Lab. Cymru seats	Plaid Dem. seats	Lib. + other	Ind. seats	Cons	Pop.	% speak Welsh	% born in Wales
1	Flint	*42	2	7	17	1	147000	15.7	BC53.0
2	Conwy	19	7	15	13	5	111900	35.8	C53.5
3	Denbigh	14	8	1	22	2	90500	29.6	BC57.3
4	Powys	6	-	7	*59	1	126000	20.4	B60.3
5	Monmouth	18	-	1	4	19	86300	7.1	BC62.1
6	Cardigan	1	13	1	30	-	70700	60.9	C64.2
7	Anglesey	4	9	-	27	-	65400	62.6	C67.7
8	Pembroke	*13	2	3	3	3	113700	20.4	C69.7
9	Gwynedd	12	*44	6	19	-	117500	74.3	C71.8
10	Wrexham	*26	-	7	15	4	125200	16.3	B73.6
11	Vale of Glam.	19	6	-	-	22	121300	9.6	C75.8
12	Cardiff	*50	1	18	1	5	320900	9.0	C79.1
13	Newport	*40	-	-	2	5	139200	8.4	BC81.1
14	Carmarthen	28	14	1	31	-	169000	53.5	C81.8
15	Swansea	*47	2	10	9	4	229,500	14.0	C84.1
16	Torfaen	*39	-	1	3	1	90200	8.3	B85.1
17	Bridgend	*41	2	5	5	1	131400	10.1	C85.2
18	Neath/P.Talb	*40	10	2	11	-	138800	19.1	C90.4
19	Caerffili	28	*39	3	3	-	169600	7.4	90.4
20	Rhondda	26	*42	2	5	-	240400	9.5	91.1
21	Merthyr	16	4	-	13	-	57000	8.1	92.0
22	Blaenau	34	-	1	8	-	72000	6.4	92.5
=	1232 seats 46%	563 17%	205 7%	92 24%	300 6%	72	2933500		

Another way of examining these statistics, and their implications for the heritage, and future, of Wales, is to see where people are retiring and unemployed, keeping the same rankings of % born in Wales, as above. It is fairly easy to see that the eight attractive areas ranked 2nd to 9th, from Conwy to Gwynedd, are retirement havens for people from outside Wales. Of these areas, Cardigan, Anglesey and Gwynedd are the traditional heart-lands of the Welsh language. It is equally easy to see why Plaid Cymru has captured Caerffili and Rhondda Cynon Taff after decades of Labour dominance. The four areas of Wales with the highest percentage of the population born in Wales have the worst deprivation statistics in Wales, and thereby the United Kingdom.

Appendix

	AREA	% ret'd	% unemp	Total % retd. + Unemp.	% in buildings B & D	B & D council tax £	% GCSE A-C	% speak Welsh	% born in Wales
1	Flint	17.3	3.8	21.1	19	592	55.3	15.7	BC53.0
2	Conwy	26.6	5.3	31.8	22	488	60.4	35.8	C53.5
3	Denbigh	23.8	4.2	28.0	20	647	59.1	29.6	BC57.3
4	Powys	21.9	3.4	25.3	17	552	63.0	20.4	B60.3
5	Monmouth	20.0	3.3	23.3	19	485	62.3	7.1	BC62.1
6	Cardigan	21.9	3.8	25.7	22	670	67.7	60.9	C64.2
7	Anglesey	21.3	8.0	29.3	22	534	59.3	62.6	C67.7
8	Pembroke	21.0	6.0	27.0	19	542	59.0	70	C69.7
9	Gwynedd	22.0	5.4	27.4	15	618	60.2	74.3	C71.8
10	Wrexham	18.8	3.8	22.6	16	633	57.6	16.3	B73.6
11	Vale/Glam.	19.2	4.4	23.6	18	532	58.5	9.6	C75.8
12	Cardiff	17.3	4.3	21.6	16	573	57.3	9.0	C79.1
13	Newport	18.7	5.0	23.7	16	531	60.8	8.4	BC81.1
14	Carmarthen	23.1	6.0	29.1	16	666	64.7	53.5	C81.8
15	Swansea	20.5	5.6	26.1	15	596	58.7	14.0	C84.1
16	Torfaen	18.6	4.4	22.8	9	564	55.1	8.3	B85.1
17	Bridgend	19.2	5.2	24.4	16	647	60.2	10.1	C85.2
18	Neath/P.Tlb	21.0	6.5	27.5	12	750	62.7	19.1	C90.4
18	Caerffili	17.6	6.8	24.4	9	633	52.5	7.4	90.4
20	Rhondda	18.2	6.5	24.7	8	686	55.2	9.5	91.1
21	Merthyr	18.6	7.7	26.3	7	712	54.1	8.1	92.0
22	Blaenau	19.5	10.0	29.5	4	640	42.0	6.4	92.5

Booklist

Author	Title	Publisher	Published
Attwater, Donald	The Penguin Dictionary of Saints	Penguin	1983
Awbery, Stan	I Searched for Llantwit Major	Barry & District News	1965
Awbery, Stan	Llancarfan, Village of a Thousand Saints	Barry & District News	1957
Awbery, Stan	Let Us Talk of Barry	Barry & District News	1954
Awbery, Stan	The Story of St Athan and Aberthaw	Barry & District News	1959
Awbery, Stan	St Donat's and the Stradlings	Barry & District News	1966
Balsom, Denis	Wales Yearbook 2000	HTV	2000
Barber, Chris	In Search of Owain Glyndŵr	Blorenge	1998
Barber, Chris and Pykitt,	David Journey to Avalon	Samuel Weiser	1997
Barber, Chris & Williams, J.G.	The Ancient Stones of Wales	Blorenge	1989
Baring-Gould, S. and Fisher, John	Lives of the British Saints	Honourable Society of Cymrodorion	1907
Blackett, Baram & Wilson, Alan	Artorius Rex Discovered	King Arthur Research	1986
Bohn H.G.	Britannia after the Romans	H.G. Bohn (250 copies)	1836
Borrow, George	Wild Wales (1862)	John Jones	1998
Bowen, E. G.	Saints, Seaways and Settlements in the Celtic Lands	University of Wales Press	1969
Bowen, E.G.	The Settlements of the Celtic Saints in Wales	University of Wales Press	1956
Bowen, E.G.	Triodd Ynys Pryden: The Welsh Triads	University of Wales Press	1961
Breverton T. D.	A History of the Parish of St Tathan: Aberddawen, Eglwys Brewys, Flemingstonand Gileston	Glyndŵr Publishing	late 2000
Breverton, T. D.	The A-Z of Wales and the Welsh	Christopher Davies Ltd.	2000
Chadwick, Nora	The Age of the Saints in the Early Celtic Church, facsimile reprint of 1960 Newcastle University Riddell Memorial Lectures	Llanerch Publishers	n.a.
Dark, K. R.	The Inscribed Stones of Dyfed	Gomer Press	1992
Davies, J.L. & Kirby, D.P.	Cardiganshire County History	University of Wales Press	1994
Davies, Janet	A Pocket Guide to the Welsh Language	University of Wales Press & Western Mail	1999
Davis, Paul R. & Lloyd-Fern, Susan	Lost Churches of Wales and the Marches	Alan Sutton	1990
Denning, R. T. W. (ed)	The Diary of William Thomas of Michaelston-super-Ely 1762-1795	South Wales Record Society	1995
Doble, G. H. (edited D. Simon Evans)	Lives of the Welsh Saints	University of Wales Press	1971
Duncan, David Ewing	The Calendar	Fourth Estate	1998
Edwards, Rev. A. G.	Landmarks in the History of the Welsh Church	John Murray	1912
Evans, C. J.	The Story of Glamorgan	The Educational Publishing Company, Cardiff	1908
Farmer, David Hugh	The Oxford Dictionary of Saints, 3rd edition	Clarendon Press	1996
Fisher, Rev. J.	The Welsh Calendar	Seaford Press	1895

Booklist

Gilbert, Adrian, with Wilson, Alan & Blackett, Baram	The Holy Kingdom – the Quest for the Real King Arthur	Bantam Press	1998
Hanning, Robert W.	The Vision of History in Early Britain from Gildas to Geoffrey of Monmouth	Columbia University Press	1966
Henken, Elissa R.	Traditions of the Welsh Saints	St Edmundsbury Press	1987
Henken, Elissa R.	The Welsh Saints – A Study in Patterned Lives	Brewer, Boydell	1991
Hopkins, Keith	A World Full of Gods	Weidenfeld	1999
Hutton, Ronald	The Pagan Religions of the Ancient British Isles – Their Nature and Legacy	Blackwell	1991
Jarman, A.O.H., & Hughes, Gwilym Rees	A Guide to Welsh Literature Vol. I	Christopher Davies	1976
Jenkins, Augusta F.	The Legend of St Tathana	in 'The Welsh Outlook'	November 1924
Jenkins, J. Geraint	Life and Tradition in Rural Wales	J. M. Dent & Sons Ltd.	1976
Jones, Francis	The Holy Wells of Wales	University of Wales Press	1954 reprinted 1998
Jones, T. Gwynne	Welsh Folklore and Folk-Custom	D. S. Brewer reissue, 1979	1930
Jowett, George F.	The Drama of the Lost Disciples	Covenant	1963
Kilvert, R. F. (ed. William Plomer)	Kilvert's Diary	Pimlico	1999
Leatham, Diana	They Built on Rock	Llanerch	1996 reprint
Lewis, Rev. Lionel Smithett	St Joseph of Arimathea at Glastonbury or The Apostolic Church of Britain	James Clarke & Co.	1955 7th edition
Lloyd, J.E. et al (editors)	The Dictionary of Welsh National Biography: Down to 1940	The Honourable Society of Cymmrodorion	1959
Llywelyn, Dorian	Sacred Place, Chosen People	University of Wales Press	1999
McMurry, Enfys	Hearst's Other Castle	Seren	1999
Merrick, Rice (ed. Corbett, James Andrew)	Morganiae Archaiographia (A Book of Glamorganshire's Antiquities)	Dryden Press 1887, reprinted in 1987 by Stewart Williams	1578
Miller, Molly	The Saints of Gwynedd	The Boydell Press	1979
Morgan, W	St Paul in Britain, or The Origin of British Christianity	Artisan Sales (abridged)	1984
Nicholas, Thomas	The History and Antiquities of Glamorganshire and its Families	Longmans	1874
Okasha, E	Corpus of Early Inscribed Stones of South-West Britain	Leicester University Press	1993
Opie, Iona Oxford & Tatem, Moira	Dictionary of Superstitions	Oxford University Press	1989
Orrin, Geoffrey R.	Medieval Churches of the Vale of Glamorgan	D. Brown & Sons	1988
Owen, Trefor M.	A Pocket Guide to the Customs and Tradition of Wales	University of Wales Press	1991
Owen, Trefor M.	Welsh Folk Customs	National Museum of Wales	1959
Parker, Rev. John (ed. Edgar W. Parry)	Tour of Wales and its Churches (1860)	Gwasg Carreg Gwalch	reprint 1998
Parry-Jones, D.	Welsh Legends	Batsford	1953
Pennant, Thomas (abridged David Kirk)	A Tour in Wales	Gwasg Carreg Gwalch	1998
Pennick, Nigel	The Celtic Saints	Thorsons	1997
Phillips, Pauline	A View of Old Montgomeryshire	Christopher Davies	1977
Pugh, T.B. (ed.)	Glamorgan County History	University of Wales Press	1971

Redknap, Mark	The Christian Celts: Treasures of late Celtic Wales	National Museum of Wales	1991
Redwood, Charles	The Vale of Glamorgan - Scenes and Tales among the Welsh	Saunders and Otley	1839
Rees Rice	An Essay on the Welsh Saints or the Primitive Christians usually considered to have been the Founders of Churches in Wales	Longman	1836
Rees, W. J.	Lives of the Cambro-British Saints	Welsh MSS Society	1853
Romilly Allen, J.	Celtic Crosses of Wales	Lanerch	1989
Salter, Mike	'The Old Parish Church' series of North Wales, Mid-Wales, South-West Wales and Gwent, Glamorgan and Gower.	Folly Publications	Various dates from 1991
Seaborne, Malcolm	Celtic Crosses of Britain and Ireland	Shire Publications	1991
Sellner, E. C.	Wisdom of the Celtic Saints	Ave Maria Press	1993
Sharkey, John	Celtic High Crosses of Wales	Carreg Gwalch	1998
Sikes, Wirt	Rambles & Studies in Old South Wales	Sampson Low etc.	1881
Stephens, Meic (ed.)	The New Companion to the Literature of Wales	University of Wales Press	1998
Styles, S	Welsh Walks and Legends	John Jones	1972
Taylor, John W.	The Coming of the Saints	Covenant Press, reprint first pub. 1906 by Methuen	1969
Thomas, D. Aneirin	The Welsh Elizabethan Catholic Martyrs	University of Wales Press	1971
Thomas, Keith	Religion and the Decline of Magic	Penguin	1995
Thomas, Patrick	Candle in the Darkness: Celtic Spirituality from Wales	Gomer	1993
Toulson, Shirley	'The Celtic Year'	Element Books	1996
Tregarneth, Anita	Founders of the Faith in Wales	Hugh Evans and Sons	1947
Trevelyan, Marie	Llantwit Major, Its History and Antiquities	John E. Southall	1910
Wall, J. Charles	The First Christians of Britain	Talbot & Co.	1910? no date
Wallis, Don (ed)	A Village in the Vale: A history of Llandow in the Vale of Glamorgan	AVC	1992
Westwood, J.O.	Lapidarium Walliae: the Early Inscribed Stones of Wales	Oxford	1876-1879
Williams, Waldo	Dail Pren	Llandysul	1956
White, James	Picturesque Excursions into South Wales (quoted in Ken Etheridge 'Welsh Costume in the 18th and 19th century')	Christopher Davies	1977

Other reading includes:

Internet websites : Catholic Online Saints; Brittannia

T. Charles-Edwards 'St Winefride and her Well: The Historical Background', publisher unknown, bought at St Winefride's Well souvenir shop, Holywell

Reverend Christopher David 'St Winefride's Well: a history and guide', publisher unknown, bought as above, reprinted 1993

Idris Davies 'The Collected Poems of Idris Davies' edited by Islwyn Jenkins, Gomer Press reprint 1993. This book should be compulsory reading in all Welsh schools. We can learn more of Welsh history and sociology in the 20th century from Davies than anyone. T.S. Eliot said of his poems: *'They are the best document I know about a particular epoch in a particular place, and I think that they really have a claim to permanence.'*

'Enjoy Medieval Denbighshire' is a free colour booklet from the County Council of great interest in describing churches and the like, and an fine example for other councils in Wales to copy, as are the 'Menter Preseli' and 'Menter Powys' leaflets.

OTHER BOOKS FROM GLYNDŴR PUBLISHING:

'The Secret Vale of Glamorgan - the Story of St Tathan, Gileston, Eglwys Brewys, Flemingston and Aberthaw', T.D. Breverton, June 2000

'The Book of 100 Great Welshmen', T.D. Breverton, November 2000

'The Dragon Entertains - 100 Welsh Stars', Alan Roderick, October 2000

'From Paths to Inexperience', David Jervis, November 2000

'The Welsh Almanac', T.D. Breverton, December 2000

'100 Great Welsh Women', T.D. Breverton, February 2001

'Another 100 Great Welsh Men', T.D. Breverton, March 2001

'Rock of Ages - A history of Welsh rock groups', T.D. Breverton & Dave Hardacre, forthcoming

'The Book of Welsh Pirates and Buccaneers', September 2001

'King Arthur and St Armel - the rediscovery', T.D. Breverton, F. Dault & D. Hamon, June 2001

T.D. Breverton is also the author of 'The A-Z of Wales and the Welsh', published by Christopher Davies Ltd., March 2000

If the above publications are not readily available in retail outlets, kindly contact the publisher for direct sales at: Wales Books, Porth Glyndŵr, St. Tathan, Vale of Glamorgan, CF62 4LW, or at www.walesbooks.com

Addenda

The following information was received after the book went to the printers. If anyone can enlighten the author with details of Thomas Capper, martyred in Cardiff, kindly do so,

ADDENDUM A - CHRISTOPHER LOVE 1618-1651

Born in Cardiff, he graduated from New Hall, Oxford in 1635, and was a staunch Presbyterian. He found difficulty in gaining ordination in the Church of England, but was offered ordination as a pastor in Scotland. However, he assumed the pastorate of St Lawrence Jury in London, where he taught theology to the children of the Sheriff of London. He met Mary Stone at the Sheriff's house, and they had five children. The two girls died very early, and the third boy was born a week after Love's death. He had been tried by Cromwell's forces for an alleged plot to raise money for the restoration of the monarchy, with several other prominent London ministers, including the notable Thomas Watson. All were released, but Love was made a convenient scapegoat for the arresting authorities and found guilty of treason. Protesting his innocence, he was beheaded on Tower Hill on August 22nd.

ADDENDUM B - ST PEIRIO

The Bedd Porius Stone was noted by Westwood, standing in a field near Trawsfynydd. In Pennant's time it had been in a farmhouse, and was rescued from being used in a field wall by on of the notable Wynne family. It is near the Llech Idris menhir. The very early inscription in Roman capitals was:

PORIVS - HIC IN TVMVLO IACIT - HOMO XPIANVS FVIT - 1245 E.

The third line is difficult to read, and one version is Homo Meirianus (a man of Meironeth), but probably means 'he was a Christian man'. The numbers are a late addition. Westwood states *'Peirio, one of the sons of Caw, also called Cato or Cadaw, was a saint of the congregation of St Illtud, to whom is dedicated a church in Anglesey. He was a contemporary with St Kebius or Kuby, (circ. 360-400).* In the text, the author made Porius the Latin name for Pyr, but this may be the grave of the saint who had a church on Barri Island.

ADDENDUM C - LLANDEILO TAL Y BONT

One has the opportunity of seeing the church of St Teilo now being erected at the Museum of Welsh Life, and there is an exhibition nearby of the history of the church, and of how the wall - paintings were painstakingly recovered and are being restored. From the leaflet available at the site: *'Most churches, and many houses, during the middle ages would have been decorated with brightly coloured wall-paintings. Church services would have been in Latin which very few ordinary people could understand: wall paintings (and pictorial stained glass windows) helped to convey the stories and messages of the Bible. Some churches had scenes showing the torments of Hell, the life or death of Christ, depictions of saints or angels, or combinations of one or more of these. They were painted directly onto the lime plaster which covered the walls, Often, after a generation or so, new paintings would be painted over these wall-paintings to bring them 'up-to-date' or to illustrate some different theme. At the time of the Reformation in the 1530's these wall-paintings fell out of favour and were painted over. Later, it became fashionable to paint religious texts and verses on the walls, as well as the coat-of-arms of the monarch (who was by then also head of the Church of England). In Victorian times the walls were again covered with whitewash, and so, for many years, centuries in fact, many wall-paintings remained hidden from view beneath layer and layer of whitewash. At Llandeilo Tal-y-Bont two major series of pre-Reformation wall-paintings were discovered, plus two later* schemes, as well as several texts and areas of decorative patterns. The two earliest paintings date from about 1400, one of which shows St Catherine. The entire church appears to have been repainted about 1500 with scenes from the life of Christ.'

ADDENDUM D - ST PASGEN

The author placed Pasgen as 5th century, but the Pascent Stone at Towyn seems to be not that of Pasgen ap Brychan but that of Pagen ap Dingad, a great grandson of Brychan, and thus 6th - 7th century.

ADDENDUM E - CIDER-MAKING

The brewing of 'seidr' (from apples) and perry (from pears) was traditional to Wales, and is still a big industry in Hereford. St Gwenole chose to live on cider as a form of penance and punishment. Gutun Owain's cywydd to Abbot Sion of Valle Crucis states:

Dir I mi gan seidr a medd
Oedi gwin a da Gwynedd
(It's no wonder, because of the plentiful cider and mead
That I linger tasting the wine and bounty of Gwynedd)

Glyndŵr had a noted cider-apple orchard at Sycharth, and St Teilo is the patron of apples in Brittany as he took trees from Wales to plant orchards there. It was made all over Wales, for instance in Flemingstone Thomas Watkin in 1696 had a *'sider house - 1 sider ring, 1 ters, 1 tubb, 1 trindle, valued at £1. 10s. 0d.'* In the 1950's, farmers were still making cider for their labourers, and the daily ration of 'scrumpy' was between 4 and 8 pints per day. This ancient Welsh tradition must be renewed as a source of extra income for farmers.

ADDENDUM F - LAMPETER

It was not made clear in the text that Lampeter was once known as Llanystyffan, possibly founded by St Ystyffan.

ADDENDUM G - EDWARD POWELL (1478?-1540)

This Welsh Catholic graduated from Oxford, becoming a Fellow of Oriel College in 1495. His livings included Salisbury, Lyme Regis and Bedminster, and he preached several times at Kenry VIII's court. However, he wrote a dissertation against Lutheran doctrine, and fiercely opposed Henry's divorce from Catherine of Aragon. In 1534 his refusal to acknowledge the succession to the throne ensured that he was found guilty of high treason. Incarcerated in the Tower of London for 6 years, he was executed at Smithfield with five other martyrs.

ADDENDUM H - THOMAS MORGAN (1543-c.1605)

Probably from Llantarnam in Monmouthshire, and educated at Oxford, he served the households of the bishop of Exeter then the archbishop of York. In 1569 he was recommended by the earls of Northumberland and Pembroke to enter the service of the Earl of Shrewsbury. Shrewsbury was holding the imprisoned Mary Queen of Scots at Tutbury Castle, and Morgan attached himself to her service. He carried the secret letters implicating her in the Ridolfi Plot, and imprisoned in the Tower of London for nine months in 1572. On his release, he made for Paris, and worked as secretary to Mary's ambassador, the Archbishop of Paris. In 1584, the libellous attack on Elizabeth I's Protestant advisors, 'Leycester's Commonwealth', appeared. Walsingham was convinced that Morgan was the anonymous author and demanded Morgan's extradition. He managed Mary's correspondence, and was accused by Dr William Parry (probably under torture) of hatching the assassination plot on Elizabeth I's life, for which Parry himself was executed in 1585. Henry III of France held off returning Morgan to English justice, for fear of Spanish reprisals, but kept Morgan in the Bastille from 1585-1590. Morgan's correspondence with Mary was constantly intercepted by Protestant spies working for Walsingham, and led to her execution in 1586. Morgan had helped to organise the Babington Plot, which gave Walsingham the concrete proof that Elizabeth needed to kill Mary. Thomas Morgan, still in the Bastille, now worked for Mary's son, the Catholic James VI of Scotland, and kept contact with Catholic friends and relations in South Wales, fomenting unrest. Released from the Bastille, Morgan had no funding, and had made enemies of the Jesuits. He advanced the cause of Owen Lewis (q.v.), bishop of Cassano, and was expelled from France. In the Spanish Netherlands, the Jesuits ensured that he was imprisoned again (1590-1592). When James VI came to power as James I of England, Morgan approached Sir Thomas Parry, the ambassador in Paris in an attempt to reconcile English Catholics against the Jesuits. In 1605 he was accused of conspiracy with the mistress of Henry IV (the lady's sister was in contact with English Catholics) and condemned to death, but was still alive in a Paris prison at the end of that year. This remarkable Catholic may have still been alive in 1611, still hoping for a legacy promised him by Mary Queen of Scots. Perhaps someone can write his biography.

ADDENDUM I - WILLIAM PARRY (d. 1585)
Mentioned in the above entry upon Thomas Morgan, William ap Harry ap David of Northop (Llaneurgain, Flintshire) escaped his creditors by entering the service of the Welshman Lord Burghley, to act as a spy upon Catholics. He was on the Continent in 1571, 1579 and 1582, and found himself so much in empathy with the British refugees that he became a Catholic himself. He now saw the need to depose Elizabeth. After he had made a speech in the House of Commons condemning a bill against Jesuits, he was betrayed by a fellow-conspirator. He was found guilty of plotting against Elizabeth's life, and executed on March 2nd, 1585. Whether the whole affair was a charade made up by Burghley and/or Walsingham to alert the state against Catholics, we may never know. It seems that poor Parry was an example 'pour les autres'.

ADDENDUM J - GWEIRYDD, ARVIRAGUS; and OFFA'S DYKE
A recent book, 'The Keys to Avalon' by S.Blake and S.Lloyd (Element Books 2000), places Arthur as a North Walian. The authors are involved in the 'development of an Arthurian Centre planned for North Wales', and all that this author can state without incurring the laws of libel is that he is strongly opposed to their findings. However, they place (St) Gweirydd as the British name of Arviragus. In the same book, they make a claim which seems substantial that Offa's Dyke was originally the third wall of Roman Britain, constructed by Severus around 205. From various sources, he built an earthwork stretching from sea to sea, 132 miles long. The wall was built between Alban (Powys) and Deira (Cheshire). The Antonine Wall of c.140 runs just 37 miles, between Stirling and Glasgow, and Hadrian's Wall of c.120 is 73 miles long between Newcastle and Carlisle.

ADDENDUM K - TEILO, TEULYDDOG
A recent edition of Cambria (Summer 2000) carries the view of the Very Rev. Wyn Evans, Dean of St David's, that Teilo and the Teulyddog who established a church in the ruins of Roman Carmarthen were the same person. Evans also makes the point that St Ystyffan was the original saint of St Anthony's Well at Llansteffan.

ADDENDUM L - FURTHER READING OMITTED FROM THE BOOKLIST
'Nennius - British History and The Welsh Annals', ed. & trans. John Morris, Phillimore & Co. 1980 (includes The Welsh Annals, Historia Brittonum and Annales Cambriae);
'Llantwit Major - a fifth century university', Alfred C. Fryer, Elliot Stock 1893

ADDENDUM L - ST ELVIS (see Ailbe)

Upon 5th June, 2000, the author took part in a GMTV breakfast news transmission from St Elvis Farm. Intense media interest was stirred up by a full-page Daily Mail article of Friday, 2nd June, Elvis the Welshman, published while Terry Breverton was working in Italy. The author received telephone calls from the BBC and other media while in Italy, and returned home to find that there were messages to contact BBC Radio 1, 2, 4, 5, BBC Wales and BBC World Service, Capital Gold, The Big Breakfast and GMTV television shows, and that there had also been articles in The Guardian and the Daily Mirror. A Mail reporter had read a short note in the author's 'An A-Z of Wales and the Welsh', and devised the article, making the author a 'professor of history at Cardiff University', rather than a Senior Lecturer in Marketing at UWIC Business School. However, the two live transmissions from St Elvis Farm, complete with an Elvis impersonator singing 'I can't help falling in love with you (ewe)' and Blue Suede Ewes (Shoes)' and the Haverfordwest Male Voice Choir, allowed the author to study the area. Speaking to the National Trust tenant farmer, Geraint Roberts, and his father Gareth, who formerly farmed the land, it was ascertained that St Elvis Parish is the smallest in Great Britain, and the title Rector of St Elvis was superior to that of the incumbent of the nearby vicar of St Teilo's in Solva. The name St Elvis has appeared on maps since at least the 16th century. On the site are the 5000 year-old St Elvis Cromlech, a huge burial chamber with two tombs, and a few yards away the foundations of a square tower, possibly a lookout post or storage barn for the monks on this site. The remains of the church are quite big, and unusually situated north-south, covered with blackthorn. Following down the valley, there is St Elvis Holy Well, that was still pumping out 360 gallons an hour during the great 1976 drought, and had to be used to water the cattle at that time. (There is potential here for bottling the water). This lies under St Elvis Farm, where a barn was built in the early 20th century from the dressed stones of St Elvis Church. The last marriages took place in St Elvis Church in the 1860's and are recorded in the Haverfordwest Archives. The area, where the Preseli Hills sweep down to the sea, in just two fields away, but hidden from Irish and Viking pirates. St Elvis Rocks off the mouth of the picturesque Solva Harbour are now known as Green Scar, Black Scar and The Mare. If any reader knows their original Welsh names, please contact the author. Two very important ley lines meet here, one going to Stonehenge, and the site is littered with graves. Gareth Roberts has said that often in building sheds etc, he has seen 'chalk-marks' in the soil, which when touched powder into dust, i.e. ancient bones. The well was not recorded by Francis Jones, but local tradition is that St David was baptised by his cousin St Elvis on this site, with water from the well, in the font at St Elvis Church. This font is now in St Teilo's in Solva. St David's is just a few miles away. A cross-marked 6th century pillar, formerly a gate-post, was taken to St Teilo's Church, but its partner post was 'lost' in 1959 when a farm laboured used it as part of a field bank. The labourer died shortly after. Even more intriguing, and of massive historical importance, is a square stone, with the simple face of a man carved into it. It is thought that National Trust employees used it to repair a field-bank. There are extremely few Dark Age facial representations among the ancient stones of Wales, and a non-intrusive survey may well find it. It was formerly in the centre of the ruined church and had holes bored into its top and bottom to hinge it to act as a door. This is the very type of information that we can gather from all over Wales, before it is lost forever. If CADW was adequately funded, there could be a proper 'dig' on the site, as should happen at Llanilltud Fawr Roman villa. The St Elvis cromlech, monastery site, ruined church, scattered and lost stones, Dark Ages holy well and Elvis connections make this an extremely attractive proposition for television's 'Time Team', which the author has contacted. The name 'Elvis' is only found here in all of Europe.

ADDENDUM L - ST TATHANA

The author published, in June 2000, a book called 'The Secret Vale of Glamorgan - the Story of St Tathan, Gileston, Eglwys Brewys, Flemingston and Aberthaw'. I looked with local man Les Dixon for the site of Tathana's cell, on the banks of the Thaw, in a field called Chapel Field, or Chapel Cross Field, where a chapel was marked on old maps. From East Orchard Castle we found a series of thick stepping slabs across the stream which flows from West Orchard castle through Rills Valley to the Thaw. They were of a different stone to that locally occurring. Local limestone would dissolve and crack over time in such a wet situation. Chapel Field is supposed to be the triangular field above the woods on Castleton Farm lands, with one edge overlooking Flemingston Moors and one edge along the Rills Valley. Not finding any traces, we cut down through the woods, finding a dead dog fox in a fork of a tree on the way, and half-way down saw a rectangular shape in the valley. Made up of a mixture of dressed stone with traces of mortar, and rubble, the ground-level walls were aligned approximately 25 feet East to West, and 15 feet North to South. The Thaw then meandered through the valley, and this would have been close to the high tide level - could this have been the site of Tathana's 6th century church? The site has recently been recorded by the Glamorgan-Gwent Archaeological Trust.

ADDENDUM M - ROMANS

It appears from recent articles that the gold at Llanpumsaint may have been the major reason for the Roman invasion, and that most of the gold had bee mined by the British prior to their operations.

ADDENDUM N

With reference to the need for Welsh 'theme-pubs', the author met the directors of Cardiff Rugby Club and an Arms Park 'tafarn' will be sited under their North Stand during the 2000-2001 season.